The Insider's Guide

to the

GRE CAT®

KARL WEBER

Author of nearly seven books offering frank and impartial test-preparation advice

THOMSON

PETERSON'S ™

Australia • Canada • Mexico • Singapore • Spain • United Kingdom • United States

About The Thomson Corporation and Peterson's

With revenues of US$7.2 billion, The Thomson Corporation (www.thomson.com) is a leading global provider of integrated information solutions for business, education, and professional customers. Its Learning businesses and brands (www.thomsonlearning.com) serve the needs of individuals, learning institutions, and corporations with products and services for both traditional and distributed learning.

Peterson's, part of The Thomson Corporation, is one of the nation's most respected providers of lifelong learning online resources, software, reference guides, and books. The Education Supersite[SM] at www.petersons.com—the Internet's most heavily traveled education resource—has searchable databases and interactive tools for contacting U.S.-accredited institutions and programs. In addition, Peterson's serves more than 105 million education consumers annually.

GRE test questions selected from *GRE: Practicing to Take the General Test, 9th Edition,* Educational Testing Service, 1994. Reprinted by permission of Educational Testing Service.

Permission to reprint GRE materials does not constitute review or endorsement by Educational Testing Service of this publication as a whole or of any other testing information it may contain.

For more information, contact Peterson's, 2000 Lenox Drive, Lawrenceville, NJ 08648; 800-338-3282; or find us on the World Wide Web at www.petersons.com/about.

ISBN 0-7689-1095-1

Printed in Canada

10 9 8 7 6 5 4 3 2 1   04 03 02

Acknowledgments

Creating this edition for *The Insider's Guide to the GRE* has been a team effort. I've been fortunate enough to have the assistance of a very talented group of educators and writers who skillfully crafted significant portions of the manuscript, drawing on both their considerable knowledge and their notable literary skills to complement my abilities beautifully. In particular, I wish to acknowledge and thank:

Dr. Harold D. Shane
Peter Lanzer
Nancy J. Brandwein
Robert A. Kaplan
Rajiv Rimal
Peter Orton
Laura A. Weber
Mary-Jo D. Weber

Naturally, any errors or inadequacies that the book may contain are mine alone.

I also want to thank Bob Schaeffer of FairTest and John Nelson and Andrea Wilson of Kaplan Educational Centers for their helpful responses to my many inquiries. Thanks, too, to Don Essig, Karen Reinisch, and Stephanie Hammett, and Bob Sehlinger.

And my gratitude especially, and always, to my wife, whose love makes it all worthwhile.

Karl Weber
Chappaqua, New York

About the Author

K arl Weber has been helping students to prepare for the GRE and other standardized exams for twenty years. He was a teacher, writer, and editor for Stanley H. Kaplan Educational Centers and later designed and taught the verbal test-preparation programs at Mathworks, a school in New York City. Weber is featured on a popular series of test-preparation videos published by Video Aided Instruction, a producer of educational materials located in Roslyn Heights, New York.

Weber is also well known in the publishing industry as an editor and book developer. He was the editor of two of the best investment books of all time, as selected in 1997 by *Worth* magazine, and also worked with former president Jimmy Carter on three best-selling books *An Hour Before Daylight*, *Living Faith*, and *Sources of Strength*. He lives with Mary-Jo Weber, his wife of 30 years, in Chappaqua, New York.

Contents

The *Insider's Guide* Declaration of Independence

In America, where advanced educational credentials are growing more and more important, the GRE has become one of the crucial hurdles in the lives of millions. Your performance on the GRE plays a major role in determining whether or not you'll be able to attend the graduate school of your choice.

Furthermore, unlike the GRE Subject Tests, which focus on the knowledge you've gained in your chosen field during college, the GRE General Test covers an arbitrary and slightly weird collection of skills you may not have used since taking the SAT or ACT Assessment. Maybe you've majored in French literature and hope to study Flaubert at the Sorbonne. No matter—you have to take a test that includes questions about plane geometry and algebra. Are you an aspiring researcher in biochemistry? Fine—here's a test that includes logic puzzles about how guests should be seated at a banquet. Does it make sense? Not much. Do you have a choice? Not really.

To survive the process—and to make it work for you—you need help.

YOU CAN'T DEPEND ON THE TEST-MAKERS

Unfortunately, it seems that almost everyone involved in the standardized testing industry (and make no mistake, it is an industry—a big one) has some kind of axe to grind.

The test-makers themselves—the Graduate Record Examinations Board, which sponsors the GRE program, and the Educational Testing Service, which writes and administers the test—have a huge vested interest in the survival and credibility of their exam. Both the GRE Board and ETS are not-for-profit organizations. That doesn't make them immune to the pressures felt by every organization in a competitive industry. They make their living by producing the GRE for use by universities as part of the student admission process. The fine salaries and nice offices enjoyed by the executives at the GRE Board and ETS are dependent on having university admission officers and the general public continue to believe that the GRE is a useful, accurate, and basically fair tool for measuring student abilities. If that belief were to vanish, universites would stop asking students to take the GRE, and the people who work for the GRE Board and ETS would have to find new jobs.

Therefore, everything the test-makers say publicly about the GRE must serve the purpose of bolstering public confidence in the accuracy and fairness of the exam. That is why, for decades, the test-makers strenuously claimed that it was impossible to improve your GRE scores significantly by preparing beforehand. They feared that, if it became generally recognized that GRE scores could be improved through study programs, the perceived fairness of the GRE program might ultimately crumble.

In recent years, under pressure from students, public advocacy groups, and politicians, the test-makers have changed their stance to some degree. For the first time, they have made some actual past exams publically available (they used to be kept strictly secret). And they admitted—however grudgingly—that study and preparation could improve GRE scores significantly. (Not missing a beat, they also began publishing and selling their own GRE preparation materials.)

Nonetheless, concerns about image and credibility still constrain the test-makers. They must be careful to avoid any suggestion that the GRE, or any part of the GRE, can be successfully negotiated by mastering a handful of relatively simple techniques. If students can score higher on the GRE by using a few easy-to-learn "tricks," then the exam begins to appear more like a gimmick than a serious educational tool. From the test-makers' point of view, that would never do.

Thus, the test-makers have a vested interest in stressing how difficult, time-consuming, and intellectually challenging it is to prepare for the GRE. They desperately want to bolster the image of the GRE as an "unbeatable" exam. It's understandable. In their shoes, most of us would feel—and behave—the same.

Don't misunderstand. We don't consider the GRE Board or ETS crass, unprofessional, or venal. They are highly competent specialists in test design and administration, and undoubtedly they sincerely believe in the value of their work. But the nature of that work makes it impossible for them to offer you the kind of disinterested, unbiased, and completely honest advice you need about the best and easiest ways to prepare for the GRE.

TEST-PREP SCHOOLS HAVE THEIR OWN AGENDA

What about the other sources of test-taking advice and information? Aren't they immune to these biases?

Yes—but most of them have other biases of their own. For example, over the last two decades, several nationwide chains of test-preparation schools have sprung up. They offer classroom courses, supplemented with printed and electronic study material, to help students prepare for the GRE and other exams. Some of these have become big businesses in their own right, owned by or affiliated with major media conglomerates. You can buy books and software bearing the names of these schools and containing some of the techniques and strategies taught in their classroom programs.

Naturally, like any business people, the executives who manage these schools are interested in keeping profits high. To do this, they must funnel as many students as possible through their classroom programs. Given a choice, they'd much rather have you buy one of their ambitious, multi-week courses than a book or even a piece of software. (The profit on a book that costs $15 to $20 can't begin to compare with the profit on a $1,000 course.) Thus, they must view their books primarily as promotional vehicles for their schools. They hope that some of the students who buy their books will be sufficiently impressed—and perhaps sufficiently intimidated—to sign up for a class.

In their case, the vested interest lies in making the GRE appear scary enough to drive you into an $800 classroom program—and in making the test-taking strategies and techniques you need to learn appear complicated and arcane enough to demand weeks of work with a teacher or tutor.

Again, don't misunderstand. Some test-preparation schools offer fine programs. And some of the books and software they produce can be quite helpful in preparing for an exam. But, just as with the test-makers themselves, we think the inherent self-interest in how the test-prep schools do business inevitably colors the kind of advice they give you and the kinds of preparation they recommend.

OUR PLEDGE

We have no such bias. We have no vested interest in the reputation or image of the GRE, and we are not selling classroom courses for any exam. Our only concern is to offer you the most efficient, accurate, and useful guidance for earning your highest possible score on the GRE. If a particular type of math question can be solved without performing any calculations, or a certain kind of analogy question can be answered even if you don't recognize some of the words, or some parts of a reading passage can be safely ignored, we're free to say so, thus letting you focus your time and energy in more effective ways—and earn a higher score in the process.

That's why we proudly bear the banner of the *Insider's Guides.* Authorized and controlled by no one, we serve only one master—you, our reader.

How This Guide Was Researched and Written

The authors of this book are specialists in test-preparation, teaching, and the writing of educational materials. We've followed the development of the GRE for twenty years, tracking and analyzing the changes in the kinds of questions used and the skills tested. We've also worked with students (and teachers) in various settings, helping them to develop the test-taking abilities and the self-confidence needed to do well on the exam.

Based on these years of experience, we've developed a keen awareness of what the GRE is like and what techniques the test-makers use to measure the strengths and weaknesses of individual students. Equally important, we've developed a strong sense as to what kinds of test-taking strategies most students find really beneficial and which ones, frankly, are more complicated or confusing than helpful. This expertise has helped to shape both the contents and the style of this guide.

All the test-taking advice in this book is based on extensive analysis of actual GRE exams. Take, for example, "The Insider's GRE Word List." Rather than simply create a vocabulary list based on instinct or on the recommendations of college English teachers, we started by compiling a list of all vocabulary words actually tested on recent GRE exams, including difficult words used in answer choices, vocabulary questions, and sentence completion and analogy questions. We then selected the words that turned up most frequently on the exam, eliminating some that would have made the list only through the quirk of appearing in a particular reading passage and are unlikely to recur any time soon.

To increase the value of the list as a learning tool, we then added not only clear, accurate definitions and sample sentences illustrating the meanings of the words but also word root explanations—we call them *origins*—that will help you to connect these words to others that have appeared on the GRE. This will make it easy for you to learn two, three, or four new words rather than one at a time. The result, we believe, is the most up-to-date, complete, and truly useful GRE vocabulary list currently available. And we've applied a similar approach to every topic on the exam.

SPECIAL FEATURES

To help you get the most out of this book quickly and easily, the text is enhanced with FYI sidebars that provide you with:

- tips and shortcuts that save you time

- cautions and warnings about pitfalls to avoid

- strategies that offer an easier or smarter way to do something

- statements from real people that can give you valuable insights

- an insider's fact or anecdote

We also recognize you need to have quick information at your fingertips and thus have provided the following Appendices at the back of the book:

A. The Insider's GRE Word List
B. The Insider's GRE Math Review
C. Resources for Further Study
D. The Insider's Stress-Buster's Guide

What To Expect on the GRE for 2002–03

NO MORE NUMBER TWO PENCIL—THE COMPUTERIZED TEST RULES

The GRE General Test administered on April 10, 1999, was the *last* paper-and-pencil GRE to be given in the United States. As of that date, the *only* version of the General Test available is the Computer-Based Test (sometimes called the Computer-Adaptive Test, or CAT).

The only paper-and-pencil GRE exams to be offered in the future are:

- General Tests in some non-U.S. locations where a complete network of computer testing centers has not yet been established.

- The Subject Tests, currently covering sixteen academic areas. These are given only in paper-and-pencil format because the relatively low numbers of students taking each test doesn't justify computerization in economic terms.

- The new GRE Analytical Writing Measure (see below), *if* you take it at the college or university test sites on a date when the Subject Tests are administered, rather than at a computer testing center.

SCHEDULE FOR THE COMPUTERIZED GRE

The computerized GRE is available at more than 600 Sylvan Learning Centers throughout the United States, U.S. territories, and Canada. Call Sylvan at 800-GRE-CALL to find the center nearest you and to schedule your exam.

During October through January, the GRE is available all month. However, during February through September, you can take the GRE only during the first three weeks of the month. We recommend that you register early. Some centers fill up quickly, and it's important to leave yourself enough time to retake the exam if you don't score high enough the first time you take it.

TWO ESSAY SECTIONS

The GRE Analytical Writing Measure includes two essay sections, which represent an entirely new type of GRE question. The purpose of this new question type is to measure your ability to write clear, well organized, grammatically correct English prose in a "real-life" writing situation. The Analytical Writing Measure was created in response to concerns from graduate school professors that too many entering students have weak writing skills.

The GRE Analytical Writing Measure includes two sections:

- **Present Your Perspective on an Issue** (45 minutes): You must write an essay giving your thoughts and reactions regarding an opinion statement presented by the test-makers.

- **Analyze an Argument** (30 minutes): You must write an essay in which you examine the strengths and weaknesses of a logical argument presented by the test-makers.

- The essays will be graded on a scale of 0 (lowest) to 6 (highest) by college teachers, based on their overall impression of how well you organize, develop, support, and express your ideas.

- See Chapter 12 of this book for a detailed guide to the GRE Analytical Writing Measure and a description of the best strategies to practice and use on this portion of the exam.

Part I

First Things First

Chapter 1

The Insider's Guide to the GRE Diagnostic Test

INSTRUCTIONS

The following Insider's Guide to the GRE Diagnostic Test will provide your first look at the format, contents, and difficulty levels of the GRE. It will also enable you to diagnose your strengths and weaknesses and help you focus on the skills and test areas where you have the greatest opportunity to boost your GRE scores.

This test is about the same length as the real GRE. Take it under true testing conditions. Complete the entire test in a single sitting. Eliminate distractions (TV, music) and clear away notes and reference materials.

Time each section of the test separately with a stopwatch or kitchen timer, or have someone else time you. If you run out of time before answering all the questions, stop and draw a line under the last question you finished. Then go on to the next test section. When you are done, score yourself based only on the questions you finished in the allotted time. Later, for practice purposes, you should answer the questions you were unable to complete in time.

The answer key and explanatory answers appear at the end of the test, beginning on page 38.

This diagnostic test includes the new GRE analytical writing measure. For this part of the diagnostic, you can write using a word-processing program or pencil and paper. Either way, stick with the time restrictions and other test conditions. Though you can't get an admissions officer's evaluation of your work, you will get a feel for how well you handle this part of the exam, and you can plan your preparation accordingly.

NOTE: If you are taking the GRE after September 30, 2002, take Sections 1 and 2 and skip Section 4. Otherwise skip Sections 1 and 2 and start with Section 3.

SECTION 1

ANALYTICAL WRITING MEASURE

Time—45 Minutes

PRESENT YOUR PERSPECTIVE ON AN ISSUE

In this section, you will have 45 minutes to plan and compose an essay that presents your perspective on an assigned topic. An essay on any other topic is not acceptable.

The topic will appear as a brief quotation that states or implies an issue of general interest. You are free to accept, reject, or qualify the quotation, so long as the ideas you present are clearly relevant to the topic. Support your views with reasons and/or examples drawn from such areas as your reading, experience, observation, or academic studies.

College and university faculty members from various subject matter areas will read your essay and evaluate its overall quality, based on how well you do the following:

- Consider the complexities and implications of the issue
- Organize, develop, and express your ideas
- Support your ideas with relevant reasons and/or examples
- Control the elements of standard written English

You may want to take a few minutes to think about the issue and to plan a response before you begin writing. Be sure to develop your ideas fully and organize them coherently, but leave time to reread what you have written and make any revisions that you think are necessary.

> **Directions:** Present your perspective on the issue below, using relevant reasons and/or examples to support your views.

"The use of surveillance cameras to monitor activity in public places is a valuable tool for fighting crime and poses no threat to the privacy of law-abiding citizens. After all, a person who is doing nothing wrong has nothing to fear from being observed."

SECTION 2

ANALYTICAL WRITING MEASURE

Time—30 Minutes

ANALYSIS OF AN ARGUMENT

In this section, you will have 30 minutes to plan and write a critique of an argument presented in the form of a short passage.

You will be asked to consider the logical soundness of the argument. A critique of any other argument is not acceptable.

College and university faculty members from various subject matter areas will read your critique and evaluate its overall quality, considering how well you do the following:

- Identify and analyze important features of the argument
- Organize, develop, and express your ideas
- Support your ideas with relevant reasons and/or examples
- Control the elements of standard written English

Before you begin writing, you may want to take a few minutes to evaluate the argument and to plan a response. Be sure to develop your ideas fully and organize them coherently, but leave time to reread what you have written and make any revisions that you think are necessary.

> **Directions:** For this task, you will read a brief argument and then discuss how well reasoned you find the argument. Note that you are *not* being asked to agree or disagree with the position taken or the conclusion reached by the argument. In your discussion, be sure to analyze the line of reasoning in the argument. You should consider what, if any, questionable assumptions underlie the thinking and, if evidence is cited, whether it supports the conclusion. You can also discuss the sort of evidence that would strengthen or refute the argument, changes in the argument that would make it more logically sound, and whether additional information would help you to evaluate its conclusion.

"More than half of the households in Citrus City are childless, and almost all of the voters in these households voted against this year's school budget bill, forcing dramatic reductions in public school spending. These voters, however, were shortsighted. Although childless people do not benefit directly from high-quality public schools, a strong educational system will make Citrus City an attractive place for families to live and help keep home values in the area high."

SECTION 3

VERBAL

30 Questions

Time—30 Minutes

Directions (Antonyms): Each question consists of a word printed in capital letters, followed by five lettered words or phrases. Choose the lettered word or phrase that is most nearly *opposite* in meaning to the word in capital letters.

Directions (Analogies): In each question, a related pair of words or phrases is followed by five lettered pairs of words or phrases. Select the lettered pair that best expresses a relationship similar to that expressed in the original pair.

Directions (Sentence Completions): Each sentence has one or two blanks, each blank indicating that something has been omitted. Beneath the sentence are five lettered words or sets of words. Choose the word or set of words for each blank that *best* fits the meaning of the sentence as a whole.

Directions (Reading Comprehension): Each passage is followed by questions based on its content. After reading a passage, choose the best answer to each question. Answer all questions following a passage on the basis of what is *stated* or *implied* in the passage.

---

1. CENSUS : POPULATION ::

   (A) index : information
   (B) catalog : salesperson
   (C) collection : specimens
   (D) inventory : merchandise
   (E) score : competition

2. PREVALENT:

   (A) weak
   (B) indecisive
   (C) vitiated
   (D) rare
   (E) notable

3. JUXTAPOSE:

   (A) discard
   (B) pronounce
   (C) vacillate
   (D) reply
   (E) separate

4. Fearing discovery, the dissenters held the meeting _____;
   those in attendance were warned not to _____ the meeting
   time, place, or the subjects of discussion.

   (A) secretly..forget
   (B) surreptitiously..suppress
   (C) quickly..reveal
   (D) clandestinely..disclose
   (E) covertly..deny

5. WOOL : SHEEP ::

   (A) down : duck
   (B) cotton : field
   (C) linen : cloth
   (D) tusk : boar
   (E) leather : shoe

6. SONG : DIRGE ::

   (A) dance : march
   (B) literature : novel
   (C) music : ditty
   (D) poem : elegy
   (E) painting : portrait

7. Although thousands of people die every year as a result of rabies, the disease is _____ in the United States thanks to the fact that dogs and other pets that are potential sources of the disease are _____.

    (A) unusual..quarantined
    (B) severe..widespread
    (C) rare..inoculated
    (D) atypical..uncommon
    (E) benign..vaccinated

8. MISCARRY:

    (A) conduct
    (B) promote
    (C) manage
    (D) succeed
    (E) transport

Questions 9–10 refer to the following passage.

Line   Community cancer clusters are viewed quite differently by citizen activists than by epidemiologists. Environmentalists and concerned local residents, for instance, might immediately suspect environmental radiation as the culprit when a high incidence of cancer cases occurs near a nuclear facility.
(5)   Epidemiologists, in contrast, would be more likely to say that the incidences were "inconclusive" or the result of pure chance. And when a breast cancer survivor, Lorraine Pace, mapped twenty breast cancer cases occurring in her West Islip, Long Island, community, her rudimentary research efforts were guided more by hope—that a specific environmental agent could be correlated
(10)   with the cancers—than by scientific method.
    When epidemiologists study clusters of cancer cases and other noncontagious conditions such as birth defects or miscarriage, they take several variables into account, such as background rate (the number of people affected in the general population), cluster size, and specificity (any notable character-
(15)   istics of the individual affected in each case). If a cluster is both large and specific, it is easier for epidemiologists to assign blame. Not only must each variable be considered on its own, but it must also be combined with others. Lung cancer is very common in the general population. Yet, when a huge number of cases turned up among World War II shipbuilders who had all worked
(20)   with asbestos, the size of the cluster and the fact that the men had had similar occupational asbestos exposures enabled epidemiologists to assign blame to the fibrous mineral.
    Furthermore, even if a cluster seems too small to be analyzed conclusively, it may still yield important data if the background rate of the condition is low
(25)   enough. This was the case when a certain vaginal cancer turned up almost simultaneously in a half-dozen young women. While six would seem to be too small a cluster for meaningful study, the cancer had been reported only once or twice before in the entire medical literature. Researchers eventually found that the mothers of all the afflicted women had taken the drug diethystilbestrol (DES)
(30)   while pregnant.

9. The "hope" mentioned in line 9 refers specifically to Pace's desire to

   (A) help reduce the incidence of breast cancer in future generations.
   (B) improve her chances of surviving breast cancer.
   (C) determine the culprit responsible for her own breast cancer case.
   (D) refute the dismissive statements of epidemiologists concerning her research efforts.
   (E) identify a particular cause for the breast cancer cases in West Islip.

10. The case of six young women with vaginal cancer (lines 25–26) is an example of a cluster that has

    (A) a high background rate and is fairly specific.
    (B) a low background rate and is fairly specific.
    (C) a high background rate and small size.
    (D) a low background rate and inconclusive cluster size.
    (E) a low background rate and is nonspecific.

11. The article presented the commander's courage as _____; it _____ his actions on the battlefield and even implied that others should follow in his footsteps.

    (A) rash..denigrated
    (B) exemplary..glorified
    (C) spurious..praised
    (D) noteworthy..analyzed
    (E) questionable..revered

12. Scientists who have been working for years to _____ the ongoing AIDS epidemic were _____ last year when a new regime of drugs was introduced that seems to lessen some of the worst symptoms.

    (A) end..successful
    (B) eliminate..surprised
    (C) overcome..cheerful
    (D) control..thwarted
    (E) combat..encouraged

13. PROSCENIUM : CURTAIN ::

    (A) fence : gate
    (B) house : facade
    (C) movie : screen
    (D) doorway : lintel
    (E) window : shade

14. REVOKE:
    (A) grant
    (B) placate
    (C) predict
    (D) deploy
    (E) lend

15. SANCTIFY:
    (A) destroy
    (B) desecrate
    (C) abominate
    (D) deny
    (E) renege

Questions 16–18 refer to the following passage.

Line The strength of the film lay in its own ingenuity and invention. And this in every instance originated in cinema's role of entertaining a large and avid public. A generation of filmmakers grew up whose essential vision belonged to no other medium than that of the cinema and whose public was a universal audience
(5) spread across the world. Like the first dramas of Shakespeare, their art was not a product of the *salon,* but of the common playhouse. This is what gave them their strength and freshness.

However, there has always been a price to be paid. The *salon* artist has only a known patron, or group of patrons, to satisfy, and if he is strong enough
(10) he can, like the painters of the Renaissance, mold their taste in the image of his own. This can also be true of the greater and more resolute artists of the cinema, from Chaplin in the 1920s to, say, Bergman or Antonioni in the sixties. But the larger the dimension of the public and the more costly the medium to produce, the greater are the pressures brought to bear on the less conventional creator to
(15) make his work conform to the pattern of the more conventional creator.

16. According to the passage, the pressures to conform that a filmmaker experiences are in proportion to the

    (A) difficulty of finding the support of a patron.
    (B) cost of producing a film.
    (C) conservatism of the viewing audience.
    (D) personal talents of the filmmaker.
    (E) diversity of the filmgoing public.

17. The reference in the passage to the dramas of Shakespeare is intended to emphasize certain filmmakers'

    (A) awareness of the role of film as a profit-making enterprise.
    (B) strength of personality and artistic convictions.
    (C) independence from the restrictions of other art forms.
    (D) enjoyment of a large and supportive audience.
    (E) plebeian family backgrounds and social origins.

18. The author refers to the films of Bergman and Antonioni primarily because they are

    (A) unconventional.
    (B) ingenious.
    (C) satisfying.
    (D) popular.
    (E) well crafted.

19. MOTORCADE : CAR ::
    (A) flotilla : ship
    (B) train : caboose
    (C) parade : bandleader
    (D) caravan : merchandise
    (E) panorama : vista

20. MONEY : IMPECUNIOUS ::
    (A) cruelty : ruthless
    (B) bias : disinterested
    (C) content : amorphous
    (D) luxury : opulent
    (E) energy : indefatigable

21. EQUANIMITY:
    (A) puzzlement
    (B) violence
    (C) skepticism
    (D) irritability
    (E) rejection

22. The city police _____ the riots relatively quickly, but the
    sometimes brutal tactics they seemed to aim particularly at
    members of certain ethnic groups gave them a reputation for
    _____ that lingers today.
    (A) investigated..bigotry
    (B) prevented..malevolence
    (C) pacified..tolerance
    (D) denounced..mediocrity
    (E) quelled..racism

Questions 23–25 refer to the following passage.

Line   If you've ever cupped your hand around a blinking firefly or noticed an eerie
       glow in the ocean at night, you are familiar with the phenomenon of
       bioluminescence. The ability of certain plants and animals to emit light has long
       been a source of fascination to humans. Why do certain species of mushrooms
(5)   glow? Why are midwater squids designed with ornate light-emitting organs
       underneath their eyes and ink glands? Why do certain particles and biological
       detritus floating in the depths of the ocean sparkle after a physical disturbance?
       Are these light displays simply an example of nature in its most flamboyant
       mode—a case of "if you've got it, flaunt it"—or do they serve any practical
(10)   purposes?

       As it turns out, the manifestations of bioluminescence are as diverse as
       they are elegant. Yet virtually all of the known or proposed ways in which
       bioluminescence functions may be classed under three major rubrics: assisting
       predation, helping escape from predators, and communicating.
(15)   Many examples of the first two uses can be observed in the ocean's
       midwaters, a zone that extends from about 100 meters deep to a few kilometers
       below the surface. Almost all of the animals that inhabit the murky depths where
       sunlight barely penetrates are capable of producing light in one way or another.
       Certain animals, when feeding, are attracted to a spot of light as a possible food
(20)   source. Hence, other animals use their own luminescence to attract them. Just in
       front of the angler fish's mouth is a dangling luminescent ball suspended from a
       structure attached to its head. What unwitting marine creatures see as food is
       really a bait to lure them into the angler fish's gaping maw.

       The uses of luminescence to elude prey are just as sophisticated and
(25)   various. Some creatures take advantage of the scant sunlight in their realm by
       using bioluminescence as a form of camouflage. The glow generated by
       photophores, light-producing organs, on the undersides of some fishes and
       squids acts to hide them through a phenomenon known as countershading: the
       weak downward lighting created by the photophores effectively erases the
(30)   animals' shadows when viewed from below against the (relatively) lighted
       waters above.

       Some marine animals use bioluminescence more actively in their own
       defense, turning their predators into prey. For instance, there is the so-called
       "burglar alarm effect," in which an animal coats an advancing predator with
(35)   sticky glowing tissue that makes the would-be attacker vulnerable to visually
       cued hunters—like bank robbers marked by exploding dye packets hidden in
       stolen currency.

23. The angler fish's use of bioluminescence in predation is most nearly analogous to
    (A) a deer hunter's use of a flashlight to find his way in a dark and overgrown forest.
    (B) an exterminator's use of insecticide to poison the insects that have infested a home.
    (C) a duck hunter's use of a reed-shielded blind as a hiding place from which to shoot at ducks.
    (D) a trout fisherman's use of a lure designed to resemble an insect that trout love to eat.
    (E) a police detective's use of a bright lamp to blind and so intimidate a suspect during questioning.

24. Each of the following statements about the use of bioluminescence in countershading is true EXCEPT
    (A) The light given off by photophores underneath certain fish and squid makes the animals appear to blend in with the sunlit waters above them.
    (B) Bioluminescence allows the parts of an animal normally in shadow to appear lighter.
    (C) Countershading is one of several ways in which bioluminescence is used to avoid predation.
    (D) Countershading is used most effectively in regions of relatively weak sunlight.
    (E) Bioluminescent animals use countershading as a way to elude predators that lurk in the sunlit waters above them.

25. The reference to bank robbers in lines 32–37 serves mainly to
    (A) distinguish between two phenomena that appear similar but are fundamentally different.
    (B) suggest a practical application for recent discoveries from natural science.
    (C) point out the weaknesses in one proposed solution to a scientific conundrum.
    (D) explain how scientists developed a theory concerning the underlying purpose of a natural phenomenon.
    (E) clarify a phenomenon of the animal world by comparing it to human behavior.

26. MORIBUND:
    (A) carefree
    (B) disdainful
    (C) mobile
    (D) sanguine
    (E) vigorous

27. APPOSITE:

    (A) similar
    (B) vague
    (C) irrelevant
    (D) noteworthy
    (E) concerned

28. ASSIDUOUS:

    (A) loquacious
    (B) deliberate
    (C) gallant
    (D) sporadic
    (E) lazy

29. The fennec uses its huge six-inch-long ears to _____ its prey by lurking and listening quietly for its whereabouts; they are also an aid to desert survival, as they help _____ the otherwise unbearable heat.

    (A) locate..dissipate
    (B) obtain..intensify
    (C) trap..radiate
    (D) scare..dispel
    (E) capture..reduce

30. IMMUNE : DISEASE ::

    (A) invisible : senses
    (B) afflicted : suffering
    (C) curable : illness
    (D) impregnable : attack
    (E) vulnerable : defense

SECTION 4

ANALYTICAL

35 Questions

Time—60 Minutes

> **Directions:** Each question or group of questions is based on a passage or set of conditions. In answering some of the questions, it may be useful to draw a rough diagram. For each question, select the best answer choice given.

1. Studies over the last 20 years have shown that virtually all babies born to drug-addicted mothers are themselves addicted to drugs. No such correlation, however, has been shown between drug-addicted fathers and their newborn children. It would appear, then, that drug addiction is a genetically inherited trait that is gender-linked and passed through the mother.

    All of the following, if true, would weaken the argument above EXCEPT

    (A) Although some biological conditions have been shown to be genetically based, drug addiction is not among them.

    (B) Drug addiction is an acquired condition that cannot be passed on from a mother to her children.

    (C) Prior to the recent development of DNA testing, while maternity was unquestionable, paternity could not be positively determined.

    (D) There have been instances in which drug-addicted babies have been born to addicted fathers and nonaddicted mothers.

    (E) Very few studies regarding fathers of drug-addicted babies have been conducted.

2. The major issue of the 1860 American presidential campaign was the extension of slavery into the territories. Of that year's four candidates, Republican Abraham Lincoln was against extension; Northern Democrat Stephen A. Douglas, Southern Democrat John C. Breckinridge, and Constitutional Union candidate John Bell all favored it. Lincoln won the popular vote with 1,800,000, but his opponents together garnered more than 2,850,000 votes. Lincoln was named president by the electoral college.

   All of the following conclusions can be reasonably drawn from the information above EXCEPT

   (A)   Lincoln won the election largely because voters who opposed his political views were split among the other three candidates.

   (B)   Despite—or due to—his stand on slavery extension, Lincoln was the most popular single candidate in the presidential election.

   (C)   None of the other issues in the campaign contributed significantly to the final result of the election.

   (D)   The Democratic party failed to win the election because its supporters were split between Douglas and Breckinridge.

   (E)   The extension of slavery was a crucial issue in the presidential election of 1860.

3. When the three original *Star Wars* films were rereleased in 1996 and 1997, their producer, George Lucas, expected them to enjoy respectable revenues at the nation's movie box offices. In fact, however, each of the three films had a commanding lead in ticket sales during the first weekend on which it was shown.

   Which of the following statements, if true, would be LEAST likely to help account for the information presented above?

   (A)   None of the other films released on the same weekends as the *Star Wars* films featured a major box-office star.

   (B)   Despite his expertise in the movie industry, Lucas seriously misjudged the extent of the public's interest in his films.

   (C)   The announced release of three new *Star Wars* movies helped rekindle the public's interest in the original films.

   (D)   It had been so long since the original *Star Wars* films had been released that there was a whole generation of moviegoers that had never seen them in theaters.

   (E)   Several actors from the original *Star Wars* films had recently appeared in highly touted but unsuccessful films.

Questions 4–7 refer to the following:

Six sculptures—C, D, E, F, G, and H—are to be exhibited in rooms 1, 2, and 3 of an art gallery.

Sculptures C and E may not be exhibited in the same room.

Sculptures D and G must be exhibited in the same room.

If sculptures E and F are exhibited in the same room, no other sculpture may be exhibited in that room.

At least one sculpture must be exhibited in each room, and no more than three sculptures may be exhibited in any room.

4. If sculpture D is exhibited in room 1 and sculptures E and F are exhibited in room 2, which of the following must be true?

   (A) Sculpture C must be exhibited in room 1.
   (B) Sculpture H must be exhibited in room 3.
   (C) Sculpture G must be exhibited in room 1.
   (D) Sculpture H must be exhibited in room 2.
   (E) Sculptures C and H must be exhibited in the same room.

5. If sculptures C and G are exhibited in room 1, which of the following may NOT be a complete list of the sculpture(s) exhibited in room 2?

   (A) Sculpture D
   (B) Sculpture E
   (C) Sculpture F
   (D) Sculptures E and H
   (E) Sculptures F and H

6. If sculpture D is exhibited in room 3 and sculptures E and F are exhibited in room 1, which of the following must be true?

   (A) Sculpture C is exhibited in room 1.
   (B) Sculpture H is exhibited in room 1
   (C) Sculpture G is exhibited in room 2.
   (D) Sculptures C and H are exhibited in the same room.
   (E) Sculptures G and F are exhibited in the same room.

7. If sculpture G is exhibited in room 2 and sculpture E is exhibited in room 3, which of the following must be true?

   (A) Sculpture C is exhibited in room 1.
   (B) No more than two sculptures are exhibited in room 3.
   (C) Sculptures F and H are exhibited in the same room.
   (D) Three sculptures are exhibited in room 2.
   (E) Sculpture H is exhibited in room 3.

8. In 1962, when the Pennsylvania Railroad announced plans to tear down New York's Pennsylvania Station, an architectural gem completed in 1910 and designed by one of America's preeminent architectural firms, civic groups rose in protest. Nevertheless, the building was demolished the following year. In 1965, New York City established its Landmarks Preservation Commission, which was followed by the establishment of similar commissions around the country.

   All of the following conclusions, if true, would help account for the events described above EXCEPT

   (A) Only the razing of a building as famous as Pennsylvania Station was sufficient to rouse the public's interest in landmark preservation.

   (B) There was no public interest in preserving America's architectural heritage prior to 1962.

   (C) Several other significant urban landmarks had been torn down in the years just prior to the railroad's announcement.

   (D) New York City is considered by other cities to be a leader in cultural affairs.

   (E) Civic groups are, on occasion, able to bring about important changes in the urban policies of American cities.

9. Anatole France's often-quoted statement, "The only books I have in my library are those which people have lent me" would seem to justify the fear of those who love books that, once lent, they are unlikely to be returned.

   Which of the following, if true, most strengthens the argument above?

   (A) France was considered by those who knew him to be unusually remiss in returning books.

   (B) Most people who borrow books return them after a reasonable period of time.

   (C) Only a small percentage of borrowed books are ever returned to their owners.

   (D) Many book lovers are eager to share their pleasure in particular books with others.

   (E) France made his statement because he thought it would be entertaining rather than because it was true.

Questions 10–13 refer to the following:

Seven trees of species M, N, O, R, T, X, and W are to be planted in a row along a garden path.

Species R must be planted third in the row.

Species X must be planted sixth in the row.

Species N and T must be planted with exactly one tree between them.

Species M and W may not be planted next to one another.

10. Which of the following is an acceptable planting sequence?
 (A) N, O, T, R, M, X, W
 (B) M, W, R, O, N, X, T
 (C) T, N, R, W, O, X, M
 (D) W, O, R, T, M, N, X
 (E) O, T, R, N, W, X, M

11. If species M is planted fifth in the row, species N could be planted
 (A) first.
 (B) second.
 (C) third.
 (D) sixth.
 (E) seventh.

12. If species W is planted first in the row and species T is planted fifth, which of the following must be true?
 (A) Species M is planted second.
 (B) Species O is planted second.
 (C) Species N is planted fourth.
 (D) Species M is planted seventh.
 (E) Species O is planted seventh.

13. If species M is planted fourth in the row, which species could be planted second?
 (A) N
 (B) O
 (C) R
 (D) T
 (E) X

14. From the time they burst onto the music scene in England in 1962 until they disbanded in 1969, the Beatles were the most popular rock group the world had ever seen. They were also the best, because while their music retained its characteristic style, each new album was different and exhibited a steadily increasing depth and sophistication.

The argument above requires all of the following assumptions EXCEPT

(A) Prior to 1962, there had never been a rock group with as large a following as the Beatles.

(B) Each member of The Beatles was individually more talented than his counterparts in other popular rock groups.

(C) Prior to the Beatles, no other rock group had retained its unique style while exhibiting the same degree of musical growth.

(D) Increasing depth and sophistication are evidence of a musical group's extraordinary talent.

(E) To attain true greatness in music, it is essential that a group develop and retain a recognizable style.

Questions 15–18 refer to the following:

A musical workshop that restores used theremins operates according to the following schedule:

A theremin is examined three calendar days after it is received in the workshop. (Thus, if it is received on the first day of the month, it is examined on the fourth.) On the next Monday following the examination, the theremin is delivered to the restoration room.

Restoration work may be finished one, two, or three calendar days after the theremin is delivered to the restoration room. On the next Wednesday following the completion of the restoration work, the theremin cover is varnished. Two calendar days later, the varnish is dry and the theremin may be shipped. All restored theremins are shipped at the close of business on the 15th or the 30th day of the month.

This year, the first day of the month of January is a Friday.

15. If the workshop receives a steady supply of used theremins, on how many days during January will theremin cover varnishing take place?

    (A) Two
    (B) Three
    (C) Four
    (D) Five
    (E) Six

16. If a used theremin is received at the workshop on Tuesday January 5th, its restoration work will be completed no later than

    (A) Monday the 11th.
    (B) Wednesday the 13th.
    (C) Thursday the 14th.
    (D) Friday the 15th.
    (E) Wednesday the 20th.

17. In order to be certain that a restored theremin will be shipped from the workshop on January 30th, what is the latest date by which it may be received at the workshop?

    (A) Thursday the 14th
    (B) Friday the 15th
    (C) Saturday the 16th
    (D) Monday the 18th
    (E) Tuesday the 19th

18. The longest delay in shipping a restored theremin will involve a theremin whose cover varnish dries on

    (A) January 1st.
    (B) January 8th.
    (C) January 15th.
    (D) January 22nd.
    (E) January 29th.

19. The Hudson River, which flows through New York State from its source in the Adirondack Mountains through New York City, was so polluted two decades ago that only the most foolhardy dared go near it. Today, however, thousands of local inhabitants and tourists engage in a wide range of water sports on the river.

Which of the following, if true, is the most likely explanation for the facts presented above?

(A) There has been a significant increase in tourism in the Hudson River region.

(B) Some twenty years ago, local conservation groups mounted a major effort to clean up the waters of the Hudson.

(C) More people today live within five miles of the banks of the Hudson River than ever before.

(D) Surveys suggest that most local residents no longer regard pollution in the Hudson as a major problem.

(E) More people are interested in water sports today than in the past.

20. One of the first American authors to use a typewriter was Mark Twain. This enabled him to write faster than other authors, make changes more easily, get his manuscripts to his publisher faster, see them published sooner, and, consequently, become one of the most popular authors of his day.

All of the following, if true, are valid objections to the argument above EXCEPT

(A) many of the other popular authors of Mark Twain's time also used typewriters to write their books.

(B) using a typewriter does not necessarily enable a writer to finish a book sooner.

(C) the means by which a manuscript is delivered to a publisher is not affected by the manner in which it is written.

(D) having books published more quickly than other authors does not ensure a writer's popularity.

(E) making changes in a typewritten manuscript is no easier than making changes in a handwritten one.

Questions 21–24 refer to the following:

At a certain resort, seven theme parks—F, G, H, J, K, L, and Q—are connected by a network of one-way monorail lines. Three trains travel these lines according to the following routes, which they repeat throughout the day:

Train 1 travels from F to J to K to Q, and then back to F.

Train 2 travels from J to G to H, and then back to J.

Train 3 travels from H to L to Q, and then back to H.

21. A tourist at K who wishes to travel by monorail to any other park at the resort must travel to

   (A) G
   (B) H
   (C) J
   (D) L
   (E) Q

22. A tourist may travel without changing trains from

   (A) G to F
   (B) H to K
   (C) H to Q
   (D) L to J
   (E) Q to G

23. What is the minimum number of intermediate stops for a tourist traveling from F to L?

   (A) One
   (B) Two
   (C) Three
   (D) Four
   (E) Five

24. A tourist at J wishes to travel to K. If she leaves J aboard train 2, the route she should follow subsequently to arrive at K with the fewest intermediate stops passes through

   (A) F
   (B) J
   (C) L
   (D) Q
   (E) None of the above

25. Compared to older houses, new houses are sure to have newer, more efficient heating and cooling units, more modern kitchen appliances, and more contemporary-style bathroom fixtures. They also generally conform to the most up-to-date code regulations. It is accordingly always advantageous to purchase a new house rather than an old one.

Which of the following is the best criticism of the argument above?

(A) When an older house is sold, correcting any code violations is the responsibility of the seller.

(B) As a rule, older houses have more of the kind of details that lend charm to a home than do new houses.

(C) Some people prefer more traditional styles of bathroom fixtures.

(D) New equipment and fixtures are not the only factors home buyers consider when choosing a house.

(E) New houses are generally more expensive than older houses of comparable size.

Questions 26–29 refer to the following:

An animal shelter houses eighteen puppies in three kennels, six puppies to a kennel. There are puppies of three colors: white, brown, and gray.

The number of white puppies in the shelter is exactly twice the number of brown puppies.

Each kennel contains at least one gray puppy.

26. Each of the following could be the number of white puppies in the shelter EXCEPT

(A) 4
(B) 5
(C) 6
(D) 8
(E) 10

27. If Kennel A contains exactly one gray puppy and no white puppies, the number of white puppies in Kennel C must be

(A) 1
(B) 2
(C) 3
(D) 4
(E) 5

28. If each kennel contains a different number of white puppies, and no kennel contains more than three white puppies, the number of gray puppies in the shelter may be

    (A) 5
    (B) 6
    (C) 9
    (D) 10
    (E) 11

29. If each kennel contains at least one brown puppy, and the number of brown puppies in Kennel A is three times the number of brown puppies in Kennel C, the number of white puppies in Kennel B must be

    (A) 1
    (B) 2
    (C) 3
    (D) 4
    (E) 5

30. In the closing days of the Civil War, President Abraham Lincoln was planning to graciously welcome the defeated Confederate states back into the Union. After Lincoln was assassinated, however, the "Radical Republicans" in Congress imposed martial law in the South, creating resentment that caused problems well into this century. Had Lincoln lived, the history of regional conflict in twentieth-century America would have been considerably different.

    All of the following assumptions underlie the argument above EXCEPT

    (A) the imposition of martial law in the South was primarily responsible for the resentment felt in the South.
    (B) had he lived, Lincoln would have treated the defeated South as he had planned.
    (C) Lincoln would have been able to prevent the Radical Republicans in Congress from imposing martial law in the South.
    (D) factors other than the imposition of martial law in the South affected the history of regional conflicts in twentieth-century America.
    (E) had Lincoln been able to carry out his plans, people in the southern states would have felt less resentment toward the Union.

Questions 31–34 refer to the following:

At a dinner party, four married couples are seated around a circular table with eight seats, numbered 1 through 8. The four couples are B and T, C and R, E and W, and F and Y. (In each case, the wife is listed first, the husband second.) In seating the eight people, wives and husbands must be seated alternately, and a married couple may not be seated together. In addition:

E and R may not be seated together.

C and Y must be seated together.

31. Which of the following is an acceptable seating arrangement, from seat 1 through seat 8?

    (A) B, E, F, R, C, Y, T, W
    (B) B, W, C, Y, E, T, F, R
    (C) C, W, R, F, T, E, Y, B
    (D) F, T, E, R, C, Y, B, W
    (E) T, E, Y, C, R, F, W, B

32. If R is in seat 1 and Y is in seat 5, which of the following may NOT be true?

    (A) B is in seat 2.
    (B) C in in seat 4.
    (C) E is in seat 8.
    (D) T is in seat 7.
    (E) W is in seat 7.

33. If C is in seat 1 and W is in seat 4, who is in seat 3?

    (A) B or E
    (B) E or F
    (C) R or R
    (D) R or Y
    (E) T or Y

34. If the husbands are seated in alphabetical order in seats 1, 3, 5, and 7, what is the order in which the wives are seated in seats 2, 4, 6, and 8?

    (A) B, C, E, F
    (B) B, E, C, F
    (C) C, B, F, E
    (D) E, F, C, B
    (E) F, C, E, B

35. Rock and roll music started in the 1950s as a young man's medium, and rock is still best performed by men in their twenties and thirties. As rock performers grow into their forties, and even fifties, they are simply less physically capable of producing the kind of exciting music they did when they were younger.

All of the following assumptions underlie the argument above EXCEPT

(A) as rock performers mature, their performances tend to become less exciting.

(B) rock music is dominated by male performers.

(C) women performers have always played a significant role in rock music.

(D) the physical demands of performing rock are better met by the young.

(E) those who played rock music in its earliest days are no longer among its best performers.

SECTION 5

QUANTITATIVE

28 Questions

Time—45 Minutes

Directions (Multiple-Choice): Each question has five answer choices. For each question, select the best of the answer choices given.

Numbers: All numbers used are real numbers.

Figures: Position of points, angles, regions, etc. can be assumed to be in the order shown; and angle measures can be assumed to be positive.

Lines shown as straight can be assumed to be straight.

Figures can be assumed to lie in a plane unless otherwise indicated.

Figures that accompany questions are intended to provide information useful in answering the questions. However, unless a note states that a figure is drawn to scale, you should solve these problems NOT by estimating sizes by sight or by measurement, but by using your knowledge of mathematics.

Directions (Quantitative Comparisons): Each question consists of two quantities, one in Column A and one in Column B. You are to compare the two quantities and choose

   (A)   if the quantity in Column A is greater;
   (B)   if the quantity in Column B is greater;
   (C)   if the two quantities are equal;
   (D)   if the relationship cannot be determined from the information given.

Note: Since there are only four choices, NEVER MARK (E).

Common Information: In a question, information concerning one or both of the quantities to be compared is centered above the two columns. A symbol that appears in both columns represents the same thing in Column A as it does in Column B.

---

1. If the fraction $\dfrac{60}{N}$ has been simplified to simplest form, which of the following numbers may be a factor of N?

   (A) 25
   (B) 27
   (C) 49
   (D) 110
   (E) 213

Column A	**Column B**

The original price of a computer was $1200

2.
The price of the computer after two 10% markdowns	The price of the computer after a 20% markdown

3. Margaret earns an average of 88 on her first four calculus exams. To get a grade of A in the course, she must have a 90 average. What grade must Margaret earn on her next calculus exam to raise her average to 90?

   (A) 98
   (B) 96
   (C) 94
   (D) 92
   (E) 90

<table>
<tr><td>Column A</td><td>Column B</td></tr>
</table>

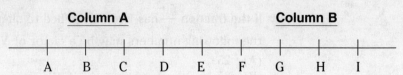

Note: The vertical marks in the figure above are equally spaced.

4.

The ratio of AF to BD	The ratio of BH to CF

---

5. The ratio of passing to failing students in a certain class is 5:2. Which of the following could be the total number of students in the class?

    (A) 12
    (B) 15
    (C) 21
    (D) 30
    (E) 34

Column A   **Column B**

$$0 < n < 1$$

6.

$n \times n \times n$	$n + n + n$

---

7. Three consecutive integers are written in increasing order. If the sum of the first and second integers and twice the third integer is 93, what is the second integer?

    (A) 37
    (B) 34
    (C) 24
    (D) 23
    (E) 22

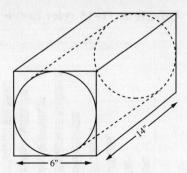

8. The block of wood shown in the figure above is a rectangular solid 14 inches long with a square base that is 6 inches on a side. A right circular cylinder is drilled out of the block as shown. To the nearest cubic inch, what is the volume of the remaining wood?

(A) 54
(B) 108
(C) 396
(D) 485
(E) 495

Column A	Column B
9.	
The cost of 12 cans of peas at 34¢ apiece	The cost of 12 cans of corn at 3 for $1.00

$$3y - 6 = 2 - y$$

10.	
y^2	$2y$

Questions 11–15 refer to the following graphs.

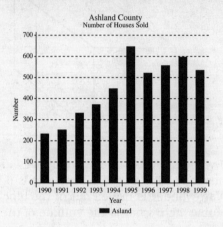

Ashland County
Number of Houses Sold

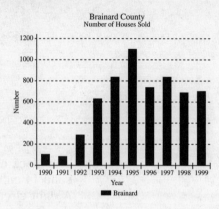

Brainard County
Number of Houses Sold

Ashland and Brainard
Sales in Millions of Dollars

11. What was the total number of houses sold in Ashland County and Brainard County in 1994?

(A) 820
(B) 1010
(C) 1070
(D) 1280
(E) 1720

12. In how many years did the number of houses sold in Ashland County exceed the number sold in Brainard County?

(A) 2
(B) 3
(C) 4
(D) 5
(E) 6

13. In which year did the average sales price per house in Ashland County fall below $100,000?

    (A) 1992
    (B) 1993
    (C) 1996
    (D) 1998
    (E) 1999

14. By approximately what percent did the number of houses sold in Brainard County decrease from 1995 to 1996?

    (A) 10%
    (B) 15%
    (C) 20%
    (D) 25%
    (E) 35%

15. What was the approximate average sales price per house in the two counties combined in 1995?

    (A) $70,000
    (B) $79,000
    (C) $91,000
    (D) $99,000
    (E) $110,000

Column A	**Column B**

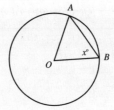

O is the center of the circle with diameter 10.
The perimeter of $AOB = 16$.

16.

x	60

Column A	Column B

In a row of blocks, the only black block is the 7th from the left end of the row and the 11th from the right end of the row.

17.

The number of blocks in the row	18

18. In a group of 20 singers and 40 dancers, 20% of the singers are under 25 years old, and 40% of the entire group are under 25 years old. What percentage of the dancers are under 25 years old?

(A) 20%
(B) 40%
(C) 50%
(D) 60%
(E) 80%

Column A	Column B

a, b, and c are positive.
$c < b$

19.

The arithmetic mean (average) of a and b	The arithmetic mean (average) of a, b, and c

Column A   **Column B**

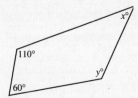

Note: Figure not drawn to scale.

20.

x	$180 - y$

---

a is chosen from the set A = {−1, −6, 3}
b is chosen from the set B = {−4, 4, 5}

21.

The largest possible value of $\dfrac{a}{b}$	1.5

---

22. The price of 4 rolls, 6 muffins, and 3 loaves of bread at a certain
bakery is $9.10. The price of 2 rolls, 3 muffins, and a loaf of bread
at the same bakery is $3.90. What is the price of a loaf of bread at
this bakery?

(A) $1.05
(B) $1.10
(C) $1.20
(D) $1.25
(E) $1.30

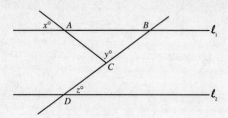

	Column A	**Column B**

$\ell_1 \parallel \ell_2$

23.

$x + y + z$	180

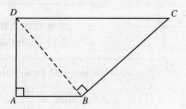

24. In the figure above, $AB = 3$, $AD = 4$, and $BC = 12$. What is the perimeter of the quadrilateral $ABCD$?

    (A) 32
    (B) 30
    (C) 28
    (D) 26
    (E) 24

Column A	Column B

Five more than twice a number n is 17.

25.

3 less than n	2 less than $\dfrac{1}{2}n$

One side of a rectangle is the diameter of a circle.
The opposite side of the rectangle is tangent to the circle.

26.

The perimeter of the rectangle	The circumference of the circle

---

$x > 0$

27.

$\sqrt{x} + 2x$	$2\sqrt{x} + x$

---

28. If x and y are positive integers, and $2x + y = 7$, which of the following is the value of $4x^2 - y^2$?

(A) 0
(B) 6
(C) 14
(D) 15
(E) 35

Answer Key

SECTIONS 1 AND 2—ANALYTICAL WRITING MEASURE

On the real GRE, your essays will be graded on a scale of 0 (lowest) to 6 (highest) by the "holistic" method—that is, a single score will be assigned to each essay based on the overall impression it makes on the reader. See Chapter 12 for more information on the holistic scoring system and how to evaluate your own writing in the light of the GRE scoring criteria.

Section 3 Verbal		Section 4 Analytical		Section 5 Quantitative	
1. D	16. B	1. D	19. B	1. C	15. C
2. D	17. D	2. C	20. A	2. A	16. B
3. E	18. A	3. E	21. E	3. A	17. B
4. D	19. A	4. C	22. C	4. A	18. C
5. A	20. B	5. A	23. C	5. C	19. D
6. D	21. D	6. D	24. B	6. B	20. A
7. C	22. E	7. B	25. D	7. D	21. C
8. D	23. D	8. B	26. B	8. B	22. E
9. E	24. E	9. C	27. E	9. A	23. C
10. B	25. E	10. E	28. C	10. C	24. A
11. B	26. E	11. B	29. D	11. D	25. A
12. E	27. C	12. B	30. D	12. B	26. B
13. E	28. E	13. B	31. B	13. C	27. D
14. A	29. A	14. B	32. C	14. E	28. E
15. B	30. D	15. C	33. B		
		16. C	34. D		
		17. A	35. C		
		18. A			

Scoring Guide

COMPUTING YOUR SCALED SCORES

Verbal

Count the number of correct answers you chose for the questions in Section 3. Write the total here: _____. This is your Verbal Raw Score.

Look up your Verbal Raw Score on the Score Conversion Table (page 40). Find the corresponding Verbal Scaled Score and write it here: _____.

Analytical

Count the number of correct answers you chose for the questions in Section 4. Write the total here: _____. This is your Analytical Raw Score.

Look up your Analytical Raw Score on the Score Conversion Table (page 40). Find the corresponding Analytical Scaled Score and write it here: _____.

Quantitative

Count the number of correct answers you chose for the questions in Section 5. Write the total here: _____. This is your Quantitative Raw Score.

Look up your Quantitative Raw Score on the Score Conversion Table (page 40). Find the corresponding Quantitative Scaled Score and write it here: _____.

Score Conversion Table

Insider's Guide to the GRE Diagnostic Test

Raw Score	Verbal Scaled Score	Analytical Scaled Score	Quantitative Scaled Score
35		800	
34		780	
33		760	
32		740	
31		720	
30	800	700	
29	780	680	
28	750	660	800
27	720	650	780
26	700	640	750
25	680	620	720
24	660	610	700
23	640	600	680
22	620	590	660
21	600	580	640
20	590	570	620
19	580	560	610
18	570	540	600
17	560	520	590
16	540	510	570
15	520	500	560
14	500	480	540
13	480	460	520
12	460	440	500
11	440	420	480
10	420	400	450
9	400	380	430
8	380	360	400
7	360	340	380
6	340	320	350
5	320	300	330
4	300	280	300
3	270	260	280
2	250	240	250
1	230	220	230
0	200	200	200

Explanatory Answers

SECTION 3

1. **The correct answer is (D).** Just as a *census* is a methodical count of a nation's population, so an *inventory* is a methodical count of the merchandise held in a store or warehouse.

2. **The correct answer is (D).** *Prevalent* means widespread, dominant, or commonplace; when we say that illiteracy was prevalent in the middle ages, we mean that most people then could not read or write. The opposite would be *unusual, uncommon,* or *rare.*

3. **The correct answer is (E).** To juxtapose two things is to put them next to each other; the opposite is to part or separate them.

4. **The correct answer is (D).** We're looking for word choices here that would fit the cause-and-effect structure of the sentence. If the dissenters were afraid of being discovered, then it would make sense for them to hold the meeting "clandestinely" and warn one another not to "disclose" information about it.

5. **The correct answer is (A).** Wool is a substance that is removed from the outside of a sheep and used in making clothing; similarly, down is a substance removed from the outside of a duck and also used in making clothing.

6. **The correct answer is (D).** A dirge is a particular kind of song—one written to express sorrow over some sad event, such as a death. An elegy is a particular kind of poem—one written to commemorate a person who has died.

7. **The correct answer is (C).** The word "Although" is a clue that the two halves of the sentence will contrast with one another. The first half speaks about how widespread rabies is; the second half makes the point that it is, in fact, "rare" in the U.S., and explains why.

8. **The correct answer is (D).** When something miscarries, it fails; hence the common use of the word "miscarriage" to refer to a failed pregnancy. (One also hears the phrase "a miscarriage of justice" to refer to any failure of justice, as when a trial results in an obviously unfair verdict.) The opposite of *miscarry,* then, is *succeed.*

9. **The correct answer is (E).** Refer back to the sentence in which the word "hope" appears. It says that Pace wanted to "correlate" something in the environment with the incidence of cancer, which is the same idea paraphrased in choice (E).

10. **The correct answer is (B).** The story told in the third paragraph involves a "low background rate" because the number of people in the general population who suffer from this kind of cancer is very small; it is a "fairly specific" cluster (according to the definition given in the second paragraph) because of the notable characteristic shared by all the victims—all had taken DES while pregnant.

11. **The correct answer is (B).** As suggested by the semicolon (;) in the middle of the sentence, the two halves of the sentence make the same point in different ways. If the article implied that others should imitate the commander, then "exemplary" is a logical adjective to describe how it portrayed his behavior.

12. **The correct answer is (E).** "Encouraged" is the logical adjective to describe how AIDS researchers would feel in reaction to good news about possible treatment of the disease. In choice (C), "cheerful" seems an odd word; it describes a passing mood rather than a response to outside events.

13. **The correct answer is (E).** In a theater, the proscenium is the front of the stage; when the curtain falls, the proscenium is "closed" and the stage is concealed. In much the same way, when the shade on a window is closed, what's beyond the window is concealed.

14. **The correct answer is (A).** To revoke something is to take it away; the word is usually used in reference to a right, a license, or a privilege. The opposite is to give or grant something.

15. **The correct answer is (B).** To sanctify something is to bless it or make it holy, as a priest may do, for example, by sprinkling holy water on a person, place, or thing. The opposite would be to remove or spoil the sacredness of something, which is what *desecrate* means.

16. **The correct answer is (B).** Look back at the last sentence of the passage. It makes clear that the pressures on the filmmaker are greater when the medium (i.e. the film) is "more costly . . . to produce."

17. **The correct answer is (D).** Shakespeare is mentioned as an example of an artist who, like the earliest filmmakers, enjoyed "a universal audience spread across the world."

18. **The correct answer is (A).** The point of the second paragraph is that movie makers must "pay a price" for their popularity. That price is bearing the pressure toward conventionality. Chaplin, Bergman, and Antonioni are mentioned as examples of filmmakers who are "greater and more resolute" and therefore able to withstand that pressure, as demonstrated by their willingness to make unconventional movies.

19. **The correct answer is (A).** A motorcade is a kind of parade in which many cars participate; a flotilla is a grand assemblage and parade of ships.

20. **The correct answer is (B).** To be impecunious is to be lacking in money; to be disinterested (as, for example, an honest judge should be) is to be lacking in bias.

21. **The correct answer is (D).** Equanimity is a sense of calm, placidity, or evenness of spirit. The opposite is excitement, irascibility, or irritability.

22. **The correct answer is (E).** The use of "brutal tactics" by the police against particular ethnic groups would logically produce a reputation for "racism."

23. **The correct answer is (D).** Just as the angler fish uses a fake piece of food as bait to capture a hungry prey, so does the trout fisherman when he lures a trout with a tasty-looking fake insect.

24. **The correct answer is (E).** Countershading is described in the fourth paragraph, where it is stated that this effect protects fish from predators *below* them, not above.

25. **The correct answer is (E).** The author mentions the "exploding dye packets" that help mark a bank robber in order to clarify how some animals coat predators with glowing tissue to mark them and make them vulnerable.

26. **The correct answer is (E).** When something is moribund, it is sickly or dying; a business about to go bankrupt, for example, might be described as moribund. By contrast, something vigorous is strong, healthy, and full of life.

27. **The correct answer is (C).** Apposite means relevant, apt, and appropriate. A speech, for instance, should include examples and quotations that are apposite. The opposite would be *irrelevant* or *inappropriate*.

28. **The correct answer is (E).** When you are assiduous, you are hardworking, disciplined, and dedicated. (The English word is related to the Latin root *sedes*, which means seat—can you see why?) The opposite is *lazy*.

29. **The correct answer is (A).** Cause-and-effect relationships are at work in both halves of this sentence. If the fennec uses its ears by "listening quietly" for its prey, then clearly the ears are helping it to "locate" the prey. Similarly, if the ears help the fennec with "desert survival," then it would be logical to conclude that they help "dissipate" the heat.

30. **The correct answer is (D).** When you are immune to a disease, it cannot harm you; when you are impregnable to attack (for example, when protected inside a very powerful fortress), the attack has no power to harm you.

SECTION 4

1. **The correct answer is (D).** Choices (A), (B), (C), and (E) all either undermine the notion that drug addiction is an inherited ailment or weaken the idea that drug addiction is a maternally linked trait. Choice (D), however, doesn't weaken the argument, since it's possible that a genetically transmitted trait might *also* be developed through other means, at least in a modest number of cases (as implied in the answer: "there have been instances . . .").

2. **The correct answer is (C).** Choice (C) *cannot* be logically inferred from the information presented because it is an overstatement. The first sentence of the passage tells us that slavery extension was "the major issue" of the campaign, but not that "none of the other issues . . . contributed significantly" to the outcome.

3. **The correct answer is (E).** All of the answers except choice (E) help to explain the discrepancy between Lucas's expectations and the actual box-office results. Choice (E), however, makes the success of the rereleased movies *more*, not less surprising.

4. **The correct answer is (C).** If sculpture D is in room 1, sculpture G must be there with it.

5. **The correct answer is (A).** Room 1 must also contain sculpture D, since D and G must be exhibited together. This leaves three sculptures, E, F, and H, to be distributed among the other two rooms. Any combination of these is possible; however, choice (A) is the answer, since sculpture D can't be in any room other than room 1.

6. **The correct answer is (D).** Room 1 contains only sculptures E and F, based on one of the puzzle rules we've been given. Room 3 contains sculpture D and also sculpture G, based on another rule. This leaves sculptures C and H. Both of these could be in room 2, or they could be split between rooms 2 and 3. Only choice (D) fits this scenario.

7. **The correct answer is (B).** If G is in room 2, so is D. If E is in room 3, then C must be in room 1 or 2 (see the rules). This leaves F and H, which may be together in room 1 or split up among rooms 1, 2, and 3. The only statement of the five that *must* be true is (B), since both F and H cannot join E in room 3—that would violate the rule that no third sculpture can be added to a room that already contains both E and F.

8. **The correct answer is (B).** What needs to be "accounted for" here is the fact that the razing of an important building, curiously, led to a surge of interest in landmarks preservation. All of the answers help suggest possible explanations except choice (B), which merely emphasizes the degree of novelty in the concept of landmark preservation without helping to explain why it became popular.

9. **The correct answer is (C).** Choices (A) and (B) suggest that most people are actually pretty good about returning books they've borrowed; choice (E) suggests that France's original statement may have been false in itself, which certainly weakens the argument based on it. And choice (D) suggests a motive for book lending without strengthening the notion that borrowed books are never returned. Only choice (C) supports that idea.

10. **The correct answer is (E).** Only choice (E) does not violate any of the planting rules we've been given. Choice (A) puts T, not R, in the third spot; choice (B) puts M and W together; choice (C) does not separate N and T properly; and choice (D) puts N, not X, in the sixth spot.

11. **The correct answer is (B).** If species M is planted fifth, then species N and T, which must be separated by one tree, must appear in the second and fourth spots—the only remaining places in the row where they can fit (in either order). Thus, N could be second or fourth, and only choice (B) works.

12. **The correct answer is (B).** If T is fifth, then N, by rule, must be two spaces away, in the seventh spot. Since M may not be next to W, which is in the first spot, it must be in the fourth spot, putting O in the second spot. Given this lineup, only choice (B) must be true.

13. **The correct answer is (B).** If M is fourth, then N and T, in order to be properly separated, must be in spots five and seven (in either order). This puts O and W in spots one and two (also in either order).

14. **The correct answer is (B).** For the group as a whole to be the world's best band needn't imply that each individual in the band was the best at his particular role; it's conceivable, for example, that the weakness of Ringo Starr on drums (as compared to, say, rival Ginger Baker) might have been more than offset by the songwriting talent of Lennon and McCartney.

15. **The correct answer is (C).** The puzzle rules tell us that varnish is applied on Wednesdays. During a January (containing 31 days) that begins on Friday, there are four Wednesdays. (Draw a little calendar—it will help you answer the remaining questions much more quickly than would otherwise be possible.)

16. **The correct answer is (C).** A theremin that comes in on the 5th will be examined on the 8th and delivered to the restoration room on Monday the 11th. Its restoration work will be finished at most three days later—the 14th.

17. **The correct answer is (A).** Work backwards from the 30th. The cover varnish dries on Friday (since it is applied on Wednesday); so in this case, we want the varnishing to be done on Wednesday the 27th. To allow enough time for the restoration work, the theremin must have been delivered to the restoration room the preceding Monday, the 18th. This means it must have been examined no later than the day before, the 17th; and if that date is three days after the arrival of the theremin, it must have arrived on the 14th.

18. **The correct answer is (A).** A theremin whose varnish dries on January 1st won't be shipped until the 15th, a fourteen-day wait.

19. **The correct answer is (B).** The newfound popularity of water sports on the Hudson is best explained by this answer because it suggests how the pollution of the river might have been alleviated in recent years. Choice (D) merely asserts in another form the fact that local residents now enjoy the cleanliness of the Hudson; it doesn't help to explain how that came to be.

20. **The correct answer is (A).** If true, choice (A) doesn't weaken the conclusion of the argument; it merely states that other writers of Twain's time enjoyed the same relative advantage he did in using the typewriter. The other answers weaken the conclusion by suggesting that the advantages asserted in the passage are more illusory than real.

21. **The correct answer is (E).** Draw a map illustrating the seven parks and the monorail routes among them. Use arrows to show the one-way paths. Your sketch might look something like this:

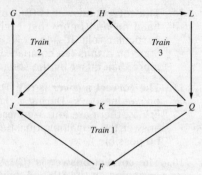

Most of the answers can be read right off this map. For question 18, you can see that a tourist at K has no choice but to travel to Q, since that is the next park on the only line available.

22. **The correct answer is (C).** One can travel from H to Q on train 3. All the other proposed trips require at least one change of trains.

23. **The correct answer is (C).** The route from F to L with the fewest stops goes: F, J (change trains), G, H (change again), L. On this trip there are three intermediate stops.

24. **The correct answer is (B).** Our unlucky tourist should have gotten on train 1, of course; it would have taken her directly to K. Her best bet for getting to K under the circumstances is to stay on train 2 until it makes the complete circuit back to J, then change to train 1. This is preferable to (for example) switching to train 3 at H.

25. **The correct answer is (D).** The passage draws the general conclusion that homebuyers should "always" buy a new house based on a couple of specific advantages that new houses offer. Choice (D) is the best criticism of the argument because it suggests that these factors are not necessarily the only factors, or the most important ones, in the homebuying decision.

26. **The correct answer is (B).** A little (extremely simple) math is involved in this puzzle. Since the number of white puppies is exactly double the number of brown puppies, there's only a limited number of possible color distributions. Here's a complete chart:

W	B	G
2	1	15
4	2	12
6	3	9
8	4	6
10	5	3

We can't have fewer than 3 gray puppies, since one of our rules is that each of the three kennels must have at least one. From the chart, it's easy to see that the correct answer is (B).

27. **The correct answer is (E).** Now you need a grid showing the three kennels and the number of dogs of each color they contain—like this:

	W	B	G
A	0		1
B			
C			

If Kennel A contains just one gray puppy and no white puppies, the rest of its quota of six must be made up by brown puppies. Now refer back to the color distribution chart. We have (at least) five brown puppies in the shelter. That's the maximum possible number. This means we must have the maximum number of white puppies, too—10. Suddenly we see that the entire grid can be quickly filled in:

	W	B	G
A	0	5	1
B	5	0	1
C	5	0	1

Now the answer to the question is easy to read.

28. **The correct answer is (C).** Our color distribution chart tells us that the only possible numbers of white puppies in the shelter are 2, 4, 6, 8, and 10. Which of these numbers can be made up of three different quantities, each no greater than 3? Only one—6, which can be made up of 1, 2, and 3. If there are 6 white puppies, then there are 3 brown ones and 9 gray ones.

29. **The correct answer is (D).** If the number of brown puppies in Kennel A is three times the number in Kennel C, what can the two quantities possibly be? Only one pair of numbers is possible—3 and 1. (Anything larger would give us too many brown puppies; remember, our maximum is five.) Start filling in the grid:

	W	B	G
A		3	
B			
C		1	

We must have five brown puppies, so Kennel B has one. If we have five brown puppies, we must have three gray ones, one to a kennel; and the rest of the grid is easy to complete:

	W	B	G
A	2	3	1
B	4	1	1
C	4	1	1

30. **The correct answer is (D).** The author of the passage emphasizes the importance of the imposition of martial law in the South as an influence on later U.S. history. Therefore, choice (D), which tends to minimize that importance, is not an assumption made by the author.

31. **The correct answer is (B).** Compare the possibilities with the rules. Choice (D) seats E and R together—no good. Choice (C) does not seat C and Y together. Choice (A) violates the rule of husband/wife alternation (it starts with three women together). And choice (E), subtly, goofs by seating husband T next to wife B. Don't you see it?—their initials come first and last in the list, meaning they are seated next to one another *at this circular table*.

32. **The correct answer is (C).** You can't infer much about the seating arrangements from the scanty facts you've been given. If Y is in seat 5, then C (her seatmate) must be in either 4 or 6. But each seat has at least two possible occupants. However, we *can* tell that E may not sit in seat 8. If she did, she'd be sitting next to the person R, which is against one of our rules. (Again, remember that the table is circular.)

33. **The correct answer is (B).** If C is in seat 1, where is her seatmate Y? There are two possibilities. He could be in seat 8, like this:

1	2	3	4	5	6	7	8
C			W				Y

In that case, R would have to be in seat 6 (to avoid sitting next to wife C), and the remaining man, T, would go in seat 2:

1	2	3	4	5	6	7	8
C	T		W		R		Y

We have three women, B, E, and F, remaining. Our clearest shot is E. She can't sit next to husband W, so she has to go to seat 7. Then B must go to seat 5 (to avoid T) and F to seat 3:

1	2	3	4	5	6	7	8
C	T	F	W	B	R	E	Y

Remember, though, there's another scenario: Y could be in seat 2. You can work out all the possibilities, but here's what your seating plan should look like:

1	2	3	4	5	6	7	8
C	Y	E	W	B/F	R	B/F	T

Considering both scenarios, seat 3 could be occupied either by E or by F.

34. **The correct answer is (D).** Alphabetical husbands would mean the following:

1	2	3	4	5	6	7	8
R		T		W		Y	

C must take seat 6, to be next to Y and away from R. Seat 4 can't be occupied by either B or E, so it has to be occupied by F. Follow similar logic with the remaining seats, and the chart looks like this:

1	2	3	4	5	6	7	8
R	E	T	F	W	C	Y	B

35. **The correct answer is (C).** Although the passage uses the (slightly sexist) term "young man" to describe the typical early performer of rock and roll, the author is not concerned with gender but with age. Therefore, the prevalence of women among rock and roll performers is irrelevant to the argument and neither underlies it nor weakens it.

SECTION 5

1. **The correct answer is (C).** If the fraction has been simplified to simplest form, N cannot have as a factor any number whose prime factorization has any numbers in common with the prime factors of 60. But $60 = (2)(2)(3)(5)$. Thus, the answer must be 49, since in this set, only choice (C), 49, has a prime factorization (namely, 7×7) lacking 2, 3, and 5.

2. **The correct answer is (A).** For Column A, marking down $1200 by 10% reduces the price by 10% of $1200 = 120$; so the new price is $1200 - 120 = 1080$. Marking that down 10% further reduces the price by 10% of $1080 = 108$, so that the final price is $1080 - 108 = 972$. For Column B, a single 20% markdown reduces the price by 20% of $1200 = 240$, to a final price of $1200 - 240 = 960$, which is less than 972.

3. **The correct answer is (A).** If Margaret's average is 88 on four exams, she must have a total of $(4)(88) = 352$. In order to average 90 on five exams, her total must be $(5)(90) = 450$. Therefore, she must score $450 - 352 = 98$ on her last exam!

4. **The correct answer is (A).** Counting spaces, we see that in Column A, we have

$$AF : BD = 5 : 2 = \frac{5}{2} = 2.5$$

but in Column B, we have

$$BH : CF = 6 : 3 = \frac{6}{3} = 2.$$

5. **The correct answer is (C).** Since $P : F = 5 : 2$, we let $P = 5k$ and $F = 2k$. The total number in the class must be $P + F = 5k + 2k = 7k$. Clearly, choice (C) 21 will work for $k = 3$. If you try the other possibilities, k will be a fraction for which neither $5k$ nor $2k$ will be a whole number. Of course, you can't have a fractional number of students, so the answer must be (C).

6. **The correct answer is (B).** In Column A, we have n^3, and in Column B, we have $3n$. Since n is between 0 and 1, cubing n makes it smaller. So n^3 is less than n. Therefore, it is certainly less than $3n$.

7. **The correct answer is (D).** Calling the smallest number x, the second is $x + 1$, and the third is $x + 2$. Therefore:

$$x + (x + 1) + 2(x + 2) = 93$$
$$x + x + 1 + 2x + 4 = 93$$
$$4x + 5 = 93$$
$$4x = 88$$
$$x = 22$$

Hence the middle number is $22 + 1 = 23$, choice (D).

8. **The correct answer is (B)**. The original volume of the solid was

$$V_B = (6)(6)(14) = 504$$

Since the circle just goes from one side to the other of the square base, it must have a diameter of 6, which means a radius of 3. Hence, the volume of the piece drilled out is

$$V_H = \pi(3)^2(14) = 126\pi$$

Since π = about $\frac{22}{7}$, 126π = about 396. Therefore, the volume of the remaining wood is $504 - 396 = 108$ in^3.

9. **The correct answer is (A)**. Looking at Column B, we see that 3 for a dollar is $33\frac{1}{3}$¢ apiece, which is less than 34¢ apiece. Naturally, it doesn't matter how many items you have; if the number of items is the same in both groups, the one with the lower price per item has the lower total price.

10. **The correct answer is (C)**. Solving the equation:

$$3y - 6 = 2 - y$$
$$4y = 8$$
$$y = 2$$

For $y = 2$, $y^2 = 2y = 4$. The quantities are the same.

11. **The correct answer is (D)**. Reading the first bar graph, we see that the number of houses sold in Ashland in 1994 was about 450. The number sold in Brainard, where the scale is twice as large, was about 830. The total is 1280.

12. **The correct answer is (B)**. Reading the bar graphs from 1993 through 1999, the number of sales in Brainard exceeds 600, while the number of sales in Ashland was less than or equal to 600 every year except 1995, when Ashland was less than 700 but Brainard was 1100. Thus, the only possible years in which Ashland sales exceed Brainard sales are 1990, 1991, and 1992. In 1992, Ashland's sales were a little over 300 and Brainard's were a little under. In the other two years, Ashland's clearly exceeded Brainard's. Hence, there were exactly three years.

13. **The correct answer is (C)**. The average sales price is the total sales divided by the number of sales. In 1992, the bar graph shows about 330 houses sold in Ashland, while the line graph shows total sales of about $40,000,000. $40,000,000 ÷ 330 = about $121,000. From this example, it is easy to see that the average will be over $100,000 if the total sales in millions is larger than the number of sales in tens. Thus, in 1993, we have $46,000,000 ÷ 370 = about $124,000. In 1996, total sales were only 43 million on about 520 sales. Since 52 > 43, the average was under $100,000 (43 ÷ 52 = about 0.83). In 1998 and 1999, the figures were 82 million on 600 and 80 million on 550, respectively. Thus, 1996, choice (C), is correct.

14. **The correct answer is (E)**. The number of houses sold in Brainard in 1995 was 1100. In 1996, the number was about 720, for a decline of $1100 - 720 = 380$. The fractional decline was $\frac{380}{1100}$, which = about 0.345 or 34.5%. Clearly, the closest choice is (E), 35%.

15. **The correct answer is (C).** From the line graphs, the total sales were 70 + 90 million = 160 million. The total number of houses sold from the bar graphs was 650 + 1100 = 1750. 160,000,000 ÷ 1750 = about 91,000, choice (C). Notice that this is *not* the same as the average of the average sales prices in the two counties separately.

16. **The correct answer is (B).** Since the diameter is 10, $\overline{OA}$ and $\overline{OB}$, being radii, both have a length of 5. Since the perimeter is 16, we see that AB has a length of 6. Hence, $\angle O$ is the largest angle in the triangle. Since the other two angles are base angles of an isosceles triangle, they must be equal and have measure x. Hence, x must be less than 60°, or the three angles would total more than 180°.

17. **The correct answer is (B).** Since the black block is seventh from the left, there are 6 blocks to its left. Similarly, there are 10 blocks to its right. Hence, there are 6 + 10 + 1 (the black one) = 17 blocks in all.

18. **The correct answer is (C).** Of the whole group of 60, 40% are under 25. 40% of 60 is (0.4)(60) = 24. For the singers, 20% of 20 = (0.2)(20) = 4 are under 25. Hence, the remaining 25 or unders must be dancers. That is, 20 dancers or half of all the dancers fall into this category. Since half is 50%, the correct answer is choice (C).

19. **The correct answer is (D).** You really can't tell. Try some numbers. For example, if $a = 2$ and $b = 12$, their average is 7. If $c = 7$, then the three still average 7. However, if $c = 10$, the average becomes 8; and if $c = 4$, the average becomes 6.

20. **The correct answer is (A).** The four angles in the quadrilateral must total 360°. The two given angles total 170°. Hence, $x + y = 190$. Therefore, $x = 190 - y$, which is certainly greater than $180 - y$.

21. **The correct answer is (C).** To find the largest possible value of $\frac{a}{b}$, you certainly want a positive number, which you can get in two ways: a positive divided by a positive, or a negative divided by a negative. The largest fraction you can form using positive numbers from A and B is $\frac{3}{4}$. However, using the negative possibilities, we have $\frac{-6}{-4} = \frac{3}{2} = 1.5$. Hence the two quantities are equal.

22. **The correct answer is (E).** Letting r, m, and b be the prices in cents of rolls, muffins, and bread respectively yields two equations:

$$4r + 6m + 3b = 910$$

and

$$2r + 3m + b = 390$$

If we multiply the second equation by -2 and add the two together, we have:

The first equation:	$4r + 6m + 3b =$	910
-2 times the second equation:	$-4r - 6m - 2b =$	-780
	$b =$	130

Hence, the price of a loaf of bread is $1.30.

23. **The correct answer is (C).** In $\triangle ABC$, the measure of $\angle A = x°$ by the property of vertical angles, and the measure of $\angle B = z°$ by the property of alternate interior angles. Hence, $x + y + z = 180$.

24. **The correct answer is (A).** This example uses two well-known right triangles. We see that in triangle ABD, one leg is 3 and one is 4, which makes BD = 5. This tells us that the lengths of the sides of triangle BDC are 5–12–13. Thus, CD is 13, and the entire perimeter is $3 + 4 + 12 + 13 = 32$.

25. **The correct answer is (A).** Five more than twice n is $2n + 5$. Thus, $2n + 5 = 17$, which we solve to get $n = 6$. Three less than 6 is 3, and 2 less than $\frac{1}{2}$ of 6 is 2 less than 3, or 1. Since $3 > 1$, the correct choice is (A).

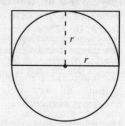

26. **The correct answer is (B).** From the description, the situation must be that shown in the diagram above. Calling the radius r, we see that the perimeter of the rectangle is $2(2r) + 2(r) = 6r$. The circumference of the circle is $2\pi r$, and $\pi > 3$. Therefore, $2\pi > 6$, and the circumference of the circle is larger.

27. **The correct answer is (D).** Try to set up the inequality:

$$\sqrt{x} + 2x > 2\sqrt{x} + x$$

Subtracting $\sqrt{x} + x$ from both sides yields $x > \sqrt{x}$. This is true if $x > 1$, but false if $x < 1$. Therefore, you do not have enough information.

28. **The correct answer is (E).** Since $4x^2 - y^2 = (2x - y)(2x + y) = 7(2x - y)$, $4x^2 - y^2$ must be divisible by 7. Therefore, 6 and 15 are not possible. If the result is to be zero, $2x - y = 0$, which means $y = 2x$, so that $2x + 2x = 4x = 7$, which is also impossible for any integral value of x. Hence, the result must be 14 or 35. If the result is to be 14, $2x - y = 2$. Adding gives us:

$$\begin{array}{r} 2x + y = 7 \\ \underline{2x - y = 2} \\ 4x = 9 \end{array}$$

This has no integer solutions. Hence, choice (E), 35, for which $x = 3$ and $y = 1$ are the only possible values.

Chapter 2

Making Your Plan

Get the Scoop On . . .

- The three levels of GRE skills, and how you can improve all three
- How to develop a personalized study plan focused on your current skill levels and needs
- How to tailor your study plan to the amount of time you have to prepare

---

HOW TO GET WHERE YOU WANT TO GO

As you decide which graduate schools you intend to apply to, your GRE goals should be based largely on the credentials needed to win admission to the school(s) of your choice.

Now we come to the heart of this book. How can you make sure that your GRE scores will be a help rather than a hindrance to you when you apply to graduate schools? What steps can you take to close the gap that may exist between your current levels of GRE skills and the ones you'll need to earn your highest possible score?

The rest of this book will help you answer those questions.

THE INSIDER'S ROUTE TO TOP SCORES

Some of the terms and topics in this explanation might not be familiar to you. Don't worry—you'll learn much more about them in Chapter 3.

There are three levels of skill that can help boost your GRE scores. Each requires a different kind of preparation. Most important, each requires a different time frame to be completely developed. If you want to reach your full potential on the GRE, you'll want to devote time and energy to all three levels of skill.

Here's how the three levels work.

Level One—Testwiseness (30 to 150 points)

This first level of test-taking skill is the "low-hanging fruit" of test-preparation: skills that are relatively quick and simple to learn that can rapidly boost your total GRE scores from 30 to 150 points.

Level One includes such skills as:

- Familiarity with the format, structure, and question types found on the exam

- Ability to budget your time wisely as you work each section of the exam
- Understanding of the Computer Adaptive Test format and how to make it work for you

Level One skills are specific to the GRE. A student who'd never seen a standardized exam before and had done no preparatory reading about the GRE would lack these skills and therefore would lose points through sheer ignorance of the game.

Fortunately, Level One skills are easy to learn. Many students pick up some of them just by taking a GRE exam. That's why, as the test-makers admit, most students increase their scores by 30 to 50 points whenever they take the exam a second time, even if they do no studying between the two tests.

If your preparation for the GRE is condensed into just a couple of weeks, you'll need to focus especially on Level One skills. Chapters 1–3 and 14–16 in this book are particularly focused on Level One.

Level Two—Topic Strategies (75 to 250 points)

The test-makers at ETS officially minimize the importance of Level One and Level Two skills and that "short-term preparation" to develop them won't earn you many points. The fact is that these skills are vital to handling GRE questions confidently and correctly. Millions of students have lost points because they were guided by ETS's denigration of "short-term preparation." We agree that long-term preparation is better: but short-term preparation is worth a lot.

Skills at this level are a bit more complex. They generally take longer to learn but have a correspondingly greater payoff. If you work to improve your Level Two skills (as well as your Level One skills), you can expect to boost your overall GRE scores by anywhere from 75 to 250 points.

Level Two includes such skills as:

- Knowing how to interpret the relationships between words on analogy questions
- Ability to recognize the logical connections between parts of a sentence or a reading passage
- Awareness of how and when to use rounding off and "guesstimating" when working on math problems
- Understanding of the technique of "plugging in numbers" in quantitative comparison questions
- Knowing how to create a simple diagram that will help you solve an analytical ability puzzle
- Gaining the ability to develop a clear, simple outline that will help you write an effective essay in 30 minutes or less.

Level Two skills relate specifically to particular question types on the GRE. However, they involve intellectual abilities that can be used in other contexts as well. For instance, if you're good at seeing the logical connections between parts of a reading passage, this will help you not only on the GRE but whenever you do any difficult reading—in a textbook or scholarly journal, for example.

You've probably developed some Level Two skills already, both in and out of school. However, you probably aren't aware of how to apply these skills directly to answering GRE questions. Because these skills are somewhat complex (and because there are many of them), it'll take you a while to master them. But the rewards can be great.

If you have four weeks or more to prepare for the GRE, you'll have enough time to delve fairly deeply into Level Two skills. Chapters 4 through 12 of this book explain them in detail.

Level Three—Broad-Based Verbal and Math Abilities (150 to 600 points)

These are the most general skills, and they take the longest time to fully develop. In a sense, Level Three skills are the ones the test-makers originally intended the GRE to focus on, and certainly your performance on the test will be heavily affected by your Level Three skills. If you devote significant time and effort to improving your Level Three skills (along with Levels One and Two), you can aim for an increase of your overall GRE scores of from 150 to 600 points.

Level Three includes such skills as:

- Knowledge of the meanings and correct usage of a large number of difficult English words

- The ability to read and understand complex passages dealing with challenging topics from science, the humanities, the social sciences, and literature

- Familiarity with the basic facts, principles, and procedures of arithmetic, algebra, and geometry

- The ability to quickly recognize numerical relationships and to manipulate them accurately and creatively

- A sophisticated understanding of logical reasoning and the fallacies that can undermine an argument

Level Three skills clearly go well beyond the requirements of the GRE exam. In fact, you probably learned and practiced skills like these in every high school and college class you ever took (well, maybe not in gym class).

You'll continue to develop and improve your Level Three skills in many ways between now and when you take the GRE: through your ongoing college course work; through challenging reading that you might do for school or any other purpose; and through the intellectual exercise you get whenever you take a test, including sample GRE exams you use as part of your test-prep program.

The more time you have between now and the exam, the greater your chances of improving your Level Three skills. In this book, Appendixes A and B specifically address these skills by offering you help in building your word knowledge and sharpening your understanding of mathematics. Appendix C includes suggestions for other resources you can turn to if you want additional help in the verbal, quantitative, or analytical areas.

In addition, you'll find that you are using and practicing your Level Three skills every time you work on an exercise or sample test from any chapter in this book. Just as regular, disciplined exercise improves your overall muscle tone and strengthens your heart, mental workouts are the key to strengthening your Level Three skills.

MAKING THE MOST OF THE TIME YOU HAVE

As with almost any form of learning, preparing for the GRE is an investment of time. The more you have, the better your chances of significantly boosting your scores. Next, we'll walk you through three different study plans, each tailored to a specific amount of preparation time. Find the plan that fits your circumstances and adapt it to your needs.

If You Have Two Weeks to Prepare

Obviously, if you plan to take the GRE in two weeks or less and are just beginning your preparation program, your time is at a premium. You'll have to make the most of every available hour between now and the day of the test. As much as you can, cut back or eliminate nonessential activities over the next two weeks (work, travel, entertainment) and focus your energies on the exam.

You can still develop a plan, leaning heavily on Level One skills, that will make a significant difference in your test scores, but you need to make it your highest priority, starting *today*. The outline shown in Table 2.1 will help.

If You Have Four to Six Weeks to Prepare

With a month or more to get ready for the GRE, you can make some major improvements in your test-taking skills. You can delve rather deeply into Level Two skills, as well as master all the key Level One skills. It'll take some discipline and some hard work, of course. Try to cut back on nonessential activities between now and the day of the exam, and set aside significant blocks of time (evenings, weekends) for reading, study, and practice. If you do this, following the steps we suggest in Table 2.2, you'll boost your scores noticeably.

Table 2.1
Your Two-Week Plan—The Steps to Take

1. If you haven't already, take the Insider's GRE Diagnostic Test (Chapter 1). Set aside 3¼ hours and take the exam under true test conditions. Then grade your performance using the Scoring Guide beginning on page 39.
2. Based on the results of your Insider's GRE Diagnostic Test, identify the *three* question types on which you need the greatest improvement.
3. Turn to Part II of this book and read Chapter 3, "Finding Your Way Around the GRE CAT." It will give you an overview of the real exam and a number of important hints about test-taking strategy that will help boost your scores significantly.
4. Then find the two chapters from chapters 4 through 12 that cover the three question types you identified in Step 2. Study those chapters, and try your hand on at least two of the practice exercises in each one. If you achieve an above-average or excellent score on both practice exercises, move on. Otherwise, reread the chapter and do as many additional practice exercises as you can.
5. Turn to Appendix B, "The Insider's GRE Math Review." This part of the book covers the 50 math topics most frequently tested on the GRE. Take 15 minutes to skim this appendix, pencil in hand. Circle the number of any topic you find new or unfamiliar. Then set aside an afternoon or evening to read those topics in detail.
6. If you have time, read the chapters in Part II that you haven't already read.
7. Sometime in the week before the GRE, set aside 3 hours. Take the Insider's GRE Sample Test (chapter 13) under true test conditions. Then grade your performance using the Scoring Guide beginning on page 416.
8. Compare your performance on the Insider's GRE Sample Test with your performance on the Insider's GRE Diagnostic Test. Is there any *one* question type where your performance still lags? If you have time, read or reread the chapter in Part II that covers that question type.
9. Two days before the GRE, read Chapter 14 and follow its advice about how to approach the weekend of the exam. Also read Appendix D and apply the tips it offers about reducing your stress level on the day of the test.
10. The evening before the GRE, read Chapter 16, "The Insider's Tip Sheet." It provides a concise review of the key test-taking strategies you need to maximize your scores on the exam.
11. After taking the GRE, read Chapter 15.

Table 2.2
Your Four- to Six-Week Plan—The Steps to Take

1. If you haven't already, take the Insider's GRE Diagnostic Test (Chapter 1). Set aside 3¼ hours and take the exam under true test conditions. Then grade your performance using the Scoring Guide beginning on page 39.

2. Based on the results of your Insider's GRE Diagnostic Test, identify the *five* question types on which you need the greatest improvement.

3. Turn to Part II of this book and read Chapter 3, "Finding Your Way Around the GRE CAT." It will give you an overview of the real exam and a number of important hints about test-taking strategy that will help boost your scores significantly.

4. As soon as possible, begin to set aside fifteen minutes each day to study Appendix A, "The Insider's GRE Word List." Plan to read the definitions and explanations of 15 words from the word list each day. At this rate, you'll have been exposed to every word on the list within five weeks.

5. Read Appendix D and practice the stress-reducing tips it offers as you prepare for the test.

6. Now, find the five chapters from chapters 4 through 12 that cover the five question types you identified in Step 2. Over the next two weeks, study those chapters and try your hand on at least two of the practice exercises in each chapter. If you achieve an above-average or excellent score on both practice exercises, move on. Otherwise, reread the chapter and do as many additional practice exercises as you can.

7. Next, turn to Appendix B, "The Insider's GRE Math Review." This part of the book covers the 50 math topics most frequently tested on the GRE. Over the next week, read this appendix thoroughly. With a pencil, circle the number of any topic you find difficult or confusing. Between now and the date of the exam, review the circled topics from time to time.

8. If you have time, read the chapters in Part II that you haven't already read.

9. Sometime in the week before the GRE, set aside 3 hours. Take the Insider's GRE Sample Test (Chapter 13) under true test conditions. Then grade your performance using the Scoring Guide beginning on page 416.

10. Compare your performance on the Insider's GRE Sample Test with your performance on the Insider's GRE Diagnostic Test. Is there any *one* question type where your performance still lags? If you have time, read or reread the chapter in Part II that covers that question type.

11. Two days before the GRE, read Chapter 14 and follow its advice about how to approach the weekend of the exam.

12. The evening before the GRE, read Chapter 16, "The Insider's Tip Sheet." It provides a concise review of the key test-taking strategies you need to maximize your scores on the exam.

13. After taking the GRE, read Chapter 15.

Table 2.3
Your Three-Month Plan—The Steps to Take

1. If you haven't already, take the Insider's GRE Diagnostic Test (Chapter 1). Set aside 3¼ hours and take the exam under true test conditions. Then grade your performance using the Scoring Guide beginning on page 39.

2. Based on the results of your Insider's GRE Diagnostic Test, rank the nine question types in order of priority, from the one on which you need the greatest improvement to the one in which you currently perform the best.

3. Turn to Part II of this book and read Chapter 3, "Finding Your Way Around the GRE CAT." It will give you an overview of the real exam and a number of important hints about test-taking strategy that will help boost your scores significantly.

4. As soon as possible, begin to set aside fifteen minutes each day to study Appendix A, "The Insider's GRE Word List." Plan to read the definitions and explanations of 15 words from the word list each day. At this rate, you'll have been exposed to every word on the list within five weeks. As suggested in the appendix, also start your own vocabulary notebook and add to it frequently.

5. Read Appendix D and practice the stress-reducing tips it offers you as you prepare for the test.

6. Now, read Chapters 4–12 in the priority sequence you identified in Step 2. Also try your hand on at least two of the practice exercises in each chapter. If you achieve an above-average or excellent score on both practice exercises, move on. Otherwise, reread the chapter and do as many additional practice exercises as you can.

7. Next, turn to Appendix B, "The Insider's GRE Math Review." This part of the book covers the 50 math topics most frequently tested on the GRE. Over the next week, read this appendix thoroughly. With a pencil, circle the number of any topic you find difficult or confusing. Between now and the date of the exam, review the circled topics from time to time.

8. Get a copy of *GRE: Practicing to Take the General Test*, an official publication of the ETS, which contains a collection of recent actual GRE exams (see Appendix C for details). During each of the four to six weeks prior to your scheduled test, find a time when you can set aside three to four hours to take one complete exam from this book under true test conditions. Score your test following the instructions in the book. As the weeks pass, keep track of your scores. They may rise and fall, but the overall trend should be upward.

9. Sometime in the week before the GRE, set aside 3 hours. Take the Insider's GRE Sample Test (Chapter 13) under true test conditions. Then grade your performance using the Scoring Guide beginning on page 416.

10. Compare your performance on the Insider's GRE Sample Test with your performance on the Insider's GRE Diagnostic Test. Is there any *one* question type where your performance still lags? If you have time, reread the chapter in Part II that covers that question type.

11. Two days before the GRE, read Chapter 14 and follow its advice about how to approach the weekend of the exam.

12. The evening before the GRE, read Chapter 16, "The Insider's Tip Sheet." It provides a concise review of the key test-taking strategies you need to maximize your scores on the exam.

13. After taking the GRE, read Chapter 15.

If You Have Three Months or More to Prepare

Congratulations! Through astute planning, admirable self-discipline, or sheer good luck, you've positioned yourself so that you have ample time to prepare thoroughly for one of the most important challenges of your academic life. With three months or more to prepare, you can improve all three levels of your GRE skills and give yourself an excellent chance of achieving or surpassing your score goals.

Take advantage of your foresight by pacing yourself intelligently. Set aside time every week to pursue your test-prep program, preferably in major chunks—2 or 3 hours at a time on an evening or a weekday. An extended study program spread out over 12 weeks or more will boost your score more than an intensive, high-pressure program with the same number of study hours crammed into fewer weeks.

The steps in Table 2.3 will guide you through the planning process.

After you've sketched your plan, turn to Chapter 3. There you'll begin developing your Level One skills by learning what to expect on the real GRE and some of the best test-taking strategies for every part of the exam.

JUST THE FACTS

- Level One skills involve Testwiseness, and can be developed quickly

- Level Two skills involve Topic Strategies, and take more time to develop

- Level Three skills involve Broad-Based Verbal, Quantitative, and Analytical Abilities, and take the longest time to develop

- Skills at all three levels can help boost your GRE scores

- Depending on your schedule, your personal study program can delve more or less deeply into all three kinds of skills

Part II

Getting Inside the GRE CAT

Chapter 3

Finding Your Way Around the GRE CAT

Get the Scoop On . . .

- The new computer-adaptive testing—a revolution in which *you* might be a pawn
- How the CAT differs from traditional paper-and-pencil tests in format, content, and scoring
- How to manage the mechanics of test-taking on the computer
- Test-taking strategies that will boost your CAT scores

GETTING THE BIG PICTURE

We are living through a revolution in standardized testing. In November, 1993, the test-makers at ETS and the GRE Board, sponsors of the GRE exam, introduced the Computer Adaptive Test (CAT) version of the GRE exam. It's an entirely new way to take a standardized test, involving changes that go far beyond whether you mark your answers with a number two pencil or the click of a mouse. As you'll see, the changes have major implications for every test-taker. It seems likely that, eventually, most other standardized tests, including ETS's famous and controversial college admission test, the SAT, will be administered via computer.

For several years, test-takers had a choice between the CAT and the traditional paper-and-pencil GRE. No more. Now, only the CAT is available.

THE OFFICIAL DESCRIPTION

How the CAT Works

When you take the CAT version of the GRE, you're tested in the same subject areas that appeared on the traditional exam. However, rather than reading questions from a printed test booklet and marking answers on a scannable sheet, you'll read questions from a computer monitor and select answers by clicking the button on a mouse.

The GRE questions are divided into three broad categories—Verbal, Quantitative, and Analytical. (In October, 1999, a separate test was added: the GRE Writing Assessment. Most students tackle this test the same day they take the rest of the GRE.) There are four specific types of Verbal questions: analogies, antonyms, sentence completions, and critical reading. There are two types of Quantitative questions: multiple-choice problems and quantitative comparisons. And there are two types of Analytical questions: analytical reasoning and logical reasoning. (You'll find a chapter in this book for each of these eight question types, filled with test-taking strategies and practice questions. There's also a chapter on the GRE Analytical Writing Measure.)

Your GRE will include a Verbal section, a Quantitative section, an Analytical section, and two Writing Assessment sections (technically considered a separate test rather than part of the GRE). There will also be two additional sections containing either Verbal, Quantitative, or Analytical questions or perhaps some new type of question that ETS is studying. These are referred to by the test-makers at ETS as "equating" or "research" sections. We'll explain their significance and purpose later.

The Map of the GRE (Table 3.1) gives a more detailed listing of the types and quantities of questions you'll probably encounter on the exam.

How the CAT Adapts to the Test-Taker

Because the CAT is tailored to each test-taker, no two students will be given the same questions. *This is the single most revolutionary feature of computer-adaptive testing. If every student takes a different test, can their performances really be fairly compared? ETS says that their statistical formulas make it possible; but whether the general public will accept this as computerized testing becomes more widespread remains to be seen.*

If the CAT were simply a matter of throwing questions on a screen rather than printing them in a booklet, the change would be relatively insignificant. But the test-makers have a far more ambitious agenda. They are using computer-adaptive testing to radically change the way standardized tests are written, administered, and scored. Here's how it works.

As you know, a standardized test like the GRE is intended to measure the level of your skills and knowledge in particular areas—in this case, what the test-makers call Verbal, Quantitative, and Analytical Ability. Each test-taker, in theory, has some "true" level of ability in each area, represented by a score from 200 to 800 on the three-digit GRE scale. To determine with fair accuracy where your ability level falls, the traditional paper-and-pencil test includes questions covering a wide range of difficulty levels, from very easy to very hard.

The number of questions you get right in a given test area is supposed to give a good indication of your "true" ability in that area. If your "true" Verbal ability, for example, is around 520—close to the average level among GRE test-takers—then, when you take the paper-and-pencil exam, you should get nearly all of the easy questions right, get nearly all of the very difficult questions wrong, and, on those questions that fall in the middle of the difficulty range, get some right and some wrong. The overall number you get right will determine your score.

Table 3.1
Map of the GRE

GRE Analytical Writing Measure—2 Sections, 75 Minutes
(after September 30, 2002)

  1   present your perspective topic (45 minutes)
  1   analyze an argument topic (30 minutes)
  ——
  2   Topics Total

Verbal Section—30 Minutes

  6   sentence completions
  7   analogies
  8   reading comprehension questions (based on three passages)
  9   antonyms
  ——
  30   Questions Total

Quantitative Section—45 Minutes

  14   quantitative comparisons
  14   multiple-choice problems
  ——
  28   Questions Total

Analytical Section—60 Minutes (before October 1, 2002)

  24   analytical reasoning questions
  11   logical reasoning questions
  ——
  35   Questions Total

Equating Sections—30 Minutes
(Verbal or Quantitative only after September 30, 2002)

  Verbal, Quantitative, or Analytical questions

On the old paper-and-pencil test, you normally had to answer a total of 76 Verbal questions to cover this wide range of difficulties. On the CAT, however, there are far fewer items. You'll have just one 30-minute Verbal section with a total of only 30 questions to answer; you'll receive a score as long as you answer at least 24 of the 30.

How is this possible? In theory, when an average-level student takes a paper-and-pencil test, he is "wasting" a lot of his time on very easy questions (nearly all of which he answers correctly) and on very hard questions (nearly all of which he answers wrong). It's the middle-level questions—where his performance is more unpredictable—that really determine this student's score.

Ideally, then, the test-makers would like to be able to give each student a test tailored to his or her specific skill level. Mr. Average would get a test made up almost entirely of middle-level questions, while Mr. Below Average would get an easier test and Mr. Above Average would get a harder one. This would save the test-taker's time and energy by focusing him on questions at the most relevant difficulty level. It would also, in theory, enable the test-makers to zero in more precisely on the test-taker's "true" skill level.

The CAT is designed to make this ideal a reality. It works like this. When you begin work on the Verbal section (for example), you'll be given a question of average difficulty, selected at random from an extensive bank of questions stored in the computer's software. If you get it right, you'll next be given a slightly harder question from the bank; if you get it wrong, you'll be given a slightly easier one. Depending on how you do with the second question, you'll be given either an easier or a harder question after that. As you continue through the section, the difficulty level of the questions will continue to be adjusted. If you're like most students, you'll eventually settle in to a specific skill range that is appropriate for you, and most of the questions you'll be given should be in that difficulty range.

Navigating the Test Section

This scoring method is fair only if you trust ETS when they say, "Don't worry—our software knows how to pick the 'right' questions to score your abilities fairly." Is this a believable claim? You decide. Unfortunately, the procedure by which the questions for your test are selected is a "black box"—an opaque process not subject to scrutiny or evaluation by anyone outside ETS.

The adaptive nature of the CAT—according to which the questions are selected, one by one, while the test is actually in progress—gives rise to a number of interesting changes in the test format:

- Question types are intermingled rather than presented in batches. In other words, rather than starting the Verbal section with a batch of analogies, followed by a batch of sentence completions, and so on, you might start with an analogy followed by a sentence completion, an antonym, a reading comprehension question, another antonym, two analogies, two reading comprehension items, an antonym . . . you get the idea. By the time you finish the section, you'll have been given a fair assortment of every question type, but rather than getting them grouped in batches, you'll get them in a seemingly random order.

- You may not work on question types in the sequence you choose. The items are presented in whatever order the software's algorithm (formula) dictates. If you prefer to start with antonyms, too bad; you must answer the questions as the computer picks them.

- You may not skip or go back to an earlier question. After you've selected an answer for question 1 and moved on to question 2,

Although the folks at ETS will never admit it, the freedom from test disclosure benefits them in another way, too. It's much easier for the test-makers to operate in secrecy rather than in the glare of publicity. When students can't review their test questions after the exam, they can't easily detect or complain about errors or ambiguities and ETS is spared the expense, effort, and embarrassment of admitting and correcting their mistakes.

you will never see question 1 again. If you decide later in the section that your answer to question 1 was wrong, you can't change it.

- You can see only one question at a time. It's not possible, as it is with the paper-and-pencil test, to compare two questions from different portions of the same test section. The software is set up to show one and only one item on the screen at any given time.

As you can imagine, these features of the CAT have important implications for test-taking strategy. We'll discuss these in detail shortly.

How the CAT Is Scored

On the traditional GRE, each question was worth the same amount. Your three-digit scaled score was determined by a formula based on the number of correct answers you chose. The formula varied depending on the overall difficulty level of the test, but it didn't differentiate among questions.

Again, the CAT is different. Your exam will include a mixture of hard, easy, and middle-level items, but most of the questions will be at a difficulty level that the computer figures is approximately right for you. The score you end up with will take into account not only the number of right answers you choose but also the difficulty rating of the individual questions. In other words, if you get a batch of difficult questions right, you'll earn more points than you would by getting a batch of easy questions right.

Is there any way to outsmart the software by focusing particularly on the questions that will earn you the most points? Yes. We'll explain the system shortly.

THE INSIDER'S REPORT

Why the Test-Makers Love the CAT

The CAT has several specific, powerful benefits for the folks at ETS:

- Because each computerized GRE requires fewer questions than the traditional test, ETS needn't write, edit, and pretest as many items, thereby saving a lot of money.

- Better still, because the test disclosure laws on the books in New York State and elsewhere apply only to test forms taken by a certain minimum number of individuals—and *no two people ever take the same CAT*—the computerized tests are exempt from disclosure. This means that ETS can use and reuse the same items over and over again. (Of course, a minimum number of new items must always be created, so that students who retake the exam don't run into a number of the same questions.)

- The fact that every student takes a different exam makes the risk of cheating—*test security*, in ETS parlance—absolutely minimal. As long as the GRE software that contains those banks of difficulty-graded questions is secure, it's almost impossible to imagine how anyone can compromise the integrity of the exam.

- Because the CAT is administered to one student at a time at centers around the country, GRE testing and score reporting is spread out through the year rather than concentrated around a few nationwide test dates. This makes the flow of paperwork much easier for ETS to manage.

- As with most "automated" processes, the computerization of the GRE reduces the number of relatively costly humans required to administer the exams—another cost saving.

- Finally, the fact that you can learn your score instantly, right off the computer screen, saves ETS the headache of fielding inquiries from anxious students during the weeks after the exam. And if instant feedback encourages more students to retake the exam once, twice, or even more often—at $105 a pop—the test-makers won't mind a bit.

Making the CAT Work for You

It's easy to see why ETS likes the CAT. But is there anything in it for you?

Some of the advantages of the CAT can work in your favor, too. Ready availability of the test on most days of each month, rather than a handful of Saturdays a year, certainly adds to your convenience. So does being able to see your test scores immediately. And the fact that the number of test questions is smaller on the CAT than it is on the paper-and-pencil test probably strikes many test-takers as a blessing. (But don't expect your time at the test center to be any shorter than in the old paper-and-pencil days. Paperwork, test sections used for equating and experimental purposes, and the computer tutorial that walks you through the workings of the testing software all combine to make the CAT at least as time-consuming overall as the traditional test.)

If you're computer literate or even a computerphile, someone who works with computers daily and enjoys using them, you might prefer the CAT to the traditional paper-and-pencil test. You might also like it if you prefer the idea of a highly intense, relatively *shorter* mental challenge as opposed to the longer, marathon-like endurance battle of the traditional exam.

In any case, there are definite steps you can take both to make the CAT experience relatively painless and to maximize your opportunity to score high under the special new conditions of computerized testing. In the next few pages, we'll outline these strategies and explain how and why they work.

What to Expect at the Testing Center

Most students take the GRE CAT at one of more than 4200 Prometric test centers in 141 countries and at many institutions of higher learning. A private company, Prometric is the subcontractor that provides this service to ETS; they were chosen largely because they have an extensive network of computerized centers in which space is generally available for testing on weekday mornings.

Testing facilities vary widely in size, quality, and amenities. Some are relatively spacious, clean, quiet, and well organized; othere are not. If you have a choice of more than one location, you may want to visit both before choosing one at which to register.

On the day of your test, you'll be asked to show up early, bearing your photo I.D. (driver's license, passport, etc.), admission card from ETS, a pen, and a pencil. You might find that you can begin the GRE process right away, or you might have to sit in a waiting room half an hour or more, depending on how well run your test center is. The administrator should provide you with a small locker in which to store your jacket, bag, or other belongings; she's not supposed to let you bring any such item into the test room with you.

After being admitted to the test room—and possibly photographed for security purposes—you'll be assigned to a carrel with a desk, a chair, and a computer with keyboard, monitor, mouse, and mouse pad. You'll be given a few pages of scrap paper, too. The GRE software will be pre-loaded and booted up, and you should be ready to go right away.

The GRE software begins with an extensive tutorial explaining how the test works, features of the testing interface (i.e., what the different items on the screen are for), how to use the mouse, and so on. Make sure you understand exactly how the program works before you plunge into the first test section.

Managing the Mechanics of the CAT

If you're familiar with the conventions of Windows- or Mac-based computing, as most students today are, you won't find the GRE software complicated. If you're not, get familiar with them *before* you sit for the CAT. Visit your college computer center or talk a friend into letting you use her desktop for a few hours; type a term paper, work up a personal budget, or manage some other mundane task using Windows- or

Mac-style software. The idea is to be comfortable with such computer basics as pointing and clicking with the mouse; scrolling up and down through a lengthy text; the use of Next, Help, Quit, and other specialized on-screen command buttons; selecting activities from a menu of choices; and the feel of reading or working with material in one window while other information appears elsewhere on the computer desktop.

There are a handful of crucial mechanical details you *must* pay attention to when you take the exam, so let's break them down.

FYI

On verbal and logical reasoning items, for which no single "perfect" answer is calculated, try this technique: scroll with the mouse arrow down through the five bubbles as you read the corresponding answer choices, and click when you come upon an answer you like better than any preceding answer. After reading all five answers, the one best *answer should be highlighted.*

Understand How to Choose, Change, and Confirm Answer Choices

For each question that appears on the screen, you'll be given five answers from which to choose. They are *not* labeled (A), (B), (C), (D), and (E), by the way; each is merely preceded by a little oval "bubble," not unlike the bubbles to be blackened in on the traditional paper-and-pencil answer sheet.

To choose an answer, move the onscreen arrow to the bubble using the mouse and click either mouse button. The bubble will be filled in. To change the answer, just click on a different bubble.

When you're satisfied with your answer, click on the Next arrow at the bottom of the screen. This will cause another box, labeled Answer Confirm, to be highlighted. Click there, your answer will be registered, and you'll move on to the next question.

Be Certain You Check Your Answer Before Hitting the Answer Confirm Button

Make sure that you've clicked correctly and highlighted the answer you really want! Remember, you'll have no opportunity to reconsider or change your answer after it has been confirmed and registered by the computer.

Be Aware of What Will Happen When You Exit A Test Section or Quit the Test

At the bottom of each screen, you'll find buttons labeled Test Quit and Section Exit. Unless you become deathly ill, *don't use these*.

If you click on Test Quit, the exam will vanish, and your scores for that day will be canceled, including your scores on any previous test sections you completed. Similarly, if you click on Section Exit without having completed *every* question in the section, you will *not* receive a score for that section.

Rather than run the risk of wasting your time and effort in this way, simply ignore those two buttons. If you finish a section with two or three extra minutes to spare, use the time to rest and relax. This will reenergize you for the sections still to come.

Keep Track of the Last Item You Are Working on and the Amount of Time You Have Left

Throughout the test, you'll see a bar across the top of the screen containing three pieces of information: the time remaining for the section; the number of the section; and the number of the item you are working on. It will look something like this:

> 00:18   GRE Section 5   14 of 35

When five minutes remain, the time indicator will flash and change to read:

> 00:05:00

which means that five minutes and zero seconds are left. For the last five minutes, seconds are counted down along with the minutes.

Glance at this information bar from time to time as you work. It will help you follow the proper timing strategy, as we'll discuss in a moment.

Use the Scroll Bar to Read Long Passages

In the Verbal section, full-length reading passages do not fit on the computer screen all at once. To read through the entire passage, you have to scroll through the material. The same might be true of graphs in the Quantitative section and occasionally other materials.

Long passages and graphs will normally be set up on the left-hand side of the screen, leaving a window on the right for a question to appear. This way, you can scan the passage simultaneously with looking at the question.

There are three different ways you can scroll through a long text: (1) by clicking on the Up and Down buttons at the top and bottom of the scroll bar; (2) by "pulling" the scroll tab up or down within the bar; or (3) by clicking anywhere within the bar to move the tab. We recommend method (1); it moves the text more smoothly and makes for much easier reading.

Test-Taking Strategies for the CAT That Really Work

Above all, get the first five questions in each section correct

The single most important thing you can do to boost your score on the GRE CAT is to answer the first five questions correctly. *The difference this makes in your overall score—regardless of your performance on the remaining questions—is significant.*

Why is this so? Let's explain.

The theory of computer-adaptive testing, you'll recall, is that the program that selects questions for your customized test is supposed to zero in fairly quickly on your general skill level for a particular test area. Starting with a question of medium difficulty, the program rapidly shifts up or down based on how well you do, settling down after just a handful of questions at the level it "thinks" is approximately right for you.

FYI

Don't overlook material that doesn't fit on a single screen. Clue: a scroll bar will appear at the right-hand margin of the window containing the lengthy text, and the word "Beginning" will appear at the top of the screen. Don't overlook these; otherwise, you'll think you can't answer the questions because you lack some of the necessary information.

Thereafter, the difficulty adjustments made by the program are much smaller. In effect, the program thinks it knows you by now: the issue now is not whether you'll earn a score of 300 or 700, but whether you'll earn 520, 540, or 560. The remaining questions will all be of roughly similar difficulty and will be chosen with the goal of "fine-tuning" your score within a range that has already been determined.

How do we know that the test works this way? See the box labeled "One Test-Taker's Story" for an account of an actual experiment. The results will surprise you.

One Test-Taker's Story

"By the time my appointment to take the CAT came along, I'd actually changed my mind about going to graduate school (figured I'd get a "real job" instead, which is another story). But I decided to take the test anyway, just to see how it worked. After reading about the theory behind computer-adaptive testing, I planned a little experiment.

"I knew from practice tests that I could score high on both the Verbal and Quantitative sections. But I wanted to see what would happen to my scores if I handled the start of the sections differently. So I made a plan. I looked up how many questions there would be in each section, and then I figured out how many questions would be 65% of the total. I decided to make that my target for the total number of questions I'd answer correctly.

"Then the kicker: I decided to deliberately get the first five Verbal questions *wrong,* while working extra hard to make sure that I'd get the first five Quantitative questions *right.* After that, I'd get some wrong and some right, in the proper numbers to add up to 65% correct answers overall. (I know it sounds obsessive, but it was all in the name of science, right?) This way, I figured, the difference in my scores on the two sections would have to be due totally to my out-the-chute performance on questions 1–5.

"The results floored me. My Quantitative score came in at the 80th percentile—in other words, I was in the top fifth of all test-takers. But my Verbal score was at the 19th percentile—in the bottom fifth.

"Remember, on both sections I got about the same overall number correct! The only difference was how I did on the first five items. Getting them right put me in the penthouse; getting them wrong put me in the basement."

What does this mean for you as a test-taker? *You should do whatever it takes to answer the first five questions in each section correctly.* Throw out all test-taking strategies that are designed to save time. Instead, tackle the first five items with extra care, even if it takes more time. Read *and reread* the questions to make sure you understand what's being asked. Double-check your calculations. Solve the same problem twice, using two different methods or approaches, to make sure that the answers match. On Quantitative items, try checking not only the right answer but also each answer you think is wrong to confirm that both direct solving and the process of elimination point to the same response. And on Verbal items, consider every answer choice carefully to make sure that one you've overlooked isn't subtly correct.

In short, treat those first five questions as if your entire test score depends on them. *To a large degree, it does.*

Start Slow; Speed Up Later

On a paper-and-pencil test, your best timing strategy is to tackle the easiest questions first, zip through them, then slow down as you try your hand at the harder items. On the CAT, *reverse* this approach. Take your time on the first few items so as to maximize your chance of getting them all right; then, gradually, speed up as you move into items that will affect your final score less significantly.

Table 3.2 shows our suggested timing pattern, based on the number of questions per section used on the typical CAT. We suggest you learn it and use it, at least roughly, as a guide when you take the exam.

Always Answer the Minimum Number of Items Needed to Earn A Score

When you begin work on a section of the CAT, you'll see a screen on which you'll be told the total number of items in the section and the minimum number you must answer to earn a score.

The minimum number will vary from one section to another and from one test administration to another. Table 3.3 shows some examples of typical minimum requirements.

Work your way through the section with the minimum requirement in mind. As you monitor the amount of time you are spending on each question, balance your need to work deliberately and carefully with the need to answer at least the minimum number of questions.

If you find yourself running short of time—two minutes remaining—without having reached the minimum requirement, *guess at random, if necessary, to reach that minimum.* You will probably get a few questions wrong in this way. However, the modest loss of points this will entail is less significant than the possibility of receiving no score at all for the section.

Table 3.2
Suggested Timing for CAT Sections

Verbal (30 Questions, 30 Minutes)
Questions 1–5:
Questions 6–15:   8–10 minutes
Questions 16–24:   8–10 minutes
Questions 25–30:   Time remaining, if any*

Quantitative (28 Questions, 45 Minutes)
Questions 1–5:   10–15 minutes
Questions 5–14:   10–15 minutes
Questions 15–23:   10–15 minutes
Questions 24–28:   Time remaining, if any*

Analytical (35 Questions, 60 Minutes)
Questions 1–5:   10–15 minutes
Questions 6–15:   15–20 minutes
Questions 16–28:   15–20 minutes
Questions 29–35:   Time remaining, if any*

* Manage your time so that you complete the minimum number of questions needed to receive a score on the section (see below). Use any time remaining at the end of the section to answer questions beyond the minimum.

Actually, the time allotments for each section of the CAT are fairly generous. If you practice the question types diligently between now and the day of the exam, you'll probably find that you have no difficulty in finishing all the questions on each section in the time permitted. But don't forget the minimum question requirement. It's important.

The Best Tips
Practice with the Test-Taking Tools as Long as You Need
The onscreen tutorial that precedes the first test section walks you through the various test-taking tools that are built into the CAT program. You're not allowed to skip this tutorial—there's no "early exit" button to

Table 3.3
Typical Minimum Answers Required for a Score

Section	Total Questions	Minimum Required
Verbal	30	24
Quantitative	28	23
Analytical	35	28

click—but it's tempting to rush through it by simply clicking the "Next" button on each screen in rote fashion.

Resist the temptation. You might be familiar with Windows- or Mac-style software, but the CAT program, like every other, has its small peculiarities of appearance and procedure. Take all the time you need to become fully comfortable with it before the test begins. It would be a shame to lose points on your GRE score because you hastily clicked the wrong button due to a misunderstanding or memory lapse.

Use Scrap Paper Freely

The test administrator should provide you with a small batch of scrap paper at the start of the test. You'll be warned that you may not carry this paper out of the center; ETS doesn't want students to copy the questions down and circulate them among future test-takers. However, you can and should use this paper freely during the exam. In fact, working back and forth between the monitor, the mouse, and your scrap paper is one of the key skills you'll need to use when you take the CAT.

In Chapters 4 through 12 of this book, we explain test-taking strategies for each question type that appears on the GRE. In those chapters, whenever we refer to making notes or sketches or jotting down information, we are talking about using your scrap paper. (On the paper-and-pencil exam, you'd use the margins of the question booklet for the same purposes.) Here are some specific ways you should expect to use the scrap paper during the CAT:

- Briefly outline each long reading passage on the Verbal section, using key words and phrases to summarize the main ideas (see Chapter 7 for details).

- Perform all necessary math calculations during the Quantitative section (Chapters 8 and 9).

- Copy the diagrams that accompany geometry problems from the Quantitative section, and add to or modify these as you develop new information based on the data provided (Chapters 8 and 9). If no diagram is provided, sketch your own.

- When tackling analytical puzzles, create a simple diagram, map, or table summarizing the puzzle conditions from which the answers can usually be read (Chapter 11).

- Create a simple outline for each of the essays you write for the GRE Analytical Writing Measure (Chapter 12).

In addition, as was suggested earlier, use the scrap paper to note the minimum number of questions you must answer in each section.

As you can see, you might need a large amount of scrap paper. Use the short break between sections to ask the test administrator for more paper; the supply is unlimited, and there's no reason to take a chance on running out.

The Most Important Warnings

Once You've Answered the Minimum Number of Items, Guess Selectively

On the paper-and-pencil GRE, there was never any penalty for guessing. You lost no points for wrong answers, so it always paid to answer every question, even if you had to guess completely at random.

Proper guessing strategy changes on the CAT. Unfortunately, it changes in a slightly complex way. You need to know and remember three separate guessing rules, depending on where you are in a given test section:

- If you have not yet answered the minimum number of questions, and you are faced with a question you can't answer, guess. Use elimination to rule out any answers you know or suspect are wrong, and then follow your best hunch in choosing from among the remaining answers. You *must* put an answer before you'll be allowed to move on to the next item, so obviously you have no option—you must guess.

- If you have not yet answered the minimum number of questions and time is running short, guess. As was discussed above, it's crucial that you reach the minimum before time runs out. Therefore, even if you only have time for random guesses, make sure you click on some response for as many questions as you need to reach the specified minimum.

- If you *have* answered the minimum number of questions, guess selectively. After you've reached the minimum, you've earned a score for that test section. It will not change dramatically no matter how you perform on the last several questions in the section. However, you could increase or decrease it by ten to thirty points based on how well you do with the final five to seven items.

Therefore, after you've attained the minimum, use your last few minutes (if any) to answer the final questions carefully. Don't guess at random. Instead, take the time to examine each item. Eliminate answers that are clearly wrong; guesstimate, work backward from individual answer choices, experiment with possible solutions, and use any other techniques you know to try to zero in on a correct answer. (Many such techniques are covered in Chapters 4–12 of this book.) Only when

FYI

Use the pauses between sections for a quick relaxation break. It will increase your alertness and efficiency as you start work on each new topic. We explain how in Chapter 14.

you've picked the right answer, or narrowed the possible choices to two, should you choose and confirm an answer.

You'll help your score in the final moments more by approaching the last few questions carefully and thoughtfully than by rushing to select any old answer.

Remember, the Clock Never Stops

After you begin work on a test section, the computer begins counting down the allotted time for that section. Time remaining appears on the upper left-hand corner of your screen, unless you choose to remove that number by clicking the Time box at the bottom.

Be aware that *nothing* that you or the test administrator can do will stop or slow the ticking of the software's internal clock. Removing the time indication from the screen; visiting the rest room or getting a drink of water; requesting extra scrap paper; opening the Help screen to refresh your memory about techniques for using the software—none of these has any effect on the inexorable march of time.

The point is obvious: don't waste your testing time on any of these activities. Instead, use the breaks between sections for any housekeeping you must do. You'll get a one-minute break between sections and a ten-minute break halfway through. If you're efficient (and if you make a pit stop *before* beginning work), those pauses will suffice.

Taming the CAT?

Having read this chapter, you know a lot about computer-adaptive testing, as well as about the test-taking strategies necessary to score your highest on the CAT.

As advocates for test-takers, we regret the demise of the paper-and-pencil exam. In part, this is for personal reasons: unfortunately, some of the test-taking strategies we've developed and taught through the years that rely on paper-and-pencil methods will have to be scrapped.

On the other hand, the CAT offers a host of opportunities for new strategies, which will keep us busy for years to come. So our work of helping students earn higher scores on the GRE won't really be dramatically affected by the change.

No, our regret over the passing of the paper-and-pencil text is really due to one fact: On the paper-and-pencil exam, the student was (largely) in control. On the CAT, the software is in control.

Earlier in this chapter, we explained some of the reasons the test-makers love the CAT. Here's another, which might be the crucial factor: For control freaks like the folks at ETS, computer-adaptive testing is a true joy.

The CAT replaces the familiar test booklet, which the student can flip through (section by section) at will, with a "black box" that presents only one question at a time, selected by a mysterious process that is completely hidden from the student.

It supposedly tailors the test to the skills of the individual, creating the specter (a false one, of course), of a machine that can "read the mind" of the student.

It forces the test-taker to answer questions as they're presented, precluding the possibility of revisiting items, tackling questions in any preferred sequence, or changing your mind on later reflection.

And it eliminates—at least under current law—the test disclosure rules that have forced the test-makers to make most past exams publicly available for scrutiny and criticism.

All of these changes, intentionally or not, have the same psychological impact: they put the test-taker in a one-down position, forced to respond passively to the agenda of a machine rather than actively managing the test- taking process. For a student who is computer illiterate or uncomfortable with machines, the same effect is heightened.

As you can see, we're not fans of computer-adaptive testing. For now, however, it is the wave of the future. And there is no reason why you can't score high on the CAT if you prepare for it in a savvy fashion.

In the chapters that follow, we'll examine each of the nine question types used on every form of the GRE, and you'll learn test-taking strategies that will help you conquer each one.

JUST THE FACTS

- You need to master both the mechanics and the special strategy of computerized testing before taking the CAT.
- Above all, aim to answer the first five questions of each CAT section correctly; they're crucial to your score.
- Use scrap paper freely to solve problems, take notes, and otherwise assist you in tackling test items.
- Adjust your guessing strategy on the CAT depending on which part of the section you're in.

Chapter 4

Antonyms

Get the Scoop On . . .

- The best techniques for tackling antonyms
- Why anticipating answers can help you find the correct choice more quickly and easily
- How to use word roots and context clues to guess difficult words
- How the backward check can help you avoid tempting wrong answers
- How connotations and secondary meanings can unlock tricky antonyms

---

THE TEST CAPSULE

What's the Big Idea?

You'll be given a word together with five answer choices—five words or phrases that are the same part of speech as the original word. Your job is to pick the answer choice whose meaning is most nearly *opposite* to the meaning of the original word.

How Many?

Of the 30 questions in your verbal section, your GRE will probably have a total of nine antonym questions.

How Much Do They Count?

Because there are nine antonyms of 30 total verbal questions, they count as 29 percent of your overall verbal score.

How Much Time Should They Take?

You need to answer antonyms at a rate of almost two per minute. Aim to finish each antonym in 40 to 45 seconds.

What's the Best Strategy?

Anticipate a possible answer *before* looking at the answer choices. This will help you avoid becoming slightly confused or off target when confronted with a series of answers that are closely related but subtly wrong.

What's the Worst Pitfall?

Grabbing the first answer that looks right without examining all five answer choices. Antonyms are "shades of gray" questions; the first answer you see might be fairly correct, but a second choice might be better, and a third choice might be better still. Because many words in English have connotations that subtly alter the implications of the word, more than one answer choice could be partly right; so scrutinize all five answers before picking one.

THE OFFICIAL DESCRIPTION

What They Are

Antonyms are designed to test both your knowledge of English vocabulary and your ability to use logic to recognize meanings that are opposite one another. The original word (the *stem word*) will appear in capital letters, followed by a colon (:). Five answer choices will follow. You must pick the answer choice that is most nearly opposite in meaning to the stem word.

Where They Are

In the typical computerized GRE, you'll have one verbal section that is 30 minutes long. It will probably include nine antonyms, interspersed seemingly at random among the other verbal question types—sentence completions, analogies, and reading comprehension questions. Reminder: the test-makers claim the right to change the format at any time! However, the typical format we just described is what you're most likely to encounter.

What They Measure

Obviously, the primary type of knowledge tested by antonyms is English vocabulary. Antonyms reward word knowledge that is both broad and precise. The more words you know, and the more exact your knowledge of their meanings, the better you're likely to do on antonym items. You're not expected to know specialized words, such as technical terminology from the sciences or a particular field of art or literature. Instead, the words tested on the GRE are drawn from the general vocabulary that most college-educated people have encountered in serious literature, textbooks, and scholarly writings.

The Insider's GRE Word List (Appendix A) is a good place to begin your vocabulary study for the exam. You might want to read the introductory material that appears there now; it discusses in a bit more detail the kinds of words that the test-makers like to include on the exam.

The Directions

> **Directions:** Each question below consists of a word printed in capital letters, followed by five words or phrases. Choose the word or phrase that is most nearly *opposite* in meaning to the word in capital letters.
>
> Since some of the questions require you to distinguish fine shades of meaning, be sure to consider all the choices before deciding which one is best.

THE INSIDER'S REPORT

FYI

Do pause long enough to scan each answer choice. On antonyms, as on all verbal questions, there are shades of gray among answers, and two or more choices may be partially correct. So it pays to read all five answer choices before marking your choice. But don't agonize; if you know a particular word well, you can probably answer the question in 15 seconds or less, which will leave you extra time for the more difficult questions that are likely to turn up elsewhere in the section.

Now that you've heard the official rap on the GRE Antonyms questions, it's time to get down to the real nitty-gritty. The following sections bring you the best strategies and tips for boosting your GRE score. And you'll also get an unofficial heads-up about pitfalls on this section of the GRE, so you can step right around them and move on to higher scores.

Strategies That Really Work

If the Answer Jumps out at You, Grab It!

You'll find that GRE antonym items vary greatly in difficulty. (As you learned in Chapter 3, that's true of every question type on the exam.) The difficulty of each item will vary depending on how well you've done on previous questions.

In any case, don't be surprised if some of the antonyms on your exam appear "obvious." You can expect that to be the case occasionally, especially early in the test section, before the computer has "figured out" your personal skill level. If the right answer jumps out at you, great! It is probably correct.

If No Answer Is Obvious, Define the Stem Word

When the answer doesn't jump out at you, start by considering the stem word—the word in capital letters whose opposite you must find. *Without focusing on the answer choices,* take a few seconds and try to define the stem word for yourself. If you can, think of a one- or two-word synonym or a defining phrase.

This is a useful step for several reasons. For one thing, the answer choices might be confusing or misleading. Remember, four of them are wrong, and only one is right. If you approach the answer choices with only a vague idea about the meaning of the stem word, you might find yourself misled by the distractors—the wrong answer choices.

Also, on many antonyms, more than one answer choice will be partly right; the differences among the answers might be quite subtle. If your idea of the meaning of the stem word is clearly focused beforehand, you'll find it easier to distinguish among several similar answer choices.

Anticipate an Answer

Next, *before scrutinizing the answer choices,* think of what the opposite of the stem word would be. Come up with your own word or a short phrase that defines the stem word's antonym. *Then* look at the answer choices. If one of these is the same as the opposite you thought of, you've found the right answer. If not, look for a synonym for the word you thought of; that will be the answer you want.

Anticipating the answer is another way of avoiding the confusion that might arise when you have to consider five often subtly differentiated answer choices. If you know what you're looking for before you begin to search, you're more likely to find it.

Here's an example of how this process might work:

PUSILLANIMOUS:

(A) noteworthy
(B) magnanimous
(C) vindictive
(D) intrepid
(E) grandiose

Start by trying to define the stem word, *pusillanimous.* If you've encountered this word in your reading, you might know that it means "cowardly, timid, fainthearted." (If you don't know the word, or have only a vague idea of its meaning, don't despair; we'll discuss later what to do with words of whose meaning you're uncertain.) What's the opposite of this? A word that means "brave, courageous, bold." That's the meaning to look for among the answer choices.

In this case, the correct answer is (D), intrepid, which one dictionary defines as "characterized by resolute fearlessness." If you know this word well, the fact that it is a close antonym of *pusillanimous* might be apparent right away. However, if your understanding of intrepid is a little shaky, then defining the opposite *before* looking at the answer choices might help you avoid picking a vaguely related wrong answer. For example, choice (B), magnanimous, has a positive meaning, just as intrepid does. However, a person who is magnanimous isn't brave; he is generous, forgiving, or compassionate. Focusing on the true opposite before looking at the answer choices should help you see that magnanimous doesn't really work—but intrepid does.

FYI

Don't be afraid to guess, even if you're not completely sure about the best answer, especially early in the test section, before you've answered the minimum number of questions needed to receive a score. See Chapter 3 for a more detailed discussion of GRE guessing strategy.

When Necessary, Use the Process of Elimination

As you might have noticed, in some antonym items, the words given as answer choices might be as difficult as the stem words. So you might find that your knowledge of the meanings of some of the answer choices may be vague or shaky.

When this happens, work by elimination. Go through the answer choices one by one. You probably know the meanings of at least a few of the words or phrases given, and it's probably possible for you to eliminate one, two, or three of them as being clearly wrong. Focus on the answers that remain—words whose meaning you aren't sure of, but which at least seem to be possible answers. Then choose arbitrarily among them, following your instincts or your best hunch, and move on to the next question.

Consider this example, which comes from a real GRE exam:

SODDEN:

(A) barren
(B) desiccated
(C) temperate
(D) expedient
(E) artificial

You might or might not know the word *sodden;* it's a fairly common word, but the lack of a context probably makes it harder to recall its meaning. As it happens, *sodden* means "thoroughly soaked, heavy with moisture"; think of a dishtowel that has been used to mop up a big spill. So the opposite would be some word meaning "very dry."

In this question, some of the answer choices are words that most people would find hard. Take a look at them. Does the right answer jump out at you? If not, see how many answers you can eliminate as clearly wrong (that is, as not meaning "very dry"). The chances are good that you can eliminate one, two, or three possibilities, even if you're not sure about the meanings of some of the answer words.

It so happens that the correct answer is choice (B), desiccated—the word that most people would probably consider hardest among the answer choices. (If it's new to you, look it up in your dictionary.) You might have been able to pick this answer strictly by means of elimination, if you could see that none of the other answer choices mean "dry." In this case, working by elimination can enable you to pick the right answer *even if you don't know its meaning.*

This is not a unique example; you'll probably find one or more antonym items on the GRE that work for you in just this way. So don't give up on an item where you can't pick the right answer; approach the problem from the other direction by eliminating the wrong answers, and so zeroing in on what *must* be correct.

Check Your Answer Backward

After choosing the answer you think is best, check your answer backward. In other words, look at the answer you've chosen and ask yourself: "What would be the opposite of *this* word?" The answer should be the same as the original word. If it is, you've chosen correctly. If not, think again.

Let's look back at the same example:

SODDEN:

(A) barren
(B) desiccated
(C) temperate
(D) expedient
(E) artificial

The closest wrong answer—the one many students find most tempting—is choice (A), barren. The backward check offers a perfect opportunity to avoid it. As you probably know, *barren* means "lifeless, without offspring, infertile." It's a tempting wrong answer, because we associate barrenness with dryness. (Think of a desert, for example.) But if you had tentatively chosen *barren* as your answer, for the backward check you'd ask: What would be the opposite of *barren?* The answer would be a word meaning something like "full of life, abundant, fertile." It's definitely *not* "sodden." The backward check makes it obvious that *barren* is wrong, since *barren* and *sodden* aren't opposites.

Here's another example:

INDIGENT:

(A) capable
(B) affluent
(C) celebrated
(D) free-spending
(E) miserly

The stem word means "poor, lacking money." Therefore, the correct antonym should mean something like "rich." If you find it easy to pick the right answer choice, great. But if not, several of the answers may be tempting, because several have to do with wealth or money. The backward check will help you distinguish among them.

Choice (A), *capable*, means "competent." The opposite would be "incompetent, unable to do things." Clearly that's not a synonym for *indigent*.

Choice (B), *affluent*, means "well-to-do, prosperous." The opposite would be "poor," which *is* a synonym for *indigent*. We seem to be on the right track here.

Choice (C), *celebrated*, means "famous." The opposite would be "unknown." No match here.

Choice (D), *free-spending*, might be tempting; a rich person is certainly more likely to have this quality than a poor person. But what's the opposite? It would be something like "miserly, cheap, or stingy." None of these means the same as *indigent*.

Finally, choice (E), *miserly*, means "stingy, greedy." The opposite would be "generous, liberal." Again, this is definitely wrong. We're driven back to choice (B), which, of course, is correct.

The Best Insider's Tips

Use Word Roots and Context Clues to Guess at Meanings

FYI

The Insider's GRE Word List (Appendix A) contains numerous mini-lessons on important word roots, under the sidebar heading "Origin." When you study the word list, take time to read about the word roots and learn as many as possible. They'll help you remember and guess word meanings on the exam.

You'll probably encounter some words on the GRE of whose meanings you're uncertain. That's normal; remember, the questions are designed to vary in difficulty, and most students will find at least a few questions in each section quite challenging.

When this happens, don't immediately give up or simply pick an answer at random. Instead, take a few moments to try to guess the meaning of the unknown word. You might be surprised to find that you can figure it out—or at least come close—quite frequently.

One of the best tools for guessing word meanings is *word roots*. These are word fragments—syllables or groups of letters—that are found in one or more English words and that generally indicate the origin of the word in Latin, Greek, or some other language. A word root conveys a fragment of meaning; if you recognize the word root, you can figure out at least part of the meaning of the word that contains it.

A second tool for guessing word meanings is *context clues*. The context of a word is the phrase, sentence, or other environment in which it is used. Every time you read or hear a word, it appears in some context, which generally helps you understand the meaning of the word.

On GRE antonym items, of course, the words are devoid of any normal context, which is one of the things that makes these questions challenging. Thus, when you can, you should provide your own context for difficult words on the exam. This means trying to recall a phrase or sentence in which you've seen the word used. Recalling a context can help you pin down the meaning of a word that seems vaguely familiar.

Here's an example of the use of context clues and word roots in guessing a word's meaning. Suppose the stem word for an antonym item is

DESECRATION. If you know its meaning, fine. But if, like most test-takers, you find this a difficult word, try to think of a context in which you've seen or heard it used. One common context for this word is in news stories about vandalism of houses of worship or cemeteries; you might have heard a reporter speak of the "desecration of a church by local teenagers," for instance. This kind of recollection might be enough to jog your memory of the word's meaning.

As an alternative, see if you can break the word down into its component parts, yielding a word root that might be helpful. *Desecration* begins with the familiar prefix *de-*, which means "away from," "out of," or "not." (Think of words like *destabilize* or *deregulate* as examples.) This is followed by *secr*, which is a variant of the word root *sacr*, found in words like *sacred, sacrifice,* and *sacrament.* What do all these words have in common? They all deal with holy things—and "holy" is the meaning of the word root *sacr.*

When you combine the prefix *de-* with the root *sacr,* you can see that the word *desecration* probably refers to "taking away the holiness of something." Clearly, that definition makes sense in the news-story context we cited a moment ago.

Of course, this is just one example. You might not recognize the root *sacr*, and you might never have encountered the word *desecration* in any helpful context. But in many cases, you'll be able to use these tools to help you remember the meanings of difficult words, or to make a guess at words you've rarely seen before.

If Necessary, Play the Good Word/Bad Word Game
When your recollection of a word is really vague, you might have to play the good word/bad word game. This means placing the word on a single, simple axis from positive to negative; in other words, is it a "good" word or a "bad" word? Even if you remember almost nothing about a word, you might remember this; and, in some instances, that might be enough to pick the right antonym.

Here's a real example from the GRE:

HACKNEYED:

(A) fresh
(B) illicit
(C) careful
(D) unpopular
(E) dissenting

Again, you might know the word well, in which case the answer might come easily. But if your recollection is vague, try to guess whether *hackneyed* is a good word or a bad word. Does it mean something positive or negative?

Most people can tell that the meaning of *hackneyed* is more negative than positive. Maybe it's because the word *hack* has a negative feeling, both as a verb meaning "to stab, slash, or chop" and as a noun meaning "a writer without talent." Whatever the reason, if you know that *hackneyed* is a bad word, you can guess that the antonym you're looking for is a good word—a word with positive rather than negative meanings.

Knowing this enables you to eliminate choice (B) and probably also choices (D) and (E). (We could argue about those, but they strike most people as more negative than positive.) This narrows the number of possible choices to two, which gives you pretty good odds of guessing correctly. The right answer is choice (A), *hackneyed,* which means "trite, unoriginal," so "fresh" is a good opposite.

The Most Important Warnings

Consider Connotations

When more than one answer to an antonym question seems right, consider the *connotations,* or feelings, of the words as well as their *denotations,* or literal meanings. For example, the word *shrewd* means "clever, smart." So a word meaning something like "foolish, dull" would be more or less opposite to *shrewd.* But *shrewd* also has the connotation of "tricky, cunning, deceitful." So the best antonym would be a word that includes the connotation of "open, innocent, sincere." A word like *simple* or *artless* would be a good choice.

Make Sure Your Answer Is "Opposite Enough"

Be certain that the answer you pick is *directly opposed* in meaning to the stem word. For example, if the stem word is *turbid,* meaning "cloudy, muddy," the opposite should be a word that means "very clear," like *pellucid* or *crystalline.* A word like *translucent* or *milky,* which refers to a partly cloudy substance, would be a poor answer; it isn't "opposite enough."

Here's another example:

REVILE:

(A) ignore
(B) tease
(C) describe
(D) evaluate
(E) laud

To revile someone is to attack or insult them in a harsh or vicious way. It's a strong word, and the antonym should be equally strong. The best answer is choice (E); to laud someone is to praise them highly. The other answers are also opposed in meaning to *revile,* but they aren't "opposite enough"; they convey either a slightly negative meaning (*tease*) or a basically neutral one rather than the highly positive meaning we need.

Don't Forget Secondary Meanings

When no answer seems correct, look at the stem word again. It might have a secondary meaning that you're forgetting. For example, *decisive* means "self-assured, definite, determined." A good opposite would be *hesitant, unsure,* or *wavering.* You might find, however, that no word like this is included among the answer choices. If so, a secondary meaning of *decisive* might be intended: "crucial, playing a deciding role," as in the sentence "Gettysburg was a decisive battle of the U.S. Civil War." The best opposite for this meaning would be a word like *insignificant, minor,* or *unimportant.*

Here's a real GRE example:

NICE:

(A) indirect
(B) indecisive
(C) imperceptible
(D) imprecise
(E) imperturbable

You'll have trouble with this question unless you know that a secondary meaning of *nice* is "precise, particular, exact, finicky." (In this sense, one of the generals who defeated Napoleon at Waterloo is supposed to have remarked about that battle, "It was a damned nice thing," meaning that it was a close call.) The correct answer is (D).

When faced with a set of answer choices, none of which seems right, don't struggle to pick one; return to the stem word and see whether some secondary meaning is in play.

JUST THE FACTS

- When tackling an antonym, first define the stem word; then anticipate a possible opposite.

- Check your answer backward to make sure you've chosen correctly.

- When in doubt, use word roots and context clues to remind you of word meanings or to help you guess them.

- Consider the connotations (feelings) of words to distinguish among subtle answer choices.

- When no answer seems correct, consider any secondary meanings of the stem word.

PRACTICE, PRACTICE, PRACTICE: ANTONYM EXERCISES

Instructions

The following exercises will give you a chance to practice the skills and strategies you've just learned for tackling antonym questions. As with all practice exercises, work under true testing conditions. Complete each exercise in a single sitting. Eliminate distractions (TV, music) and clear away notes and reference materials.

Time yourself with a stopwatch or kitchen timer, or have someone else time you. If you run out of time before answering all the questions, stop and draw a line under the last question you finished. Then go ahead and tackle the remaining questions. When you are done, score yourself based only on the questions you finished in the allotted time.

Understanding Your Scores

0–3 correct: A poor performance. Study this chapter again, and start spending time each day studying the Insider's GRE Word List (Appendix A).

4–6 correct: A below-average score. Study this chapter again.

7–9 correct: An average score. You may want to study this chapter again. Also be sure you are managing your time wisely (as explained in Chapter 3) and avoiding errors due to haste or carelessness.

10–12 correct: An above-average score. Depending on your personal target score and your strength on other verbal question types, you may or may not want to devote additional time to antonym study.

13–15 correct: An excellent score. You are probably ready to perform well on GRE antonym items.

EXERCISE 1

15 Questions

Time—10 Minutes

> **Directions:** Each question below consists of a word printed in capital letters, followed by five lettered words or phrases. Choose the lettered word or phrase that is most nearly *opposite* in meaning to the word in capital letters.
>
> Since some of the questions require you to distinguish fine shades of meaning, be sure to consider all the choices before deciding which one is best.

1. ORNATE:
    - (A) monochromatic
    - (B) balding
    - (C) garish
    - (D) severe
    - (E) brackish

2. IMMATURE:
    - (A) in preparation
    - (B) in excellent condition
    - (C) subject to decay
    - (D) intelligent
    - (E) fully developed

3. TEMPERANCE:
    - (A) sloth
    - (B) hospitality
    - (C) dissipation
    - (D) miserliness
    - (E) callousness

4. VACILLATE:
    - (A) make vulnerable
    - (B) reach a firm decision
    - (C) refuse allegiance
    - (D) remain confident
    - (E) affirm belief in

5. BANE:

(A) source of benefit
(B) abundant supply
(C) highest point
(D) chief virtue
(E) heavy burden

6. SUNDRY:

(A) contiguous
(B) indescribable
(C) numerous
(D) identical
(E) relative

7. DISPERSE:

(A) incite
(B) announce
(C) seize
(D) muster
(E) touch

8. PROPAGATE:

(A) uproot
(B) soften
(C) desert
(D) saturate
(E) prune

9. ANATHEMA:

(A) fortitude
(B) benediction
(C) distinction
(D) convalescence
(E) rectitude

10. EQUANIMITY:

(A) lassitude
(B) terror
(C) malignity
(D) wrath
(E) passion

11. PERPETUAL:

   (A) passe
   (B) deceased
   (C) motionless
   (D) versatile
   (E) fleeting

12. SPURN:

   (A) begrudge
   (B) persist
   (C) inject
   (D) embrace
   (E) praise

13. VALIANT:

   (A) modest
   (B) despicable
   (C) diminutive
   (D) ill-favored
   (E) timorous

14. UNTENABLE:

   (A) stable
   (B) competent
   (C) defensible
   (D) occupied
   (E) frangible

15. DEPRECIATE:

   (A) repair
   (B) inveigle
   (C) overrate
   (D) intensify
   (E) despoil

EXERCISE 2

15 Questions

Time—10 Minutes

> **Directions:** Each question below consists of a word printed in capital letters, followed by five lettered words or phrases. Choose the lettered word or phrase that is most nearly *opposite* in meaning to the word in capital letters.
>
> Since some of the questions require you to distinguish fine shades of meaning, be sure to consider all the choices before deciding which one is best.

1. BRUSQUE:
   - (A) serious
   - (B) gay
   - (C) alluring
   - (D) talkative
   - (E) congenial

2. ASSIDUOUS:
   - (A) casual
   - (B) slothful
   - (C) unintentional
   - (D) nominal
   - (E) slow

3. KINDRED:
   - (A) orphaned
   - (B) alien
   - (C) simulated
   - (D) paternal
   - (E) disjointed

4. MITIGATE:
   - (A) exacerbate
   - (B) sanction
   - (C) postpone
   - (D) retain
   - (E) commend

5. MOOT:

   (A) illegal
   (B) unarguable
   (C) digressive
   (D) valid
   (E) formative

6. SPURIOUS:

   (A) inappropriate
   (B) complimentary
   (C) genuine
   (D) mild
   (E) impetuous

7. CURSORY:

   (A) considerable
   (B) laudatory
   (C) repeated
   (D) exhaustive
   (E) monotonous

8. STULTIFYING:

   (A) enervating
   (B) astonishing
   (C) encouraging
   (D) mortifying
   (E) disquieting

9. EXTIRPATE:

   (A) extend
   (B) nurture
   (C) predominate
   (D) broadcast
   (E) infuse

10. PENURY:

   (A) wealth
   (B) generosity
   (C) fame
   (D) grandiosity
   (E) nobility

11. BELITTLE:

   (A) appraise
   (B) extol
   (C) support
   (D) nominate
   (E) defend

12. LISTLESS:

   (A) earnest
   (B) mobile
   (C) living
   (D) vigorous
   (E) essential

13. RETARD:

   (A) revivify
   (B) educate
   (C) release
   (D) intensify
   (E) accelerate

14. SOLUBLE:

   (A) deceptive
   (B) unanswerable
   (C) indecisive
   (D) unmentionable
   (E) invulnerable

15. DISCREPANCY:

   (A) normality
   (B) reliability
   (C) agreement
   (D) consensus
   (E) proximity

EXERCISE 3

15 Questions

Time—10 Minutes

> **Directions:** Each question below consists of a word printed in capital letters, followed by five lettered words or phrases. Choose the lettered word or phrase that is most nearly *opposite* in meaning to the word in capital letters.
>
> Since some of the questions require you to distinguish fine shades of meaning, be sure to consider all the choices before deciding which one is best.

1. VEHEMENT:
   - (A) halfhearted
   - (B) minuscule
   - (C) meandering
   - (D) forced
   - (E) dull

2. REND:
   - (A) unite
   - (B) depict
   - (C) transform
   - (D) pierce
   - (E) embellish

3. ADULTERATED:
   - (A) clarified
   - (B) pure
   - (C) antiseptic
   - (D) sinless
   - (E) transmuted

4. DOGMATIC:
   - (A) imprecise
   - (B) whimsical
   - (C) flexible
   - (D) inarticulate
   - (E) unorthodox

5. CREDULOUS:

   (A) visionary
   (B) atheistic
   (C) skeptical
   (D) amazing
   (E) disloyal

6. MALIGNANT:

   (A) unimposing
   (B) soothing
   (C) beneficent
   (D) ineffectual
   (E) allied

7. REPUDIATE:

   (A) verify
   (B) suggest
   (C) account
   (D) glean
   (E) espouse

8. INCHOATE:

   (A) shrilly whistling
   (B) in steady motion
   (C) easily noticed
   (D) vividly colored
   (E) fully formed

9. PERSPICACITY:

   (A) dullness
   (B) timidity
   (C) restraint
   (D) composure
   (E) optimism

10. INGENUOUS:

   (A) new
   (B) sophisticated
   (C) inane
   (D) foolish
   (E) innocuous

11. RESOURCEFUL:

   (A) inept
   (B) weary
   (C) fearful
   (D) single-minded
   (E) bland

12. STRESS:

   (A) deny
   (B) de-emphasize
   (C) soften
   (D) undermine
   (E) assail

13. SPONTANEOUS:

   (A) rehearsed
   (B) regulated
   (C) willful
   (D) insincere
   (E) dour

14. INFERNAL:

   (A) redeemable
   (B) useful
   (C) celestial
   (D) laudatory
   (E) notable

15. GREGARIOUS:

   (A) eccentric
   (B) asocial
   (C) inimitable
   (D) intent
   (E) platitudinous

EXERCISE 4

15 Questions

Time—10 Minutes

> **Directions:** Each question below consists of a word printed in capital letters, followed by five lettered words or phrases. Choose the lettered word or phrase that is most nearly *opposite* in meaning to the word in capital letters.
>
> Since some of the questions require you to distinguish fine shades of meaning, be sure to consider all the choices before deciding which one is best.

1. REQUISITE:
   - (A) scorned
   - (B) paltry
   - (C) flawed
   - (D) insignificant
   - (E) needless

2. IMPLICATE:
   - (A) support
   - (B) disprove
   - (C) convict
   - (D) demonstrate
   - (E) exonerate

3. FORBEARANCE:
   - (A) indication
   - (B) response
   - (C) harshness
   - (D) impatience
   - (E) punishment

4. VITIATE:
   - (A) undermine
   - (B) deaden
   - (C) rescind
   - (D) perfect
   - (E) enforce

5. CONFOUND:

(A) convey
(B) praise
(C) distinguish
(D) shatter
(E) verify

6. BONDAGE:

(A) liberalization
(B) emancipation
(C) revolt
(D) expulsion
(E) loosening

7. FLAUNT:

(A) obey
(B) conceal
(C) refrain
(D) languish
(E) abase

8. DOGGED:

(A) easily discouraged
(B) unusually intelligent
(C) slow to anger
(D) impossible to trace
(E) deeply depressed

9. SEVER:

(A) approach
(B) apply
(C) mollify
(D) link
(E) promise

10. TRITE:

(A) dissimilar
(B) characteristic
(C) grotesque
(D) unlawful
(E) novel

11. DEFILE:

   (A) decorate
   (B) dampen
   (C) purify
   (D) edify
   (E) regulate

12. EGREGIOUS:

   (A) divorced from society
   (B) inclined to argue
   (C) not readily noticeable
   (D) deviating from the norm
   (E) extremely cooperative

13. QUELL:

   (A) instigate
   (B) surge
   (C) baffle
   (D) augment
   (E) repeal

14. ALIENATE:

   (A) provoke
   (B) attract
   (C) convene
   (D) appease
   (E) renounce

15. INFAMY:

   (A) futurity
   (B) reputation
   (C) anonymity
   (D) honor
   (E) ignorance

EXERCISE 5

15 Questions

Time—10 Minutes

> **Directions:** Each question below consists of a word printed in capital letters, followed by five lettered words or phrases. Choose the lettered word or phrase that is most nearly *opposite* in meaning to the word in capital letters.
>
> Since some of the questions require you to distinguish fine shades of meaning, be sure to consider all the choices before deciding which one is best.

1. GLOWER:
   - (A) grimace
   - (B) gaze
   - (C) snicker
   - (D) beam
   - (E) sneer

2. PREDILECTION:
   - (A) innovation
   - (B) modesty
   - (C) concern
   - (D) prophecy
   - (E) distaste

3. REJUVENATE:
   - (A) grow
   - (B) elate
   - (C) age
   - (D) weaken
   - (E) depress

4. PIQUE:
   - (A) defy
   - (B) withdraw
   - (C) embolden
   - (D) please
   - (E) scatter

5. RECONDITE:

   (A) obvious
   (B) impartial
   (C) frequent
   (D) irrational
   (E) indeterminate

6. ALLAY:

   (A) exacerbate
   (B) dismay
   (C) terrorize
   (D) invoke
   (E) blacken

7. ARTICULATE:

   (A) casual
   (B) obscure
   (C) incoherent
   (D) simpering
   (E) dull

8. OPAQUE:

   (A) prismatic
   (B) diaphanous
   (C) visible
   (D) refulgent
   (E) intangible

9. FETTER:

   (A) free
   (B) rebel
   (C) escape
   (D) extend
   (E) revive

10. PROFICIENT:

   (A) careless
   (B) inexperienced
   (C) inappropriate
   (D) unskilled
   (E) hesitant

11. NONPARTISAN:
    (A) variegated
    (B) undivided
    (C) nominal
    (D) illicit
    (E) factional

12. ATROCIOUS:
    (A) fierce
    (B) admirable
    (C) normal
    (D) vivid
    (E) mottled

13. NULLIFY:
    (A) restate
    (B) notify
    (C) validate
    (D) promulgate
    (E) sign

14. PALATABLE:
    (A) culinary
    (B) garish
    (C) noxious
    (D) unflavored
    (E) bland

15. EMINENT:
    (A) unlikely
    (B) ill-favored
    (C) depressed
    (D) little-known
    (E) mythical

Answer Key

Exercise 1	Exercise 2	Exercise 3	Exercise 4	Exercise 5
1. C	1. E	1. A	1. E	1. D
2. E	2. B	2. A	2. E	2. E
3. C	3. B	3. B	3. D	3. C
4. B	4. A	4. C	4. D	4. D
5. A	5. B	5. C	5. C	5. A
6. D	6. C	6. C	6. B	6. A
7. D	7. D	7. E	7. B	7. C
8. A	8. C	8. E	8. A	8. B
9. B	9. B	9. A	9. D	9. A
10. E	10. A	10. B	10. E	10. D
11. E	11. B	11. A	11. C	11. E
12. D	12. D	12. B	12. C	12. B
13. E	13. E	13. A	13. A	13. C
14. C	14. B	14. C	14. B	14. C
15. C	15. C	15. B	15. D	15. D

Explanatory Answers

EXERCISE 1

1. **The correct answer is (C).** *Ornate* means "elaborately decorated." *Severe,* which in one sense means "austerely plain," is a good antonym.

2. **The correct answer is (E).** *Immature* is sometimes used to characterize behavior that is stupid and foolish, the opposite of choice (D), but its basic meaning is "not ripe," that is, "not fully developed." Thus, choice (E) is an exact opposite.

3. **The correct answer is (C).** *Temperance* means "moderation, restraint, especially in the use of alcohol"; *dissipation* means "intemperance, lack of moderation, especially in the use of alcohol."

4. **The correct answer is (B).** *Vacillate* means "to waver, hesitate, or go back and forth between choices." The opposite is to *reach a firm decision.*

5. **The correct answer is (A).** A *bane* is a source of harm or ruin. The opposite is a *source of benefit.*

6. **The correct answer is (D).** *Sundry* means "various, varied, diverse, miscellaneous." *Identical* is a good antonym; it means "exactly the same."

7. **The correct answer is (D).** To *disperse* is to scatter or spread apart, as in "*disperse* the crowd." By contrast, to *muster* is to gather or collect, as in "*muster* the troops for battle."

8. **The correct answer is (A).** To *propagate* something is to help it grow, spread, or multiply. One could *propagate* a plant, for instance, by taking a cutting from it and starting a new plant; or one could propagate a belief or an idea by speaking or writing about it. *Uproot* is a good opposite. Meaning "to dig up, destroy, or prevent from growing," it, too, can be applied both to living things and to ideas and beliefs.

9. **The correct answer is (B).** *Anathema* means "ban, curse, solemn denunciation"; *benediction* means "blessing."

10. **The correct answer is (E).** *Equanimity* means "evenness of mind or temper, calm, composure." *Passion,* which refers to any strong feeling, excitement, or emotion, is a good opposite. *Terror* (choice B), *malignity* (choice C), and *wrath* (choice D), because they name particular passions, are too specific.

11. **The correct answer is (E).** *Perpetual* means "eternal, lasting forever"; *fleeting* means "transitory, passing quickly."

12. **The correct answer is (D).** To *spurn* something is to reject it scornfully or disdainfully. The opposite is to *embrace* it—that is, to welcome it or to accept it gladly.

13. **The correct answer is (E).** *Valiant* means "brave, courageous, strong of mind and spirit." *Timorous* means "fearful, timid, lacking in courage or self-confidence."

14. **The correct answer is (C).** *Untenable* means "unreasonable; not able to be held, maintained, or defended." The opposite is *defensible.*

15. **The correct answer is (C).** One definition of *depreciate* is to underrate, disparage, or belittle—that is, to speak of something as being less valuable than it really is. The opposite is to *overrate* something—that is, to speak of it as being more valuable than it really is.

EXERCISE 2

1. **The correct answer is (E).** A *brusque* manner is abrupt, curt, blunt, or rude. By contrast, a *congenial* manner is warm, friendly, and sociable.

2. **The correct answer is (B).** *Assiduous* means "hard-working." The opposite is *slothful*, which means lazy.

3. **The correct answer is (B).** *Kindred* means "related, allied, connected." A *kindred* spirit, for example, is anyone whose heart and mind seem sympathetic to one's own. *Alien* is a good opposite; it means "foreign, remote, unrelated."

4. **The correct answer is (A).** *Mitigate* means "to relieve, to make less severe"; *exacerbate* means "to intensify, to make more severe."

5. **The correct answer is (B).** A *moot* point is subject to discussion or argument. A point that is not subject to question or dispute is *unarguable* or *indisputable.*

6. **The correct answer is (C).** *Spurious* means "false" or "counterfeit." Opposites include *genuine, true,* and *authentic.*

7. **The correct answer is (D).** *Cursory* means "fast and usually superficial"; *exhaustive* means "thorough."

8. **The correct answer is (C).** *Stultifying*, at least in one sense, means "impairing, frustrating; rendering useless, futile, or ineffectual." *Encouraging*, which means "stimulating, fostering, giving help or support to," is a reasonable antonym.

9. **The correct answer is (B).** To *extirpate* something is to root it out and destroy it. By contrast, to *nurture* something is to take care of it and help it to survive and grow.

10. **The correct answer is (A).** *Penury* is poverty; the opposite is *wealth*.

11. **The correct answer is (B).** To *belittle* is to mock or disparage. The opposite is to *extol* or *praise*.

12. **The correct answer is (D).** *Listless* means "lacking energy." *Vigorous*, which means "strong, spirited, energetic," is a good opposite.

13. **The correct answer is (E).** To *retard* something is to slow it down. The opposite is to *accelerate* something, or speed it up.

14. **The correct answer is (B).** A *soluble* problem is one that can be solved. One that cannot be solved is *insoluble, inexplicable,* or *unanswerable*.

15. **The correct answer is (C).** A *discrepancy* is a disagreement or a failure of two things to match as expected. The opposite is *agreement*. Use the backward check to eliminate choice (A): the opposite of *normality* is *abnormality*, which is not the same as *discrepancy*.

EXERCISE 3

1. **The correct answer is (A).** *Vehement* means "forceful, strong, ardent." A good opposite would be *weak, diffident,* or *halfhearted*.

2. **The correct answer is (A).** To *rend* something is to tear it apart; to *unite* something is to put it together.

3. **The correct answer is (B).** *Adulterated* means "polluted, corrupted, debased, or made impure by the addition of a foreign substance." The opposite is *pure*. Don't be misled by choice (D); adulterated isn't directly connected with the sin of adultery, although both words derive from the same root.

4. **The correct answer is (C).** A *dogmatic* person is rigid or inflexible in his or her beliefs and opinions. Good opposites include *flexible, accommodating,* and *open-minded*.

5. **The correct answer is (C).** *Credulous* means "gullible, overwilling to believe." The opposite is *skeptical,* which means "doubtful, questioning, unwilling to believe."

6. **The correct answer is (C).** As the root *mal* should tell you, *malignant* means "doing evil or harm." *Beneficent* means "doing good."

7. **The correct answer is (E).** To *repudiate* a cause or belief is to reject it. The opposite is to *accept, support,* or *espouse* it.

8. **The correct answer is (E).** *Inchoate* means "imperfectly formed" or "not fully developed"; one speaks of a vague thought or mental image as inchoate. The opposite is *fully formed*.

9. **The correct answer is (A).** *Perspicacity* refers to keenness of perception, understanding, and discernment. The opposite is *dullness* or *stupidity*.

10. **The correct answer is (B).** *Ingenuous* means "innocent, unsophisticated, naive." *Sophisticated, worldly,* and *urbane* are all good antonyms.

11. **The correct answer is (A).** *Resourceful* means "capable of meeting situations and solving problems." The opposite is *incapable, incompetent,* or *inept.*

12. **The correct answer is (B).** To *stress* something is to emphasize it. Thus, *de-emphasize* is a natural antonym.

13. **The correct answer is (A).** Something *spontaneous* is unplanned. By contrast, something *rehearsed* is planned and practiced beforehand.

14. **The correct answer is (C).** *Infernal* means "hellish"; *celestial* means "heavenly."

15. **The correct answer is (B).** A *gregarious* person is one who likes to be with other people. The opposite is a person who prefers to be alone. *Asocial, unfriendly,* and *reclusive* might all serve as antonyms.

EXERCISE 4

1. **The correct answer is (E).** *Requisite,* which is related to *required,* means "necessary." *Needless,* which means "unneeded" or "unnecessary," is a good antonym.

2. **The correct answer is (E).** To *implicate* someone is to connect, involve, or entangle that person with something that is usually unpleasant: "The witness's testimony may *implicate* several others in the crime." The opposite is to *exonerate* someone, that is, to disentangle that person from any blame or involvement in a misdeed.

3. **The correct answer is (D).** *Forbearance* is patience, restraint, or self-control under provocation. The opposite is *impatience.*

4. **The correct answer is (D).** To *vitiate* something is to make it imperfect; to spoil, ruin, or corrupt it. The opposite is to *perfect* something.

5. **The correct answer is (C).** To *confound* two things is to confuse them, to mistake one for the other. Thus *distinguish,* which means "to make a clear distinction between things," is a good opposite.

6. **The correct answer is (B).** *Bondage* means "slavery" or "captivity"; *emancipation* means "liberation" or "the act of setting free." Choices (A), (C), and (E), though tempting, don't specifically and clearly relate to the act of freeing someone from bondage.

7. **The correct answer is (B).** To *flaunt* something is to display it in a showy and conspicuous fashion. By contrast, to *conceal* something is to hide it.

8. **The correct answer is (A).** *Dogged* means "persistent, stubborn, or determined." *Easily discouraged* is a reasonable antonym.

9. **The correct answer is (D).** To *sever* is to divide or separate; to *link* is to join or connect.

10. **The correct answer is (E).** Something *trite* is old hat, commonplace, or overfamiliar. Something *novel* is new, unusual, or modern.

11. **The correct answer is (C).** To *defile* something is to dirty it or sully it. To *purify* something is to clean it or make it pure.

12. **The correct answer is (C).** *Egregious* means "flagrant, outrageous, conspicuously bad": "The defense attorney destroyed the testimony of the witness by exposing several *egregious* errors in his statement." Though not an exact opposite, *not readily noticeable,* meaning "inconspicuous," is fairly close.

13. **The correct answer is (A).** To *quell* something—such as a riot—is to calm it or bring it under control. To *instigate* something is to stir it up, arouse it, or initiate it. Bottle-throwing crowds may *instigate* a riot; the police may *quell* it.

14. **The correct answer is (B).** To *alienate* people is to drive them away or repel them. The opposite is to *attract* them.

15. **The correct answer is (D).** *Infamy* is shame or disgrace. *Honor* is a suitable antonym.

EXERCISE 5

1. **The correct answer is (D).** To *glower* is to scowl or stare menacingly. To *beam*, on the other hand, is to wear an expression of happiness, friendliness, and good feeling.

2. **The correct answer is (E).** A *predilection* is a fondness, inclination, or preference for something. The opposite is a *distaste* or *dislike* for something.

3. **The correct answer is (C).** *Rejuvenate* means "to make young again" (the fountain of youth for which Ponce de Leon searched was supposed to *rejuvenate* the old). *Age,* which means "to make old," is a near opposite.

4. **The correct answer is (D).** As a verb, *pique* has two meanings: "to stimulate or arouse" (as in "*pique* one's curiosity") and "to annoy or irritate" (as in "*piqued* by their indifference"). *Please* is a good opposite for the second meaning.

5. **The correct answer is (A).** *Recondite* means "profound, abstruse, or difficult to understand" (modern physics is considered by many to be a *recondite* subject). *Obvious* is a good antonym.

6. **The correct answer is (A).** To *allay* something, such as pain or fear, is to make it less bad, to relieve it, or to calm it. The opposite is to make it worse or to intensify it, which is the meaning of *exacerbate*.

7. **The correct answer is (C).** As an adjective, *articulate* means "expressing oneself clearly and logically." An *articulate* person states his or her ideas understandably and well. The opposite is *incoherent,* which means "difficult to understand" or "confused."

8. **The correct answer is (B).** Something *opaque* can't be seen through; light does not pass through it at all. A brick wall is *opaque.* By contrast, something *diaphanous* can be seen through—for example, a piece of thin, filmy fabric.

9. **The correct answer is (A).** To *fetter* someone is literally to put him or her in chains; the word is used to refer to any kind of imprisonment or slavery. To *free* someone is the opposite.

10. **The correct answer is (D).** *Proficient* means "skilled, skillful, or adept." The opposite is *unskilled* or *incompetent.* Choice (B) is tempting, but the opposite of *inexperienced* is *experienced,* not proficient. A person can be experienced without being skilled.

11. **The correct answer is (E).** *Factional* means "pertaining to a faction," which is a party or interest group. The word is a good antonym for *nonpartisan,* which describes an action or policy that can be supported by all, regardless of their party or interest group.

12. **The correct answer is (B).** Something *atrocious* is awful, horrible, extremely wicked, or outrageous. The opposite would have to be a word expressing strong approval; *admirable* is a good choice.

13. **The correct answer is (C).** To *nullify* something is to negate it, to take away its power or effect. The opposite is to strengthen, enforce, or uphold something—to *validate* it.

14. **The correct answer is (C).** Literally, *palatable* means "able to be tasted or eaten"; figuratively, it means "acceptable." The word *noxious* combines the opposites of these two meanings well. It means both "revolting or disgusting to taste" and "hateful, odious."

15. **The correct answer is (D).** *Eminent* means "well-known, prominent." (Justice Holmes was an *eminent* legal authority.) The opposite is *little-known* or *obscure.*

Chapter 5

Analogies

Get the Scoop On . . .

- Proven strategies for acing analogies
- The top nine analogy types used on the GRE
- How to guess the meaning of analogy words you don't know
- The most common analogy traps and how to avoid them

THE TEST CAPSULE

What's the Big Idea?

You'll be given a pair of words (the stem pair) that have a certain logical relationship to one another. You have to pick the pair of words from five answer choices that has the same logical relationship.

How Many?

Of the 30 questions in your verbal section, your GRE will probably have a total of seven analogies questions.

How Much Do They Count?

Because analogies are seven out of 30 total verbal questions, they count as 23 percent of your overall verbal score.

How Much Time Should They Take?

You need to answer analogies at a rate of better than one per minute. Aim to finish each *antonym* in 40 to 45 seconds.

What's the Best Strategy?

Build a bridge—a sentence that defines the logical relationship between the two words in the question stem. Then test the bridge with each pair of words in the five answer choices. Only one will work!

What's the Worst Pitfall?

Picking an answer because the words it contains are similar on the surface to those in the question stem. (Maybe both the stem words and the answer words have to do with cooking, for instance.) Ignore surface similarities and look deeper to find the most similar logical relationship.

THE OFFICIAL DESCRIPTION

What They Are

Analogies test your ability to recognize the relationships between pairs of words. You'll be given a pair of words in capital letters (the stem pair) that have a particular relationship to one another. You'll then be given five additional pairs of words (the answer choices). Your job is to select that answer choice with a pair of words whose relationship is most similar to the relationship between the words in the stem pair.

Where They Are

In the typical computerized GRE, you'll have one verbal section that is 30 minutes long; another verbal section will be 15 minutes long. It will probably include seven analogies, interspersed seemingly at random among the other verbal question types—antonyms, sentence completions, and reading comprehension questions. Reminder: the test-makers claim the right to change the format at any time! However, the typical format just described is what you're most likely to encounter.

What They Measure

To answer an analogy correctly, you need to know the meaning of the words in the stem pair and in the answer choices. You also need to understand the logical relationships between words, and at times these can be subtle. So analogies measure both your vocabulary knowledge and your understanding of logical relationships among ideas.

The Directions

> **Directions:** In each of the following questions, a related pair of words or phrases is followed by five other pairs of words or phrases. Select the pair that best expresses a relationship similar to that expressed in the original pair.

THE INSIDER'S REPORT

Strategies That Really Work

Build a Bridge

A bridge is a short sentence that contains both words in the stem pair and shows how they are related. Let's call the two words in the stem pair "X" and "Y." A typical bridge would define X in terms of Y. Consider this example—a real analogy from the test-makers at ETS:

CRUMB : BREAD : :

- (A)   ounce : unit
- (B)   splinter : wood
- (C)   water : bucket
- (D)   twine : rope
- (E)   cream : butter

For the stem pair in this example, the bridge might say, "A CRUMB is a very small piece that falls off or breaks off a piece of BREAD." Notice how this sentence explains the relationship between the two words. It also defines CRUMB (tells what a crumb is) in terms of BREAD. A lovely bridge! (No wonder: it's the test-makers' own example.)

Here are a couple of other examples. Suppose the stem pair was "OPERA : MUSIC." (By the way, you would read this aloud, "opera is to music.") The bridge might say, "An OPERA is a long, elaborate, classical work of MUSIC." If the stem pair was "SURGEON : SCALPEL," the bridge might be, "A SURGEON is a professional who uses a SCALPEL." Get the idea?

Plug in the Answer Choices

After you've created a bridge, turn to the answer choices. One by one, try to plug in the words from the answer choices into the same sentence. If your bridge is a strong one, only one pair of words will make sense.

Try this with the five answer choices for the sample question above. Only the words in choice (B) fit comfortably into the bridge: "A SPLINTER is a very small piece that falls off or breaks off of a piece of WOOD." Think about the others. Is an OUNCE a very small piece of a UNIT (choice A)? No; an ounce is a kind of unit—a unit of weight. Is WATER a very small piece of a BUCKET (choice C)? No; water might be carried in a bucket. The same with the other answers. So choice (B) is correct. (By the way, you would read the stem pair and the correct answer this way: "CRUMB is to BREAD as SPLINTER is to WOOD.")

What if our stem pair is OPERA : MUSIC?

Which of these five answer choices fits the same bridge?

(A) novel : artistry
(B) painting : landscape
(C) oboe : instrument
(D) epic : poetry
(E) microphone : recording

The correct answer is (D), because only that word pair fits into the same bridge: "An EPIC is a long, elaborate, classical work of POETRY."

Get as Narrow as Needed

Sometimes the differences among the answer choices will be subtle—so subtle that the first bridge you've built won't eliminate the wrong answers. When that's the case, two or more answer choices might fit the bridge. Here's an example:

SURGEON : SCALPEL : :

(A) judge : gavel
(B) painter : canvas
(C) executive : computer
(D) farmer : fertilizer
(E) carpenter : saw

If you built the bridge, "A SURGEON is a professional who uses a SCALPEL" and then tried plugging each of the answer pairs (A) through (E), you'd be dismayed to find that all five answer pairs could fit the bridge! A judge uses a gavel (it's the hammer a judge uses to pound on the bench); a painter (often) uses a canvas; an executive (often) uses a computer; a farmer uses fertilizer; and a carpenter uses a saw. Based on this bridge, all five answer choices could be considered correct! Now what?

Solution: narrow your bridge—that is, add details to the sentence to make it more specific.

In this case, you might narrow the bridge in this way: "A SURGEON is a professional who uses a SCALPEL as a tool for cutting." Now plug in the answer choices. Only one fits the new, narrower bridge: choice (E). That's the correct answer.

Of course, picking the correct answer depends on your narrowing the bridge correctly. You could concoct a misleading bridge that included details that pointed to a different answer. For example, you could say, "A SURGEON is a professional who wears a protective smock while using a SCALPEL." With that bridge, choice (B) is arguably correct, because artists, like surgeons, do often wear protective smocks. (The robe a judge wears isn't "protective," so choice (A) doesn't work. And the people in the other choices don't wear smocks at all.) Does this mean that choice (B) is just as good as choice (E)?

No—in fact, if you think about it, you probably find choice (B), and the bridge we made up that points to it, a little silly. The smock that a surgeon (or an artist) wears isn't central to his or her work; and it certainly has little to do with the use of the scalpel. The first narrow bridge we created—the one that refers to the scalpel as a cutting tool—seems more sensible. It defines exactly what the scalpel does in the hands of the surgeon—which is similar to what the saw does in the hands of the carpenter.

The point is that it takes a bit of judgment to build the right bridge. You want to focus on the central, basic nature of the relationship between the two words—not on side issues that are irrelevant (like the surgeon's smock). It's a little subjective, yes. But nine times out of ten, devising the right bridge will strike you as a matter of "common sense."

In fact, in the example we've been looking at, you may have been able to "see" the similarity between SURGEON : SCALPEL and carpenter : saw even without consciously building the new, narrow bridge. That's fine; if the correct answer jumps out at you, go for it! But as you prepare for the test, practice your bridge-building technique. It'll give you crucial help on the handful of really tough analogies your test will contain.

Look for the Test-Makers' Favorite Relationships

FYI

If the correct answer "jumps out at you" without the bridge-building step, great! But the more you practice bridge-building, the faster your instincts will supply answers on GRE day.

Pity the drudges at ETS. They write test questions by the hundred, week in and week out. Like anyone else, they eventually start to repeat themselves. (Ever notice how the third album by your favorite rock band sounds a lot like the first and second albums—only less interesting?) But this is a good thing for you, the test-taker. It means that analogies fall into repeated patterns that you can practice and learn. If you know and understand the test-makers' favorite analogy relationships, you'll quickly pounce on them if they pop up on your exam. And they will, they will!

Here are the top nine analogy relationships we've found on past and current GREs. (If any of the examples that follow contain words you're not sure about, you know what to do: grab your dictionary!)

Part : Whole

In this kind of analogy, one word names something that is part of what's named by the other word—usually a specific kind of part. Here are a couple of examples:

LID : POT : : roof : house
MOVEMENT : SYMPHONY : : scene : play

Opposites

Here, the two words in the pair are opposite or opposed in meaning. Examples:

NAIVE : SOPHISTICATED : : untutored : educated
WATER : DROUGHT : : food : famine

Actor : Action

This kind of analogy links a person or thing with what they commonly do. Examples:

COUNTERFEITER : FAKE : : blackmailer : extort
DETERGENT : CLEAN : : bleach : whiten

Actor : Acted Upon

The word pair includes a person or thing and another person or thing that is commonly acted upon or affected by the first. Examples:

TEACHER : CLASS : : orator : audience
NET : FISH : : trap : game

Action : Acted Upon

Here, an action is paired with the person or thing that commonly receives or is affected by the action. Examples:

ALPHABETIZE : FILES : : catalog : books
RAZE : BUILDING : : fell : tree

Action : Emotion

One of the words describes an action, the other an emotion commonly associated with it. Examples:

LOSS : MOURN : : triumph : celebrate
TREMBLE : FEAR : : shiver : cold

Thing : Description

This kind of word-pair includes one word that names a person or thing, another that describes it. Examples:

MISER : STINGY : : spendthrift : wasteful
GLADE : SHADY : : clearing : open

Description : Quality

Here, an adjective that describes a particular quality is paired with a noun that names the quality. Examples:

LIFELIKE : VIVIDNESS : : truthful : honesty
ARROGANT : PRIDE : : modest : humility

Differing Connotations

In this kind of analogy, two words are linked that have similar meanings but different feelings, moods, or nuances—in other words, different connotations. Examples:

CAR : JALOPY : : house : shanty
HIGH : SHRILL : : bright : blinding

Not every analogy on your exam will fit into one of these nine categories, but three-quarters of them will. Those that don't will embody "miscellaneous" relationships of their own, like these examples:

MUSICIAN : CONCERT : : poet : reading

Here, a type of artist is paired with an event at which he or she might perform.

BOTANY : PLANT : : astronomy : star

A field of science is paired with a typical object that is studied in that field.

GAUNTLET : HAND : : helmet : head

A gauntlet is an armored glove worn, of course, on the hand; a helmet is an armored hat worn on the head.

The Best Tips

Use the Analogy Structure to Guess Words You Don't Know

FYI

More students hurt themselves on the GRE by shunning the "obvious." Don't be shy about guessing at word relationships! The test-makers are predictable, and the obvious connection is usually the right one.

On some analogies, you might encounter words of whose meaning you aren't sure. Don't worry. You can use the analogy structure to help you guess the meaning of the unknown words. First, realize that all the word pairs contain words that are the same parts of speech. For example, if the stem pair contains a noun and a verb, like this:

TYRANT : OPPRESS

then each of the other word pairs will also contain a noun and a verb, in that order. So in any analogy with an unknown word, by looking at any of the other word pairs, you can tell whether the unknown word is a noun, verb, adjective, or any other part of speech—which in itself can be helpful in guessing its meaning.

Next, try using what you know about analogy relationships—and the words in the question that you *do* understand—to make a smart guess as to the meaning of the unknown word. Look at this example:

ETYMOLOGY : WORD : :

(A) etiology : disease
(B) history : event
(C) literature : author
(D) microscopy : microbe
(E) psychology : insanity

(We've deliberately included some difficult, specialized words in this analogy, to illustrate a point; actually, a word like *etiology* is unlikely to be used in an analogy on the real GRE.) You might or might not know what ETYMOLOGY means in the stem pair, but you can tell by glancing at the other word pairs that it must be a noun, since the first word in every pair is a noun. And you can probably guess, from the way the word looks, that it refers to a study or science of some kind. (Words that end in *-ology*, like *biology* and *anthropology*, usually do.)

Now, ETYMOLOGY is paired with WORD. From what you know of analogy relationships, you obviously know that ETYMOLOGY has something to do with a word or words. Given that fact, what's a possible meaning of ETYMOLOGY? Your first guess is likely to be that ETYMOLOGY is "the science or study of words." As it happens, that's not quite correct; but never mind. This guess is probably close enough to enable you to eliminate choices (B), (C), and (E) as clearly wrong.

History can't be defined as "the science of events"; it's the study of the past, including events, people, forces, trends, and so on. Literature isn't "the science of authors"; it's the study of what authors produce, namely books and other writings. And psychology is not "the science of insanity"; psychology studies the mind and human behavior, including both sane and insane subjects. So by sheer guesswork—and a modicum of word sense—you can narrow your choices to two, giving you great odds for guessing, even if you have little or no idea what *etiology* and *microscopy* mean.

The correct answer, by the way, is (A). ETYMOLOGY is actually the study of word origins—where words come from. Similarly, *etiology* is the study of the origins of disease—where particular illnesses come from. So the analogy is close. (Microscopy has nothing to do with the origin of microbes, if you're wondering.)

Not every obscure word in an analogy will be positioned quite so well for guessing. But many will be. Don't let one or more unknown words in a question alarm you; work from what you do know to make reasonable guesses as to the meaning of the new words, and don't be afraid to base your answer choice on these guesses.

FYI

On some analo-
gies, you might
find that your
bridge enables you
to eliminate two or
three answer
choices, leaving
two or three pos-
sible answers. If
that happens, try
working backward
from each of the
live possibilities.
Look at each word
pair, build a
bridge that defines
their relationship,
and then try to
plug the stem pair
into that bridge.
It'll probably work
with only one of
the answer pairs—
and that, of
course, is the cor-
rect answer.

Don't Fear the Flip-Flop

The logical relationship in the stem pair will "run" a certain way; the relationships in the answer choices will run the same way. For example, suppose you face this stem pair:

PROLIFIC : CREATOR

The relationship here is "Description : Thing," and it might be summarized by the bridge, "A PROLIFIC CREATOR is one that produces a lot (of offspring, ideas, artwork, or whatever)." Your job would be to find the answer choice with the same "Description : Thing" relationship, preferably using words that fit nicely into the same bridge. Choosing the right answer, as you've already seen, might at times be subtle, even tricky. But one kind of trick you *don't* have to worry about is the "flip-flop." The test-makers do *not* try to trick you by giving you a correct word pair in reverse order, like this:

SOURCE : ABUNDANT

As we said before, on the GRE, you'll find that all the answer choices match the stem pair in their parts of speech. Similarly, you'll find that relationship reversals are not used to try to trick you. (Frankly, the test-makers at ETS disdain *mere* trickery. They prefer really *sneaky* tricks!) So don't worry about flip-flops—they don't turn up on the GRE.

When all Else Fails, Don't Be Afraid to Guess

Sometimes—it should be rare—you won't be able to find the one best answer for an analogy question. And you might encounter words whose meaning you don't know, and can't guess, even using the clues provided by the analogy structure. When this happens, work by elimination. Build the best bridge you can and plug in the answer choices. Eliminate any answer pairs that don't seem to fit, and guess from among the remaining answers.

Occasionally you might find that you've eliminated all the answers you understand, leaving only an answer that contains words you don't know. Don't be afraid—choose it!

The Most Important Warnings

Ignore the Topics of the Word Pair

It's easy to go wrong by focusing on the surface meanings of the words in the word pairs rather than on their underlying relationship. Consider this example:

WING : FEATHER : :

(A) turtle : shell
(B) eagle : talon
(C) fish : fin
(D) wall : shingle
(E) bird : flight

FYI

Test-makers call wrong answers "distractors." You can see why. The wrong answers are deliberately designed to "distract" the unwary test-taker from the correct answer—which, on its surface, may appear far-fetched. Don't focus on the surface. Go deeper, focusing on the logical relationship between the words. That's what counts.

The words in the stem pair refer to parts of a bird, of course. A hasty glance at the answer choices shows that four of them also refer to animals of one kind or another, and two choices (B) and (E) refer specifically to birds. So you might be tempted to pick one of these answers, misled by the surface similarity.

Don't! The correct answer is (D). A well thought-out bridge will tell you why. The relationship between the words in the stem pair might be described this way: "The WING of a bird is covered by many small, overlapping segments, each called a FEATHER." Only choice (D) fits the same bridge: "The WALL of a house is [or may be] covered by many small, overlapping segments, each called a SHINGLE." Can you picture the similarity? No such similarity exists when you picture the turtle and its shell, the eagle and its talon (or claw), or any of the other items named in the answer choices.

Be Prepared to Jump from the Concrete to the Abstract

The test-makers sometimes like to make you connect a pair of words that are concrete—related to the physical world—with a pair that are abstract—related to the world of ideas. Practice recognizing such analogies. Here are a couple of examples:

SPARK : FIRE : : inspiration : invention

SPARK and FIRE are concrete, physical things; a SPARK is a small thing that helps to create a larger, more powerful force, a FIRE. *Inspiration* and *invention* are abstract ideas that have much the same relationship.

RETRACE : PATH : : reiterate : argument

When you RETRACE a PATH, you are walking over the same steps you took before, in a physical sense. When you *reiterate* an *argument*, you are repeating the same ideas you stated before, in an abstract sense.

JUST THE FACTS

- You need to answer analogies quickly—faster than one per minute. Practice makes it possible.

- Building a bridge that defines the analogy relationship is the basic, proven strategy.

- Look for the test-makers' nine favorite relationships—they come up again and again.

- When unfamiliar words are used, guess at their meanings based on familiar analogy relationships.

- Be ready for analogies that compare concrete relationships to abstract ones.

PRACTICE, PRACTICE, PRACTICE: ANALOGY EXERCISES

Instructions

The following exercises will give you a chance to practice the skills and strategies you've just learned for tackling analogy questions. As with all practice exercises, work under true testing conditions. Complete each exercise in a single sitting. Eliminate distractions (TV, music) and clear away notes and reference materials.

Time yourself with a stopwatch or kitchen timer, or have someone else time you. If you run out of time before answering all the questions, stop and draw a line under the last question you finished. Then go ahead and tackle the remaining questions. When you are done, score yourself based only on the questions you finished in the allotted time.

Circle the letter of the correct response. In addition, any time your answer is a guess—that is, any time you enter a response about which you are not certain—circle the number of that question. After you've completed the exercises, count the number of circled items and the number of these items that you answered correctly. Then divide the number of correct answers by the number of circled items. The result is your Guessing Quotient (G.Q.). If your G.Q. is higher than .20, you will probably boost your overall score by guessing on the real GRE.

Understanding Your Scores

0–3 correct: A poor performance. Study this chapter again, and start spending time each day studying the Insider's GRE Word List (Appendix A).

4–6 correct: A below-average score. Study this chapter again; especially make sure that you understand the nine most common analogy relationships used on the GRE.

7–9 correct: An average score. You may want to study this chapter again. Also be sure you are managing your time wisely (as explained in Chapter 3) and avoiding errors due to haste or carelessness.

10–12 correct: An above-average score. Depending on your personal target score and your strength on other verbal question types, you may or may not want to devote additional time to analogy study.

13–15 correct: An excellent score. You are probably ready to perform well on GRE analogy items.

EXERCISE 1

15 Questions

Time—10 Minutes

Directions: In each of the following questions, a related pair of words or phrases is followed by five lettered pairs of words or phrases. Select the lettered pair that *best* expresses a relationship similar to that expressed in the original pair.

1. PROTECT : HELMET::

 (A) fit : cap
 (B) adorn : headdress
 (C) attract : wig
 (D) wear : armor
 (E) doff : hat

2. LETTER : ALPHABET::

 (A) note : scale
 (B) word : poem
 (C) drop : water
 (D) hue : palette
 (E) symbol : code

3. FLORIST : BOUQUET::

 (A) painter : easel
 (B) haberdasher : wardrobe
 (C) chef : dinner
 (D) gardener : bed
 (E) author : royalty

4. GENERAL : ADMIRAL::

 (A) squadron : platoon
 (B) commander : follower
 (C) soldier : sailor
 (D) captain : officer
 (E) leader : manager

5. DELUGE : TRICKLE::

 (A) flood : abundance
 (B) upheaval : serenity
 (C) downpour : drizzle
 (D) tornado : hurricane
 (E) wealth : plenty

6. TRAITOR : ALLEGIANCE::

   (A) musician : harmony
   (B) opponent : friendship
   (C) thief : imprisonment
   (D) spy : espionage
   (E) adulterer : fidelity

7. RUDDER : SHIP::

   (A) steering wheel : automobile
   (B) aileron : plane
   (C) wing : eagle
   (D) engine : locomotive
   (E) scale : fish

8. ACHE : ANALGESIC::

   (A) fever : influenza
   (B) sleep : sedative
   (C) sensation : anesthetic
   (D) pleasure : narcotic
   (E) loneliness : nostalgia

9. AD LIB : REHEARSAL::

   (A) random : foresight
   (B) accidental : preparation
   (C) unnecessary : intention
   (D) improvised : logic
   (E) aleatory : plan

10. SUPPRESS : REACTION::

    (A) enlarge : photograph
    (B) stifle : sneeze
    (C) release : prisoner
    (D) foresee : accident
    (E) defy : command

11. OVERTURE : CODA::

    (A) symphony : movement
    (B) preface : afterword
    (C) introduction : foreword
    (D) prologue : intermission
    (E) kickoff : touchdown

12. PROSCENIUM : CURTAIN::
    - (A) fence : gate
    - (B) house : facade
    - (C) movie : screen
    - (D) doorway : lintel
    - (E) window : shade

13. PAINT : DAUB::
    - (A) sculpt : carve
    - (B) pluck : strum
    - (C) sing : caterwaul
    - (D) versify : compose
    - (E) dance : perform

14. BEWILDERMENT : FLUMMOXED::
    - (A) ease : abashed
    - (B) perplexity : nonplussed
    - (C) originality : altered
    - (D) equanimity : embarrassed
    - (E) fear : undaunted

15. APPOINTMENT : TRYST::
    - (A) song: serenade
    - (B) meeting : conference
    - (C) arrangement : commitment
    - (D) letter : note
    - (E) engagement : betrothal

EXERCISE 2

15 Questions

Time—10 Minutes

> **Directions:** In each of the following questions, a related pair of words or phrases is followed by five lettered pairs of words or phrases. Select the lettered pair that *best* expresses a relationship similar to that expressed in the original pair.

1. FOOT : ANKLE::
   - (A) arm : elbow
   - (B) hand : wrist
   - (C) finger : toe
   - (D) knee : joint
   - (E) head : neck

2. ACTOR : SCRIPT::
   - (A) architect : design
   - (B) painter : mural
   - (C) musician : score
   - (D) judge : brief
   - (E) student : textbook

3. LIBRARY : SHELF::
   - (A) grocery : food
   - (B) bookstore : book
   - (C) museum : case
   - (D) auditorium : seat
   - (E) office : desk

4. CHAUFFEUR : DRIVE::
   - (A) pilot : propel
   - (B) painter : refurbish
   - (C) engineer : tinker
   - (D) captain : launch
   - (E) mechanic : repair

5. PLAIN : ORNATE::
   - (A) austere : luxurious
   - (B) simple : logical
   - (C) obvious : unconcealed
   - (D) embellished : beautiful
   - (E) garish : gaudy

6. INGEST : GORGE::

(A) devour : envelop
(B) swallow : engulf
(C) grasp : seize
(D) imbibe : guzzle
(E) respire : breathe

7. ROADBLOCK : TRAVEL::

(A) detour : route
(B) impediment : progress
(C) filibuster : legislature
(D) arrest : criminal
(E) illness : physician

8. LACE : SHOE::

(A) cuff : trouser
(B) drawstring : hood
(C) zipper : pouch
(D) clasp : brooch
(E) brim : hat

9. FERVENT : ZEALOT::

(A) savory : epicure
(B) foreign : xenophobe
(C) lustful : lecher
(D) charismatic : politician
(E) patriotic : citizen

10. FIREARM : MUSKET::

(A) vessel : galleon
(B) domicile : apartment
(C) tool : pliers
(D) vehicle : sled
(E) appliance : dishwasher

11. SALVAGE : WRECK::

(A) bury : treasure
(B) paint : antique
(C) sink : vessel
(D) retrieve : property
(E) excavate : ruin

12. TEMPERAMENTAL : STOLID::
    (A) moody : brusque
    (B) hostile : sedate
    (C) vivacious : lively
    (D) mercurial : impassive
    (E) intellectual : thoughtful

13. ENIGMA : MYSTIFIED::
    (A) problem : apathetic
    (B) deception : misinterpreted
    (C) mistake : worried
    (D) dilemma : undecided
    (E) threat : irritated

14. SALT : BRINE::
    (A) flavor : broth
    (B) seasoning : meal
    (C) thyme : herb
    (D) pepper : meat
    (E) sugar : syrup

15. ETHIC : NICETY::
    (A) preference : whim
    (B) morality : scruple
    (C) creed : belief
    (D) dogma : teaching
    (E) doubt : misgiving

EXERCISE 3

15 Questions

Time—10 Minutes

> **Directions:** In each of the following questions, a related pair of words or phrases is followed by five lettered pairs of words or phrases. Select the lettered pair that *best* expresses a relationship similar to that expressed in the original pair.

1. STEEPLE : CHURCH::
   - (A) mast : schooner
   - (B) pillar : edifice
   - (C) summit : mountain
   - (D) altar : chapel
   - (E) statute : pedestal

2. GONG : HAMMER::
   - (A) organ : pedal
   - (B) oboe : reed
   - (C) cymbal : sound
   - (D) piano : key
   - (E) drum : drumstick

3. CURE : MEDICATION::
   - (A) diagnose : drug
   - (B) poison : antidote
   - (C) treat : examination
   - (D) prevent : vaccination
   - (E) relieve : physician

4. STIFFNESS : RIGID::
   - (A) tangibility : rough
   - (B) malleability : pliant
   - (C) brittleness : soft
   - (D) solidity : fluid
   - (E) transparency : bright

5. HAIR : LOCK::
   - (A) species : specimen
   - (B) quarry : ore
   - (C) fabric : swatch
   - (D) hand : thumb
   - (E) branch : limb

6. SKINFLINT : MISERLINESS:

(A) philanthropist : wealth
(B) spendthrift : wastefulness
(C) pauper : indigence
(D) investor : shrewdness
(E) tightwad : generosity

7. JAM : BROADCAST::

(A) drown out : speech
(B) misquote : statement
(C) distort : image
(D) paint over : damage
(E) reroute : traffic

8. GRACEFUL : DANCER::

(A) powerful : athlete
(B) stentorian : orator
(C) harmonious : musician
(D) vocal : singer
(E) dexterous : juggler

9. RECRUIT : SOLDIER::

(A) elect : officer
(B) appoint : committee
(C) attract : audience
(D) enroll : member
(E) deploy : troop

10. GLAD : EUPHORIC::

(A) grateful ; appreciative
(B) unhappy : miserable
(C) mournful : joyous
(D) depressed : downcast
(E) pleased : gratified

11. VINDICTIVE : FORGIVE::

(A) jealous : embrace
(B) scornful : revile
(C) eager : pause
(D) insatiable : gratify
(E) unyielding : compromise

12. POACHER : GAME::

    (A) embezzler : bank
    (B) trespasser : privacy
    (C) burglar : window
    (D) arsonist : fire
    (E) plagiarist : text

13. QUARRY : MARBLE::

    (A) mine : coal
    (B) ocean : tuna
    (C) silo : grain
    (D) well : gusher
    (E) reservoir : water

14. TYRO : EXPERIENCE::

    (A) apprentice : mastery
    (B) elder : wisdom
    (C) journeyman : proficiency
    (D) rookie : talent
    (E) ingenue : charm

15. CATACLYSM : UPHEAVAL::

    (A) colossus : statue
    (B) avalanche : earthquake
    (C) oppression : rebellion
    (D) disaster : calamity
    (E) casualty : war

EXERCISE 4

15 Questions

Time—10 Minutes

> **Directions:** In each of the following questions, a related pair of words or phrases is followed by five lettered pairs of words or phrases. Select the lettered pair that *best* expresses a relationship similar to that expressed in the original pair.

1. PATH : HIGHWAY::
   - (A) yard : alley
   - (B) vein : artery
   - (C) branch : tree
   - (D) walkway : ramp
   - (E) brook : river

2. HOPELESS : DESPAIR::
   - (A) listless : enervation
   - (B) careless : melancholy
   - (C) tireless : fatigue
   - (D) heedless : solemnity
   - (E) feckless : gaiety

3. GRAIN : SAND::
   - (A) leaf : forest
   - (B) stone : mountain
   - (C) bird : aviary
   - (D) knife : cutlery
   - (E) drop : water

4. PIPES : PLUMBER::
   - (A) houses : carpenter
   - (B) brushes : painter
   - (C) seeds : farmer
   - (D) tools : gardener
   - (E) wiring : electrician

5. WHIRLPOOL : WATER::
   - (A) explosion : noise
   - (B) tornado : air
   - (C) hurricane : wind
   - (D) vortex : movement
   - (E) orbit : satellite

6. BIRD : NEST::

 (A) salmon : lake
 (B) beaver : lodge
 (C) canary : cage
 (D) raccoon : forest
 (E) eagle : mountainside

7. FILTER : PURIFY::

 (A) screen : project
 (B) drain : empty
 (C) sieve : sift
 (D) grate : pulverize
 (E) net : envelop

8. HAND : WATCH::

 (A) mercury : thermometer
 (B) length : yardstick
 (C) needle : gauge
 (D) dial : radio
 (E) blade : sword

9. PLAUSIBLE : EXPLANATION::

 (A) gullible : deception
 (B) watertight : alibi
 (C) attractive : proposal
 (D) defensible : theory
 (E) unlikely : coincidence

10. CAST : ACTOR::

 (A) drama : protagonist
 (B) statue : sculptor
 (C) script : author
 (D) orchestra : musician
 (E) score : composer

11. IMMACULATE : STAIN::

 (A) colorless : hue
 (B) eternal : change
 (C) hermetic : seal
 (D) formless : edge
 (E) impervious : touch

12. HARBINGER: AFTERMATH::

    (A)   precursor : ancestor
    (B)   omen : fulfillment
    (C)   genesis : progeny
    (D)   forebear : descendant
    (E)   prediction : accuracy

13. SATIATE : DESIRE::

    (A)   bite : hunger
    (B)   quench : thirst
    (C)   relax : tension
    (D)   appease : hostility
    (E)   suppress : longing

14. DELAY : DILATORY::

    (A)   punctuality : punctilious
    (B)   threat : menacing
    (C)   authority : officious
    (D)   sleep : soporific
    (E)   activity : quiescent

15. KEEP : IMPREGNABLE::

    (A)   message : indecipherable
    (B)   compartment : sealed
    (C)   code : unbreakable
    (D)   warrior : invincible
    (E)   safe : massive

EXERCISE 5

15 Questions

Time—10 Minutes

> **Directions:** In each of the following questions, a related pair of words or phrases is followed by five lettered pairs of words or phrases. Select the lettered pair that *best* expresses a relationship similar to that expressed in the original pair.

1. WINDMILL : BREEZE::
   - (A) pinwheel : rotation
   - (B) pump : well
   - (C) dynamo : energy
   - (D) water wheel : current
   - (E) plow : oxen

2. PILOT : NAVIGATE::
   - (A) fireman : ignite
   - (B) oarsman : propel
   - (C) captain : commandeer
   - (D) midshipman : obey
   - (E) helmsman : dock

3. SHIVER : COLD::
   - (A) swelter : aridity
   - (B) pant : anxiety
   - (C) tremble : uncertainty
   - (D) fan : heat
   - (E) droop : fatigue

4. CLEAT : TURF::
   - (A) sock : carpet
   - (B) galosh : puddle
   - (C) sandal : footprint
   - (D) spike : sand
   - (E) boot : heal

5. SPECTRUM : COLOR::
   - (A) prism : hue
   - (B) wave : frequency
   - (C) form : shape
   - (D) scale : tone
   - (E) texture : sensation

6. WEAK : POWER::
   - (A) modest : eloquence
   - (B) tired : endurance
   - (C) craven : courage
   - (D) frail : fragility
   - (E) careless : intelligence

7. PATTERN : GARMENT::
   - (A) blueprint : structure
   - (B) fashion : dress
   - (C) design : execution
   - (D) mentor : student
   - (E) shape : sculpture

8. SKEPTICAL : DOUBT::
   - (A) indecisive : resolution
   - (B) hesitant : disbelief
   - (C) oblivious : euphoria
   - (D) inquisitive : suspicion
   - (E) sure : certainty

9. CURMUDGEONLY : GROUCH::
   - (A) irascible : philanthropist
   - (B) whimsical : gallant
   - (C) egotistical : altruist
   - (D) criminal : trickster
   - (E) maudlin : sentimentalist

10. RESIGNATION : SIGH::
   - (A) hope : wish
   - (B) faith : pray
   - (C) surprise : gasp
   - (D) terror : fear
   - (E) despair : plunge

11. BRIEF : LEGAL::
   - (A) spreadsheet : financial
   - (B) review : theatrical
   - (C) letter : administrative
   - (D) formula : mathematical
   - (E) journal : daily

12. IMPREGNABLE : ASSAULT::

   (A) invincible : control
   (B) independent : conquest
   (C) inimitable : modification
   (D) immutable : alteration
   (E) intractable : destruction

13. LION : PRIDE::

   (A) bird : vanity
   (B) cow : pasture
   (C) animal : zoo
   (D) fish : school
   (E) dog : kennel

14. ALLOY : METAL::

   (A) aluminum : copper
   (B) compound : element
   (C) oxygen : gas
   (D) pair : individual
   (E) amalgam : silver

15. CAVE : SPELUNKER::

   (A) trail : climber
   (B) ocean : diver
   (C) forest : woodcutter
   (D) wilderness : settler
   (E) moon : astronaut

Answer Key

Exercise 1	Exercise 2	Exercise 3	Exercise 4	Exercise 5
1. B	1. B	1. C	1. E	1. D
2. A	2. C	2. E	2. A	2. B
3. C	3. C	3. D	3. E	3. E
4. C	4. E	4. B	4. E	4. B
5. C	5. A	5. C	5. B	5. D
6. E	6. D	6. B	6. B	6. C
7. B	7. B	7. A	7. C	7. A
8. C	8. B	8. E	8. C	8. E
9. E	9. C	9. D	9. D	9. E
10. B	10. A	10. B	10. D	10. C
11. B	11. E	11. E	11. A	11. A
12. E	12. D	12. E	12. D	12. D
13. C	13. D	13. A	13. B	13. D
14. B	14. E	14. A	14. B	14. B
15. A	15. B	15. D	15. C	15. B

Explanatory Answers

EXERCISE 1

1. **The correct answer is (B).** The purpose of a *helmet* is to *protect* your head; the purpose of a *headdress* is to *adorn* (that is, to decorate or beautify) your head.

2. **The correct answer is (A).** A *letter* is one of the items that is arranged in a particular sequence to form the *alphabet*. Similarly, a *note* is one of the items arranged in a sequence to form a musical *scale*.

3. **The correct answer is (C).** A *bouquet* is one of the standard or customary things produced by the craftsperson known as a *florist*. In the same way, a *dinner* is one of the customary things produced by a *chef*.

4. **The correct answer is (C).** Whereas a *general* is a military leader of soldiers who operate mainly on land, an *admiral* is a military leader whose troops operate mainly on the sea. Similarly, a *soldier* is based mainly on land, while a *sailor* is based mainly on the sea.

5. **The correct answer is (C).** A *deluge* is huge flow of water, while a *trickle* is a tiny one; in the same way, a *downpour* is a huge and forceful rain, while a *drizzle* is a tiny one.

6. **The correct answer is (E).** A *traitor* is someone who betrays his *allegiance* (usually to his country); an *adulterer* is someone who betrays his *fidelity* (to a spouse).

7. **The correct answer is (B).** The *rudder* of a ship is a moving device that sticks into the medium through which the *ship* travels (the water) and helps to guide its movement. Likewise, the *aileron* on the wing of a plane sticks into the medium through which the *plane* travels (the air) and helps to guide its movement.

8. **The correct answer is (C).** An *ache* can be reduced or removed by means of an *analgesic* (a pain medication). Similarly, a *sensation* can be reduced or removed by means of an *anesthetic,* which dulls the nerves.

9. **The correct answer is (E).** Something that is *ad lib* (like a theatrical performance) is done without *rehearsal*—it's improvised. Something that is *aleatory* (meaning driven by chance, like a toss of a pair of dice) is done without a *plan.*

10. **The correct answer is (B).** To *suppress* one's *reaction* is to deliberately hide it or to prevent it from being expressed. In the same way, to *stifle* a *sneeze* is to hold it in and prevent it from "exploding."

11. **The correct answer is (B).** An *overture* is the opening movement or section of a musical piece; a *coda* is a concluding section to a musical piece. Similarly, the *preface* to a book comes at the start, while an *afterword* comes at the very end.

12. **The correct answer is (E).** A *proscenium* is the opening at the front of a stage, which is covered or concealed by a *curtain*; a *window* is the opening in the side of a house, which is covered or concealed by a *shade.*

13. **The correct answer is (C).** To *daub* is to *paint* in a haphazard way, showing little care or talent for the art of painting. Similarly, to *caterwaul* is to *sing* without care or talent, the way a cat in a back alley howls at the moon.

14. **The correct answer is (B).** A person who is *flummoxed* is overwhelmed by *bewilderment*; a person who is *nonplussed* is overwhelmed by *perplexity* (or confusion).

15. **The correct answer is (A).** A *tryst* is a special kind of *appointment*—one made between lovers, often in secret. A *serenade* is a special kind of *song*—one sung by a lover to his beloved, sometimes also in secret.

EXERCISE 2

1. **The correct answer is (B).** The *ankle* is the joint just above the *foot*, on which the foot rotates and moves; the *wrist* is in a similar relationship to the *hand.*

2. **The correct answer is (C).** An *actor's* performance is guided by a *script*, which is a written account of her part in the play. Similarly, a *musician's* performance is guided by the *score*, which is the written music she follows when playing a piece.

3. **The correct answer is (C).** Items in a *library* are stored and displayed on one of many *shelves*; items in a *museum* are stored and displayed in one of many *cases*.

4. **The correct answer is (E).** The job of a *chauffeur* is to *drive* a car; the job of a *mechanic* is (often) to *repair* a car.

5. **The correct answer is (A).** Something that is *plain* is the opposite of *ornate*—the former means simple, the latter means fancy. Similarly, *austere* and *luxurious* are opposites—something *austere* is plain and severe; something *luxurious* is rich and comfortable.

6. **The correct answer is (D).** To *gorge* oneself is to eat, or *ingest*, without restraint (think of Thanksgiving dinner). To *guzzle* is to drink, or *imbibe*, without restraint.

7. **The correct answer is (B).** A *roadblock* stops *travel* from taking place (at least along that particular path); an *impediment* is an obstacle that prevents *progress* from being made.

8. **The correct answer is (B).** A *lace* is a string that is pulled and tied to hold a *shoe* in place. In the same way, a *drawstring* is pulled and tied to hold a *hood* in place.

9. **The correct answer is (C).** A *zealot* is a person who is *fervent*—that is, deeply passionate about his beliefs. A *lecher* is someone who is *lustful*—that is, full of unrestrained sexual desire.

10. **The correct answer is (A).** A *musket* is a particular kind of *firearm*—an old-fashioned one dating back to the seventeenth or eighteenth centuries. (Pictures of the Pilgrims often show them carrying muskets.) Similarly, a *galleon* is an old-fashioned kind of *vessel*, a ship that was used by explorers and merchants in the seventeenth and eighteenth centuries.

11. **The correct answer is (E).** To *salvage* a *wreck* is to explore it (by diving) and remove valuable or historic items from it for sale or safekeeping. In the same way, to *excavate* a *ruin* is to explore it (by digging) and remove valuable or historic items from it for sale or safekeeping.

12. **The correct answer is (D).** *Temperamental* and *stolid* describe opposite qualities; a *temperamental* person is filled with moods that rapidly change and that he expresses freely, while a *stolid* person has few moods and keeps his feelings mostly to himself. *Mercurial* and *impassive* have much the same relationship; a *mercurial* person is flighty and changeable, while an *impassive* person rarely changes his demeanor.

13. **The correct answer is (D).** An *enigma* (a difficult puzzle) is likely to leave you feeling *mystified*; a *dilemma* (a difficult choice) is likely to leave you feeling *undecided.*

14. **The correct answer is (E).** *Brine* is water saturated with *salt* (like ocean water, or the water pickles are cured in); *syrup* is water saturated with *sugar* (for use in making drinks or some kinds of sweets).

15. **The correct answer is (B).** An *ethic* is an important personal value, while a *nicety* is a minor one—a fine point that most people are willing to overlook from time to time. Similarly, *morality* refers to one's major beliefs, while a *scruple* is a small moral concern.

EXERCISE 3

1. **The correct answer is (C).** A *steeple* is the very highest part of a *church*; the *summit* is the very highest part of a *mountain*.

2. **The correct answer is (E).** A *gong* is played by being struck with a *hammer*; a *drum* is played by being struck with a *drumstick*.

3. **The correct answer is (D).** A *medication* is given (usually by a doctor), in hopes that it will *cure* some disease or condition. In the same way, a *vaccination* is given in hopes that it will *prevent* some disease from ever occurring.

4. **The correct answer is (B).** *Stiffness* is the quality of being *rigid* (that is, difficult or impossible to bend). *Malleability* is the quality of being *pliant* (that is, very easy to bend).

5. **The correct answer is (C).** A *lock* is a small piece of one's *hair* (often kept as a souvenir or remembrance of someone special). A *swatch* is a small piece of *fabric* (usually used as a sample by a tailor or designer).

6. **The correct answer is (B).** A *skinflint* is a person who exhibits *miserliness* (that is, stinginess) in the way he handles money. Similarly, a *spendthrift* exhibits *wastefulness* in the way he handles money.

7. **The correct answer is (A).** To *jam* a (radio or TV) *broadcast* is to block it or prevent it from being heard, usually by drowning out the signal with electronic "noise." Likewise, to *drown* out a *speech* is to prevent it from being heard by making noise.

8. **The correct answer is (E).** When a *dancer* is skillful, he performs in a way that is *graceful*; when a *juggler* is skillful, we might call him *dexterous* (that is, quick and sure-handed).

9. **The correct answer is (D).** To *recruit* a *soldier* is to convince someone to sign up for military service. Similarly, to *enroll* a *member* is to convince someone to join a club, a school, or some other organization.

10. **The correct answer is (B).** To be *euphoric* is to feel extremely *glad*; to be *miserable* is to feel extremely *unhappy*.

11. **The correct answer is (E).** A *vindictive* (that is vengeful) person is unwilling to *forgive*—instead, she seeks revenge. Likewise, an *unyielding* person is unwilling to *compromise*—instead, she insists upon having her own way.

12. **The correct answer is (E).** A *poacher* is someone who illegally catches someone else's *game* (that is, wild animals) for his own use. A *plagiarist* is someone who illegally steals someone else's *text* (that is, writing) and passes it off as his own.

13. **The correct answer is (A).** A *quarry* is a hole in the ground from which stone of various kinds, including *marble*, is extracted for use by builders or sculptors. A *mine* is a hole in the ground from which ores and metals, including *coal*, are extracted for use in industry.

14. **The correct answer is (A).** A *tyro* is a complete beginner at something, a person with virtually no *experience*. Similarly, an *apprentice* is someone who is learning a new art or craft, a person with no *mastery* of the skill he wants to practice.

15. **The correct answer is (D).** A *cataclysm* is a particularly intense, severe, and overwhelming *upheaval*; a *disaster* is a particularly intense, severe, and overwhelming *calamity*.

EXERCISE 4

1. **The correct answer is (E).** A *path* is a little road (often so small that only one person can use it at a time), while a *highway* is a large road with room for thousands. A *brook* and a *river* have a similar size relationship.

2. **The correct answer is (A).** *Despair* is the state of feeling *hopeless*; *enervation* (that is, complete lack of energy) is the state of feeling *listless*.

3. **The correct answer is (E).** A *grain* is a single, tiny piece of *sand*; one normally finds thousands or millions of grains of sand together (as at the beach). Similarly, a *drop* is a single, tiny bit of *water*, and one normally finds millions of drops of water together (as in a stream or lake).

4. **The correct answer is (E).** A *plumber* can often be found installing, fixing, or working with *pipes* in a house; an *electrician* can often be found doing the same kinds of things with the *wiring* in a house.

5. **The correct answer is (B).** A *whirlpool* is a violent, rapidly rotating spiral of *water*, which can seize or drag anything in its path (a ship, for instance). A *tornado* is a similarly violent and powerful rotating column of *air*, which can be equally dangerous.

6. **The correct answer is (B).** A *bird* builds and lives in a *nest*; a *beaver* builds and lives in a *lodge*. (The other answer choices refer to places where animals may live, but none of those creatures build the homes mentioned.

7. **The correct answer is (C).** The purpose of a *filter* is to *purify* what flows through it, which may be air, water, or some other substance. Similarly, the purpose of a *sieve* is to *sift* what flows through it, which may be flour, sand, or some other granular substance.

8. **The correct answer is (C).** The *hand* of a *watch* is the pointer that indicates the time and that one looks at when using the watch; the *needle* on a *gauge* (a car's gasoline gauge, for instance) plays the same role. (The mercury in a thermometer is a little different; more than just a pointer, it is the substance that expands or contracts as temperature changes and therefore is the controlling mechanism of the entire device.)

9. **The correct answer is (D).** An *explanation* that is *plausible* is one that is possible or believable—it may or may not be true, but at least it doesn't fly in the face of logic. Similarly, a *theory* that is *defensible* is one that knowledgeable people can advocate—it may or may not be true, but at least it makes basic sense.

10. **The correct answer is (D).** An *actor* is one member of a *cast*, which is the group of people who participate in a theater performance. In the same way, a *musician* is one member of an *orchestra*, the group that puts on a musical concert.

11. **The correct answer is (A).** Something *immaculate* is very clean, completely without a *stain*; something *colorless* is completely without a *hue*.

12. **The correct answer is (D).** The two words here have a time relationship: a *harbinger* comes before an event and helps to foretell or predict it (crocuses are harbingers of spring), while the *aftermath* is what follows an event and bears its traces. In the same way, a *forebear* is an ancestor, one who comes before a certain person or time; a *descendant* follows or comes after.

13. **The correct answer is (B).** To *satiate* is to completely satisfy a *desire*; to *quench* is to completely satisfy a *thirst*.

14. **The correct answer is (B).** Someone who is *dilatory* makes a habit of *delay*; someone who is *menacing* frequently offers *threats*.

15. **The correct answer is (C).** A *keep* is the central stronghold of a castle; a valuable one would be *impregnable,* that is, nearly impossible to break into. Similarly, a valuable *code* is one that is *unbreakable,* that is, nearly impossible to decipher.

EXERCISE 5

1. **The correct answer is (D).** A *windmill* is a simple machine that generates energy when it is moved by the *breeze;* a *water wheel* is a simple machine that generates energy when it is moved by a *current* (of water).

2. **The correct answer is (B).** The job of a *pilot* is to *navigate* (a ship or plane); the job of an *oarsman* is to *propel* (that is, to power) a boat.

3. **The correct answer is (E).** When you *shiver*, your body is expressing the fact that it is suffering from excessive *cold*; when you *droop*, your body is suffering from *fatigue*.

4. **The correct answer is (B).** A *cleat* is a special kind of footwear designed especially for use on *turf* (that is, a grassy field); a *galosh* is a special kind of footwear for walking through a *puddle*.

5. **The correct answer is (D).** The *spectrum* is made up of a series of *colors* arranged in a particular pattern; a musical *scale* is made up of a series of *tones* that are also arranged in a fixed pattern.

6. **The correct answer is (C).** To be *weak* is to be lacking in *power*; to be *craven* is to be lacking in *courage*.

7. **The correct answer is (A).** A *pattern* is a drawing that is used as a guide by a tailor or seamstress when making a *garment*. Likewise, a *blueprint* is a drawing that is used as a guide by a builder when making a *structure*.

8. **The correct answer is (E).** To be *skeptical* is to feel and to express *doubt* about the truth of something; to be *sure* is to feel and express *certainty*.

9. **The correct answer is (E).** A *grouch* is someone who is *curmudgeonly* (that is, argumentative, gloomy, and sarcastic); a *sentimentalist* is someone who is *maudlin* (that is, excessively soft-hearted or "mushy").

10. **The correct answer is (C).** A *sigh* is a particular kind of breath that often expresses the emotion of *resignation* (that is, acceptance of what can't be helped). A *gasp* is a particular kind of breath that often expresses the emotion of *surprise*.

11. **The correct answer is (A).** A *brief* is a *legal* document (prepared by an attorney for use in connection with a court case); a *spreadsheet* is a *financial* document (prepared by an accountant for use in business).

12. **The correct answer is (D).** To be *impregnable* is to be able to withstand almost any kind of *assault*; to be *immutable* is to be unchangeable and therefore able to turn away virtually any kind of *alteration*.

13. **The correct answer is (D).** A group of *lions* is a *pride*; a group of *fish* is a *school*.

14. **The correct answer is (B).** An *alloy* is a chemical mixture or blend of several *metals*; a *compound* is a chemical mixture or blend of several *elements*.

15. **The correct answer is (B).** A *spelunker* is a person who travels through and explores *caves* for fun, adventure, or for scientific reasons; a *diver* travels through and explores the *ocean* for similar reasons.

Chapter 6

Sentence Completions

Get the Scoop On . . .

- Proven strategies for mastering sentence completions
- The five kinds of sentence connections that unlock most sentence completions
- How signpost words can help you anticipate the missing words
- How you can choose the right answer even when you don't understand the sentence

THE TEST CAPSULE

What's the Big Idea?

You'll be given a sentence from which one or two words or phrases have been left out. You have to pick the words or phrases from five answer choices that best complete the sentence.

How Many?

Of the 30 questions in your verbal section, your GRE will probably have a total of six sentence completions.

How Much Do They Count?

Because sentence completions are 6 out of 30 total verbal questions, they count as 20 percent of your overall verbal score.

How Much Time Should They Take?

You need to answer sentence completions at a rate of one per minute.

What's the Best Strategy?

Learn to recognize key words that show how the parts of the sentence are connected. After you understand this connection, you can guess the meaning of the missing word or words.

What's the Worst Pitfall?

Picking an answer just because the words "make sense" when you plug them into the sentence. To some degree, *all the answers will make sense.* The best answer will not only make sense, but will also *complete* the meaning of the rest of the sentence without adding any *new* ideas.

THE OFFICIAL DESCRIPTION

FYI

Sentence completions are written to be self-contained. That is, each sentence expresses a complete idea that you can understand without any outside information. Some of the words used in the sentences and in the answer choices are challenging, but they are general vocabulary words that a well-rounded college graduate should know rather than specialized terms from science, art, or other fields.

What They Are

Sentence completions are kinds of reading comprehension questions. In this case, the items you'll be reading are quite short: single sentences that are just around 10 to 25 words long. Each sentence will contain one or two blanks, which stand for words or phrases that have been left out. You'll then be given five words or phrases, or five pairs of words or phrases, to consider. Your job is to pick the word or phrase, or the pair of words or phrases, that fits best into the blanks.

Where They Are

In the typical computerized GRE, you'll have one verbal section that is 30 minutes long. It will probably include six sentence completions, interspersed seemingly at random among the other verbal question types—antonyms, analogies, and reading comprehension questions. Reminder: the test-makers claim the right to change the format at any time! However, the typical format we just described is what you're most likely to encounter.

What They Measure

To answer a sentence completion correctly, you need to understand the main idea of the sentence as well as its logical structure—that is, how the parts of the sentence are connected. You also need to know the meanings of the words in the answer choices. So sentence completions measure both your reading ability and your vocabulary knowledge.

The Directions

> **Directions:** Each sentence below has one or two blanks, each blank indicating that something has been omitted. Beneath the sentence are five lettered words or sets of words. Choose the word or set of words for each blank that *best* fits the meaning of the sentence as a whole.

THE INSIDER'S REPORT

Strategies That Really Work

Figure out How the Parts of the Sentence Are Connected

Maybe you don't usually think about sentences as having "parts." They do, though. Most sentences contain not only a collection of words but also a number of *ideas* that are connected to one another in various ways. When you understand how these ideas are connected, you can say that you really understand the sentence.

FYI

On the real GRE CAT, the answer choices will not *be lettered. But we'll letter them throughout this book simply for ease of reference.*

Look at the following sample sentence completion, which comes from a real exam by the test-makers at ETS:

Medieval kingdoms did not become constitutional republics overnight; on the contrary, the change was _____.

(A) unpopular
(B) unexpected
(C) advantageous
(D) sufficient
(E) gradual

You can probably see that the sentence is made up of two main parts. (The semicolon (;) in the middle helps make this obvious: that's where the two parts divide.) Now, how are the two parts connected—that is, how do the ideas in the two parts fit together? The first part talks about a certain historical event—namely, the change of some governments from "kingdoms" to "constitutional republics." It says that this event did not happen "overnight." The second part talks about the same event, referring to it as "the change." It says something about that event that we can't be sure of until we've chosen an answer, because the crucial word—the last word in the sentence—has been omitted.

But by thinking about the words that *do* appear, we can see the connection between the two parts of the sentence. Both parts talk about "the change." The first part tells us something about what the change was *not* (namely, it was *not* a change that happened overnight). The second part will tell us something about what the change *was*. Do you see the difference?

The two parts of the sentence, then, talk about the same topic—this historical change—but they approach the topic differently. You might say that the first half expresses the idea negatively, the second half expresses it positively. (As we'll discuss later, this is one common type of connection found in sentence completions.) After you see this, you can easily guess the meaning of the missing word. If the change was *not* an overnight change, then what kind of change was it? The word we want should describe the *opposite* of "overnight"; it should mean something like *slow, long-drawn-out, lengthy.* The only answer choice close to this in meaning is choice (E), *gradual*—so that's the correct answer.

As you see, it's possible to figure out the connections between the parts of a sentence even when some of the words are actually missing. And after you recognize the connections, you can guess the words that are needed to complete the structure of the sentence. It's a little like those puzzles you find on the kids' comics pages: "Finish this drawing of a horse." If three of the horse's legs and one of his ears are already there, you can tell that you need one leg and one ear to complete the picture. Sentence completions work the same way.

Look for the Test-Makers' Favorite Connections
As in every part of the GRE, the test-makers often get repetitive with sentence completions. After writing hundreds of sentences for the test, they start to follow similar patterns—patterns that are commonly found in sentences anyway, which involve particular types of connections among sentence parts. If you develop a feeling for these common connections, you'll spot them easily on the exam.

Here are the test-makers' five favorite kinds of sentence connections.

1. Contrast

Quite often, one part of the sentence contains an idea that is in contrast to, opposed to, or different from an idea in another part of the sentence. The sample sentence we looked at, dealing with the change of medieval kingdoms into constitutional republics, is an example; the idea of "overnight change" in the first part of the sentence is opposed to the idea of "gradual change" in the second part. Here's another example:

> Unlike Wordsworth, who wrote his best poetry during _____, Yeats wrote some of his finest poems when he was over seventy years old.
>
> (A) illness
> (B) war
> (C) youth
> (D) marriage
> (E) convalescence

You don't need to know anything about Wordsworth or Yeats to answer this question. You just need to recognize that the first part of the sentence tells you something about Wordsworth that contrasts with what the second part tells you about Yeats. Because the second part says that Yeats wrote his best poetry when he was old ("over seventy years old"), then Wordsworth must have written his best poetry when he was young. The only answer that says so is choice (C).

2. Similarity

In this kind of sentence, one part of the sentence describes something that is similar to something described in another part of the sentence. Here's an example:

> Just as musicians in the 1970s were amazed by the powers of the electronic synthesizer, so musicians in the time of Bach _____ the organ, the technical wonder of its day.
>
> (A) railed against
> (B) marveled at
> (C) were troubled by
> (D) strove to master
> (E) practiced on

In this sentence, the words "Just as . . . so" tell you that the first part of the sentence and the second part of the sentence are describing two situations that are similar. The point is that musicians reacted to the organ in Bach's time the same way musicians reacted to the synthesizer in the 1970s. The sentence says that musicians in the 1970s "were amazed by" the synthesizer, so the words to fill in the blank should say something similar about the reaction to the organ. Only choice (B), "marveled at," says that, so it's the correct answer.

3. Example

In a sentence with this kind of organization, one part of the sentence states an idea, and another part gives an example of that idea. Look at this sentence:

> Biologists have often gained special insights by examining the lifeforms that develop in _____ regions, as illustrated by Darwin's studies of evolution among the finches on certain _____ Pacific islands.
>
> (A) arid..lush
> (B) harsh..tropical
> (C) typical..unusual
> (D) crowded..deserted
> (E) isolated..remote

You can tell by the words "as illustrated by" that the second part of this sentence gives an example of the idea presented in the first part of the sentence. What is that idea? It's a little hard to tell, because those darn test-makers have left out one of the crucial words. But you can see that the author is talking about how biologists have learned a lot by studying living things in some particular kind of location ("_____ regions"). Then, in the second part of the sentence, she cites Darwin's work "on certain _____ Pacific islands" as an example. If Darwin's work is an example of the idea from the first part of the sentence, then the missing words in both parts should say more or less the same thing. (Otherwise, Darwin's work wouldn't illustrate or explain the idea.) So the "regions" being discussed in both parts of the sentence have to be similar.

Having figured this out, look at the five choices. Only choice (E) works. "Isolated" and "remote" mean approximately the same thing. In the other choices, the two words either have no clear relationship with one another or are almost opposite in meaning. None of them would fit the Example connection that we find in this sentence.

4. Restatement

In this kind of sentence, one part of the sentence restates or repeats (in different words) what is said in another part of the sentence. (Sometimes writers will do this to make a new or complicated idea a little clearer.) Here's an example:

Public attitudes toward business _____ are deeply _____; most people resent intrusive government rules, yet they expect government to prevent businesses from defrauding, endangering, or exploiting the public.

(A) ethics..cynical
(B) investment..divided
(C) practices..emotional
(D) regulation..ambiguous
(E) leaders..hostile

In this sentence, the second part—following the semicolon (;)—is complete, with no missing words. It describes in some detail the public's attitude about government rules in business. As you can see, the attitude described is pretty confused. On the one hand, people don't like having government involved in their lives ("intrusive government rules"). On the other hand, people expect government to stop businesses from doing bad things—which is impossible, of course, unless government *is* somewhat intrusive. It's a self-contradictory attitude (but sometimes people are like that).

The first part of the sentence sums up this attitude in a few words—two of which are missing. Your job is to pick words to insert that will make this first part sum up, describe, or restate what the second part of the sentence says. You might begin by looking at the second word in each choice. We're looking for an adjective that describes the public attitude accurately. Choices (B) and (D) work best: "divided" and "ambiguous" both convey the idea that the public wants two things that don't go together very well. So we can more or less eliminate choices (A), (C), and (E), since the second word in each of those choices doesn't describe the public attitude nearly so well.

What about the first word to be inserted? We want a word that will complete the phrase, "Public attitudes toward business _____." So the missing word should accurately describe what the second part of the sentence describes. Of the choices we're given, choice (D) fits best: the attitudes described have to do with "business regulation," that is, rules laid down for business by government. Two other choices, "ethics" and "practices," work all right in the first blank space, but we've already eliminated choices (A) and (C) because the second word in each is a poor fit. So the best answer is choice (D). When the two words are plugged into the sentence, the first part accurately restates the point made in more detail in the second part.

FYI

Some sentences will have combinations of two (or even more) kinds of connections. For example, we saw a moment ago how the sentence about politics drew a contrast between "incumbent politicians" and "outside challengers." So you could say that this sentence has both a Contrast connection and a Cause and Effect connection. Both connections are worth noticing—and both help you to understand the meaning of the sentence.

5. Cause and Effect

In this kind of sentence, one part describes something that causes, produces, or influences what's described in another part. Here's an example:

> Because of the power and recognition that go with public office, incumbent politicians have enormous _____ when waging election campaigns against outside challengers.

(A) difficulties
(B) expenses
(C) advantages
(D) budgets
(E) concerns

The first part of this sentence describes something—the "power and recognition" of being in government—that causes or influences what's described in the second part. To fully understand the sentence, it helps to know that an "incumbent politician" is one who is already in office; but even if the word "incumbent" isn't already part of your vocabulary, you might be able to figure out its meaning from the rest of the sentence. "Incumbent politicians" are depicted here as running against "outside challengers." So to be "incumbent" is to be an "insider."

Logically, what effects would be caused by the "power and recognition" of public office? Would power and recognition make it easier to run for re-election, or harder? Easier, of course. So the best answer is choice (C): the natural effect of the cause described in the first part of the sentence is "advantages" for the incumbent. The closest wrong answer is probably choice (D); but "enormous budgets" wouldn't necessarily be a logical effect of having "power and recognition," would they? A candidate with a lot of power and recognition could perhaps spend as much, or as little, as he would like.

Naturally, not every sentence correction on your GRE will have one of these five kinds of connections. But most of them will.

Clue in to the Signpost Words That Mark the Connections

It will help you to recognize the common connections used in sentence completions if you learn to notice certain key words that the test-makers habitually use to mark them.

Here are examples of the signpost words to watch for.

1. Contrast

In the Contrast sentence about Wordsworth and Yeats (page 147), the key word is "Unlike." By using that word to introduce part of the sentence, the author is deliberately signaling to you, "Watch out! A Contrast is coming!" Here are some other signpost words that are used to signal Contrast connections:

although	nevertheless
but	nonetheless
by contrast	on the other hand
despite	whereas
however	yet

2. Similarity

The sample Similarity sentence about the synthesizer and the organ (page 147) used the linked words "Just as . . . so" to signal the Similarity. Here are some other words and phrases that work as Similarity signposts:

as . . . as	resembles
in the same way	same
like	similarly
likewise	

3. Example

The sample sentence about Darwin's finches on page 148 used the signpost words "as illustrated by" to make it obvious that an Example was being given. Here are some other signpost words that can play the same role:

as in the case of	specifically
for example	such as
for instance	

4. Restatement

Our example of this kind of connection—the sentence about business regulation on page 149—didn't contain a signpost word. However, it did contain a different kind of telltale mark: the semicolon (;) that divided the sentence into two parts. A semicolon often indicates that what follows the mark is a restatement of what precedes it. The same is also true of the colon (:). Watch for these two punctuation marks. Think of them as "signposts": wordless warnings that Restatement might be taking place nearby.

Also look for these words and phrases, which often mark Restatement connections:

in fact	namely
in other words	so to speak
in short	that is

FYI

Think of signpost words as being like the "Yield," "Dangerous Curve," and "One Way" signs you look for when driving. They direct you as you read, making it obvious where you—and the sentence—are headed.

---

5. Cause and Effect

The signpost words "Because of" appeared at the start of our sample Cause and Effect sentence (the one about politics on page 150). Here are some other typical signpost words that mark this kind of connection:

as a result	produces
causes	results in
consequently	therefore
due to	thus
leads to	

Notice that signpost words are often short, seemingly unimportant words. They don't contain much obvious information. Yet they are, in a sense, the most important words in any sentence!

Check Your Answer by Plugging in the Missing Word(s)

After you've picked an answer choice, read the sentence with the word or words you've chosen inserted in the blank spaces. The sentence *will* make grammatical sense; all the answers are designed that way. The deeper question is whether the sentence sounds logical, consistent, and complete. The connections among the parts should be clear and correct. If signpost words signal a Contrast between two parts of the sentence, then those two parts should obviously contrast with one another. The same with the other kinds of connections. If a certain type of connection is signaled by one or more signpost words, but not carried out in the words you've plugged in, then you've picked the wrong answer. Try again!

The Best Tips

Read Any Tough Words as "Yadda Yadda Yadda"

We said something before that's worth repeating: If you notice the signpost words and understand the connections they mark, you'll understand how the parts of the sentence fit together—*even if you know nothing about the topic of the sentence.* Now we'll go one step further: if you understand how the parts of the sentence fit together, you can usually pick the right answer—*even if you don't understand a lot of the sentence.*

If you don't believe us, think back to our very first sample sentence:

> Medieval kingdoms did not become constitutional republics overnight; on the contrary, the change was _____.

You'll recall that the correct answer is "gradual." Now, what do you know about medieval European history, the transition from monarchies to republican government, the development and evolution of the concept of a national constitution, and so on? Maybe a lot, probably only a little. It doesn't matter. For all you care, the sentence could read like this:

> *Yadda yadda yadda* did not become *yadda yadda yadda* overnight; on the contrary, the change was _____.

Who cares what the *yadda yadda yaddas* stand for? They could be anything: two styles of architecture, two scientific theories, a caterpillar and a butterfly, anything. The other words in the sentence—especially the signpost words—tell you all you need to know to pick the right answer.

Therefore, don't worry if the sentences contain words you don't understand or deal with topics you've never heard of (or, worse, took courses in and *failed*). It probably doesn't matter. Substitute *yadda yadda yadda* for the tough ideas and focus on the words that connect those ideas. In most cases, you'll still be able to answer correctly.

Anticipate the Answer with Your Eyes Shut

As we discussed the various sample questions in this chapter, you might have noticed that we examined the sentences in detail before ever discussing the choices. We did that on purpose. When you take the GRE, you shouldn't look at the choices until you've read the sentence carefully, looked for the connections among the parts of the sentence (using signpost words as clues), and then tried to guess the missing word or words—or at least what the missing words mean.

We call this anticipating the answer with your eyes shut. (Oh, all right, you can leave them open. But don't let us catch you looking at the answers!)

Why bother with this guessing game? Because—remember—four of the five choices are *wrong*. They are distractors, designed specifically to draw your attention away from the correct answer. And they'll do just that if you give them half a chance. If you read the question and jump right down to the choices, you'll probably find the first choice pretty plausible—after all, the test-makers are good at writing plausible answers. But the second choice might be even a little better. And what about the third choice ? It means something totally different than either the first or second choices, but it seems to fit the sentence, doesn't it? Then again, what *was* it that the original sentence said? Better read it over . . . By now, a minute and a half has passed, and you're more confused than when you started.

Instead, after studying the sentence, guess the meaning of the missing word or words. Then *scan* the answers, looking simply for one that means the same as your guess. Chances are, it will jump out at you. Guessing first will keep you focused—and keep the distractors at bay.

FYI

Most GRE sentence completions—about two thirds—have two blanks rather than one. This provides another way of working by elimination. Sometimes you can guess the meaning of one blank, but not the other. Good! Scan the choices, looking only for the word you've guessed. Eliminate the answers that don't include it (or a near synonym). Then guess from what remains.

Work by Elimination

As with any question type, some items will appear harder than others. If you can't find an obvious answer—perhaps because you don't understand all of the words in the choices—eliminate answers that are clearly wrong or that you have a strong hunch are wrong. Then guess from what remains. It usually pays to guess, especially in the early parts of the verbal section. (See Chapter 3 for a fuller discussion of proper guessing strategy for the GRE.)

The Most Important Warnings

Be Consistent!

It's crucial to look for an answer whose meaning is *consistent* with the rest of the sentence. Distractors are marked—sometimes subtly—by words whose meanings don't quite carry out the plan marked out by the rest of the sentence (especially by the signpost words). Here's an example:

> In addition to being statesmen, Jefferson and Franklin were noted for their _____ interests, as exemplified by Jefferson's writings on the botany of Virginia and Franklin's experiments with electricity.
>
> (A) varied
> (B) literary
> (C) artistic
> (D) scientific
> (E) multifarious

It so happens that Jefferson and Franklin had incredibly diverse interests and accomplishments, and if you are aware of this you may be tempted to select choice (A) or (E), either of which would be factually true. Choices (B) and (C) could be defended on the ground of historical accuracy, too. But choice (D) is correct *simply because it's the only answer that is completely consistent with the rest of the sentence.* The second part of the sentence, beginning with the words "as exemplified by," gives two examples of Jefferson's and Franklin's interests—and both have to do with science. (The sentence illustrates the Example connection, of course.) Thus, choice (D), scientific, is the best choice.

So the right answer to a sentence completion isn't just factually accurate, nor does it just fit logically and grammatically into the sentence. All five answers will do that. The best answer also ties in closely with the main idea of the rest of the sentence. That's what we call being consistent.

Don't Get Creative!

The flip side of being consistent is *not* to introduce any new ideas into the sentence. GRE sentences aren't terribly artistic or even necessarily interesting. They're more like very efficient little machines: precisely crafted to perform one function, with no unnecessary parts. Some distractors will be perfectly plausible words that fit the sentence and are wrong only because they introduce new ideas that aren't strictly necessary to complete the thought. An example:

Several of the mountaineers, _____ by the _____ of the icy slopes, lost their way and had to be led to safety by one of the guides.

(A) awe-struck..grandeur
(B) frightened..loneliness
(C) overcome..frigidity
(D) unnerved..slipperiness
(E) dazzled..brightness

As always, all five choices fit the sentence grammatically. What's more, all five are logically plausible. The "icy slopes" of a high mountain are quite likely to be grand, lonely, frigid, slippery, *and* bright, just as the choices state, and the reactions named ("awe-struck," "frightened," "overcome," and so on) are also plausible. The trouble with four of the answers is that they're just *too creative*. They tell us something about the mountain experience that the rest of the sentence doesn't say or imply. In short, they introduce new ideas—a no-no!

The right answer is choice (E) because the rest of the sentence talks about how the mountaineers "lost their way and had to be led to safety." So this is a sentence primarily about getting lost. We want to fit words into the blanks that relate closely to the idea of getting lost, and choice (E) does that; it explains that the mountaineers got lost because the brightness of the icy slopes temporarily blinded ("dazzled") them. It completes the idea given in the rest of the sentence without adding anything new to it.

That's the sort of answer the test-makers like: straightforward, consistent, a little dull, and perfectly correct. Not the sort of person you want to date, maybe, but the kind your parents always wanted you to marry.

JUST THE FACTS

- The key to most sentence completions is recognizing how the parts of the sentence are connected.

- Get to know the signpost words that mark the five most common sentence connections.

- Try to anticipate the answer before looking at the choices.

- Check your chosen answer by plugging it into the sentence.

- Look for answers that are consistent with the rest of the sentence and don't add new information.

PRACTICE, PRACTICE, PRACTICE: SENTENCE COMPLETION EXERCISES

Instructions

The following exercises will give you a chance to practice the skills and strategies you've just learned for tackling sentence completions. As with all practice exercises, work under true testing conditions. Complete each exercise in a single sitting. Eliminate distractions (TV, music) and clear away notes and reference materials. Time yourself with a stopwatch or kitchen timer, or have someone else time you. If you run out of time before answering all the questions, stop and draw a line under the last question you finished. Then go ahead and tackle the remaining questions. When you are done, score yourself based only on the questions you finished in the allotted time.

Circle the letter of the correct response.

Understanding Your Scores

0–3 correct: A poor performance. Study this chapter again, as well as Chapter 7 (since sentence completions and reading comprehension are closely related).

4–6 correct: A below-average score. Study this chapter again; especially make sure that you understand the five most common sentence connections used on the GRE.

7–9 correct: An average score. You may want to study this chapter again. Also be sure you are managing your time wisely (as explained in Chapter 3) and avoiding errors due to haste or carelessness.

10–12 correct: An above-average score. Depending on your personal target score and your strength on other verbal question types, you may or may not want to devote additional time to sentence completion study.

13–15 correct: An excellent score. You are probably ready to perform well on GRE sentence completion items.

EXERCISE 1

15 Questions

Time—15 Minutes

> **Directions:** Each sentence below has one or two blanks, each blank indicating that something has been omitted. Beneath the sentence are five lettered words or sets of words. Choose the word or set of words for each blank that *best* fits the meaning of the sentence as a whole.

1. Friends of the theater have long decried the _____ of the New York drama critics, whose reviews can determine the fate of a play in a single night.

   (A) insensitivity
   (B) provinciality
   (C) intelligence
   (D) power
   (E) inaccuracy

2. The _____ manner in which the teacher candidate addressed the school board was a key factor in his rejection; the school board members agreed that enthusiasm is an essential quality in a teacher.

   (A) pretentious
   (B) solicitous
   (C) superficial
   (D) perfunctory
   (E) combative

3. His _____ writing style made it difficult to follow his thought processes—no surprise to his colleagues, who were familiar with his _____ manner of speech.

   (A) precise..arcane
   (B) laborious..tedious
   (C) trite..flippant
   (D) convoluted..circumlocutory
   (E) ambiguous..affected

4. The giant squid is still _____ marine biologists, as it has never been seen alive, making it impossible to study in its natural habitat.

   (A) fascinating to
   (B) enigmatic to
   (C) dangerous to
   (D) exploited by
   (E) famous among

5. Advertising can increase sales of a _____ product, but it cannot create demand for a bad one; consumers may buy a _____ item because of advertising—but only once.

   (A) good..new
   (B) reliable..costly
   (C) useful..valuable
   (D) needless..single
   (E) well-made..badly made

6. Like Truman, who was never considered a major national figure until Roosevelt's death made him president, Ford attained national prominence only after _____ thrust him into the presidency.

   (A) personal ambition
   (B) outside circumstances
   (C) popular acclaim
   (D) political intrigue
   (E) public demand

7. Thus far predictions that global _____ would lead to mass starvation have proven false; however, in the years to come, population _____ may yet prove to be one of the world's greatest problems.

   (A) pollution..expansion
   (B) overcrowding..growth
   (C) poverty..density
   (D) deforestation..control
   (E) warfare..stabilization

8. Representative Bunker's speech at the town meeting was quite _____, as it appeared to _____ the religious beliefs held by many members of the community.

   (A) cogent..attack
   (B) tactless..defend
   (C) inflammatory..ridicule
   (D) enthralling..denigrate
   (E) devious..belittle

9. The idea of "children's literature" _____ in the late eighteenth century, when educators first decided that children needed
   special _____ of their own.

   (A) emerged..books
   (B) changed..reading
   (C) grew..treatment
   (D) developed..training
   (E) receded..teaching

10. In some of the poorest neighborhoods of New York City, commu-
    nity gardens are springing up as _____ the filth and desola-
    tion of their urban surroundings.

    (A) an affirmation of
    (B) a validation of
    (C) a reaction to
    (D) an amplification of
    (E) a celebration of

11. The neighborhood group's rendering of the proposed office
    complex _____ the _____ of the project: as they ap-
    peared on the drawing, the proposed office buildings appeared to
    dwarf the rest of the downtown area.

    (A) minimized..grandiosity
    (B) accentuated..beauty
    (C) underscored..vastness
    (D) trivialized..enormity
    (E) revealed..immensity

12. Twentieth-century Japan faced the question of how to _____
    the best of modern civilization without losing the benefits of
    Japan's _____ way of life.

    (A) reject..ancient
    (B) adopt..outmoded
    (C) assimilate..traditional
    (D) incorporate..contemporary
    (E) reshape..historic

13. The proposal to forbid the use of indoor furniture on front porches has divided the town along _____ lines: the affluent feel the old couches are eyesores, while those who cannot afford new outdoor furniture are _____ about what they feel is an attempt to restrict their lifestyle.

   (A) political..nonplussed
   (B) aesthetic..dismayed
   (C) class..pleased
   (D) racial..angry
   (E) socioeconomic..incensed

14. In his *Politics*, Aristotle characterizes Plato's support of collectivism as _____ and _____ the unity of the city; not only would it be difficult to institute and enforce, but the absence of private property would lead to bickering among the citizens.

   (A) commendable..deleterious to
   (B) controversial..essential to
   (C) impractical..detrimental to
   (D) divisive..indifferent toward
   (E) unattainable..supportive of

15. The bright coloration of American coot chicks is an anomaly: although colorful plumage is usually _____ to newborn birds because it may attract predators, among this species it appears to be _____, because parents are more likely to notice and care for brightly-colored offspring.

   (A) pernicious..fatal
   (B) dangerous..unnecessary
   (C) limited..favorable
   (D) beneficial..advantageous
   (E) detrimental..helpful

EXERCISE 2

15 Questions

Time—15 Minutes

> **Directions:** Each sentence below has one or two blanks, each blank indicating that something has been omitted. Beneath the sentence are five lettered words or sets of words. Choose the word or set of words for each blank that *best* fits the meaning of the sentence as a whole.

1. Whereas Mary's _____ personality made it difficult for her classmates to accept her, June ingratiated herself with her sweetness and modesty.
   - (A) gregarious
   - (B) sociable
   - (C) pretentious
   - (D) cloying
   - (E) winning

2. The myths of any tribe serve to explain and embody their _____; by examining a people's favorite _____, one can determine the things they most deeply cherish.
   - (A) origins..legends
   - (B) religion..pastimes
   - (C) beliefs..occupations
   - (D) history..rituals
   - (E) values..stories

3. Although Paul and Philip grew up a few blocks apart and had virtually the same educational background, their adult lives took _____ paths.
   - (A) parallel
   - (B) divergent
   - (C) improbable
   - (D) intriguing
   - (E) coinciding

4. The structure of social life among gibbons is _____ that of humans: they live in _____ groups consisting of a pair and their offspring and may associate with other similar groups, but spend the majority of their time with their nuclear family.

   (A) related to..nomadic
   (B) unlike..diurnal
   (C) parallel to..gargantuan
   (D) similar to..monogamous
   (E) identical to..nocturnal

5. Whereas privately owned delivery companies can _____ services that are unprofitable, the U.S. Postal Service, because it is _____, must serve the entire country.

   (A) increase..nationwide
   (B) concentrate..a monopoly
   (C) eliminate..government-sponsored
   (D) reduce..nonprofit-making
   (E) provide..federally subsidized

6. Because frogs have no hair, scales, or feathers to _____ their paper-thin skin, they are _____ changes in the quality of the air and water in their environment.

   (A) cover..invigorated by
   (B) conceal..unaffected by
   (C) warm..chilled by
   (D) protect..hypersensitive to
   (E) adorn..responsive to

7. As the war dragged on, with increased casualties and few signs of _____, morale among the soldiers _____.

   (A) victory..stabilized
   (B) progress..plummeted
   (C) concern..collapsed
   (D) hope..improved
   (E) dismay..dwindled

8. Amelia Earhart's hope of being the first woman to fly around the globe was _____ when she disappeared in the middle of her _____ journey.

   (A) thwarted..ill-fated
   (B) realized..triumphant
   (C) fulfilled..historic
   (D) controversial..hazardous
   (E) postponed..famous

9. The fact that the President's illness had been _____ was not uncovered for several months; when he suddenly and unexpectedly fell ill again, the doctors realized that his previous malady had not been a simple case of influenza.

   (A) misdiagnosed
   (B) remedied
   (C) contagious
   (D) deleterious
   (E) inconsequential

10. Just as the advent of television failed to _____ the demand for motion pictures, so cable television and the older broadcast television seem likely to _____ for years to come.

    (A) eliminate..coexist
    (B) diminish..reciprocate
    (C) alter..decline
    (D) increase..expand
    (E) affect..develop

11. Although the community was usually considered a safe haven for _____, some who expressed beliefs contrary to those of the majority were _____.

    (A) dissenters..applauded
    (B) free speech..disgruntled
    (C) democracy..disagreed with
    (D) freedom..necessary
    (E) individuality..persecuted

12. The circadian rhythms of some breeds of hamsters are so _____ that, regardless of their surroundings, they _____ function according to the same twenty-four-hour cycle.

    (A) irregular..sometimes
    (B) precise..unfalteringly
    (C) anomalous..regularly
    (D) unusual..continuously
    (E) predictable..rarely

13. In classical literature, love was depicted not as an ennobling passion but as an unfortunate _____ that disabled the judgment, almost a kind of _____.

    (A) condition..virtue
    (B) sickness..retribution
    (C) emotion..crime
    (D) malady..insanity
    (E) occurrence..insecurity

14. The birth of septuplets this year has led to a wave of newspaper articles presenting _____ accounts of the medical problems associated with multiple births, _____ the joyful stories about the septuplets that at first dominated the press.

    (A) morose..minimizing
    (B) perfunctory..reinforcing
    (C) sobering..counterbalancing
    (D) empathetic..obscuring
    (E) grim..substantiating

15. The _____ of the human brain is extraordinary, as illustrated by the fact that, when an infant becomes blind, regions of the cerebral cortex that usually contribute to sight are taken over by another sensory system, as if to _____ the use of every region of the cortex.

    (A) complexity..reduce
    (B) versatility..prevent
    (C) rigidity..regulate
    (D) durability..simplify
    (E) adaptability..maximize

EXERCISE 3

15 Questions

Time—15 Minutes

> **Directions:** Each sentence below has one or two blanks, each blank indicating that something has been omitted. Beneath the sentence are five lettered words or sets of words. Choose the word or set of words for each blank that *best* fits the meaning of the sentence as a whole.

1. Unlike the American worker, who expects to work for several different firms during his or her career, until recently the Japanese worker regarded employment as a _____ commitment.
   - (A) lifetime
   - (B) significant
   - (C) bilateral
   - (D) economic
   - (E) moral

2. Andre's gift for music seemed to be _____; both his mother and grandfather before him had been famed concert pianists.
   - (A) simulated
   - (B) innate
   - (C) accidental
   - (D) inexplicable
   - (E) prodigious

3. The many obvious lapses in the author's research make it _____ to accept the _____ of his conclusions.
   - (A) easy..accuracy
   - (B) impossible..meaning
   - (C) attractive..logic
   - (D) questionable..structure
   - (E) difficult..validity

4. Her wildlife movies unflinchingly capture the _____ of the animal kingdom: predators stalking their prey, singling out the weak, young, and very old as easy kills, and the cold-blooded killing that is a necessity of life in the wild.

   (A) brutality
   (B) romance
   (C) color
   (D) mystery
   (E) grandeur

5. Although the Internet was originally created to facilitate scientific research and emergency communication, today most people consider it _____ enterprise, offering services marketed as sources of information and entertainment.

   (A) a commercial
   (B) a private
   (C) an obsolete
   (D) an insidious
   (E) an institutional

6. The qualities expected of a professional musician seem _____, for she must be studious, disciplined, and technically impeccable while bringing passion and _____ to each performance.

   (A) ambiguous..capriciousness
   (B) ephemeral..impulsiveness
   (C) paradoxical..spontaneity
   (D) varied..virtuosity
   (E) impossible..emotion

7. Homer is considered by many the _____ of the Western literary tradition; the work of poets, playwrights, and writers for many subsequent centuries drew upon themes and structures _____ his epic poems.

   (A) originator..divergent from
   (B) progenitor..derived from
   (C) forefather..leading to
   (D) pariah..based upon
   (E) catalyst..described in

8. Although he had been a _____ child, Roosevelt went on to become one of our nation's most _____ presidents, both mentally and physically.

    (A) precocious..able
    (B) sickly..vigorous
    (C) healthy..stalwart
    (D) typical..competent
    (E) feeble..unusual

9. Considering today's high divorce rate and the growing number of single-parent households, it is _____ to learn that the majority of Americans still accept the _____ belief in the importance of an intact nuclear family.

    (A) surprising..traditional
    (B) encouraging..obsolete
    (C) curious..unpopular
    (D) illuminating..controversial
    (E) astonishing..superficial

10. The apparent discovery of _____ on Europa, one of Jupiter's moons, has led to speculation that there may be _____ there, on the assumption that water and life are linked elsewhere as they are on Earth.

    (A) oxygen..vegetation
    (B) craters..toxins
    (C) an atmosphere..precipitation
    (D) ice..rivers
    (E) an ocean..life

11. The _____ the popular music scene by artists with a _____ amount of musical talent has led many to conclude that success in music has less to do with creativity than with image and advertising.

    (A) appearance on..disproportionate
    (B) control of..vast
    (C) rejection of..minuscule
    (D) domination of..minimal
    (E) exploitation of..noticeable

12. Some kinds of technological advances are easy to _____; television, space flight, and robots were _____ concepts decades before they became realities.

    (A) understand..scientific
    (B) achieve..little-known
    (C) foresee..familiar
    (D) denounce..theoretical
    (E) predict..unimaginable

13. Along with hunting and pollution, the _____ of eucalyptus trees, the koala's prime habitat and food source, is one of many _____ to the species.

    (A) delicacy..rivals
    (B) nurturance..dangers
    (C) razing..threats
    (D) leveling..advantages
    (E) life span..perils

14. As a result of increased _____ the connection between nutrition and health, many Americans are planning their _____ more carefully than in the past.

    (A) concern over..diets
    (B) awareness of..exercise
    (C) ignorance of..meals
    (D) publicity about..lives
    (E) controversy concerning..careers

15. As the whale shark plows through a dense clump of the small fish on which it feeds, its stomach is _____ the food, causing a _____ clearly visible to any observer.

    (A) glutted with..discomfort
    (B) processing..digestion
    (C) engulfing..sensation
    (D) distended with..swelling
    (E) gorged with..predation

EXERCISE 4

15 Questions

Time—15 Minutes

> **Directions:** Each sentence below has one or two blanks, each blank indicating that something has been omitted. Beneath the sentence are five lettered words or sets of words. Choose the word or set of words for each blank that *best* fits the meaning of the sentence as a whole.

1. The _____ of the judges was ensured by giving each contestant a code number by which alone he or she was identified.
   - (A) impartiality
   - (B) confusion
   - (C) authority
   - (D) accuracy
   - (E) preparation

2. The doctor's _____ gave the patient new hope; now that someone had finally identified his illness, he was optimistic that a cure could be found.
   - (A) examination
   - (B) prescription
   - (C) treatment
   - (D) diagnosis
   - (E) hypothesis

3. The _____ and _____ lifestyle of certain types of primates is widely divergent from the habits of most other primate species, who are active during the day and who form societies based on interrelationships that are quite complex.
   - (A) sedentary..omnivorous
   - (B) inactive..monogamous
   - (C) nomadic..lonely
   - (D) nocturnal..solitary
   - (E) diurnal..gregarious

4. The marshes of Cape Cod, with their varied and plentiful plant and animal life, are of special interest to the _____.

   (A) geographer
   (B) painter
   (C) naturalist
   (D) vacationer
   (E) developer

5. The plan for a new shopping mall has come as an unpleasant surprise to many local residents, who _____ their small, quiet community and _____ the increased traffic and noise that the mall is likely to bring.

   (A) appreciate..anticipate
   (B) venerate..appreciate
   (C) enjoy..trivialize
   (D) deplore..recognize
   (E) cherish..dread

6. George Orwell began his career as a writer of party propaganda, and even after he turned to fiction, his work continued to serve many of the same _____ ends.

   (A) satirical
   (B) aesthetic
   (C) political
   (D) personal
   (E) religious

7. The biography depicts the well-known actress as _____ and ruthless, _____ the already widespread belief that she attained stardom through a series of unpalatable maneuvers.

   (A) scheming..questioning
   (B) charismatic..fostering
   (C) power-mad..verifying
   (D) vindictive..injuring
   (E) cruel..challenging

8. Some consider animal experimentation inhumane while others defend it, but this _____ method of testing medicines continues because the benefits to human life are generally considered to _____ the harm done to animals.

   (A) antiquated..imbalance
   (B) misunderstood..mitigate
   (C) inappropriate..exacerbate
   (D) controversial..outweigh
   (E) powerful..underscore

9. Because of the vulnerability of Japanese cities to _____, officials there have developed extensive safety plans for dealing with natural disasters.

    (A) terrorism
    (B) overcrowding
    (C) civil disorder
    (D) invasion
    (E) earthquakes

10. Although William Shakespeare of Stratford-on-Avon is generally _____ to have created some of the most brilliant plays in the English language, some scholars are _____ about his authorial credentials.

    (A) believed..dubious
    (B) thought..biased
    (C) predicted..unsure
    (D) said..convinced
    (E) known..certain

11. At the time of its construction, the gymnasium was highly _____; the students and faculty for whom it was planned were _____, but the community members who faced losing their neighborhood park were outraged.

    (A) controversial..gratified
    (B) warranted..skeptical
    (C) fortuitous..euphoric
    (D) unnecessary..impartial
    (E) desirable..numerous

12. Even a _____ and apparently _____ invention may depend on an inexplicable stroke of genius, as the fact that some great civilizations never developed the wheel suggests.

    (A) vital..essential
    (B) simple..obvious
    (C) profound..brilliant
    (D) primitive..ancient
    (E) complex..obscure

13. The fact that many public accommodations, such as movie theaters and shopping malls, are inaccessible to wheelchairs is often _____, just as the loss of revenues to the proprietors of these businesses is _____.

    (A) deleterious..minimal
    (B) unnoticed..ignored
    (C) intentional..unwitting
    (D) protested..unseen
    (E) obvious..suppressed

14. Researchers have concluded that many of the _____ connections between cells in the brain are formed during the first three months after birth, suggesting that postnatal stimulation may have a _____ effect on an infant's development.

    (A) temporary..lasting
    (B) necessary..negative
    (C) trivial..pervasive
    (D) essential..profound
    (E) vital..minimal

15. Artists benefit from corporate support of the arts, but when they receive such support, they must also _____ some degree of corporate _____.

    (A) consider..responsibility
    (B) forfeit..freedom
    (C) accept..control
    (D) condone..generosity
    (E) reject..power

EXERCISE 5

15 Questions

Time—15 Minutes

> **Directions:** Each sentence below has one or two blanks, each blank indicating that something has been omitted. Beneath the sentence are five lettered words or sets of words. Choose the word or set of words for each blank that *best* fits the meaning of the sentence as a whole.

1. As a possible presidential contender, the governor found herself subject to intense public _____; every speech she made was widely reported on television and in newspapers.

   (A) attack
   (B) adulation
   (C) manipulation
   (D) criticism
   (E) scrutiny

2. Although many of the board members were _____ about the impending deal, others were _____ the benefits it would bring to the company.

   (A) euphoric..confident of
   (B) chagrined..unsure about
   (C) pleased..disturbed by
   (D) optimistic..dubious about
   (E) angry..skeptical of

3. The cause of the altercation remains _____: although the two men are neighbors, the police have been unable to find a link between them that might explain their mutual _____.

   (A) speculative..ambivalence
   (B) controversial..affection
   (C) secret..attraction
   (D) unknown..animosity
   (E) obvious..animus

4. Although Mark Twain and Garrison Keillor are both humorists from the American Midwest, their themes, styles, and attitudes are basically _____.

(A) comic
(B) different
(C) timeless
(D) unremarkable
(E) identical

5. General dislike of the CEO was _____ in the _____ comments made at the board meeting.

(A) implied..ambivalent
(B) obvious..glowing
(C) apparent..impartial
(D) absent..contemptuous
(E) noticeable..concise

6. Just as Mozart's music broke new ground in the world of classicism, so Beethoven's work also _____ the unspoken rules of the classical period and _____ changes that eventually led to a new style called romanticism.

(A) obeyed..implemented
(B) overturned..initiated
(C) conformed to . .supported
(D) evaded..resisted
(E) eradicated..avoided

7. The members of any profession naturally seek to defend and protect one another; police officers, for instance, testify for one another in court, and doctors rarely _____ one another's medical decisions.

(A) examine
(B) criticize
(C) applaud
(D) explain
(E) review

8. As the global acreage of rain forest becomes more and more _____, the _____ among its inhabitants becomes ever more intense.

(A) polluted..communication
(B) inadequate..distance
(C) scarce..competition
(D) deficient..collaboration
(E) overpopulated..mating

9. The candidate _____ many of the causes that her opponent supports, leading some to question the necessity for her candidacy.

   (A) espouses
   (B) ignores
   (C) opposes
   (D) questions
   (E) derides

10. The _____ that computers are _____ educational tools has led many parents to believe that children don't need to be monitored when using the computer, as they do when watching TV or seeing a movie.

    (A) belief..malicious
    (B) hypothesis..powerful
    (C) misrepresentation..modern
    (D) misconception..benign
    (E) myth..dangerous

11. The remarkable fact that many inventions had their birth as toys suggests that people philosophize more freely when they know that their _____ leads to no _____ results.

    (A) cogitation..trivial
    (B) persistence..satisfactory
    (C) speculation..weighty
    (D) creativity..measurable
    (E) conjecture..inconsequential

12. As the cost of living rises and wages _____, it becomes more _____ for young adults entering the work force to support themselves, forcing greater numbers of adults between the ages of twenty-five and thirty-four to live with their parents.

    (A) vary..affordable
    (B) decline..advantageous
    (C) fall..prudent
    (D) increase..unusual
    (E) stagnate..difficult

13. Just as her older sister's _____ academic record had enabled her to attend a prestigious university, Martha was also _____ in hopes of securing admission to Columbia University.

    (A) impeccable..studious
    (B) perfect..presumptuous
    (C) modest..diligent
    (D) exemplary..optimistic
    (E) unparalleled..hard-working

14. Although the techniques used to monitor the active volcano were _____ and evacuation procedures were started _____, many of the island's inhabitants were killed by the eruption, as they refused to leave their homes when urged to do so by the foreign scientists.

    (A) useless..belatedly
    (B) comprehensive..gradually
    (C) effective..promptly
    (D) disruptive..immediately
    (E) exemplary..slowly

15. Personality is rooted as deeply in the need for _____, or at least personal interaction, as _____ well-being is rooted in chemical needs.

    (A) love..physical
    (B) hope..biological
    (C) affection..social
    (D) self-respect..bodily
    (E) companionship..natural

Answer Key

Exercise 1	Exercise 2	Exercise 3	Exercise 4	Exercise 5
1. D	1. C	1. A	1. A	1. E
2. D	2. E	2. B	2. D	2. D
3. D	3. B	3. E	3. D	3. D
4. B	4. D	4. A	4. C	4. B
5. E	5. C	5. A	5. E	5. A
6. B	6. D	6. C	6. C	6. B
7. B	7. B	7. B	7. C	7. B
8. C	8. A	8. B	8. D	8. C
9. A	9. A	9. A	9. E	9. A
10. C	10. A	10. E	10. A	10. D
11. C	11. E	11. D	11. A	11. C
12. C	12. B	12. C	12. B	12. E
13. E	13. D	13. C	13. B	13. A
14. C	14. C	14. A	14. D	14. D
15. E	15. E	15. D	15. C	15. A

Explanatory Answers

EXERCISE 1

1. **The correct answer is (D).** The missing word must fit the description of the critics given in the second half of the sentence. If they "can determine the fate of a play in a single night," then clearly they have a lot of "power."

2. **The correct answer is (D).** Remember that a semicolon (;) often indicates that the two halves of the sentence restate or paraphrase the same idea. The second half of this sentence tells us that the members of the school board wanted "enthusiasm" in a teacher candidate. Therefore, the word that describes the candidate they *rejected* should mean the opposite of "enthusiastic." "Perfunctory" fits the bill.

3. **The correct answer is (D).** Since both blanks here describe something similar—the way this unnamed person communicates—the two words should be near synonyms. And the words "difficult to follow his thought processes" make it clear that both missing words should mean "hard to understand, unnecessarily complicated."

4. **The correct answer is (B).** This sentence has a cause and effect relationship, as indicated by the word "as." If the squid "has never been seen alive," one could logically conclude that it would be "enigmatic."

5. **The correct answer is (E).** Both halves of the sentence make much the same point—that people will buy good products but not bad ones. Only the words in choice (E) fit this idea.

6. **The correct answer is (B).** Obviously, the structure of this sentence is similarity. We want a phrase to fit in the blank that will match the description of how both Truman and Ford attained prominence. You don't need to know history; just realize that Ford's case must have resembled Truman's, in which pure accident (or "outside circumstances") made him president.

7. **The correct answer is (B).** The word "however" tells you that the two halves of the sentence contrast with one another. The first half says that "predictions" of "mass starvation have proven false"; the second half says that, in the future, (something) "may yet prove to be one of the world's greatest problems." Thus, the contrast involves the idea that a problem that doesn't exist now may come to exist in the future; the same problem is being discussed in both parts of the sentence. Choice (B), then, makes sense because "global overcrowding" and "population growth" describe the same problem.

8. **The correct answer is (C).** The word "as" shows that the first half of the sentence describes the effect, the second half the cause. Choice (C) is right because the two words it contains work well together as a cause/effect pair: a speech that "ridicules" others would indeed be "inflammatory."

9. **The correct answer is (A).** If it wasn't until the late eighteenth century that educators decided children needed books of their own, then that must have been when the idea of children's literature "emerged"—choice (A).

10. **The correct answer is (C).** Only "reaction" makes sense as a description of the relationship between a garden and surroundings that are full of "filth and desolation."

11. **The correct answer is (C).** The second half of the sentence shows that "vastness" is the dominant quality of the proposed office complex.

12. **The correct answer is (C).** The sentence describes something that twentieth-century Japan *wanted* to do; therefore, it must be referring to a desirable combination of the best of the old and the new. Choice (C) makes sense because it refers to "assimilating" (that is, absorbing) what is good in modern life while retaining what is "traditional." A negative word like "outmoded" (choice B) wouldn't fit this context.

13. **The correct answer is (E).** Because the second half of the sentence contrasts "the affluent" with "those who cannot afford new outdoor furniture," we can see that the first blank should be filled with a word referring to class or economic differences. This narrows the possibilities to choices (C) and (E). Choice (C) doesn't work because an attempt to restrict someone's lifestyle wouldn't logically make them feel "pleased."

14. **The correct answer is (C).** The two words in this choice nicely paraphrase the two points made later in the sentence: "impractical" = "difficult to institute," and "detrimental to . . . unity" = "lead[ing] to bickering."

15. **The correct answer is (E).** The words "anomaly" and "although" both suggest that the second half of the sentence is built around a contrast between the role colorful plumage usually plays among birds and the role it actually plays in this particular species. Thus, the two words we want must be nearly opposite in meaning, as the two words in choice (E) are.

EXERCISE 2

1. **The correct answer is (C).** The word "Whereas" shows that the sentence describes a contrast between Mary and June. Therefore, we want a word whose meaning is strongly opposed to "sweetness and modesty." "Pretentious" works well in that role.

2. **The correct answer is (E).** The two parts of this sentence paraphrase the same idea. Therefore, the first blank should correspond to the idea of "the things they most deeply cherish" in the second half of the sentence, while the second blank should correspond to "myths." "Values" and "stories" both work.

3. **The correct answer is (B).** The word "Although" tells you to look for a contrast of some kind—something that is surprising or that apparently contradicts another idea in the sentence. It does seem surprising that two men with so many similarities should have "divergent" (i.e., widely different) lives.

4. **The correct answer is (D).** The description of gibbon life in this sentence suggests a "monogamous" family base, which in turn is roughly "parallel to" the dominant structure of human social life.

5. **The correct answer is (C).** "Whereas" alerts you to look for a contrast in the sentence. We then read that the U.S. Postal Service "must serve the entire country"; the first blank, to convey the needed contrast, must suggest that private companies can "eliminate" services they don't want to provide.

6. **The correct answer is (D).** If frogs are lacking in structures to "protect" their skin, it would make sense that they would be "hypersensitive to" their environments.

7. **The correct answer is (B).** Clearly, the second blank must contain a word meaning something like "fell"; so only choices (B), (C), and (E) qualify. Of these, choices (C) and (E) can be eliminated because, in both, the first word brings in a new idea that isn't required or justified by the rest of the sentence.

8. **The correct answer is (A).** If she disappeared during the journey, then clearly her hope of flying around the globe was "thwarted" (choice A). "Ill-fated" is the logical word to use to describe a trip that ends this way (worse than losing your luggage).

9. **The correct answer is (A).** Looking only at the first half of the sentence, any of the five choices could work; however, the second half of the sentence makes it clear that the President's doctors had made a mistake in interpreting his symptoms, a situation described only by the word "misdiagnosed."

10. **The correct answer is (A).** The words "Just as . . . so" make it clear that parallel situations are being described in the two halves of the sentence. Only the words in choice (A) logically establish the expected similarity.

11. **The correct answer is (E).** The contrast between the two halves of the sentence is signaled by the word "Although." Choice (E) makes sense because the contradiction between "a safe haven for individuality" and the fact that those who disagree were sometimes "persecuted" is clear and sharp.

12. **The correct answer is (B).** You don't need to know the slightly arcane word "circadian" to understand the sentence. Even without that word, you can tell that these hamsters are behaving in a very regular fashion since they "function according to the same twenty-four hour cycle." Thus, their rhythms are certainly "precise."

13. **The correct answer is (D).** If love was thought to "disable the judgment" (i.e., to confuse one's brains), then clearly the word "insanity" is an apt description.

14. **The correct answer is (C).** The word we want for the second blank must suggest how the articles about "medical problems" related to the "joyful stories" that first appeared. Only "counterbalancing" really makes sense.

15. **The correct answer is (E).** The phenomenon described in the sentence, in which parts of the brain change their function, clearly illustrates the "adaptability" of the brain.

EXERCISE 3

1. **The correct answer is (A).** The word "Unlike" of course shows us that the two halves of the sentence will contrast with one another. The idea of a "lifetime" commitment nicely contrasts with the idea of changing jobs several times.

2. **The correct answer is (B).** If musical talent runs in Andre's family, then it would be logical to consider his gift inborn, inherited, or "innate."

3. **The correct answer is (E).** A simple cause and effect relationship is required here; if the research contains "many obvious lapses," then accepting its conclusions would certainly be "difficult."

4. **The correct answer is (A).** All we need here is a word that summarizes the tone of the second half of the sentence. A word like "violence," "bloodthirstiness," or "brutality" will work.

5. **The correct answer is (A).** If the Internet today offers "services" that are "marketed," then it is clearly a "commercial" (that is, for-profit) enterprise.

6. **The correct answer is (C).** We can see that the sentence is suggesting contradictory or opposing qualities that a musician has, since "discipline" and "passion" are usually thought of as very different. The first blank, "paradoxical," captures this sense of contradiction, while the second blank, "spontaneity," fits nicely with "passion" and contrasts appropriately with "disciplined."

7. **The correct answer is (B).** Obviously, the sentence is discussing the effect Homer had on later writers. Therefore, "progenitor" makes sense for the first blank, and "derived from" logically fits the relationship of the later work to that of Homer.

8. **The correct answer is (B).** The word "Although" tells us to look for two words that are contradictory or opposite in meaning. "Sickly" and "vigorous" fill the bill nicely.

9. **The correct answer is (A).** Second blank first: since the "nuclear family" is being contrasted to "today's" marital trends, it's clear that the nuclear family is being discussed as something out of the past; thus, a word like "traditional" or "obsolete" (choice B) is needed. Choice (A) is the better answer because the sentence clearly suggests that the belief in the nuclear family is "surprising," whereas the idea that it is "encouraging" drags in a value judgment unsupported by the rest of the paragraph.

10. **The correct answer is (E).** The second half of the sentence tells us that water and life are being linked; hence, "an ocean" and "life" make sense for the first half of the sentence.

11. **The correct answer is (D).** If the author believes that "image and advertising" are more important than "creativity," then the artists he is discussing must have little talent or, as the second word in choice (D) puts it, "minimal" talent.

12. **The correct answer is (C).** The fact that television and the other advances named were concepts long before they were realities suggests that they were easy to "foresee."

13. **The correct answer is (C).** We can tell that the second blank must be a word like "dangers" or "threats," since it is describing some phenomenon that resembles "hunting and pollution." Then, it's easy to see that the first blank must refer to the "razing" (i.e., destruction) of the koala's habitat and food.

14. **The correct answer is (A).** Since the sentence is discussing "nutrition," we can see that the second blank must refer to food. And if Americans are planning their diets more carefully, then what must have increased is their "concern over" nutrition.

15. **The correct answer is (D).** The two blanks must be filled with words that go together logically and that, in combination, describe something that would be "clearly visible to any observer." Only a "swelling" of the stomach would be visible in this way.

EXERCISE 4

1. **The correct answer is (A).** The use of a code number to keep the contestants' identities secret is clearly designed to maintain the judges' "impartiality."

2. **The correct answer is (D).** The two halves of the sentence make the same point. Thus, the blank should be filled with a word that corresponds to the idea of "identifying his illness"—diagnosis.

3. **The correct answer is (D).** We want words here that suggest a contrast to the second half of the sentence, as indicated by the phrase "widely divergent from." Choice (D) works because "nocturnal" opposes "active during the day," and "solitary" opposes the idea of "interrelationships that are quite complex."

4. **The correct answer is (C).** All of the choices are inherently plausible, but only the "naturalist" would automatically be interested in "varied and plentiful plant and animal life." Remember, don't bring in any new ideas that aren't strictly required by the rest of the sentence.

5. **The correct answer is (E).** The words "unpleasant surprise" make it clear that the residents don't want the mall. Therefore, the first blank should contain a positive word to describe their feelings about the community as it now exists, while the second blank should contain a negative word to describe how they feel about the "increased traffic and noise" they expect.

6. **The correct answer is (C).** We want a word that goes naturally with the idea of "party propaganda." While such writing *may* be "satirical" or "personal" or even "religious," we can only say for sure that it *must* be "political."

7. **The correct answer is (C).** The first blank must match up with "ruthless," while the second blank must describe how the image in the biography fits with "the already widespread belief" about the actress. Clearly, it will "verify" what people already believe about her.

8. **The correct answer is (D).** The word for the first blank, "controversial," summarizes the point made in the first nine words of the sentence; the word for the second blank logically explains why animal experimentation "continues."

9. **The correct answer is (E).** The missing word must describe a kind of "natural disaster," since that is what the sentence is about.

10. **The correct answer is (A).** To complete the expected contrast (signaled by the word "Although"), we need a word like "dubious" or "unsure" for the second blank. Choice (C) is wrong because "predicted" makes no sense with reference to a past event.

11. **The correct answer is (A).** The word "but" shows that the reaction of the students and faculty was different from that of the community members (hence, "gratified"); and the word "controversial" describes the fact that the two groups had such opposite opinions.

12. **The correct answer is (B).** The word "Even" tells us that the kind of invention being described here is one that we normally *wouldn't* assume would depend on "an inexplicable stroke of genius." To create the maximum amount of contrast, we want the words "simple" and "obvious," which do in fact make sense as descriptions of the wheel.

13. **The correct answer is (B).** We can tell that the two parts of the sentence describe similar occurrences because of the words "just as" in the middle of the sentence. So we want words for the two blanks that are similar in meaning, which "unnoticed" and "ignored" certainly are.

14. **The correct answer is (D).** The words "suggesting that" show that the two halves of the sentence have a cause and effect relationship; what's in the first half suggests what's in the second half. The two nearly synonymous words "essential" and "profound" carry out the expected relationship.

15. **The correct answer is (C).** It's logical to conclude that, if artists are supported by corporations, they will also be influenced by those corporations.

EXERCISE 5

1. **The correct answer is (E).** All of the answer choices are plausible, but only "scrutiny" describes the governor's experience as described in the sentence without bringing in any new ideas.

2. **The correct answer is (D).** These two words carry out the required contrast between the reactions of the two groups of board members. Choice (C) is wrong because it makes no sense to imagine the board members being "disturbed by the benefits" the deal would produce.

3. **The correct answer is (D).** If "police have been unable" to find an explanation, then the cause remains "unknown"; since an "altercation" (i.e., an argument) is being discussed, the relationship between the two men must have involved some kind of "animosity."

4. **The correct answer is (B).** Since the word "Although" tells us to look for a contrast between the two halves of the sentence, we can see that the blank must be filled with a word that mentions differences between the two writers rather than another similarity.

5. **The correct answer is (A).** The two words to be inserted here must suggest a logical relationship between the comments made and the attitude the board members felt. Only the words in choice (A) make sense: "ambivalent" comments might well "imply" negative feelings about the head of the company.

6. **The correct answer is (B).** The words "Just as . . . so" tell us that Beethoven, like Mozart, was a musical revolutionary. Therefore, to say that he "overturned" the rules and "initiated" changes makes good sense.

7. **The correct answer is (B).** We need a word that makes the behavior of the doctors parallel to the behavior of the police officers, since the two are given as examples of the same general principle.

8. **The correct answer is (C).** The missing words must logically suggest a cause and effect relationship. If room in the rain forests is becoming more "scarce," then it's logical that "competition" among its inhabitants would increase.

9. **The correct answer is (A).** If some "question the necessity for her candidacy," then her political positions must seem insignificant or pointless in some way. This would only be true if her positions are just the same as those of her opponent; that could make it seem silly for her to oppose him.

10. **The correct answer is (D).** We want words that suggest a feeling about computers that would lead parents to let their children use the devices without being watched. Only choice (D) works, because only "benign" is sufficiently positive to suggest that idea.

11. **The correct answer is (C).** To fit the idea of inventions originating as toys, we want the second blank to suggest "results" that are *not* serious or important—the opposite of what we think about toys. Hence, "weighty."

12. **The correct answer is (E).** If more young adults are being forced to live with their parents, then their economic condition must be generally bad. To fit this notion, it makes sense to speak about wages "stagnating" (that is, failing to increase) and self-support being "difficult."

13. **The correct answer is (A).** To attend a "prestigious" university would obviously require a good academic record, so the first word must be one that means something like "excellent." And for the second blank, the word we want should relate to what's needed to achieve such a record; "studious" is the choice that makes the most sense.

14. **The correct answer is (D).** Clearly, the fact that the inhabitants were killed by the eruption contradicts the description needed of the monitoring and evacuation procedures (the word "Although" tells us this). Only the words in choice (D) create the necessary degree of contrast.

15. **The correct answer is (A).** The first blank should contain an idea that fits the concept of "personal interaction"; the second blank should contain a word that describes the kind of "well-being" that would have a "chemical" basis. Only "love" and "physical" fit both requirements.

Chapter 7

Reading Comprehension

Get the Scoop On . . .

- How the three-stage reading method can help you master the passages and get more questions right
- How to separate main ideas from supporting details
- How to recognize the vital connections among ideas in the passages
- Why you should read with pencil in hand
- The kinds of deceptive wrong answers the test-makers love to use—and how to avoid them

THE TEST CAPSULE

What's the Big Idea?

In reading comprehension, you'll be given a passage to read, which will read like an excerpt from a scholarly discussion of a topic from the natural sciences, the social sciences, or the humanities. You'll then have to answer a group of two to four questions about the passage, testing how well you've understood its content.

How Many?

Of the 30 questions in your verbal section, your GRE will probably have a total of 8 reading comprehension questions.

How Much Do They Count?

Because reading comprehension questions are 8 out of 30 total verbal questions, they count as 27 percent of your overall verbal score.

How Much Time Should They Take?

You should spend about five minutes on any group of reading passages. Expect to spend about half of that time reading and the other half answering the questions.

What's the Best Strategy?

Use the *three-stage method* when reading passages: preview, read, and review. With this approach, you'll gather much more information from the passage than with conventional one-step reading, and you'll be able to answer the questions that follow faster and more correctly.

What's the Worst Pitfall?

Choosing answers merely because they sound familiar or are factually true. The answers you pick must not only be plausible and true but must also relate directly to the question and be drawn from the most relevant portion of the passage.

THE OFFICIAL DESCRIPTION

What They Are

Reading on the GRE involves two steps. The first step is reading a passage of nonfiction prose, usually between 150 and 400 words long, that might deal with almost any subject from the natural sciences, the social sciences, and the humanities. The second step is answering a group of two to four questions dealing with the content, form, and style of the passage.

Where They Are

In the typical computerized GRE, you'll have one verbal section that is 30 minutes long. It will probably include three reading comprehension passages with a total of eight questions, interspersed seemingly at random among the other verbal question types—antonyms, analogies, and sentence completions. Reminder: the test-makers claim the right to change the format at any time! However, the typical format we just described is what you're most likely to encounter.

What They Measure

Reading comprehension is designed to measure your ability to handle the varied kinds of sophisticated, complex, and subtle readings that graduate students are called upon to do. To answer the questions, it's not enough to understand the basic facts presented in the passage; you also need to notice the more elusive *implications* in the passage (that is, ideas that are suggested rather than directly stated) as well as the *form, structure,* and *style* of the passage (that is, how the author has chosen to present her ideas).

What They Cover

GRE reading passages consist of edited excerpts from scholarly or serious nonfiction books about almost any subject from the natural sciences (chemistry, biology, physics, geology, astronomy, and so on), the social sciences (history, sociology, psychology, anthropology, and so on), and the humanities (literature, art, music, architecture, philosophy, and so on). The three passages you'll probably be given on your GRE will normally include one passage from each category.

The Directions

> **Directions:** Each passage is followed by questions based on its content. After reading a passage, choose the best answer to each question. Answer all questions following a passage on the basis of what is *stated* or *implied* in that passage.

THE INSIDER'S REPORT

Strategies That Really Work

Read Each Passage in Three Stages: Previewing, Reading, Reviewing
Reading comprehension on the GRE poses a special time-management problem. Unlike the other verbal question types, reading comprehension requires you to spend a large chunk of time doing something *before* you look at the questions—namely, reading the passage itself. Under the circumstances, with time pressure a real concern for most students, it's easy to get impatient. The temptation to rush through the passage in your haste to start filling in answers might be very great.

Don't do it! Unless you invest some time in getting to know the passage well, your chances of answering most of the questions right are pretty slim. In fact, we'll go further. We'll recommend that you spend *more time* reading the passages than you normally would. Whereas most people ordinarily read something once and once only, we suggest that you read (or at least scan) each passage on the GRE *three* times before answering a single question.

We have good reason for this recommendation. The three-stage reading method is a proven technique long taught and used by skilled readers as the best way of getting the most possible information out of anything in writing. Paradoxically, you'll find—we can virtually guarantee it—that if you practice the three-stage method, you'll soon find that you're gathering more information out of what you read *more quickly than ever before*.

Here's how the three-stage method works.

1. Previewing
First, preview the passage in one of two ways. You can skim its contents by letting your eyes quickly scroll down the screen, picking up as much information as you can. Or you can actually read selected sentences from the passage: specifically, the *first* sentence of each paragraph in the

passage, and the *last* sentence of the entire passage. Either of these methods works well; we suggest you experiment with both and choose the one you prefer.

What's the point of previewing? It's to give you some idea of what the passage is about and, generally, how it is organized, *before* you actually read it. Think about it: when you know, in general, what a teacher will be teaching, don't you find it easier to understand and absorb the lesson? (Educational researchers have proven it's true.) The same idea applies here: if you know generally what the passage is about before reading it, you'll understand it better.

Don't spend a long time previewing—on the average GRE reading passage, this stage should take about 30 seconds. Practice with a watch until you get a feel for it.

2. Reading

Having previewed the passage, go ahead and read it through, more or less in the conventional way. (Actually, we'll be suggesting some special reading techniques for this stage in a moment, but for now, just think of stage two as the familiar reading process you've always done.)

3. Reviewing

The third stage involves scanning the passage one more time, reminding yourself of its main ideas, most important details, and overall structure. Like previewing, this should be a fast process—spend no more than 30 seconds to review an average GRE passage.

Why bother with reviewing? There are three main reasons:

- First, by the time you finish reading a complex, subtle, or confusing GRE passage, you might find that you don't really remember how the passage began. Reviewing refreshes your memory for the structure of the entire passage, making it easier for you to "hold it in mind" as a unit.

- Second, reviewing can help you understand the earlier parts of the passage better than you did when you first read them. Quite often, a point made in the first or second paragraph isn't fully explained until the third or fourth paragraph. Reviewing the whole thing ties together loose ends that otherwise might have remained slightly confusing.

- Third, reviewing helps you remember which topics are discussed in which parts of the passage. This will make it easier when you need a specific detail to answer a question. Rather than scanning the whole passage, you'll probably be able to zero in on the right paragraph quickly.

Here's how the timing of the three-stage method works. Let's say the reading passage is 350 words long (toward the high end for GRE passages). The average student reads about 250 words per minute. So the three stages would take a total of two and a half minutes:

Stage Number	Stage	Time
Stage 1	Previewing	½ minute
Stage 2	Reading	1½ minutes
Stage 3	Reviewing	½ minute
Total time		2½ minutes

FYI

Some students wonder whether they should learn "speed reading" to improve their GRE performance. For most students, it's unnecessary. If you can read at an average rate of 250 words per minute, as most college students do, you'll have plenty of time for the passages on the exam. If you're not sure of your current reading speed, test yourself with a sample GRE passage and a watch. Just count the words and divide by the number of minutes spent to determine your words-per-minute rate.

You'd spend about two minutes on the two or three questions that follow the passage, making a total of under five minutes for the passage and questions. On the exam, you'll find that this kind of timing works well and will leave you with ample time for the other verbal questions in the section.

Focus on Big Ideas, Not Little Details

Almost everything you read—on the GRE or elsewhere—can be broken down into two kinds of information: *main ideas* and *supporting details*. It's important to distinguish between the two when reading for the exam. The main ideas are worth focusing on; the supporting details are usually not.

How can you recognize the main ideas in a passage? There are several clues to look for:

- Main ideas tend to be broad and general; supporting details tend to be narrow and specific.

- Often, each paragraph of a passage is centered on a single main idea that is explicitly stated somewhere in the paragraph.

- The main idea often appears first or last in the paragraph; supporting details usually appear in the middle of the paragraph.

Consider the following example. It's a paragraph excerpted from a reading passage on an actual exam:

Line

(5)

The myth of the infallible scientist evaporates when one thinks about the number of great ideas in science whose originators were correct in general but wrong in detail. The English physicist John Dalton (1766–1844) gets credit for modern atomic theory, but his mathematical formulas for calculating atomic weights were incorrect. The Polish astronomer Copernicus, who corrected Ptolemy's ancient concept of an Earth-centered universe, nevertheless was mistaken in the particulars of the planets' orbits.

There are three sentences in this paragraph. Of the three, which expresses a broad, general idea rather than a narrow, specific detail?

The answer: the first sentence. It makes a general point—that scientists, even great ones, are not infallible. The second and third sentences give details to support and explain this idea: the second sentence describes the example of John Dalton, and the third sentence adds the example of Copernicus. Both are interesting and help to clarify the overall theme, but neither is as important as the first sentence, which states the author's main point.

Here's another real example:

Line "Popular art" has a number of meanings, impossible to define with any precision, which range from folklore to junk. The poles are clear enough, but the middle tends to blur. The Hollywood Western of the 1930s, for example, has elements of folklore, but is closer to junk than to high art or folk art. There can
(5) be great trash, just as there is bad high art. The musicals of George Gershwin are great popular art, never aspiring to high art. Schubert and Brahms, however, used elements of popular music—folk themes—in works clearly intended as high art. The case of Verdi is a different one: he took a popular genre—bourgeois melodrama set to music (an accurate definition of nineteenth-century
(10) opera)—and, without altering its fundamental nature, transmuted it into high art. This remains one of the greatest achievements in music, and one that cannot be fully appreciated without recognizing the essential trashiness of the genre.

This paragraph starts with a broad, general idea—that "popular art" has a number of meanings. The next five sentences give a series of examples to illustrate this idea—Hollywood Westerns and the works of Gershwin, Schubert, and Brahms.

Then we see a shift. The author signals us, in the next sentence, that Verdi will be considered as more than just another example of the use of elements of popular art ("The case of Verdi is a different one"). He devotes the next two sentences to explaining what is unique about Verdi; and, in fact, the rest of the passage deals exclusively with Verdi. (A glance at the remaining paragraphs would make this obvious; just run your eye down the column of text, and a host of capital Vs jump out at you!)

This paragraph is almost *two* paragraphs in one. The first half of the paragraph deals with various definitions of popular art and offers a number of examples—none of them very important in itself, but illustrating the ways popular art can be used by "fine" artists. All of this helps to introduce the *real* topic of the passage, which is Verdi's use of popular motifs and forms in his great operatic works. The second half of the paragraph (starting with "The case of Verdi") makes the transition into this idea.

In this paragraph, as in the paragraph about the "infallible scientist," the details are interesting; they certainly add to the experience of reading the passage, and they help make the author's point vivid and understandable. *But the details are of secondary importance.* Don't spend a lot of time struggling to understand the details of a passage if they are tricky, and certainly don't try to memorize them. Instead, read them quickly, and make a mental note of where they are in case a question is asked about them. *It probably won't happen.*

Look for the Connections among the Parts of the Passage

Think of a reading passage as a *structure of ideas*. Most passages are devoted to conveying a number of ideas that are connected to one another in some way. If you understand these ideas *and* the connections among them, you truly understand the passage as a whole.

Quite often, the structure of ideas will be made explicit, even obvious. Consider, for example, a reading passage containing five paragraphs that begin with the following five sentences:

(1)   Historians have long debated the reasons for the defeat of the Confederacy in the American Civil War.

(2)   For decades, the dominant theory held that the North's victory was due primarily to the superior economic resources available to the Union armies.

(3)   A second school of historians pointed instead to the geographic advantages enjoyed by the Northern generals.

(4)   In recent years, however, more and more historians have begun to claim that, contrary to traditional Southern belief, the Northern generalship was consistently superior.

(5)   In the end, perhaps the most likely explanation of the Northern victory is that it was caused by a combination of several factors.

Simply by reading these five sentences you can get a very good idea of the content and structure of the whole passage. The passage deals with the issue of why the North won the Civil War. Its structure is clear-cut. Paragraph (1) sets forth the question to be discussed. Paragraphs (2), (3), and (4) each suggest a different answer to the question. And paragraph (5) concludes the passage by suggesting a possible resolution of the disagreement.

Why is it helpful to recognize the logical structure of a reading passage? It helps you in several ways:

■ It makes it easy to see the main ideas of the passage. In this case, the main ideas are the three separate theories being presented and discussed.

■ It tells you the *purpose* of the supporting details—even when you don't know what those details are. In this passage, for example, we've looked at only the first sentence of paragraph (2).

Nonetheless, we can easily imagine what kind of supporting details will be given in the rest of the paragraph. The missing sentences will probably give examples of the superior economic resources enjoyed by the North (coal mines, factories, or railroad lines, for instance).

If, in reading the complete passage, the actual details turned out to be complex or tricky, that would be okay. We'd still understand their purpose and basic thrust, even if the fine points were elusive. In most cases, that would be enough to answer any questions.

- The logical structure *organizes* all the information in the passage, making it easy to locate any detail about which you might be asked. In this passage, if a question focuses on some detail related to the third of the three theories (Northern generalship), you'll be able to find the relevant paragraph quickly.

- The structure explains how the main ideas are related to one another. In this case, the main ideas are three different, conflicting explanations of the same historical event. One or more questions are likely to focus on the relationships among these ideas; for example, how they differ from one another and why the earlier theories have been superseded by later ones.

GRE passages don't always boast such clear-cut logical structures, but a structure of some kind is usually present. With practice, you can learn to recognize it.

Table 7.1 will help. It lists several of the most common types of logical structures found in GRE reading passages. Either alone or in combination, these structures underlie many of the passages you'll encounter on the exam. Practice looking for them whenever you read.

Make Notes on the Passage as You Read
When tackling reading comprehension on the GRE, read with your pencil in hand. Use it to note key points and logical connections as you find them by jotting a brief outline of the passage on your scrap paper.

This will help you in two ways: the physical act of copying particular words and phrases will strengthen your memory of the ideas you've highlighted, and the rudimentary outline created in this way will make it easier to find key parts of the passage if you need to locate them later.

Here are some specific suggestions about what to look for and note as you read:

- **Look for the main idea of the passage as a whole.** This is one sentence that summarizes the central theme of the passage.

Table 7.1
Types of Logical Structures Often Used in GRE Reading Passages

1. Several theories or approaches to a single question or topic (often one theory or approach per paragraph)

2. One theory or idea illustrated with several detailed examples or illustrations (often one example or illustration per paragraph)

3. One theory or idea supported by several arguments (often one argument per paragraph)

4. Pro-and-con arguments presented on both sides of a single issue

5. A comparison or contrast between two events, ideas, phenomena, or people

6. A cause-and-effect sequence showing how one event led to another (presented either in chronological order or via "flashback," with later events named *before* the earlier ones)

Most passages contain such a sentence. It often appears near the beginning of the passage, to introduce the key idea; in other cases, it appears near the end as a kind of summary or conclusion. When you find it, jot down a few words that sum it up on your scrap paper outline.

■ **Look for the main idea of each paragraph.** Remember the idea of the topic sentence? You might have had a high school English teacher who taught you to include one in every paragraph you write. GRE paragraphs often contain such a sentence that summarizes the central point of the paragraph. When you find one, jot a couple of words from it on your scrap paper.

■ **Look for the logical structure of the passage, and use numbers, symbols, or words to annotate it.** For example, if a passage is organized as a pro-and-con presentation of arguments on both sides of an issue, label each argument with the word "pro" or "con" in the margin. If a passage presents a series of historical events, showing how one led to the next, jot the date of each key event or list the events, numbered in sequence in the margin—1, 2, 3, and so on.

Practice making notes on reading passages each time you work on reading comprehension between now and the day of the test.

Truth is, the *process* of making notes on the passage is as important as the notes themselves. It encourages an active approach to reading as

FYI

Making notes on the passage helps you in another way: It provides a simple guide for stage 3 of the three-stage reading method. Before you review the passage, quickly scan the outline you created. In a jiffy, you'll refresh your memory as to the main ideas in the passage as well as the connections among them.

opposed to a passive one. Using this as part of the three-stage reading method will help you delve more deeply into the meaning of a passage than you ever did with conventional ways of reading.

Keep your notes simple and very brief; only you need to understand them, and only for the next few minutes. For example, for the passage we discussed above dealing with the American Civil War, the paragraphs might be summarized with these key words:

1. reason South lost?
2. Northern economy
3. geography
4. maybe better generals?
5. combination

These notes will help you remember the structure and main ideas of the passage, and they'll help you find key details when they're needed to answer a question.

The Best Tips
Try Previewing the Question Stems along with the Passage
Remember, the question stem is the part of the question that precedes the answer choices: "The author of the passage includes the details concerning Picasso's father primarily in order to emphasize . . ." would be an example of a question stem.

By previewing the stems, some students feel they get an advance look at the main themes of the passage and the details on which the test-makers plan to focus. Other students, however, find this strategy more time-consuming than useful. Our recommendation: try this technique a couple of times and decide whether or not you find it helpful. If you do, use it.

When Answering Reading Comprehension Questions, Refer Back to the Passage as Often as You Need To
Most questions will focus on a particular paragraph or sentence of the passage. Many of the questions will contain explicit references to specific line numbers in the passage; others will simply mention particular details and expect you to locate them.

When this happens, you'll usually need to look back at the passage to answer the question correctly. Don't try to answer from memory. Quite often the wrong answer choices will be *subtly* wrong; only a careful review of the specific detail being asked about will enable you to see which answer is correct and why the others are not.

FYI

If you do preview the question stems, remember these two important don'ts. (1) Don't try to memorize the question stems—it's too much to keep in mind and might distract you when you're trying to read the passage. (2) Don't preview the answer choices. Remember, 80 percent of those choices are wrong! Why clutter your mind with falsehoods, distortions, and inaccuracies? Read the question stems only, and save the answer choices for later.

The Most Important Warnings

Don't Pick the First Answer Choice that Sounds Good

On all verbal questions, there are *degrees* of right and wrong. (By contrast, on math questions, correctness is much more black and white: if the right answer to a math problem is 16, then the answer 13 isn't "partially right" or "arguably right," it's just plain *wrong*.)

The "grayness" of verbal answer choices is especially noticeable on reading comprehension questions. The test-makers are highly skilled at crafting wrong answer choices (distractors) that are plausible and attractive. So if you begin reading the answers to a reading comprehension question and find that the first answer sounds good, *don't* just select it. Read on. The third answer might sound even better, and the fifth answer might be best of all. You always have to read all five answers to a reading comprehension item before making your choice.

Don't Pick an Answer Just Because It Sounds Familiar

One popular trick used by ETS in crafting distractors is to draw the information for wrong answers from the passage itself. This makes for distractors that are especially tempting because they sound (and are) familiar. Your reaction might be, "Oh, yes, it says that right here in paragraph 2. This must be the right answer."

Such reasoning might be flawed. The correct answer for the particular question might be found in paragraph 4, and paragraph 2 might simply be irrelevant. Don't fall for this.

The best way to avoid this trap is to refer back to the portion of the passage being asked about before you pick an answer. Make sure the answer you choose comes from *there*, not from some other part of the passage.

Don't Pick an Answer Just Because It's True

Most of the passages you'll read on the GRE will be about topics you know only a little about. That's okay. The test-makers don't expect you to have any background knowledge, and none is needed to answer the questions.

Occasionally, however, you might encounter a passage on a topic you're familiar with. It might even be a topic you personally are fascinated by. This can be helpful—reading about something you like and care about is fun, and you'll probably find the passage easy to understand.

However, this situation can also be dangerous. The danger lies in bringing your own outside knowledge and opinions to the questions. You might be tempted to pick an answer choice because you happen to know it's true or because you personally agree with it. Those aren't good reasons. The correct answer must be based specifically on the information in the passage, and it must reflect accurately the opinions and ideas expressed there—even if you happen to disagree with them.

FYI

Some students have been taught that certain words or phrases mark wrong answers to reading comprehension questions. For instance, some teachers say that answer choices with words like "all," "every," "always," "none," and "never" are usually wrong. False! ETS test-makers are specifically trained not to fall into giveaway patterns like these. There are no such simple rules you can count on— unfortunately.

So set aside your own knowledge and beliefs when reading a passage on a topic you care about. Pick answers based solely on what you find in the passage—not on anything else you happen to know.

JUST THE FACTS

- Use the three-stage method—previewing, reading, reviewing—to get the most out of every passage on the GRE.

- As you read, look for the main ideas in the passage and the connections among them.

- Read with pencil in hand and make notes on scrap paper.

- Learn the most common types of wrong answers used by the test-makers and how to avoid choosing them.

PRACTICE, PRACTICE, PRACTICE: READING COMPREHENSION EXERCISES

Instructions

The following exercises will give you a chance to practice the skills and strategies you've just learned for tackling critical reading questions. As with all practice exercises, work under true testing conditions. Complete each exercise in a single sitting. Eliminate distractions (TV, music) and clear away notes and reference materials. Time yourself with a stopwatch or kitchen timer, or have someone else time you. If you run out of time before answering all the questions, stop and draw a line under the last question you finished. Then go ahead and tackle the remaining questions. When you are done, score yourself based only on the questions you finished in the allotted time.

Understanding Your Scores

0–2 correct: A poor performance. Study this chapter again, and (if you haven't already) begin spending time each day in building your vocabulary using the Insider's GRE Word List in Appendix A.

3–4 correct: A below-average score. Study this chapter again, focusing especially on the skills and strategies you've found newest and most challenging.

5–7 correct: An average score. You may want to study this chapter again. Also be sure you are managing your time wisely (as explained in Chapter 3) and avoiding errors due to haste or carelessness.

8–9 correct: An above-average score. Depending on your personal target score and your strength on other verbal question types, you may or may not want to devote additional time to reading comprehension.

10–11 correct: An excellent score. You are probably ready to perform well on GRE reading comprehension.

EXERCISE 1

11 Questions

Time—15 Minutes

> **Directions:** Each passage in this group is followed by questions based on its content. After reading a passage, choose the best answer to each question. Answer all questions following a passage on the basis of what is *stated* or *implied* in that passage.

Line The delegates to the Constitutional Convention were realists. They knew that the greatest battles would follow the convention itself. The delegates had overstepped their bounds. Instead of amending the Articles of Confederation by which the American states had previously been governed, they had proposed an
(5) entirely new government. Under these circumstances, the convention was understandably reluctant to submit its work to the Congress for approval.

Instead, the delegates decided to pursue what amounted to a revolutionary course. They declared that ratification of the new Constitution by nine states would be sufficient to establish the new government. In other words, the
(10) Constitution was being submitted directly to the people. Not even the Congress, which had called the convention, would be asked to approve its work.

The leaders of the convention shrewdly wished to bypass the state legislatures, which were attached to states' rights and which required in most cases the agreement of two houses. For speedy ratification of the Constitution,
(15) the single-chambered, specially elected state ratifying conventions offered the greatest promise of agreement.

Battle lines were quickly drawn. The Federalists, as the supporters of the Constitution were called, had one solid advantage: they came with a concrete proposal. Their opponents, the Antifederalists, came with none. Since the
(20) Antifederalists were opposing something with nothing, their objections, though sincere, were basically negative. They stood for a policy of drift while the Federalists were providing clear leadership.

Furthermore, although the Antifederalists claimed to be the democratic group, their opposition to the Constitution did not necessarily spring from a
(25) more democratic view of government. Many of the Antifederalists were as distrustful of the common people as their opponents. In New York, for example, Governor George Clinton criticized the people for their fickleness and their tendency to "vibrate from one extreme to another." Elbridge Gerry, who refused to sign the Constitution, asserted that "the evils we experience flow from the
(30) excess of democracy," and John F. Mercer of Maryland professed little faith in his neighbors as voters when he said that "the people cannot know and judge the character of candidates."

1. The best title for the passage would be

   (A) "The U.S. Constitution: Its Strengths and Weaknesses."
   (B) "The Battle for Ratification of the Constitution."
   (C) "Divided Leadership at the Constitutional Convention."
   (D) "The Views of the Antifederalists on Democracy."
   (E) "How the Constitution Became Law."

2. According to the passage, the delegates to the Constitutional Convention did not submit their work to Congress for approval because

(A) they believed that Congress would not accept the sweeping changes they had proposed.

(B) they knew that most members of Congress gave little weight to the concept of states' rights.

(C) it was unclear whether Congress had the legal right to offer or withhold such approval.

(D) they considered it more democratic to appeal directly to the citizens of the separate states.

(E) Congress was dominated by a powerful group of Antifederalist leaders.

3. In stating that the Antifederalists "were opposing something with nothing" (line 20), the author suggests that the Antifederalists

(A) based most of their arguments on their antidemocratic sentiments.

(B) lacked leaders who were as articulate as the Federalist leaders.

(C) were unable to rally significant support for their position among the populace.

(D) had few reasonable arguments to put forth in support of their position.

(E) offered no alternative plan of government of their own.

4. The words of John F. Mercer are quoted in lines 31–32 primarily to illustrate

(A) the antidemocratic sentiments of some Antifederalist spokesmen.

(B) the concern for states' rights shared by most leaders from the smaller states.

(C) some of the weaknesses of the plan of government proposed by the Federalists.

(D) the "policy of drift" advocated by the Antifederalists.

(E) the kinds of arguments to which the Federalists were forced to reply.

5. The author implies that, by comparison with the position of the Antifederalists, the position of the Federalists was which of the following?

I. More decisive
II. More democratic
III. More sincere

(A) I only
(B) I and II only
(C) I and III only
(D) II and III only
(E) I, II, and III

Line   Although Alfred Wegener was not the first scientist to propose the idea that the
continents have moved, his 1912 outline of the hypothesis was the first detailed
description of the concept and the first to offer a respectable mass of supporting
evidence for it. It is appropriate, then, that the theory of continental drift was
(5)   most widely known as "Wegener's hypothesis" during the more than fifty years
of debate that preceded its ultimate acceptance by most earth scientists.

In brief, Wegener's hypothesis stated that, in the late Paleozoic era, all of
the present-day continents were part of a single giant land mass, Pangaea, that
occupied almost half of the earth's surface. About 40 million years ago, Pangaea
(10)   began to break into fragments that slowly moved apart, ultimately forming the
various continents we know today.

Wegener supported his argument with data drawn from geology,
paleontology, zoology, climatology, and other fields. So impressive was his array
of evidence that his hypothesis could not be ignored. However, until then 1960s,
(15)   most scientists were reluctant to accept Wegener's ideas. There are several
reasons why this was so.

First, although Wegener showed that continental movement was consistent with much of the geological and other evidence—for example, the apparent
family relationships among forms of plants and animals now separated by vast
(20)   expanses of ocean, once geographically united on the hypothetical Pangaea—he
failed to suggest any causal mechanism for continental drift sufficiently powerful
and plausible to be convincing.

Second, while the period during which Wegener's theory was propounded
and debated saw rapid developments in many branches of geology and an
(25)   explosion of new knowledge about the nature of the earth and the forces at work
in its formation, little of this evidence seemed to support Wegener. For example,
data drawn from the new science of seismology, including experimental studies
of the behavior of rocks under high pressure, suggested that the earth has far
too much internal strength and rigidity to allow continents to "drift" across its
(30)   surface. Measurements of the earth's gravitational field made by some of the
early scientific satellites offered further evidence in support of this view as late
as the early 1960s.

Third, and perhaps most significant, Wegener's theory seemed to
challenge one of the most deeply-held philosophical bases of geology—the
(35)   doctrine of uniformitarianism, which states that earth history must always be
explained by the operation of essentially unchanging, continuous forces. Belief
in the intervention of unexplained, sporadic, and massive shaping events—
known as catastrophism—was considered beyond the pale by mainstream
geologists.
(40)   Wegener was not, strictly speaking, a catastrophist—he did not suggest
that some massive cataclysm had triggered the breakup of Pangaea—but his
theory did imply a dramatic change in the face of the earth occurring relatively
late in geologic history. Such a belief, viewed as tainted with catastrophism, was
abhorrent to most geologists throughout the first half of this century.

6. According to the passage, Wegener believed that Pangaea

   (A) was destroyed in a massive cataclysm occurring about 40 million years ago.
   (B) consisted of several large land areas separated by vast expanses of ocean.
   (C) was ultimately submerged by rising oceans at the end of the Paleozoic era.
   (D) has gradually drifted from its original location into its current position.
   (E) contained in a single land mass the basic material of all the continents that exist today.

7. It can be inferred from the passage that, by the end of the Paleozoic era,

   (A) early human beings existed on earth.
   (B) many forms of plant and animal life existed on earth.
   (C) the land mass of Pangaea no longer existed.
   (D) a series of unexplained catastrophes had changed the face of the earth.
   (E) most of today's land forms had taken their current shape.

8. The passage provides information to answer which of the following questions?

   I.   What geological forces caused the breakup of Pangaea?
   II. What evidence discovered in the 1960s lent support to Wegener's hypothesis?
   III. When did Wegener's hypothesis win acceptance by most earth scientists?

   (A) I only
   (B) II only
   (C) III only
   (D) I and III only
   (E) II and III only

9. The passage implies that the most significant reason for the opposition to Wegener's hypothesis on the part of many scientists was its

   (A) indirect challenge to a fundamental premise of geology.
   (B) lack of supporting evidence from fields other than geology.
   (C) impossibility of being tested by experimental means.
   (D) conflict with data drawn from the fossil record.
   (E) failure to provide a comprehensive framework for earth history.

10. The author refers to the scientific information gathered by satellites in order to suggest the
    (A) philosophical changes that ultimately led to the acceptance of Wegener's hypothesis.
    (B) dramatic advances in earth science during the 1960s.
    (C) differing directions taken by various earth scientists in the decades following Wegener.
    (D) nature of the some of the evidence that appeared to refute Wegener.
    (E) need for experimental demonstration before any new geological theory can be accepted.

11. It can be inferred from the passage that the ultimate acceptance of Wegener's hypothesis by most geologists could not have occurred unless
    (A) the catastrophic event that destroyed Pangaea had been conclusively demonstrated.
    (B) Wegener had renounced his efforts to attack the doctrine of uniformitarianism.
    (C) uniformitarianism had been shown to be demonstrably false.
    (D) the general bias against catastrophism had moderated.
    (E) the empirical evidence in its favor had been uniform and overwhelming.

EXERCISE 2

11 Questions

Time—15 Minutes

> **Directions:** Each passage in this group is followed by questions based on its content. After reading a passage, choose the best answer to each question. Answer all questions following a passage on the basis of what is *stated* or *implied* in that passage.

Line With the ascendance of Toni Morrison's literary star, it has become commonplace for critics to deracialize her by saying that Morrison is not just a "black woman writer," that she has moved beyond the limiting confines of race and gender to larger "universal" issues. Yet Morrison, a Nobel laureate with six

(5) highly acclaimed novels, bristles at having to choose between being a writer or a black woman writer, and willingly accepts critical classification as the latter.

To call her simply a writer denies the key roles that Morrison's African-American roots and her black female perspective have played in her work. For instance, many of Morrison's characters treat their dreams as "real,"

(10) are nonplussed by visitations from dead ancestors, and generally experience intimate connections with beings whose existence isn't empirically verifiable. While critics might see Morrison's use of the supernatural as purely a literary device, Morrison herself explains, "That's simply the way the world was for me and the black people I knew."

(15) Just as her work has given voice to this little-remarked facet of African-American culture, it has affirmed the unique vantage point of the black woman. "I really feel the range of emotion and perception I have had access to as a black person and a female person are greater than that of people who are neither," says Morrison. "My world did not shrink because I was a black female

(20) writer. It just got bigger."

1. The author of the passage is chiefly concerned with

    (A) explaining Morrison's own viewpoint on the role of her race and gender in her novels.

    (B) assessing the significance of the black female perspective in the modern American novel.

    (C) acknowledging Morrison's success in giving voice to unknown aspects of the African-American experience.

    (D) presenting a counter-argument to critics who seek to "deracialize" Morrison.

    (E) explaining why being a writer and being a black female writer are distinct critical classifications.

2. Morrison's use of the supernatural in her novels is mentioned by the author in order to explain

(A) why some critics categorize her as a "writer" but not a "black woman writer."

(B) the distinction between drawing from one's personal experience and using a literary device.

(C) the enormous critical acclaim Morrison's novels have received.

(D) one way in which Morrison's novels are rooted in her experience as an African-American woman.

(E) one of the universal themes that is woven throughout Morrison's novels.

3. The author suggests that critics who seek to deny Morrison's racial and gender identity are motivated by a desire to

(A) emphasize the broad human interest of the themes she writes about.

(B) explain the popular and commercial success her work has achieved.

(C) ignore the contributions of African-American writers to modern culture.

(D) downplay the role of the supernatural in her work.

(E) disparage her writing for its parochialism and narrowness.

4. The passage suggests that the author would be most likely to agree with which of the following statements?

(A) The intelligent critic often has a more profound understanding of art than the artist himself.

(B) The true artist transcends her origins by transforming the personal into the universal.

(C) For African Americans, the psychological importance of race will always outweigh that of gender.

(D) The differences among human cultures are trivial by comparison with what they have in common.

(E) The most universal art is often that which is most deeply rooted in a particular culture.

Line In the summer of 1904, the great Russian Empire was, unlike most of the countries of Europe by that time, still under the control of one man, the 36-year-old Tsar Nicholas II, who had ruled since the death of his father, Alexander III, ten years before. By many accounts a kind man with a genuine love
(5) for his country, Nicholas was nevertheless beginning to be pictured as a ruthless dictator by those who wished to see the empire democratized, and the complaints of his people were very much in the Tsar's thoughts that summer. One event, however, took Nicholas' mind away from his political difficulties. On August 12, he wrote in his diary "A great, never-to-be-forgotten day when the
(10) mercy of God has visited us so clearly. Alix gave birth to a son at one o'clock. The child has been called Alexis."

Married to Nicholas since 1894, the former Princess Alix of Hesse-Darmstadt and one of Queen Victoria's numerous grandchildren, the Tsarina (called Alexandra after her marriage), had given birth to four daughters—Olga,
(15) Tatiana, Marie, and Anastasia—between 1897 and 1901. But the laws of succession decreed that only a male could succeed the Tsar, so the birth of Alexis, which assured the continuation of the three-hundred-year-old Romanov dynasty, was a cause of great rejoicing for his parents as well as throughout the vast empire.

(20) But within a few months it became clear that the apparently healthy child was not healthy at all—he had hemophilia, a disease he had inherited through his mother from his great-grandmother, Queen Victoria, many of whose other descendants also had the disease. Hemophilia is a blood disorder in which the blood does not clot properly. A small, external scratch or cut presents no real
(25) problem as the bleeding can be stopped relatively quickly, but bumps and bruises, such as children are prone to, create internal bleeding. This blood, in turn, gathers in knee and elbow joints, causing excruciating pain and, sometimes, permanent injury. Once Alexis' diagnosis was confirmed, however, it was decided that, for the good of the dynasty and the country, the boy's illness
(30) would remain a family secret. That decision may have changed history.

Despite his joy at the birth of an heir, Nicholas' political problems continued. Just a few months later, in January, 1905, government troops fired on a crowd of unarmed petitioners at the Winter Palace in St. Petersburg, killing over one hundred and wounding hundreds more. This in turn set off
(35) countrywide demonstrations against the government. Despite halfhearted efforts on Nicholas' part to satisfy the dissidents, notably the October Manifesto of 1905, which converted Russia into a constitutional monarchy with an elected parliament called the *Duma*, these problems would plague him for another dozen years.

(40) In the meantime, in her anguish over her son's illness, Alexandra turned to religion and to a newcomer to the Russian court for help. Grigory Rasputin, born in Siberia in 1871, was an Eastern Orthodox mystic who had been introduced to the court by one of the Tsar's numerous relatives. Although it was well known that he led a dissolute life, he had mesmerizing eyes that captivated many of the
(45) Tsar's courtiers. More important, he was able—although to this day no one knows how—to calm the young Alexis when he had hurt himself and, apparently, to ease his pain considerably. For the Tsarovich's distraught mother, this was sufficient, and for the rest of their lives Alexandra heeded Rasputin's advice, both personal and, more important, political.

(50) For nearly a decade after Alexis' birth, the political situation in Russia grew worse. Even the great patriotic fervor that greeted the empire's entry into the First World War took a downturn when the nation's early victories gave way to progressively greater defeats and the loss of hundreds of thousands of Russian lives. In an effort to stem the tide, Nicholas decided it was his duty to

(55)   lead the army himself, and in 1915 he left St. Petersburg and took up residence at Army Headquarters, in effect leaving Alexandra to rule the country with Grigory Rasputin at her side.

    The increasingly dire situation at the front resulted in a repudiation of the war by many in Russia, which led to even more demonstrations at home by

(60)   dissidents, most importantly the Bolsheviks, who wanted not a constitutional monarchy but, rather, a fully democratic state answering only to the people. The Tsar and Tsarina came increasingly under personal attack, as did Rasputin. The Russian people, not knowing of the Tsarovich's hemophilia, could not understand why the mystic seemed to have so much power over the imperial

(65)   family, and both he and Alexandra were much reviled in the press. Rasputin had also made important enemies at court. On December 16, 1916, he was assassinated by three courtiers.

    Three months later, on March 15, 1917, the Tsar abdicated his throne, and on November 7th the Bolshevik Revolution brought the communists to power.

(70)   Less than a year later, on July 29, 1918, Nicholas and his family, including Alexis, who would have been the next Tsar, were executed on orders of Bolshevik authorities at Ekaterinburg in the Ural Mountains, ending the three-hundred-year-old Romanov dynasty.

5. The passage implies that those who in 1904 regarded Nicholas II as a "ruthless dictator" (lines 5–6) primarily objected to

    (A)   the excessive influence of Rasputin over court affairs.

    (B)   his refusal to consider establishment of an elected parliament for Russia.

    (C)   the alliance between the Romanovs and the family of Queen Victoria.

    (D)   his maintenance of an autocratic form of government in Russia.

    (E)   the failure of the Tsar and his wife to produce a male heir to the throne.

6. The author implies that the October Manifesto of 1905 failed to placate those who advocated reform of the Russian government because it was

    (A)   never fully carried out as written into law.

    (B)   unaccompanied by religious, economic, and social changes.

    (C)   undermined by the continuing dictatorial behavior of Nicholas.

    (D)   unable to prevent the onset of the First World War.

    (E)   only a partial step toward the establishment of full democracy.

7. The author implies that the decision of Nicholas to assume personal leadership of the Russian army stemmed mainly from his

    (A)   sense of responsibility.

    (B)   political desperation.

    (C)   inability to trust other leaders.

    (D)   growing megalomania.

    (E)   fear of popular revolt.

8. The "downturn" mentioned in line 52 refers most directly to
   - (A) the growing popular concern over the political power of Rasputin.
   - (B) personal attacks on the Tsar and Tsarina in the Russian press.
   - (C) national disaffection with Russia's undemocratic form of government.
   - (D) the Tsar's distraction from civic duties by his son's illness.
   - (E) public dismay over Russian military failures.

9. The author implies that, if the Russian people had known of Rasputin's ability to ease the symptoms of the Tsarovich, they would have
   - (A) demanded that Rasputin relinquish his authority over the imperial family.
   - (B) insisted that the Romanov dynasty abdicate in favor of a more democratic regime.
   - (C) sympathized with the motives of the Tsarina in relying on Rasputin.
   - (D) renewed their support of the Tsar and the war effort he was leading.
   - (E) been won over to the religious and mystical views Rasputin advocated.

10. It can be inferred from the passage that, during World War I, newspapers in Russia were
    - (A) under the strict control of the imperial family and its supporters.
    - (B) generally enthusiastic in their support of the war effort.
    - (C) relatively free to criticize the government and its actions.
    - (D) mainly opposed to the growing pacifism among some elements of Russian society.
    - (E) severely restricted by military censors in order to protect state security.

11. The passage suggests that the murder of Rasputin was motivated primarily by.
    - (A) the growing demand among the Russian populace for true democracy.
    - (B) disagreements over religious doctrine.
    - (C) hostility in the popular press against both Rasputin and the imperial couple.
    - (D) intrigues and jealousies among the Tsar's retinue.
    - (E) increasing disaffection with the war among many Russians.

EXERCISE 3

11 Questions

Time—15 Minutes

> **Directions:** Each passage in this group is followed by questions based on its content. After reading a passage, choose the best answer to each question. Answer all questions following a passage on the basis of what is *stated* or *implied* in that passage.

Line   In the early years of the twentieth century, astrophysicists turned their attention to a special category of stars, known as cepheid variables. A variable star is one whose apparent brightness changes from time to time. Among some variables, the change in brightness occurs so slowly as to be almost imperceptible; among
(5)   others, it occurs in sudden, brief, violent bursts of energy. Cepheid variables (which take their name from the constellation Cepheus, where the first such star was discovered) have special characteristics that make them a useful astronomical tool.

   It was Henrietta Leavitt, an astronomer at the Harvard Observatory, who
(10)   first examined the cepheid variables in detail. She found that these stars vary regularly in apparent brightness over a relatively short period of time—from one to three days to a month or more. This variation in brightness could be recorded and precisely measured with the help of the camera, then still a new tool in astronomy.

(15)   Leavitt also noticed that the periodicity of each cepheid variable—that is, the period of time it took for the star to vary from its brightest point to its dimmest, and back to its brightest again—corresponded to the intrinsic or absolute brightness of the star. That is, the greater the star's absolute brightness, the slower its cycle of variation.

(20)   Why is this so? The variation in brightness is caused by the interaction between the star's gravity and the outward pressure exerted by the flow of light energy from the star. Gravity pulls the outer portions of the star inward, while light pressure pushes them outward. The result is a pulsating, in-and-out movement that produces increasing and decreasing brightness. The stronger
(25)   the light pressure, the slower this pulsation. Therefore, the periodicity of the cepheid variable is a good indication of its absolute brightness.

   Furthermore, it is obvious that the apparent brightness of any source of light decreases the further we are from the light. Physicists had long known that this relationship could be described by a simple mathematical formula, known
(30)   as the inverse square law. If we know the absolute brightness of any object—say, a star—as well as our distance from that object, it is possible to use the inverse square law to determine exactly how bright that object will appear to be.

   This laid the background for Leavitt's most crucial insight. As she had discovered, the absolute brightness of a cepheid variable could be determined
(35)   by measuring its periodicity. And, of course, the apparent brightness of the star when observed from the earth could be determined by simple measurement. Leavitt saw that with these two facts and the help of the inverse square law, it would be possible to determine the distance from earth of any cepheid variable. If we know the absolute brightness of the star and how bright it appears from
(40)   the earth, we can tell how far it must be.

Thus, if a cepheid variable can be found in any galaxy, it is possible to measure the distance of that galaxy from earth. Thanks to Leavitt's discovery, astronomical distances that could not previously be measured became measurable for the first time.

1. The primary purpose of the passage is to explain

    (A) the background and career of the astronomer Henrietta Leavitt.
    (B) how and why various categories of stars vary in brightness.
    (C) the development of the inverse square law for determining an object's brightness.
    (D) important uses of the camera as an astronomical tool.
    (E) how a particular method of measuring astronomical distances was created.

2. According to the passage, the absolute brightness of a Cepheid variable

    (A) depends upon its measurable distance from an observer on earth.
    (B) may be determined from the length of its cycle of variation.
    (C) changes from time to time according to a regular and predictable pattern.
    (D) indicates the strength of the gravitation force exerted by the star.
    (E) is a result of the periodicity of the star.

3. According to the passage, Leavitt's work provided astronomers with the means of determining which of the following?

    I. The absolute brightness of any observable Cepheid variable
    II. The apparent brightness of any object a given distance from an observer
    III. The distance from earth of any galaxy containing an observable Cepheid variable

    (A) I only
    (B) III only
    (C) I and II only
    (D) I and III only
    (E) I, II, and III

4. It can be inferred from the passage that a Cepheid variable of great absolute brightness would exhibit

   (A) a relatively rapid variation in brightness.
   (B) a correspondingly weak gravitational force.
   (C) brief, violent bursts of radiant energy.
   (D) slow and almost imperceptible changes in brightness.
   (E) a strong outward flow of light pressure.

5. The passage implies that Leavitt's work on Cepheid variables would NOT have been possible without the availability of

   (A) the camera as a scientific tool.
   (B) techniques for determining the difference between stars
   (C) a method of measuring a star's gravitational force
   (D) an understanding of the chemical properties of stars
   (E) a single star whose distance from earth was already known.

Line From the opening days of the Civil War, one of the Union's strategies in its efforts to defeat the rebelling southern states was to blockade their ports. Compared to the Union, relatively little was manufactured in the Confederacy—either consumer goods or, more important, war materials—and it was believed that a
(5) blockade could strangle the South into submission. But the Confederacy had 3,500 miles of coastline and, at the start of the war, the Union had only 36 ships to patrol them.

Even so, the Confederate government knew that the Union could and would construct additional warships and that in time all its ports could be
(10) sealed. To counter this, the Confederacy decided to take a radical step—to construct an ironclad vessel that would be impervious to Union gunfire. In doing so, the South was taking a gamble because, though the British and French navies had already launched experimental armor-plated warships, none had yet been tested in battle.

(15) Lacking time as well as true ship-building capabilities, rather than construct an entirely new ship, in July, 1861, the Confederacy began placing armor-plating on the hull of an abandoned U.S. Navy frigate, the steam-powered *U.S.S. Merrimack*. Rechristened the *C.S.S. Virginia*, the ship carried ten guns and an iron ram designed to stave in the wooden hulls of Union warships.

(20) Until then, Union Secretary of the Navy Gideon Welles had considered ironclads too radical an idea, and preferred to concentrate on building standard wooden warships. But when news of the *Virginia* reached Washington, the fear it engendered forced him to rethink his decision. In October, 1861, the Union began construction of its own ironclad—the *U.S.S. Monitor*—which would
(25) revolutionize naval warfare.

Designed by John Ericson, a Swede who had already made substantial contributions to marine engineering, the *Monitor* looked like no other ship afloat. With a wooden hull covered with iron plating, the ship had a flat deck with perpendicular sides that went below the waterline and protected the propeller
(30) and other important machinery. Even more innovative, the ship had a round, revolving turret that carried two large guns. Begun three months after work started on the conversion of the *Virginia*, the *Monitor* was nevertheless launched in January, 1862, two weeks before the Confederacy launched its ironclad.

On March 8th, now completely fitted, the *Virginia* left the port of Norfolk,
(35) Virginia, on what was expected to be a test run. However, steaming into Hampton Roads, Virginia, the Confederate ship found no fewer than five Union

ships at the mouth of the James River—the *St. Lawrence, Congress, Cumberland, Minnesota,* and *Roanoke.* The first three of these were already obsolete sailing ships, but the others were new steam frigates, the pride of the Union navy.

(40)   Attacking the *Cumberland* first, the *Virginia* sent several shells into her side before ramming her hull and sinking her. Turning next to the *Congress,* the southern ironclad sent broadsides into her until fires started by the shots reached her powder magazine and she blew up. At last, after driving the *Minnesota* aground, the *Virginia* steamed off, planning to finish off the other

(45) ships the next day. In just a few hours, she had sunk two ships, disabled a third, and killed 240 Union sailors, including the captain of the *Congress*—more naval casualties than on any other day of the war. Although she had lost two of her crew, her ram, and two of her guns and sustained other damage, none of the nearly 100 shots that hit her had pierced her armor.

(50)   The *Monitor,* however, was already en route from the Brooklyn Navy Yard, and the next morning, March 9th, the two ironclads met each other for the first—and only—time. For nearly four hours the ships pounded at each other, but despite some damage done on both sides, neither ship could penetrate the armor-plating of its enemy. When a shot from the *Virginia* hit the *Monitor*'s pilot

(55) house, wounding her captain and forcing her to withdraw temporarily, the Confederate ship steamed back to Norfolk.

     Although both sides claimed victory, the battle was actually a draw. Its immediate significance was that, by forcing the withdrawal of the *Virginia,* it strengthened the Union blockade, enabling the North to continue its ultimately

(60) successful stranglehold on the South. Even more important, it was a turning point in the history of naval warfare. Although neither ship ever fought again, the brief engagement of the *Monitor* and *Virginia* made every navy in the world obsolete, and, in time, spelled the end of wooden fighting ships forever.

6. According to the passage, the Confederacy wanted an ironclad vessel for all the following reasons EXCEPT

   (A)   an ironclad vessel might be able to withstand Union attacks.
   (B)   it needed open ports in order to receive supplies from overseas.
   (C)   the British and French navies already had ironclads.
   (D)   it knew that the Union would be building more warships.
   (E)   without an ironclad, it would probably be unable to break the Union blockade.

7. The passage implies that the South was vulnerable to a naval blockade because of its

   (A)   limited manufacturing capabilities.
   (B)   relatively short coastline.
   (C)   weak and ineffectual navy.
   (D)   lack of access to natural resources.
   (E)   paucity of skilled naval officers.

8. All of the following were unusual design features of the *Monitor* EXCEPT its

    (A) armor plating.
    (B) perpendicular sides.
    (C) revolving gun turret.
    (D) flat deck.
    (E) wooden hull.

9. It can be inferred from the passage that, by comparison with the design of the *Monitor*, that of the *Virginia* was more

    (A) offensively oriented.
    (B) radical.
    (C) costly.
    (D) versatile.
    (E) traditional.

10. It can be inferred from the passage that the *Virginia* was able to sink or disable the *St. Lawrence, Congress*, and *Cumberland* for which the following reasons?

    (A) It carried more guns.
    (B) Its armor plating was virtually impervious to gunfire.
    (C) Its steam-powered engines made it highly maneuverable.
    (D) Its armor plating made it fireproof.
    (E) It was capable of greater speed than the Union warships.

11. The author suggests that the most important long-term result of the battle between the *Virginia* and the *Monitor* was that it

    (A) enabled the Union to maintain its blockade of southern ports.
    (B) demonstrated that ironclad ships represented the future of naval warfare.
    (C) saved the Union navy from destruction by the *Virginia*.
    (D) demonstrated the superior technological prowess of the North.
    (E) effectively ended the naval career of the captain of the *Monitor*.

EXERCISE 4

11 Questions

Time—15 Minutes

> **Directions:** Each passage in this group is followed by questions based on its content. After reading a passage, choose the best answer to each question. Answer all questions following a passage on the basis of what is *stated* or *implied* in that passage.

(This passage is from an article published in 1976.)

Line
The idea of building "New Towns" to absorb growth is frequently considered a cure-all for urban problems. It is erroneously assumed that if new residents can be diverted from existing centers, the present urban situation at least will get no worse. It is further and equally erroneously assumed that since European New
(5) Towns have been financially and socially successful, we can expect the same sorts of results in the United States.

Present planning, thinking, and legislation will not produce the kind of New Towns that have been successful abroad. It will multiply suburbs or encourage developments in areas where land is cheap and construction profitable rather
(10) than where New Towns are genuinely needed.

Such ill-considered projects not only will fail to relieve pressures on existing cities but will, in fact, tend to weaken those cities further by drawing away high-income citizens and increasing the concentration of low-income groups that are unable to provide tax revenues. The remaining taxpayers,
(15) accordingly, will face increasing burdens, and industry and commerce will seek escape. Unfortunately, this mechanism is already at work in some metropolitan areas.

The promoters of New Towns so far in the United States have been developers, builders, and financial institutions. The main interest of these
(20) promoters is economic gain. Furthermore, federal regulations designed to promote the New Town idea do not consider social needs as the European New Town plans do. In fact, our regulations specify virtually all the ingredients of the typical suburban community, with a bit of political rhetoric thrown in.

A workable American New Town formula should be established as firmly
(25) here as the national formula was in Britain. All possible social and governmental innovations as well as financial factors should be thoroughly considered and accommodated in this policy. Its objectives should be clearly stated, and both incentives and penalties should be provided to ensure that the objectives are pursued. If such a policy is developed, then the New Town approach can play an
(30) important role in alleviating America's urban problems.

1. The passage implies that New Town projects are often considered a possible solution to the problem of

   (A) poverty in the central cities.
   (B) excessive suburban population.
   (C) urban crime.
   (D) declining property values.
   (E) uncontrolled urban growth.

2. It can be inferred from the passage that the author regards past and present New Town projects in the United States as

   (A) largely successful.
   (B) socially innovative.
   (C) hampered by government regulation.
   (D) financially sound.
   (E) poorly planned.

3. According to the passage, as compared with American New Towns, European New Towns have been designed with greater concern for

   (A) social needs.
   (B) typical suburban lifestyles.
   (C) the profits of developers and builders.
   (D) the needs of high-income residents.
   (E) financial conditions.

4. It can be inferred from the passage that the author considers present American New Town regulations to be

   (A) overly restrictive.
   (B) insufficiently innovative.
   (C) politically expedient.
   (D) unrealistically idealistic.
   (E) highly promising.

5. The author cites the British experience with the construction of New Towns as an example of

   (A) the difficulties New Town projects face in a socially traditional environment.
   (B) a New Town policy wisely tailored to national needs.
   (C) the economic weaknesses that have generally plagued New Town projects.
   (D) a political system in which New Town projects are likely to achieve success.
   (E) the use of both penalties and incentives in controlling New Town development.

Line   For years, the contents of a child's sandbox have confounded some of the
nation's top physicists. Sand and other granular materials, such as powders,
seeds, nuts, soil, and detergent, behave in ways that seem to undermine natural
laws and cost industries ranging from pharmaceuticals to agribusiness and
(5)   mining billions of dollars.

Just shaking a can of mixed nuts can show you how problematic granular
material can be. The nuts don't "mix"; they "unmix" and sort themselves out,
with the larger Brazil nuts on top and the smaller peanuts on the bottom. In this
activity and others, granular matter's behavior apparently goes counter to the
(10)   second law of thermodynamics, which states that entropy, or disorder, tends to
increase in any natural system.

Mimicking the mixed-nut conundrum with a jar containing many small
beads and one large bead, one group of physicists claimed that vibrations
causing the beads to percolate open up small gaps rather than larger ones.
(15)   Thus, when a Brazil nut becomes slightly airborne, the peanuts rush in
underneath and gradually nudge it to the top. Another group of physicists
color-coded layers of beads to track their circulation in the container and
achieved a different result. Vibrations, they found, drive the beads in circles up
the center and down the sides of the container. Yet downward currents, similar
(20)   to convection currents in air or water, are too narrow to accommodate the larger
bead, stranding it on top.

One industrial engineer who has studied the problem says that both the
"percolation" and "convection current" theories can be right, depending upon
the material, and that percolation is the major factor with nuts. Given the
(25)   inability of scientists to come up with a single equation explaining unmixing, you
can see why industrial engineers who must manage granular materials go a little,
well, "nuts." Take pharmaceuticals, for instance. There may be six types of
powders with different-sized grains in a single medicine tablet. Mixing them at
some speeds might sort them, while mixing at other speeds will make them
(30)   thoroughly amalgamated. One aspirin company still relies on an experienced
employee wearing a latex glove who pinches some powder in the giant mixing
drum to see if it "feels right."

Granular material at rest can be equally frustrating to physicists and
engineers. Take a tall cylinder of sand. Unlike a liquid, in which pressure exerted
(35)   at the bottom increases in direct proportion to the liquid's height, pressure at
the base of the sand cylinder doesn't increase indefinitely. Instead it reaches a
maximum value and stays there. This quality allows sand to trickle at a nearly
constant rate through the narrow opening separating the two glass bulbs of an
hourglass, thus measuring the passage of time.

(40)   Physicists have also found that forces are not distributed evenly
throughout granular material. It is this characteristic that may account for the
frequent rupturing of silos in which grain is stored. In a silo, for instance, the
column's weight is carried from grain to grain along jagged chains. As a result,
the container's walls carry more of the weight than its base, and the force is
(45)   significantly larger at some points of contact than at others.

Coming up with equations to explain, much less, predict, the distribution
of these force chains is extremely difficult. Again, using beads, physicists
developed a simple theoretical model in which they assume that a given bead
transmits the load it bears unequally and randomly onto the three beads on
(50)   which it rests. While the model agrees well with experimental results, it doesn't
take into account all of the mechanisms of force transmission between grains of
sand or wheat.

In the struggle to understand granular materials, sand-studying physicists
have at least one thing in their favor. Unlike particle physicists who must secure

(55) billions of dollars in government funding for the building of supercolliders in which to accelerate and view infinitesimal particles, they can conduct experiments using low-cost, low-tech materials such as sand, beads, marbles, and seeds. It is hoped that more low-tech experiments and computer simulations will lead to equations that explain the unwieldy stuff and reduce
(60) some of the wastage, guesswork, and accidents that occur in the various industries that handle it.

6. Which of the following titles most accurately describes the above passage?

   (A) "New Theories about the Physical Properties of Sand"

   (B) "The Behavior of Granular Matter in Motion and at Rest"

   (C) "The Percolation Theory versus the Convection Current Theory of Unmixing"

   (D) "Theoretical and Practical Problems in Handling Granular Matter"

   (E) "How Physicists Are Helping to Solve Industrial Problems"

7. The percolation theory of unmixing is best illustrated by which of the following examples?

   (A) Larger rocks rising to the surface in a garden after a period of frost

   (B) Currents of small beads blocking the upward movement of large beads in a shaken container

   (C) Contents settling in a bag of potato chips so that the package appears less full after handling

   (D) Large nuts blocking the upward movement of small nuts in a shaken container

   (E) A can of multi-sized beads sorting into layers of large and small beads upon shaking

8. In saying that the percolation and convection current theories may both be right (line 23), the industrial engineer means that

   (A) neither theory is supported by an adequate mathematical basis.

   (B) both theories are still unproven, since they have not been tested on a variety of material.

   (C) though the theories have different names, they describe the same physical mechanisms.

   (D) the mechanism causing unmixing varies depending upon the type of granular material.

   (E) both mechanisms are involved in all instances of unmixing.

9. Which of the following appears to be the best solution for combatting the "unmixing" problem faced by pharmaceutical manufacturers that must prepare large quantities of powders?

   (A) To craft powders so that all the grains have similar sizes and shapes
   (B) To craft powders in which every grain weighs the same amount
   (C) To mix all the powders together at the same speed
   (D) To hire only engineers who have years of experience in powder mixing
   (E) To analyze and control the pattern of force chains in a vat of powder

10. The passage implies that, if the top bulb of an hourglass were filled with water instead of sand, the pressure pushing the water through the opening would

    (A) increase as water trickles through the opening.
    (B) decrease as water trickles through the opening.
    (C) remain constant as water trickles through the opening.
    (D) be directed at the walls of the container rather than the base.
    (E) make the water trickle down in drops rather than a stream.

11. In lines 53–58, the author implies that physicists studying granular material

    (A) are grappling with issues that are less complicated than those confronting particle physicists.
    (B) are fortunate in having available a selection of relatively easy means of crafting experiments.
    (C) are less likely to receive government funding than are particle physicists.
    (D) are likely to develop a complete predictive model for the behavior of granular material in the near future.
    (E) know less about grains of sand than particle physicists know about infinitesimal forms of matter.

EXERCISE 5

11 Questions

Time—15 Minutes

> **Directions:** Each passage in this group is followed by questions based on its content. After reading a passage, choose the best answer to each question. Answer all questions following a passage on the basis of what is *stated* or *implied* in that passage.

Line   Urodeles, a class of vertebrates that includes newts and salamanders, have the enviable ability to regenerate arms, legs, tails, heart muscle, jaws, spinal cords, and other organs. Planaria, simple worms, can be sliced and diced in hundreds of pieces, with each piece giving rise to a completely new animal. However, while

(5)   both urodeles and planaria have the capacity to regenerate, they use different means of accomplishing this feat.

In effect, urodeles turn back the biological clock. First the animal heals the wound at the site of the missing limb. Then various specialized cells at the site, such as bone, skin, and blood cells, lose their identity and revert to cells as

(10)   unspecialized as those in the embryonic limb bud. This process is called dedifferentiation, and the resulting blastema, a mass of unspecialized cells, proliferates rapidly to form a limb bud. Ultimately, when the new limb takes shape, the cells take on the specialized roles they had previously cast off.

In contrast, planaria regenerate using cells called neoblasts. Scattered

(15)   within the planarian body, these neoblasts remain in an unspecialized, stem-cell state, which enables them at need to differentiate into any cell type. Whenever planaria are cut, the neoblasts migrate to the site and form a blastema by themselves. It is interesting to note that this mechanism is similar to that following reproductive fission in these animals, and that species incapable of this

(20)   form of asexual reproduction have poorly developed regenerative capacities.

1. The primary purpose of the passage is to

   (A) describe the roles of blastema in regenerating urodeles and planaria.

   (B) describe how urodeles use the process of dedifferentiation to regenerate.

   (C) contrast the mechanisms by which urodeles and planaria accomplish regeneration.

   (D) show how methods of cellular regeneration have evolved in different animal species.

   (E) explain the link between reproductive fission and regeneration in simple worms.

2. All of the following are true of dedifferentiation in regenerating urodeles EXCEPT

   (A) the cells recover their specialized roles after the limb bud takes shape.

   (B) it involves a regression by cells to an earlier stage of development.

   (C) specialized cells migrate to the site of the blastema and proliferate rapidly.

   (D) the healing of the wound at the site of the injury is the first step of the process.

   (E) dedifferentiation is characterized by a loss, and then recovery, of cellular identity.

3. The author says that urodeles "turn back the biological clock" (line 6) because they can

   (A) revert the cells in a severed part to a nearly embryonic state.

   (B) regrow body parts from existing cells.

   (C) produce a new limb bud from formerly differentiated cells.

   (D) create a blastema from unspecified cells.

   (E) develop specified cells from a blastema.

4. In the final sentence of the passage, the author implies that

   (A) those planaria that reproduce by splitting themselves in two are more likely to regenerate using the same mechanism.

   (B) planaria that reproduce sexually use the process of dedifferentiation to regenerate entirely new animals.

   (C) asexual reproduction is related to regeneration in planaria, but not in urodoles.

   (D) the genetic makeup of planaria created through regeneration would be the same as in those created through reproductive fission.

   (E) reproductive fission and regeneration in certain planaria differ solely in the quantity of new planaria produced.

Line   As the climate in the Middle East changed beginning around 7000 B.C.E.,
        conditions emerged that were conducive to a more complex and advanced form
        of civilization in both Egypt and Mesopotamia. The process began when the
        swampy valleys of the Nile in Egypt and of the Tigris and Euphrates Rivers in
(5)   Mesopotamia became drier, producing riverine lands that were both habitable
        and fertile, and attracting settlers armed with the newly developed techniques
        of agriculture. This migration was further encouraged by the gradual
        transformation of the once-hospitable grasslands of these regions into deserts.
        Human population became increasingly concentrated into pockets of settlement
(10)   scattered along the banks of the great rivers.
            These rivers profoundly shaped the way of life along their banks. In
        Mesopotamia, the management of water in conditions of unpredictable drought,
        flood, and storm became the central economic and social challenge. Villagers
        began early to build simple earthworks, dikes, canals, and ditches to control the
(15)   waters and reduce the opposing dangers of drought during the dry season
        (usually the spring) and flooding at harvest time.
            Such efforts required a degree of cooperation among large numbers of
        people that had not previously existed. The individual village, containing only a
        dozen or so houses and families, was economically vulnerable; but when several
(20)   villages, probably under the direction of a council of elders, learned to share
        their human resources in the building of a coordinated network of water-control
        systems, the safety, stability, and prosperity of all improved. In this new
        cooperation, the seeds of the great Mesopotamian civilizations were being sown.
            Technological and mathematical invention, too, were stimulated by life
(25)   along the rivers. Such devices as the noria (a primitive waterwheel) and the
        Archimedean screw (a device for raising water from the low riverbanks to the
        high ground where it was needed), two forerunners of many more varied and
        complex machines, were first developed here for use in irrigation systems.
        Similarly, the earliest methods of measurement and computation and the first
(30)   developments in geometry were stimulated by the need to keep track of land
        holdings and boundaries in fields that were periodically inundated.
            The rivers served as high roads of the earliest commerce. Traders used
        boats made of bundles of rushes to transport grains, fruits, nuts, fibers, and
        textiles from one village to another, transforming the rivers into the central
(35)   spines of nascent commercial kingdoms. Trade expanded surprisingly widely;
        we have evidence suggesting that, even before the establishment of the first
        Egyptian dynasty, goods were being exchanged between villagers in Egypt and
        others as far away as Iran.
            Similar developments were occurring at much the same time along the
(40)   great river valleys in other parts of the world—for example, along the Indus in
        India and the Hwang Ho in China. The history of early civilization has been
        shaped to a remarkable degree by the relationship of humans and rivers.

5. The primary purpose of the passage is to explain

   (A) how primitive technologies were first developed in the ancient Middle East.
   (B) how climatic changes led to the founding of the earliest recorded cities.
   (C) the influence of river life on the growth of early civilizations.
   (D) some of the recent findings of researchers into early human history.
   (E) the similarities and differences among several ancient societies.

6. According to the passage, the increasing aridity of formerly fertile grasslands in Egypt and Mesopotamia caused settlement patterns in those regions to become

   (A) less stable.
   (B) more sparse.
   (C) more concentrated.
   (D) less nomadic.
   (E) more volatile.

7. According to the passage, the unpredictability of water supplies in Mesopotamia had which of the following social effects?

   I.   It led to warfare over water rights among rival villages.
   II. It encouraged cooperation in the creation of water-management systems.
   III. It drove farmers to settle in fertile grasslands far from the uncontrollable rivers.

   (A) I only
   (B) II only
   (C) III only
   (D) II and III only
   (E) Neither I, II, nor III

8. The passage implies that the earliest geometry was patronized primarily by

   (A) Mesopotamian monarchs.
   (B) mechanical artisans.
   (C) traders and merchants.
   (D) farm laborers.
   (E) landowners.

9. According to the passage, the earliest trade routes in the ancient Middle East

(A) were those between various centrally ruled commercial kingdoms.
(B) were those that linked villages in Egypt with others in Iran.
(C) were created to ease the transfer of technological and mathematical knowledge among villages.
(D) served to link the inhabitants of small villages with the dynastic kings who ruled them.
(E) connected villages that were scattered along the banks of the same river.

10. It can be inferred from the passage that the emergence of complex civilizations in the Middle East was dependent upon the previous development of

(A) basic techniques of agriculture.
(B) symbolic systems for writing and mathematical computation.
(C) tools for constructing houses quickly and easily.
(D) a system of centralized government.
(E) a method of storing and transferring wealth.

11. The author refers to emerging civilizations in India and China primarily to emphasize the

(A) importance of water transportation in the growth of early trade.
(B) relatively advanced position enjoyed by the Middle East in comparison to other regions.
(C) rapidity with which social systems developed in the Middle East spread to other places.
(D) crucial role played by rivers in the development of human cultures around the world.
(E) significant differences in social systems among various groups of early humans.

Answer Key

Exercise 1	Exercise 2	Exercise 3	Exercise 4	Exercise 5
1. B	1. A	1. E	1. E	1. C
2. A	2. D	2. B	2. E	2. C
3. E	3. A	3. D	3. A	3. C
4. A	4. E	4. E	4. B	4. A
5. A	5. D	5. A	5. B	5. C
6. E	6. E	6. C	6. D	6. C
7. B	7. A	7. A	7. D	7. B
8. C	8. E	8. E	8. D	8. E
9. A	9. C	9. E	9. A	9. E
10. D	10. C	10. B	10. B	10. A
11. D	11. D	11. B	11. B	11. D

Explanatory Answers

EXERCISE 1

1. **The correct answer is (B).** The passage focuses specifically on some of the key issues that arose during the early stages of the battle for ratification of the Constitution. All of the other answer choices are either off the point, choices (A), (C), and (E), or are too narrow, choice (D).

2. **The correct answer is (A).** See the first paragraph. Having exceeded the mandate given to them by Congress, the delegates to the convention naturally feared that Congress would not approve of the sweeping changes they were proposing.

3. **The correct answer is (E).** The fourth paragraph explains that the Federalists had the advantage of "a concrete proposal," i.e. the Constitution itself. The Antifederalists had no such specific plan to offer in its place.

4. **The correct answer is (A).** The Mercer quotation is one of several offered in the last paragraph to illustrate the general point that "Many of the Antifederalists were distrustful of the common people as their opponents."

5. **The correct answer is (A).** The author says that both the Federalists and the Antifederalists had doubts about the virtues of democracy; and he credits the Antifederalists with being just as "sincere" as the Federalists (see the fourth paragraph). However, the Federalists were more "decisive," since they offered a program, while the Antifederalists offered only "a policy of drift."

6. **The correct answer is (E).** The first sentence of the second paragraph makes this point clearly.

7. **The correct answer is (B).** In the fourth paragraph, the passage explains that Wegener used the existence of similar plants and animals on widely separated continents as evidence that all the Earth's land masses were formerly connected in the supercontinent of Pangaea. For this evidence to be valid, it would have to mean that many plants and animals existed prior to the breakup of Pangaea, which paragraph two tells us began late in the Paleozoic era.

8. **The correct answer is (C).** The first paragraph tells us that Wegener's hypothesis was accepted some fifty years after it was first proposed in 1912—in the early 1960s. This answers question III. Question I is not answered; the passage only says that Wegener himself had no answer for this question (end of paragraph four). Question II is not answered; in fact, paragraph five refers to evidence from the 1960s that seemed to undermine, rather than support, Wegener's hypothesis.

9. **The correct answer is (A).** See the first sentence of the sixth paragraph. The "perhaps most significant" reason for many scientists' discomfort with Wegener's hypothesis was that it seemed to challenge their deep-seated belief in uniformitarianism.

10. **The correct answer is (D).** You'll find this stated in the last sentence of the fifth paragraph.

11. **The correct answer is (D).** Clearly, the discomfort felt by most geologists at the notion of accepting an idea "tainted with catastrophism" must have become less strong by the 1960s; otherwise, Wegener's hypothesis could never have been ultimately accepted. However, choices (A) and (C) are too strong; it's not necessary for uniformitarianism to have been utterly abandoned, merely that one exception to the principle should be considered plausible. Choice (E) is wrong because, as paragraph 5 explains, some of the new evidence in the 1960s seemed to undermine Wegener's theory, not support it.

EXERCISE 2

1. **The correct answer is (A).** Notice that the first paragraph says that Morrison "bristles" at how her work is sometimes described and that the second and third paragraphs quote her own comments. Clearly, the passage is mainly concerned with presenting Morrison's own viewpoint about her writing.

2. **The correct answer is (D).** See the first sentence of the second paragraph, which makes clear the underlying point being made by the author in citing the use of the supernatural in Morrison's writing.

3. **The correct answer is (A).** The first sentence of the entire passage suggests this answer. The author seems to be saying that those who want to "deracialize" Morrison are trying to pay her the compliment of calling her work "universal"—though the author of the passage considers this a mistake.

4. **The correct answer is (E).** In the first paragraph, the author suggests that a writer should not "have to choose" between universal and particular identities. The implication is that a great writer can be both rooted in a particular culture and universal in her appeal.

5. **The correct answer is (D).** The first paragraph attributes the opposition to "those who wished to see the empire democratized," and it has already explained that Russia was, at this time, one of the few countries in Europe still ruled by a single individual—in other words, "an autocratic form of government."

6. **The correct answer is (E).** The fourth paragraph describes the October Manifesto as one of Nicholas's "halfhearted efforts . . . to satisfy the dissidents." There's no implication that the Manifesto was "never fully carried out" (choice A), only that it was an inadequate step toward full democracy.

7. **The correct answer is (A).** See paragraph six: "Nicholas decided it was his duty to lead the army himself."

8. **The correct answer is (E).** The sentence that mentions the "downturn" attributes it specifically to "progressively greater defeats" in the war.

9. **The correct answer is (C).** The latter portion of the seventh paragraph makes this clear. It says that Rasputin and Alexandra "were much reviled in the press" because the Russian people did not understand the health concerns that had driven the Tsarina to rely on Rasputin.

10. **The correct answer is (C).** Since we're told that the press harshly criticized the royal family, it's clear that a large measure of freedom—at least in this regard—was enjoyed by the Russian press.

11. **The correct answer is (D).** We're told in the last two sentences of the seventh paragraph that Rasputin's murder came about because he "had also made important enemies at court."

EXERCISE 3

1. **The correct answer is (E).** The last paragraph of the passage neatly summarizes the significance of Leavitt's work with cepheid variables.

2. **The correct answer is (B).** The third paragraph describes the important relationship Leavitt discovered: that the cepheid variable's periodicity (its cycle of variation) and its absolute brightness vary together. Thus, each one can be determined from the other.

3. **The correct answer is (D).** As the last sentence of paragraph four makes clear, statement I is true; from its periodicity (which is easily observable), we can determine the absolute brightness of a cepheid variable. Statement III is supported by the last paragraph of the passage. Statement II is false because the passage doesn't suggest that Leavitt developed the method by which astronomers measured stars' apparent brightness; in fact, in paragraphs two and six, Leavitt appears to take this method for granted and build upon it.

4. **The correct answer is (E).** Paragraph four explains that a star with a great absolute brightness is also a star with relatively stronger light pressure; hence, the slower in-and-out pulsation and the longer periodicity that Leavitt observed.

5. **The correct answer is (A).** See the last sentence of the second paragraph. It seems clear that the camera was a necessary tool for Leavitt's work to be possible.

6. **The correct answer is (C).** Although it's true that the British and French already had ironclad ships, the passage doesn't imply that this was a motivation for the Southern leaders; after all, neither the British nor the French were enemies of the South (as you can tell from the passage, even if your knowledge of Civil War history is a little shaky).

7. **The correct answer is (A).** This point is made in the second sentence of the passage.

8. **The correct answer is (E).** The last sentence of the third paragraph makes it obvious that wooden hulls were the rule, not the exception, among ships of the period.

9. **The correct answer is (E).** The *Virginia* was created simply by armor-plating a traditional wooden boat, whereas the *Monitor* had an entirely new design that "looked like no other ship afloat."

10. **The correct answer is (B).** See the last sentence of the seventh paragraph: "none of the nearly 100 shots that hit her had pierced her armor."

11. **The correct answer is (B).** Choice (B) restates the idea found in the last sentence of the passage.

EXERCISE 4

1. **The correct answer is (E).** The first two sentences of the passage imply that New Towns are viewed as a way of "diverting" population from existing cities and thereby preventing the problems of those cities from getting worse. Thus, uncontrolled growth appears to be the problem that New Towns are supposed to relieve.

2. **The correct answer is (E).** See the first sentence of the second paragraph, which summarizes the author's skepticism about American New Towns.

3. **The correct answer is (A).** The last paragraph-and-a-half of the passage is devoted to praising European-style New Towns in contrast to American-style New Towns because they "consider social needs."

4. **The correct answer is (B).** The author criticizes U.S. regulations governing New Towns because they "specify virtually all the ingredients of the typical suburban community" (paragraph four). In other words, they contain no new ideas and instead merely replicate the problems of existing towns.

5. **The correct answer is (B).** In the last paragraph, the author holds up the British "formula" for New Towns as the kind of successful model American planners ought to imitate.

6. **The correct answer is (D).** Choices (A) and (C) are too narrow; choices (B) and (E) are too broad. Choice (D) is good because it brings out the *practical* slant of the passage, which focuses on the industrial use of granular matter and the role played by science in facilitating it.

7. **The correct answer is (D).** Review the first two sentences of the third paragraph. The percolation theory deals with how small and large objects interrelate when a mass of granular material is shaken, as in a can of nuts.

8. **The correct answer is (D).** See the first sentence of the fourth paragraph; the engineer says that both theories can be right, "depending on the material."

9. **The correct answer is (A).** As the fourth paragraph makes clear, the problem pharmaceutical firms face in dealing with granular materials is based mainly on the fact that different-sized grains are present in a single product. Clearly, it would help matters if all the grains could be made the same size.

10. **The correct answer is (B).** The fifth paragraph explains that, unlike with sand, the pressure in a liquid "increases in direct proportion to the liquid's height." In other words, the higher (or deeper) the mass of liquid, the greater the pressure at the bottom. Therefore, as the water trickled through (getting shallower, of course), the pressure would decrease.

11. **The correct answer is (B).** Notice the way the granular scientists' "low-cost, low-tech" experiments are contrasted with the complicated and expensive studies that particle physicists must somehow fund.

EXERCISE 5

1. **The correct answer is (C).** The last sentence of the first paragraph sets forth this central theme. The paragraphs that follow give the relevant details.

2. **The correct answer is (C).** As paragraph two explains, the specialized cells "lose their identity and revert" to being unspecialized cells, forming a blastema. *Only after this* do they proliferate; so it's wrong to say that the "specialized cells . . . proliferate rapidly," as choice (C) does.

3. **The correct answer is (C).** Urodeles "turn back the clock" because the specialized cells revert to the embryonic state of a limb bud. Choice (A) is wrong because it is not the cells "in a severed part" that revert but rather the cells near the site where the severed part formerly existed.

4. **The correct answer is (A).** The sentence says that those species of planaria that engage in "reproductive fission" (i.e., splitting) are the ones that are more likely to regenerate themselves in the same way.

5. **The correct answer is (C).** The last sentence of the passage neatly summarizes its main theme.

6. **The correct answer is (C).** The last two sentences of the first paragraph explain that the transformation of the grasslands into deserts made the human population "increasingly concentrated . . . along the banks of the great rivers."

7. **The correct answer is (B).** The third paragraph of the passage describes how the need for water-management systems encouraged cooperation among large groups of Mesopotamian villagers. Statement I is not supported by the passage, and Statement III is contradicted by the last sentence of the first paragraph.

8. **The correct answer is (E).** The last sentence of the fourth paragraph says that geometry was developed in response to "the need to keep track of land holdings and boundaries in fields."

9. **The correct answer is (E).** See the first sentence of the fifth paragraph.

10. **The correct answer is (A).** In the first paragraph, we're told that the development of great civilizations in the Middle East began when the river valleys attracted "settlers armed with the newly developed techniques of agriculture."

11. **The correct answer is (D).** The last paragraph, where India and China are mentioned, is used to make the point that life along river valleys has played a crucial role in the development of civilization in many parts of the world.

Chapter 8

Multiple-Choice Math

Get the Scoop on . . .

- Proven strategies for tackling multiple-choice math problems
- How rounding off and guesstimating can save time and help avoid errors
- How to work backwards to untangle challenging questions
- How to find answers in the diagrams provided by the test-makers
- How to master the numerical data buried in charts and graphs

THE TEST CAPSULE

What's the Big Idea?

Multiple-choice math questions are designed to test your knowledge of the basic math facts and skills most students learn in high school. You'll be given a varied mixture of problem types, including some word problems, problems that involve reading and interpreting graphs and charts, geometry problems with and without diagrams, and a few straightforward arithmetic and algebra problems. For each question, five answer choices are provided; you just have to pick the right one.

How Many?

Of the 28 questions in the quantitative section, your GRE will probably have a total of 14 multiple-choice math problems.

How Much Do They Count?

Because multiple-choice problems are 14 out of 28 total quantitative questions, they count as 50 percent of your overall quantitative score.

How Much Time Should They Take?

Plan to answer multiple-choice math problems at a rate of about 90 seconds per problem. This will leave you ample time to complete the quantitative section, and you should find it a reasonably comfortable pace for working.

What's the Best Strategy?

When in doubt, try something. The problem itself will often suggest a procedure you often used in a high school (or college) math class. If so, use it, even if you can't see how it will lead to the answer you want. Quite often, this sort of "tinkering with the numbers" will quickly lead you toward the solution.

What's the Worst Pitfall?

Don't get bogged down in lengthy or complex calculations. Most GRE math questions are deliberately designed to make complicated calculations unnecessary: the test-makers are more interested in seeing whether you understand the basic structure of the problem than whether you can correctly complete a series of computations. If you find yourself starting a complicated set of calculations, stop—you're probably overlooking a simple shortcut.

THE OFFICIAL DESCRIPTION

What They Are

Multiple-choice math problems are designed to test your skill at "quantitative reasoning," which is your ability to use knowledge of specific math facts, formulas, techniques, and methods to solve problems. Basic information about the procedures of math is needed, but the questions focus more on the underlying concepts than on the procedures themselves.

Where They Are

In the typical computerized GRE, you'll have one quantitative section that is 45 minutes long. It will include 14 multiple-choice math problems, interspersed seemingly at random with 14 quantitative comparisons. Reminder: the test-makers claim the right to change the format at any time! However, the typical format we just described is what you're most likely to encounter.

What They Measure

To score high, it's important to be very comfortable with the basic operations of arithmetic—not only addition, subtraction, multiplication, and division, but also such procedures as working with fractions and decimals, figuring out averages, and the like. You'll also need to be skilled at the basic operations of algebra, including solving equations, using negative numbers and square roots, and factoring. Finally, many of the basic principles of geometry are tested, including such concepts as the properties of triangles, circles, and quadrilaterals and determining the areas and volumes of simple figures.

What They Cover

The math areas tested on the GRE, including the multiple-choice items, are those studied by virtually every high school student: arithmetic, basic algebra, and plane and coordinate geometry. Many advanced and specialized math topics are *not* covered on the GRE, including trigonometry and calculus. See Appendix B, "The Insider's GRE Math Review," for a detailed review of the math concepts most frequently tested on the exam.

The Directions

Numbers: All numbers used are real numbers.

Figures: Position of points, angles, regions, etc., can be assumed to be in the order shown; and angle measures can be assumed to be positive.

Lines shown as straight can be assumed to be straight.

Figures can be assumed to lie in a plane unless otherwise indicated.

Figures that accompany questions are intended to provide information useful in answering the questions. However, unless a note states that a figure is drawn to scale, you should solve these problems NOT by estimating sizes by sight or by measurement, but by using your knowledge of mathematics.

Directions: Each of the following questions has five answer choices. For each of these questions, select the best of the answer choices given.

THE INSIDER'S REPORT

Strategies That Really Work

Focus on What's Actually Being Asked

Read the question carefully and make sure you know the answer being sought.

Most GRE math problems will include a series of interrelated facts. The kinds of facts will vary depending on the kind of question.

In a word problem, these facts might include the speed of a train, the distance between two cities, and the time when the train leaves the station.

In a geometry problem, the facts might include the degree measures of two angles in a triangle, the length of one side of the triangle, and the diameter of a circle in which the triangle is inscribed.

In a graph-reading problem (called *data interpretation* questions by the test-makers), the facts might include an entire series of numbers as depicted in the graph—monthly inches of rainfall in a particular county over a one-year period, for example.

One key to tackling any of these kinds of problems is to make sure you know which fact is being asked about and what form the answer should take. If you read hastily, you might *assume* a particular question when, in fact, the test-makers want to focus on a different one. Rather than asking about when the train will arrive at City B, they might ask when the train will reach the one-third point of the trip. Rather than asking about the area of either the triangle or the circle, they might ask instead about the area of the odd-shaped shaded region that falls between them. And rather than asking about the amount of rainfall in any particular month, they might ask about the *difference* between two of the months—a number that doesn't appear directly on the graph itself.

When in Doubt, Try Something

Occasionally, you'll find yourself staring at a problem without knowing how to begin solving it. If you're at a loss—try something. Often the numbers stated in the problem will suggest a starting point by reminding you of operations and procedures you often used in high school (or college) math class.

If fractions are involved, for example, try simplifying them to the simplest form or multiplying them out to rename them as whole numbers. Or rename them as decimals or percentages if they lend themselves easily to that process (for example, $\frac{1}{10} = 10\%$).

If a geometry diagram appears, work from what you know (such as the degree measures of certain angles) to fill in information that you don't know: the complementary angle alongside the angle that's marked, for example, or the angle on the other side of the transversal that must be equal to the angle you know.

If you're given a problem involving probability or permutations (varying combinations of things), just start listing all the possibilities.

FYI

Don't overlook the little words in the question, which can make a huge difference in what's being asked. "Which of the following may be true?" has a very different meaning from "Which of the following must be true?" And both, of course, are very different from "Which of the following may not be true?" So don't skim!

Quite often, seemingly random experimenting like this will lead you quickly toward the right answer. Why? It's because of the peculiar way in which GRE math problems are designed. The test-makers want to test you on a wide array of math topics in a short period of time. That means they want to ask you lots of questions that you can do quickly—in just one to two minutes each. Therefore, the questions are written so that the numbers themselves are generally "obvious." What's tricky is the underlying connection among the numbers. As soon as you "see" that connection, the math is usually simple.

As a result, GRE math tends to reward students who are willing to "mess around" with the numbers in the problem until an insight into the solution emerges. After that "Aha!" moment happens, the answer is usually close at hand.

Round Off and "Guesstimate" Freely

FYI

When tackling math problems, you have about one to two minutes per question. Don't get too lost in experimenting with the numbers. If no solution emerges after a minute or so, make your best guess and move on. But remember that you might need to adjust your guess strategy depending on where you are in the quantitative section. See Chapter 3 for details.

It's not always necessary to work with exact numbers in solving the math problems in the GRE. Sometimes the fastest and even the most accurate way to an answer is to guesstimate. Here's an example, using a real math problem from a past exam:

A total of 60 advertisements were sold for a school yearbook. If 20 percent of the first 20 sold were in color, 40 percent of the next 30 sold were in color, and 80 percent of the last 10 sold were in color, what percent of the 60 advertisements were in color?

(A) 30%

(B) $33\frac{1}{3}$%

(C) 40%

(D) $46\frac{2}{3}$%

(E) 60%

Obviously, you can solve this problem precisely with a few calculations. If you're adept with percentages, you might be able to work it out in your head rather quickly; if you're not, but you have plenty of time, you can handle it slowly and carefully and come up with the exact answer after a minute or so.

However, if you're short on time and don't have the facility with numbers to figure it quickly in your head, here's a simple way to "see" the answer using approximations only. Look back at the facts in the problem. Of the first 20 ads, 20 percent were in color; of the next 30, 40 percent were in color. Obviously, the overall average for these two groups will be between 20 percent and 40 percent. Now, the size of the two groups isn't the same, so we can't just average 20 percent and 40 percent to come up with the overall average—but we can see that the overall average for the first 50 ads will be fairly *close* to 30 percent, and a little higher (because there are more ads in the 40 percent group than in the 20 percent group).

That just leaves the last 10 ads, of which 80 percent were in color. All you need to realize about this is two things. First, since the percentage for this group is 80 percent, which is higher than 30 percent, it will raise the overall average somewhat. Second, this is a small group—just ten ads—so it won't affect the overall average very much.

So without doing any calculations, we can guesstimate that the correct answer will be a percentage somewhat higher than 30 percent—but not too much higher. This immediately eliminates choices (A) and (E), and it makes choices (B) and (D) look a little low and a little high, respectively. It so happens that the correct answer, if you work it out in detail, is choice (C), 40 percent—pretty much what we figured, based on sheer guesstimating.

Rounding off and guesstimating isn't necessary on most GRE items; in many cases, the numbers used are so few and so simple that you might as well work with them directly. But the chances are that you'll encounter several problems on your exam that will be made easier and quicker by guesstimating.

If Stymied, Plug in an Answer and Work Backward

On some questions, a quick route to the answer will jump out at you within a few seconds. In other cases, experimenting in some obvious way with the numbers will quickly direct you toward a solution. If neither of these works, try grabbing an answer from the five multiple-choice options and plugging it into the question. This will often lead you to the right answer quickly.

Here's an example, based on a question from an actual exam.

> A ball is dropped from 192 inches above level ground, and after the third bounce it rises to a height of 24 inches. If the height to which the ball rises after each bounce is always the same fraction of the height reached on its previous bounce, what is this fraction?
>
> (A) $\dfrac{1}{8}$
>
> (B) $\dfrac{1}{4}$
>
> (C) $\dfrac{1}{3}$
>
> (D) $\dfrac{1}{2}$
>
> (E) $\dfrac{2}{3}$

It helps if you can picture what's happening here. Think of a handball or a tennis ball, repeatedly bouncing, but each time rising less high until at last it settles on the ground, motionless. The problem suggests that, on each bounce, the ball will rise to a height that is some particular fraction of the previous bounce. The question is, what is that fraction—is it $\dfrac{1}{8}$, $\dfrac{1}{4}$, or what?

The fastest way to a solution is to plug in an answer. Try choice (C) and see what happens. If the ball bounces up one third as high as it started, then after the first bounce it will rise up one third as high as 192 inches. If you're fast with numbers, you'll know that this is 64 inches. (A precise number isn't essential; if you can tell it's "around 60," you're close enough.)

After the second bounce, it'll rise one third as high as that, which is $21\dfrac{1}{3}$ inches (or, if you're guesstimating, "around 20"). *Stop!* The problem says that the ball rises to 24 inches after the *third* bounce. Obviously, if the ball rises less than that after *two* bounces, it'll be way too low after three! So choice (C) cannot be the answer.

We can see that the ball must be bouncing higher than one third of the way; so the correct answer must be a larger fraction, meaning either choice (D) or choice (E). If you're pressed for time, choose one and move on (you have a 50 percent chance of being right). If you have time, plug in either and see whether it works. If you do, you'll see that choice (D) is right.

Would it be possible to develop a formula to answer this question? Probably—some physicist has done it, we'd bet. But it would be crazy to try to devise a formula for the exam. Remember the unique advantage of a test like the GRE: *All the correct answers have been provided.* When it's not obvious which one is correct, pick one and try it. Even if the one you pick first is wrong, this method will usually let you hone in on the best choice fairly quickly.

The Best Tips

For Word Problems, Build an Equation That Will Yield the Answer You Want

For some students, word problems pose the toughest math challenge. You know the kind: they deal with planes traveling at certain speeds, pipes filling vats with liquid at a particular rate, workers painting walls at so many square feet per hour, and so on.

Curiously enough, in most word problems, the math itself is not difficult. You might have a couple of fractions to multiply or divide or a simple equation to solve, but the computations will be easy. What's tricky is setting up the math in the first place—in other words, turning the words into numbers and symbols. Here are some pointers that will help:

- Let the unknown quantity equal what you want to solve for. If the question asks "What fraction of the entire job will be completed after three hours?" begin writing your equation with $J =$, where J represents that fraction of the job. Conversely, if the question asks, "How many hours will it take to do $\frac{3}{7}$ of the entire job?" then begin your equation with H, which should equal the hours of work needed. This way, after you've solved the equation, you automatically have your answer, with no further conversions needed.

- Break the problem down into phrases, and translate each into a numerical expression. Word problems can be intimidating because of their length and complexity. Your strategy: divide and conquer. Break the problem down into its component parts, and give each an appropriate number or symbol. Then devise an equation or formula that describes the relationship among these parts, and go ahead with the math.

FYI

When plugging in a number, start with the third answer. The answer choices are normally in size order, so the third answer will be the middle-size choice. If it is wrong, you can usually tell whether the correct answer is probably larger or smaller—so you've already narrowed the possibilities to just two remaining answers.

Here's an example, using one typical kind of word problem—an age problem:

> Paul is eight years older than Sarah. Four years ago, Sarah was half the age Paul is now. How old is Sarah now?

FYI

When creating an equation for a word problem, use obvious letter symbols T *for Ted's age,* H *for hours worked,* P *for price, etc.) rather than "textbook" letters like* x, y, *or* z. *They're easier to remember and less likely to cause you confusion.*

First, notice that what you're looking for is Sarah's age now. So try to set up your equation making S (Sarah's age now) the unknown for which you will solve. The only other letter we'll need is P, which stands for Paul's age now. Now create a couple of simple equations that state in symbols and numbers what the sentences in the problem say.

"Paul is eight years older than Sarah" becomes: $P - 8 = S$.

"Four years ago, Sarah was half the age Paul is now" becomes $S - 4 = \dfrac{P}{2}$.

To get rid of the fraction (usually a good idea), multiply this equation through by 2: $2S - 8 = P$.

Now you can solve for S by substituting the expression $2S - 8$ for P in the first equation:

$$(2S - 8) - 8 = S$$
$$2S - 16 = S$$
$$-16 = -S$$
$$S = 16$$

So Sarah's age today is 16 (Paul is 24).

Check out Table 8.1. It gives you some of the most common translations of words and phrases into mathematical operations. Learn the list—it'll work as a kind of "foreign phrasebook" for turning English into numbers on the exam.

Table 8.1
Words and Phrases With Mathematical Translations

Equals	*is, amounts to, is the same as*
Addition	*and, with, along with, added to, in addition to, increased by, more than, greater than, larger than*
Subtraction	*less than, fewer than, without, take away, difference, decreased by, reduced by, smaller than*
Multiplication	*times, each, per, by, of, product*
Division	*divided by, part of, fraction, piece, portion*

Rename All Quantities as Units That Are Easier to Work With
Don't feel locked into the numbers presented in the problem. If you can see that a different number that you can easily get to will be simpler to work with, go for it by changing the units of measurement.

In particular, when you can, look for opportunities to rename working units as the units in which the answer is wanted. So, for example, if you see that the answers are all stated in terms of square feet, and one of the numbers in the problem is in square yards, rename it as square feet before beginning your work. (One square yard equals nine square feet.)

On Geometry Problems, Search the Diagram for Clues to the Answer
Most geometry problems on the GRE are accompanied by diagrams. They are there for a reason. You can usually leap from what you know—the facts you are given—to what you need to know simply by using the parts of the diagram as "stepping stones." Here's an example:

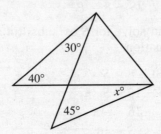

In the figure above, what is the value of *x*?

(A) 65
(B) 45
(C) 40
(D) 30
(E) 25

The diagram gives you three explicit facts: the degree measures of the angles that are marked as 30°, 40°, and 45°. However, a host of implicit facts are also contained there. If you recall some basic facts about geometric figures, they'll fall into your lap one by one. Quickly, as you'll see, they'll lead you to the answer.

First, you should remember that the number of degrees in the three (interior) angles of a triangle will always sum to 180°. This enables us to calculate the size of the third, unmarked angle in the upper-right triangle; it must measure 110°.

FYI

Basic geometry facts and formulas, like the number of degrees in the angles of a triangle and how to calculate the area of a circle, are crucial for success on the GRE. All the relevant data are covered in the Insider's GRE Math Review (Appendix B). You should know these facts backward and forward so they come to mind quickly and easily on the day of the exam.

Next, you should recall that, when two straight lines intersect (cross), the opposite angles formed are equal. (This is easy to remember—the angles in such a figure *look* equal.) Based on this, we can see that the "top" angle in the bottom triangle must also measure 110°, like its twin.

From this fact, we can now figure out the size of the angle in question. Since 110° + 45° = 155°, there are just 25° left for the third angle of the triangle; so the right answer is choice (E).

Solving a geometry problem like this one is easy. Just fill in the blank parts of the diagram using what you can deduce from the information you're given. (You'll need to quickly replicate the diagram on a piece of scrap paper and mark in the new information as you deduce it.) After you get to the fact being asked about, you're home free.

In some geometry questions, studying the diagram can make "math" totally unnecessary:

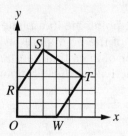

In the figure above, which two sides of polygon *ORSTW* have the same slope?

(A) $\overline{OR}$ and $\overline{OW}$
(B) $\overline{OW}$ and $\overline{ST}$
(C) $\overline{RS}$ and $\overline{ST}$
(D) $\overline{RS}$ and $\overline{WT}$
(E) $\overline{ST}$ and $\overline{WT}$

When you studied coordinate geometry in high school, you learned that the slope of a line is often expressed as a fraction. You also learned a formula for calculating the slope of a line from its endpoints. It's possible you may need to use that formula for one question on the GRE. (If you've forgotten it, don't worry; you can refresh your memory of it in Appendix B.)

However, *the formula is totally unnecessary for this problem—and so are any numbers whatsoever.* You can tell which two sides have the same slope just by looking at the diagram and deciding which two sides of the polygon "go in the same direction." It's easy—the only possibility is choice (D), sides *RS* and *WT*, which are obviously parallel to one another.

As long as you have even a vague idea as to what the word *slope* means, you can scarcely get this question wrong. The diagram does all the work for you.

If No Diagram Is Given, Sketch One

Sometimes, a question without a diagram simply cries out for one. That's what your pencil is for—and that's also why the test-makers will provide you with as much scrap paper as you want. Draw your own diagram and read the answer right off of it.

Here's an example:

> Five distinct points lie in a plane such that 3 of the points are on line *ℓ* and 3 of the points are on a different line, *m*. What is the total number of lines that can be drawn so that each line passes through exactly 2 of these 5 points?
>
> (A) Two
> (B) Four
> (C) Five
> (D) Six
> (E) Ten

Can you picture this in your mind's eye? Me neither. Grab your pencil and start sketching. The only tricky thing to notice is the discussion of the number of points involved. You're told that three points lie on one line and three points lie on another line—and that the total number of points is five. $3 + 3 = 6$, not 5; obviously something funny is going on here. What's the solution?

The answer is that one of the points must lie on *both* lines, as shown in the figure below.

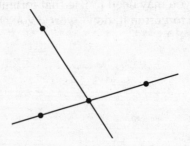

Now, how did we know how to draw these lines—the angle at which they cross, for example—and where to place the other four points? We didn't know; we just took a guess. Notice that the question strongly implies that *it doesn't matter* exactly how these details are drawn—there is one and only one answer, no matter what the sketch looks like.

(If several answers were possible, the question would have to say something like, "Which of the following *is a possible number of lines* . . . ?" or "*What is the the greatest possible number of lines* . . . ?" But it doesn't say that. It just says, "What is the number . . . ?" So you can tell that there's only one possible answer.)

Now that we have our basic drawing, we just have to figure out how many lines can be drawn that pass through two of the five points. Don't agonize over it—just start drawing. In a flash, you'll have your answer. (The lines in question are the *dotted* lines in the figure below.)

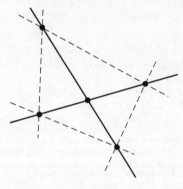

I can't think of any other way to fit in more lines here—can you? So the answer is choice (B), Four. (Don't get confused and pick choice (D), Six. The original two lines don't count—because they pass through three dots each, not two.)

This question is considered fairly hard by GRE standards. But that's true only because many students allow the wording to confuse them and don't think to make a picture. After you do, the answer almost jumps off the screen.

On "Weird Operation" Questions, Just Plug in Numbers
Perhaps the most intimidating GRE math problems of all are what we call "weird operation" problems, in which the test-makers create some new way of manipulating or mangling numbers and ask you to imitate it.

Like many GRE math problems, these are really tests of your reasoning ability, not your number skills. If you calmly and methodically plug in the simple numbers they give you, you'll usually find these problems laughably easy. Here's an example:

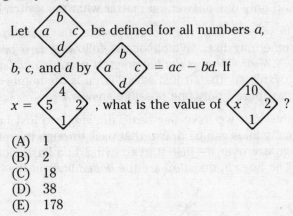

Let $\langle\begin{smallmatrix}&b&\\a&&c\\&d&\end{smallmatrix}\rangle$ be defined for all numbers a, b, c, and d by $\langle\begin{smallmatrix}&b&\\a&&c\\&d&\end{smallmatrix}\rangle = ac - bd$. If

$x = \langle\begin{smallmatrix}&4&\\5&&2\\&1&\end{smallmatrix}\rangle$, what is the value of $\langle\begin{smallmatrix}&10&\\x&&2\\&1&\end{smallmatrix}\rangle$?

(A) 1
(B) 2
(C) 18
(D) 38
(E) 178

This looks weird, all right. Arranging letters or numbers in a diamond and then treating this as a math computation? You never learned *this* back in tenth grade!

Nonetheless, don't get nervous. The test-makers tell you precisely what to do, though in slightly cryptic style. When they "define" the diamond-shaped figure as "$ac - bd$," what they are saying is that, whenever you see four numbers in a diamond like this, you should plug them into the mathematical expression shown in the order given. The question itself then requires you to perform this simple task twice.

First, let's figure out the value of x. If x is the diamond labeled as x, then $a = 5$, $b = 4$, $c = 2$, and $d = 1$. Now we plug those numbers into the simple math computation:

$x = (5 \times 2) - (4 \times 1)$
$x = 10 - 4$
$x = 6$

There, that wasn't so bad, was it? Now the second step. Having figured out the value of x, we can plug it into our second diamond, where $a = 6$ (our old friend x, that is), $b = 10$, $c = 2$, and $d = 1$. Again, plug in the numbers:

$(6 \times 2) - (10 \times 1)$
$12 - 10$
2

So the answer is choice (B), 2. *Notice how ridiculously easy the math itself is.* You could have done these calculations when you were seven years old! The only "trick" is understanding what the test-makers are doing, which is "defining" a new math operation, and then patiently plugging in the numbers.

With a little practice, you'll never get a "weird operation" problem wrong.

On Data Interpretation Problems, Spend 30 Seconds Analyzing the Graph(s) before Tackling the Questions

Your GRE quantitative ability sections will probably include one set of data interpretation questions, which are designed to test your ability to understand and use information presented in a table or graph. Again, the math involved is usually not hard. The key is knowing how to find the relevant information and separating it from the mass of other information in which it is embedded.

Think of these problem sets as resembling reading comprehension questions. Spend 30 seconds "reading" the graph(s) first, noting their structure and basic contents. Then turn to the questions, referring back to the details—the specific data in the graph(s)—as often as necessary.

There are many different types of graphs. Three kinds commonly appear on the GRE: *bar graphs*, *line graphs,* and *circle graphs*.

Bar Graphs

Bar graphs are good for making simple comparisons, such as comparing a single set of statistics (birth rates, for example) for different countries or different years. Here's an example.

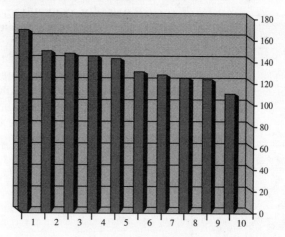

In this graph, each bar represents the annual sales of a different major industrial corporation. This type of graph makes the differences in size from one corporation to another very clear. However, if the data were more complex, this graph would be more difficult to look at and understand. (You wouldn't use a bar graph, for example, to show the sales of the entire *Fortune* 500, for example!) A bar graph also has limitations when it comes to spotting trends.

Line Graphs

Line graphs, by contrast, can be both precise and intricate. Large numbers of data points can be shown in one or more lines on a graph, and trends of increase or decrease can be easily and quickly "read" on a line graph. For these reasons, line graphs are the kind of graph most often used by scientists and statisticians.

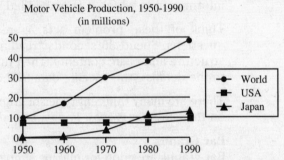

Motor Vehicle Production, 1950-1990
(in millions)

Both bar and line graphs have certain features in common:

All bar and line graphs have two *axes*, the *horizontal* (or *x*) *axis* and the *vertical* (or *y*) *axis*. By convention, the independent variable in an experiment or a statistical study is usually placed on the horizontal axis, and the dependent variable on the vertical axis. For example, if a chemist were studying the effect of temperature on the solubility of a substance, the independent variable would be temperature, and the dependent variable would be solubility. When the experiment was documented later, a graph of the data would have temperature along the horizontal axis and solubility on the vertical axis.

Circle Graphs

Circle graphs are used to show the breakdown of some large quantity into smaller quantities. The larger the relative size of a particular "slice of the pie," the larger the fraction of the overall quantity represented by that sector of the circle. Typical uses of a circle graph would include the division of the budget of a nation, business, or family into portions representing either different sources of income or different types of spending, and the division of a general population into particular categories (by age, religion, or occupation, for example).

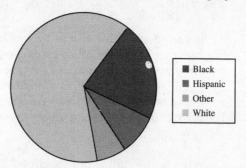

- Black
- Hispanic
- Other
- White

FYI

The structural features of the graph—the labels on the axes, the units of measurement, information in the key—are more important than the data. If you understand the structure of the graph, you'll understand the kind of information it presents and the nature of the questions that the graph is designed to answer. Once you know these things, the details provided by the data—the answers to the questions, in effect—are easy to look up when you need them.

All properly designed graphs are clearly labeled with the names of the variables being studied and the units of measurement (degrees, centimeters, percent, etc.). The divisions along the axes should be clearly numbered. All graphs should also have a title. Many graphs have a *key* providing additional information about the graph or the data. The key is usually found in one corner of the graph, or outside the limits of the graph altogether. A key is most often used when more than one line (or bar, or set of points) is plotted on one graph. Because it would be otherwise impossible for the viewer to know what is meant by the data in such a case, different sets of data are distinguished from each other by using different shadings or patterns for each line, bar, or set of points. The key explains to the viewer what each of the colors or patterns represents. You should always be sure to examine all of these features carefully whenever you encounter a graph on the GRE.

The Most Important Warning

Avoid lengthy calculations and working with big numbers. We've already seen examples of how straightforward the mathematical computations on the GRE generally are. You can count on this. In fact, if you find yourself getting involved in long, complicated, or tricky calculations—especially ones using big numbers—stop working! You've probably overlooked a shortcut or trick that would make the calculations unnecessary.

Here's an example:

> The tip of a blade of an electric fan is 1.5 feet from the axis of rotation. If the fan spins at a full rate of 1,760 revolutions per minute, how many miles will a point at the tip of a blade travel in one hour? (1 mile = 5,280 feet)
>
> (A) 30π
> (B) 40π
> (C) 45π
> (D) 48π
> (E) 60π

If you're doubtful where to begin, glance at the answer choices. The presence of π should remind you that the blades of a fan travel in a circular path (since π gets involved only when circles are involved). The point we are following is going round and round, ticking off 1,760 circles every minute. Thus, the relevant geometric formula is the equation for the circumference of a circle:

$$C = 2\pi r.$$

What is the radius of this circle? The "axis of rotation" is a fancy way of saying "the point the blade spins around"—or, in even simpler words, the middle of the fan. So the 1.5-foot measurement casually mentioned is the same as the radius of the circle. This makes it easy to figure the circumference :

$$C = 2\pi(1.5) = 3\pi.$$

So every time the blade goes around once, a point at its tip travels 3π feet. How many miles will it travel in an hour? Your instinct might be to grab your pencil and start working out the number of feet it will travel in an hour, then divide that by the number of feet in a mile (which the test-makers have kindly provided) . . . but stop! Remember our warning: don't get bogged down with big numbers! Instead, look for a shortcut.

Here's where it's hiding. The curious number 1,760 for the number of revolutions per minute wasn't chosen at random. (Curious numbers never are on the GRE.) It happens to be exactly one third the number of feet in a mile. (Try it out by multiplying. You'll confirm it's true.) Remember, the tip of the blade travels 3π feet for every revolution. Because $3 \times 1,760$ equals the number of feet in a mile, we can see that the blade tip will travel $\pi \times$ one mile every minute.

Now, just multiply this by 60 minutes to get the total distance traveled in an hour:

60π miles.

If you'd worked this out the long way—figuring out, to start with, that the tip traveled 316,800 feet per hour—you could have gotten the right answer. But it would have taken longer. And working with big numbers raises the risk of careless, easy-to-overlook math errors.

The lesson: avoid long calculations, and especially shun working with big numbers. The test-makers usually don't want you to mess with them.

JUST THE FACTS

- On GRE multiple-choice math problems, guesstimate and look for shortcuts; most questions have them.
- Break word problems into simple phrases that you can translate into numbers or symbols.
- Mine geometry diagrams for answer clues—and sketch your own when necessary.
- On "weird operation" problems, just plug in numbers and work out the solutions carefully.
- On data interpretation questions, spend 30 seconds examining the graph(s) before tackling the questions.

PRACTICE, PRACTICE, PRACTICE: MULTIPLE-CHOICE MATH EXERCISES

Instructions

The following exercises will give you a chance to practice the skills and strategies you've just learned for tackling multiple-choice math problems. As with all practice exercises, work under true testing conditions. Complete each exercise in a single sitting. Eliminate distractions (TV, music) and clear away notes and reference materials. Time yourself with a stopwatch or kitchen timer, or have someone else time you.

If you run out of time before answering all the questions, stop and draw a line under the last question you finished. Then go ahead and tackle the remaining questions. When you are done, score yourself based only on the questions you finished in the allotted time.

Understanding Your Scores

0–3 correct: A poor performance. Study this chapter again, as well as the Insider's GRE Math Review (Appendix B).

4–6 correct: A below-average score. Study this chapter again, as well as all portions of the Insider's GRE Math Review (Appendix B) that cover topics you find unfamiliar or difficult.

7–9 correct: An average score. You may want to study this chapter again. Also be sure you are managing your time wisely (as explained in Chapter 3) and avoiding errors due to haste or carelessness.

10–12 correct: An above-average score. Depending on your personal target score and your strength on other quantitative question types, you may or may not want to devote additional time to multiple-choice math problems.

13–15 correct: An excellent score. You are probably ready to perform well on GRE multiple-choice math problems.

EXERCISE 1

15 Questions

Time—15 Minutes

> **Directions:** Each of the following questions has five answer choices. For each of these questions, select the best of the answer choices given.

1. On the number line shown, which point corresponds to the number 2.27?

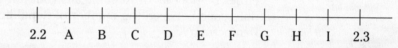

(A) I
(B) H
(C) G
(D) F
(E) Not a labelled point

2. If $m = 121 - 5k$ is divisible by 3, which of the following may be true?

I. m is odd
II. m is even
III. k is divisible by 3

(A) I only
(B) II only
(C) II and III only
(D) I and II only
(E) I, II, and III

3. The cost of 4 rolls, 6 muffins, and 3 loaves of bread is $9.10. The cost of 2 rolls, 3 muffins, and a loaf of bread is $3.90. What is the cost of a loaf of bread?

(A) $1.05
(B) $1.10
(C) $1.20
(D) $1.25
(E) $1.30

4. If $3x + 4y$ is an odd number, which of the following CANNOT be true?

 I. x is odd and y is odd
 II. x is even and y is even
 III. x is even and y is odd

 (A) I only
 (B) I and II only
 (C) II only
 (D) III only
 (E) II and III only

5. The ratio of Democrats to Republicans in a certain state legislature is 5:7. If the legislature has 156 members, all of whom are either Democrats or Republicans (but not both), what is the difference between the number of Republicans and the number of Democrats?

 (A) 14
 (B) 26
 (C) 35
 (D) 37
 (E) 46

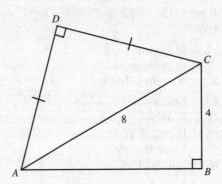

6. The area of the region shown above is

 (A) $16 + 8\sqrt{3}$
 (B) $8 + 8\sqrt{3}$
 (C) $12 + 4\sqrt{3}$
 (D) 16
 (E) $8\sqrt{3}$

7. If $A < 2 - 4B$, which of the following is true?

   (A) $\dfrac{2 - A}{4} > B$

   (B) $\dfrac{2 - A}{4} < B$

   (C) $B > 4A + 2$

   (D) $B < 4A + 2$

   (E) None of the above

8. A box contains five blocks numbered 1, 2, 3, 4, and 5. Johnnie picks a block and replaces it. Lisa then picks a block. What is the probability that the sum of the numbers they picked is even?

   (A) $\dfrac{9}{25}$

   (B) $\dfrac{2}{5}$

   (C) $\dfrac{1}{2}$

   (D) $\dfrac{13}{25}$

   (E) $\dfrac{3}{5}$

9. If a fleet of m buses uses g gallons of gasoline every two days, how many gallons of gasoline will be used by 4 buses every 5 days?

   (A) $\dfrac{10g}{m}$

   (B) $10gm$

   (C) $\dfrac{10m}{g}$

   (D) $\dfrac{20g}{m}$

   (E) $\dfrac{5g}{4m}$

10. If x and y are positive integers and $x + y = 10$, what is the value of $|x - y|$ when $x^2 + y^2$ is as small as possible?

(A) 8
(B) 6
(C) 4
(D) 2
(E) 0

Questions 11–15 refer to the following graphs.

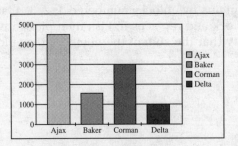 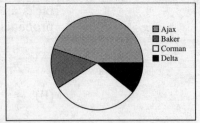

ONE MONTH'S PAYMENTS BY XYZ CORPORATION TO FOUR SUPPLIERS

11. By how much did payments made to Corman exceed the combined payments to Baker and Delta?

(A) $0
(B) $500
(C) $1000
(D) $1500
(E) $2000

12. If the company took half of the business it gives to Ajax and gives it to Delta, which of the following would be true?

 I.   Delta would get the largest payment.
 II. Ajax would get less than Baker.
 III. Ajax and Corman would have a smaller total than Baker and Delta.

(A) I only
(B) I and III only
(C) II and III only
(D) Neither I, II, nor III
(E) I, II, and III

13. How many degrees are there in the angle of the sector of the circle chart representing Corman?

    (A) 36
    (B) 60
    (C) 100
    (D) 108
    (E) 120

14. If XYZ transfers 25% of its business to a new supplier, Excorp, taking equal amounts from Ajax and Corman, what percent of its business will Ajax be left with?

    (A) 40
    (B) 32.5
    (C) 30
    (D) 25
    (E) 12.5

15. If Corman goes out of business and XYZ divides up its payments to Corman among the three suppliers Ajax, Baker, and Delta in the ratio of 3:2:1, how many degrees in the new pie chart will be in the sector representing Baker?

    (A) 25
    (B) 45
    (C) 60
    (D) 75
    (E) 90

EXERCISE 2

15 Questions

Time—15 Minutes

> **Directions:** Each of the following questions has five answer choices. For each of these questions, select the best of the answer choices given.

1. On the number line shown, where is the number that is less than D and half as far from D as D is from G?

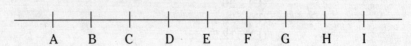

(A) A
(B) B
(C) C
(D) D
(E) Not a labeled point

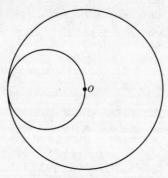

2. In the figure above, the larger circle shown has an area of 36π. What is the circumference of the smaller circle?

(A) 2π
(B) 4π
(C) 6π
(D) 8π
(E) 12π

3. A faucet is dripping at a constant rate. If, at noon on Sunday, 3 ounces of water have dripped from the faucet into a holding tank and, at 5 P.M. on Sunday, a total of 7 ounces have dripped into the tank, how many ounces will have dripped into the tank by 2:00 A.M. on Monday?

   (A) 10

   (B) $\dfrac{51}{5}$

   (C) 12

   (D) $\dfrac{71}{5}$

   (E) $\dfrac{81}{5}$

4. If A and B are positive integers and $24AB$ is a perfect square, then which of the following CANNOT be possible?

   I.   Both A and B are odd.
   II. AB is a perfect square.
   III. Both A and B are divisible by 6.

   (A) I only
   (B) II only
   (C) III only
   (D) I and II only
   (E) I, II, and III

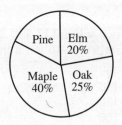

TREES ON MAIN STREET

5. There are 300 trees altogether on Main Street. According to the graph above, how many of the trees are pine trees?

   (A) 45
   (B) 54
   (C) 60
   (D) 70
   (E) 90

6. If $r = -2$, then $r^4 + 2r^3 + 3r^2 + r =$
   (A) -8
   (B) -4
   (C) 0
   (D) 6
   (E) 10

7. $[3(a^2b^3)^2]^3 =$
   (A) $27a^{12}b^{18}$
   (B) $729a^{12}b^{18}$
   (C) $27a^7b^8$
   (D) $3a^8b^{12}$
   (E) $3a^{12}b^{18}$

$$\begin{array}{r} 7x \\ xy \\ \underline{xx} \\ 117 \end{array}$$

8. Shown above is a correct problem in addition, with x and y representing certain digits. What is the value of y?
   (A) 1
   (B) 2
   (C) 3
   (D) 4
   (E) 5

9. How many liters of 50% antifreeze must be mixed with 80 liters of 20% antifreeze to get a mixture that is 40% antifreeze?
   (A) 160
   (B) 140
   (C) 120
   (D) 100
   (E) 80

10. Horace averaged 70 on his first m exams. After taking n more exams, he had an overall average of 75 for the year. In terms of n and m, his average for his last n exams was

(A) $\dfrac{5m + 75}{n}$

(B) $\dfrac{5m}{n} + 75$

(C) $\dfrac{5n}{m} + 75$

(D) $\dfrac{70m + 75n}{m + n}$

(E) 80

Questions 11–15 refer to the following graphs.

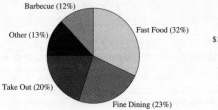

Dinner On Anniversary
Survey of 500 Couples

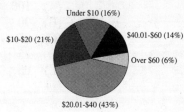

Cost of Anniversary Dinner
Survey of 500 Couples

11. How many of the couples surveyed ate at a fast food restaurant?

(A) 16
(B) 32
(C) 64
(D) 160
(E) 320

12. Which of the following dining categories most nearly totaled $\dfrac{1}{3}$ of the couples surveyed?

(A) Barbecue and other
(B) Fast food
(C) Take out and other
(D) Fine dining and barbecue
(E) Fine dining and other

13. How many of the couples surveyed spent more than $10 but not more than $60 on their anniversary dinner?
    - (A) 420
    - (B) 390
    - (C) 360
    - (D) 300
    - (E) 280

14. If everyone surveyed who spent over $60 on their anniversary dinner spent it on fine dining, approximately what percentage of the people who experienced fine dining did so for $60 or less?
    - (A) 74
    - (B) 66
    - (C) 58
    - (D) 50
    - (E) 26

15. If a total of 300 couples surveyed ate fast food or spent in the $20.01 to $40 range when paying for their anniversary dinner, how many did both?
    - (A) 100
    - (B) 90
    - (C) 85
    - (D) 75
    - (E) 65

EXERCISE 3

15 Questions

Time—15 Minutes

> **Directions:** Each of the following questions has five answer choices. For each of these questions, select the best of the answer choices given.

1. Which of the following numbers is evenly divisible by 3, 4, and 5, but not by 9?
   - (A) 15,840
   - (B) 20,085
   - (C) 23,096
   - (D) 53,700
   - (E) 79,130

2. If $a = -1$ and $b = -2$, what is the value of $(2 - ab^2)^3$?
   - (A) 343
   - (B) 216
   - (C) 125
   - (D) 64
   - (E) 27

3. Which of the following expressions is equivalent in value to $9y - \dfrac{6y^3}{2y^3}$?
   - (A) $\dfrac{3y}{4}$
   - (B) $\dfrac{3}{y}$
   - (C) $3y$
   - (D) $6y$
   - (E) $-6y$

4. If x and y are positive integers, and $x - 2y = 5$, which of the following could be the value of $x^2 - 4y^2$?
   - (A) -3
   - (B) 0
   - (C) 14
   - (D) 45
   - (E) 51

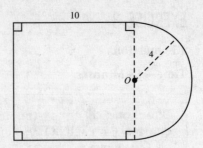

5. Find the area of the region shown in the figure above. Note: The curved side is a semicircle.

   (A) $20 + 4\pi$
   (B) $20 + 6\pi$
   (C) $40 + 6\pi$
   (D) $60 + 8\pi$
   (E) $80 + 8\pi$

6. If the result of squaring a number n is less than twice the number, then the value of n must be

   (A) negative
   (B) positive
   (C) between -1 and $+1$
   (D) greater than 1
   (E) between 0 and 2

Questions 7 and 8 are based on the following definition:

$$n^\wedge = \frac{2n}{n-1}$$

7. If $n = p + 1$, what is the value of $n^\wedge$?

   (A) 2

   (B) $\dfrac{2p}{p-1}$

   (C) $\dfrac{2p+1}{p-1}$

   (D) $2 + \dfrac{1}{p}$

   (E) $2 + \dfrac{2}{p}$

8. For which non-zero value of n is $n^\wedge = n$?

   (A) 1
   (B) 2
   (C) 3
   (D) 4
   (E) 5

9. You roll a fair six-sided die twice. What is the probability that the die will land with the same side facing up both times?

   (A) $\dfrac{1}{6}$

   (B) $\dfrac{1}{12}$

   (C) $\dfrac{2}{36}$

   (D) $\dfrac{1}{36}$

   (E) 0

10. The ratio of the arithmetic mean of two numbers to one of the numbers is 3:5. What is the ratio of the smaller number to the larger?

   (A) 1:5
   (B) 1:4
   (C) 1:3
   (D) 1:2
   (E) 2:3

Questions 11–15 refer to the following graph.

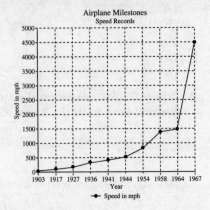

11. By how many miles per hour did the airplane speed record increase from 1903 to 1964?

    (A) 530
    (B) 770
    (C) 970
    (D) 1,170
    (E) 1,470

12. In what year did a plane first fly over 500 miles per hour?

    (A) 1940
    (B) 1941
    (C) 1943
    (D) 1948
    (E) 1950

13. At what average rate per year did the airplane speed record increase from 1964 to 1967?

    (A) 500
    (B) 800
    (C) 1,000
    (D) 1,200
    (E) 1,500

14. Approximately how many years did it take for the airplane speed record to double from its 1941 level?

    (A) 26
    (B) 20
    (C) 18
    (D) 13
    (E) 6

15. The air distance from New York to Los Angeles is about 3,000 miles. How much longer (in hours) would it take a plane flying at record speed in 1944 than in 1964 to fly that distance?

    (A) 6
    (B) 4
    (C) 3
    (D) 2.5
    (E) 2

EXERCISE 4

15 Questions

Time—15 Minutes

> **Directions:** Each of the following questions has five answer choices. For each of these questions, select the best of the answer choices given.

1. The advertised price of potatoes is 35¢ per pound. If a 3-pound bag actually weighs $3\frac{1}{4}$ pounds, what is the closest approximation in cents to the actual price per pound for that bag?

    (A) 36
    (B) 35
    (C) 34
    (D) 33
    (E) 32

2. If $\left(\dfrac{-2}{5}\right)^3$ is equal to N thousandths, what is N?

    (A) −100
    (B) −64
    (C) −32
    (D) 32
    (E) 64

3. In the figure above, the centers of all three circles lie on the same line. The medium-sized circle has twice the radius of the smallest circle. The smallest circle has radius 1. What is the length of the boundary of the shaded region?

   (A) 12π
   (B) 6π
   (C) 12
   (D) 3π
   (E) 6

4. What is the perimeter of a rectangle that is twice as long as it is wide and has the same area as a circle of diameter 8?

   (A) $8\sqrt{\pi}$
   (B) $8\sqrt{2\pi}$
   (C) 8π
   (D) $12\sqrt{2\pi}$
   (E) 12π

5. If the negative of the sum of two consecutive odd numbers is less than -35, which of the following may be one of the numbers?

   (A) 17
   (B) 16
   (C) 15
   (D) 13
   (E) 11

6. How many gallons of milk that is 2% butterfat must be mixed with milk that is 3.5% butterfat to get 10 gallons that is 3% butterfat?

 (A) 3

 (B) $\dfrac{10}{3}$

 (C) $\dfrac{7}{2}$

 (D) $\dfrac{11}{3}$

 (E) 4

7. If the arithmetic mean of x and y is m, and $z = 2m$, then the arithmetic mean of x, y, and z is

 (A) m

 (B) $\dfrac{2m}{3}$

 (C) $\dfrac{4m}{3}$

 (D) $\dfrac{3m}{4}$

 (E) $\dfrac{3}{4m}$

8. Which of the following is a common factor of both $x^2 - 4x - 5$ and $x^2 - 6x - 7$?

 (A) $x - 5$
 (B) $x - 7$
 (C) $x - 1$
 (D) $x + 5$
 (E) $x + 1$

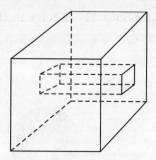

9. The figure above shows a cube 3 units on a side with a 1 × 1 square hole cut through it. How many square units is the total surface area of the resulting solid figure?

    (A) 66
    (B) 64
    (C) 60
    (D) 54
    (E) 52

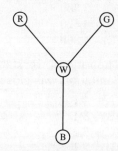

10. In a certain computer game, a light starts at the center (white) at time zero and moves once every second in the following pattern: from white to blue, back to white, then to green, back to white, then to red, in a counterclockwise direction. If the light continues to move in this way, what will be the color sequence at times 208–209?

    (A) white to green
    (B) white to blue
    (C) white to red
    (D) red to white
    (E) green to white

Questions 11–15 refer to the following graphs.

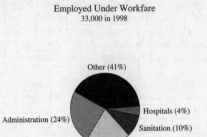

Employed Under Workfare
33,000 in 1998

Other (41%)
Hospitals (4%)
Sanitation (10%)
Administration (24%)
Park (21%)

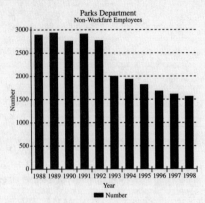

Parks Department
Non-Workfare Employees

■ Number

11. The number of workfare employees in Sanitation or Hospitals totaled

(A) 462
(B) 1,320
(C) 3,300
(D) 4,620
(E) 4,860

12. The ratio of workfare employees in Administration to those in Sanitation was closest to

(A) 4:1
(B) 3:1
(C) 5:2
(D) 2:1
(E) 1.5:1

13. The percent decline in non-workfare Parks Department employees from 1992 to 1995 was closest to

(A) 36
(B) 40
(C) 45
(D) 50
(E) 67

14. In which year between 1988–1998 did the Parks Department employ the median number of non-workfare employees?

    (A) 1992
    (B) 1993
    (C) 1994
    (D) 1995
    (E) 1996

15. In 1998, the percent of Parks Department employees in 1998 who were not employed under workfare was closest to

    (A) 50
    (B) 44
    (C) 32
    (D) 23
    (E) 19

EXERCISE 5

15 Questions

Time—15 Minutes

> **Directions:** Each of the following questions has five answer choices. For each of these questions, select the best of the answer choices given.

1. For which n is the remainder largest when the number 817,380 is divided by n?

   (A)   4
   (B)   5
   (C)   6
   (D)   8
   (E)   9

2. The towns of Andover and Diggstown are 840 miles apart. On a certain map, this distance is represented by 14 inches. The towns of Lincoln and Charleston are 630 miles apart. On the same map, the distance between them in inches is

   (A) $9\frac{1}{2}$

   (B)   10

   (C) $10\frac{1}{2}$

   (D)   11

   (E) $11\frac{1}{2}$

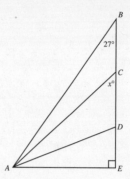

3. In the figure above, $\overline{AC}$ and $\overline{AD}$ trisect $\angle A$. What is the value of x?

    (A) 21
    (B) 27
    (C) 42
    (D) 48
    (E) 60

4. If the radius of a cylinder is tripled while its height is halved, its volume will be

    (A) halved.
    (B) unchanged.
    (C) doubled.
    (D) increased by 350%.
    (E) four times as large.

5. Through how many degrees does the minute hand of a clock turn from 3:50 P.M. to 4:15 P.M. on the same day?

    (A) 25
    (B) 45
    (C) 90
    (D) 120
    (E) 150

6. Harvey paid $400 for a used car that travels 28 miles per gallon on the highway and 20 miles per gallon in the city. If he drove twice as many highway as city miles last month while using 34 gallons of gasoline, how many miles did he drive altogether?

    (A) 1,000
    (B) 840
    (C) 400
    (D) 340
    (E) 280

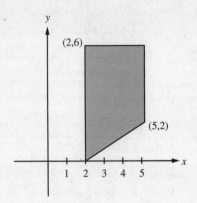

7. The area of the shaded region in the figure above is

   (A)   15
   (B)   16
   (C)   17
   (D)   18
   (E)   20

8. What is the perimeter of a rectangle that is three times as long as it is wide and has the same area as a circle of circumference 6?

   (A) $8\sqrt{3\pi}$

   (B) $8\sqrt{\pi}$

   (C) $4\sqrt{3\pi}$

   (D) $\dfrac{8\sqrt{3}}{\sqrt{\pi}}$

   (E) $\dfrac{8}{\sqrt{3\pi}}$

9. A plane is flying from City A to City B at m mph. Another plane flying from City B to City A travels 50 mph faster than the first plane. The cities are R miles apart. If both planes depart at the same time, in terms of R and m, how far are they from City A when they pass?

(A) $\dfrac{R}{m} + 50$

(B) $\dfrac{Rm}{2m} - 50$

(C) $\dfrac{Rm}{2m + 50}$

(D) $\dfrac{R + 50}{m + 50}$

(E) $\dfrac{m + 50}{R}$

10. P percent of $20\sqrt{3}$ is 3. $P =$

(A) $\sqrt{3}$

(B) 3

(C) $5\sqrt{3}$

(D) $10\sqrt{3}$

(E) 20

Questions 11–15 refer to the following graphs.

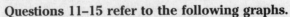

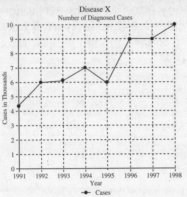

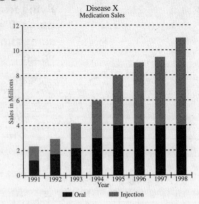

11. The percent increase in diagnosed cases of disease X from 1997 to 1998 was closest to

    (A) 8
    (B) 9
    (C) 10
    (D) 11
    (E) 12

12. The second greatest percent increase in diagnosed cases of disease X occurred between which two years?

    (A) 1991–1992
    (B) 1992–1993
    (C) 1993–1994
    (D) 1994–1995
    (E) 1995–1996

13. By how much did the total sales of medication for disease X in 1998 exceed total sales in 1994?

    (A) $5,000,000
    (B) $4,200,000
    (C) $3,800,000
    (D) $3,000,000
    (E) $2,500,000

14. In which year were the sales of oral and injection medication for disease X most nearly the same?

   (A) 1992
   (B) 1993
   (C) 1994
   (D) 1995
   (E) 1996

15. How did the percent increase in number of cases of disease X diagnosed from 1995 to 1998 compare to the percent increase in sales of injection medication for disease X for the same period?

   (A) It was 18% less.
   (B) It was 8% less.
   (C) It was about the same.
   (D) It was 10% more.
   (E) It was 20% more.

Answer Key

Exercise 1	Exercise 2	Exercise 3	Exercise 4	Exercise 5
1. C	1. E	1. D	1. E	1. D
2. D	2. C	2. B	2. B	2. C
3. E	3. D	3. D	3. B	3. D
4. E	4. D	4. D	4. D	4. D
5. B	5. A	5. E	5. A	5. E
6. A	6. E	6. E	6. B	6. B
7. A	7. A	7. E	7. C	7. A
8. D	8. C	8. C	8. C	8. D
9. A	9. A	9. A	9. B	9. C
10. E	10. B	10. A	10. C	10. C
11. B	11. D	11. E	11. D	11. D
12. A	12. C	12. C	12. C	12. A
13. D	13. B	13. C	13. A	13. A
14. B	14. A	14. D	14. B	14. C
15. E	15. D	15. B	15. E	15. B

Explanatory Answers

EXERCISE 1

1. **The correct answer is (C).** Since the labeled end points are 2.2 and 2.3, the ten intervals between must each be one-tenth of the difference. Hence the "tick marks" must represent hundredths. That is, A = 2.21, B = 2.22, and so on. Thus, we know that G = 2.27.

2. **The correct answer is (D).** The fact that a number is divisible by 3 does not make it odd. (Think of 6 or 12.) Therefore, $121 - 5k$ could be either odd or even. However, k cannot be divisible by 3, because 121 is not. Hence, only I or II is possible.

3. **The correct answer is (E).** Let r, m, and b be the prices in cents of rolls, muffins, and bread respectively This yields two equations:

$$4r + 6m + 3b = 910$$

and

$$2r + 3m + b = 390$$

If we multiply the second equation by -2 and add the two together, we have:

$$\text{The first equation:} \quad 4r + 6m + 3b = 910$$
$$-2 \text{ times the second equation:} \quad -4r - 6m - 2b = -780$$
$$b = 130$$

Hence, the price of a loaf of bread is $1.30, which is choice (E).

4. **The correct answer is (E).** $4y$ must be even, so for the sum of $3x$ and $4y$ to be odd, $3x$ must be odd. Since 3 is odd, $3x$ will be odd only if x is odd. Hence, x is odd and y can be anything. So II and III cannot be true.

5. **The correct answer is (B).** Let the number of Democrats be $5m$ and the number of Republicans be $7m$, so that D:R :: $5m : 7m = 5$:7. The total is $5m + 7m = 12m$, which must be 156. Therefore, $12m = 156$, and $m = 13$. Of course, the difference is $7m - 5m = 2m = 2(13) = 26$. Hence, the answer is choice (B).

6. **The correct answer is (A).** Since $BC = 4$ and $AC = 8$, we know that $\triangle ABC$ is a $30°$–$60°$–$90°$ right triangle. Hence, we know $AB = 4\sqrt{3}$, and taking one-half the product of the legs, the triangle has area $\frac{1}{2}(4)(4\sqrt{3}) = 8\sqrt{3}$. Since $\triangle ADC$ is an isosceles right triangle with hypotenuse 8, each leg must be $\frac{8}{\sqrt{2}}$. Again, taking one-half the product of the legs, the triangle has area $\frac{1}{2}\left(\frac{8}{\sqrt{2}}\right)\left(\frac{8}{\sqrt{2}}\right) = \frac{64}{4} = 16$. Adding the two areas, we have $16 + 8\sqrt{3}$.

7. **The correct answer is (A).** Add -2 to both sides, thus:

$$A < 2 - 4B$$
$$\underline{-2 = -2}$$
$$A - 2 < -4B$$

Divide by -4, remembering to reverse the inequality, thus: $\frac{A-2}{4} > B$; that is, $\frac{2-A}{4} > B$, which is choice (A).

8. **The correct answer is (D).** Since each person had 5 choices, there are 25 possible pairs of numbers. The only way the sum could be odd is if one person picked an odd number and the other picked an even number. Suppose that Johnnie chose the odd number and Lisa the even one. Johnnie had 3 possible even numbers to select from, and for each of these, Lisa had 2 possible choices, for a total of $(3)(2) = 6$ possibilities. However, you could have had Johnnie pick an even number and Lisa pick an odd one, and there are also 6 ways to do that. Hence, out of 25 possibilities, 12 have an odd total, and 13 have an even total. The probability of an even total, then, is choice (D), $\frac{13}{25}$.

9. **The correct answer is (A).** Running m buses for 2 days is the same as running one bus for $2m$ days. If we use g gallons of gasoline, each bus uses $\frac{g}{2m}$ gallons each day. So, if you multiply the number of gallons per day used by each bus by the number of buses and the number of days, you should get total gasoline usage. That is, $\frac{g}{2m} \times (4)(5) = \frac{10g}{m}$.

10. **The correct answer is (E).** If $x = 5$ and $y = 5$, $x^2 + y^2 = 50$. For any other choice, say 6 and 4, the sum is larger. Hence, $x^2 + y^2$ is at a minimum when $x = y$ and $|x - y| = 0$.

11. **The correct answer is (B).** Baker gets $1,500 and Delta $1,000, for a total of $2,500. Corman gets $3,000, and $3,000 − $2,500 = $500.

12. **The correct answer is (A).** Set up a table:

	Now	**After Switch**
Ajax	4500	2250
Baker	1500	1500
Corman	3000	3000
Delta	1000	3250

Now it is easy to see that I is true: Delta is the largest. However, Ajax still gets more business than Baker, so II is false. And the sum of A and C is $5,250, while the sum of B and D is only $4,750, so III is false. Hence, choice (A) is correct.

13. **The correct answer is (D).** Totaling the payments made to all four suppliers, you have 4,500 + 1,500 + 3,000 + 1,000 = $10,000. Of this total, 3,000 was paid to Corman—that is, 30% of the total. Hence, the sector representing Corman must be 30% of 360° = 108°.

14. **The correct answer is (B).** 25% of 10,000 is 2,500. Taking equal shares from Ajax and Corman takes 1,250 away from Ajax, leaving 4,500 − 1,250 = 3,250, or 32.5% of the total.

15. **The correct answer is (E).** Corman's total was 3,000. Let Delta's share be k. Then Baker gets $2k$ and Ajax $3k$, for a total of $6k = 3,000$. Thus, $k = 500$, and Baker gets $2(500) = 1,000$ in additional business added to its present 1,500. Baker's new total is 2,500 out of 10,000, or 25% of the total. 25% of the circle is 90°.

EXERCISE 2

1. **The correct answer is (E).** Any number less than D must lie to the left of D. The distance from D to G is 3 units. Thus, the point we want must be $1\frac{1}{2}$ units to the left of D, that is, halfway between B and C. Since this is not a labeled point, the correct choice is (E).

2. **The correct answer is (C).** The larger circle has area $A_L = \pi(r)^2 = 36\pi$. That means that $r^2 = 36$, and $r = 6$. The diameter of the smaller circle equals the radius of the larger one, so its radius is $\frac{1}{2}(6) = 3$. Its circumference must be $C_S = 2\pi(3) = 6\pi$, choice (C).

3. **The correct answer is (D).** In 5 hours, 4 ounces $(7 - 3)$ have dripped. Therefore, the "drip rate" is $\frac{4}{5}$ of an ounce per hour. From 5:00 P.M. on Sunday until 2:00 A.M. on Monday is 9 hours, causing the total to be:

$$7 = \frac{4}{5} \times 9 = 7 + \frac{36}{5} = \frac{71}{5}$$

4. **The correct answer is (D).** The prime factorization of 24 is $2^3 3$; hence, if $24AB$ is a perfect square, then AB must have a factor of 2 and a factor of 3. This means, first of all that both A and B cannot be odd. So I cannot be possible. II also cannot be possible, because if AB were a perfect square and $24AB$ were also a perfect square, then 24 would be a perfect square, which it is not. Of course, if, for example, A were 6 and B were 36, $24AB$ would be a perfect square with both A and B divisible by 6, so III is possible. Hence, the correct choice is (D).

5. **The correct answer is (A).** Totaling the other three tree types (elm, maple, and oak), we see that they make up 85% of the trees on Main Street. This leaves 15% of the trees to be pine trees, and 15% of 300 is 45.

6. **The correct answer is (E).** Substituting: $(-2)^4 + 2(-2)^3 + 3(-2)^2 + (-2) = 16 - 16 + 12 - 2 = 10$.

7. **The correct answer is (A).** Working outward from the inner parentheses, $[3(a^2 b^3)^2]^3 = [3a^4 b^6]^3 = 27a^{12} b^{18}$.

8. **The correct answer is (C).** The only way that $7 + x + x$ in the left column can total 11 is if x is 2, since if there were a "carry" of 1, x would not be a whole number; and if you try for a "carry" of 2, x would be 1, and $x + y + x$ in the right column would be at most 11, with a carry of only 1. Since $x = 2$, the only way $2x + y$ could have a units digit of 7 is if $y = 3$. So, in other words, the original addition must have been $72 + 23 + 22$.

9. **The correct answer is (A).** Let x be the unknown number of liters of 50% antifreeze. Now, the final mixture will have $(x + 80)$ liters, and the amount of antifreeze will be:

$$0.50x + 0.20(80) = 0.40(x + 80)$$
$$0.5x + 16 = 0.4x + 32$$
$$0.1x = 16$$
$$x = 160$$

10. **The correct answer is (B).** Since Horace's average overall was 75, he had a total overall of $75(m + n) = 75m + 75n$ on $n + m$ exams. Since he averaged 70 on m exams, he had a total of $70m$ on the first m. That means that his total on the last n exams was $75m + 75n - 70m = 5m + 75n$, and his average was $(5m + 75n) \div n = \frac{5m}{n} + 75$.

11. **The correct answer is (D).** 32% of 500 is 160.

12. **The correct answer is (C).** The choices total 25%, 32%, 33%, 35%, and 36% respectively. 33% is closest to $\frac{1}{3}$.

13. **The correct answer is (B).** The "under $10" and "over $60" groups totaled 22% or 110 couples. The remainder was 390 couples.

14. **The correct answer is (A).** The number who spent over $60 was 6% of 500 = 30. The number who chose fine dining was 23% of 500 = 115. Hence, 85 of 115 satisfied the condition, and $\frac{85}{115} \approx 0.739$. Choice (A), 74%, is closest.

15. **The correct answer is (D).** The number who ate fast food was 32% of 500 = 160. The number in the given price range was 43% of 500 = 215. Adding these two together, we get 375. But the combined total was only 300. Hence, 75 were counted twice and must have been in both groups.

EXERCISE 3

1. **The correct answer is (D).** The easiest thing to look for is divisibility by 5. Does the number end in 5 or 0? By inspection, we eliminate 23,096, which ends in 6. We want the number to be divisible by 4, which means it must be even, and its last two digits must form a number divisible by 4. That knocks out the one ending in 5 (which is odd), and also 79,130, because 30 is not divisible by 4. This leaves 15,840 and 53,700. The digits of 15,840 add up to 18, while those of 53,700 total 15. Both are divisible by 3, but 15,840 is also divisible by 9. Therefore, only choice (D), 53,700, meets all the conditions.

2. **The correct answer is (B).** Substituting: $[2 - (-1)(-2)^2]^3 = [2 - (-4)]^3 = 6^3 = 216$.

3. **The correct answer is (D).** The fraction simplifies to $3y$, and $9y - 3y = 6y$.

4. **The correct answer is (D).** Since $x^2 - 4y^2 = (x - 2y)(x + 2y) = 5(x + 2y)$, $x^2 - 4y^2$ must be divisible by 5. Therefore, -3, 14, and 51 are not possible. If the result is to be zero, $x + 2y = 0$, which means $y = -2x$, so that both numbers cannot be positive. Hence, the expression must equal 45, which you get for $x = 7$ and $y = 1$.

5. **The correct answer is (E).** The dotted line divides the region into a rectangle and a semicircle. Since the radius of the circular arc is 4, the diameter is 8, and that is the width of the rectangle. The length is 10. Hence, its area is 80. The area of the whole circle would be $\pi r^2 = \pi(4^2) = 16\pi$. Hence, the area of the semicircle is half of that, or 8π. Therefore, the total area is choice (E), $80 + 8\pi$.

6. **The correct answer is (E).** If $n^2 < 2n$, that means that $n^2 - 2n < 0$, or $n(n - 2) < 0$. Clearly, if n is any positive number less than 2, then n is positive and $(n - 2)$ is negative, making the result true.

7. **The correct answer is (E).** Substituting $(p + 1)$ for n, we have:

$$n^\wedge = \frac{2(p + 1)}{(p + 1) - 1} = \frac{2p + 2}{p} = 2 + \frac{2}{p}$$

8. **The correct answer is (C).** It is easiest to try plugging in the values offered. You'll find that, for $n = 3$, $n^\wedge = \frac{2(3)}{3 - 1} = \frac{6}{2} = 3$.

9. **The correct answer is (A).** It really doesn't matter what number you roll on the first roll; the chance of matching it the next time is always $\frac{1}{6}$.

10. **The correct answer is (A).** Calling the numbers x and y, $\frac{x+y}{2} : x = \frac{3}{5}$. That is, $\frac{x+y}{2} = \frac{3}{5}$. Cross-multiplying:

    $$5x + 5y = 6x; \; 5y = x$$

    Hence, one number is five times as large as the other, so their ratio is 1:5.

11. **The correct answer is (E).** The record in 1964 was 1,500. The record in 1903 was nearly zero. (It's almost impossible to read the exact number on the graph; in fact, it was 30.) Choice (E), 1,470, is clearly the only plausible choice.

12. **The correct answer is (C).** In 1941, the record was under 500, and in 1944, it was over 500. The line graph seems to cross the 500 grid line at about 1943.

13. **The correct answer is (C).** The record was 1,500 in 1964 and about 4,500 in 1967, for an increase of 3,000 over a 3-year period. The average annual rate of increase was $3,000 \div 3 = 1,000$.

14. **The correct answer is (D).** The 1941 record was about 400, and the 1954 record was about 800. The number of years it took to double was about 13.

15. **The correct answer is (B).** The 1964 record was 1,500 mph. To fly 3,000 miles at that speed would take 2 hours. In 1944, the speed record was 500 mph. To fly 3,000 miles at that speed would take 6 hours, or 4 hours longer.

EXERCISE 4

1. **The correct answer is (E).** At 35¢ per pound, the 3-pound bag will be marked $1.05 or 105¢. Dividing this by the weight of the bag, we have $105 \div 3.25$. Hence, choice (E), 32, is the closest.

2. **The correct answer is (B).** Cubing, $\left(\frac{-2}{5}\right)^3 = \frac{-8}{125}$. To rename this fraction as thousandths, multiply both the numerator and the denominator by 8 to get $\frac{-64}{1000}$. Hence, $N = -64$.

3. **The correct answer is (B).** Since the smallest circle has radius of 1, the medium circle has radius 2, and the diameter of the large circle must be 6, which makes its radius 3. The length of a semicircle is half that of a circle, that is, πr. So the length of the boundary of the shaded region is the sum of the lengths of the three semicircles: $\pi + 2\pi + 3\pi = 6\pi$.

4. **The correct answer is (D).** The area of a circle of diameter 8 is $\pi 4^2 = 16\pi$, since its radius is 4. Let the width of the rectangle be w. Its length is $2w$ and its area is $2w^2$, which must equal 16π. Thus:

$$2w^2 = 16\pi$$
$$w^2 = 8\pi$$

and
$$w = \sqrt{8\pi}$$
$$= 2\sqrt{2\pi}$$

Thus, $L = 4\sqrt{2\pi}$

The perimeter is $2L + 2W = 8\sqrt{2\pi} + 4\sqrt{2\pi} = 12\sqrt{2\pi}$.

5. **The correct answer is (A).** Calling the numbers x and $(x + 2)$, the negative of the sum is $-[x + (x + 2)]$, and this should be less than -35. That is, $-[2x + 2] < -35$. Solving the inequality:

$$-2x - 2 < -35$$
$$-2x \quad < -33$$

Dividing by -2 reverses the inequality:
$$x > 16.5$$

Looking at the choices, we need an odd number. $x = 17$ will work, because $(x + 2) = 17 > 16.5$.

6. **The correct answer is (B).** Let g be the number of gallons that is 2% butterfat. Then $10 - g$ will be the amount that is 3.5% butterfat. The total amount of butterfat is:
$$0.02g + 0.035(10 - g) = 0.03(10)$$
$$0.02g + 0.35 - 0.035g = 0.3$$

Let's multiply by 1,000 to clear out the decimals:
$$20g + 350 - 35g = 300$$
$$-15g = -50; g = \frac{10}{3}$$

7. **The correct answer is (C).** The arithmetic mean of x and y is $\frac{x + y}{2} = m$, which means that $x + y = 2m$ and $x + y + z = 4m$. Dividing by 3 to get the arithmetic mean of x, y, and z, we get $\frac{x + y + z}{3} = \frac{4m}{3}$.

8. **The correct answer is (C).** $x^2 - 4x - 5 = (x - 5)(x + 1)$, and $x^2 - 6x - 7 = (x - 7)(x + 1)$. The common factor is $x + 1$.

9. **The correct answer is (B).** Each side of the cube has an area of $3 \times 3 = 9$. Since there are 6 sides, the original cube had a surface area of 54 square units. Two 1×1 squares are missing, making the outside area 52. The "hole" has four 3×1 rectangular sides with a total area of 12, giving us a final total of 64.

10. **The correct answer is (C).** The sequence is:

0	1	2	3	4	5	6	7	8	9	10	11	12
W	B	W	G	W	R	W	B	W	G	W	R	W

Every time you reach a time divisible by 6, the sequence starts over with W and proceeds: WBWGWR. 204 is divisible by 6; hence, we must have the sequence:

204	205	206	207	208	209
W	B	W	G	W	R

Times 208–209 are W–R.

11. **The correct answer is (D).** 14% of the workers were in one of the two units named. 14% of 33,000 = 4,620.

12. **The correct answer is (C).** The ratio of 24:10 = 2.4, which is closest to 5:2 = 2.5.

13. **The correct answer is (A).** In 1992, there were 2,800 such workers. In 1995, there were 1,800. The decline was 1,000 out of 2,800 or 1,000 ÷ 2,800 = .357, which is closest to 36%.

14. **The correct answer is (B).** As it happens, for the five years before 1993, the number of employees was higher than in 1993, and for the five years after 1993, the number of employees was less than in 1993. Hence, the median was in 1993.

15. **The correct answer is (E).** From the bar graph, the number of non-workfare employees was 1,600. From the pie chart, the number of workfare employees was 21% of 33,000 = 6,930, for a total of 1,600 + 6,930 = 8,530. $\frac{1600}{8530} = 0.1875 \approx 19\%$.

EXERCISE 5

1. **The correct answer is (D).** 817,380 is divisible by all the numbers in the list except 8. Hence, 8 must give the largest remainder, because it is the only one that is not zero. To start, 817,380 is divisible by 5 because its last digit is 0. It is divisible by 2 because it is even, and by 4 because 80 is divisible by 4. However, it is not divisible by 8 because 380 isn't. In addition, the sum of its digits is 27, which is divisible by 3 and by 9. Since it is divisible by both 2 and 3, it is also divisible by 6.

2. **The correct answer is (C).** The actual distance and the distance on the map must be in the same proportion. That is, 630:840 = x : 14, where x is the unknown distance. In fractions:

$$\frac{630}{840} = \frac{x}{14}; \frac{3}{4} = \frac{x}{14}$$

Cross-multiplying: $4x = 42$; $x = 10.5$.

3. **The correct answer is (D).** Looking first at $\triangle ABE$, we have a right triangle with one angle 90° and one 27°. Thus, m∠A must be 63°. Hence, m∠BAC is one-third of that, or 21°. So looking at $\triangle ABC$, ∠BCA must be 180° − 21° − 27° = 132°. Since x is the supplement to that angle, $x = 48$.

4. **The correct answer is (D).** The volume is $V = \pi r^2 h$. Replacing r by $3r$ and h by $\frac{1}{2}h$, we have $V = \pi(3r)^2 \left(\frac{1}{2}h\right) = \frac{9}{2}\pi r^2 h$. That is, it is 4.5 times as large, which means it is 350% larger than it was.

5. **The correct answer is (E).** The clock hand has moved through 25 minutes, which is $\frac{25}{60} = \frac{5}{12}$ of the full circle. Thus, in degrees:

$$\frac{5}{12}(360) = 150°$$

6. **The correct answer is (B).** Let x be the number of city miles Harvey drove, and let $2x$ be the number of highway miles. Miles divided by miles per gallon should give the number of gallons of gas used. Thus:

$$\frac{x}{20} + \frac{2x}{28} = 34$$

$$\frac{x}{20} + \frac{x}{14} = 34$$

Multiply the equation by the LCD 140 to get:

$$7x + 10x = 4760$$
$$17x = 4760$$
$$x = 280$$

Since Harvey drove a total of $3x$ miles, the correct choice is $3(280) = 840$.

7. **The correct answer is (A).** If we drop a perpendicular line from the point (5,2) to the x-axis, it will hit the axis at (5,0), and we will have a rectangle that is 3 units wide and 6 units high (since it goes from the x-axis, where $y = 0$, to the height of (2,6), which is 6 units.) The area of this rectangle is 18 square units. Subtracting the area of the missing triangle, which is $\frac{1}{2}(2)(3) = 3$, we see that the area of the shaded portion is 15.

8. **The correct answer is (D).** If the circle has a circumference of 6, its radius is given by $6 = 2\pi r$, so that $r = \frac{3}{\pi}$. The area of a circle of radius $\frac{3}{\pi}$ is $\pi\left(\frac{3}{\pi}\right)^2 = \frac{9}{\pi}$. Let the width of the rectangle be w. Its length is $3w$, and its area is $3w^2$, which must equal $\frac{9}{\pi}$. Thus:

$$3w^2 = \frac{9}{\pi}$$
$$w^2 = \frac{3}{\pi}$$

and

$$w = \sqrt{\frac{3}{\pi}} = \frac{\sqrt{3}}{\sqrt{\pi}}$$

The perimeter is $2L + 2W = 6W + 2W = 8W = \frac{8\sqrt{3}}{\sqrt{\pi}}$.

9. **The correct answer is (C).** The planes pass at the time when the sum of the distances travelled by both is R. Call this time t. The first plane, going m miles per hour, has travelled mt miles. The second plane, going $(m + 50)$ miles per hour, has travelled $(m + 50)t$ miles. The two sum to R. Thus:

$$R = mt + mt + 50t$$
$$R = (2m + 50)t$$

Thus:

$$t = \frac{R}{2m + 50}$$

Hence, the planes' distance from City A is m times this time, or:

$$mt = \frac{Rm}{2m + 50}$$

10. **The correct answer is (C).** P percent means $\frac{P}{100}$. Hence, $\frac{P}{100} \times 20\sqrt{3} = 3$ must be solved for P. Thus, $\frac{P\sqrt{3}}{5} = 3$. Multiply by $\frac{5}{\sqrt{3}}$, and notice that $\frac{3}{\sqrt{3}} = \sqrt{3}$ gives $P = 5\sqrt{3}$.

11. **The correct answer is (D).** In 1997, there were 9,000 cases. In 1998, there were 10,000 cases. The increase was 1,000 on a base of 9,000, or $\frac{1}{9} = 0.1111\ldots \approx 11\%$.

12. **The correct answer is (A).** The most sizeable increase in absolute terms was from 1995 to 1996, when the number of cases went up 3,000 from a level of 6,000, for a 50% increase. The second greatest was the increase from about 4,400 cases to 6,000 cases from 1991 to 1992.

13. **The correct answer is (A).** Total sales in 1998 were $11,000,000, up from $6,000,000 in 1994, for an increase of $5,000,000.

14. **The correct answer is (C).** In 1994, both were equal to $3 million.

15. **The correct answer is (B).** The number of diagnosed cases increased from 6,000 to 10,000, or about 67%. The sales of injection medication increased from $4 million to $7 million, or 75%. Hence, the number of diagnosed cases increased about 8% less than sales.

Chapter 9

Quantitative Comparisons

Get the Scoop On . . .

- Proven strategies for scoring high on quantitative comparisons
- Shortcuts for saving time and minimizing complex calculations
- How the "plug-in" technique can help you decipher unknown quantities
- The most common traps set by the test-makers and how to avoid them

THE TEST CAPSULE

What's the Big Idea?

You'll be given two quantities—that is, numbers, formulas, or other statements that define a value. You have to decide how the quantities compare with one another: whether one quantity is greater than the other, the quantities are equal, or you've been given too little information to decide.

How Many?

Of the 28 questions in your quantitative section, your GRE will probably have a total of 14 quantitative comparisons.

How Much Do They Count?

Because quantitative comparisons are 14 out of 28 total math questions, they count as 50 percent of your overall math score.

How Much Time Should They Take?

You need to answer quantitative comparisons at a rate of about one per minute.

What's the Best Strategy?

Don't sweat the details! Remember, these aren't conventional math problems: you aren't required to find the *exact* value of any quantity. All you need is enough information to determine which quantity is greater—and in most cases you can do that with approximate values or with *no definite values at all.*

What's the Worst Pitfall?

Making assumptions about information you haven't been given. Only a small handful of facts is provided for each Quantitative Comparison item; you have to make the comparison based solely on these data. Be careful not to unconsciously assume additional facts or details that the test-makers haven't explicitly provided.

THE OFFICIAL DESCRIPTION

What They Are

Quantitative comparisons test your ability to recognize the relationships between pairs of mathematical quantities. You'll be given quantities in two columns, called Column A and Column B. Your job is to decide whether the quantity in Column A is greater, the quantity in Column B is greater, the two quantities are equal, or the information given is not enough to determine which quantity is greater.

Where They Are

In the typical computerized GRE, you'll have one math section that is 45 minutes long. It will include 14 quantitative comparisons, interspersed seemingly at random with 14 multiple-choice problems. Reminder: the test-makers claim the right to change the format at any time! However, the typical format we just described is what you're most likely to encounter.

What They Measure

Unlike the other math questions on the exam, quantitative comparisons don't require you to figure out the exact answer to any question. In fact, for many quantitative comparison items, you'll have no calculations to do: you'll find that estimating, rounding, eliminating needless information, and other tricks (which you'll learn in this chapter) can enable you to choose the right answer without knowing the *precise* value of either quantity. Rather than your skill at calculating, quantitative comparison items test your knowledge of mathematical concepts and your quickness, creativity, and accuracy at applying those concepts.

What They Cover

The math areas tested on the GRE, including the quantitative comparison items, are those studied by virtually every high school student: arithmetic, basic algebra, and plane and coordinate geometry. Many advanced and specialized math topics are *not* covered on the GRE, including trigonometry and calculus. Thus, even if you took few or no math courses in college, you have almost certainly learned the math that's covered on the GRE. See Appendix B, "The Insider's GRE Math Review," for a detailed review of the math concepts most frequently tested on the exam.

The Directions

Directions: Each question consists of two quantities, one in Column A and one in Column B. You are to compare the two quantities and indicate whether

the quantity in Column A is greater;

the quantity in Column B is greater;

the two quantities are equal;

the relationship cannot be determined from the information given.

Common Information: In a question, information concerning one or both of the quantities to be compared is centered above the two columns. A symbol that appears in both columns represents the same thing in Column A as it does in Column B.

THE INSIDER'S REPORT

Strategies That Really Work

Make the Columns Look Alike

Start by doing whatever it takes to make the columns resemble one another. Only when the columns look alike—and therefore are comparable—can you easily tell which is greater. Here's a simple example:

Column A	Column B

a is 30% of *b*
b is 40% of *c*

Percent that *a* is of *c*	11

FYI

Although the answer choices for each question do not have letter labels on the CAT, for our convenience we'll refer to them as if they do. Thus, the first answer choice will be called choice (A), the second answer choice will be called choice (B), and so on. The test-makers will not change the sequence of answer choices, so it's perfectly safe to think of them as choices (A), (B), (C), and (D).

First, let's be clear about what you're looking at. This question starts with two lines of information that are centered between Column A and Column B. This information isn't part of either column but, instead, is provided to help you interpret the values given in the columns. You're to assume that this information is true and that it applies to whatever quantities appear in the columns underneath.

Now look at the two quantities that you're supposed to compare. Column A *describes* a quantity: the "percent that *a* is of *c*." Column B, by contrast, *states* a quantity, in the simplest possible form: it's the integer 11. Can you tell, at a glance, which is greater? Probably not. The reason is that the two quantities are named in terms so different that they're not readily comparable.

To compare them, you need to make them look alike. Since Column B is already stated in the simplest possible form, your plan should be to make Column A look like Column B—that is, turn it into a simple number as well. To do that, you'll have to use your math skills. Since the shared information tells you that *a* is 30% of *b* and *b* is 40% of *c*, you can tell that *a* must be 30% of 40% of *c*. What is 30% of 40%? Multiply:

$$.30 \times .40 = .12$$

So you can tell from the information given that *a* is 12% of *c*. Now we have a quantity for Column A—12—which can easily be compared with the quantity in Column B. Because 12 is greater than 11, Column A is greater, and choice (A) is the answer for this question.

FYI

When in doubt, try something! It might not be obvious what the test-makers want you to do with either quantity. If so, start messing around with the quantities, using whatever mathematical techniques strike you as natural or logical. Chances are good that some method you've used dozens of times in a math class will yield the result the test-makers are looking for—even if you can't anticipate it when you start work.

Here's another example:

Column A	Column B

x and y are negative

$(x + y)(x + y)$	$x^2 + y^2$

In this question, neither column contains a quantity that's easy to measure—especially since we don't know the value of either unknown, x or y. But don't despair! It might still be possible to figure out how the two quantities compare if we can make them appear similar and therefore comparable.

Which column can more easily be made to resemble the other? In this case, you can probably see how Column A can be made to look something like Column B. Two quantities contained in parentheses, like those in Column A, are practically crying out to be multiplied together. And you can probably tell that, when you multiply them out, you'll end up with a quantity that includes x^2 and y^2, not unlike Column B. Here's what happens to the comparison when the multiplication in Column A is carried out:

Column A	Column B

$x^2 + 2xy + y^2$	$x^2 + y^2$

We've used a basic algebra process here: when you multiply two binomials, like those in Column A, you end up with a trinomial like the one we've now created. See Appendix B, the Insider's GRE Math Review, if this procedure seems unfamiliar.

Now the two columns resemble one another, and we can compare them more easily. But to determine which is greater, we need to use the second basic strategy for quantitative comparisons.

Eliminate Whatever the Columns Share

Remember, you're interested in figuring out the *difference* between the two quantities. That means that anything that the two quantities have in common—anything they share—is *irrelevant*.

Here's an analogy. Suppose you're trying to decide which of two used cars to buy. Also suppose that both cars are four-door models, about the same size, made in the same model year, with roughly the same amount of mileage on them. Since all of those factors are the *same*, they are all *irrelevant* to your choice—none of these will help you decide which car is better. Instead, you'll have to choose based on ways in which the two cars *differ*—price, for example, or appearance.

In the same way, when comparing two mathematical quantities on the GRE, you can eliminate as irrelevant anything both quantities share. Let's go back to the item we've been considering, with Column A transformed by having been multiplied out:

Column A	Column B
$x^2 + 2xy + y^2$	$x^2 + y^2$

At a glance, you can see that both columns now have two terms in common: x^2 and y^2. We don't know the numeric value of either of these terms, since we don't know the value of either x or y. Nonetheless, we can eliminate both x^2 and y^2 from the comparison because they appear in both columns. The *difference* between the columns can't be contained in what they have in common!

After we eliminate—remove—these two terms from both sides of the comparison, we can compare what remains:

Column A	Column B
$2xy$	0

Having eliminated x^2 and y^2 from Column A, all that's left there is $2xy$. And having made the same elimination from Column B, all that's left there is nothing—zero! So to answer the question, we simply have to decide whether $2xy$ is greater, less than, or equal to zero.

By using the information given above the two quantities, you can determine this. If both unknowns are negative, then when the two are multiplied together, the result is positive. (A negative times a negative is always a positive—a basic algebra principle you need to remember). So xy is positive, and $2xy$, of course, will also be positive—which means it is greater than zero. So the answer to this question is choice (A): Column A is greater than Column B. The quickest way to determine this is to eliminate what both columns have in common and then compare what's left—which is easy.

FYI

In many quantitative comparison items, it's impossible to determine the precise value of one or both quantities. This might tempt you to opt for choice (D), "the relationship can not be determined." Not necessarily! Even imprecise or vague quantities can sometimes be compared. (You know the Sears Tower is taller than your local post office, even if you don't know the actual height of either building.)

Here's another example of the principle of eliminating what the columns share:

Column A	Column B
$35 \times 112 \times 76$	$78 \times 56 \times 2 \times 35$

Whatever you do, *don't* start multiplying. It's time-consuming and may lead to a careless mistake—especially if you start rushing. Quantitative comparison items are generally written to minimize calculations, and this question is no exception; you can answer it with no figuring whatsoever.

First, notice that both "multiplication chains" have one factor in common—35. Eliminate it from both sides. Now the comparison looks like this:

Column A	Column B
112×76	$78 \times 56 \times 2$

Now what? Do you have to start multiplying after all? Not if you're observant. The two columns now have something else in common. The term 112 in Column A is exactly the same in value as the two terms 56×2 in Column B! (You can probably "see" this even without calculating it.) So these values can be eliminated from the two columns as well. All that's left to compare now is:

Column A	Column B
76	78

Obviously, Column B is greater. Not a single multiplication is required.

One more example:

Column A	Column B
The number of prime numbers between 10 and 30	The number of prime numbers between 20 and 40

To answer this question, you need to figure out how many prime numbers there are between 10 and 30 and how many there are between 20 and 40—right? Not quite. Notice that there is an area of overlap between the range of numbers included in these two groups. Primes between 20 and 30 would fall into *both* categories. Therefore, they can be ignored! All you really need to consider is the primes between 10 and 20 (Column A) and the primes between 30 and 40 (Column B).

If you know the definition of a prime number—a number that has exactly two factors, namely 1 and itself—enumerating them isn't too hard. The primes between 10 and 20 are 11, 13, 17, and 19. (Primes, except for 2, must be odd, of course, because all other even numbers are divisible by two.) The primes between 30 and 40 are 31 and 37. There are more primes between 10 and 20, so the answer to this item is choice (A). Notice the time we saved by, in effect, ignoring half of the question—the half that covered the overlap!

Plug in Values for x
Many quantitative comparisons include algebra-style unknowns: x, y, a, n, and so on. Often the quantitative comparison item itself will naturally suggest some algebraic operation; we saw an example in the second problem above, where it seemed natural to multiply out the binomials so as to produce a quantity that would be easier to compare with its counterpart.

After you've taken all the obvious steps, however—multiplying to remove parentheses, simplifying fractions, consolidating like terms, and so on—you will usually still have the mysterious unknown quantity to reckon with. When this happens, take a few seconds to try plugging in a couple of possible values for the unknown and see what happens. Often the correct answer will jump out at you as a result.

Here's an example:

Column A	Column B

$$3r - 4 > 11$$

5	r

FYI

On the real exam, you will have time to plug in possible values on most quantitative comparison items. The math calculations are deliberately kept simple, because the test-makers are more concerned with whether you grasp the underlying arithmetic concepts rather than your ability to carry out the additions, subtractions, multiplications, and divisions. So unless you encounter an unusually complicated problem, don't hesitate to plug in numbers—on most quantitative comparison items you can do the figuring in your head within a few seconds.

Of course, you need to understand the inequality sign here: it means, "is greater than," since it points toward the right side. If $3r - 4$ is greater than 11, what is a possible value of r? Could it be greater than the quantity you're supposed to compare it to, which is 5? Try plugging in an arbitrary value—6, for example—in place of r in the original inequality, and see whether it works:

$$3(6) - 4 > 11$$
$$18 - 4 > 11$$
$$14 > 11$$

Yes, that's correct—14 is greater than 11; so r could equal 6. But to make sure B is the right answer, also try plugging in a value of r that is less than 5:

$$3(4) - 4 > 11$$
$$12 - 4 > 11$$
$$8 > 11?\ \text{NO WAY}$$

Or try making r equal to 5 itself:

$$3(5) - 4 > 11$$
$$15 - 4 > 11$$
$$11 > 11?\ \text{NOPE}$$

(The value 11 is not greater than *itself*, obviously.) So by plugging in three possible values for the unknown—one greater than, one less than, and one equal to the quantity given in the "opposite" column—you can determine that the answer to this question is choice (B).

Note: We've printed out the steps in our calculations here just for clarity's sake, to make it easy for you to follow. But notice how easy the calculations are. Most likely, you won't have to write anything on your scrap paper at all.

Here's one more example of plugging in numbers:

<u>Column A</u>	<u>Column B</u>

$$0 < m < 1$$

m^2	m^3

Again, we don't know the precise value of the unknown m. It doesn't matter. If you're not sure which of the two comparable quantities is greater, plug in a possible value and see what happens. In this case, we know that m is a positive fraction less than 1. Let's plug in the simplest possible value for m, $\frac{1}{2}$. (That will make the calculations a breeze.) If m is $\frac{1}{2}$, then $m^2 = \left(\frac{1}{2}\right)\left(\frac{1}{2}\right) = \left(\frac{1}{4}\right)$, and $m^3 = \left(\frac{1}{2}\right)\left(\frac{1}{2}\right)\left(\frac{1}{2}\right) = \frac{1}{8}$. Since $\frac{1}{4}$ is greater than $\frac{1}{8}$, Column A is greater.

But before filling in the answer space, stop and ask: will the answer be different if the value of m is different? In this case, no. If m is $\frac{1}{4}, \frac{3}{5}, \frac{11}{26}$, or any other positive fraction less than 1, the same relationship will exist—the value continues to go down as the fraction is multiplied repeatedly by itself. (That fact is what the question is designed to test.) But always ask that crucial question—will the answer be different if the value of the unknown is different?—when you plug in a number. That way, you won't be misled by an answer that just *happens* to be true with a particular value for *x*.

FYI

You need to work quantitative comparison items at the rate of about one per minute. That's pretty fast, but it's doable, provided you don't get bogged down in lengthy calculations. If you find, after examining an item for one minute, that you can't see a way of tackling it, make your best guess and move on. As in every part of the GRE CAT, you might need to adjust your guessing strategy depending on where in the test section you are; see Chapter 3 for details.

The Best Tips

Memorize the Answer System

You should practice quantitative comparisons enough before the day of the test so that the weird multiple-choice answer system begins to feel like second nature. You shouldn't have to read the directions or spend any time during the section thinking about which answer comes first, second, third, or fourth.

Look for Math Shortcuts and Use Them Whenever You Find Them

We've already seen that most quantitative comparisons require few calculations and simple ones. This is deliberate: the test-makers are eager to measure your understanding of the underlying concepts rather than your ability to handle the calculations. (And keeping the math simple enables them to throw more questions at you in the same amount of time!) So avoid lengthy or complicated figuring; if a question seems to require it, you've probably overlooked a built-in shortcut.

Here's an example:

Column A	Column B

The average (arithmetic mean) of 5 integers, *m, n, o, p,* and *q,* is 19.

The average (arithmetic mean) of *m, n, o, p, q,* and 17.5	19

On the principle of "When in doubt, try something," your first instinct might be to start working with the definition of "average." As you know, an average is calculated by taking the sum of a set of numbers and dividing it by the number of numbers in the set. In this case, if five integers have an average of 19, it would be possible to calculate the sum of those integers by multiplying the average by the number of numbers ($19 \times 5 = 95$). Then you could go ahead and calculate the sum of the set of six numbers shown in Column A, with the sixth number 17.5 thrown in, and finally divide that new sum by 6 to come up with the new average.

But stop! None of this is necessary. Look at the quantities being compared. All you need to figure out is whether the new average is more or less than 19—the old average. Now, what makes the new average different from the old average? It's simply the new member of the set, the sixth number, 17.5. And will that new member raise or lower the overall average? Because 17.5 is below the old average, it will drag the average down—it will lower it. Therefore, *with no calculations at all*, you can see that the answer will be choice (B): the old average, 19, is greater than the new average, *whatever it is.*

The Most Important Warnings
Assume Nothing!
Quantitative comparisons are designed to test how quickly, creatively, and accurately you can think about a wide range of what might be called "math situations." As you've seen, these situations can be drawn from every area of math: arithmetic, algebra, geometry, word problems, and so on, enabling the test-makers to test your knowledge of techniques in all these areas. One key aspect of accuracy under these conditions is the ability to separate the *facts* you've been given from the *assumptions* you might make—which might or might not be correct.

Let's consider a few examples.

Column A	Column B

In 1990, the price of a certain item was $50.00.

The price of the same item in 1998	$50.00

It's tempting to answer this question based on what you know about the real world. Because of the economic phenomenon known as inflation, prices of most things tend to go up over time (although this is not true of everything: computers, for example, consistently fell in price during the 1990s). Therefore, it's extremely likely that the "certain item" that cost $50.00 in 1990 cost more than that in 1998. The right answer, in that case, would be choice (A).

The logic is tempting—and wrong. You can't assume that inflation applies to this item *because you haven't been told to assume it.* We're not in the "real world" now but rather in GRE territory, where only the facts as stated in the question can be assumed to be true. The correct answer for this item is choice (D)—the relationship can't be determined.

Column A	Column B

Parking is legal on Pine Street only on even-numbered calendar days.

Number of legal parking days in a calendar month	15

Obviously, the number of legal parking days in a calendar month will be somewhere around 15—since half the days are even-numbered days, and most months have around 30 days. But which month are we talking about? The question doesn't specify, so let's think it through. The month could be January or July, with 31 days, of which 15 are even-numbered (the 2nd, the 4th, the 6th, . . . the 30th); it could be June or September, with 30 days, of which the same 15 are even-numbered. The correct answer then would be choice (C): the number of legal parking days (Column A) would be equal to the number 15 (Column B). But the month could also be February, which has only 28 days (except in leap year), of which just 14 are even-numbered. In that case, the correct answer would be choice (B).

FYI

The real meaning of choice (D) is slightly hidden by its wording ("the relationship cannot be determined"). Don't think of it as meaning, "I don't know what the answer is." Instead, think of it as meaning, "More than one answer could be true." If any two choices—(A) and (B), (A) and (C), or (B) and (C)— are both possible, then the correct answer for the item is choice (D).

FYI

Be careful about assumptions when plugging in numbers for an unknown quantity. We're so accustomed to the "counting numbers"—1, 2, 3, and so on—that we easily forget that x may equal zero, a negative number, or a fraction. Any of these possibilities might change the outcome of the comparison. So when plugging in possible values, be sure to include one of each of these number types unless they have been specifically ruled out.

So there are two possible answers—choices (B) and (C)—and we don't know which is correct, because the question doesn't tell us. Sure, there are 11 chances out of 12 that the month is *not* February, but we can't make that assumption. Because choice (C) is correct under one possible assumption and choice (B) is correct under another, the correct answer is choice (D)—it cannot determined.

One more example of the danger of making assumptions:

Column A	**Column B**

On a certain day, 30 percent of the females were absent and 50 percent of the males were present in a history class.

Number of females present	Number of males present

From the information given, you can tell that the percentage of females present was greater than the percentage of males present (70 versus 50). But notice what you are being asked to compare: not the percentage of females and males present, but the *number* present. We know nothing about this because we don't know *how many* females or males were enrolled in the history class. You might, without much thought, assume that the number of females and males is approximately equal—but that's simply an assumption, with no special validity. The correct answer for this item is choice (D)—it cannot be determined.

Strictly speaking, there *are* a few—a very few—facts you can safely assume on quantitative comparison items:

- Everyday facts like the number of inches in a foot and the number of days in a week are fair game.

- The basic formulas from geometry (for calculating the area of a circle or a triangle, for example) are not only assumed—you should know them by heart. (You'll find them in Appendix B, of course.)

- And you can assume, as the test-makers state in the general notes that precede each quantitative section, that all the numbers used (including unknowns, like *x*), are "real numbers" (as opposed to "imaginary numbers," a special kind of number used only in certain quite specialized and advanced math operations).

Other than these facts, however, you should avoid assuming anything—as you've seen, it's dangerous.

When There's No Unknown, Don't Guess Choice (D)
On quantitative comparison items, as on every other kind of question, there might be times when you have to guess. Perhaps you will find yourself running out of time with several questions still left to answer, or perhaps a couple of items will call for math skills you just can't recall. General guessing strategy for quantitative comparisons should be much the same as for other question types: follow a hunch, if you have one; when you can, eliminate answers and guess from what remains; and guess more cautiously and selectively toward the end of the test section than near the beginning.

However, there's one special rule about guessing that applies only to quantitative comparisons. On about one third of quantitative comparison items, no unknown quantity is involved: there is no algebraic x or n, nor is there any geometric quantity (the degree measure of an angle or the length of a line segment, say) that is unknowable. Whenever this is true, the answer cannot be choice (D). Even if you, for whatever reason, can't figure out which quantity is greater, it is theoretically *possible* to figure it out—so choice (D) is an incorrect option.

Here's an example:

Column A	Column B
Price of a $320 stereo after a discount of 15%	$275

If you've run out of time or have momentarily forgotten how to multiply by a percentage, you may not be able to answer this question. (Since $320 \times 85\% = \$272$, the answer is choice (B).) However, the question itself does not contain any unknown quantity. Therefore, if you have to guess on a question like this, don't guess (D). Because there is no unknown, only choices (A), (B), and (C) are possible answers.

JUST THE FACTS

- Quantitative Comparisons feature a weird multiple-choice answer system that you must understand and memorize.

- Do whatever you can to make the two quantities to be compared look as similar as possible.

- Simplify the comparison by eliminating what both quantities have in common.

- Use math shortcuts whenever you can.

- Never assume any information not explicitly stated in the question.

PRACTICE, PRACTICE, PRACTICE: QUANTITATIVE COMPARISON EXERCISES

Instructions

The following exercises will give you a chance to practice the skills and strategies you've just learned for tackling quantitative comparisons. As with all practice exercises, work under true testing conditions. Complete each exercise in a single sitting. Eliminate distractions (TV, music) and clear away notes and reference materials.

Time yourself with a stopwatch or kitchen timer, or have someone else time you. If you run out of time before answering all the questions, stop and draw a line under the last question you finished. Then go ahead and tackle the remaining questions. When you are done, score yourself based only on the questions you finished in the allotted time.

Write the letter of your response next to each question.

Understanding Your Scores

0–3 correct: A poor performance. Study this chapter again, as well as the Insider's GRE Math Review (Appendix B).

4–6 correct: A below-average score. Study this chapter again, as well as all portions of the Insider's GRE Math review (Appendix B) that cover topics you find unfamiliar or difficult.

7–9 correct: An average score. You may want to study this chapter again. Also be sure you are managing your time wisely (as explained in Chapter 3) and avoiding errors due to haste or carelessness.

10–12 correct: An above-average score. Depending on your personal target score and your strength on other quantitative question types, you may or may not want to devote additional time to quantitative comparisons.

13–15 correct: An excellent score. You are probably ready to perform well on GRE quantitative comparison items.

EXERCISE 1

15 Questions

Time—15 Minutes

> **Directions:** Compare the two quantities and choose
>
> (A) if the quantity in Column A is greater;
> (B) if the quantity in Column B is greater;
> (C) if the two quantities are equal;
> (D) if the relationship cannot be determined from the information given.

Column A	Column B

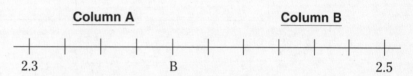

Note: The vertical marks in the figure above are equally spaced.

1.

2.37	B

2.

The price of a coat that cost $200 wholesale sold at a 40% markup	The price of a coat listed at $300 on sale at 10% off

Column A	Column B

3.
$$n^3$$

$$n^2$$

$$n > 7$$

4.
$$\frac{n}{6}$$

$$\frac{6}{n}$$

5.

The area of a circle with a diameter of 10	The area of a square with a diagonal of 12

Column A   **Column B**

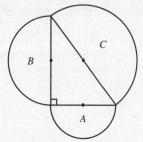

The sides of the triangle are the diameters of the semicircles.

6.

| The area of semicircle C | The sum of the areas of semicircles A and B |

$$2n - 5 < 7$$

7.

| n | 6 |

Column A	**Column B**

In $\triangle ABC$, $\angle B$ is $50°$ more than $\angle A$, and the degree measure of $\angle C$ is three times the degree measure of $\angle A$.

8.

The degree measure of $\angle B$	The degree measure of $\angle C$

9.

n^4	4^n

$$n = m - 2$$
$$m = s + 4$$

10.

n	s

Column A	Column B

$$2n - m = 6$$
$$2n + m = 10$$

11.

m	2

12.

$3^2 3^3$	$(3^2)^3$

One negative number is 5 more than another.
Their product is 23 more than their sum.

13.

The sum of the numbers	-10

	Column A	**Column B**

$$xyz = 18$$
$$x < 0$$

14.

z	0

$$x \neq -1$$

15.

$\dfrac{3x + 1}{x + 1}$	2

EXERCISE 2

15 Questions

Time—15 Minutes

> **Directions:** Compare the two quantities and choose
>
> (A)   if the quantity in Column A is greater;
> (B)   if the quantity in Column B is greater;
> (C)   if the two quantities are equal;
> (D)   if the relationship cannot be determined from the infor-
>   mation given.

Column A		Column B

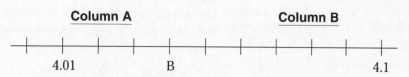

4.01   B   4.1

Note: The vertical marks in the figure above are equally spaced.

1.

The distance from B to 4.1	0.07

2.

The price of a $300 item marked up 10% and then marked down 20%	The price of a $300 item marked down 20% and then marked up 10%

Column A	Column B

3. | n^3 | $3n^2$ |

In a group of 18 students taking Spanish or German, 12 are taking Spanish, and 4 are taking both Spanish and German.

4. | The number taking Spanish but not German | The number taking German but not Spanish |

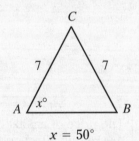

$x = 50°$

5. | AB | 7 |

	Column A	**Column B**

$$5r - 2s = 2$$

6. $\quad(-1)^{(10r - 4s)}$ $\qquad\qquad$ $(-1)^{(15r - 6s)}$

The number of miles from A to B by train is 42. The number of miles from B to C by train is 62.

7.
The number of stations between A and B	The number of stations between B and C

Column A	Column B

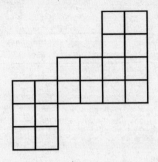

All the small squares are the same size.
The area of the region shown is 72.

8.

The perimeter of the region shown	50

$x = 2$

9.

1.10	$x^0 + x^{-4}$

Column A	**Column B**

$$10 - x > x$$

10.

x	5

Seven less than half a number n is 5.

11.

One third of n	8

A circle of diameter d and a square of side s have the same area.

12.

s	d

	Column A	**Column B**

$$t > 0$$

13.

$\dfrac{t^2 + 5t}{t}$	$t + 5$

$$x^2 + 2y^2 = 1$$
$$x = \frac{1}{2}$$

14.

$|y|$	$\dfrac{1}{2}$

$$0 < n < 1$$

15.

$3n^3$	$3^3 n$

EXERCISE 3

15 Questions

Time—15 Minutes

> **Directions:** Compare the two quantities and choose
>
> (A)   if the quantity in Column A is greater;
> (B)   if the quantity in Column B is greater;
> (C)   if the two quantities are equal;
> (D)   if the relationship cannot be determined from the information given.

Column A	Column B
1. The remainder when 6,037,854 is divided by 6	The remainder when 3,521,912 is divided by 8

$$x - 5 = 2$$

2. $x + 3$	11

Column A	Column B

Arnold's car used 22 gallons of gas last week.
Marla's car used 16 gallons of gas last week.

3.
The number of miles Arnold drove last week.	The number of miles Marla drove last week.

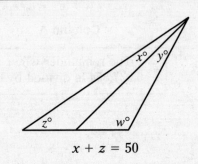

$$x + z = 50$$

4.
$y + w$	130

Column A	**Column B**

$$x > 2$$

5.

x^2	2^x

$$r < s < t$$
The average (arithmetic mean) of r, s, and t is 90.

6.

The average of s and t	90

$$xy = 21$$
$$x < 3$$

7.

7	y

Column A	Column B

$$S = \{1,2,2,2,3,5,6,7,8\}$$

8.

The mean minus the median of S	The median minus the mode of S

$$x - 4 = -2$$
$$2 - y = 4$$

9.

y	x

$$3x + 9 > 6$$

10.

$x + 2$	1

| **Column A** | **Column B** |

The cost of 4 rolls, 6 muffins, and 3 loaves of bread is $9.10.
The cost of 2 rolls, 3 muffins, and a loaf of bread is $3.90.

11.

| The cost of a roll | The cost of a muffin |

12.

| $(x - 1)^2$ | $x^2 - 1$ |

13.

| $\sqrt{13}$ | $2\sqrt{3}$ |

	Column A	Column B

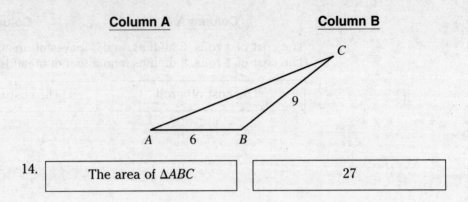

14.

The area of $\triangle ABC$	27

A marble is drawn at random from a box containing 4 red marbles and 6 white marbles.

15.

The probability that the marble is white	$\dfrac{2}{3}$

EXERCISE 4

15 Questions

Time—15 Minutes

> **Directions:** Compare the two quantities and choose
>
> (A)   if the quantity in Column A is greater;
> (B)   if the quantity in Column B is greater;
> (C)   if the two quantities are equal;
> (D)   if the relationship cannot be determined from the information given.

Column A	Column B
$\dfrac{-6}{11}$	$\dfrac{13}{-22}$

$x < 0$ and $y > 0$

2.

$-4x^4y^3$	0

	Column A	Column B

Apples sell for $2 a dozen.
Pears sell for $3 a dozen.

3.

The price of 18 apples and 24 pears	$9

$$5 - t = 3t$$

4.

$2t$	2

$$xy^2 = 4$$
$$x = 9$$
$$y > 0$$

5.

y	$\dfrac{2}{3}$

Column A	**Column B**

$$y > 0$$

6.

$9y - \dfrac{6y^3}{2y^2}$	$6y$

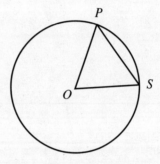

Arc *PS* in the figure above has a degree measure of 62°.
The diameter of the circle is 18.

7.

The length of chord *PS*	9

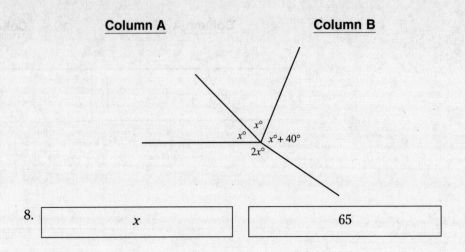

Column A	Column B

8.

x	65

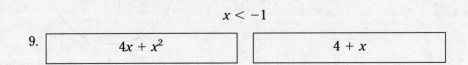

$$x < -1$$

9.

$4x + x^2$	$4 + x$

Column A	Column B

p percent of 120 is less than 90

10.

p	80

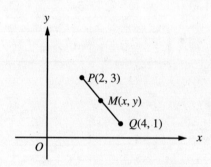

M is the midpoint of $\overline{PQ}$

11.

x	y

	Column A	Column B

$$4x - 2y = 2$$

12. | $(2x - y)^2$ | 1 |

$$x < -2$$

13. | x^2 | $-2x$ |

Column A	Column B

$$x^2 + 2y^2 = 1$$
$$y = \frac{1}{2}$$

14.

$|x|$	1

15.

The median of the set 1,2,2,2,2,3,4,4,4,4,4	4

EXERCISE 5

15 Questions

Time—15 Minutes

> **Directions:** Compare the two quantities and choose
>
> (A) if the quantity in Column A is greater;
> (B) if the quantity in Column B is greater;
> (C) if the two quantities are equal;
> (D) if the relationship cannot be determined from the information given.

Column A	Column B

Twelve boxes of crackers cost $4.80.
Eight boxes of cookies cost $4.00.

1.
The price of one box of crackers	The price of one box of cookies

2.
$(2 + x)^2$	$(2x)^2$

Column A	**Column B**
$m < n < 0$	
3.	
$3m^2 n^3$	0

Column A	**Column B**
$x > y$	
4.	
x^2	y^2

Column A	**Column B**
$z + 3 = 5$	
5.	
$2z + 7$	10

Column A   **Column B**

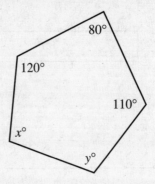

6.

$x + y$	220

a is chosen from set $A = \{-1, -3, 2\}$
b is chosen from set $B = \{-4, 6, 8\}$

7.

The largest possible value of $\dfrac{a}{b}$	1

Column A	**Column B**
8. The volume of a rectangular solid that has height 6 feet and has a square base of side 4	The volume of a cylinder with a length of 7 feet and a diameter of 4

$$\sqrt{5} \cdot \sqrt{x} = 10$$

9. $\sqrt{x}$	$2\sqrt{5}$

$$x < 0 < y$$

10. $\dfrac{\dfrac{x}{y}}{\dfrac{y}{x}}$	$\dfrac{x}{y}$

	Column A	Column B

$$x = y + 3$$
$$y = 1 - z$$

11.

	x		z

The cost of 4 cookies, 6 doughnuts, and 3 boxes of doughnut holes is $8.15.

The cost of 2 cookies, 3 doughnuts, and 4 boxes of doughnut holes is $7.20.

12.

The cost of one box of doughnut holes	$1.25

	Column A	Column B

$$x \neq \frac{1}{2}$$

13.

$\dfrac{x}{2x-1}$	$\dfrac{1}{2} - x$

14.

The length of the hypotenuse of a triangle with legs of lengths 3 and 5	6

$$x + 2y - 3z = 5$$
$$2x + 2y + 3z = 8$$

15.

$9x + 12y$	39

Answer Key

Exercise 1	Exercise 2	Exercise 3	Exercise 4	Exercise 5
1. B	1. B	1. C	1. A	1. B
2. A	2. C	2. B	2. B	2. D
3. D	3. D	3. D	3. C	3. B
4. A	4. A	4. C	4. A	4. D
5. A	5. A	5. A	5. C	5. A
6. C	6. C	6. A	6. C	6. A
7. B	7. D	7. D	7. A	7. B
8. B	8. B	8. C	8. B	8. A
9. D	9. A	9. B	9. D	9. C
10. A	10. B	10. A	10. B	10. A
11. C	11. C	11. D	11. A	11. D
12. B	12. B	12. D	12. C	12. C
13. A	13. C	13. A	13. A	13. D
14. D	14. A	14. B	14. B	14. B
15. D	15. B	15. B	15. B	15. C

Explanatory Answers

EXERCISE 1

1. **The correct answer is (B).** The vertical marks are spaced at intervals of 0.02, so B=2.38 > 2.37.

2. **The correct answer is (A).** 40% of 200 = 0.4(200) = 80, so with the markup, the value in Column A = 200 + 80 = 280. In Column B, subtracting 10% of 300 (which equals 30) leaves only 270.

3. **The correct answer is (D).** The answer for this item depends entirely upon what x is. If x is 0 or 1, the two columns are equal. If $x > 1$, then $x^3 > x^2$, while the reverse is true if x is between 0 and 1.

4. **The correct answer is (A).** Since $n > 7$, $\frac{n}{6} > 1$, and $\frac{6}{n} < 1$.

5. **The correct answer is (A).** A circle with a diameter of 10 has a radius of 5 and an area of $\pi 5^2 = 25\pi$. A square with a diagonal of 12 has a side of $\frac{12}{\sqrt{2}}$ and an area of $\left(\frac{12}{\sqrt{2}}\right)^2 = 72$. Since $\pi > 3$, the area of the circle is greater than 75.

6. **The correct answer is (C).** Since the area of a circle is πr^2, the area of a semicircle is $\frac{1}{2}\pi r^2$. Since $r = \frac{1}{2}d$, we know that the area of the semicircle is $\frac{\pi d^2}{8}$. Calling the sides of the triangles a, b, and c, we know that $a^2 + b^2 = c^2$, which we multiply by $\frac{\pi}{8}$ to see that the two columns are equal.

7. **The correct answer is (B).** Adding 5 to both sides of the inequality, we see that $2n < 12$, and dividing by 2, that $n < 6$.

8. **The correct answer is (B).** The sum of the angles in the triangle must be 180. Letting the degree measure of $\angle A$ be x, we have $x + 50$ for $\angle B$, and $3x$ for $\angle C$. Now:

$$x + (x + 50) + 3x = 180$$
$$5x + 50 = 180$$
$$x = 26$$

Hence, m$\angle B = 76°$, and m$\angle C = 78°$.

9. **The correct answer is (D).** This depends upon what n is. For example, if n is 1, then $n^4 = 1$, and $4n = 4$. But if $n = 2$, both are equal to 16, and if $n = 3$, the first quantity is 81, while the second is 64.

10. **The correct answer is (A).** Substituting from the second equation into the first gives us $n = s + 4 - 2$, and $n = s + 2$. Hence, $n > s$.

11. **The correct answer is (C).** Adding the two equations gives us $4n = 16$, so $n = 4$. Knowing that $n = 4$, the second equation tells us that $8 + m = 10$, and $m = 2$.

12. **The correct answer is (B).** $3^2 3^3 = 3^{2+3} = 3^5 = 243$, but $(3^2)^3 = 3^{2 \times 3} = 3^6 = 729$.

13. **The correct answer is (A).** Letting the smaller number be x, the larger is $(x + 5)$. Hence:

$$x(x + 5) = x + (x + 5) + 23$$
$$x^2 + 5x = 2x + 28$$
$$x^2 + 3x - 28 = 0$$

This factors as:

$$(x + 7)(x - 4) = 0$$
$$x + 7 = 0 \text{ or } x - 4 = 0$$

Hence, $x = -7$ and $x + 5 = -2$, with sum -9, or $x = 4$ and $x + 5 = 9$, with sum 13. We must choose the negative value, $-9 > -10$.

14. **The correct answer is (D).** The fact that $xyz = 18$ means that the product of x, y, and z is positive. Since x is negative, then yz must be negative. That means that either y or z is negative, but we do not know which, so we cannot tell the relationship between z and 0.

15. **The correct answer is (D).** If $x = 0$, then Column A is 1, which is less than 2; but if $x = 10$ (for example), Column A is $\frac{31}{11}$, which is greater than 2.

EXERCISE 2

1. **The correct answer is (B).** The vertical marks are spaced at intervals equal to 0.01, so B = 4.04. The distance from 4.04 to 4.10 is $4.10 - 4.04 = 0.06 < 0.07$.

2. **The correct answer is (C).** In the Column A case, you take 300(1.10) (0.80). In the Column B case, you take 300 (0.80) (1.10). The result in both cases is the same: 264.

3. **The correct answer is (D).** This depends entirely upon what x is. For example, if x is 1 or 2, $x^3 < 3x^2$. If $x = 4$, $x^3 > 3x^2$.

4. **The correct answer is (A).** Of the 12 students taking Spanish, 4 are taking both languages, leaving 8 taking only Spanish. Since 12 of the 18 are taking Spanish, just 6 are taking only German. Thus, the number in Column A is larger.

5. **The correct answer is (A).** Since $AC = BC = 7$, the triangle is isosceles. Hence, the base angles are both 50°, making the vertex angle 80°. Since the side opposite the larger angle is the longer side, $AB > 7$.

6. **The correct answer is (C).** Since $5r - 2s = 2$, $10r - 4s = 2(5r - 2s) = 4$. Then, $(-1)^4 = 1$; $15r - 6s = 3(5r - 2s) = 6$. And $(-1)^6 = 1$.

7. **The correct answer is (D).** There is no information about the spacing of stations. So you cannot tell which quantity might be larger.

8. **The correct answer is (B).** There are 18 small squares with a total area of 72. Thus, each has an area of 4 square units and sides of length 2. Counting the sides that make up the perimeter, there are 24, for a length of 48.

9. **The correct answer is (A).** If $x = 2$, $x^0 = 2^0 = 1$; and $x^{-4} = 2^{-4} = \frac{1}{2^4} = \frac{1}{16} = 0.0625$. Hence, $x + x^{-4} = 1.0625$, which is less than 1.10.

10. **The correct answer is (B).** Adding x to both sides of the inequality, we see that $10 > 2x$, and dividing both sides by 2, $5 > x$.

11. **The correct answer is (C).** The verbal description leads to the equation $\frac{1}{2}n - 7 = 5$, for which $n = 24$. So one-third of 24 is 8.

12. **The correct answer is (B).** The radius of a circle is $\frac{1}{2}d$. Hence, the area of the circle is $\frac{1}{4}\pi d^2$. The area of the square is s^2. If the two are equal, $\frac{1}{4}\pi d^2 = s^2$; that is, $\pi d^2 = 4s^2$. Since $\pi < 4$, the two can only be equal if $d > s$. Geometrically, unless $d > s$, the entire circle can be fitted inside the square and therefore must have less area.

13. **The correct answer is (C).** As long as $t \neq 0$, we can divide out the common factor of t in the numerator and denominator of $\frac{t^2 + 5t}{t}$ to get $t + 5$. Hence, the two are equal.

14. **The correct answer is (A).** If $x = \frac{1}{2}$, then $x^2 + 2y^2 = \frac{1}{4} + 2y^2 = 1$ implies that $2y^2 = \frac{3}{4}$ and $y^2 = \frac{3}{8}$. Now, $|y| = \sqrt{\frac{3}{8}} = \sqrt{0.375} \approx 0.6 > 0.5$.

15. **The correct answer is (B).** Taking the difference, $3n^3 - 3^3n = 3n^3 - 27n = 3n(n^2 - 9)$. Since n is between 0 and 1, $n^2 < 9$, and $3n(n^2 - 9) < 0$. Thus, $3n^3 < 3^3n$.

EXERCISE 3

1. **The correct answer is (C).** 6,037,854 is divisible by 6, and 3,521,912 is divisible by 8. Hence, both give remainder 0.

2. **The correct answer is (B).** We solve $x - 5 = 2$, getting $x = 7$. Column A is now $x + 3 = 10 < 11$.

3. **The correct answer is (D).** Since we do not know how many miles per gallon each car gets, and they may not be the same, we cannot tell.

4. **The correct answer is (C).** $x + y$ is the measure of the top angle in the large triangle. Hence, $x + y + z + w = 180$. Since $x + z = 50$, $y + w = 130$.

5. **The correct answer is (A).** Since $x > 2$, $xx > 2x$, that is, $x^2 > 2x$.

6. **The correct answer is (A).** The average of a group of numbers must increase if you take out the smallest number in the group. Thus, the average of s and t must be larger than 90.

7. **The correct answer is (D).** If $x < 3$, and x is positive, then $xy = 21$ implies that $y > 7$. However, x could be negative, in which case, so is y.

8. **The correct answer is (C).** The median (middle number) is 3, the mode is 2, and the mean is $(1 + 2 + 2 + 2 + 3 + 5 + 6 + 7 + 8) \div 9 = 4$. Thus, the mean minus the median is $4 - 3 = 1$, and the median minus the mode is $3 - 2 = 1$. Thus, the two quantities are equal.

9. **The correct answer is (B).** Solving the first equation: $x = -2 + 4 = 2$. Solving the second equation: $-4 + 2 = y$, $y = -2$. Hence, $x > y$.

10. **The correct answer is (A).** Solving the inequality: $3x > 6 - 9$, $3x > -3$, $x > -1$. Adding 2 to both sides now yields: $x + 2 > 1$.

11. **The correct answer is (D).** Using the obvious notation:

    $$4r + 6m + 3b = 910$$
    $$2r + 3m + b = 390$$

    Multiplying the second equation by -2 and adding the two together, we have $b = 130$. Hence, we know the price of the bread; but that leaves us two identical equations relating r and m—namely, $2r + 3m = 260$—and we have no way of knowing whether r or b is larger.

12. **The correct answer is (D).** If $x = 1$, the two quantities are equal. However, when $x = 0$, the Column A quantity is positive, while the Column B quantity is negative and is thus smaller. If $x = 2$, the inequality goes the other way.

13. **The correct answer is (A).** $2\sqrt{3} = \sqrt{12} < \sqrt{13}$.

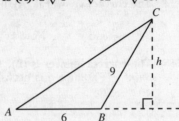

14. **The correct <u>answer</u> is (B).** Dropping the perpendicular from C down to the extension of AB (as in figure above), we see that the altitude of the triangle, h, is less than 9, and the area of $\triangle ABC$ is thus less than $\frac{1}{2}(6)(9) = 27$.

15. **The correct answer is (B).** The probability that the marble is white is given by the number of white marbles (6) divided by the total number of marbles (10); that is, $\frac{3}{5} < \frac{2}{3}$.

EXERCISE 4

1. **The correct answer is (A).** First of all, it does not matter where you put the negative sign—numerator, denominator, or opposite the fraction bar; if there is one negative sign, the fraction is negative. Remember, in comparing negative numbers, the one with the larger absolute value is the least number. So start by ignoring the signs, and compare the absolute values of the fractions. If the two fractions had a common denominator (or numerator) it would be easy. So multiply the numerator and denominator of $\frac{6}{11}$ by 2 to yield $\frac{12}{22}$ and it is easy to see that $\frac{13}{22}$ is the larger. Hence, $\frac{-6}{11}$ is the greater number.

2. **The correct answer is (B).** x^4 is positive, because it has an even power. y^3 is positive, because y is, and -4 is obviously negative. The product of two positives and a negative is negative. Thus, $-4x^4y^3 < 0$.

3. **The correct answer is (C).** 18 apples is $1\frac{1}{2}$ or 1.5 dozen. At \$2 per dozen, that totals \$3. 24 pears is 2 dozen. At \$3 per dozen, that totals \$6. The grand total is \$9.

4. **The correct answer is (A).** Solving the given equation, $5 = 4t$, $t = \frac{5}{4}$, and $2t = \frac{5}{2} = 2.5 > 2$.

5. **The correct answer is (C).** Since $x = 9$, the given equation is $9y^2 = 4$, or $y^2 = \frac{4}{9}$; $y = \pm\frac{2}{3}$. Since $y > 0$, it must be $y = \frac{2}{3}$.

6. **The correct answer is (C).** $\frac{6y^3}{2y^2} = 3y$ and $9y - 3y = 6y$.

7. **The correct answer is (A).** The triangle is isosceles, because all radii of the same circle are equal in length. Therefore, the base angles are equal, and each is 59°. This implies that the chord is longer than the radius, which is 9.

8. **The correct answer is (B).** The sum of the angles around a point must be 360°. Thus:

$$x + x + (x + 40) + 2x = 360$$
$$5x + 40 = 360$$
$$5x = 320$$
$$x = 64$$

9. **The correct answer is (D).** Factoring: $4x + x^2 = x(4 + x)$. The quantities are thus equal if $x = -4$, but not otherwise. For example, if $x = -2$, A > B, but if $x = -6$, B > A.

10. **The correct answer is (B).** p percent is $\dfrac{p}{100}$. Hence, "p percent of 120 is less than 90" means $\dfrac{p}{100}(120) < 90$. That is, $\dfrac{6p}{5} < 90$. Multiplying by 5: $6p < 450$; and dividing by 6: $p < 75$.

11. **The correct answer is (A).** x is the average of 2 and 4, that is, $x = 3$. y is the average of 3 and 1, that is, $y = 2$.

12. **The correct answer is (C).** Dividing the given equation by 2, we get $2x - y = 1$. Thus, $(2x - y)^2 = 1$.

13. **The correct answer is (A).** If $x < -2$, then x is negative; so $x(x) > x(-2)$, that is, $x^2 > -2x$.

14. **The correct answer is (B).** If $y = \dfrac{1}{2}$, $x^2 + 2y^2 = x^2 + \dfrac{1}{2} = 1$ implies that $x^2 = \dfrac{1}{2}$, and $|x| = \sqrt{\dfrac{1}{2}} = \sqrt{0.5} \approx 0.7 < 1$.

15. **The correct answer is (B).** The median is the middle number. In this case, there are 11 numbers, and the middle one is 3.

EXERCISE 5

1. **The correct answer is (B).** From the first line, each box of crackers cost $4.80 \div 12 = .40$ or 40¢. From the second line, each box of cookies costs $4.00 \div 8 = 0.50$ or 50¢.

2. **The correct answer is (D).** You really cannot tell. For example, if $x = 0$, in Column A you have 4, and in Column B you have 0. But if $x = -2$, Column A is 0 and Column B is 16.

3. **The correct answer is (B).** m^2 must be positive, since m is not zero. n^3 is negative, because n is. Hence, $3m^2n^3 < 0$.

4. **The correct answer is (D).** $x^2 > y^2$ if $x > y$ and if both are positive. But either or both variables could be negative, so you need more information.

5. **The correct answer is (A).** Solving the equation: $z = 2$. Now, $2z + 7 = 11 > 10$.

6. **The correct answer is (A).** If you divide a pentagon into triangles, you should convince yourself that the sum of the angles it contains must be 540°. Since the three given angles total 310°, the other two must total 230°.

7. **The correct answer is (B).** The largest possible value of $\frac{a}{b}$ using positive numbers in the numerator and denominator is $\frac{2}{6}$. Using negative numbers, the largest value is $\frac{-3}{-4} = \frac{3}{4}$. In either case, it is smaller than 1.

8. **The correct answer is (A).** The volume of the rectangular solid is $V = (4)(4)(6) = 96$. The radius of the cylinder is 2, so its volume is $V_C = \pi(2)^2(7) = 28\pi$. Since π equals around $\frac{22}{7}$, 28π equals around 88. Therefore, the rectangular solid is larger.

9. **The correct answer is (C).** Since $10 = \sqrt{100}$ and $\sqrt{5} \cdot \sqrt{x} = \sqrt{5x}$, we know that $5x = 100$, and $x = 20$. But $20 = 4 \times 5$, so $\sqrt{20} = 2\sqrt{5}$. Hence, the two quantities are equal.

10. **The correct answer is (A).** $\dfrac{\frac{x}{y}}{\frac{y}{x}} = \frac{x}{y} \times \frac{x}{y} = \frac{x^2}{y^2} = \left(\frac{x}{y}\right)^2$. So the question is, which is larger, $\left(\frac{x}{y}\right)^2$ or $\frac{x}{y}$? But x and y have opposite signs, so the fraction $\frac{x}{y}$ is negative. The square of the fraction is positive and is thus larger than the fraction itself.

11. **The correct answer is (D).** Substituting from the second equation into the first gives us $x = 1 - z + 3$ and $x = 4 - z$. This tells us that $x + z = 4$, but, for example, x could be 3 and z could be 1, or the reverse. Either way, both conditions would be satisfied.

12. **The correct answer is (C).** Using the obvious notation, we have:

$$4c + 6d + 3h = 815$$
$$2c + 3d + 4h = 720$$

Multiplying the second equation by -2 and adding them yields:

$$-5h = -625$$
$$h = 125$$

13. **The correct answer is (D).** You cannot tell. For example, if $x = 0$, Column A is 0 and Column B is $\frac{1}{2}$. However, if $x = 1$, Column A is 1 and Column B is $-\frac{1}{2}$.

14. **The correct answer is (B).** By the Pythagorean Theorem, $c^2 = \sqrt{3^2 + 5^2} = \sqrt{34} < 6$.

15. **The correct answer is (C).** Adding the two equations, we have $3x + 4y = 13$. Multiplying by 3, we have $9x + 12y = 39$.

Chapter 10

Logical Reasoning

Get the Scoop On . . .

- Tested techniques for conquering logical reasoning questions
- How to recognize the three key elements in every logical argument
- The six types of logical fallacies most often tested on the GRE
- The four question types you'll encounter, and how to answer each one
- The dangers of "creative" and "sophisticated" thinking, and how to avoid them

THE TEST CAPSULE

What's the Big Idea?

You'll be given a short reading passage, 50–100 words long, which presents a logical argument designed to prove a point of some kind. You'll then have to answer a question that requires you to evaluate the logic of the passage.

How Many?

Of the 35 total questions in the analytical section, your GRE will probably have a total of 11 logical reasoning questions.

How Much Do They Count?

Because logical reasoning questions are 11 out of 35 total analytical questions, they count as 31 percent of your overall analytical score.

How Much Time Should They Take?

You need to answer logical reasoning questions at a rate of about two minutes per question.

What's the Best Strategy?

Learn to look for the six most common types of fallacies—logical errors—that are built into most logical reasoning passages. If you can recognize these, you'll be able to demolish the faulty arguments that turn up on the exam and ace the questions related to them.

What's the Worst Pitfall?

Responding to a logical reasoning passage or to the accompanying question on the basis of what you know or believe to be true. You might have strong opinions or extensive personal knowledge about some of the topics discussed in this part of the exam. Forget it all! A worthy point of view might be defended ineptly in a logical reading passage, while a despicable position may be argued ably. All you should care about is the strength or weakness of the argument on the screen—not the validity of the underlying opinions.

THE OFFICIAL DESCRIPTION

What They Are

Logical reasoning is a specialized kind of reading comprehension in which the emphasis is placed on your ability to understand and analyze the logic behind an argument. You'll be given a short passage to read, which may resemble an excerpt from a magazine article, a book, a newspaper editorial, a political speech, an advertisement, or even a snippet of conversation. In every case, the passage presents an argument—that is, an attempt to persuade the reader of the truth of some statement. You'll then be asked to answer a question that focuses in one way or another on the strength or weakness of the argument.

Where They Are

On the typical GRE, you'll have one analytical section that is 60 minutes long. It will include eleven logical reasoning questions interspersed seemingly at random among several analytical reasoning puzzles that make up the rest of the section. Reminder: The test-makers claim the right to change the format at any time! However, the typical format we just described is what you're most likely to encounter.

What They Measure

You're not expected to bring any special background knowledge to logical reasoning questions. The passages contain all the information necessary to answer the questions; so even if a passage deals with a topic you know absolutely nothing about (the second law of thermodynamics, say, or drunk driving laws in Oregon), don't be concerned—you'll be told everything you need to know.

In addition, formal logic is not tested on the GRE. You won't be required to solve a syllogism or use specialized terms or symbols from logic. If you've taken a logic course, fine—it won't hurt; but you're not at a disadvantage if you haven't. The key skill being tested is the ability to think clearly and to see the flaws in the fuzzy thinking of others.

The Directions

> **Directions:** Each question or group of questions is based on a passage or set of conditions. In answering some of the questions, it may be useful to draw a rough diagram. For each question, select the best answer choice given.

THE INSIDER'S REPORT

Strategies That Really Work

Learn to Recognize the Key Elements of Any Argument

The word *argument* as used here might be a bit misleading. We don't mean a quarrel (the way "argument" is usually used in everyday life: "My aunt and uncle had another argument, and she threw his clothes out all over the front lawn again"). Instead, we're using the word to mean any attempt to persuade you of a particular fact, idea, or opinion.

In this sense, you encounter arguments by the dozens every day. Your spouse or best friend tries to talk you into taking a vacation in the mountains instead of by the shore; she marshals arguments to persuade you that her plan will be more fun, more affordable, more whatever. A commentator on the radio holds forth about the latest political controversy; he fires arguments at you in an attempt to convince you of his point of view. And what is an advertisement if not an argument designed to persuade you that a certain product or service is the best available and that you'll be happy if you buy it?

The fact is, you're constantly bombarded by arguments. Some are sound and valid (maybe a cabin in the Rockies *would* be a nice change this year); others are laughably inept (think of the last TV commercial whose idiocy made you snort). In most cases, however, you probably don't bother to analyze the arguments you hear carefully—nor should you. A quick "gut check" is often enough in real life to tell you whether or not you believe a particular argument, and in most cases you won't go far wrong making decisions on that basis.

Logical reasoning on the GRE attempts to test your ability to evaluate arguments in a more formal, rigorous fashion. The gut instinct for baloney that most of us develop through a lifetime of exposure to TV commercials, newspaper editorials, and political rhetoric will be your main weapon in tackling these questions. But it also helps to have at your disposal a few basic tools for analyzing and understanding arguments in a consistent, formal fashion. When the questions on the exam get tricky, subtle, or complicated, these tools can help you.

Table 10.1
Clue Words That Signal Conclusions

therefore	we can conclude
consequently	which shows that
hence	it can be inferred that
thus	it is apparent that
so	we must agree that

The first tool you need is a knowledge of the basic structure of any argument. As presented on the GRE, almost every argument has three elements: a *conclusion*; *evidence* to support the conclusion; and one or more *hidden assumptions* on which the argument rests. Let's consider each more closely.

The *conclusion* is what the author of the argument is trying to get you to believe or agree with. It will normally be stated explicitly somewhere in the passage (though not always, as we'll discuss later). The conclusion might sound like a statement of fact ("One third of the physicians in the Denver area own foreign sports cars"); it might sound like an opinion ("The new Alberghetti convertible is fun to drive!"); it might even sound like a call to action ("You should test-drive the new Alberghetti today"). In each case, the conclusion is what the rest of the argument is intended to support or prove.

FYI

Don't be misled by the word conclusion. *The conclusion of an argument need not appear at or near the end of the argument. It might appear anywhere— beginning, end, or middle. You'll recognize the conclusion by looking for the clue words that usually mark its presence.*

The conclusion is often signaled by one or more *clue words* inserted specifically to alert the reader to the fact that the main point of the argument is coming. We've listed some of the most common examples in Table 10.1. Practice looking for them whenever you read.

The *evidence* is the material that the author of the argument is using to try to convince you to agree with the conclusion. In GRE logical reasoning (as in real life), evidence isn't necessarily like evidence in a court of law. It might include all manner of ideas, statements, and information, relevant or irrelevant.

The evidence used in a logical reasoning passage may include facts ("The Alberghetti convertible goes from zero to sixty in 1.2 milliseconds"), quotations ("Sports-car driver Jim Crashtest says, 'I love the new Alberghetti convertible!'"), statistics ("The Alberghetti is the fastest-selling convertible in America"), emotional appeals ("The sleek lines of the Alberghetti ooze sex appeal!"), and so on. What they all have in common is that they are intended to help win you over to the author's conclusion. Anything that plays this role in a GRE argument is called evidence.

Sometimes, the evidence is also signaled by clue words. Table 10.2 lists some examples to watch for.

Table 10.2
Clue Words That Signal Evidence

Because	Inasmuch as
Since	Insofar as
As	Given the fact that
Due to	As demonstrated by

The *hidden assumptions* are facts or ideas, *not stated in the passage,* that must be true if the argument is to be considered valid. Hidden assumptions underlie every argument. This is inevitable because no argument can state explicitly every single fact or idea that's needed to support a particular conclusion. (Life is too short.) However, assumptions are the secret pitfall of many an argument. If they are true, the argument might be sound, valid, and convincing. If they are false, the argument is likely to break down completely. And because they are unstated—"hidden" in that sense—they are easy to overlook, though crucial.

Because assumptions don't actually appear in the passage, no clue words mark them. Instead, you must "read between the lines" to recognize what is not being said but what *must* be true if the argument is valid.

Here's how it works. Suppose that an argument is being made to support the conclusion, "You should buy the new Alberghetti convertible." As we've already seen, many kinds of evidence could be presented on behalf of this conclusion. Almost every one involves one or more hidden assumptions.

Evidence: "The Alberghetti convertible goes from zero to sixty in 1.2 milliseconds."

Assumption: You need or want a car that can accelerate obscenely fast.

If this assumption is true, then the evidence does support the notion that the Alberghetti is a good car to buy; if not, then the evidence is worthless.

Evidence: "Sports-car driver Jim Crashtest says, 'I love the new Alberghetti convertible!' "

Assumptions: You should care what Jim Crashtest says. The opinion of a professional sports-car driver as to which car is best is relevant to your needs as a driver.

FYI

Here's another way to think about assumptions: They are often necessary links between the evidence and the conclusion. If the assumption is sound, then the evidence leads inexorably to the conclusion. If the assumption is weak—like a crumbling footbridge—then there's no real connection between the evidence and the conclusion, and the argument collapses.

If you too are a sports-car driver, then Jim's opinion might actually be relevant to your driving needs. But if you spend most of your driving hours stuck in five-mile-per-hour traffic, or if you use your car mainly to shuttle a three-year-old to day care, then Jim's tastes might mean nothing to you.

Evidence: "The Alberghetti is the fastest-selling convertible in America."

Assumptions: If a car sells quickly, it must be good. If other people are buying a car, it must be right for you, too.

Obviously, sheer popularity isn't proof of quality. After all, lots of people bought Spice Girls albums, too.

Evidence: "The sleek lines of the Alberghetti ooze sex appeal!"

Assumption: You want or need a car whose design is sexy.

Whatever that means, exactly.

When you read a logical reasoning argument on the GRE, start by looking for the conclusion. The most important thing you can do is to be clear on exactly what the author is trying to convince you of.

Then consider the evidence. How convincing is it? How strong is the connection between the evidence and the conclusion? What hidden assumptions underlie that connection? Are those assumptions plausible? These are the issues that determine whether or not the argument is logical, valid, and convincing. In almost every case, the question that follows the passage will focus on these issues.

Look for Fallacies—the Logical Weaknesses that Can Cripple an Argument

As we've already suggested, the arguments presented on the GRE aren't always watertight in their logic (to say the least). Like advertisements, political speeches, newspaper letters to the editor, and the dinner-table pronouncements of your father-in-law, they are often marred by lapses in reasoning, implausible assertions, and illogical connections. These, of course, are fodder for the questions that follow.

Logic is an ancient discipline, and philosophers dating back to classical Greece have studied, diagnosed, and cataloged dozens of specific types of logical flaws. These are often called *fallacies*. If you've ever taken a course in what's usually called "informal logic," you've learned about these. They're sometimes taught in English or writing classes as well. However, if you've never studied the topic, no matter. As with every area on the GRE, the test is designed so that no particular college course is necessary to do well. And only a handful of the many types of fallacies studied by philosophers appear frequently on the exam.

In what follows, we'll explain the most common fallacies found in logical reasoning passages and give an example or two of each.

FYI

The names we use for the common fallacies are not tested on the exam, nor is any other terminology from the study of logic. To do well on the GRE, you need to recognize when an argument is flawed; you don't *need to be able to classify the flaw according to any specific or formal system of logic.*

Scanty Evidence

This is probably the single most common fallacy found on the GRE. In an argument with this fallacy, the amount of evidence offered in support of the conclusion is inadequate. The fallacy can take several forms:

- The conclusion might be a sweeping generalization, while the evidence might be one or two specific facts that fall short of justifying the broad conclusion.
- The evidence might consist of a few handpicked facts that tend to support the conclusion, while other facts that might tend to undermine the conclusion are (deliberately?) ignored.
- The evidence might involve statistics, a survey, or an experiment that is too limited in scope to justify the conclusion drawn.

Here are a couple of examples:

> Despite what people say, there are plenty of teaching opportunities for Ph.D.'s in the humanities. Windsor College recently had to cancel plans to hire two teachers for its English department because of a lack of qualified candidates.

One anecdote isn't sufficient evidence to support the general conclusion stated in the first sentence. Maybe Windsor College is an exceptionally unattractive employer—located on the Arctic tundra, for example.

> Samothrace Shoes is deeply committed to fair treatment of all workers, including those in third world countries. The company recently announced a new policy of refusing to do business with any Asian supplier that hires children to work in its factories.

Only one fact is mentioned, while facts that might reflect badly on the business methods of Samothrace Shoes aren't mentioned. Is it because they don't exist, or because the author wants to bury them?

Post Hoc Reasoning

The name of this fallacy comes from a Latin phrase, *post hoc, ergo propter hoc,* which means "After this, therefore because of this." The phrase describes the fallacy: It occurs whenever the author of an argument assumes that, because one event occurs *after* another event, it therefore occurs *because of* that other event. (You might also call this fallacy "faulty cause-and-effect reasoning.")

Because the world is a complicated place, cause-and-effect relationships are rarely simple or obvious. Arguments that assume that one cause is the sole cause of one effect are often oversimplified or misleading; more often, a combination of factors lies behind any significant event or trend. Arguments that commit the post hoc fallacy ignore this reality.

Here are a couple of examples of the post hoc fallacy:

> Fifty years ago, American schools were safe havens for the young. Students' persons and property were rarely assaulted, and serious crimes of violence were almost unheard-of. Over the past four decades, ever since the U.S. Supreme Court banned voluntary prayer in public schools, the rate of violent crime in schools has risen steadily. It's time to bring back prayer in schools and so restore them to morality and safety.

Undoubtedly, many factors have contributed to the increasing amount of crime in schools. Is the absence of prayer such a factor—even the major factor, as the author apparently believes? Maybe, but the argument presented certainly doesn't prove it.

> In a study of 200 families with school-age children, those families that had received family counseling from a psychologist or social worker reported significantly higher rates of drug, alcohol, and sexual abuse than those that had not received such counseling. Clearly, family counseling does more harm than good.

This argument has probably gotten cause and effect backwards. It seems more logical to assume that the families with problems are the ones who seek counseling rather than to assume that the counseling *causes* the problems.

The Straw Man

A logical argument sometimes must respond to opposing points of view by showing how and why they are wrong. Occasionally, however, an argument designed to respond to an opponent goes awry. In an argument with the straw man fallacy, the opposing point of view is presented in an unfairly simplified, exaggerated, or distorted form. (Hence the name of the fallacy: rather than battling a flesh-and-blood opponent, the author props up a "straw man" and beats *that* to a pulp.)

A simple version of this fallacy appears constantly in politics, where candidates on the right call their opponents "way-out liberals," while candidates on the left call their opponents "right-wing extremists." Here's a slightly more subtle version, taken from a real exam, complete with the accompanying question:

> Asserting that newspapers should reflect the needs of their readers, a group of newspaper publishers conducted a survey to

determine how readers felt newspapers could be improved. The readers made two recommendations: newspapers should emphasize events closer to the readers' lives and should feature articles about the reporters. If we take the publishers and their survey seriously, readers will be asked which events in their own lives they wish to read about, and these articles, overlaid with autobiographical vignettes, will be produced by the reporters. In this closed world, writers and readers will hold forth in an uninterrupted one-to-one dialogue from which events of the larger world—what used to be called news—are shut out.

The author's response to the survey is flawed because the author

(A) fails to consider alternative explanations of the data.
(B) fails to define what he means by the term "news."
(C) considers only one of the recommendations made by the survey respondents.
(D) misinterprets the intention of the survey respondents' recommendations.
(E) assumes that newspapers do not need to be improved.

Whatever you might think about the survey described in the passage, the author's description of the "closed world" that would be created if newspapers followed the recommendations made there is certainly exaggerated. The readers who asked for more coverage of events close to their lives and expressed an interest in knowing more about the reporters surely didn't mean to imply that "events of the larger world" should be completely *eliminated* from the news. Yet that is what the author seems to think. He is guilty of turning the point of view he dislikes into a straw man, as explained in other words by choice (D).

The Ad Hominem Argument

This is another Latin phrase borrowed from scholarly logicians; *ad hominem* means "against the person." An ad hominem argument attacks an opposing point of view, not by pointing out logical or factual flaws in the opposing argument but by criticizing the opponent on personal grounds.

Again, politics is a fruitful source of examples. But an ad hominem argument can crop up in almost any field. Here's an example:

The Energy Resources Council has issued a report advocating the use of ethanol as a fuel additive, claiming that it will help clean our atmosphere and reduce our reliance on fossil fuels. But the Council receives a portion of its annual budget from a large grain-processing firm, which will benefit financially from the use of ethanol, so the claims in the report must be discounted.

Notice how one might respond logically to the information presented here. In the real world, we know that people *are* influenced by their pocketbooks, so an awareness of the Council's funding sources and any *possible* bias they might promote is important. Knowing that the Council's supporters might have a stake in promoting ethanol should prompt informed readers (especially those competent to judge the claims made in the report, such as scientists) to examine the data in the report with an especially skeptical eye.

However, to simply dismiss the report because of the Council's funding source is to go too far. It's not enough to show that an opponent *might* be biased; it's also necessary to refute the actual arguments raised by the opponent in order to demonstrate that *possible* bias has become real. As written, the argument is guilty of the ad hominem fallacy because it assumes that merely attacking the credibility of the opponent is sufficient.

The Excluded Middle

Not some sort of flab-fighting exercise plan, the excluded middle is a fallacy that involves reducing disagreements to black-and-white terms. An excluded-middle argument assumes, literally, that there is no middle ground and tries to force anyone with a different position to occupy one of two diametrically opposed camps.

Debates over deeply held moral convictions often generate excluded-middle arguments: Think of abortion, for example, where opposing groups, both sincerely convinced of their moral rightness, seem unable to view one another in any light but the most uncompromisingly negative one.

Here's an example from a field that is only slightly less contentious:

> The U.S. Department of Justice has prosecuted a leading software manufacturer for what it calls "anti-competitive" practices. Far from benefiting consumers, this action will, in the long run, harm them and our nation. The government has no business interfering in the operations of the free market, and when it does so it inevitably produces a mess that is worse than the one it intended to "fix." One need only look at the disastrous effects of government-run markets in the former Soviet bloc to recognize this.

The author of this argument lumps together a Justice Department prosecution of a software company for anti-competitive practices with all the problems of the former Soviet economy—as if *any* government role in the economy is tantamount to communism. This is a classic example of excluded-middle reasoning—persuasive at a glance, but without nuance and, ultimately, divorced from reality.

The Dubious Assumption

As we've seen, every argument rests on one or more hidden assumptions. There's nothing sinister about this; because there's never enough time to say *everything*, it's inevitable that any author must take for granted certain basic concepts. If these are valid, there's no problem. The trouble starts when an argument is based on assumptions that are logically flawed or factually dubious. When this is true, the entire argument is likely to collapse.

Here's a fairly obvious example, complete with the accompanying question:

> Employees at Wall Street financial firms earn higher salaries than those at most other companies. Wilma is an office manager at a Wall Street financial firm, so she must be earning a very impressive salary.

The primary weakness of this argument is its

(A) attempt to isolate a single cause for a phenomenon that might have many causes.

(B) failure to clearly define what is meant by an "impressive salary."

(C) assumption that what is true about a group as a whole must also be true about each member of that group.

(D) apparent confusion between the cause of a phenomenon and an effect of that phenomenon.

(E) reliance on a single example to demonstrate the truth of a generalization.

The answer to the question is choice (C). The conclusion is true only if the assumption stated in choice (C) is correct. If it *is* correct, then the connection between the evidence stated in the first sentence of the passage and the conclusion stated in the second sentence is a strong one.

But that assumption is obviously false. We all know that (virtually) every generalization has its exceptions—although we all forget this at times, as when we stereotype people on the basis of one characteristic. So the problem with the logic in the passage is its reliance on a false assumption, and the question is designed to ferret this out.

Here's a more subtle example:

> The essence of the United States president's relationship with members of the executive branch is that he must persuade them to believe that what the president wants of them is what their own appraisal of their own responsibilities requires them to do in their own interest, not the president's. For persuasion deals in the coin of self-interest, and people always have some freedom to reject what they find counterfeit.

FYI

The six fallacies we've just discussed certainly don't exhaust the possibilities you'll encounter on the GRE; but you'll probably find that most of the logical reasoning passages on the exam do contain fallacies of one kind or another and that most of these are variations on our top six list.

The claim about the nature of persuasion advanced above is weakened if it is true that some members of the executive branch

(A) are subject to persuasion not only by appeals to self-interest but also by reasoned argument.

(B) are appointed by the president and therefore are likely to be like-minded agents who require no persuasion.

(C) are appointed by the president and therefore are beholden to the president for their jobs.

(D) do not appraise their own interests and responsibilities accurately.

(E) do what they consider to be in their own interest regardless of the president's attempts at persuasion.

Notice that, in this case, neither the question nor the answer explicitly uses the word "assumption." Nonetheless, this is a question about the faulty assumption underlying the argument. The author assumes—without offering evidence to prove it—that people only and always act in accordance with their self-interest. This *might* be true—it's a large philosophical question—but it depends, in large measure, on how you define "self-interest" and on what sorts of seemingly altruistic or unselfish acts one is willing to consider exceptions to the rule. In any case, it's a sweeping generalization that is certainly open to question, if not clearly erroneous.

Because this is the major flaw in the argument, the best way to "weaken" the claim it makes (as asked for in the question) is to expose that flaw—which choice (A) does by suggesting that the assumption might be false.

FYI

All four question types have one thing in common: Each, in its own way, probes the relationship among the three key elements of the argument—the evidence, the conclusion, and the hidden assumptions. Each question type is simply a different way of focusing on this relation-ship.

The Best Tips

Recognize and Practice the Four Most Common Question Types

As with every question type, logical reasoning items fall into definite patterns. We've found that the test-makers generally use variations on four basic types of questions. If you understand what the test-makers are looking for in a response to each of these four question types, none of the items on the exam is likely to mystify you.

Pick the Rebuttal

As we've seen, most (not all) logical reasoning passages contain fallacies of some kind. A pick-the-rebuttal question asks you to recognize the kind of fallacy the passage exhibits and choose an answer that brings it clearly to the fore.

Here are some of the typical question stems that are used to introduce pick-the-rebuttal items:

Which of the following is the most serious weakness in the argument above?

All of the following are valid objections to the argument above EXCEPT

Which of the following is the best criticism of the argument above?

Unearth the Assumption

This kind of question asks you to recognize one or more of the hidden assumptions that underlie the argument. You might have to recognize the difference between a truly *crucial* assumption—an idea that *must* be true to keep the entire argument from collapsing—and a minor assumption whose falsehood would affect the argument only marginally.

Here are some of the typical question stems to expect for an unearth-the-assumption item:

Which of the following assumptions is most pivotal to the argument above?

Which of the following must be true if the conclusion of the argument above is valid?

Which of the following is an assumption underlying the conclusion of the passage above?

Weigh New Evidence

Here, the question presents you with one or more new pieces of evidence—facts, ideas, or other information. Your job is to decide how each piece of new evidence would affect the argument. Does it agree with or bolster the evidence given in the argument, and thereby strengthen the conclusion? Or does it undermine or contradict the evidence presented and thereby weaken the conclusion?

Here are some of the ways that a weigh-new-evidence item might be worded:

Which of the following, if true, most weakens [*or* strengthens] the argument above?

The answer to which of the following questions would be most helpful in evaluating the argument above?

Which of the following, if true, provides evidence to support [*or* refute] the claim made in the argument above?

Draw Your Own Conclusion

Occasionally, you'll be presented with a passage that contains no conclusion. Instead, a number of facts, ideas, opinions, or other pieces of evidence will be offered, and your job will be to decide what kind of conclusion might logically be based on this evidence. The correct answer choice will be one that states a conclusion that grows naturally from the evidence; wrong answers will normally exhibit one or more logical fallacies like the ones we illustrated previously.

The Most Important Warnings

Forget What You Know; Forget What You Think

The passages appearing in GRE logical reasoning will deal with a wide variety of topics: social issues, business concerns, political and economic disputes, scientific theories, and purely personal matters. If you happen to know or care about a particular topic that pops up on the exam, *forget what you know or think.*

It's likely that the conclusion reached by the author of the argument on the exam will be different from your own opinion; it's quite possible that the evidence presented will be inaccurate, outdated, or completely fictitious. You mustn't let any of this bother you. Base your answer strictly on the logical strengths and weaknesses of the passage as written, and don't bring your personal knowledge or beliefs into the equation.

Don't Think Outside the Box

Remember that each passage on the GRE represents an argument as presented by an author, either real or fictitious. The argument may be valid, invalid, or a little of both; but in any case, your job is to respond to the question *in terms of the argument presented,* not in broader terms of right and wrong, truth and falsehood.

Consider this example, from a real GRE:

Between 1950 and 1965, the federal government spent one-third more on research and development than industry did from its own funds. In 1980, for the first time, industry spent more on research and development than the federal government did. Representatives of industry claim that these statistics show an increased commitment on the part of industry to develop competitive products.

Which of the following, if true, would help to refute the claim of the representatives of industry?

(A) In 1980, the federal government spent half as much on research and development as it spent in 1965.

(B) Between 1965 and 1980, industry in the United States experienced increasing competition from industry in other countries.

(C) In 1979, the federal government shifted research allocations from pharmaceuticals to electronics.

(D) Since 1965, industry has developed major product innovations, such as the personal computer.

(E) Before 1985, money spent by industry on research and development was not taxed by the federal government.

This passage reads like part of the ongoing debate over American business competitiveness. Is American industry doing enough to ensure its competitive strength versus foreign companies into the next century? What role should the government play in this effort? As a nation, are we investing enough in R&D, education, capital improvements, worker training, and other efforts to bolster the productivity and creativity of business? These issues have been debated for years, and people with interests on all sides have traded criticisms and rebuttals freely.

In this context, we might read the claim made by "representatives of industry" in the passage as part of a larger defense of U.S. business interests against the attacks of those who consider American executives shortsighted, self-serving, or inept. And this larger context actually exists in the real world. *However, it's completely irrelevant to the question as written* and is likely to mislead you when you try to answer the question. Here's why.

If you think of this passage as part of the ongoing pro-and-con debate about American business, you might be tempted to select choice (B) or (E). Choice (B) could be relevant because it suggests that U.S. industry was under siege from foreign competition during the 1970s (as in fact it was), and that only because of this intense, unprecedented pressure did American business increase its R&D investments. Therefore, one might conclude, industrial leaders don't really deserve any credit for spending more on R&D—it was a "no-brainer" decision that might in any case have been too little, too late.

Similarly, choice (E) might seem relevant because it suggests an important secondary motive for businesspeople in spending money on R&D—to get the tax breaks provided for such spending by Uncle Sam. Again, this statement, if true, could be regarded as taking away much of the credit the executives might otherwise deserve.

In a debate about the wisdom or foolishness of American business leadership, both of these ideas might well be relevant. In the context of the GRE question, however, both are irrelevant. The question does *not* ask about the larger issues of the quality of American business management, the proper role of government in the economy, laissez-faire versus government intervention, and so on. It simply asks for the best refutation of the *specific* claim in the passage.

That claim relates only to the argument cited by the "representatives of industry"—namely, the fact that, in 1980, industry spent more on R&D than government. What is the weakness in the use of this fact as evidence of an increased commitment to competitiveness by industry? It's simple. The fact that industry spent more than government might not reflect increased spending on the part of industry; rather, it might reflect *decreased* spending by government. Industry's spending could have remained the same, or even fallen, so long as it fell by less than government spending. Without the actual numbers, we can't tell. The answer that focuses on this very narrow, specific issue is choice (A), and that's the only answer the test-makers will accept.

The point? Be careful not to broaden the question by including it in a wider, more general, or more sophisticated intellectual, social, or conceptual context. The GRE doesn't reward creative or sophisticated thinking! Stick closely and single-mindedly to the specific question asked and the specific facts cited; that's what the test-makers like to see.

JUST THE FACTS

- Every argument has three key elements—evidence, a conclusion, and hidden assumptions.

- Six types of fallacies are commonly found in logical reasoning passages; you should learn to recognize each.

- Each of the four question types featured on the exam focuses differently on the relationship among the key elements of the argument.

- Avoid interpreting the questions in a creative, sophisticated way or applying outside knowledge; stick closely to what's on the page.

PRACTICE, PRACTICE, PRACTICE: LOGICAL REASONING EXERCISES

Instructions

The following exercises will give you a chance to practice the skills and strategies you've just learned for tackling logical reasoning questions. As with all practice exercises, work under true testing conditions. Complete each exercise in a single sitting. Eliminate distractions (TV, music) and clear away notes and reference materials.

Time yourself with a stopwatch or kitchen timer, or have someone else time you. If you run out of time before answering all the questions, stop and draw a line under the last question you finished. Then go ahead and tackle the remaining questions. When you are done, score yourself based only on the questions you finished in the allotted time.

Understanding Your Scores

0–2 correct: A poor performance. Study this chapter again.

3–4 correct: An average score. You may want to study this chapter again. Also be sure you are managing your time wisely (as explained in Chapter 3) and avoiding errors due to haste or carelessness.

5–6 correct: An above-average score. Depending on your personal target score and your strength on the other analytical question type, you may or may not want to devote additional time to logical reasoning study.

EXERCISE 1

6 Questions

Time—10 Minutes

> **Directions:** Each question or group of questions is based on a passage, graph, table, or set of conditions. In answering some of the questions, it may be useful to draw a rough diagram. For each question, select the best answer choice given.

1. Due, in part, to the success of African-American Alex Haley's book *Roots* in 1976 and the popular television miniseries based on it, interest in genealogy has increased significantly in the United States over the past 20 years.

   Since the book's publication, the average age of Americans has also increased, due to the millions of Americans born during the "baby boom" who, by the mid-90s, were reaching middle age, and many of whom are now interested in discovering their own "roots."

   If the information in the statement above is true, which of the following must also be true?

   (A) African Americans are more interested than other Americans in their family histories.
   (B) Prior to the publication of Haley's book, the American public had little interest in genealogy.
   (C) Middle-aged Americans are more likely to have an interest in genealogy than are younger people.
   (D) White Americans are more interested in genealogy than African Americans.
   (E) Television is chiefly responsible for the current increase in interest in genealogy.

2. In 1939, when the film *Gone With the Wind*, based on Margaret Mitchell's best-selling book, was about to be released, Hollywood's censors were very strict about permitting off-color language to be used in the movies. Nevertheless, David O. Selznick, the film's producer, was able to convince the censors to allow Clark Gable's now-famous line, "Frankly, my dear, I don't give a damn."

Knowledge of all of the following would potentially be useful in explaining the events described above EXCEPT

(A) the status of Selznick in the film industry at the time.
(B) whether the line in question had appeared in the original best-selling book.
(C) the degree of Selznick's concern over public reaction to the use of the word "damn."
(D) whether the censors had banned the use of the word "damn" in other films.
(E) the popularity of Clark Gable among the movie-going public.

3. Neither archaeologists nor historians have found any written texts in the Hebrew language dating from before the tenth century B.C. This means that the story of the Israelites' exodus from Egypt as recorded in the Old Testament, which occurred before that date, must have been originally preserved not as a written text but by means of oral tradition.

All of the following are valid objections to the argument above EXCEPT

(A) the story of the exodus may have been originally written down in a language other than Hebrew.
(B) texts in Hebrew from before the tenth century B.C. may have existed at some time in the past.
(C) texts composed in an earlier form of Hebrew may have been found but not recognized as such.
(D) texts in Hebrew from before the tenth century B.C. may exist without having come to the attention of historians or archaeologists.
(E) oral tradition is not as reliable a means of preserving stories of the past as written accounts.

4. Arthur Conan Doyle's fictional detective Sherlock Holmes is renowned as a master of deductive reasoning. On more than one occasion, when Holmes was confronted with an apparently insoluble problem, he was quoted as saying, "When you have eliminated the impossible, whatever remains, *however improbable*, must be the truth."

   All of the following are valid criticisms of Holmes's argument EXCEPT

   (A) "the truth" may involve a combination of possibilities rather than a single fact.
   (B) the improbability of an explanation makes it unlikely to be the truth.
   (C) there may be a possibility of which the reasoner is unaware.
   (D) a reasoner may be unable to determine with certainty whether or not a particular explanation is possible.
   (E) improbability is a subjective rather than objective criterion.

5. Many film critics have called Sir Laurence Olivier the greatest actor of the twentieth century. However, his participation in such ill-conceived and poorly executed films as *The Betsy, Clash of the Titans*, and *Bunny Lake Is Missing* seriously undermines his claim to any such exalted title.

   All of the following assumptions underlie the conclusion of the passage above EXCEPT

   (A) the three films cited were in fact ill-conceived and poorly executed.
   (B) if a particular film was poor, then Olivier's performance in it must have been equally poor.
   (C) the three films cited are representative of Olivier's acting career.
   (D) film critics frequently make inflated claims about actors whom they admire.
   (E) even a few poor performances by an otherwise fine actor can suffice to undermine his claim to true greatness.

6. Dr. O: Extensive clinical trials of the new drug Pilogro have demonstrated that Pilogro is effective in slowing the rate of hair loss associated with male pattern balding in men between the ages of 35 and 65 years old.

   Dr. T: I disagree. A recent study suggests that Pilogro is also useful in restoring hair growth among women who have suffered hair loss due to chemotherapy or other cancer treatments.

   Dr. T.'s response suggests that she has interpreted Dr. O.'s statement to mean that

   (A) Pilogro is effective only in treating male pattern balding.
   (B) not all men who suffer from male pattern balding should be treated with Pilogro.
   (C) Pilogro should be available to either men or women who suffer from hair loss.
   (D) women rarely suffer hair loss sufficient to justify the use of a drug like Pilogro.
   (E) Pilogro is the only drug that has been found effective in treating male pattern balding.

EXERCISE 2

6 Questions

Time—10 Minutes

> **Directions:** Each question or group of questions is based on a passage, graph, table, or set of conditions. In answering some of the questions, it may be useful to draw a rough diagram. For each question, select the best answer choice given.

1. As a rule, those who work in the book publishing industry are underpaid, overworked, and subject to being fired without warning at any time. Moreover, as more and more people turn to computers for both information and entertainment, books are rapidly becoming outdated. It is accordingly inadvisable for young people to choose careers in book publishing.

   All of the following are valid objections to the argument above EXCEPT

   (A) despite the recent increase in the use of computers, overall book sales have continued to grow.
   (B) individuals in the publishing industry are no more subject to being fired than are those in many other industries.
   (C) there are numerous fields other than book publishing in which workers are underpaid and overworked.
   (D) for a significant minority, book publishing careers prove to be both enjoyable and lucrative.
   (E) those interested in literary endeavors find book publishing to be an ideal working environment.

2. In 1861, the fossilized remains of an unknown and rather strange creature were discovered in a geological stratum dating from the latter years of the age of the dinosaurs. Although it resembled a small dinosaur, it was clear that the creature had wings and feathers. Consequently, it was named *archaeopteryx*, which means "ancient wing." Largely on the basis of this discovery, Thomas Henry Huxley, among others, argued that modern-day birds must be descended from dinosaurs.

Which of the following is NOT an assumption on which Huxley's argument was based?

(A) An animal that resembles a dinosaur is most likely related to dinosaurs.

(B) Modern-day animals have evolved from earlier forms of life.

(C) The biological connection between birds and dinosaurs is at best a tenuous one.

(D) *Archaeopteryx* lived during the age of the dinosaurs.

(E) An animal exhibiting features resembling those of birds is most likely related to birds.

3. Frank Lloyd Wright was the designer of such notable buildings as Fallingwater in Pennsylvania; his own homes in Spring Green, Wisconsin, and Scottsdale, Arizona; and the Guggenheim Museum in New York City. Based on this body of work, Wright is considered by most American architects, as well as many critics around the world, as the preeminent architect of the twentieth century.

Which of the following assumptions is most pivotal to the argument above?

(A) The buildings mentioned are outstanding examples of modern architecture.

(B) American architects generally agree with the critical assessments of architects from around the world.

(C) Architects put more care into designing their own homes than they put into other buildings.

(D) There are many twentieth-century architects who have designed notable buildings.

(E) The buildings mentioned are the best known of those Wright designed.

4. Many individuals take antihistamine medications to alleviate the symptoms of allergies. Although all antihistamines are essentially similar, there is sufficient variation among the available formulations to make some more effective for a particular individual than others. Therefore, if an allergy sufferer keeps trying different antihistamine formulations, she will eventually find one that is effective in her case.

All of the following assumptions underlie the conclusion of the passage above EXCEPT

(A) at least one antihistamine will relieve any individual's allergy symptoms.

(B) the effectiveness of an antihistamine is partially determined by an individual's unique characteristics.

(C) the effectiveness of an antihistamine is partially determined by the drug's specific formulation.

(D) no factors other than body chemistry and antihistamine formulation significantly alter the effectiveness of an antihistamine in alleviating allergy symptoms.

(E) some allergy sufferers have symptoms that will not respond to any available antihistamine treatment.

5. Although the extent of the Holocaust, the murder of six million Jews by the Nazis during World War II, became apparent with the war's end in 1945, it wasn't until the early 1990s, due to the success of Steven Spielberg's film *Schindler's List* and the opening of the U.S. Holocaust Memorial Museum in Washington, D.C., that it became a topic of general conversation among Americans.

Which of the following conclusions can properly be drawn from the statement above?

(A) Prior to the 1990s, the American public was largely unaware of the Holocaust.

(B) *Schindler's List* would not have been a success if the Holocaust museum had not opened at the same time.

(C) Prior to the opening of the museum in Washington, the U.S. government had taken no official notice of the Holocaust.

(D) The museum would not be as popular as it has been if Spielberg's film had not been so successful.

(E) The success of Spielberg's film and the museum opening were instrumental in bringing the subject of the Holocaust to the public's attention.

6. Ernest Hemingway is considered by many literary critics to be one of the greatest American writers of the twentieth century, if not of all time. However, his sexist attitude toward women and his macho posturings have made him less popular than some of his contemporaries among today's readers.

If the statements above are true, all of the following must also be true EXCEPT

(A) Hemingway's more popular contemporaries do not exhibit his sexist and macho attitudes.

(B) Hemingway's outdated attitudes are a major reason for his relative lack of popularity.

(C) many modern readers find Hemingway's sexist and macho attitudes distasteful.

(D) most of Hemingway's contemporaries exhibited the same sexist and macho attitudes.

(E) most of the general reading public does not agree with the critics' estimation of Hemingway's work.

EXERCISE 3

6 Questions

Time—10 Minutes

> **Directions:** Each question or group of questions is based on a passage, graph, table, or set of conditions. In answering some of the questions, it may be useful to draw a rough diagram. For each question, select the best answer choice given.

1. Although we may be exposed to all the various types of music—classical, folk, jazz, rock, and country—over the course of a lifetime, the type of music we loved as adolescents will always be our favorite.

   Which of the following, if true, would most seriously weaken the argument above?

   (A) Some people who are exposed to folk music only late in life learn to enjoy it.

   (B) Some people who love rock as adolescents come to prefer classical music later in life.

   (C) Those who are exposed to jazz only as children never learn to appreciate it.

   (D) Those who enjoy country music as adolescents always favor it over other types of music.

   (E) Some people who are exposed to classical music as adolescents never learn to enjoy it.

2. Due to outdated marine regulations, when the supposedly "unsink-able" R.M.S. *Titanic* struck an iceberg and sank in April 1912, there were enough lifeboats aboard to accommodate fewer than half of the passengers and crew, and more than 1,500 lives were lost. The public was shocked by the sinking and appalled at the loss of life. Shortly after the disaster, marine regulations were changed to require all passenger ships to carry enough lifeboats for everyone on board.

All of the following conclusions can be properly drawn from the statement above EXCEPT

(A) prior to the sinking, the public was unaware of the inad-equacy of the marine lifeboat regulations.

(B) until the disaster, the public had little interest in marine regulations.

(C) the individuals responsible for marine lifeboat regulations were unaware of their inadequacy.

(D) the public's reaction to the *Titanic* disaster was a contribut-ing factor in changing the marine lifeboat regulations.

(E) the public's reaction to the *Titanic*'s sinking was due in part to the ship's reputation as "unsinkable."

3. First editions of books by famous authors have long found a ready market among serious book collectors, some of them fetching extremely high prices. Curiously, though, first editions of books by the contemporary horror novelist Stephen King, who is not generally considered a significant literary figure, bring higher prices at auction than books by such esteemed American authors as Faulkner and Fitzgerald.

Which of the following, if true, would be most helpful in account-ing for the phenomenon described above?

(A) Neither Faulkner nor Fitzgerald was as popular in his time as King is today.

(B) Most serious book collectors are not interested in the books of contemporary authors.

(C) On average, collectors of Faulkner and Fitzgerald have about as much discretionary income as collectors of King.

(D) Because of King's popularity, many more people collect first editions of his books than those of other authors.

(E) Books sold at auction today invariably bring higher prices than they did in the past.

4. Because cable television networks rely on subscribers rather than advertisers for their income and are subject to less stringent censorship, they are able to offer programs with more explicit sexual content than their broadcast counterparts. This provides cable networks with an unfair competitive advantage over broadcast networks, which should be eliminated by the Federal Communications Commission.

Knowledge of which of the following would be LEAST useful in evaluating the argument made in the passage above?

(A) The extent of the public demand for shows with explicit sexual content
(B) The difference between the censorship exerted on cable and broadcast networks
(C) The nature of the FCC's regulations, if any, regarding competition between networks
(D) The amount of programming on cable networks with explicit sexual content
(E) The extent of the influence exerted by advertisers on the contents of television programming

5. *Publishers Weekly* is the most important and widely read magazine in the book industry, providing news about trade publishing (that is, the publishing of books primarily for sale in bookstores). It is accordingly essential for all those involved in publishing, and anyone interested in the field, to read each issue as soon as it is available.

All of the following are valid criticisms of the conclusion stated above EXCEPT

(A) those not directly involved in publishing do not have to keep up with the latest news in that industry.
(B) some publishers produce books to be sold mainly through direct mail rather than bookstores.
(C) publishers can generally function effectively without being aware of the latest news.
(D) there are several areas of publishing that are concerned with products other than books.
(E) news about publishing is rarely so timely that a delay in reading it causes a significant disadvantage.

6. Company spokesperson: It is true that specimens of five rare or endangered animals have died within two months of the opening of our new Animal World theme park. However, the over 1,000 other animals at the park are in healthy condition, and park management has taken every reasonable precaution to insure their continued survival and good health.

   Which of the following, if true, would most strengthen the claim above?

   (A) The five animals that died succumbed to infectious diseases spread through unclean drinking water.
   (B) Most zoos and other facilities that house rare animals experience several fatalities within two months of opening.
   (C) Over $2 million was spent by the management of Animal World on health facilities for the animals at the park.
   (D) The rare or endangered animals living at Animal World were obtained through legally sanctioned conservation programs.
   (E) One of the world's most famous zoo directors was hired by Animal World as a consultant on animal health.

EXERCISE 4

6 Questions

Time—10 Minutes

> **Directions:** Each question or group of questions is based on a passage, graph, table, or set of conditions. In answering some of the questions, it may be useful to draw a rough diagram. For each question, select the best answer choice given.

1. Suburban home owners have more living space than city apartment dwellers; they are buying something—their homes—with the money they spend for housing, rather than merely paying rent; they save on taxes because they can deduct part of their mortgage payments from their taxable incomes; they have greater access to the outdoors; and they live in quieter surroundings. For all these reasons, owning a suburban home is always preferable to living in a city apartment.

   All of the following assumptions underlie the conclusion of the passage above EXCEPT

   (A) all city apartment dwellers rent rather than buy their apartments.
   (B) everyone wants to have greater access to the outdoors.
   (C) city apartments dwellers prefer not having to commute to downtown jobs.
   (D) everyone prefers living in quieter surroundings.
   (E) all suburban houses contain more or larger rooms than do city apartments.

2. In his book *A Moveable Feast*, Ernest Hemingway claimed that when fellow writer F. Scott Fitzgerald remarked to him, "The rich are different from you and I," Hemingway responded by saying, "Yes, they have more money."

   All of the following conclusions can be reasonably drawn from the above EXCEPT

   (A) Fitzgerald believed that there was some fundamental difference between the rich and everyone else.
   (B) Hemingway believed that the difference between those with and without money was simply financial.
   (C) Hemingway had a sardonic sense of humor.
   (D) neither of the authors had as yet achieved significant commercial success.
   (E) having at one time been wealthy, Hemingway knew firsthand that Fitzgerald was wrong in his estimation of the rich.

3. When visiting a house of worship of a faith other than your own, it is respectful to follow the customs of that faith. When attending a service in an orthodox Jewish synagogue, it would be appropriate, for example, for a non-Jewish woman to sit in the women's section and a non-Jewish man to wear a *yarmulke* (skullcap) but not a *talis* (prayer shawl).

   If the statements above are true, all of the following statements must also be true EXCEPT

   (A) men of the Jewish faith generally cover their heads during orthodox services.
   (B) men and women generally do not sit together in orthodox Jewish synagogues.
   (C) only Jewish men are supposed to wear prayer shawls in an orthodox synagogue.
   (D) only those of the Jewish faith are allowed to attend orthodox synagogue services.
   (E) it would be considered disrespectful for a man to appear bareheaded in an orthodox synagogue.

4. Beginning at the end of World War II, the enormous expenditure on arms that the Cold War forced on both the United States and the Soviet Union, while having no obvious effect on the quality of life in America, resulted in a considerable diminution of that quality in the Soviet Union. This, in turn, led to general dissatisfaction, disappointment in the Communist system, and ultimately the dismantling of the Soviet Union.

Which of the following, if true, most seriously weakens the argument above?

(A) Although it was not obvious, the arms expenditures of the Cold War did affect the quality of life in America.

(B) The quality of life in the Soviet Union was relatively poor even prior to the end of World War II.

(C) Overall, the quality of life actually improved in America during the years after the conclusion of World War II.

(D) There was widespread political and economic dissatisfaction in the Soviet Union prior to the onset of World War II.

(E) Dissatisfaction with the quality of life was only one of many factors that contributed to the Soviet people's disillusionment with communism.

5. Collectors—whether they collect books, CDs, dolls, spoons, or anything else—would be well advised to purchase one of the various computer database programs available, because any such program will enable them to create catalogs of their collections from which information can be accessed quickly and easily.

All of the following are valid objections to the argument above EXCEPT

(A) some database programs may be more appropriate for creating catalogs of collection than others.

(B) entering information into a computer database can be extremely time consuming.

(C) not every collector has or is comfortable using a computer.

(D) not all collectors are interested in cataloging their collections.

(E) a catalog of a collection may be created using handwritten index cards instead of a computer.

6. Many, if not most, people find history uninteresting and are unable to see the point of making the effort to learn about it. However, in his book *Reason and Common Sense*, philosopher George Santayana argued that "Those who cannot remember the past are condemned to repeat it."

   Which of the following assumptions is most pivotal to the argument above?

   (A) Mistakes can be avoided by one who knows about similar mistakes made in the past.

   (B) Fate determines the decisions people make, regardless of their knowledge of the past.

   (C) Understanding what occurred in the past provides no real help in planning for an unpredictable future.

   (D) The lessons learned by individuals in the past are not directly transferable to those living in the present.

   (E) Both fortunate and unfortunate events of the past can be sources of knowledge for those who study history.

EXERCISE 5

6 Questions

Time—10 Minutes

> **Directions:** Each question or group of questions is based on a passage, graph, table, or set of conditions. In answering some of the questions, it may be useful to draw a rough diagram. For each question, select the best answer choice given.

1. The two men who led the North and South during the Civil War were as different as they could have been. Abraham Lincoln was easy to talk to, extremely communicative, and skilled at efficiently delegating authority. Jefferson Davis, president of the southern Confederacy, was difficult to approach, kept things to himself, and insisted on being involved in every decision. It is clear, then, that Lincoln's leadership skills were the decisive factor in the North's winning the war.

   All of the following, if true, weaken the argument above EXCEPT

   (A) the number of men available for military service in the North was much greater than in the South.
   (B) before the Civil War, Jefferson Davis had served with distinction in the U.S. Senate, a higher post than any Lincoln had held.
   (C) the North's superior manufacturing capabilities gave it a significant military advantage over the South.
   (D) the South's military officers were less skilled than those of the North.
   (E) during most of his presidency, Lincoln was strongly disliked by many citizens of the North.

2. Senator C: I oppose the use of statistical techniques by the U.S. Census Bureau to estimate how many Americans have been mistakenly omitted from the population tally and add them into the official count for each state. The clause in the U.S. Constitution that provides for a census calls for "an actual enumeration," not an estimate, so the Bureau has no right to make its guesswork part of the official count.

    Senator M: Senator C's opposition is without merit. It is solely based on the fact that the political party he opposes is likely to gain seats in Congress based on the newly adjusted population figures.

    Which of the following is the most serious weakness in Senator M's response?

    (A) It criticizes Senator C on personal grounds without responding to the argument he has made.
    (B) It fails to focus on the vagueness of Senator C's description of the Census Bureau's statistical techniques.
    (C) It assumes that those listening are more likely to be members of Senator M's party than of Senator C's.
    (D) It does not raise the possibility of amending the relevant clause of the U.S. Constitution.
    (E) It assumes a degree of knowledge concerning statistical methods that most listeners are unlikely to have.

3. In 1893, Arthur Conan Doyle, having wearied of writing about Sherlock Holmes, his popular fictional detective, wanted to drop the character. Fearing that his public would demand more Holmes stories, Doyle wrote "The Final Problem," a story in which Holmes and his newly invented archrival, Professor Moriarty, plunge to their deaths at the Reichenbach Falls. Doyle eventually brought Holmes back to life, in "The Empty House," and wrote 30 more Holmes stories, but critics have said that after the Reichenbach Falls, Holmes was never the same man.

    All of the following may be properly concluded from the information above EXCEPT

    (A) Doyle killed Holmes because he considered this the best way to justify writing no more stories about him.
    (B) after the Reichenbach Falls, Doyle was less interested in writing about Sherlock Holmes than he had been earlier in his career.
    (C) it was egotism that led Doyle to believe that the reading public would demand that he continue to write about Holmes.
    (D) Doyle in all likelihood created the character of Professor Moriarty as a means of bringing about Holmes's death.
    (E) the reading public reacted positively to Holmes's reappearance in "The Empty House."

4. During the Renaissance, many people in western Europe apparently believed that those of the Jewish faith had horns on their heads. In fact, Michelangelo's famous statue of Moses, part of the tomb he sculpted for Pope Julius II between 1520 and 1534, depicts the Jewish patriarch with a pair of clearly discernible horns.

   All of the following, if true, would help account for the information presented above EXCEPT

   (A) some of the Jews living in western Europe at the time actually had horns.
   (B) a mistranslation in a passage of the Bible most commonly read in western Europe at the time suggested that Jews had horns.
   (C) anti-Jewish prejudice among non-Jews in western Europe at the time encouraged the proliferation of false beliefs about Jews.
   (D) there were so few Jews living in western Europe at the time that most non-Jewish people had never met one.
   (E) none of the Jews living in western Europe at the time actually had horns.

5. Although many ghost sightings have been claimed by people of questionable veracity, there have been a significant number of sightings by people who are highly intelligent, honest, and reputable. It is reasonable, therefore, to assume that there are such things as ghosts and that they do make themselves known to the living.

   All of the following, if true, would serve to weaken the conclusion of the argument above EXCEPT

   (A) those who believe in ghosts are likely to interpret any ambiguous or inexplicable sight as a ghost sighting.
   (B) there is no demonstrable correlation between intelligence and honesty.
   (C) highly intelligent people are often more imaginative than others.
   (D) even people who are normally honest may lie on occasion.
   (E) a good reputation is no assurance of accurate eyesight.

6. Due to a misunderstanding, U.S. President Andrew Jackson married his wife Rachel before she was legally divorced from her previous husband. Although the divorce was finalized shortly after the wedding, in the presidential election of 1828, Jackson's opponents used this bigamous marriage to smear the couple. Although Jackson won the election, Rachel died before he took office, and the new president blamed his wife's death on the personal attacks she had suffered during the campaign.

   Which of the following assumptions must be true if Jackson's claim about his wife's death is true?

   (A) Jackson's opponents were trying to smear him through attacks on his wife.
   (B) Rachel Jackson would not have died when she did had it not been for the attacks on her.
   (C) The couple were attacked by Jackson's enemies despite the fact that Rachel's divorce had been finalized.
   (D) Rachel's previous husband was behind the attacks on the couple.
   (E) Rachel was ill during the presidential campaign and would probably have died shortly anyway.

Answer Key

Exercise 1	Exercise 2	Exercise 3	Exercise 4	Exercise 5
1. C	1. C	1. B	1. C	1. B
2. C	2. C	2. C	2. E	2. A
3. E	3. A	3. D	3. D	3. C
4. B	4. E	4. D	4. E	4. E
5. D	5. E	5. A	5. E	5. B
6. A	6. D	6. B	6. A	6. B

Explanatory Answers

EXERCISE 1

1. **The correct answer is (C).** The last sentence of the passage draws a direct connection between the arrival of the baby-boom generation at middle age and their increasing interest in genealogy.

2. **The correct answer is (C).** Choice (C) is not relevant to explaining Selznick's success in winning the approval of the movie censors; if anything, it relates merely to Selznick's willingness to include the controversial line in the movie script despite the possibility of public disapproval. The other choices suggest possible explanations as to why the censors might have been willing to make an exception to their usual rule concerning "off-color language."

3. **The correct answer is (E).** Choices (A) through (D) all offer possible explanations as to how the story of the exodus might have been preserved in writing without any current trace of that writing. Choice (E) is unrelated to this point; it merely suggests that the story of the exodus is likely to have been changed as a result of oral rather than written transmission.

4. **The correct answer is (B).** Choice (B) fails to undermine Holmes's reasoning because it ignores the fact that, according to the detective, all possibilities other than the improbable have already been eliminated. If this is so, then even the improbable is relatively likely since it is the only remaining possibility.

5. **The correct answer is (D).** All of the other answer choices represent beliefs that the author of the passage must accept if his conclusion—that Olivier is not really a great actor—is to be sound. Choice (D) might help to explain why critics exaggerate their praise of Olivier, but it doesn't support the conclusion of the passage.

6. **The correct answer is (A).** When Dr. T. says that he "disagrees" with Dr. O.'s statement because of the fact that women find the drug effective, the strong implication is that Dr. T. has interpreted Dr. O.'s statement as meaning that only men can use Pilogro.

EXERCISE 2

1. **The correct answer is (C).** Choice (A) is an effective response to the argument offered in the second sentence of the passage; choices (B), (D), and (E) are all logical responses to the points made in the first sentence. However, choice (C) merely suggests that other careers may be just as bad as book publishing, which doesn't demonstrate that book publishing is a desirable career.

2. **The correct answer is (C).** Rather than supporting Huxley's argument, the point made in choice (C) would tend to undermine it.

3. **The correct answer is (A).** The argument is supposed to demonstrate the greatness of Wright as an architect on the basis of the specific buildings mentioned—Fallingwater and the others. This argument makes sense only if the buildings referred to are in fact great works of architecture; if they are not, then Wright's reputation, based upon them, will surely suffer.

4. **The correct answer is (E).** Choices (A) through (D) all support the conclusion of the passage that every allergy sufferer can be helped by one or another antihistamine. By contrast, choice (E), if true, weakens the conclusion; it suggests that there are some allergy sufferers who cannot be helped by any antihistamine formulation.

5. **The correct answer is (E).** The phrase "due to" in the middle of the passage clearly implies that the movie and the opening of the museum played pivotal roles in making the Holocaust a topic of popular conversation among Americans.

6. **The correct answer is (D).** If the information in the passage is true, then the statement in choice (D) is probably false. The passage says that Hemingway's sexism had made him "less popular than some of his contemporaries," clearly implying that many of Hemingway's contemporaries had attitudes free of sexism—otherwise, their work would suffer from the same disfavor as Hemingway's.

EXERCISE 3

1. **The correct answer is (B).** The statement in choice (B) directly contradicts the argument by showing that some people do *not* continue to prefer the music of their adolescence later in life.

2. **The correct answer is (C).** Each of the other answer choices is strongly implied in the passage. However, the passage offers no evidence one way or another concerning the awareness of those responsible for lifeboat regulations of their inadequacy, or lack thereof.

3. **The correct answer is (D).** Answers (A) and (E) are irrelevant to the question of why King first editions draw higher prices than Faulkner and Fitzgerald when all the books in question are sold today. Choices (B) and (C) undermine potential explanations. Only choice (D) suggests a possible explanation, by showing that the potential market for King first editions is greater than that for more esteemed authors, thereby increasing the competition to buy and, consequently, the prices fetched.

4. **The correct answer is (D).** Choices (B), (C), and (E) all call into question some of the factual statements made in the passage; choice (A) challenges the author's contention that cable's freedom from sexual censorship gives it "an unfair competitive advantage." Only choice (D) bears no direct relationship to the argument being offered in the passage; whether or not cable operators take full advantage of their "competitive advantage" by showing a lot of sexy programming doesn't affect whether or not that advantage exists.

5. **The correct answer is (A).** Choice (A) is irrelevant to the conclusion of the passage, since the author claims only that "those involved in publishing" ought to read *Publishers Weekly*; he makes no assertions about anyone else.

6. **The correct answer is (B).** If statement (B) is true, it suggests that the track record of Animal World is comparable to that of other similar facilities and therefore that the management of the park has probably been reasonably careful about its treatment of the animals. Choices (C), (D), and (E) do not in and of themselves significantly support the general claim that the park management has been responsible. For example, to evaluate the importance of choice (C), one would have to know whether $2 million is an adequate sum for such facilities. The passage doesn't tell us that.

EXERCISE 4

1. **The correct answer is (C).** Each of the other answer choices states a fact that supports the arguments made in the passage. Choice (C), however, points in the opposite direction; it suggests an advantage for city apartment dwelling rather than an advantage of suburban home life.

2. **The correct answer is (E).** Choices (A) through (D) are all implied by one part of the exchange or the other. However, we can't tell from the information provided in the passage whether or not Hemingway had ever been rich, so choice (E) is the best answer.

3. **The correct answer is (D).** This is the only *false* answer choice; the passage is based on the assumption that non-Jews may attend orthodox Jewish services, which choice (D) contradicts.

4. **The correct answer is (E).** The passage states that one and only cause—the costs of the arms race—produced the collapse of the Soviet system. Choice (E) points out the weakness of this argument by suggesting what is probably true—that so massive an effect was probably the result of a combination of factors rather than just one.

5. **The correct answer is (E).** Choices (B) through (D) all suggest reasons why a collector might not want to use a computer to create a catalog. Choice (A) undermines the author's point that "any such program" can be used. Only choice (E) is beside the point; the author does not assert that *only* a computer is capable of creating a catalog, merely that a computer database is a quick and easy way of doing so.

6. **The correct answer is (A).** This statement accurately summarizes the point of the famous Santayana quotation. Choices (B), (C), and (D) run counter to Santayana's point, and choice (E) makes a fundamentally irrelevant point.

EXERCISE 5

1. **The correct answer is (B).** The other answer choices all weaken the point that Lincoln's leadership skills were the decisive factor in the North's victory—choices (A), (C), and (D)—by suggesting other factors, and choice (E) by undermining the contention that Lincoln was a popular leader. Choice (B) is irrelevant because in itself the fact that Davis had served in the Senate does not demonstrate that he was an effective leader.

2. **The correct answer is (A).** Whether or not one agrees with Senator C, he makes an argument based on the language of the Constitution that deserves a response. However, rather than offer a response, Senator M merely attacks Senator C's motivations, a logical weakness that choice (A) reveals.

3. **The correct answer is (C).** The passage does not suggest that Doyle's belief in the popularity of Holmes was egotistical—if anything, the opposite, since there was evidently sufficient demand for stories about Holmes to justify Doyle's writing of 30 such stories after the character's supposed death.

4. **The correct answer is (E).** Choices (A) through (D) all suggest possible reasons why the weird belief described in the passage might have been held by some Europeans. (Choice (A), of course, is clearly very improbable; however, "if true," as specified in the question stem, it *would* help to explain the belief.) Choice (E) merely underscores the irrationality of the belief; it doesn't help to explain it.

5. **The correct answer is (B).** Each of the other answer choices helps to show why people who are "intelligent, honest, and reputable" may nonetheless believe in something as apparently unlikely as ghosts. Choice (B) is irrelevant, since the passage doesn't assume any connection between intelligence and honesty; it merely bases its conclusion on the testimony of people who happen to exhibit both qualities.

6. **The correct answer is (B).** If Jackson blamed his wife's death on the personal attacks she suffered, then he must have believed the statement given in choice (B)—that she died because of those attacks rather than because of more "natural" causes.

Chapter 11

Analytical Reasoning

Get the Scoop On . . .

- Powerful techniques for mastering analytical reasoning puzzles
- How to create a simple diagram to unravel even the most complex puzzle
- The most common puzzle types used and the best approach for each
- Methods for answering questions correctly even when the puzzle remains partially unsolved
- How to avoid making false assumptions that lead to confusion and wrong answers

---

THE TEST CAPSULE

What's the Big Idea?

Analytical reasoning involves puzzles in which the relationships among a group of people, things, places, or activities are described. The puzzles may deal with such things as the seating of people around a table at a dinner party, the scheduling of performances in a series of concerts, or possible travel routes along roads that connect a group of towns. After reading several statements that outline the rules governing these relationships, you'll have to answer between three and five questions about them.

How Many?

Of 35 total questions in the analytical section, your GRE will probably have a total of 24 analytical reasoning questions.

How Much Do They Count?

Because analytical reasoning questions are 24 out of 35 total analytical questions, they count as 69 percent of your overall analytical score.

How Much Time Should They Take?

You need to answer analytical reasoning questions at a rate of five to seven minutes for each group of items. Since each puzzle contains between three and five items, this will give you a bit more than a minute per question.

What's the Best Strategy?

Using your pen and pencil and the scrap paper provided at the test center, create a simple diagram, chart, map, or calendar that summarizes the relationships described. In some cases, the answers to the questions may be read directly from this diagram. In other cases, the questions will add extra information that you can use to modify, clarify, or complete the diagram. The correct answer will then appear on the modified diagram.

What's the Worst Pitfall?

Making unwarranted assumptions about the puzzle relationships that aren't explicitly stated in either the original conditions or the questions. Anything that is not stated directly may or may not be true and cannot be relied on in answering the questions.

THE OFFICIAL DESCRIPTION

What They Are

Analytical reasoning is a test of logical thinking based on a set of arbitrary, interlocking relationships described in a series of statements. After reading and analyzing the statements, you'll be asked to answer three to five questions about the relationships described, which require you to accurately interpret the information given as well as to draw logical inferences about the relationships that go beyond what is explicitly stated.

Where They Are

On the typical GRE, you'll have one analytical section that is 60 minutes long. It will probably include six analytical reasoning puzzles, each with three to five questions (four is average). Interspersed among the puzzles will be eleven logical reasoning items, which make up the remainder of the section. Reminder: the test-makers claim the right to change the format at any time! However, the typical format we just described is what you're most likely to encounter.

What They Measure

The skills tested by analytical reasoning are akin to those used in solving brain teasers, assembling jigsaw puzzles, playing with construction toys, and competing in strategy board games like chess, checkers, and backgammon. If you enjoy activities like these, you may find analytical puzzles on the GRE entertaining and fun. Although connections can be drawn between analytical reasoning on the GRE and certain topics from formal logic and mathematics (the math field known as *combinatorics*, for example), no knowledge from either area is assumed or required.

The Directions

> **Directions:** Each question or group of questions is based on a passage or set of conditions. In answering some of the questions, it may be useful to draw a rough diagram. For each question, select the best answer choice given.

THE INSIDER'S REPORT
Strategies That Really Work

Create a Diagram or Chart That Summarizes the Puzzle Conditions

Analytical reasoning is probably the single weirdest question type on the GRE and the least like anything you're familiar with from past academic work. However, that doesn't mean that you've never done anything like it before. You have—only not in a classroom.

Think back to the last time you had to plan any complicated activity. Maybe it was seating family members at a Thanksgiving dinner—keeping Cousin Edna away from Uncle Bert (who can't stand Edna's bragging about her kids) and separating three sets of ex-spouses, while making sure that each child under ten had an adult on either side to maintain order. Maybe it was registering for your last semester at college, fitting in three required courses and two marathon lab sessions while allowing time for a two-mile trek across campus between your chemistry and history classes. Or maybe it was planning a vacation, figuring out how to transfer between flights at O'Hare when your jet from Newark is landing two terminals away from the gate where your jet to Seattle is departing twenty minutes later. Analytical puzzles on the GRE resemble this sort of exercise.

Does it resemble the work you'll be doing in graduate school? Probably not. But ETS has decreed that this is part of what the aspiring grad student needs to know, so here goes.

For most students, the crucial challenge in analytical puzzles is simply keeping straight the relationships described. The key is to work them out on paper, creating a diagram, chart, table, map, or list that reflects accurately the information given in the puzzle statements. Once you've sketched a clear and accurate puzzle diagram, answering the questions is usually not terribly difficult. Many can be answered simply by reading the necessary information from the diagram; in some cases, you'll need to modify the diagram slightly for each question. Either way, working on paper is essential to maintain clarity and to keep your sanity as you juggle the complicated rules and conditions on which the puzzle is based.

You'll create the diagram using some of the scrap paper provided at the test center. Begin each puzzle on a fresh piece of paper and sketch the basic diagram on the top half of the page. This will leave you space to create variations on the diagram for individual questions if that proves to be necessary.

Here are some specific pointers to bear in mind as you practice creating puzzle diagrams:

1. Be Flexible

Before you begin creating the diagram, read quickly through the entire group of puzzle statements with which the question set begins. This will give you a sense of the nature of the relationships described and will enable you to picture the kind of diagram that's appropriate. Every puzzle on the GRE is slightly different, and each requires a different type of diagram.

Generally, the first one or two puzzle statements outline the overall structure of the relationships, which suggests the kind of diagram needed. For example, suppose a particular puzzle begins with these sentences:

> Five singers—F, G, H, J, and K—are to be scheduled to perform in a certain sequence at a concert. They must be scheduled according to certain conditions.

You can see from this statement that the diagram you'll need to create will resemble a concert program with five slots to be filled, like this:

1.

2.

3.

4.

5.

The remaining puzzle statements will give you clues as to when each singer may perform; as you read each statement, you can fill in parts of the program based on the information provided.

Here's another example:

> Six towns, known as Millwood, Northport, Peterville, Redmond, Smithtown, and Truman, are connected by one-way roads only as follows.

You can see from this statement that the diagram needed will look like a road map. From the information given so far, you don't know the exact spatial relationships among the towns (which town is farthest north, for example), *and you may never be given that information.* However, you can begin sketching a map with the six towns placed in an arbitrary fashion—say, in a rough circle—leaving room for roads to be drawn in as described in the later statements. Your diagram might look like this:

M

T   N

S

R   P

The one-way roads themselves will be drawn in later, based on the additional puzzle statements. Depending on what those statements say, the final diagram might look something like this:

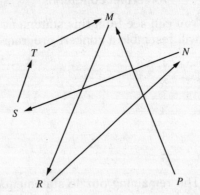

(You can see one-way roads running from Millwood to Redmond, from Redmond to Northport, from Northport to Smithtown, etc.)

Later in this chapter, we'll explain the most common puzzle types that appear on the GRE and show examples of how to create diagrams for each. However, it's always possible that the test-makers will spring some new type of puzzle on you, so you need to be prepared to create new types of diagrams as needed. The best preparation is practice; the more sample puzzles you try, the more adept you'll become at devising diagram styles to fit particular puzzles.

2. Keep the Diagram Simple

Remember, the puzzle diagram is only for your benefit, and you need to be able to use it only for the five to seven minutes it will take to answer the questions. Therefore, don't make it elaborate. Abbreviate freely. Don't draw any more lines, circles, or rules than are essential. Ignore neatness, the straightness of lines, and penmanship—all are unimportant.

3. Skip around among the Conditions as Needed

As you work on your diagram, you may find that some of the puzzle statements are easier to diagram than others. Feel free to skip around among the statements, diagramming those that are clearer and simpler first and then filling in the more complicated ones later.

Here's an example. Think back to the puzzle sample we presented earlier, beginning with this statement:

> Five singers—F, G, H, J, and K—are to be scheduled to perform in a certain sequence at a concert. They must be scheduled according to certain conditions.

Now suppose that the remaining puzzle statements are as follows:

> H   must sing immediately after K.
>
> J   may not sing either immediately before or immediately after F.
>
> G   must sing second.
>
> F   must sing third.

When you read the first statement ("H must sing immediately after K"), it's hard to see how this should be fitted into the diagram. K and H could sing, in that order, in slots 1 and 2, of course; but they could also sing in slots 2 and 3, 3 and 4, or 4 and 5. So the first statement doesn't help us much in filling out the puzzle diagram.

Neither does the second statement; it, too, leaves many possible scheduling slots for singers J and F.

With the third statement, however, we hit pay dirt. It gives us a single, definite piece of information that we can fill in on our diagram easily. If "G must sing second," then we can add that fact to our concert program like this:

1.

2. G

3.

4.

5.

The fourth statement ("F must sing third") is equally easy to diagram:

1.
2. G
3. F
4.
5.

We can now work backward to the other statements. The first statement says that H must sing immediately after K. The only place on the schedule in which these two may sing together is now slots 4 and 5:

1.
2. G
3. F
4. K
5. H

Of course, this leaves only slot 1 for the remaining singer, J:

1. J
2. G
3. F
4. K
5. H

FYI

Try starting your diagram with an anchor condi-tion—*the single most definite puzzle statement that establishes one clear and unvarying relationship independent of any other puzzle fact. Not every puzzle will offer such an anchor condition, but many do; look for it and use it as a starting point for your diagram.*

Our diagram is now complete, and the questions that follow are likely to be easy to answer.

Practice the Most Common Puzzle Types

With every GRE question type, the test-makers fall into habits and patterns over time, and analytical reasoning is no exception. Certain kinds of puzzles appear again and again on the exam, and after you've tackled a few sample tests (or the practice exercises at the end of this chapter), you should be familiar with these "classics." Not every puzzle you'll find on the exam will fit one of the four categories we present below, but more than half of them will; so understanding these four common patterns will give you a definite leg up in tackling the puzzles you'll encounter on your real GRE.

Ducks in a Row

This is our name for any puzzle in which items are arranged in a linear sequence.

The sequence may be spatial, a literal "line": for example, the puzzle could deal with a group of houses, each painted a different color, arranged in a particular order along a certain street.

The line could also be temporal (that is, a time sequence): the sample puzzle we've already considered, involving the arrangement of singers in a particular order for a concert, is a ducks-in-a-row puzzle based on a temporal sequence.

Finally, the line could represent some other kind of sequence: for example, a group of basketball players could be arranged by height ("Michael is taller than Scottie; Scottie is taller than Tony; Tony is shorter than Dennis," etc.).

No matter what the nature of the sequence, what all ducks-in-a-row puzzles have in common is the relatively simple nature of the relationships and the diagram needed to represent them: a line, either horizontal or vertical, with a series of slots to be filled in based on the puzzle statements and the information provided in the questions themselves.

Here's a sample ducks-in-a-row puzzle typical of the ones you may encounter on the GRE:

> Six race horses—G, H, J, L, M, and N—are to be housed in a row of seven stalls numbered 1 through 7, one horse to a stall, with one stall left empty. The horses must be housed according to the following restrictions:
>
> Horse M must be in stall 6.
>
> Horses H and L must be in adjacent stalls.
>
> Horses G and N must not be in adjacent stalls.
>
> Horses G and J must have exactly one stall between them.

We can see from the puzzle statements that the diagram needed will contain seven slots, representing a row of seven stalls, like this:

$$1 \qquad 2 \qquad 3 \qquad 4 \qquad 5 \qquad 6 \qquad 7$$

For this puzzle, there's an anchor condition—one statement that provides a clear and definite relationship that's easy to fit into the diagram: "Horse M must be in stall 6":

$$1 \qquad 2 \qquad 3 \qquad 4 \qquad 5 \qquad 6 \qquad 7$$
$$ M$$

However, *none of the other statements can be fitted into the basic diagram without further information.* As we'll discuss later, this is a common situation on GRE puzzles. Don't worry—the questions can still be answered, as you'll see in a moment.

However, the remaining puzzle statements *can* be represented in graphic form on your scrap paper, which can be a useful memory device. Here's how.

"Horses H and L must be in adjacent stalls."

This means that H and L must be together, in either order (that is, either H L or L H). You can represent this by writing on your scrap paper, next to the basic seven-slots diagram, this note:

(H L)

The parentheses mean that H and L must go together. *You must remember that H and L could be flip-flopped; that is, their order could be reversed.* It shouldn't be too hard to recall this variation for the few moments you'll be working on the puzzle.

"Horses G and N must not be in adjacent stalls."

This is, in a way, the opposite of the preceding statement; it tells us that two horses must be separated. This can be represented by the following note:

G / N

The vertical bar or "slash" mark means that the two items listed must be separated. Finally:

Horses G and J must have exactly one stall between them.

Represent this as follows:

G _ J

The blank space indicates the stall that must appear between the stalls containing horses G and J. *Again, you must remember that G and J could be flip-flopped.*

So the puzzle statements in this case yield a seven-slot diagram with only one slot filled in (slot 6), and a set of three notes that are symbolic representations of the remaining puzzle conditions, jotted down next to the diagram. You'll find you can answer the questions that follow simply by referring to this diagram and the notes.

FYI

On the real GRE CAT, the answer choices will not be lettered. But we'll letter them throughout this book simply for ease of reference.

Here's how, using a couple of typical sample questions.

1. Which of the following is an acceptable arrangement of horses in stalls, from stall 1 through 7?

   (A) G, N, J, L, H, M, empty
   (B) H, L, N, empty, G, M, J
   (C) J, L, H, G, empty, M, N
   (D) L, H, J, M, G, empty, N
   (E) N, L, G, empty, J, M, H

This is a common type of analytical reasoning item that often appears first in the puzzle set. It is asking you simply to apply the puzzle conditions you've been given to determine which of the five answer arrangements suggested does *not* break any of the rules.

One easy way to solve a question like this is to go through the puzzle statements one at a time and eliminate any answer choice that violates the condition stated. Let's apply that method here.

First, we're told that horse M is in stall 6. Glance quickly down through the five answer choices to see whether any of them violates this rule. Choice (D) does—it puts horse M in the fourth stall. So we can eliminate choice (D) immediately.

Second, we're told that horses H and L must be in adjacent stalls. Do any of the answer choices violate this rule? Yes, choice (E) does—so we can eliminate that answer as well.

Third, we know that horses G and N must not be in adjacent stalls. This allows us to eliminate choice (A).

Finally, G and J must be separated by a single stall. This eliminates choice (C). The correct answer is choice (B), the only arrangement that doesn't violate any of the rules.

Our second sample question involves a different problem-solving strategy:

2. If J is in stall 3, then which of the following must be true?

   (A) G is in stall 1.
   (B) H is in stall 4.
   (C) L is in stall 5
   (D) N is in stall 7.
   (E) Stall 2 is empty.

It's not unusual for individual questions to introduce new puzzle conditions, as this item does. We're told, for the purposes of this question, to assume that horse J is in stall 3. We can fill this new fact into the diagram as follows:

1	2	3	4	5	6	7
		J			M	

But when we consider the original puzzle rules again, we can see that certain other relationships fall into place as a result of the new information.

First of all, we know that G must be separated from J by exactly one stall. That means that G must be in either stall 1 or stall 5. So there are now two possible arrangements that need to be diagrammed:

The labels "Arrangement I" and "Arrangement II" are for our benefit in discussing the puzzle; on the real exam, you would not bother with such labels, which are strictly unnecessary.

Arrangement I:

1	2	3	4	5	6	7
G		J			M	

Arrangement II:

1	2	3	4	5	6	7
		J		G	M	

Now, since we know that H and L must be together (that is, in adjacent stalls), we can place those two horses in either of our two possible arrangements:

Arrangement I:

1	2	3	4	5	6	7
G		J	HL	HL	M	

Arrangement II:

1	2	3	4	5	6	7
HL	HL	J			G	M

(Notice that we've used "HL" to indicate that each of the two adjacent stalls may contain either H or L, since the horses could fit into those stalls in either order.)

Finally, we can use the fact that horses G and N must be separated to determine that N must go into slot 7 in either arrangement:

Arrangement I:

1	2	3	4	5	6	7
G		J	HL	HL	M	N

Arrangement II:

1	2	3	4	5	6	7
HL	HL	J		G	M	N

These, then, are the four possible arrangements under the condition specified in question 2—that horse J is in stall 3. (Yes, *four* possible arrangements. Remember, Arrangement I and Arrangement II both represent two possibilities, since H and L can flip-flop in both cases.)

Now the question is not too hard. Notice that it asks "which of the following *must* be true?" Of the five answer choices, only choice (D) is true under every possible scenario: horse N must be in stall 7, no matter what.

Pigs in a Poke

This is our name for puzzles that involve the assembling of groups of items according to specified rules.

There are many possible variations on this kind of puzzle. A pigs-in-a-poke puzzle could describe how teams (of athletes, workers, or volunteers) may be assembled for a particular assignment; it could describe how collections of books, records, or works of art may be selected; it could describe how groups of tourists may be organized for a trip.

In any case, the puzzle will provide you with rules by which the groups are to be organized. Your job will be to make sure you understand the rules and then to apply them accurately in answering the questions that follow. Here's a sample pigs-in-a-poke puzzle:

> A gourmet store sells gift baskets containing assortments of unusual fruit, including carambolas, kiwis, loquats, mangos, pomegranates, and quinces. Each basket contains four varieties of fruit, selected according to certain rules.
>
> If a basket contains carambolas, it may not contain quinces.
>
> If a basket contains loquats, it must also contain pomegranates.
>
> If a basket contains kiwis, it must also contain either carambolas or mangos.

As you can probably see, this is a rather open-ended puzzle. The conditions are few and simple, and there is a wide array of possible "solutions" (i.e., assortments of fruit that fit the specified rules). The diagram (really more a set of symbolic notes) you might make before tackling the questions would probably be correspondingly simple. The notes might look like this (each line of notes followed by our explanation for your benefit):

C K L M P Q

(Simply the initials of the exotic fruits to be used. No need to write out the whole names, of course!)

C × Q

(C and Q may *not* be used together.)

L → P

(When L is used, P must be used also.)

K → C or M

(When K is used, C or M must also be used.)

These four lines of notes will make it easy to answer the questions that follow. Here are two samples.

FYI

Be careful not to confuse one-way relationships with two-way relationships. The statement "If a basket contains loquats, it must also contain pomegranates" does not imply the reverse; a basket containing pomegranates need not contain loquats. Hence, the arrow in our note runs only in one direction.

3. If a basket contains loquats and carambolas, how many possible different assortments of fruit may the basket contain?

   (A) One
   (B) Two
   (C) Three
   (D) Four
   (E) Five

Since L → P, the basket must also contain pomegranates. How many possible choices are there for the fourth fruit? Just two: mangos and kiwis. Quinces are not an option, since C and Q can't go together. So the number of possible combinations is choice (B), Two: L, C, P, M and L, C, P, K.

4. If a basket contains kiwis and quinces, which of the following must be the other fruits in the basket?

   (A) Carambolas and loquats
   (B) Carambolas and mangos
   (C) Loquats and mangos
   (D) Loquats and pomegranates
   (E) Mangos and pomegranates

Since C and Q can't go together, C is ruled out—eliminate choices (A) and (B). K requires either C or M, but we've just ruled out C, so M must be included—eliminate choice (D). Choice (E) works without breaking any rule, but what about choice (C)? No good—you can't have loquats without pomegranates. So the answer is choice (E).

Roads Less Traveled

This is our name for a puzzle that involves moving between one place, event, or activity and another. Sometimes a roads-less-traveled puzzle literally involves roads, which may connect buildings, parks, towns, etc. Sometimes it involves less tangible connections; for example, the puzzle may describe a series of interrelated activities in a process so as to suggest how a person might "move" from one activity to another to complete the entire process (you might need to visit six different government offices in order to get a passport, for example).

The usual strategy for a roads-less-traveled puzzle is to create a simple map. Each place, event, or activity will appear on the map, usually as a letter or some other abbreviation, with lines connecting the letters to illustrate how one might move between them. If the sequence of moves is a one-way sequence or otherwise restricted, arrows or other symbols may be added. Here's an example.

An underground depository for sensitive government records contains eight storage chambers, numbered 1 through 8. The chambers are accessible only through two elevators, A and B, which travel between the earth's surface and chambers 3 and 7, respectively. The chambers are connected only by underground walkways in the following pattern:

Chamber 1 is connected to chambers 4, 7, and 8.

Chamber 2 is connected to chambers 6 and 7.

Chamber 3 is connected to chambers 4 and 5.

Chamber 5 is connected to chamber 6.

Each of the walkways between one chamber and another is the same length.

Generally speaking, the best approach is to start your diagram by placing the various items to be interconnected in a rough circle on your paper. In this case, the eight chambers might be depicted like this:

```
          1
  8                 2

7                       3

  6                 4
          5
```

(Placing the items in a circle usually makes it easy to draw the connections among them.) Then draw in the additional information—in this case, the pattern of walkways connecting the chambers:

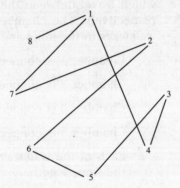

Finally, we can indicate the locations of the two elevators, A and B:

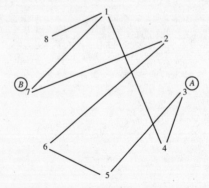

In many cases, the answers to the questions for a roads-less-traveled puzzle may be read directly off the map, with little fuss. Here are a couple of examples.

5. A government worker who enters the depository through elevator B would have to walk through which of the following chambers in order to reach chamber 5 by the shortest route?

    (A) Chamber 1
    (B) Chamber 3
    (C) Chamber 4
    (D) Chamber 6
    (E) Chamber 8

The shortest route from chamber 7 (where elevator B arrives) to chamber 5 goes through chambers 2 and 6. (Now we see why the puzzle specifies that all of the walkways are the same length. If that were not the case, one couldn't be sure which route is the *shortest*.) The alternative route, through chambers 1, 4, and 3, involves an extra walkway and therefore is longer.

6. Which of the following gives the first two steps of the shortest route from the earth's surface to chamber 8?

    (A) Descend in elevator A; walk to chamber 1.
    (B) Descend in elevator A; walk to chamber 4.
    (C) Descend in elevator A; walk to chamber 5.
    (D) Descend in elevator B; walk to chamber 1.
    (E) Descend in elevator B; walk to chamber 2.

From the map, it's easy to see that the best route to chamber 8 is to descend to chamber 7 in elevator B and then walk to chamber 1, from which chamber 8 can be reached immediately.

Days of Our Lives

This kind of puzzle involves a schedule of events or activities that must be fitted into a weekly or monthly calendar of some sort. As you might expect, the best strategy is normally to create a simple calendar and fill in the events according to the conditions specified. Here's an example.

Five guides—R, S, T, V, and W—are to be scheduled to lead tours of an art museum. The tours are given Monday through Friday, one tour in the morning and one tour in the afternoon. The guides must be scheduled in accordance with the following conditions:

Each guide leads exactly two tours every week, and no guide may lead two tours on the same day. S leads the Tuesday afternoon tour. V leads the Friday morning tour. R and W may not lead tours on the same day. T -must lead a tour the day after W leads a tour (except when W leads a tour on Friday).

Here's what our diagram and notes for this puzzle might look like:

	M	T	W	T	F
morn					V
aft		S			

R W

W → T next day

The calendar is probably self-explanatory. The notes mean, first, that R and W may not lead tours on the same day, and that W must be followed the next day by T.

As with some of the puzzles we've seen before, much of the diagram is blank at this point. But the questions themselves will provide additional information from which answers can be derived.

7. If W leads tours on Monday and Wednesday morning, which of the following must be true?
   - (A) R leads the Thursday morning tour.
   - (B) R leads the Friday afternoon tour.
   - (C) S leads the Monday afternoon tour.
   - (D) T leads the Thursday morning tour.
   - (E) V leads the Wednesday afternoon tour.

Start by filling in W in the two indicated slots on the calendar:

	M	T	W	T	F
morn	W		W		V
aft		S			

From this, and from the original rules given, we can make certain deductions. Since T must lead a tour the day after W, we know that T must lead the morning tour on Tuesday and one of the tours on Thursday:

	M	T	W	T	F
morn	W	T	W	T	V
				or	
aft		S		T	

Since R and W cannot lead tours the same day, R must be slotted into Friday afternoon and one of the tours on Thursday (remember, each guide must lead two tours during the week):

	M	T	W	T	F
morn	W	T	W	T	V
				or	
aft		S		R	R

That leaves an additional tour for S and one for V. These two will fit somehow into the Monday and Wednesday afternoon slots:

	M	T	W	T	F
morn	W	T	W	T	V
				or	
aft	SV	S	SV	R	R

Now look at the answer choices: which one *must* be true? Only choice (B): R leads the Friday afternoon tour. The others *may* be true, but could be false.

Another, slightly harder item for the same puzzle:

8. If R leads tours on Monday and Friday, on which days must W lead tours?

   (A) Monday and Tuesday
   (B) Monday and Wednesday
   (C) Tuesday and Wednesday
   (D) Tuesday and Thursday
   (E) Wednesday and Friday

Begin by slotting in R as indicated:

	M	T	W	T	F
morn	R				V
aft		S			R

(On Monday, R could be either in the morning or the afternoon; for simplicity's sake, we've written him in for the morning, but remember that there are two options possible.) Given this schedule, and remembering the rule that R and W may not lead tours on the same day, which days are possible for W? Monday doesn't work, because R leads a tour that day; and Thursday doesn't work, since there's no slot available on Friday for the required tour by T (the day after W, as prescribed by the rules). So W must lead tours on Tuesday and Wednesday. The resulting schedule might look like this:

	M	T	W	T	F
morn	R	W	W	T	V
aft	VS	S	T	VS	R

The correct answer is (C).

The Best Tips

Modify the Diagram as You Go

As you've seen, each puzzle begins with a series of statements describing the conditions that govern the puzzle relationships. These statements will be the basis for your initial diagram. However, some of the puzzle items may add new information—new conditions, in effect—that fill in further detail about those relationships.

When this happens, you'll need to modify or add to the diagram, using the additional information. This new data, in turn, may enable you to make new inferences based on the original rules. Work back and forth between the original statements and the new information, and use the conclusions you reach to fill in the diagram further. Then answer the question based on the modified diagram you've created.

Remember: new information provided in a particular question applies to that question only. When you move on to the next item, you must revert to the original set of puzzle conditions.

Study Your Options Methodically

Some items will require you to consider two or more possible "solutions" to the puzzle or even to count the number of solutions that may exist. For example, a roads-less-traveled puzzle may include an item asking, "Which route between point X and point Y is the shortest?" This requires you to consider all of the possible routes in search of the one that is shortest. Similarly, a pigs-in-a-poke puzzle may include an item asking, "How many possible combinations satisfy all of the conditions described?"

When this happens, study the options methodically. You may want to use your scrap paper to list the possibilities one by one, using abbreviations to jot them down quickly and succinctly. An easy way to make sure that you consider all the options without overlooking any is to use alphabetical order. Thus, if you are listing possible combinations among three items designated by letters B, C, and D, the most methodical approach is to list them alphabetically, the way they'd be arranged in a dictionary:

> BCD
>
> BDC
>
> CBD
>
> CDB
>
> DBC
>
> DCB

This is a better system than simply jotting down possibilities as they occur to you; the random approach makes it easy to inadvertently overlook an option or list it twice without realizing it.

FYI

Bring both a pen and a pencil (with eraser) to the test center, and use both when tackling analytical puzzles. Use the pen to create the basic puzzle diagram, incorporating all the information given in the original puzzle statements. Use the pencil to modify the diagram with new information provided for a particular question. Then, when you've finished that question, erase the pencil markings, and you'll be left with the original pen diagram you created in the first place, ready to tackle the next question.

The Most Important Warnings

Don't Be Afraid of Uncertainty

As you've already seen, many analytical puzzles are deliberately written so that the original conditions do *not* provide all the information needed to create a complete and detailed diagram. Furthermore, even when additional information is provided for a particular question, it may not suffice to eliminate all but one of the puzzle "solutions"; in other words, more than one combination of relationships may satisfy the rules and conditions of the puzzle.

Don't let this uncertainty bother you. Despite the open-ended nature of such puzzles, for which several equally correct solutions may exist, all of the information you need to answer the questions will always be provided.

Assume Nothing That Isn't Stated

The puzzle conditions are written to be complete and all-inclusive; everything you need to know is stated explicitly or clearly inferrable, and *nothing that is not stated explicitly is to be assumed.*

You'll find that language is used in GRE analytical puzzles a little more precisely than it is generally used in everyday, colloquial speech; some of the connections we might assume when reasoning loosely are not intended by the test-makers. Here are a few examples of GRE "puzzle-speak" and the ways in which it should and should not be intepreted:

> "If Richard attends the Friday performance, Yoko must attend also."

This is *not* the same as saying that Richard and Yoko must always attend the same performance. Yoko could attend the Friday performance *without* Richard; the requirement runs one way, not both. Also, of course, Richard could attend a performance on any day other than Friday without Yoko.

> "Six companies are located on various floors of a six-story building."

This sentence does *not* explicitly state that only one company is located on each floor, or that each company occupies only a single floor (although those may seem like natural assumptions to make). Unless these conditions are stated elsewhere in the puzzle, you must assume that they are not necessarily true.

> "Company A is located on a floor above company B."

This does *not* necessarily mean that company A is *immediately* above company B. If company B is on floor 2, then company A could be on *any* higher floor—floor 3, floor 4, etc.

"There is an empty seat at the dais between Dr. T and Dr. Y."

This does *not* necessarily mean that the empty seat is the *only* seat between Dr. T and Dr. Y. There could be one or more additional occupied or unoccupied seats between them as well.

As you can see, GRE puzzle-speak must be read and interpreted with care. However, you should also use your common sense in analyzing the puzzle conditions, and don't feel compelled to question assumptions that are truly everyday conventions.

For instance, it is safe to assume that, when a puzzle refers to the days of the week, an ordinary calendar is used, in which Monday follows Sunday, Tuesday follows Monday, etc.

Similarly, if a puzzle stipulates that a college committee is to be assembled including both faculty members and students, it's safe to assume that the two groups are mutually exclusive—that is, don't agonize over the unstated possibility that someone is actually *both* a faculty member and a student.

The test-makers aren't interested in trying to deceive you with dirty tricks of that kind. Analytical puzzles are weird enough—and hard enough—as it is without invoking such far-fetched and unlikely possibilities. Again, some practice with typical puzzles (like those in the exercises that follow) will help you develop a sound instinct as to how "finicky" the test- makers are in their use of language.

JUST THE FACTS

- Every analytical reasoning puzzle begins with a series of statements that describes a complex set of interrelationships.

- Start each puzzle by creating a simple diagram, chart, map, or calendar that summarizes the puzzle information.

- If need be, skip among the puzzle statements, starting with the anchor statement and filling in the other facts around it.

- As required, modify the diagram with any additional information provided in a question—but don't carry extra information from one item to the next.

- Avoid unwarranted assumptions not specifically supported by the puzzle statements or questions.

PRACTICE, PRACTICE, PRACTICE: ANALYTICAL REASONING EXERCISES

Instructions

The following exercises will give you a chance to practice the skills and strategies you've just learned for tackling analytical reasoning questions. As with all practice exercises, work under true testing conditions. Complete each exercise in a single sitting. Eliminate distractions (TV, music) and clear away notes and reference materials.

Time yourself with a stopwatch or kitchen timer, or have someone else time you. If you run out of time before answering all the questions, stop and draw a line under the last question you finished. Then go ahead and tackle the remaining questions. When you are done, score yourself based only on the questions you finished in the allotted time.

Understanding Your Scores

0–4 correct: A poor performance. Study this chapter again.

5–8 correct: A below-average score. Study this chapter again; especially make sure that you understand the most common puzzle types used on the GRE.

9–12 correct: An average score. You may want to study this chapter again. Also be sure you are managing your time wisely (as explained in Chapter 3) and avoiding errors due to haste or carelessness.

13–15 correct: An above-average score. Depending on your personal target score and your strength on other analytical question types, you may or may not want to devote additional time to studying analytical puzzles.

16–20 correct: An excellent score. You are probably ready to perform well on GRE analytical reasoning items.

EXERCISE 1

20 Questions

Time—20 minutes

> **Direcions:** Each question or group of questions is based on a passage, graph, table, or set of conditions. In answering some of the questions, it may be useful to draw a rough diagram. For each question, select the best answer choice given.

Questions 1–6 refer to the following:

A landlord owns a two-story apartment complex. The complex has four adjacent ground floor apartments, numbered 111, 112, 113, 114, respectively, and four upstairs apartments numbered 211, 212, 213, 214, such that 211 is directly above 111, 212 is directly above 112, and so on. The landlord keeps one apartment empty where he stays when he visits town, and rents out six others.

Nan lives in 114.

Hal won't live in 214, and Kit won't live next to Liz on the same floor.

Inga lives directly above Joe.

Unit 112 is being renovated and can't be rented.

1. If Kit rents 213, then which apartment must Liz rent?
    (A) 211
    (B) 212
    (C) 214
    (D) 111
    (E) 113

2. If Hal rents 111 and Joe rents 113, then which of the following CANNOT happen?
    (A) 211 is empty.
    (B) 212 is empty.
    (C) 214 is empty.
    (D) Inga lives in 213.
    (E) Kit lives in 211.

3. Which two tenants live on the same floor?

    (A) Inga and Liz
    (B) Liz and Kit
    (C) Hal and Joe
    (D) Nan and Kit
    (E) Nan and Joe

4. Which of the following CANNOT be true if Hal lives next to Nan?

    (A) Kit lives in 212.
    (B) Kit lives in 213.
    (C) Liz lives in 214.
    (D) Liz lives in 212.
    (E) Inga lives in 211.

5. If Inga insists on living next to Hal, then where must Hal live?

    (A) 211
    (B) 212
    (C) 213
    (D) 214
    (E) On the ground floor

6. If Liz lives in 213, and Nan moves to the apartment that was being renovated, then

    (A) Hal lives in 113 or 212.
    (B) Kit lives in 211 or 113.
    (C) Kit lives in 113.
    (D) Inga lives in 211 or 214.
    (E) Hal cannot live in 212.

Questions 7–10 refer to the following:

A candy factory offers a package containing exactly one dozen (12) candies. The factory has seven types of candy: A, B, C, D, E, F, and G. The contents of each package are determined by these considerations:

> If a package contains one of any type of candy, then it contains a second of that type of candy.
>
> A, B, or D cannot be in a package containing F.
>
> A or G cannot be in a package containing C.
>
> E cannot be in a package containing B.
>
> The maximum number of Cs in a package is 4.
>
> At least two As must be in every package containing two Gs.

7. Which of the following could be the candy types contained in a package of exactly three different types of candy?
   - (A) D, C, and B
   - (B) C, B, and E
   - (C) F, G, and C
   - (D) F, C, and A
   - (E) G, D, and C

8. Candy G can be in the same package along with which of the following types of candy?
   - (A) F, C
   - (B) F, B
   - (C) D, C
   - (D) D, A
   - (E) C, A

9. Suppose a package contains only six Bs and one other type of candy. Which of the following could be that other type of candy?
   - (A) F
   - (B) G
   - (C) D
   - (D) C
   - (E) E

10. Which of the following will never be in a package containing exactly four different types of candy?

    (A) D
    (B) B
    (C) F
    (D) G
    (E) E

Questions 11–14 refer to the following

The countries of Eton, France, Geo, Hartz, Ibiz, Jonia, and Kenya form alliances. Each alliance contains no fewer than two and no more than four countries.

Each country enters into one and only one alliance.

Only one of Hartz or Kenya allies with Ibiz.

Kenya allies with just two other countries.

Eton and Hartz do not ally together.

11. If Geo, Ibiz, and Kenya do not ally amongst themselves either altogether or individually, then Hartz is in an alliance with

    (A) France.
    (B) Geo.
    (C) Ibiz.
    (D) Jonia.
    (E) Kenya.

12. If Kenya allies with Jonia in an "Alliance of Friendship" and just one other alliance is formed, which other country joins the "Alliance of Friendship"?

    (A) Eton
    (B) France
    (C) Geo
    (D) Hartz
    (E) Ibiz

13. If Kenya accepts the invitation from France and Geo to join their single alliance, Eton must join an alliance

    (A) with only Ibiz.
    (B) with only Jonia.
    (C) with Hartz and three other countries.
    (D) with Ibiz and two other countries.
    (E) with Jonia and four other countries.

14. Which of the following sets of alliances does not violate the conditions specified?

   (A) Eton/Hartz   France/Ibiz/Kenya   Geo/Jonia

   (B) Eton/Ibiz   Geo/Hartz   France/Jonia/Kenya

   (C) Eton/Jonia   Geo/Hartz   France/Ibiz/Kenya

   (D) Eton/Kenya   Hartz/Jonia   France/Geo/Ibiz

   (E) Eton/Jonia/Kenya   Hartz/France   Geo/Ibiz

Questions 15–20 refer to the following

The city arena has five events—a basketball tournament, a hockey tournament, a concert series, an opera series, and a truck show—scheduled over five consecutive months. These events are scheduled as follows:

   The events are scheduled March through July, one per month.

   The basketball tournament is scheduled earlier than the opera series and the truck show.

   Both the hockey series and opera series are scheduled after the concert series.

15. Which of the following is an acceptable schedule for the five months?

	March	April	May	June	July
(A)	Basketball	Concert	Hockey	Opera	Truck
(B)	Opera	Hockey	Basketball	Truck	Concert
(C)	Truck	Opera	Basketball	Concert	Hockey
(D)	Truck	Opera	Basketball	Concert	Basketball
(E)	Concert	Hockey	Opera	Hockey	Concert

16. In which month can any of the events be scheduled and still allow all five events to be scheduled?

   (A) March
   (B) April
   (C) May
   (D) June
   (E) July

17. If the truck show is scheduled before the concert series, which of the following must also be true?

    (A) The basketball tournament is scheduled after the opera series.
    (B) The concert series is scheduled after the basketball tournament.
    (C) The concert series is scheduled after the hockey tournament.
    (D) The opera series is scheduled after the hockey tournament.
    (E) The truck show is scheduled after the opera series.

18. Which of the following pairs of events could be scheduled for March and April, in that order?

    (A) Basketball tournament and opera series
    (B) Concert series and basketball tournament
    (C) Concert series and truck show
    (D) Hockey tournament and opera series
    (E) Opera series and concert series

19. Which of the following events could be scheduled in the month indicated?

    (A) Hockey tournament in March
    (B) Opera series in March
    (C) Truck show in April
    (D) Hockey tournament in June
    (E) Basketball tournament in July

20. If the truck show is scheduled in June and the hockey tournament is scheduled in July, which of the following must be true?

    (A) The concert series is scheduled for March.
    (B) The basketball tournament is scheduled for April.
    (C) The opera series is scheduled for April.
    (D) The basketball tournament is scheduled for May.
    (E) The opera series is scheduled for May.

EXERCISE 2

20 Questions

Time—20 minutes

> **Directions:** Each question or group of questions is based on a passage, graph, table, or set of conditions. In answering some of the questions, it may be useful to draw a rough diagram. For each question, select the best answer choice given.

Questions 1–4 refer to the following:

Sarah invites some friends—A, B, C, D, E, F, and G—to her home to eat. She will serve breakfast, lunch, and dinner, and each friend stays for one or more meals. The following rules will determine when the friends visit:

Two consecutive meals may not be served to the same friend.

Each meal is served to two or more friends.

Whenever A stays for a meal, B stays for that meal, too.

F visits for the meal immediately before D's meal.

F won't come for the same meal as G.

1. Which of the following is an accurate list of visitors who could stay for breakfast?
    (A) A, C
    (B) D, F
    (C) A, F, G
    (D) C, E, F
    (E) A, B, F, G

2. Which of the following friends will NOT come for breakfast?
    (A) C
    (B) D
    (C) E
    (D) F
    (E) G

3. If only B, C, and D stay for dinner, then which of the following will stay for lunch?

(A)   E, A
(B)   E, F
(C)   E, G
(D)   F, B
(E)   G, A

4. If only B, C, and G come for breakfast, which of the following will come for dinner?

(A)   B
(B)   C
(C)   E
(D)   F
(E)   G

Questions 5–11 refer to the following:

At Bob's birthday party, the children play a game of musical chairs with five chairs placed from left to right. When the music stops, the children (Zoe, Bob, Chris, Dan, Ed, Fran, Geo, and Hap) try to sit in the chairs until all the chairs are filled. For each game, the following always happens:

Each chair holds only one child.

Three children are always left standing.

The middle chair is occupied by either Ed or Fran.

Geo and Chris sit next to each other if they are both seated.

If Geo gets a chair, then Chris won't be left standing.

Zoe and Hap are never both left standing.

If Zoe gets seated, she's in the first chair on the left.

5. Which of the following could be the result of one round of musical chairs, seating from left to right?

(A)   Bob   Geo   Fran   Hap   Dan
(B)   Chris   Geo   Fran   Ed   Hap
(C)   Geo   Chris   Ed   Fran   Zoe
(D)   Hap   Bob   Dan   Chris   Geo
(E)   Zoe   Ed   Geo   Chris   Dan

6. If Chris sits in the second chair from the left and Hap is left standing, which of these children could be sitting next to each other?

   (A) Zoe and Ed
   (B) Bob and Chris
   (C) Chris and Geo
   (D) Fran and Ed
   (E) Fran and Geo

7. Suppose Hap sits in the second chair from the right. Who cannot be in the chair on the right end?

   (A) Bob
   (B) Chris
   (C) Dan
   (D) Ed
   (E) Geo

8. If the second chair from the left holds Geo, who CANNOT be standing?

   (A) Bob
   (B) Ed
   (C) Fran
   (D) Hap
   (E) Zoe

9. If Ed is in the first chair on the left, which of the following must be true?

   (A) Chris is in the chair second from the right.
   (B) Fran is in the middle chair.
   (C) Geo is in the chair second from the right.
   (D) Geo is in the chair on the right end.
   (E) Hap is in the chair second from the right.

10. If Dan sits next to Ed, and Fran sits next to Dan, which of the following is correct?

    (A) Bob must be in a chair on the end.
    (B) Dan must be in chair second from an end.
    (C) Ed must be in the middle chair or the chair on the right end.
    (D) Fran must be in chair on the end.
    (E) Hap must be in second to the left chair or the right end.

11. If Chris is left standing and Ed sits in the chair on the left end, which of the following children are left standing?

    (A) Zoe and Bob
    (B) Zoe and Dan
    (C) Zoe and Geo
    (D) Zoe and Hap
    (E) Fran and Bob

Questions 12–17 refer to the following:

A bank has six employees—R, S, T, U, V, W—who deal with new accounts, which are either personal accounts or corporate accounts. Personal accounts are initially handled by R, T, or S, and corporate accounts are initially handled by R, T, or U. If an employee has a problem with an account, it will be passed on to another employee, until the problem is solved and the account is established. Rules governing the passing order are limited to the following:

> R to T if the account is personal.
>
> R to U if the account is corporate.
>
> T to U if the account is personal.
>
> T to V if the account is corporate.
>
> S to either R or T.
>
> U to either T or V.
>
> V to W.
>
> W will solve all problems.

12. Which of the following employees must have worked on all the accounts that W has worked on?

    (A) R
    (B) S
    (C) T
    (D) U
    (E) V

13. Which of the following is false?

    (A) A personal account is passed from S to R.
    (B) A personal account is passed from S to T.
    (C) A personal account is passed from R to T.
    (D) A personal account is passed from U to T.
    (E) A personal account is passed from T to V.

14. A corporate account could pass through which people before reaching W?

    (A) T, S, and U
    (B) T, R, U, and V
    (C) R, U, and V
    (D) R, T, and U
    (E) R, S, and V

15. At least how many people, besides W, must have handled an account that reaches W?

    (A) 1
    (B) 2
    (C) 3
    (D) 4
    (E) 5

16. Which employee can receive the same account a second time?

    (A) R
    (B) S
    (C) U
    (D) V
    (E) W

17. All six employees could have worked on which of the following kind of account?

    (A) A corporate account initiated by R
    (B) A corporate account initiated by T
    (C) A corporate account initiated by U
    (D) A personal account initiated by R
    (E) A personal account initiated by S

Questions 18–20 refer to the following:

A truck driver passes straight through six cities on his way north. The names of the cities, in no particular order, are Larkdale, Hillbrook, Pikeston, Millview, Bedford, and Greenham.

Three towns south of Greenham is Larkdale.

Greenham is not one of the last two towns traversed by the truck.

Millview is just north of Bedford.

The truck passes through Pikeston just after it passes through Hillbrook.

18. It starts raining while the truck is in Greenham. The rain continues through the next town, and only after the driver comes to the following town, Pikeston, does he turn on his wipers. Knowing this, which of the following must be true?
    - (A) Millview is the second-most southern town.
    - (B) Greenham is the third-most southern town.
    - (C) Pikeston is the most northern town.
    - (D) Hillbrook is the third-most northern town.
    - (E) Bedford is the most southern town.

19. Suppose the second town that the truck passes through is Bedford. In that case, which town does the truck next come to after it leaves Greenham?
    - (A) Bedford
    - (B) Millview
    - (C) Pikeston
    - (D) Larkdale
    - (E) Hillbrook

20. If Millview is the last town that the truck passes through, which of the following towns does the truck pass through immediately after leaving Greenham?
    - (A) Bedford
    - (B) Larkdale
    - (C) Hillbrook
    - (D) Millview
    - (E) Pikeston

EXERCISE 3

20 Questions

Time—20 minutes

> **Directions:** Each question or group of questions is based on a passage, graph, table, or set of conditions. In answering some of the questions, it may be useful to draw a rough diagram. For each question, select the best answer choice given.

Questions 1–5 refer to the following:

A corporation occupies all ten floors of a building. Each floor is completely occupied by a department: legal occupies one floor, marketing occupies two floors, research occupies three floors, and acquisitions occupies four floors.

Marketing occupies adjacent floors.

Marketing and acquisitions are not on adjacent floors.

The top and bottom floors are occupied by research.

Legal and research are not on adjacent floors.

1. If legal is on floor 5 and marketing is on floor 4, which of the following must be true?
   - (A) Floor 2 is occupied by acquisitions.
   - (B) Floor 6 is occupied by research.
   - (C) Floor 7 is occupied by research.
   - (D) Floor 8 is occupied by research.
   - (E) Floor 9 is occupied by acquisitions.

2. Which of the following are departments that CANNOT occupy floors 2, 3, and 4, respectively?
   - (A) Marketing, marketing, research
   - (B) Acquisitions, acquisitions, legal
   - (C) Acquisitions, acquisitions, acquisitions
   - (D) Research, acquisitions, legal
   - (E) Research, marketing, marketing

3. If floor 2 is a research floor and floors 3 and 4 are acquisitions floors, then legal must be on which floor?

   (A) 5
   (B) 6
   (C) 7
   (D) 8
   (E) 9

4. If floor 3 is occupied by research and floor 4 by marketing, then legal must be on which floor?

   (A) 2
   (B) 5
   (C) 6
   (D) 7
   (E) 9

5. If acquisitions occupy four consecutive floors, then legal and marketing could occupy which floors, respectively?

   (A) 1 and 2
   (B) 3 and 4
   (C) 4 and 5
   (D) 5 and 6
   (E) 6 and 7

Questions 6–10 refer to the following:

Four women visit a tailor, and at least three want to order two dresses each, one for a wedding and one for a graduation. The tailor has five different fabrics to choose from—solid blue, solid green, solid red, patterned polka dots, and patterned stripes—and each woman who orders wants each of her two dresses to be made with a different fabric. In addition, at least one of the wedding dresses and at least one of the graduation dresses must be a solid color fabric. Finally, if a woman wants a red dress for the wedding, then she also wants a patterned dress for the graduation.

6. Suppose all four women order dresses. What is the greatest number of solid-color graduation dresses that can be made?

   (A) One
   (B) Two
   (C) Three
   (D) Four
   (E) Five

7. All four women order dresses, and two of them order red dresses for the wedding. Which of the fabrics CANNOT be used for the wedding?

   (A) Any of the fabrics available can be used.
   (B) Blue
   (C) Green
   (D) Polka-dotted
   (E) Striped

8. If exactly three women order two red dresses and one striped dress for the wedding, they could order which dresses for the graduation (in the same order)?

   (A) Green, green, and striped
   (B) Striped, red, and red
   (C) Striped, green, and green
   (D) Polka dots, striped, and striped
   (E) Polka dots, polka dots, blue

9. If exactly three women order dresses, they CANNOT order which of the following three dresses for the wedding?

   (A) Blue, green, striped
   (B) Red, polka dots, blue
   (C) Green, green, green
   (D) Red, red, red
   (E) Blue, blue, blue

10. If nobody orders a red dress for one of the occasions, then what must be true of that particular occasion?

   (A) Both polka dot and green dresses must be made.
   (B) Both polka dot and striped dresses must be made.
   (C) Either blue or green dresses or both must be made.
   (D) Either polka dot or striped dresses, but not both, must be made.
   (E) Either blue or striped dresses must be the only ones made.

Questions 11–16 refer to the following:

A rock band tours five cities—Albany, Boston, Chicago, Detroit, and Evanston. The tour schedule follows these rules:

The tour stops at Boston before either Detroit or Evanston.

The tour stops at one city after Albany before stopping at Detroit.

The tour does not stop in Chicago second.

11. Evanston cannot be visited
    (A) first.
    (B) second.
    (C) third.
    (D) fourth.
    (E) fifth.

12. Suppose the first stop on the tour is Albany. Which of the following must be true?
    (A) The band visits Chicago before it visits Boston.
    (B) The band visits Chicago before it visits Detroit.
    (C) The band visits Chicago fourth.
    (D) The band visits Boston second.
    (E) The band visits Evanston fourth.

13. Every one of the cities can be scheduled for which particular spot on the tour?
    (A) First
    (B) Second
    (C) Third
    (D) Fourth
    (E) Fifth

14. Which of the following must be true if the band visits Albany immediately before Chicago?
    (A) The third city on the tour is Albany.
    (B) The first city on the tour is Boston.
    (C) The fourth city on the tour is Chicago.
    (D) The fifth city on the tour is Detroit.
    (E) The second city on the tour is Evanston.

15. Suppose three consecutive stops on the tour are Boston, Detroit, and Evanston, respectively. When can Albany be visited?

    (A) Either first or second
    (B) Either first or fifth
    (C) Either second or third
    (D) Either third or fifth
    (E) Either fourth or fifth

16. If the band decides to play Detroit last, then

    (A) Albany must be third.
    (B) Boston must be second.
    (C) Chicago must be first.
    (D) Chicago must be fourth.
    (E) Evanston must be fourth.

Questions 17–20 refer to the following:

A ski resort has a lodge at the top of the mountain and six scenic points: Evergreen, Frost Forest, the Gorge, Heavenly, Ice Palace, and Joker's Peak. The following ski trails are open with lifts: between Evergreen and Forest, between Ice Palace and Forest, between Heavenly and Forest, between Heavenly and Joker's Peak, between Joker's Peak and Evergreen, between the lodge and Joker's Peak, and between the lodge and Ice Palace.

In addition, there are trails between the lodge and Heavenly and between Heavenly and the Gorge, and a one-way trail that goes only *from* the Gorge *to* the lodge. Because of lines involved at each stop, a skier wants to make the fewest number of stops.

17. A skier is at the Ice Palace and wants to go to the Gorge with as few stops as possible. The first two stops will be

    (A) Frost Forest and then Heavenly.
    (B) the lodge and then the Gorge.
    (C) Frost Forest and then Evergreen.
    (D) the lodge and then Joker's Peak.
    (E) the Gorge and then Heavenly.

18. A skier is at Joker's Peak and wants to go to the Ice Palace. Her next stop must be

    (A) Ice Palace.
    (B) Evergreen.
    (C) Heavenly.
    (D) the lodge.
    (E) Frost Forest.

19. Suppose a skier is at the lodge, and she wants to go to Joker's Peak and the Gorge in no particular order but with the fewest possible stops. What will the order of her first two stops?

(A) the Gorge, Heavenly
(B) Heavenly, the Gorge
(C) Heavenly, Joker's Peak
(D) Joker's Peak, Heavenly
(E) Joker's Peak, the lodge

20. A skier at Evergreen heads to the Ice Palace, but not through Frost Forest and in the fewest number of stops. The first two stops have to be

(A) Joker's Peak and then Heavenly.
(B) Frost Forest and then the Gorge.
(C) Joker's Peak and then the lodge.
(D) the Gorge and then Heavenly.
(E) Heavenly and then the lodge.

EXERCISE 4

20 Questions

Time—20 minutes

> **Directions:** Each question or group of questions is based on a passage, graph, table, or set of conditions. In answering some of the questions, it may be useful to draw a rough diagram. For each question, select the best answer choice given.

Questions 1–6 refer to the following:

Five houses on one side of a street—numbered 101, 103, 105, 107, and 109—are going to be painted by a painting company. There are six colors to choose from—white, blue, chartreuse, yellow, green, and tan. The houses are painted based on these rules:

A house adjacent to one painted in one color can be painted in the same color.

No more than three houses can be painted the same color.

No more than one house can be painted chartreuse.

If 101 is painted chartreuse, no house can be painted yellow.

If a house numbered higher than a house painted green is painted blue, then there are exactly two houses which are painted blue.

House 109 is painted white.

1. Which of the following is an acceptable order of colors for the houses, from 101 to 111, respectively?
   - (A) Chartreuse, tan, blue, green, white
   - (B) Chartreuse, tan, green, blue, white
   - (C) Yellow, chartreuse, tan, chartreuse, blue
   - (D) Green, white, white, white, white
   - (E) White, tan, chartreuse, chartreuse, white

2. Three houses can be painted blue if house 101 is painted in any of the following colors EXCEPT
   - (A) green.
   - (B) chartreuse.
   - (C) tan.
   - (D) white.
   - (E) yellow.

3. Suppose the houses are painted using the most number of different colors, and that 101 is painted chartreuse and 103 is painted tan. Which of the following sets of colors must be used?

   (A) 105: blue 107: green

   (B) 105: blue 107: white

   (C) 105: green 107: blue

   (D) 105: green 107: yellow

   (E) 105: white 107: yellow

4. If houses 101, 103, and 105 are painted tan, chartreuse, and green, respectively, it must be true that

   (A) no house is painted blue.
   (B) no house is painted white.
   (C) no house is painted yellow.
   (D) the houses are painted using four colors.
   (E) the houses are each painted differently.

5. If houses 101 and 103 are both painted yellow, which of the following CANNOT be the colors used to paint the three other houses?

   (A) White, white, white
   (B) Tan, chartreuse, white
   (C) Chartreuse, white, white
   (D) Green, blue, white
   (E) Yellow, blue, white

6. If all the houses are painted using only two colors, which of the following statements must be true?

   (A) No house is painted blue.
   (B) No house is painted green.
   (C) No house is painted tan.
   (D) No house is painted chartreuse.
   (E) No house is painted yellow.

Questions 7–10 refer to the following:

Lindsay offers private piano lessons in her home on Sunday, Monday, and Tuesday from 3 p.m. to 4 p.m., and from 4 p.m. to 5 p.m. Her six students are Adam, Brooke, Carina, David, Elizabeth, and Fred.

Her students have the following scheduling requirements:

Adam needs his lesson to start at 4 p.m.

Brooke has basketball practice Monday and Tuesday afternoons, so she needs to schedule her lessons on Sunday.

Carina and David are siblings and want their lessons on the same day.

Elizabeth can never have her lesson on Sunday.

Fred needs his lesson to start at 3 p.m.

7. Which of the following represents a feasible schedule for lessons to be held at Sun. 3 p.m., Sun. 4 p.m., Mon. 3 p.m., Mon. 4 p.m., Tues. 3 p.m., and Tues. 4 p.m.?
   (A) Brooke, Adam, Elizabeth, Fred, David, Carina
   (B) Brooke, Adam, Fred, Carina, Elizabeth, David
   (C) Carina, David, Fred, Adam, Brooke, Elizabeth
   (D) Elizabeth, Brooke, Fred, Adam, Carina, David
   (E) Fred, Brooke, Carina, David, Elizabeth, Adam

8. Which of the following must be true?
   (A) Adam and Fred must have their lessons on the same day.
   (B) Brooke and Elizabeth must have their lessons on the same day.
   (C) Brooke must have her lesson at 4 p.m.
   (D) Carina and David must have their lessons both on Monday or Tuesday.
   (E) Fred must have his lesson on Sunday.

9. If Elizabeth's lesson is at 3 p.m. on Tuesday, who must be scheduled for the 4 p.m. on the same day?
   (A) Adam
   (B) Brooke
   (C) Carina
   (D) David
   (E) Fred

10. If Fred is scheduled on Tuesday at 3 p.m., which of the following statements must be true?

    (A)   Adam can be scheduled on Tuesday.
    (B)   Brooke can be scheduled at 4 p.m. on Sunday.
    (C)   Carina can be scheduled on Sunday.
    (D)   David can be scheduled on Tuesday.
    (E)   Elizabeth must be scheduled on Tuesday at 4 p.m.

Questions 11–17 refer to the following:

Four girl scout leaders (listed in order from most experienced to least experienced) are A, B, C, and D, and four boy scout leaders (listed in the same order) are E, F, G, and H. These leaders are offering two workshops to their troops— basketweaving and fishing—and each workshop is taught by three leaders based on these rules:

All three districts must be represented at every workshop.

B and F are from district 1.

A, D, and H are from district 2.

C, E, and G are from district 3.

Two or more of the girl scout leaders must teach basketweaving because they are more experienced at it.

Not less than two boy scout leaders must teach fishing because they are more experienced at it.

The leader with the most experience in each workshop is responsible for that workshop.

Should one of the leaders be absent, then the replacement leader must also fulfill all the rules.

Each leader can teach at most one workshop.

11. If G is responsible for the fishing workshop, who must also be teaching that workshop?

    (A)   A, F
    (B)   B, D
    (C)   B, H
    (D)   C, H
    (E)   D, E

12. Which of the following pairs includes at least one leader who must teach a workshop?

   (A) A, D
   (B) C, E
   (C) B, F
   (D) C, G
   (E) A, H

13. The three teachers of the fishing workshop could be

   (A) A, B, and E.
   (B) B, D, and G.
   (C) C, F, and H.
   (D) D, E, and H.
   (E) E, G, and H.

14. The three teachers for the basketweaving workshop could be

   (A) A, B, and G.
   (B) A, E, and F.
   (C) B, C, and F.
   (D) B, E, and H.
   (E) C, D, and G.

15. Suppose the teachers for the fishing workshop are D, F, and G. If E is not teaching a workshop, which of the following is not necessarily true?

   (A) B is teaching basketweaving.
   (B) C is teaching basketweaving.
   (C) Only one of A or H is teaching basketweaving.
   (D) C is responsible for the basket-weaving workshop.
   (E) F is responsible for the fishing workshop.

16. Suppose C, D, and F teach the basketweaving workshop, and suppose G replaces someone to teach the fishing workshop. Which of the leaders must now be responsible for the fishing workshop?

   (A) B
   (B) E
   (C) F
   (D) G
   (E) H

17. If C and F, but not D, teach basketweaving, and a third leader is appointed, which of the following will now be responsible for that workshop?

    (A) A
    (B) B
    (C) C
    (D) F
    (E) H

Questions 18–20 refer to the following:

Williams High School is closing, and its best teachers may be transferred to either of two other schools, Allendale Academy and Fleetwood High. The transferrable teachers are four women (Ms. Flint, Ms. James, Ms. Chang, Ms. Heckels) and four men (Mr. Barson, Mr. Davis, Mr. Garcia, Mr. Peters).

At least seven of the eight teachers must be placed in a new school.

Ms. James and Mr. Peters work as partners and must be assigned to the same school.

Mr. Barson and Mr. Davis are both drama teachers; neither of the new schools needs more than one drama teacher.

Mr. Barson and Ms. Flint are married and must be placed in the same school.

Each of the two schools must receive at least one new teacher.

18. If the only male teacher assigned to Allendale is Mr. Davis, which of the following must be true?

    (A) No more than five teachers are assigned to Fleetwood.
    (B) At least three of the male teachers are assigned positions.
    (C) Exactly two teachers are assigned to Allendale.
    (D) Each school is assigned two of the female teachers.
    (E) All of the female teachers are assigned positions.

19. Which of the following could be the entire list of teachers assigned to Allendale?

    (A) Ms. Chang, Mr. Peters, Ms. Flint, Mr. Davis, Ms. James, Mr. Garcia
    (B) Mr. Davis, Mr. Garcia, Mr. Peters, Ms. Chang, Mr. Barson
    (C) Ms. Flint, Mr. Peters, Mr. Garcia, Mr. Barson
    (D) Ms. Chang, Mr. Barson, Ms. Heckels, Ms. Flint, Mr. Garcia
    (E) Mr. Barson, Ms. Chang, Ms. Flint, Ms. James

20. Suppose we know that Mr. Davis is transferred to one of the two schools, and that only Mr. Barson and one other teacher are assigned to Allendale. Which of the following must be transferred to Fleetwood?

(A) Ms. Heckels, Mr. Peters, Mr. Davis, but not Ms. Chang
(B) Ms. James, Mr. Davis, Mr. Peters, and at least two others
(C) Mr. Davis, Ms. James, Mr. Peters, Ms. Chang, but not Ms. Heckels
(D) Mr. Davis, Ms. Chang, Ms. Heckels, Mr. Peters
(E) Ms. Chang, Mr. Davis, Ms. Heckels, and at least two others

EXERCISE 5

20 Questions

Time—20 minutes

> **Directions:** Each question or group of questions is based on a passage, graph, table, or set of conditions. In answering some of the questions, it may be useful to draw a rough diagram. For each question, select the best answer choice given.

Questions 1–5 refer to the following:

The local race track is a square with four turns. In order to measure a racer's performance, four timers—Aaron, Bill, Chad, Derek—are positioned around the track as follows:

Each timer is positioned between two turns.

No two timers are between the same two turns.

The starting post is also considered the fourth turn.

Aaron is adjacent to the first turn.

Bill is adjacent to the third turn.

Derek is adjacent to the fourth turn.

Aaron is not adjacent to the fourth turn.

1. The timers can be around the racetrack in which of the following order, beginning after the first turn?
   (A) Aaron/Chad/Derek/Bill
   (B) Aaron/Chad/Bill/Derek
   (C) Aaron/Derek/Bill/Chad
   (D) Chad/Bill/Derek/Aaron
   (E) Chad/Aaron/Bill/Derek

2. Which of the following situations will allow the other three timers to be positioned in more than one way?
   (A) Chad is positioned between the fourth and first turns.
   (B) Derek is positioned between the fourth and first turns.
   (C) Bill is positioned between the third and fourth turns.
   (D) Chad is positioned between the third and fourth turns.
   (E) Derek is positioned between the third and fourth turns.

3. Who can be positioned between the third and fourth turns?

   (A) Bill only
   (B) Chad only
   (C) Either Bill or Chad
   (D) Either Bill or Derek
   (E) Either Bill, Chad, or Derek

4. Which of the following must be true if Chad is adjacent to the third turn?

   (A) Bill is adjacent to the second turn.
   (B) Bill is adjacent to the fourth turn.
   (C) Chad is adjacent to the second turn.
   (D) Derek is adjacent to the first turn.
   (E) Derek is adjacent to the third turn.

5. If one of the timers nearest Chad is Derek, which of the following cannot be true?

   (A) Bill is adjacent to the fourth turn.
   (B) Chad is adjacent to the first turn.
   (C) Chad is adjacent to the fourth turn.
   (D) Derek is adjacent to the first turn.
   (E) Derek is adjacent to the third turn.

Questions 6–10 refer to the following:

There are four tellers—A, B, C, D—working at the bank, which is open from Monday through Friday. Each teller works according to the following rules:

   On Mondays, only A or B works.

   On Tuesdays, B works alone or with one of the other tellers, but not A.

   On Wednesdays, C works alone or with one of the other tellers.

   On Thursdays, two tellers work together, but B is not one of them.

   On Fridays, three tellers work together.

6. B must work on which of the following days?

   (A) Monday
   (B) Tuesday
   (C) Wednesday
   (D) Thursday
   (E) Friday

7. If only B and D are working on a certain day, which day must
    it be?

    (A) Monday
    (B) Tuesday
    (C) Wednesday
    (D) Thursday
    (E) Friday

8. If only one teller is working on a particular day, which of the
    following must be true?

    (A) The day is Monday or Tuesday.
    (B) The day is Monday, Tuesday, or Wednesday.
    (C) The day is Tuesday, Wednesday, or Thursday.
    (D) The day is Tuesday, Thursday, or Friday.
    (E) The day is Wednesday, Thursday, or Friday.

9. If we know that D is working on a particular day but don't know
    whether anyone else is working, that day could be all of the
    following EXCEPT

    (A) Monday.
    (B) Tuesday.
    (C) Wednesday.
    (D) Thursday.
    (E) Friday.

10. If two tellers are working on a particular day, and neither of them
    is C, which of the following must be true?

    (A) It is Monday or Tuesday.
    (B) It is Tuesday or Wednesday.
    (C) It is Tuesday or Thursday.
    (D) It is Wednesday or Thursday.
    (E) It is Wednesday or Friday.

Questions 11–15 refer to the following:

Four men (A, B, C, D) and four women (W, X, Y, Z) are going rafting in two rafts. Each raft holds exactly four people, and the groups of people in the two rafts follow these conditions:

There are exactly two men and two women in each raft.

Either A or B, but not both, must be in the first raft.

If W is in the first raft, then C must also be in the first raft.

If Y is in the first raft, then B cannot be in the first raft.

11. If W is in the first raft, which of the following must be in the second raft?

(A) C
(B) D
(C) X
(D) Y
(E) Z

12. If B is in the first raft, which of the following can be the other three people in the first raft?

(A) A, X, Z
(B) C, D, W
(C) C, W, X
(D) C, X, Y
(E) D, W, Z

13. If B, D, and X are in the first raft, which of the following CANNOT be in the second raft?

(A) A
(B) C
(C) W
(D) Y
(E) Z

14. If X and Z are in the second raft, which of the following men must be in the first raft?

(A) B and C
(B) B and D
(C) A and B
(D) A and C
(E) A and D

15. Suppose Y is in the first raft and C is in the second raft. Which of the following statements, if true, makes it possible to identify all the people in both rafts?
    (A) B is in the second raft.
    (B) W is in the second raft.
    (C) Z is in the second raft.
    (D) A is in the first raft.
    (E) D is in the first raft.

Questions 16–20 refer to the following:

At the Magic Castle club, a psychic's assistant has distributed nine balls among four people, as follows:

Three of the balls are green.

Three of the balls are red.

The remainder of the balls are blue.

Each of the four people holds at least two balls.

No one person holds two or more balls of the same color.

At her show, the psychic tried to guess what each person held.

She guesses as follows:

"David has a red ball and a green ball."

"Caroline has one of each of the three colors."

"Chuck has a red ball and a blue ball."

"Bonnie has a green ball and a blue ball."

The psychic guessed correctly on two of the people but interchanged the balls held by the two other people.

16. If Bonnie has two balls but neither are red, what also must be true?
    (A) The psychic guesses what David has correctly.
    (B) David has no red balls.
    (C) The psychic guesses what Chuck has correctly.
    (D) Chuck has no green balls.
    (E) The psychic guesses what Bonnie has correctly.

17. If the psychic guesses wrong on David and Caroline, it must be true that

    (A) Bonnie does not have a green ball.
    (B) Bonnie does not have a blue ball.
    (C) David has one each of a red, green, and blue ball.
    (D) Chuck has one each of a red, green, and blue ball.
    (E) Bonnie has one each of a red, green, and blue ball.

18. Suppose Caroline does not hold a red ball. If so, which of the following must be true?

    (A) The psychic's guess about David is wrong.
    (B) The psychic's guess about Chuck is wrong.
    (C) The psychic's guess about Bonnie is wrong.
    (D) The psychic's guess about Bonnie is right.
    (E) The psychic's guess about Caroline is right.

19. If the guess about David is correct, what must also be true?

    (A) Chuck does not have a red ball.
    (B) Chuck does not have a green ball.
    (C) Chuck does not have a blue ball.
    (D) Caroline has a red ball.
    (E) Caroline has a blue ball.

20. Which of the following must be true if David and Caroline are the two people who the psychic guessed correctly about?

    (A) Chuck has a red ball.
    (B) David and Chuck each has a green ball.
    (C) Bonnie has a green ball.
    (D) Chuck does not have a blue ball.
    (E) Bonnie does not have a red ball.

Answer Key

Exercise 1	Exercise 2	Exercise 3	Exercise 4	Exercise 5
1. E	1. D	1. E	1. A	1. B
2. C	2. B	2. D	2. A	2. B
3. E	3. B	3. C	3. A	3. E
4. B	4. A	4. C	4. A	4. D
5. B	5. B	5. E	5. D	5. A
6. E	6. D	6. D	6. D	6. B
7. A	7. E	7. A	7. E	7. B
8. D	8. D	8. E	8. D	8. B
9. C	9. B	9. D	9. A	9. A
10. C	10. B	10. C	10. E	10. C
11. C	11. C	11. A	11. C	11. B
12. A	12. E	12. D	12. C	12. C
13. B	13. E	13. C	13. C	13. E
14. C	14. C	14. B	14. A	14. E
15. A	15. B	15. A	15. D	15. C
16. C	16. C	16. A	16. D	16. E
17. B	17. E	17. A	17. A	17. C
18. B	18. C	18. D	18. B	18. C
19. C	19. E	19. D	19. D	19. E
20. E	20. A	20. C	20. B	20. B

Explanatory Answers

EXERCISE 1

1. **The correct answer is (E).** From the conditions, you can set up a chart:

    211 _____   212 _____   213 _____   214 __   I
                                                      | KL
    111 _____   112 _x_   113 _____   114 _N_   J

    For this question, you are told that Kit rents 213, so temporarily put her in:

    211 _____   212 _____   213 _K_   214 _____
    111 _____   112 _x_   113 _____   114 _N_

    Notice that now the only free upstairs-downstairs pair available to Inga and Joe are 211 and 111. So put them in:

    211 _I_   212 _____   213 _K_   214 _____
    111 _J_   112 _x_   113 _____   114 _N_

    Since Liz cannot be on the same floor with Kit, Liz cannot be in 212 or 214. So what room does that leave Liz? That's right: 113.

2. **The correct answer is (C).** Let's sketch a diagram for this question:

   211 _____   212 _____   213 _I___   214 _____
   111 _H___   112 _x___   113 _J___   114 _N__

   That leaves 211, 212, and 214 for Kit and Liz. Since Kit and Liz are not adjacent, either Kit or Liz must take 214. So 214 cannot be empty.

3. **The correct answer is (E).** We see that Nan is restricted to the ground floor. Is anyone else?

   Your conditions tell you: Inga above Joe. But there are only two floors. That means Joe always lives on the ground floor. So Nan and Joe always live on the same floor.

4. **The correct answer is (B).** For this problem:

   211 _____   212 _____   213 _____   214 ___   I
                                                | KL
   111 _____   112 _x___   113 _H___   114 _N_   J

   Put Hal in 113 and the only two upstairs-downstairs vacancies are 111 and 211. So Inga and Joe get them. Plug them in.

   Since Kit and Liz don't live adjacent on the same floor, one of them must take 212 and one must take 214. Which means 213 is empty. So choice (B) *cannot* be true.

5. **The correct answer is (B).** For this question, Hal lives next to Inga. So, where's Inga? In 211 or 213 because 211–111 and 213–113 are the only upstairs-downstairs available (for Inga above Joe).

   Then if Inga is in 211 or 213 and next to Hal, Hal is in 212.

6. **The correct answer is (E).** For this question you need to adjust your diagram because the conditions have changed.

   211 _____   212 _____   213 _L___   214 _   I
                                              | KL
   111 _____   112 _N___   113 _____   114 _   J

   This restricts Inga and Joe to 211–111 or 214–114 (Inga above J). Which means Inga lives in 211 or 214.

7. **The correct answer is (A).** From the conditions, we can make the following notes:

   2 each
   FD
   FB
   FA
   CG
   CA
   BE
   CCCC no more
   G → A

   For this choice, there are no conflicts if there are four candies of each type:
   DDDDCCCCBBBB

8. **The correct answer is (D).** If G is in a package, then A must also be in the package. D does not conflict with either A or G.

9. **The correct answer is (C).** D does not conflict with B in the same package, does not require another type of candy to be included in the package, and a package can contain 3 or more of it.

10. **The correct answer is (C).** Since type F conflicts with types D, B, and A, the only possibility for a box with exactly four types of candy including F is F, G, C, and E. However, if a package includes G, then it must also include A, which conflicts with F.

11. **The correct answer is (C).** From the conditions, we have

    EH IHK
    K _ _

    For this question, we have

Alliance 1	Alliance 2	Alliance 3
G _	I _	K _ _

    I must be in the same alliance as either K or H. Since I and K are in different alliances, then I and H must be in the same alliance.

12. **The correct answer is (A).** For this question, we have

Friendship	Alliance 2
K J _	_ _ _ _

    The third country in "Alliance of Friendship" must be either E or H because they cannot be in the same alliance together. If the third country is H, then I cannot be in the same alliance as either H or K. I must be in the same alliance as exactly one of those two, so the third country must be E.

13. **The correct answer is (B).** For this question, we have

Alliance 1
F, G, K

    The four countries left are E, H, I, and J. Since E and H cannot be in the same alliance, then the four countries must form two alliances of two. I must be in the same alliance as H, so E and J must make up the other alliance.

14. **The correct answer is (C).** In this choice, E is not in the same alliance as H; I is in the same alliance as K but not H; and K is in a three-country alliance.

15. **The correct answer is (A).** From the conditions, we have

    B |← O →
        |← T →
    C |← H →
        |← O →

    For this choice, the basketball tournament is scheduled before the opera series and the truck show, and the concert series is scheduled before the hockey tournament and the opera series.

16. **The correct answer is (C).** We arrive at this answer by eliminating all the other choices. For this choice, we could have the following five schedules:

```
-  -  -  -  -    -  -  -  -  -
C  H  B  O  T    B  T  C  H  O
-  -  -  -  -    -  -  -  -  -
C  B  H  O  T    C  B  O  T  H
-  -  -  -  -
C  B  T  O  H
```

17. **The correct answer is (B).** We know that the truck show is scheduled before the concert series. Since the truck show must be scheduled after the basketball tournament, the concert series must also be scheduled after the basketball tournament.

18. **The correct answer is (B).** For this choice, we could have the following schedule:

```
-  -  -  -  -
C  B  O  T  H
```

19. **The correct answer is (C).** For this choice, the truck show must be scheduled after the basketball tournament, so it can be scheduled in April if the basketball tournament is scheduled in March. For instance:

```
-  -  -  -  -
B  T  C  O  H
```

20. **The correct answer is (E).** We know that the truck show and the hockey tournament are scheduled for June and July. This means that the basketball tournament, the concert series, and the opera series must be scheduled during the first three months. Since the opera series must be scheduled after both the basketball tournament and the concert series, it must be scheduled on the last of the three available months—May.

EXERCISE 2

1. **The correct answer is (D).** From the conditions, we have

```
A → B
F
D
FG
X
X
Breakfast: _ _ . .
Lunch: _ _ . .
Dinner: _ _ . .
```

There are no conditions at prevent C, E, and F from attending breakfast. For instance, we could have the following:

Breakfast:	C, E, F
Lunch:	G, D
Dinner:	A, B

2. **The correct answer is (B).** D cannot come for breakfast because F must come for the meal immediately preceding D, and there are no meals before breakfast.

3. **The correct answer is (B).** For this question, we have

    Dinner: B, C, D

    We know that F must come for lunch because F must come for the meal immediately before D. G cannot come for lunch because F is coming for lunch. Neither B, C, nor D can come for lunch because they all come for dinner, and nobody can come for two consecutive meals. A cannot come for lunch because B does not come for lunch. Thus, the only other person who can come for lunch is E. Thus, F and E must be the only ones coming for lunch.

4. **The correct answer is (A).** For this question, we have

    Breakfast: B, C, G

    F cannot come for lunch because if he comes for lunch, then B must also come for lunch, which violates the fact that a friend cannot come for two consecutive meals. However, F must come for a meal, so he must come for dinner, which means that B must also come for dinner.

5. **The correct answer is (B).** From the conditions, you can draw the following notes:

    Chairs: 1   2   3   4   5
                      E/F
    If G ⟶ GC or CG
    Z or/and H
    If Z, then Z in 1

    An elimination strategy works well for this question. Eliminate the choices that violate the conditions:

    Choices (D) and (E) violate the first fact. They don't have E or F in chair 3. Choice (C) puts Z in chair 5, which violates the last fact. Choice (A) has G but without C next to G. That leaves (B) as the correct choice.

6. **The correct answer is (D).** If H is left standing, then Z must be in chair 1. (Z or H is a must.) (If Z, then Z in 1.)

    From the question conditions, you know C is in chair 2. And chair 3 must have E or F. So the first three chairs are ZCE or ZCF. That rules out choices (A), (B), and (C).

    It also eliminates choice (E) because C is already sandwiched and if G wants to sit anywhere, G must be next to C. You're left with choice (D).

7. **The correct answer is (E).** Put H in chair 4 and plug each of the choices into chair 5. You get HB, HC, HD, HE, and HG.

    HG isn't possible because of the fact: If G then GC or CG. (You would need a sixth chair for HGC.)

8. **The correct answer is (D).** You know who must have a chair. C must because if G gets one, then C sits next to G. But C isn't a choice.

Since G is in chair 2, C must sit in chair 1 or 3. But only E and F can sit in chair 3. So, you know C is in chair 1.

Chairs: 1   2   3   4   5
            C   G   E/F

If chair 1 is full, Z can't sit anywhere. This means H *must* sit somewhere because either Z or H always get a seat.

9. **The correct answer is (B).** Rule 1 says only E or F can sit in chair 3. If E sits in chair 1, then F must sit in chair 3 or it will be empty. That's choice (B).

10. **The correct answer is (B).** If D sits next to E, and F sits next to D, you get E D F or F D E. Since either E or F must sit in chair 3, you have four possibilities:

E D F = 1 2 3 or 3 4 5.
F D E = 1 2 3 or 3 4 5.

Combining both, E = 1, 3, or 5; D = 2 or 4; F = 1, 3, or 5.

11. **The correct answer is (C).** Remember, the question is . . . who *doesn't* get a chair?

If no C, then no G because G always means C has a seat.

If E is in chair 1 then Z can't sit anywhere. (If Z then Z1.)

So, C, G, and Z don't get chairs.

12. **The correct answer is (E).** From the conditions, we have

personal
IN → R, T, or S;

personal
R → T

corporate

V
R, T, or U

corporate

V
U

personal
T → U

corporate

V
V
    both   both
S → R or T;   U → T or V;   V → W
W → DONE

Since the only person that can pass an account to W is V from the chart above, any account that reaches W must pass through V.

13. **The correct answer is (E).** We can see from above that T passes personal accounts to U, not to V. Thus, choice (E) is false.

14. **The correct answer is (C).** We arrive at this answer by eliminating the answer choices that have flaws. For example, in choice (A), T to S is not allowed. In choice (B), T cannot pass a corporate account to R. In choice (C), R to U is allowed, and U to V is allowed. So this is correct. In choice (D), R can pass corporate accounts only to U, not to T. In choice (E), R to S is not allowed.

15. **The correct answer is (B).** W cannot begin an account. The person who handles the account before W must be V. However, V is not one of the people who can begin an account. U, who can pass an account to V, can begin a corporate account. Thus, the shortest possible sequence to W is: U → V → W.

16. **The correct answer is (C).** If the account is personal, U can receive it from T and pass it to T, who can then pass it back to U.

17. **The correct answer is (E).** Notice that S cannot receive accounts; S can only pass accounts to someone else. So, to include all employees, S should be the initiater of the account, which means choice (E) must be the answer.

   $$S \rightarrow R \rightarrow T \rightarrow U \rightarrow V \rightarrow W$$

18. **The correct answer is (C).** From the conditions, we can make the following diagram:

   SOUTH $\_\ \_\ \_\ \_\ \_\ \_$ NORTH   BM
   $\qquad\qquad\quad$ G G

   $\qquad\qquad\qquad$ HP
   $\qquad\qquad$ → TRUCK-MOVES-NORTH →   L $\_\ \_$ G

   from which we deduce the only possible placement of Larkdale and Greenham:

   SOUTH   L $\_\ \_$ G $\_\ \_$ NORTH   BM
   $\qquad\qquad\qquad\qquad\qquad\qquad\qquad$ HP

   Since this question tells us that the truck passes through Pikeston two towns after Greenham, and since Greenham is the third from the north, Pikeston must be the most northern:

   SOUTH   L $\_\ \_$ G $\_$ P   NORTH   BM
   $\qquad\qquad\qquad\qquad\qquad\qquad\qquad$ HP

   Now Hillbrook must be just south of Pikeston, and of the two remaining, Bedford is more northern, giving us the final configuration:

   SOUTH   L B M G H P   NORTH

   Thus choice (C), which says that Pikeston is the most northern town, is the correct response.

19. **The correct answer is (E).** In this question we also know the location of Bedford:

   SOUTH   L B $\_$ G $\_\ \_$ NORTH   BM
   $\qquad\qquad\qquad\qquad\qquad\qquad\qquad$ HP

   Thus Hillbrook and Pikeston can only be in the last two positions. So the truck comes to Hillbrook just after leaving Greenham.

Peterson's ■ *The Insider's Guide to*
the GRE CAT
www.petersons.com

20. **The correct answer is (A).** This question also stipulates that Millview is northernmost:

SOUTH   L _ _ G _ M   NORTH BM
                                               HP

From which follows the placement of Bedford, which we know is directly south of Millview, and the placement of the remaining two:

SOUTH   L H P G B M   NORTH

Thus, the truck passes through Bedford immediately upon leaving Greenham.

EXERCISE 3

1. **The correct answer is (E).** From the conditions, we have

```
1L        2M   3R   4A
R         R
-    . .  -
1         10
MM
MA
LR
```

For this question, legal is on 5 and marketing is on 4. So the two marketing departments must be on floors 3 and 4 because they are on adjacent floors.

```
R   M   M   L           R
-   -   -   -   -   -   -   -   -   -
1   2   3   4   5   6   7   8   9   10
```

We also know that marketing cannot be adjacent to acquisitions. Thus, floor 2 must be the third floor of research.

```
R   R   M   M   L           R
-   -   -   -   -   -   -   -   -   -
1   2   3   4   5   6   7   8   9   10
```

Thus, acquisitions must occupy floors 6–9.

2. **The correct answer is (D).** In this case, we would have the following arrangement:

```
R   R   A   L           R
-   -   -   -   -   -   -   -   -   -
1   2   3   4   5   6   7   8   9   10
```

Which would leave two consecutive marketing floors and three floors of acquisitions for 5–9. But since acquisitions cannot be adjacent to marketing, as would result from this arrangement, this choice is not possible.

3. **The correct answer is (C).** For this question, we know:

R	R	A	A						R
-	-	-	-	-	-	-	-	-	-
1	2	3	4	5	6	7	8	9	10

In order for the marketing not to be adjacent to acquisitions, the four acquisitions floors have to be consecutive, i.e., floors 3–6, and legal must be on floor 7.

R	R	A	A	A	A	L	M	M	R
-	-	-	-	-	-	-	-	-	-
1	2	3	4	5	6	7	8	9	10

4. **The correct answer is (C).** For this question, we have

R		R	M	M					R
-	-	-	-	-	-	-	-	-	-
1	2	3	4	5	6	7	8	9	10

Since legal cannot be on an adjacent floor to research, legal cannot be on floors 2 or 9. Since marketing and acquisitions cannot be on adjacent floors, legal must be on floor 6.

5. **The correct answer is (E).** For this choice, we would have:

R					L	M	M		R
-	-	-	-	-	-	-	-	-	-
1	2	3	4	5	6	7	8	9	10

We could put acquisitions on floors 2–5 and floor 9 would be the third research floor.

6. **The correct answer is (D).** From the conditions, we can make the following notes:

Wedding	Graduation
1 or more is Solid	1 or more is Solid

For each woman: Wedding = Graduation

If Wedding (red) → Grad (striped or polka-dotted)

As long as the solid-colored wedding dresses are not red, then all of the dresses could be solid colored, either green and blue. For example, if the wedding dress for the first woman is blue, then her graduation dress could be green or red. If her wedding dress is green, then her graduation dress could be either blue or green. And so on for the other three women. So there may be a total of four solid-colored graduation dresses.

7. **The correct answer is (A).** The only information we have is that two of the dresses for the wedding are red. This means that two of the dresses for the graduation must be either polka dot or striped. One of the remaining wedding dresses can be any fabric, as long as the fourth is not red (so that a graduation dress can be solid).

8. **The correct answer is (E).** For this choice, we have

Wedding	Graduation
R R S	P P B
- - -	- - -
1 2 3	1 2 3

All the other choices have flaws. For this choice, since the dresses for the wedding for the first two women are red, their dresses for the graduation are polka dot and polka dot. Since there needs to be a solid-colored dress for the graduation, the third dress is solid blue.

9. **The correct answer is (D).** If the three women all order red dresses for the wedding, then they all must have either polka dots or striped dresses for the graduation. This means that no woman has a solid-colored dress for graduation, which was one of the requirements.

10. **The correct answer is (C).** Since there are no red dresses made, and there has to be at least one solid-colored dress made for each occasion, either blue dresses or green dresses, or both, must be made for that occasion.

11. **The correct answer is (A).** From the conditions, we have

$$C \neq 2; \ B \ . \ . \ D; \ B \ . \ . \ E; \ A \_ D$$

The band must tour Boston before they tour Evanston. Thus, Evanston cannot be toured first.

12. **The correct answer is (D).** If the band tours Albany first, then they must tour Detroit third. Since they must tour Boston before they tour Detroit, Boston must be toured second.

13. **The correct answer is (C).** We arrive at this answer by eliminating all the other choices. The band can tour Boston third since there is time for the band to tour Detroit and Evanston afterward. Albany can be toured third if Evanston is toured fifth. Detroit and Evanston can both be toured third as long as Boston is toured before. Finally, Chicago can also be toured third.

14. **The correct answer is (B).** Since we know that the band toured Albany immediately before they toured Chicago, we know that they toured Albany, Chicago, and Detroit one after each other in that order. Since the band must tour Boston before they tour Detroit, they must also tour Boston before they tour Albany and Chicago. Since the band must tour Boston before they tour Evanston, Boston must be toured first.

15. **The correct answer is (A).** We arrive at this answer by eliminating all the other choices. For this choice, two possible schedules could be:

A	B	D	E	C		C	A	B	D	E
-	-	-	-	-	AND	-	-	-	-	-
1	2	3	4	5		1	2	3	4	5

16. **The correct answer is (A).** The band must tour Albany two cities before they tour Detroit. Thus, if they tour Detroit last, or fifth, then they must tour Albany third.

17. **The correct answer is (A).** From the description of the ski resort, we can construct the following diagram of the ski trails:

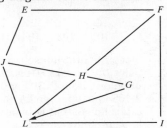

In order to reach the Gorge, the skier must pass by Heavenly. The two shortest paths from the Ice Palace to Heavenly are either I → L → H or I → F → H. Since the lodge and then Heavenly is not one of the choices, the correct choice is Frost Forest and then Heavenly.

18. **The correct answer is (D).** As you can see, the shortest route from Joker's Peak to Ice Palace is going directly through the lodge, which is the one and only intermediate stop. All the other routes involve at least two stops.

19. **The correct answer is (D).** Since the skier cannot go directly from the lodge to the gorge, the shortest path she can take to reach both Joker's Peak and the Gorge from the lodge is L → J → H → G. Any other way would require more stops than that. Thus, Joker's Peak and Heavenly are the first two stops, respectively.

20. **The correct answer is (C).** The shortest path involving going to the Gorge and not through T is E → J → L → I. Thus, her first two stops are Joker's Peak and the lodge.

EXERCISE 4

1. **The correct answer is (A).** From the conditions, we have

    No more than 3 same color.

    No more than 1 chartreuse.

    if   C————————————→Y
                                      W

    $\underline{\quad}$ $\underline{\quad}$ $\underline{\quad}$ $\underline{\quad}$ $\underline{\quad}$
    101   103   105   107   109
    if G . . B   ⇒ 2B

    We arrive at this answer by eliminating all the other choices. In this choice, house 101 is painted chartreuse, so there are no houses painted yellow. In addition, house 109 is painted white. There are no other rules that apply to this choice.

2. **The correct answer is (A).** If the first house is painted green, the rules require in such a case that, if any house is painted blue, there be exactly *two* houses painted blue.

3. **The correct answer is (A).** In this question, we have

C	T		W	
___	___	___	___	___
101	103	105	107	109

Since the first house is painted chartreuse, yellow cannot be used to paint the houses. Thus, in order for the houses to use the most number of colors, houses 105 and 107 are painted using green and blue. However, if 105 is painted green and 107 is painted blue, then there must be another house that is painted blue. Thus, 105 must be painted blue and 107 is painted green.

4. **The correct answer is (A).** For this question, we have

T	C	G		W
-	-	-	-	-
101	103	105	107	109

House 107 cannot be painted blue because if it is painted blue, then there must be another house painted blue because house 105 (a lower-numbered house) is painted green.

5. **The correct answer is (D).** For this question, we have

Y	Y			W
-	-	-	-	-
101	103	105	107	109

If houses 105 and 107 are painted green and blue respectively, then there must be a second house that is painted blue.

6. **The correct answer is (D).** Chartreuse can be used to paint only one house. Since the second color, which must be white, can only be used to paint up to three houses, it is impossible to paint all the houses with only two colors if just one house is painted chartreuse.

7. **The correct answer is (E).** Based on the conditions, you may have made the following notes:

	B E		
	SUN	MON	TUES

F → 3 p.m.
A → 4 p.m.

C D on same day

Choice (E), satisfies these requirements:

	SUN	MON	TUES
3 p.m.	F	C	E
4 p.m.	B	D	A

An effective way of getting to this answer is to apply a fact from the original information to each of the choices, and eliminate those that violate that fact. Then try the next fact, and so on, until you have only one choice remaining—the correct choice.

8. **The correct answer is (D).** Since Brooke must meet on Sunday, and Carina and David want their lessons on the same day, their lessons must both be scheduled on Monday or both on Tuesday.

9. **The correct answer is (A).** From the question, we get

	B E SUN	MON	TUES
F → 3 p.m. A → 4 p.m.			E

C D on same day

Therefore, C and D must have their lessons on Monday as this is the only day open for two lessons. (Remember, B is taking one of the Sunday lessons.) Since F can only have a 3 p.m. lesson, this leaves A for the Tuesday 4 p.m. lesson.

	B E SUN	MON	TUES
3 p.m.	F	C/D	E
4 p.m.	B	C/D	A

So Adam is the only one who can be scheduled for 4 p.m. on Tuesday.

10. **The correct answer is (E).** If Fred is scheduled for Tuesday at 3 p.m., this gives us:

	B E SUN	MON	TUES
F →3 p.m. A →4 p.m.			F

Since B will be taking one of the Sunday lessons, C and D must both be scheduled on Monday.

	B E SUN	MON	TUES
F → 3 p.m.		C/D	F
A → 4 p.m.		C/D	

That puts E in the Tuesday at the 4 p.m. slot.

	SUN	MON	TUES
F → 3 p.m.		C/D	F
A → 4 p.m.		C/D	F

Which now means that A must be on Sunday at 4 p.m., and B must be on Sunday at 3 p.m.

11. **The correct answer is (C).** From the conditions, we have

GS: A > B > C > D   District 1:   B, F

BS: E > F > G > H   District 2:   A, D, H

District 3:   C, E, G

Basketweaving: GS   GS   AND   1   2   3

               -     -   -   -   -   -

Fishing: BS   BS   AND   1   2   3

               -     -   -   -   -   -

Responsible for a class = largest in a workshop

For this question, we know that G is the most experienced in the fishing workshop. Since there must be two boy scout leaders and only H is less experienced than G, H is the second teacher. The third teacher must come from district 1 and must be a girl scout leader, so the third teacher is B.

12. **The correct answer is (C).** Because one leader from district 1 must teach in each workshop, and there are only two leaders from district 1 and there are two workshops, both of them, B and F, must teach in a workshop.

13. **The correct answer is (C).** If F and H are the two boy scouts teaching the fishing workshop, then the third teacher must come from district 3, and C is a valid choice.

14. **The correct answer is (A).** Two girl scout leaders, A and B, are teaching basketweaving. This means that the third teacher must come from district 3, and G is a valid choice.

15. **The correct answer is (D).** If E is not teaching any workshops and D, F, and G are teaching the fishing workshop, then the teachers for the basketweaving workshop must include B and C to satisfy the district requirements. Thus, C is not the most experienced girl scout leader and thus cannot be responsible for the workshop.

16. **The correct answer is (D).** The four possible original teachers for the fishing workshop are A, B, E, and H. Since A and H are from the same district, and since there must be two boy scout leaders teaching fishing, the three original teachers are B, E, and H. G can only replace E because they are from the same district. Thus, the new teachers are B, G, and H. Since G is the more experienced of the boy scout leaders, he is responsible for the fishing workshop.

17. **The correct answer is (A).** The replacement must also be a girl scout leader and come from district 2, and the only choice to satisfy both is A. Since A has the most experience of the girl scout leaders, she is now responsible for the basketweaving workshop.

18. **The correct answer is (B).** From the conditions, we can make the following notes:

    JP BD BF

    At least 7 transferred

    Each school gets at least 1

    For this question we may set up a chart, showing that Mr. Davis goes to Allendale:

Allendale	Fleetwood
D	

    Since Mr. Davis is the only male teacher assigned to Allendale, the male teachers who must be assigned in pairs must all go to Fleetwood (since seven teachers must be assigned, neither of the pairs may be let out):

Allendale	Fleetwood
D	J, P, B, F

    Thus, at least three of the male teachers are assigned: Mr. Davis, Mr. Peters, and Mr. Barson.

19. **The correct answer is (D).** Since Ms. James and Mr. Peters must be assigned together, (B), (C) and (E) are impossible. Since choice (A) does not assign Mr. Barson and Ms. Flint to the same school, the only valid answer is choice (D).

20. **The correct answer is (B).** And for this question, we may create a chart:

Allendale	Fleetwood
B __	_ _ _ _ _ (_) D

    Since F must go with B, and since D must be stored, we have:

Allendale	Fleetwood
B F	D _ _ _ _ _ (_)

    Since J and P must go together and neither of them going to Fleetwood would mean less than seven transfers, we have:

Allendale	Fleetwood
B F	D J P _ _ (_)

EXERCISE 5

1. **The correct answer is (B).** From the conditions, we have

   1A or A1; 3B or B3; 4D or D4; 4A and A4

   We can most easily arrive at this answer by eliminating all the other choices: Apply the conditions one by one to the choices and knock out those choices that violate a fact. For this choice, Aaron is next to the first turn, Bill is next to the third turn, Derek is next to the fourth turn, and Aaron is not next to the fourth turn.

2. **The correct answer is (B).** If Derek is positioned between turns 1 and 4, then Aaron must be between turns 1 and 2. Now the only fact that needs to be satisfied is Bill must be next to the third turn, and he can be on either side of the third turn. Thus, there is more than one arrangement of the timers.

3. **The correct answer is (E).** Bill must be positioned next to the third turn, and Derek must be positioned next to the fourth turn, so both of these can be placed between turns 3 and 4. If Bill is positioned between turns 2 and 4 and Derek is positioned between turns 1 and 4, then Chad can also be positioned between turns 3 and 4. However, Aaron cannot be positioned between turns 3 and 4 because he must be next to the first turn.

4. **The correct answer is (D).** If Chad is also one of the closest to the third turn, then the two between turns 2 and 3 and between turns 3 and 4 are Bill and Chad (not necessarily in that order). This means that Derek must be between turns 1 and 4, which means he must be one of the timers closest to the first turn.

5. **The correct answer is (A).** If Bill is one of the timers closest to the fourth turn, then it must be between turns 3 and 4. This forces Derek to be between turns 1 and 4 and Aaron to be between turns 1 and 2. This means that Chad and Derek cannot be separated by exactly one turn.

6. **The correct answer is (B).** From the conditions, you can make the following notes:

Monday:	A	or	B
Tuesday:	B	or	B A
Wednesday:	C	or	C
Thursday:	_ _	B B	
Friday:	_ _ _		

   From the table above, we can see that B must work on Tuesday.

7. **The correct answer is (B).** On Tuesdays, B can work with one other teller provided that person is not A. This is the only day that B and D can be the only ones working.

8. **The correct answer is (B).** From the conditions above, we can see that only one teller works on Mondays. In addition, B can work alone on Tuesdays and C can work alone on Wednesdays. Thus, if there's only one teller working, that day could be Monday, Tuesday, or Wednesday.

9. **The correct answer is (A).** We can see from the conditions that only A and B can work on Mondays, so if D is working, then it cannot be Monday.

10. **The correct answer is (C).** It cannot be Monday because only one teller works on Mondays. It cannot be Friday because three tellers work on Fridays. It cannot be Wednesday because C must work on Wednesdays. Thus, it must either be Tuesday or Thursday.

11. **The correct answer is (B).** From the conditions, we have

    ABCD = Men
    WXYZ = Women
    - - - - ← 2M 2W → - - - -
    A <u>or</u> B
                 If W ⟶ C
    If Y ————————→ B

    For this question, we know that W is in the first raft, which implies that C must also be in the first raft. Since one of A or B must be in the first raft, this means that D cannot be in the first raft.

12. **The correct answer is (C).** For this question, we know that B is in the first raft, which implies that Y cannot be in the first raft. Nor can A be in the first raft. For this choice, W is in the raft, which means that C is the second man in the raft. Having X in the raft does not conflict with any rules.

13. **The correct answer is (E).** For this question, we know that B, D, and X are in the raft. Y must be in the second raft because B is in the first raft. W must be in the second raft because C is not in the first raft. Since the fourth person in the first raft must be a woman, then Z must be in the first raft and cannot be in the second.

14. **The correct answer is (E).** For this question, we know that X and Z are in the second raft, which means the women in the first raft are W and Y. Since W is in the raft, C must also be in the raft. Since Y cannot be in the same raft as B, B must be in the second raft, which means that A must be in the first raft.

15. **The correct answer is (C).** For this question, we know that Y is in the first raft, which means that B is in the second raft, and we know C is in the second raft, which means that W is not in the first raft.

    Y   B C W

    Thus, we know the men in the raft are A and D.

    Y A D   B C W

    However, either X or Z could be the fourth person in either raft. If we know where Z is, then we also know where X is.

16. **The correct answer is (E).** From the conditions, we can make the following notes:

    Red: - - -   — three people.
    Green: - - -   — three people.
    Blue: - - -   — three people.
    David: R, G
    Caroline: R, G, B
    Chuck: R, B   — two of these are correct,
    Bonnie: G, B   two are switched.

    The psychic guesses that Bonnie is the only one without red balls, and since this question states that Bonnie does not have a red ball, the psychic guesses about Bonnie correctly.

17. **The correct answer is (C).** If the psychic guessed David and Caroline incorrectly, the correct content for David is R, G, B. This means that David has balls of all three colors.

18. **The correct answer is (C).** If Caroline does not have a red ball, then she must have a green and blue ball. Thus, the psychic did not guess Bonnie correctly.

19. **The correct answer is (E).** If David is correctly guessed, then he is the one out of the four who does not have a blue ball. That means the other three people each have a blue ball, including Caroline.

20. **The correct answer is (B).** If the psychic guesses David and Caroline correctly, then she must have flip-flopped Chuck and Bonnie. The correct content for Chuck is green and blue balls. Thus, David and Chuck each have a green ball.

Chapter 12

The GRE Analytical Writing Measure

Get the Scoop On . . .

- How to ace the new GRE essay-writing sections
- The four-step writing process that quickly and easily budgets your time and energy
- How to come up with ideas to write about, no matter what the topic
- Professionals' proven techniques for sounding smart whenever you write
- Ways to make your essay as nearly error free as possible

THE TEST CAPSULE

What's the Big Idea?

On the GRE Analytical Writing Measure, you'll be given two essay assignments, one requiring you to develop your own point of view on a particular issue, the other asking you to critique the reasoning behind someone else's argument on an issue. For each assignment, you'll have to write an essay that presents an intelligent response to the topic, uses facts or examples to support that response, and is clear, well-organized, and correct according to the rules of standard written English.

How Many?

The GRE Analytical Writing Measure will have two essay questions; you'll have forty-five minutes to complete one, which asks you to present your own perspective on an issue, and thirty minutes to complete the other, which asks you to analyze someone else's argument.

How Much Do They Count?

Each of your essays will be graded by two readers, using a scale ranging from 0 (worst) to 6 (best). Your final analytical writing score is an average of all four grades. This average does *not* contribute to your GRE verbal score or any other GRE score but is reported separately, to be interpreted by the schools to which you're applying as they see fit.

How Much Time Should They Take?

You'll have 30 or 45 minutes to complete each essay. However, as we'll explain, you should plan on devoting just 20 to 30 minutes to actual writing. This will leave you 5 minutes for prewriting and 5 minutes to proofread and check your work.

What's the Best Strategy?

Use the four-step writing process to organize and budget your time:

1. Brainstorm (3 minutes)
2. Outline (2 minutes)
3. Write (20 to 30 minutes)
4. Revise (5 minutes)

If you follow this four-step plan, you'll end up with a much better essay much more easily than if you'd just plunged in and started writing without a plan.

What's the Worst Pitfall?

Beware of getting overly complicated in your ideas or your essay's structure. The simpler your outline, the better; a simple plan will enable you to develop each idea in interesting detail and produce a clear, coherent essay in which the ideas sound well-connected and you come across as a smart, logical thinker.

THE OFFICIAL DESCRIPTION

What They Are

The test-makers describe the GRE Analytical Writing Measure as consisting of two "writing tasks" designed to test "the kinds of high-level thinking and writing skills generally recognized as essential for success in many graduate programs." Within the time provided, you'll have to decide on your approach to the assigned topic, plan an essay, write your essay (using the computer's simple word processing program), and put your essay into final form after proofreading or checking it in any way you wish.

Where They Are

In the typical computerized GRE Analytical Writing Measure, you'll have two writing assessment sections, each containing one essay assignment. Reminder: the test-makers claim the right to change the format at any time! However, the typical format we just described is what you're most likely to encounter.

What They Measure

The readers who grade your essays will be instructed to assign each essay a one-digit score, ranging from 0 (worst) to 6 (best), considering four main factors: (1) how fully you considered and analyzed the topic; (2) how well you organized, developed, and expressed your ideas; (3) how well you provided relevant reasons and examples to support and explain your ideas; and (4) how correctly you followed the rules of standard written English.

What They Cover

You'll be given a topic about which to write; if you fail to write on the assigned topic, you'll receive a grade of 0 for that essay. The topics deal with mildly controversial issues from various social, political, and ethical fields, on which almost anyone could be expected to have some opinions or ideas. No outside knowledge or background information is provided, and none is needed. You'll almost certainly have enough facts and ideas to write the required essays if you draw upon information you've gathered from your reading for school and pleasure and the general background knowledge you derive from newspapers, magazines, and other media.

The Directions

There are two types of analytical writing assessment assignments: "Present Your Perspective on an Issue" and "Analysis of an Argument." Each has a slightly different set of directions.

Present Your Perspective on an Issue

In this section, you will have 45 minutes to plan and compose an essay that presents your perspective on an assigned topic. An essay on any other topic is not acceptable.

The topic will appear as a brief quotation that states or implies an issue of general interest. You are free to accept, reject, or qualify the quotation, so long as the ideas you present are clearly relevant to the topic. Support your views with reasons and/or examples drawn from such areas as your reading, experience, observation, or academic studies.

College and university faculty members from various subject matter areas will read your essay and evaluate its overall quality, based on how well you do the following:

- Consider the complexities and implications of the issue
- Organize, develop, and express your ideas
- Support your ideas with relevant reasons and/or examples
- Control the elements of standard written English

You may want to take a few minutes to think about the issue and to plan a response before you begin writing. Be sure to develop your ideas fully and organize them coherently, but leave time to reread what you have written and make any revisions that you think are necessary.

Directions: Present your perspective on the issue below, using relevant reasons and/or examples to support your views.

Analysis of an Argument

In this section, you will have 30 minutes to plan and write a critique of an argument presented in the form of a short passage.

You will be asked to consider the logical soundness of the argument. A critique of any other argument is not acceptable.

College and university faculty members from various subject matter areas will read your critique and evaluate its overall quality, considering how well you do the following:

- Identify and analyze important features of the argument.
- Organize, develop, and express your ideas
- Support your ideas with relevant reasons and/or examples
- Control the elements of standard written English

Before you begin writing, you may want to take a few minutes to evaluate the argument and to plan a response. Be sure to develop your ideas fully and organize them coherently, but leave time to reread what you have written and make any revisions that you think are necessary.

Directions: For this task, you will read a brief argument and then discuss how well reasoned you find the argument. Note that you are *not* being asked to agree or disagree with the position taken or the conclusion reached by the argument. In your discussion, be sure to analyze the line of reasoning in the argument. You should consider what, if any, questionable assumptions underlie the thinking and, if evidence is cited, whether it supports the conclusion. You can also discuss the sort of evidence that would strengthen or refute the argument, changes in the argument that would make it more logically sound, and whether additional information would help you to evaluate its conclusion.

THE INSIDER'S REPORT

What You Need to Know about the GRE Analytical Writing Measure

The Analytical Writing Measure differs from the rest of the GRE in several ways:

- Unlike the rest of the GRE, the Analytical Writing Measure is graded subjectively rather than objectively. Trained readers will scrutinize your essays and assign them scores based solely on their opinions of your writing. No two readers are likely to score you the same.

- Unlike the rest of the GRE, the Analytical Writing Measure is graded "holistically" rather than item-by-item. The readers will assign your essay a single number based on their overall assessment of your work. By contrast, your scores in other areas of the GRE are based on a mass of detailed plusses and minuses—right and wrong answers to individual test questions.

- And, unlike the rest of the GRE, your Analytical Writing Measure score will have only a minor impact, if any, on your graduate school admission decision.

Strategies That Really Work

The teachers who read and score the writing assessment essays work under intense time pressure. On average, they have only two minutes to spend on each essay. This has a definite impact on the writing strategies that will and will not make a difference in the score you receive.

The GRE Analytical Writing Measure was created at the request of the graduate schools that sponsor the exam. They'd found that too many of their entering students—including some who scored high on the GRE—were unable to write clear and coherent English prose. True, almost every graduate school applicant must submit a personal statement in essay form; but this doesn't necessarily reflect the applicant's own writing ability since it's always possible to enlist outside editing and rewriting help. Forcing the applicant to write two essays within time constraints at the same time that he takes the GRE was their solution.

The way graduate schools evaluate and interpret Analytical Writing Measure scores varies, but it's rare for a writing score to make or break a candidate. Most schools think of the Analytical Writing Measure as an extra way of checking the applicant's writing ability. If a student has good overall credentials and earns a high GRE verbal score, a low Analytical Writing Measure score (3 or less) may make a school ask: Is there some reason why this student might have trouble expressing himself in writing? Would a remedial writing course be advisable? But it's unlikely that a student who otherwise would be accepted would be rejected because of a poor Analytical Writing Measure score. By the same token, a student with poor or marginal credentials isn't going to be accepted to graduate school because of a high score on the Analytical Writing Measure.

Therefore, we'd recommend you *not* agonize over the Analytical Writing Measure. Review the writing tips in this chapter, and practice the essay questions when you take the sample tests in this book. Beyond that, most students don't need to focus on this part of the exam. The other sections of the GRE are more important and deserve more attention.

Having said that, there are definite strategies you can use to improve your performance on this part of the exam. In fact, they're largely the same strategies that savvy test-takers use whenever they work on an essay exam. If you've been successful on essay tests in history, English, or other college courses, you may find that the ideas in this chapter sound familiar—even if you never consciously learned them. They reflect smart essay-writing practice as used by many students over the years.

Use the Four-Step Writing Process to Make the Most of Your Time
The thirty or forty-five minutes allowed to write each essay isn't much time. Of course, the expectations of the readers who grade your paper will reflect that fact. Almost no one is capable of writing a profound, thoroughly developed, well-crafted, technically perfect essay in just half an hour or so, and you *don't* need to achieve this to earn a high score (5 or 6) on the Analytical Writing Measure.

However, you do need to use your time wisely. It's best to have a clear game plan in mind, which will enable you to tackle each step of the essay-writing process with self-confidence and inner calm. The four-step process we're about to describe is such a game plan. Practice it between now and the day of the exam, and it'll help you feel organized and in control when you tackle the Analytical Writing Measure.

Step 1: Brainstorm (three minutes)
For each of the two essay topics, you'll need to come up with some things to write about.

For the Present Your Perspective on an Issue essay, you'll probably be asked to agree or disagree with someone's opinion. This opinion (we'll call it the *stimulus,* since it serves to stimulate your own writing) will be stated in such broad, general terms that almost anyone can find some facets of the opinion with which to quibble or to agree.

For the Analysis of an Argument essay, the assignment is slightly different: you'll be asked to evaluate the strength or weakness of someone's argument regarding a particular topic. Again, the stimulus you must respond to will be so general in scope that almost anyone can come up with something to say about it.

Your first step in developing your essay is to brainstorm ideas about what to say. There's no magic formula for this process. Just take about three minutes to jot down on a piece of scrap paper a handful of ideas that are relevant to the topic.

You may begin with a clear idea as to whether you agree or disagree with the stimulus. (Perhaps as soon as you read the opinion in the question, you'll have a strongly positive or negative reaction.) If so, that's fine. Just spend your three minutes imagining all the points you could raise to support your point of view. List them as they occur to you, without evaluating how "good" or "bad" they are. Brainstorming is a nonjudgmental activity.

If you begin without feeling any clear agreement or disagreement with the stimulus, that's okay too. Just start jotting down ideas on *either* side of the argument as they come to you. You'll probably find that you think of more ideas on one side than the other. Bingo!—that's your opinion. Since there's truly no "right" or "wrong" opinion, just pick whichever opinion you have the most things to say about and run with it.

Here's an example of a typical Present Your Perspective topic like those you'll find on the real GRE:

> Present your perspective on the issue below, using relevant reasons and/or examples to support your views.

> "Schools should be responsible only for teaching academic skills and not for teaching ethical and social values."

Notice how broad the stimulus is. You can define "schools," "academic skills," and "ethical and social values" any way you like. You could write about teaching kindergarten kids to get along with one another; about whether high school students should be allowed to have organized prayer in public schools; about "speech codes" on college campuses, or any of several dozen other possible variations. The writing measure topics are deliberately designed so that any conscious person can probably think of something intelligent and thoughtful to say about them.

Notice, too, that the question that precedes the stimulus is designed to jog your thinking about ideas to discuss. Refer to that question if you find yourself at a loss. It suggests that you provide "reasons and/or examples to support your views." Again, a very wide net is being cast—deliberately. You can come up with supporting ideas based upon:

- classroom discussions in which you've participated
- things you learned in school
- movies or TV shows
- books, essays, or other writings
- the lives of famous people
- your own experiences
- stories people have told you
- current events
- episodes from history

And so on. Again, almost anyone can come up with a few relevant things to mention by simply drawing on one or more of these sources.

Here's an example of what a student's brainstorming notes for the topic above might look like:

```
Whose values?
       Amish
       suburbanites
       yuppies
       Southern Baptists
pluralism
schools need focus
sex education
classroom cooperation vs. competition
teachers set example—indirectly
```

The first several lines reflect one train of thought: if schools were to teach ethical values, *whose* values would they teach? Those of the Amish? Suburban values (family togetherness, peace and harmony, leisure)? Yuppie values (greed, ambition)? Those of Southern Baptists (tradition, piety, respect for authority)? Since America is pluralistic, it may be impractical for schools to teach values; consequently, they need to focus on academics.

The other notes reflect other random ideas:

Should sex education be academic in focus (the biology of sex) or values-based?

Most schools encourage classroom competition rather than cooperation (if you look at a neighbor's test paper, you're "cheating"); is that ethically proper?

Teachers set ethical examples every day by what they do and say.

Finally, would the problems of drugs and violence in schools be less serious if ethics were deliberately taught?

The notes, obviously, are somewhat of a hodgepodge. *That's all right.* The point of brainstorming is just to generate a bunch of ideas. There'll be time in a moment to winnow and organize them.

Naturally, no two people will write notes that look alike. The point is to keep this first step in the writing process simple and straightforward: generate raw material for your essay by writing down whatever comes to mind in a matter of three minutes or less. It'll almost certainly provide plenty of fodder for the remaining steps and for the essay that's your ultimate goal.

Step 2: Outline (two minutes)

Now spend two minutes organizing the raw, random notes you created by brainstorming into a simple outline for your essay.

This can be done quite quickly. Here's how.

First, if you haven't already, decide on a point of view (pro or con) that you want to defend in your essay.

Then, look at your notes and pick the three or four ideas you like best. They should be ideas that you think (1) make sense, (2) relate to the topic, (3) support your point of view reasonably well, and (4) you know enough about to write a few sentences on. Put a check or other mark next to those ideas. You'll use these in your essay.

If there aren't enough good ideas that fit these criteria, take one or two of the ideas you like and elaborate on them. Think of related ideas, add details or examples, and use these to fill out your list.

Finally, decide on a sequence for the ideas. This can be done in several ways. Occasionally, a sequence will be obvious: one idea may be the cause of all the others and therefore should clearly come first; or the ideas may all reflect historic events that took place in a definite time sequence, which it would be natural to follow. If there's an obvious sequence, use it.

If there is no obvious sequence, decide which idea you like *best*. It may be the idea you find most interesting; it may be the idea you consider most convincing; it may be an idea you were recently talking about with a friend or wrote a paper about for school, so you happen to know a lot about it. Whatever the reason, put your favorite idea *first*. Then, put your second favorite idea *last,* and then stick the remaining idea(s) in between, in an arbitrary order.

What's the rationale for this strategy? The most emphatic parts of any essay—the parts the reader is most likely to remember—are the beginning and the end. What appears in the middle is most likely to be half-forgotten. Therefore, your best material ought to come either at the start or the end of your essay. In those locations, it'll have the greatest positive effect on your grade.

Once you've decided on a sequence for your ideas, just mark the items with numbers in the appropriate sequence, right there on your notes: 1, 2, 3, 4. That's your outline. Simple, no?

Here's an example of how the brainstorming notes from above might be turned into a simple outline:

2. ✔ <u>Whose values?</u>
    Amish
    suburbanites
    yuppies
    Southern Baptists

1. ✔ pluralism

3.   schools need focus
    sex education
    classroom cooperation vs. competition
    teachers set examples—indirectly

4.   drugs & violence

The test-taker who produced the original notes decided that (for the purposes of the writing measure) he would agree with the argument presented—that schools should teach academics only, not ethical values. (Why did he decide that? Maybe that's his sincere belief. More important, he has a few good notes he can use to defend that point of view! That's all that really matters when tackling the Analytical Writing Measure.)

Having decided this, he scanned his notes and found that the first three points listed all seemed to fit nicely into his argument. He also thought of a fourth idea that might make a good ending, so he jotted this at the end: "U.S. schools lag." (The idea here is that American schools are already behind most other countries in academic standards—at least, so most people believe—so why take precious teaching time away from academic subjects to teach ethics? This seems like a reasonably effective argument to close with.) He marked all four ideas with a check.

Finally, he decided, somewhat arbitrarily, on a logical order for the four ideas. He'll start with the idea that America is pluralistic. From that, it makes sense to ask, "Whose values would be taught in schools?" and use the Amish/suburban/etc. examples. This leads nicely into the point about focusing on academics and, finally, the argument about how American students lag behind others. Wham, bam, the outline is done.

Again, no two students will produce the same outline based on any given topic. It doesn't matter. All that matters is that you come up with a few ideas you feel able to write about and put them into a more-or-less logical sequence.

FYI

If you're used to using a computer for writing, you'll be completely comfortable with the GRE word-processing program. If not, you should practice beforehand on a computer equipped with standard word-processing software (such as Microsoft Word or WordPerfect). You shouldn't have to waste energy mastering the sheer mechanics of computerized typing while trying to write your essays.

Now you're ready to do some actual writing.

Step 3: Write (twenty to thirty minutes)

Five minutes have passed, and you haven't yet typed a single word of your essay. Don't get nervous! The time you've spent getting organized is about to pay dividends. Writing your essay will go much more smoothly than it otherwise would because you've invested a few minutes in picking the best ideas to write about and in coming up with a logical sequence for them.

Go ahead and begin writing your essay. You'll be typing it on the test center computer, of course. The test-makers have equipped your machine with a simple word-processing program, able to handle most of the basic maneuvers found in other such programs. You can move from place to place in the essay using the arrow keys; you can delete, insert, and move text; you can use the mouse to jump to a particular word, etc.

As you write, follow the simple outline you created a moment ago, with these two added elements:

- Begin the essay with a brief introductory paragraph that sets forth your point of view and, if you like, suggests the nature of the ideas you'll be using to defend it.

- End the essay with a brief concluding paragraph that summarizes your point of view in a clear, concise, forceful way.

Use the paragraph as your structural unit. That is, think of each idea as occupying a single, fully developed paragraph, three to six sentences long. This isn't a rigid rule: a "big" idea may develop into two paragraphs, and two simple ideas may nestle comfortably in a single longish paragraph. But, in general, the simplest and clearest structure for writing is to start a new paragraph each time you begin a new idea. This makes your writing easy to follow and makes you sound clear-headed—something the weary, harried readers of your GRE essays will appreciate.

Here's how the notes from above might be turned into a first-draft essay. (The numbers at the start of each paragraph are included for our ease in discussing the essay.)

[1]   Schools, especially in a pluralistic nation like America, should stick to teaching academic subjects and leave ethics for the home and the church, temple, or synagogue. To do otherwise is to invite trouble, as this essay will show.

[2]   The most important question to be answered, if our schools are to teach values, is: *whose* values would they teach? After all, not all ethical values are the same. Let's consider two examples that illustrate, in an extreme form, how divergent American values can be. The Amish, who practice their traditional way of life in farming communities in Pennsylvania, Ohio,

FYI

If you abhor the idea of writing your essays on the computer, you do have another option. You can take the Analytical Writing Measure in paper-and-pencil format on any day when the GRE Subject Tests are offered at college testing sites around the country. See the GRE Web site at www.gre.org for more information.

FYI

"Tell 'em what you're going to tell 'em; then tell 'em; then tell 'em what you told 'em."—Old maxim for writers. This traditional advice isn't always best—it produces formulaic writing—but on the GRE Analytical Writing Measure, a handy formula is exactly what you want. Try it!

and other states, have a value system that stresses simplicity and austerity; they avoid modern conveniences, including many forms of technology that most Americans take for granted, and even shun dancing.

[3] By contrast, the typical young urban family—"yuppies," as they're sometimes called—believes in buying the latest electronic gadgets, going on expensive vacations, and enjoying a wide range of current entertainment, from the newest movies and TV shows to the current best-selling books. Both the Amish and the yuppies are representative American social groups, yet either might be deeply offended by the values of the other.

[4] True, Amish and yuppie children aren't likely to attend the same schools; but what about Jewish kids and fundamentalist Christians? These two groups may live in the same town or neighborhood, and either one would be incensed to have the other group's moral teachings imposed on them. This example isn't merely fanciful. In some southern towns where prayers from the Christian Bible are still recited in public schools, Jewish families have had to go to court to protect their right to abstain without suffering ridicule. Conversely, non-Jewish families in a New York town dominated by orthodox Jews have recently been protesting the fact that the local schools were presenting traditional Jewish teachings in the classroom. In instances like these, bringing ethics into the schools causes divisiveness, not harmony.

FYI

As you read this essay, compare it to the brainstorming notes and outline that appeared earlier. See how the notes and outline became the basis for the essay?

[5] The only way to avoid the inevitable conflicts that teaching ethics would bring to our schools is by allowing teachers to focus on what they're paid to do: to teach academics. We send children to school to learn math, English, history, and science. How would we feel if our children came home ignorant about geometry but filled with someone else's religious or ethical ideas? Justly annoyed, I think.

[6] Given the fact that American schoolchildren lag behind most other nations in academic achievement, it would be foolish for us to divert precious classroom time to teaching morality. This is not to say that the ethical dimensions of topics in history, English, or other subjects must be banned from the classroom. Students and teachers should be free to reflect on moral themes in their own papers and in classroom discussions. But the curriculum shouldn't aim to inculcate any particular ethical point of view, and dialogues regarding morality should always be focused on the underlying educational purpose—that is, to teach history, English, or whatever.

[7] Ironically, then, the most ethical thing our schools can do for our children is to avoid getting entangled in ethical issues. Stick to academics, and let families teach morality in their own way, and on their own time.

Notice a few features of this essay:

- Paragraphs 1 and 7 succinctly summarize the writer's point of view. They make the argument clear and easy to follow and give the essay a forthright tone that suggests a clear, self-confident mind.

- Paragraphs 2 through 6 reflect the numbered points from the outline. Each time the writer completed an idea from the outline, he started a new paragraph. The result is a logical sequence of paragraphs, laying out the points of the essay in easy-to-follow fashion.

- The writer adapted his outline slightly as he wrote, using new ideas and new approaches as they occurred to him. For example, point 2 in the outline ("whose values?") became the basis for three paragraphs in the final essay, not just one (paragraphs 2, 3, and 4). Furthermore, after writing about the Amish and the yuppies in paragraphs 2 and 3, the writer seemed to realize that the contrast between these two groups was a little exaggerated; hence, paragraph 4 offers a more down-to-earth pairing as well as two real-life examples of community conflicts over ethical teaching in schools. This greatly strengthens the argument. The suburbanites got left out altogether, since they seemed unnecessary.

- Is this essay a masterful piece of writing, worthy of standing beside Thoreau or Orwell in an anthology of fine English prose? Not really. But it's a clear, workmanlike, reasonably well-thought-out defense of the writer's point of view, and as such it's likely to earn a high score on the GRE Analytical Writing Measure. Mission accomplished.

Step 4: Revise (five minutes)
The last of the four writing steps is revision—literally, a "re-seeing" of your work. After you finish writing your first draft, pause for a moment; shut your eyes, lean back in your chair, stretch your arms, take a deep breath, and relax. Then scroll back up to the top of your essay and spend the last five minutes rereading it, finding and fixing as many errors and imperfections as possible.

A little later in this chapter, we'll offer some tips and warnings that will help you polish the style and mechanics of your essay. For now, these general suggestions:

- Reread your essay slowly, line by line, to make sure you spot any places where you accidentally left out words, garbled phrases, or made typographical errors.

- Try to read the essay with fresh eyes, as though you'd never seen it before. Make sure you've really said what you intended to say: as William Strunk and E. B. White's classic writing guide *The Elements of Style* puts it, "Your chances of having said it are only fair."

- Don't get drawn into drastic rewriting. Your essay is what it is; you don't have time to rethink it substantially. Tinker around the edges, but don't try to rebuild the house.

Keep Your Essay Simple

Throughout this chapter, we've emphasized the need to avoid getting complicated. The point is worth stressing. In a half hour to forty-five minutes, you have time to write an essay of only 300 to 600 words. That means, at most, 5 or 6 paragraphs expressing 3 or 4 main ideas. Trying to get more complicated will lead you into trouble in several ways: it may cause you to run out of time before finishing your essay; it may cause you or your reader to lose track of your point of view, producing confusion and a sense of incompetence; it may force you to streamline your discussion of each point so drastically as to make it seem simple to the point of inanity.

A few ideas, each one developed in a few interesting sentences: that's the formula for a winning GRE essay.

Make Sure Your Point of View Comes through Clearly

Surprisingly often, student essays (on the GRE and elsewhere) fail to clearly express a strong and distinctive point of view. True, the GRE readers don't particularly care about your point of view; there's no right or wrong opinion that you can express about any of the topics, and one can write a technically correct essay without expressing a forceful opinion. But *an essay with a clear point of view sounds smarter.* When you write as if you know what you're talking about and have the facts to back up what you believe, your writing carries conviction and authority; and such writing is apt to earn a higher score from your readers.

So lean toward an opinionated rather than a wishy-washy tone in your essay; it's more interesting and more impressive.

The Best Tips

So far, we've focused mainly on *what* to say in your essay: how to come up with ideas to write about and how to organize those ideas. Now, let's consider *how* to say it: specifically, how to tailor your writing style for the most positive effect on your readers.

The stylistic challenge on the GRE Analytical Writing Measure is actually a simple one: *to sound smart.* As we've mentioned, each writing measure essay is read and graded in about two minutes. This means that your reader will probably never notice or appreciate any subtle irony your essay may contain, any clever metaphor you use, any profound observation you make, or any moving self-revelation you share. There's no time for that. About all the reader has time to notice is whether you sound smart or dumb. Your score is a snap judgment about that.

But not to worry. There are several proven techniques you can use to make sure you sound smart, even when writing under the gun. These are techniques developed and used by professional writers—craftsmen who must sound at least reasonably smart even when cranking out reams of prose (for newspapers, magazines, and TV broadcasts) on deadline. The same techniques will work for you.

Here are a few to try. In particular, as you revise your essays, look for ways to incorporate these writing techniques. You'll find that making just a few changes in your essay in accordance with these ideas can make a big difference in its overall effectiveness.

Guide the Reader Using Signpost Words

These are words that draw connections among the ideas in your essay. There are many examples. An illustrative story may be introduced by signpost words such as *For instance* or *For example*. A series of three arguments might be introduced by the words *First . . . Second . . . Finally*. When two ideas contrast with one another, signpost words like *On the other hand* or *However* can be used.

Signpost words are valuable in many ways. They help the reader follow your argument more easily. They make the purpose of each detail, fact, story, or example you use more obvious. Most important, they make your essay sound well organized. By emphasizing the structure of your argument, they make it obvious that you've thought it through; rather than rambling aimlessly from one idea to another, you've got a plan and you are following it intelligently.

Look for opportunities to use these four kinds of signpost words in your essays:

- Words that show a contrast or change in idea:

    although, but, by contrast, despite, however, nevertheless, nonetheless, on the other hand, unlike, yet

- Words that show a similarity or the continuation of an idea:

    also, as well, equally, in the same way, likewise, parallel, similarly, so, thus, too

- Words that show a time sequence:

    after, before, earlier, later, next, previous, prior, subsequently, then

- Words that show a cause-and-effect relationship:

    as a result, because, consequently, due to, led to, produced, resulted in, since, therefore

The more evident your essay's logical structure, the more logical you'll sound—and that's a good thing.

Be Specific

Most writers—especially when writing hastily—tend to be vague. They fail to make it really clear what they are talking about. The result is prose that sounds poorly thought out, or even devoid of ideas.

To sound smart, make a deliberate effort to express each of your ideas in as specific and detailed a way as possible. Here are a couple of illustrations of what we mean. Suppose you wanted to refer to the contributions of Arab cultures to western civilization (a point that could be relevant to any number of essay topics). Here's a vague way of doing so, which is typical of many quickly written student essays:

Many important ideas in science and other areas were brought to the western world from other regions during the years following the Middle Ages.

Here's a more specific way, using a couple of details to make the point much more vivid and interesting:

Such vital scientific principles as the concept of zero and the geographical teachings of Ptolemy were imported to western Europe from Arabic culture during the fourteenth and fifteenth centuries.

Another example of the vague:

Some people in the nineteenth century felt that modern science had called into question basic concepts concerning the relationship between human beings and God.

As compared to the specific:

The writings of authors such as Matthew Arnold and Alfred Tennyson reflected the feeling that Darwin's theory of evolution had weakened belief in Christian doctrines about the creation of humans by God.

True, you need to know and use some actual facts in order to write specifically rather than vaguely. But it's not as hard as it looks. Consider the first example above, about Arabic science. It contains just two examples—the concept of zero and the geography of Ptolemy—which may be all the student author happens to remember from a semester-long course in the history of science; and since he's unclear about his dates, he carefully fudges by referring to "the fourteenth and fifteenth centuries." Sounds impressive, though, doesn't it?

Anyway, no one is going to check your facts; remember, your poor reader has just two minutes to spend. The important thing is that you *sound* as though you know something. Grab a fact or two that you do know and insert them in your essay. The result will sound much smarter than if you merely generalize.

Vary the Length of Your Sentences

There's nothing really *wrong* with an essay in which all the sentences are about the same length. Most readers won't consciously notice. But the effect is monotonous, and the result is often an essay that sounds dull, lifeless, and uninteresting.

Instead, consciously try to vary the length of your sentences. Make some of your sentences fairly long and complicated in grammatical form, as we've done with the sentence you're reading now. Keep others short, like this one. The changing rhythms of your writing will help keep your reader alert and interested and give your prose a snappy, intelligent tone.

In particular, use short sentences for emphasis. A great way to highlight a significant idea is to express it in a sentence of only five to eight words. It's especially effective when the short sentence appears among several longer ones. The bluntness of the short sentence stands out.

Here's an example of how this works. Notice how the short sentence toward the end of this paragraph draws your attention:

> In the nineteenth century, when the science of psychology was founded, its methods were generally, by modern standards, unscientific. Rather than considering only evidence that could be objectively verified or data drawn from experiments that could be repeated by other scientists, psychologists often based their theories on evidence that was highly subjective. Today, this has largely changed. Psychologists are now learning to restrict themselves to studying phenomena that can be directly observed and objectively analyzed.

The rhythm of the sentences emphasizes the historic change in the nature of psychology, which is the main point the author of this paragraph wants the reader to remember.

This is an easy trick to use whenever you write, even when the time pressures of an exam force you to work quickly. Just write a short sentence every now and then, particularly when you have a key concept you want to stress. The result is a crisp, smart-sounding style.

Make Concessions as Needed

A final way of sounding smart is to show that you recognize the limitations of your own arguments. We attribute intelligence to the judicious person—one who weighs arguments thoughtfully, seeing shades of gray rather than mere black-and-white truths. Make a point of introducing this tone into your essays by making at least one or two concessions to the opposing point of view.

You can insert a concession almost anywhere in an essay, except at the very end. (In that spot, it will make your essay sound unresolved, as though you're not sure *what* you believe.) As you may have noticed, our earlier essay, about teaching ethics in schools, contained a concession stated in two sentences from paragraph 6:

This is not to say that the ethical dimensions of topics in history, English, or other subjects must be banned from the classroom. Students and teachers should be free to reflect on moral themes in their own papers and in classroom discussions.

The same essay could also effectively *begin* with a concession:

Sometimes it seems as if our society is at the brink of ethical chaos. Violence is all too common on our streets and even in our schools; politicians and businesspeople seem to get away with deceit and crime. Under the circumstances, it's understandable that many people would like our schools to fill the moral gap. Teach ethics in schools, they say, and the next generation will have a better moral grounding.

It's an appealing idea, but one that would hurt our society more than it would help.

Notice how these sentences, presenting the opposing point of view in a sympathetic, understanding way, actually *strengthen* the writer's position by making him sound eminently reasonable. Try this technique. It really works.

The Most Important Warning

Take Steps to Eliminate Errors in Spelling, Grammar, and Usage

Theoretically, the writing measure is not mainly a test of writing mechanics. Rather it's intended to focus on your ability to structure and develop a well-organized, intelligent essay. Thus, you might assume that minor details such as spelling, grammar, and word usage "don't count." They don't—in the sense that your reader is not keeping a running tally of technical errors and then deducting (for example) one grade for every five mistakes. The writing measure scoring doesn't work like that.

On the other hand, the teachers who read and grade the GRE essays have their biases, like anyone else. And most teachers share the assumption that errors in spelling, grammar, and usage suggest ignorance, laziness, or both. Consciously or unconsciously, they can't help being influenced by this when they read and score your paper.

Therefore, when you revise your essay, follow these tips:

- Catch and fix as many spelling errors as possible. (No, the GRE software doesn't include a spell-check program—sorry.)

- If you're in doubt about a word's proper spelling, instead pick a word you *do* know, even if its meaning is a trifle less apt.

- Catch and fix as many grammar and usage errors as you can. If this is a weakness of yours, consult a book like Strunk and White's *Elements of Style,* which was mentioned earlier; it offers concise explanations of most of the grammar rules that commonly cause problems for student writers. (Appendix C suggests some other books you may find helpful as well.)

- When in doubt about the grammatical structure of a sentence, simplify it: break one long, unwieldy sentence into two, or trim away extra phrases until you're sure the remaining structure is sound.

Perfection isn't the goal; almost no one can write a perfect, error-free essay in thirty to forty-five minutes, and your work will be judged against that of other students laboring under the same time pressure. But an essay that's relatively free of grammar and spelling bugs will—even subconsciously—provoke a more respectful response, and a higher score, from your reader.

JUST THE FACTS

- Use the four-step writing process on the Analytical Writing Measure to manage your time and effort effectively.

- Keep your essay simple and make sure your point of view comes through clearly.

- To sound smart, use signpost words, be specific, vary sentence length, and make concessions where needed.

- Although mechanical errors "don't count," they really do; find them, fix them, or avoid them.

Part III

The Insider's GRE Sample Test

Chapter 13

The Insider's GRE Sample Test

INSTRUCTIONS

The following Insider's GRE Sample Test will give you a chance to practice the skills and strategies you've just learned throughout this book. As with all practice exercises, work under true testing conditions. Complete the entire test in a single sitting. Eliminate distractions (TV, music) and clear away notes and reference materials.

Time each section of the test separately with a stopwatch or kitchen timer, or have someone else time you. If you run out of time before answering all the questions, stop and draw a line under the last question you finished. Then go on to the next test section. When you are done, score yourself based only on the questions you finished in the allotted time. Later, for practice purposes, you should answer the questions you were unable to complete in time.

The answer key and explanatory answers appear at the end of the test, beginning on page 507.

This sample test includes the Analytical Writing Measure sections. If you are taking the GRE before October 1, 2002, you can skip the AWM. If you are taking the GRE after September 30, 2002, you should skip the Analytical Reasoning Section. (See Chapter 12 for more information on the GRE Analytical Writing Measure.) For this part of the diagnostic, you can write using a word-processing program or pencil and paper. Either way, stick with the time restrictions and other test conditions. Although you can't get an admissions officer's evaluation of your work, you will get a feel for how well you handle this part of the exam, and you can plan your preparation accordingly.

SECTION 1

ANALYTICAL WRITING MEASURE

Time—45 Minutes

Present Your Perspective on an Issue
In this section, you will have 45 minutes to plan and compose an essay that presents your perspective on an assigned topic. An essay on any other topic is not acceptable.

The topic will appear as a brief quotation that states or implies an issue of general interest. You are free to accept, reject, or qualify the quotation, so long as the ideas you present are clearly relevant to the topic. Support your views with reasons and/or examples drawn from such areas as your reading, experience, observation, or academic studies.

College and university faculty members from various subject matter areas will read your essay and evaluate its overall quality based on how well you do the following:

- Consider the complexities and implications of the issue
- Organize, develop, and express your ideas
- Support your ideas with relevant reasons and/or examples
- Control the elements of standard written English

You may want to take a few minutes to think about the issue and to plan a response before you begin writing. Be sure to develop your ideas fully and organize them coherently, but leave time to reread what you have written and make any revisions that you think are necessary.

Directions: Present your perspective on the issue below, using relevant reasons and/or examples to support your views.

"People often complain that the introduction of new labor-saving machines costs workers their jobs. However, most new technologies actually create more jobs than they destroy."

SECTION 2

ANALYTICAL WRITING MEASURE

Time—30 Minutes

Analysis of an Argument

In this section, you will have 30 minutes to plan and write a critique of an argument presented in the form of a short passage.

You will be asked to consider the logical soundness of the argument. A critique of any other argument is not acceptable.

College and university faculty members from various subject matter areas will read your critique and evaluate its overall quality based on how well you do the following:

- Identify and analyze important features of the argument.
- Organize, develop, and express your ideas
- Support your ideas with relevant reasons and/or examples
- Control the elements of standard written English

Before you begin writing, you may want to take a few minutes to evaluate the argument and to plan a response. Be sure to develop your ideas fully and organize them coherently, but leave time to reread what you have written and make any revisions that you think are necessary.

Directions: For this task, you will read a brief argument and then discuss how well reasoned you find the argument. Note that you are *not* being asked to agree or disagree with the position taken or the conclusion reached by the argument. In your discussion, be sure to analyze the line of reasoning in the argument. You should consider what, if any, questionable assumptions underlie the thinking and, if evidence is cited, whether it supports the conclusion. You can also discuss the sort of evidence that would strengthen or refute the argument, changes in the argument that would make it more logically sound, and whether additional information would help you to evaluate its conclusion.

The following appeared as part of plan proposed by an executive of the Stan Doncé Magazine Group to the company's president.

"Our need for printing services varies from month to month, depending on the size of our magazines and variations in scheduling. Working with outside printers has necessitated a constant scramble for adequate press time at reasonable prices. If we were to buy and operate our own printing operation, we would be better able to control both the availability and the cost of printing our magazines, which would have a favorable impact on the efficiency and profitability of our business."

SECTION 3

VERBAL

30 Questions

Time—30 Minutes

Directions (Antonyms): Each question consists of a word printed in capital letters, followed by five lettered words or phrases. Choose the lettered word or phrase that is most nearly *opposite* in meaning to the word in capital letters.

Directions (Analogies): In each question, a related pair of words or phrases is followed by five lettered pairs of words or phrases. Select the lettered pair that best expresses a relationship similar to that expressed in the original pair.

Directions (Sentence Completions): Each sentence has one or two blanks, each blank indicating that something has been omitted. Beneath the sentence are five lettered words or sets of words. Choose the word or set of words for each blank that *best* fits the meaning of the sentence as a whole.

Directions (Reading Comprehension): Each passage is followed by questions based on its content. After reading a passage, choose the best answer to each question. Answer all questions following a passage on the basis of what is *stated* or *implied* in the passage.

1. VALID:
    (A) openly expressed
    (B) not coherent
    (C) without force
    (D) incapable of speech
    (E) difficult to obtain

2. PROGRAM : BROADCAST ::
    (A) crime : investigate
    (B) opera : compose
    (C) lecture : attend
    (D) news : confirm
    (E) book : publish

3. HAUGHTY : PRIDE ::
    (A) timid : boldness
    (B) grandiose : beauty
    (C) humble : honesty
    (D) rash : bravery
    (E) bigoted : prejudice

4. Today it is hard to believe that there remains any _____ region on earth, as the advent of television has made it possible to travel to virtually every corner of the globe from our living rooms.
    (A) unexplored
    (B) fertile
    (C) uninhabited
    (D) undeveloped
    (E) unspoiled

5. ELOQUENT:
    (A) illiterate
    (B) sincere
    (C) inarticulate
    (D) restrained
    (E) dry

6. PROPONENT:
    (A) contender
    (B) foe
    (C) liege
    (D) suppliant
    (E) confidant

7. Harold went back to school to escape the _____ of his job, which consisted of nothing but endless, _____ paperwork.

   (A) pressure..boring
   (B) rigor..intimidating
   (C) tedium..mindless
   (D) onerousness..fascinating
   (E) oppressiveness..ever-changing

Questions 8–10 refer to the following passage.

Line   The Impressionist painters expressly disavowed any interest in philosophy, yet their new approach to art had far-reaching philosophical implications.

       For the view of matter that the Impressionists assumed differed profoundly from the view that had previously prevailed among artists. This view (5) helped to unify the artistic works created in the new style.

       The ancient Greeks had conceived of the world in concrete terms, even endowing abstract qualities with bodies. This Greek view of matter persisted, so far as painting was concerned, into the nineteenth century. The Impressionists, on the other hand, viewed light, not matter, as the ultimate visual reality. The (10) philosopher Taine expressed the Impressionist view of things when he said, "The chief 'person' in a picture is the light in which everything is bathed."

       In Impressionist painting, solid bodies became mere reflectors of light, and distinctions between one object and another became arbitrary conventions; for by light all things were welded together. The treatment of both color and outline (15) was transformed as well. Color, formerly considered a property inherent in an object, was seen to be merely the result of vibrations of light on the object's colorless surface. And outline, whose function had formerly been to indicate the limits of objects, now marked instead merely the boundary between units of pattern, which often merged into one another.

       (20) The Impressionist world was composed not of separate objects but of many surfaces on which light struck and was reflected with varying intensity to the eye through the atmosphere, which modified it. It was this process that produced the mosaic of colors that formed an Impressionist canvas. "Light becomes the sole subject of the picture," writes Mauclair. "The interest of the (25) object upon which it plays is secondary. Painting thus conceived becomes a purely optic art."

       From this profoundly revolutionary form of art, then, all ideas—religious, moral, psychological—were excluded, and so were all emotions except certain aesthetic ones. The people, places, and things depicted in an Impressionist (30) picture do not tell a story or convey any special meaning; they are, instead, merely parts of a pattern of light drawn from nature and captured on canvas by the artist.

8. According to the passage, the Impressionist painters differed from the ancient Greeks in that they

   (A) considered color to be a property inherent in objects.
   (B) regarded art primarily as a medium for expressing moral and aesthetic ideas.
   (C) treated the object depicted in a painting as isolated, rather than united in a single pattern.
   (D) were unconcerned with the psychological aspects of artistic expression.
   (E) treated light, rather than matter, as the ultimate reality.

9. According to the passage, an Impressionist painting is best considered

   (A) a harmonious arrangement of solid physical masses.
   (B) a pattern of lights of varying intensities.
   (C) a mosaic of outlines representing the edges of objects.
   (D) an analysis of the properties of differing geometric forms.
   (E) an experimental combination of several types of space.

10. The passage suggests that the Impressionist painters regarded the distinctions among different kinds of objects to be painted as

    (A) primarily of psychological interest.
    (B) arbitrary and essentially insignificant.
    (C) reflecting social and political realities.
    (D) to be captured on canvas by the artist.
    (E) suggestive of abstract truths.

11. ECCENTRIC:

    (A) conventional
    (B) predicted
    (C) logical
    (D) accurate
    (E) similar

12. Carpenter's attempt to smear her opponent with false accusations of adultery was _____, and when her duplicity was discovered many voters were understandably _____.

    (A) contemptible..bemused
    (B) despicable..appalled
    (C) disreputable..ambivalent
    (D) ingenious..jubilant
    (E) exemplary..disgusted

13. BARGE : VESSEL ::

  (A) truck : vehicle
  (B) yacht : rowboat
  (C) bicycle : wheel
  (D) caboose : train
  (E) sailboat : liner

14. PRINT : VISIBLE ::

  (A) meaning : plausible
  (B) form : tangible
  (C) reality : understandable
  (D) speech : audible
  (E) message : transcribable

Questions 15–16 refer to the following passage.

Line

Do women tend to devalue the worth of their work? Do they apply different standards to rewarding their own work than they do to rewarding the work of others? These were the questions asked by Michigan State University psychologists Lawrence Messe and Charlene Callahan-Levy. Past experiments

(5)   had shown that when women were asked to decide how much to pay themselves and other people for the same job, they paid themselves less. Following up on this finding, Messe and Callahan-Levy designed experiments to test several popular explanations of why women tend to shortchange themselves in pay situations.

(10)   One theory the psychologists tested was that women judge their own work more harshly than that of others. The subjects for the experiment testing this theory were men and women recruited from the Michigan State undergraduate student body. The job the subjects were asked to perform for pay was an opinion questionnaire requiring a number of short essays on

(15)   campus-related issues. After completing the questionnaire, some subjects were given six dollars in bills and change and were asked to decide payment for themselves. Others were given the same amount and were asked to decide payment for another subject who had also completed the questionnaire.

The psychologists found that, as in earlier experiments, the women paid

(20)   themselves less than the men paid themselves. They also found that the women paid themselves less than they paid other women and less than the men paid the women. The differences were substantial. The average paid to women by themselves was $2.97. The average paid to men by themselves was $4.06. The average paid to women by others was $4.37. In spite of the differences, the

(25)   psychologists found that the men and the women in the experiment evaluated their own performances on the questionnaire about equally and better than the expected performances of others.

On the basis of these findings, Messe and Callahan-Levy concluded that women's attachment of a comparatively low monetary value to their work

(30)   cannot be based entirely on their judgment of their own ability. Perhaps, the psychologists postulated, women see less of a connection than men do between their work (even when it is superior) and their pay because they are relatively indifferent to receiving money for their work.

15. According to the passage, the work of Messe and Callahan-Levy tends to weaken the notion that
    (A) people will tend to over-reward themselves when given the opportunity to do so.
    (B) women are generally less concerned with financial rewards for their work than are men.
    (C) men are willing to pay women more than women are willing to pay themselves.
    (D) payment for work should generally be directly related to the quality of the work.
    (E) women judge their own work more critically than they judge the work of men.

16. The experiment designed in the passage would be most relevant to the formulation of a theory concerning the
    (A) generally lower salaries received by women workers in comparison to men.
    (B) reluctance of some women to enter professions that are traditionally dominated by men.
    (C) low prestige given by society to many traditionally female-dominated professions.
    (D) anxiety expressed by some women workers in dealing with male supervisors.
    (E) discrimination often suffered by women in attempting to enter the workforce.

17. The flooding of the river banks, _____ occurrence in this lush region of South America, always causes _____, for if the event is mistimed, all of the community's life-sustaining crops may be destroyed.
    (A) a perennial..rejoicing
    (B) an unprecedented..turmoil
    (C) an annual..apprehension
    (D) a constant..fear
    (E) a novel..consternation

18. SUSTAIN:
    (A) attempt to forestall
    (B) greatly diminish
    (C) produce by accident
    (D) fail to support
    (E) willfully revoke

19. ANIMOSITY:
    - (A) moderation
    - (B) friendship
    - (C) proximity
    - (D) orthodoxy
    - (E) normality

20. VAT : STORE ::
    - (A) warehouse : put
    - (B) pool : swim
    - (C) pipe : convey
    - (D) bin : gather
    - (E) tub : fill

Questions 21–23 refer to the following passage.

(The article from which this passage was taken appeared in 1987.)

Line   A major goal of the Viking spacecraft missions was to determine whether the soil
of Mars is dead, like the soil of the moon, or teeming with microscopic life, like
the soils of Earth. Soil samples brought into the Viking lander were sent to three
separate biological laboratories to be tested in different ways for the presence
(5)   of life.

    The tests were based on two assumptions. First, it was assumed that life
on Mars would be like life on Earth, which is based on the element carbon and
thrives by chemically transforming carbon compounds. Second, on Earth, where
there are large life-forms (like human beings and pine trees), there are also small
(10)   ones (like bacteria), and the small ones are far more abundant, with thousands
or millions of them in every gram of soil. To have the best possible chance of
detecting life, an instrument should look for the most abundant kind of life.

    The Viking instruments were designed, therefore, to detect carbon-based
Martian microbes or similar creatures living in the soil. The three laboratories in
(15)   the lander were designed to warm and nourish any life in the Martian soil and to
detect with sensitive instruments the chemical activity of the organisms.

    One characteristic of earthly plants is that they transform carbon dioxide
in the air into the compounds that make up their roots, branches, and leaves.
Accordingly, one Viking experiment, called the carbon assimilation test, added
(20)   radioactive carbon dioxide to the atmosphere above the soil sample. The
sample was then flooded with simulated Martian sunlight. If any Martian
life-forms converted the carbon dioxide into other compounds, the compounds
could be detected by their radioactivity.

    Living organisms on Earth give off gases. Plants give off oxygen, animals
(25)   give off carbon dioxide, and both exhale water. A second experiment on each
lander, the gas exchange test, was designed to detect this kind of activity. Nutrients and water were added to the soil, and the chemical composition of the gas
above the soil was continuously analyzed for changes that might indicate life.

    A third experiment on each lander was based on the fact that earthly
(30)   animals consume organic compounds and give off carbon dioxide. The labeled
release test added a variety of radioactive nutrients to the soil and then waited
to see whether any radioactive carbon dioxide would be given off.

21. According to the passage, the tests conducted on the Viking lander were designed to search for microbes in the Martian soil because

    (A) the gas exchange activities of microbes would be readily detectable.
    (B) previous exploratory missions had suggested the presence of microbes on Mars.
    (C) microbes were assumed to be the most abundant form of life on Mars.
    (D) microbes are the most primitive form of life on Earth.
    (E) the small size of microbes would make them easily transportable.

22. According to the passage, the Viking instruments were designed to detect possible life-forms on Mars by their

    (A) chemical activity.
    (B) motion.
    (C) radioactivity.
    (D) reproductive patterns.
    (E) purposeful activity.

23. It can be inferred from the passage that radioactive carbon dioxide was used in the carbon assimilation test primarily because

    (A) radioactive carbon dioxide is commonly found in the Martian atmosphere.
    (B) the chemical changes induced by radioactivity would be a certain indication of the presence of life on Mars.
    (C) radioactivity is found on Earth only in areas where life also exists.
    (D) radioactive carbon dioxide was considered likely to be absorbed more readily than nonradioactive carbon dioxide.
    (E) radioactivity would be detectable by the Viking instruments.

24. Many students were _____ to learn the university had decided to cut back on funding dedicated to scholarships, and their _____ was visible in the protests they staged during the week following the announcement.

    (A) dubious..ambivalence
    (B) embittered..candor
    (C) euphoric..jubilation
    (D) chagrined..anger
    (E) incensed..support

25. CONTROVERT:

    (A) misconstrue
    (B) predict
    (C) affirm
    (D) praise
    (E) intend

26. OMNIPOTENCE : POWER ::

    (A) omnivorousness : life
    (B) panacea : illness
    (C) omniscience : knowledge
    (D) holocaust : fire
    (E) omnipresence : proximity

27. ADVOCATE : ARGUE ::

    (A) arbiter : judge
    (B) orator : defend
    (C) accuser : deny
    (D) actor : personify
    (E) debater : shout

28. MALADROIT:

    (A) polite
    (B) meaningful
    (C) graceful
    (D) casual
    (E) well-timed

29. IMPETUOUS:

    (A) meek
    (B) inactive
    (C) tenacious
    (D) cautious
    (E) dull

30. The belief that humans are not the only intelligent life-form in the universe is _____, as is evidenced by the _____ of stories about UFO sightings and alien abductions.

    (A) common..proliferation
    (B) increasing..scarcity
    (C) widespread..plausibility
    (D) preposterous..diversity
    (E) verifiable..suppression

SECTION 4

ANALYTICAL

35 Questions

Time—60 Minutes

> **Directions:** Each question or group of questions is based on a passage or set of conditions. In answering some of the questions, it may be useful to draw a rough diagram. For each question, select the best answer choice given.

1. The high level of violence in children's television programming today has often been cited as an explanation for the increased violence in our society as a whole. And, in fact, some recent studies show that the level of TV violence has increased considerably over the past twenty years. However, other studies indicate that the level, while high, is only slightly greater than it was twenty years ago.

   All of the following, if true, would be useful in explaining the above EXCEPT

   (A) Numerous studies of TV violence have been conducted in the past twenty years, and their results were not always in agreement.

   (B) All those involved in conducting the studies cited had the same perception of what constitutes "violence" in TV programming.

   (C) Despite their best efforts at impartiality, those who conduct studies of TV violence sometimes allow their preconceived ideas to affect their findings.

   (D) Many factors other than TV violence have a significant effect on the level of violence in society.

   (E) The methodology generally used in studies of TV violence has changed considerably over the past twenty years.

2. The United States, which was founded mainly by people who had emigrated from northern Europe, had an essentially open-door immigration policy for the first 100 years of its existence. But starting in the 1880s and continuing through the 1920s, Congress passed a series of restrictive laws that led, ultimately, to a quota system for immigration based on the number of individuals of each national origin reported in the 1890 census.

    All of the following, if true, would help account for the above EXCEPT

    (A) The American economy was weak in the 1880s, and many Americans were afraid that new immigrants would further weaken it.

    (B) Political upheavals in Europe in the late nineteenth century encouraged many left-wing radicals to emigrate to America.

    (C) Most of those emigrating to America in the 1880s were central and eastern Europeans, against whom many Americans were prejudiced.

    (D) Throughout American history, most Americans have been sympathetic toward those living under repressive regimes in Europe and seeking refuge abroad.

    (E) Most of the U.S. population in the 1880s were members of Protestant churches, while many of the new immigrants were Catholics and Jews.

3. Prior to the development of the "horseless carriage" around the start of the twentieth century, horses in our cities left tons of unsightly, messy, and malodorous manure on our streets. Based on this fact alone, there is no question that by any measure, the automobile has been a boon to humankind.

    Which of the following, if true, most seriously weakens the argument above?

    (A) Air pollution caused by automobile exhaust is less deleterious to health than that caused by horse manure.

    (B) In the nineteenth century, almost as many people were killed each year by horse-drawn conveyances as are killed today by automobiles.

    (C) In many cities, automobile traffic has been banned from large downtown areas to provide room for pedestrian malls.

    (D) Compared to horse-drawn carriages, automobiles are less efficient in terms of the energy required to operate them.

    (E) Automobiles enable people to travel greater distances in less time than did horse-drawn conveyances.

4. A recent study showed that parents whose children under the age of ten go to bed by nine o'clock in the evening have sexual relations an average of three times a week, while those whose children under ten do not go to bed until ten o'clock do so only once a week on average. Clearly, then, there is a cause-and-effect relationship between childrens' bedtimes and their parents' level of sexual activity.

Knowledge of which of the following would be LEAST useful in evaluating the claim made in the passage above?

(A) The number of families that participated in the study
(B) Whether the study differentiated between parents in their twenties, thirties, and forties
(C) The parents' level of sexual activity prior to the birth of their children
(D) Whether any of the parents in the study had additional children over ten years of age
(E) Whether the study differentiated between those parents who had to get up early in the morning and those who could sleep late

Questions 5–8 refer to the following:

Six varieties of exotic birds are to be housed in a zoo. The birds—varieties J, Q, S, V, X, and Z—will be housed one variety to a cage in two rows of three cages, which face each other across Aviary Place. The cages in the row on the west side of Aviary Place are numbered 1, 2, and 3 from north to south; the cages on the east side are numbered 4, 5, and 6 from north to south.

Variety V is housed in cage 5.

Varieties S and X must be housed in cages that face one another.

Varieties J and Q must be housed in different rows.

5. Which of the following is an acceptable housing arrangement for the six varieties of birds in the six cages, listed in numerical order?

(A) J, Z, Q, X, V, S
(B) Q, Z, V, J, X, S
(C) S, Q, Z, X, V, J
(D) S, X, J, Z, V, Q
(E) X, Q, Z, J, V, S

6. If variety S is housed in cage 4 and variety Q is housed in cage 3, which of the following must be true?
   - (A) Variety J is housed in cage 2.
   - (B) Varieties J and X are housed in cages that face one another.
   - (C) Variety Q is housed in a cage next to variety X.
   - (D) Variety S is housed in a cage that faces variety J.
   - (E) Variety Z is housed in a cage between varieties Q and X.

7. If variety Z is housed in cage 1 and variety X is housed in a cage next to variety V, which of the following must be true?
   - (A) Variety J is housed in cage 2.
   - (B) Variety Q is housed on the east side.
   - (C) Variety S is housed in cage 3.
   - (D) Variety S is housed on the west side.
   - (E) Variety X is housed in cage 4.

8. In how many different cages could variety Z possibly be housed?
   - (A) Two
   - (B) Three
   - (C) Four
   - (D) Five
   - (E) Six

9. Under current U.S. tax laws, while those with higher incomes theoretically pay a higher percentage of their earnings to the federal government, loopholes in the law often make it possible for the wealthy to pay *less* taxes than those with lower incomes. If the government created a flat tax, under which every citizen's income was taxed at the same rate and eliminated the loopholes, everyone would pay his fair share and the government would receive ample revenues.

   If the statements above are true, which of the following must be true?
   - (A) Under a flat tax, all of the wealthy would pay higher taxes than they do at present.
   - (B) Under a flat tax, every wage earner would pay the same amount in taxes.
   - (C) Under a flat tax, the wealthy would not be able to use loopholes to avoid paying their share of taxes.
   - (D) Under a flat tax, the wealthy would bear a larger share of the government's expenses than the middle class.
   - (E) Under a flat tax, lower-income wage earners would pay less in income taxes than they do now.

Questions 10–13 refer to the following:

Six rock and roll acts—N, P, R, T, V, and Y—are to perform in two amphitheater concerts, one on Friday night and one on Saturday night. To assuage the performers' intense competitiveness, the sequence of acts for the two concerts will be randomly determined, with the following provisions.

The act that performs first on Friday night must perform fourth on Saturday night.

The act that performs sixth on Friday night must perform third on Saturday night.

If act R performs first, act V must perform sixth.

If act P performs fourth, act T must perform second.

Acts N and Y may not perform consecutively in either order.

10. Which of the following is a possible sequence of acts for the Friday night concert?
    (A) N, T, R, P, Y, V
    (B) R, Y, T, P, V, N
    (C) R, T, Y, N, P, V
    (D) T, V, N, Y, P, R
    (E) Y, R, V, P, T, N

11. If the sequence of acts on Friday night is Y, T, N, P, R, and V, which of the following is a possible sequence of acts on Saturday night?
    (A) N, V, R, Y, T, P
    (B) R, T, V, Y, N, P
    (C) T, R, V, Y, P, N
    (D) T, Y, V, R, N, P
    (E) V, T, R, Y, P, N

12. If the sequence of acts on Friday night is P, N, V, T, R, and Y, which of the following must be true about the sequence of acts on Saturday night?
    (A) N performs first.
    (B) R performs fourth.
    (C) T performs second.
    (D) If V performs first, N performs fifth.
    (E) If V performs sixth, R performs first.

13. If P performs sixth on Friday night and, on Saturday night, T performs second and Y performs fifth, which of the following must perform first on Saturday night?

    (A) N
    (B) P
    (C) R
    (D) V
    (E) It cannot be determined from the information provided.

14. At the end of the nineteenth century, most Americans lived in houses in rural areas, and dogs were by far the most popular type of pet. Today, however, the majority of Americans live in urban apartments, and more people keep cats than any other animal.

    Which of the following conclusions is most strongly supported by the statements above?

    (A) City life is more congenial than country life for people and their pets.
    (B) Cats are more appropriate as pets for apartment dwellers than are dogs.
    (C) Today as compared to the past, more people prefer having cats as pets than dogs.
    (D) Dogs who live in city apartments are often unhealthy and unhappy.
    (E) Dogs have decreased in popularity due to city ordinances restricting the maintenance of pets in apartments.

Questions 15–18 refer to the following:

An office building houses seven companies, known as C, D, E, F, G, H, and K. Each floor of the building has space for exactly one company, and the building has a total of exactly seven floors, numbered from 1 (lowest) to 7 (highest).

    Company G is three floors above company D.

    Company F is one floor below company K.

    Company E is above company C.

15. Which of the following is a possible arrangement of companies in the building, from the seventh floor to the first?

    (A) C, E, G, K, F, D, H
    (B) E, C, K, F, G, H, D
    (C) F, K, G, E, C, D, H
    (D) G, K, F, D, E, H, C
    (E) H, E, K, F, G, C, D

16. If company H is on the seventh floor and company C is on the fifth floor, which of the following must be true?

    (A) Company D is on the second floor.
    (B) Company E is on the sixth floor.
    (C) Company F is on the first floor.
    (D) Company G is one floor above company F.
    (E) Company K is two floors below company H.

17. If company D is one floor above company K, company H could be on any of the following floors EXCEPT the

    (A) first.
    (B) third.
    (C) fourth.
    (D) sixth.
    (E) seventh.

18. If company F is two floors above company H, how many possible different arrangements of companies in the building are possible?

    (A) Three
    (B) Four
    (C) Five
    (D) Six
    (E) Seven

19. There are more lawyers per capita in the United States than in any other country in the world. The best possible explanation of this is that our legal system is more complicated than those of many other countries, and we are accordingly in greater need of professional help in dealing with it.

    All of the following, if true, weaken the argument above EXCEPT

    (A) Great Britain has a much simpler legal system but almost as many lawyers per capita as the United States.
    (B) The law is a very lucrative profession and is accordingly attractive to many people.
    (C) France has a more complicated legal system but has many fewer lawyers per capita than the United States.
    (D) The number of lawyers in the United States, both in absolute terms and as a percentage of the population, has grown steadily over the past twenty years.
    (E) Americans are by nature litigious, so that more lawsuits are brought against individuals in the United States than in any other nation.

Questions 20–23 refer to the following:

Ten people will be riding in three cars for a photo safari. The group includes three guides, F, G, and H; three assistants, J, K, and L; and four clients, M, N, P, and R.

Each car has a front seat and a back seat, and each seat has room for up to two people. A guide and an assistant must ride in each car.

  G and J must ride in different cars.

  H and P must ride in different cars.

  L and N must ride in different cars.

  K and R must ride in the same car.

20. If K rides in the same car with F, which of the following must ride in the same car with H?
    (A) J
    (B) L
    (C) M
    (D) N
    (E) P

21. If R rides in the same car with H, and G rides in a car with exactly three other people, which of the following must be true?
    (A) F rides in the same car with L.
    (B) G rides in the same car with N.
    (C) K and N ride in different cars.
    (D) N rides in the same car with either F or R.
    (E) P rides in the same car with either L or J.

22. If N rides in the same car with G, which of the following must ride in the same car with them?
    (A) F
    (B) J
    (C) L
    (D) M
    (E) R

23. If F and L ride in the same car, which of the following is a complete list of the additional people who could ride in the same car with them?
    (A) J and M
    (B) M and N
    (C) M and P
    (D) M, N, and P
    (E) N, P, and R

24. In the 1964 presidential campaign, Lyndon Johnson, campaigning on a promise not to escalate the then-small war in Vietnam, ran against Barry Goldwater, who was widely portrayed as a war hawk, and defeated him soundly. Despite his promises, as president, Johnson did escalate the war, and by 1968 public protests over this action forced him to decide against running for president again.

All of the following are assumptions underlying the conclusion of the passage above EXCEPT

(A) Johnson would probably have run for president in 1968 if there had been no protests against his conduct of the war.

(B) The war in Vietnam was a major campaign issue in both the 1964 and 1968 elections.

(C) If the war in Vietnam had been won by 1968, Johnson would probably have run for president again.

(D) The portrayal of Goldwater as a war hawk was an accurate one.

(E) Johnson was either unable or unwilling to keep his campaign promise concerning the war in Vietnam.

Questions 25–28 refer to the following:

The manager of a theater is planning a seven-day festival of movies from the 1950s. A total of fourteen movies will be shown, each as part of a double bill to run for one day of the festival. The fourteen movies will include examples of five genres: three westerns, two musicals, three films noirs, two science fiction movies, and four dramas. The schedule for the festival is subject to the following restrictions.

Two movies of the same genre may not appear on the same double bill, and movies of the same genre may not be shown three days in succession.

Day 1 of the festival must include a musical.

Day 3 must include a science fiction movie.

Day 4 must include a film noir.

Day 5 may not include a drama.

25. Which of the following is a possible schedule of double features for days 3, 4, and 5?

    (A) Drama and science fiction; western and film noir; musical and western
    (B) Drama and musical; science fiction and film noir; drama and western
    (C) Western and musical; film noir and drama; science fiction and drama
    (D) Western and science fiction; film noir and western; musical and western
    (E) Musical and science fiction; film noir and drama; western and musical

26. If a musical is scheduled for day 5 and a science fiction movie for day 6, which of the following could be scheduled for day 7?

    (A) Film noir and musical
    (B) Film noir and western
    (C) Musical and western
    (D) Science fiction and drama
    (E) Two dramas

27. If a musical and a western are scheduled for day 2 and a science fiction movie and a western are scheduled for day 6, which of the following must be scheduled for day 5?

    (A) Drama and western
    (B) Film noir and science fiction
    (C) Film noir and western
    (D) Musical and western
    (E) Science fiction and western

28. If a musical must always be scheduled on the same double bill as a science fiction movie, which of the following must be FALSE?

    (A) A drama is scheduled on day 2.
    (B) A drama is scheduled on day 7.
    (C) A film noir is scheduled on day 6.
    (D) A musical is scheduled on day 3.
    (E) A science fiction movie is scheduled on day 1.

29. Although the Framers of the United States Constitution provided for the direct election of members of the House of Representatives, U.S. senators were originally elected by state legislatures, and to this day the president is elected not directly by the people but by the Electoral College. It appears that the Framers believed that democracy is a good thing, but that you can have too much of a good thing.

If the statements above are true, all of the following must be true EXCEPT

(A) The Framers did not believe in direct election of the president by the people.

(B) The Framers did not believe in direct election of the members of the Senate by the people.

(C) Today, U.S. Senators are no longer elected by state legislatures.

(D) The Framers believed in direct election of members of the House of Representatives by the people.

(E) The Framers believed that direct election of representatives by the people would represent an excess of democracy.

Questions 30–33 refer to the following:

A college campus consists of six buildings—B, G, L, R, X, and Z—connected by five paths—I, II, III, IV, and V—that follow these routes:

Path I connects G and R only.

Path II connects X and Z only.

Path III connects B and X only.

Path IV connects G and Z only.

Path V connects L and Z only.

Daily tours of the campus are conducted by guides who are careful to travel only on the five paths listed above. The five paths are each 100 yards in length.

30. Which building must be visited at least twice on a campus tour that visits every building?

(A) B

(B) G

(C) L

(D) R

(E) Z

31. If a tour starts at G and travels first on path IV, how long, in yards, is the shortest possible route that visits every building on the campus?
    (A) 700
    (B) 800
    (C) 900
    (D) 1,000
    (E) 1,100

32. If a tour is to visit every building by the shortest possible route, starting from which building will the tour be longest?
    (A) B
    (B) G
    (C) L
    (D) X
    (E) Z

33. If a new path, VI, is built connecting B and G only, which of the following is a complete list of the buildings from which the shortest possible tour that visits every building may start?
    (A) B only
    (B) G only
    (C) L only
    (D) L and R only
    (E) R and X only

34. In the past, business people were generally content to use the U.S. Postal Service (USPS) to deliver written communications. However, due to the institution of overnight delivery by private carriers, and the subsequent development of facsimile machines and electronic mail, most business people now feel their communications must be delivered as quickly as possible, if not instantly, neatly illustrating the economic adage that "Supply creates demand."

    All of the following are valid objections to the conclusion drawn above EXCEPT

    (A) Many changes in the business environment have led business people to feel they need information more quickly than in the past.
    (B) A decline in the quality of service provided by the USPS has led business people to seek other means of communication.
    (C) In many fields of business, there has always been a real need to have communications delivered instantly.
    (D) Most businesses do not actually require immediate delivery of written communications to operate efficiently.
    (E) The vast majority of business communications today are delivered by the USPS and other traditional, low-speed carriers.

35. Compared to the salaries of lower-level employees, the compensation of chief executive officers in American corporations is proportionately much higher than that of their counterparts in other countries. As a result, there is considerably more resentment toward CEOs in American companies than exists in other nations.

All of the following are assumptions underlying the conclusion of the passage above EXCEPT

(A) The proportionate difference between the compensation of American and foreign CEOs is substantial.

(B) Compensation is among the most important work-related issues among American employees.

(C) Differences in compensation are a major cause of resentment among American employees.

(D) Work-related issues other than compensation are of equal importance to employees outside America.

(E) In general, American workers are no more likely to be resentful about their jobs than their foreign counterparts.

SECTION 5

QUANTITATIVE

28 Questions

Time—45 Minutes

Directions (Multiple Choice): Each question has five answer choices. For each question, select the best of the answer choices given.

Numbers: All numbers used are real numbers.

Figures: Position of points, angles, regions, etc. can be assumed to be in the order shown; and angle measures can be assumed to be positive.

Lines shown as straight can be assumed to be straight.

Figures can be assumed to lie in a plane unless otherwise indicated.

Figures that accompany questions are intended to provide information useful in answering the questions. However, unless a note states that a figure is drawn to scale, you should solve these problems NOT by estimating sizes by sight or by measurement, but by using your knowledge of mathematics.

Directions (Quantitative Comparisons): Each question consists of two quantities, one in Column A and one in Column B. You are to compare the two quantities and choose

- (A)   if the quantity in Column A is greater;
- (B)   if the quantity in Column B is greater;
- (C)   if the two quantities are equal;
- (D)   if the relationship cannot be determined from the information given.

Note: Since there are only four choices, NEVER MARK (E).

Common Information: In a question, information concerning one or both of the quantities to be compared is centered above the two columns. A symbol that appears in both columns represents the same thing in Column A as it does in Column B.

	Column A	**Column B**
1.	The remainder when 3,458,064 is divided by 4	The remainder when 5,559,063 is divided by 9

2. A faucet is dripping at a constant rate. If, at noon on Sunday, 3 ounces of water have dripped from the faucet into a holding tank, and if, at 5:00 p.m. on Sunday, a total of 7 ounces have dripped into the tank, how many ounces will have dripped into the tank by 2:00 a.m. on Monday?

   (A) 10

   (B) $\dfrac{51}{5}$

   (C) 12

   (D) $\dfrac{71}{5}$

   (E) $\dfrac{81}{5}$

	Column A	**Column B**
3.	x	$2x$

4. If A and B are positive integers and $24AB$ is a perfect square, which of the following are NOT possible?

    I.   Both A and B are odd.

    II. AB is a perfect square.

    III. Both A and B are divisible by 6.

    (A) I only

    (B) II only

    (C) III only

    (D) I and II only

    (E) I, II, and III

Column A	**Column B**

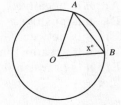

O is the center of the circle with diameter 10.
The perimeter of $AOB = 16$.

5.	x	60

Column A	Column B

a is chosen from the set $A = \{-1, -6, 3\}$

b is chosen from the set $B = \{-4, 4, 5\}$

6.

The largest possible value of $\dfrac{a}{b}$	1.5

7. If the result of squaring a number n is less than twice the number, which of the following must be true?

(A) n is negative.

(B) n is positive.

(C) n is between -1 and $+1$.

(D) n is greater than 1.

(E) n is between 0 and 2.

8. If the arithmetic mean of x and y is m, and $z = 2m$, then the arithmetic mean of x, y, and z is

(A) m

(B) $\dfrac{2m}{3}$

(C) $\dfrac{4m}{3}$

(D) $\dfrac{3m}{4}$

(E) $\dfrac{3}{4m}$

<u>**Column A**</u>   <u>**Column B**</u>

$$y = \frac{1}{2}$$

9.

1.2

$y^0 + y^2$

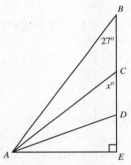

10. In the figure above, lines AC and AD trisect $\angle A$. What is the value of x?

(A)   21
(B)   27
(C)   42
(D)   48
(E)   60

Questions 11–15 refer to the following graphs.

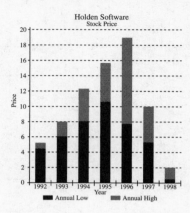

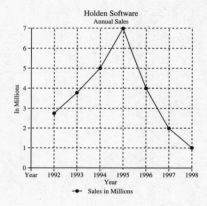

11. In which year shown was the lowest stock price for the year the highest?

    (A) 1993
    (B) 1994
    (C) 1995
    (D) 1996
    (E) 1997

12. In how many years was the lowest price of the stock higher than the highest price in 1992?

    (A) 1
    (B) 2
    (C) 3
    (D) 4
    (E) 5

13. The lowest price of the stock in 1994 was what percent higher than the highest price in 1998?

    (A) 400
    (B) 300
    (C) 200
    (D) 50
    (E) 25

14. The median annual sales (in millions) of Holden Software for the seven years covered was
   (A) 5
   (B) 3.8
   (C) 3.4
   (D) 2.8
   (E) 2

15. Which of the following may be inferred from the combined graphs?
   I.   The stock value reached its high the year after sales reached their high.
   II. The steepest decline in sales followed the year of highest sales.
   III. The greatest spread in stock price came in the year after the year of highest sales.

   (A) I only
   (B) I and II only
   (C) II and III only
   (D) I and III only
   (E) I, II, and III

Column A	**Column B**

Of 42 horses in a stable, $\frac{1}{3}$ are black and $\frac{1}{6}$ are white. The rest are brown.

16. The number of brown horses	21

Column A	Column B

Five more than twice the number n is 17.

17.

3 less than n	2 less than $\frac{1}{2}n$

18. What is the perimeter of a rectangle that is twice as long as it is wide and has the same area as a circle of diameter 8?

(A) $8\sqrt{\pi}$
(B) $8\sqrt{2\pi}$
(C) 8π
(D) $12\sqrt{2\pi}$
(E) 12π

Column A	Column B

19.

The perimeter of a square with an area of 36 square feet	The circumference of a circle with a radius of 6

Column A	Column B

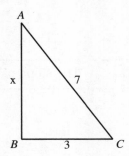

20.

The area of $\triangle ABC$	9

$$x + 6 > 7 > 2x$$

21.

3	x

22. If the negative of the sum of two consecutive odd integers is less than -35, which of the following could be one of the two integers?

   (A) 18
   (B) 16
   (C) 15
   (D) 13
   (E) 11

Column A	**Column B**

$$\text{Point } P = (-1, 2)$$
$$\text{Point } Q = (3, 5)$$
$$\text{Point } R = (2, 3)$$

23.

The slope of $\overline{PQ}$	The slope of $\overline{QR}$

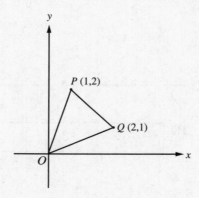

24. In the figure above, the perimeter of $\triangle OPQ$ is

(A) $2\sqrt{5} + \sqrt{2}$

(B) $\sqrt{5} + 2\sqrt{2}$

(C) $\sqrt{5} + \sqrt{2}$

(D) 3

(E) $\sqrt{7}$

Column A	Column B

Marbles are drawn at random from a bag containing
marbles of various colors.
A blue marble is drawn three times in a row.

25.

The number of blue marbles in the bag	The number of red marbles in the bag

---

26. If $N = 3^P$ and $M = P - 1$, then in terms of M, $\dfrac{3}{N} =$

(A) $\dfrac{1}{3^M}$

(B) 3^M

(C) $\dfrac{9}{3^M}$

(D) 3^{2M}

(E) 3^{1-M}

Column A	Column B

$$x \neq -2$$

27.

$\dfrac{x}{x+2}$	$1 + \dfrac{x}{2}$

(2,6) is the midpoint of the line segment connecting point $(-1, 3)$ to point $P(x, y)$.

28.

y	$2x$

Answer Key

SECTIONS 1 AND 2—ANALYTICAL WRITING MEASURE

On the real GRE, your essays will be graded on a scale of 0 (lowest) to 6 (highest) by the "holistic" method—that is, a single score will be assigned to each essay based on the overall impression it makes on the reader. See Chapter 12 for more information on the holistic scoring system and how to evaluate your own writing in the light of the GRE scoring criteria.

Section 3 Verbal		Section 4 Analytical		Section 5 Quantitative	
1. C	16. A	1. B	19. D	1. B	15. E
2. E	17. C	2. D	20. A	2. D	16. C
3. E	18. D	3. D	21. D	3. D	17. A
4. A	19. B	4. D	22. E	4. D	18. D
5. C	20. C	5. C	23. C	5. B	19. B
6. B	21. C	6. E	24. D	6. C	20. A
7. C	22. A	7. E	25. A	7. E	21. D
8. E	23. E	8. B	26. B	8. C	22. C
9. B	24. D	9. C	27. C	9. B	23. B
10. B	25. C	10. A	28. C	10. D	24. A
11. A	26. C	11. C	29. B	11. C	25. D
12. B	27. A	12. C	30. E	12. E	26. A
13. A	28. C	13. A	31. C	13. B	27. D
14. D	29. D	14. C	32. E	14. B	28. B
15. E	30. A	15. D	33. D		
		16. B	34. D		
		17. B	35. D		
		18. C			

Scoring Guide

COMPUTING YOUR SCALED SCORES

Verbal

Count the number of correct answers you chose for the questions in Section 3. Write the total here: _____. This is your Verbal Raw Score.

Look up your Verbal Raw Score on the Score Conversion Table (page 509). Find the corresponding Verbal Scaled Score and write it here: _____.

Analytical

Count the number of correct answers you chose for the questions in Section 4. Write the total here: _____. This is your Analytical Raw Score.

Look up your Analytical Raw Score on the Score Conversion Table (page 509). Find the corresponding Analytical Scaled Score and write it here: _____.

Quantitative

Count the number of correct answers you chose for the questions in Section 5. Write the total here: _____. This is your Quantitative Raw Score.

Look up your Quantitative Raw Score on the Score Conversion Table (page 509). Find the corresponding Quantitative Scaled Score and write it here: _____.

Score Conversion Table

Insider's Guide to the GRE Diagnostic Test

Raw Score	Verbal Scaled Score	Analytical Scaled Score	Quantitative Scaled Score
35		800	
34		780	
33		760	
32		740	
31		720	
30	800	700	
29	780	680	
28	750	660	800
27	720	650	780
26	700	640	750
25	680	620	720
24	660	610	700
23	640	600	680
22	620	590	660
21	600	580	640
20	590	570	620
19	580	560	610
18	570	540	600
17	560	520	590
16	540	510	570
15	520	500	560
14	500	480	540
13	480	460	520
12	460	440	500
11	440	420	480
10	420	400	450
9	400	380	430
8	380	360	400
7	360	340	380
6	340	320	350
5	320	300	330
4	300	280	300
3	270	260	280
2	250	240	250
1	230	220	230
0	200	200	200

Explanatory Answers

SECTION 3

1. **The correct answer is (C).** Something valid—a valid belief, for example, or a valid driver's license—is in effect or in force. The opposite is invalid, which means without effect or force.

2. **The correct answer is (E).** To broadcast a program is to disseminate it or make it publicly available; in the same way, to publish a book is to disseminate it or make it publicly available.

3. **The correct answer is (E).** To be haughty is to think and behave in a way that is marked by the quality of extreme pride; to be bigoted is to think and behave in a way marked by extreme prejudice.

4. **The correct answer is (A).** "Unexplored" fits the ideas in the sentence without adding any new ones. The sentence emphasizes the fact that almost every corner of the globe is easy to visit and see.

5. **The correct answer is (C).** Eloquent means able to express one's ideas clearly and gracefully. The opposite would be inarticulate, which means unable to communicate clearly or effectively.

6. **The correct answer is (B).** A proponent of an idea is someone who argues or battles on its behalf; the opposite would be an opponent, enemy, or foe.

7. **The correct answer is (C).** The words "tedium" and "mindless" both fit each other and make sense in the context, which tells us that Harold was eager to "escape" his job.

8. **The correct answer is (E).** The second paragraph of the passage expresses this idea: see lines 8–9 in particular ("The Impressionists, on the other hand, viewed light, not matter, as the ultimate visual reality").

9. **The correct answer is (B).** The third and fourth paragraphs make this point clear, especially the first sentence of the fourth paragraph, which refers to "light . . . reflected with varying intensity to the eye."

10. **The correct answer is (B).** The last sentence of the passage makes this point.

11. **The correct answer is (A).** To be eccentric is to vary from the norm; someone eccentric behaves in ways that are considered unusual, odd, or strange. The opposite is to be normal, predictable, or conventional.

12. **The correct answer is (B).** Here, the two halves of the sentence make similar or parallel points. Choice (B) makes sense because the word meanings are consistent: if what Carpenter did was "despicable," it makes sense that voters would be "appalled."

13. **The correct answer is (A).** A barge is a particular type of vessel, one dedicated to carrying cargo. A truck is a particular type of vehicle, also used to carry cargo.

14. **The correct answer is (D).** To be useful and to convey a meaning clearly, print must be visible. In the same way, speech must be audible if anyone is to understand it.

15. **The correct answer is (E).** The first sentence of the second paragraph says that Messe and Callahan-Levy wanted to test the theory "that women judge their own work more harshly than that of others." Their experiment seemed to challenge this belief, since the women evaluated their own work as highly as men did (see the last sentence of the third paragraph).

16. **The correct answer is (A).** Since the entire experiment focuses on the pay demanded and received by women and their perception of the value of their work, it seems clear that the most relevant social issue would be inequities in the pay of women vis-à-vis men.

17. **The correct answer is (C).** The second half of the sentence shows that the flooding can be dangerous; hence, "apprehension" is a logical reaction. The word "always" tells us that the flooding is a frequent event; hence, "annual" makes sense as a description.

18. **The correct answer is (D).** To sustain something is to uphold, strengthen, or support it.

19. **The correct answer is (B).** Animosity means hostility, hatred, or ill-will. The opposite is amity, love, or friendship.

20. **The correct answer is (C).** A vat is used specifically to store liquids; a pipe is used to convey (that is, to carry or transport) liquids. Choice (D) is wrong because a bin isn't used to gather anything; a person may gather things and put them in a bin, but that's not quite the same thing.

21. **The correct answer is (C).** The last two sentences of the second paragraph explain this point. Since microbes are the most common form of life on Earth, the Viking scientists assumed that the same would be true on Mars, so that looking for microbes would be the most likely way to find living things.

22. **The correct answer is (A).** See the last sentence of the third paragraph, which explains this point.

23. **The correct answer is (E).** Radioactive carbon dioxide was used because, if Martian life-forms converted it into other compounds (as living things on Earth would do), the radioactivity would be found on those compounds and would be detectable by the Viking instruments. The fourth paragraph explains this.

24. **The correct answer is (D).** We're looking for words that would describe how students might be expected to react to a reduction in scholarship funding. "Chagrined" and "anger" make sense in this context and also match one another appropriately.

25. **The correct answer is (C).** To controvert an idea or a statement is to deny it or disagree with it. The opposite would be to agree with it or to affirm it.

26. **The correct answer is (C).** Omnipotence means the quality of being all-powerful (that is, able to do anything—like God, or perhaps Bill Gates). Omniscience means the quality of being all-knowing (able to know anything). Omnipresence, choice (E), means the quality of being everywhere; proximity is the wrong word for the second part of the relationship, since it means "nearness," not "presence."

27. **The correct answer is (A).** An advocate is someone who argues (a lawyer, for instance); an arbiter is someone who judges (a judge or a sports referee, for instance). None of the other answer choices have an equally clear-cut relationship.

28. **The correct answer is (C).** Maladroit means clumsy, awkward, or graceless, either physically (tripping over one's own feet) or socially (accidentally insulting someone). The opposite is graceful, which can also be used in either a physical or social sense.

29. **The correct answer is (D).** Someone impetuous behaves in a rash, thoughtless, careless manner, doing things without first considering the consequences. The opposite is careful, thoughtful, or cautious.

30. **The correct answer is (A).** The phrase "as is evidenced" shows that what is stated in the second half of the sentence must help demonstrate or illustrate what is stated in the first half of the sentence. If UFO sightings are experiencing a "proliferation," then it would be logical to say that the belief in alien life-forms is "common."

SECTION 4

1. **The correct answer is (B).** Each of the other answer statements could help to explain either the discrepancy between the various studies of TV violence or the apparent cause-and-effect relationship between TV violence and real-life violence. Only choice (B) does neither; instead, it sharpens the apparent contradiction among the various studies without helping to explain it.

2. **The correct answer is (D).** Choices (A), (B), (C), and (E) all help to account for the restrictions on immigration that were put in place starting in the 1880s. Choice (D) does not; in fact, it suggests that these restrictions are an anomaly in need of some explanation not provided in the passage.

3. **The correct answer is (D).** Choice (D) is the only answer that clearly suggests a drawback to our reliance on automobiles rather than horses for transportation.

4. **The correct answer is (D).** It seems irrelevant whether or not additional, older children are part of the same family. All of the other answer choices, however, raise issues that could be relevant to determining whether or not the study's conclusion is valid.

5. **The correct answer is (C).** Go through the three rules, and compare each to the answer choices, eliminating those that violate a rule. Choice (B) violates the rule that says that variety V is housed in cage 5. Choices (A), (D), and (E) fail to put varieties S and X in cages facing one another. (Draw a little map. Cages 1 and 4, 2 and 5, and 3 and 6 face each other.)

6. **The correct answer is (E).** If S is in cage 4, then X must be in cage 1. If Q is in cage 3, then J must be in cage 6 (the only cage in the opposite row still available). That leaves Z in cage 2. Map it like this:

   X   S
   Z   V
   Q   J

   Then just compare the answer choices with the map. Only choice (E) is true.

7. **The correct answer is (E).** Since S and X must be opposite one another, X must be in cage 6 and S must be in cage 3. Varieties J and Q are interchangeably housed in cages 2 and 4. Only statement (E) *must* be true under these conditions.

8. **The correct answer is (B).** We know that Z can't be in cage 5, since that's occupied by V. Z also can't be in cage 4 or cage 6. Why not? Because S and X must face one another, and J and Q must be in opposite rows. If Z is in either cage 4 or cage 6, that will leave no possible combination of four cages to house S, X, J, and Q. So Z must be in a cage on the west side, giving that bird only three possible homes.

9. **The correct answer is (C).** Only this statement *must* be true given the information presented. Choice (D) is wrong because the truth of the statement would depend, in part, on how many wealthy people there are as compared to middle-class people.

10. **The correct answer is (A).** Compare the five answer choices with the rules as stated. Only one answer violates no rule. Choice (B) is wrong because it puts act V fifth, despite the fact that act R performs first. Choice (E) is wrong because it fails to put act T second, despite the fact that act P performs fourth. And choices (C) and (D) put acts N and Y together—a no-no.

11. **The correct answer is (C).** On Saturday night, Y must perform fourth (since Y performed first on Friday), and V must perform third (since V performed sixth on Friday). Since N and Y cannot perform consecutively, N may not perform fifth. These rather sketchy requirements suffice to eliminate four of the five answer choices.

12. **The correct answer is (C).** On Saturday night, Y must perform third, P must perform fourth, and (as a consequence of P's location) T must perform second.

13. **The correct answer is (A).** If P performs sixth on Friday, P performs third on Saturday. If Y is fifth and T is second on Saturday, then N must be first, since that's the only remaining location in which N avoids performing before or after Y.

14. **The correct answer is (C).** The exact nature of the relationship between the shift from rural to urban living and the change in Americans' choice of pets can't be determined based simply on the information given. All we can tell is that, in fact, more Americans are choosing cats as pets than dogs as pets.

15. **The correct answer is (D).** Choices (B) and (E) both violate the rule that G must be three floors above D. Choice (C) illegally puts F above K. And choice (A) illegally puts C above E.

16. **The correct answer is (B).** If H is on the seventh floor and C is on the fifth floor, G must be on the fourth floor and D must be on the first floor (the only way they can be three floors apart). The other companies also fall inexorably into place, like this (from highest to lowest): H, E, C, G, K, F, D.

17. **The correct answer is (B).** The condition stated puts companies D, K, and F on three floors together (highest to lowest). Since G must be three floors above D, we have this sequence of six floors (highest to lowest): G, -, -, D, K, F. Now, G could be on either the seventh floor or the sixth floor. Depending on these two choices, there are several possible locations for the remaining companies C, E, and H. Only the third floor is impossible (of the five answer choices); it must be occupied either by D or by K.

18. **The correct answer is (C).** The condition stated gives us two sequences that must exist in the building (from highest to lowest): G, -, -, D, and K, F, -, H. These two sequences must interlock in one of two ways. They could interlock to form a sequence of five floors, as follows (highest to lowest): G, K, F, D, H. Or they could interlock to form a sequence of six floors: K, F, G, H, -, D.

Given the first of these possibilities, there are three variations possible (once the remaining companies, E and C, have been plugged in): E, C, G, K, F, D, H; E, G, K, F, D, H, C; and G, K, F, D, H, E, C. Given the second possibility, there are two ways E and C could be plugged in: E, K, F, G, H, C, D; and K, F, G, H, E, D, C. Thus, there are five possibilities altogether.

Notice that this is clearly the hardest and most time-consuming question for this puzzle. If you found yourself spending a lot of time on it, you should have made a guess and moved on to the next item.

19. **The correct answer is (D).** All of the other answer choices either suggest reasons other than the complications of our legal system for the proliferation of lawyers in the U.S. or else undermine the argument by showing that the same cause-and-effect relationship doesn't seem to hold up elsewhere.

20. **The correct answer is (A).** Start each question with the observation that F, G, and H must be in three separate cars (since each car needs a guide). Work from there. If K is with F, then one car will have F, K, and R (since K and R must ride together). Now, where will the other two assistants, J and L, go? Since J can't ride with G, he must ride with H.

21. **The correct answer is (D).** If R is with H, so is K. Then J must be with F (to avoid being with G). That leaves assistant L to ride with G. And since N can't be with L, he must be in one of the other two cars, like this:

Car 1: H, R, K (and maybe N)
Car 2: G, L
Car 3: F, J (and maybe N)

If G must have three other riders, then M and P must join him in car 2. Compare this arrangement with the answer choices and you'll find that only choice (D) must be true.

22. **The correct answer is (E).** If N rides with G, L and J are excluded. That means K must join N and G, and K always brings R along for the ride.

23. **The correct answer is (C).** If F and L are together, then G, K, and R must be together and H and J must be together. M, N, and P remain to be placed, and we know that N cannot join L.

24. **The correct answer is (D).** Whether or not Goldwater was really a "war hawk" is irrelevant to the conclusion of the passage, which is that Johnson's withdrawal from the 1968 election was prompted by the controversy over the war in Vietnam.

25. **The correct answer is (A).** Start by listing, by initials, all the movie types that must be scheduled:

    W W W
    M M
    F F F
    S S
    D D D D

    Then create a starter schedule that includes the requirements established by the rules:

1	2	3	4	5	6	7
M		S	F	no D		

    For each question, add to or modify this schedule as needed, "pulling down" the movie types from your list and filling them in on the schedule as you go.

    For question 25, you can eliminate the wrong answers because they violate the basic parameters established. Choice (B), for example, does not feature a science fiction movie on day 3, as required, and it includes a drama on day 5, which is forbidden.

26. **The correct answer is (B).** Based on the information given here, the two musicals and the two science fiction movies are completely spoken for, so neither of those genres can be scheduled on day 7—eliminating choices (A), (C), and (D); and it's against the rules to schedule two movies of the same genre on a given day, eliminating choice (E).

27. **The correct answer is (C).** Plug in the information given:

1	2	3	4	5	6	7
M	M	S	F	no D	S	
	W				W	

    Now, our four dramas *must* be inserted as shown here:

1	2	3	4	5	6	7
M	M	S	F	no D	S	D
D	W	D	D		W	

    We're left with two films noirs and a western. We can't put two films noirs together, so day 5 must have one of each. Our final schedule looks like this:

1	2	3	4	5	6	7
M	M	S	F	F	S	D
D	W	D	D	W	W	F

    Just read the answer to the question from this completed schedule.

28. **The correct answer is (C).** If a musical and a science fiction movie must always go together, we know the following:

1	2	3	4	5	6	7
M		S	F	no D		
S		M				

Again, this forces us to schedule our dramas in a fixed pattern:

1	2	3	4	5	6	7
M	D	S	F	no D	D	D
S		M	D			

For day 5, the only remaining possible combination is film noir and western:

1	2	3	4	5	6	7
M	D	S	F	F	D	D
S		M	D	W		

And because of the rule against "threepeats," our last two westerns and final film noir must be inserted this way:

1	2	3	4	5	6	7
M	D	S	F	F	D	D
S	W	M	D	W	W	F

Now just read the answer from the completed schedule.

29. **The correct answer is (B).** Only this answer choice is false, since the framers clearly intended for representatives to be chosen directly by the people.

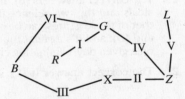

30. **The correct answer is (E).** Based on the puzzle information, you can draw a simple map like the one shown above. Most of the answers can be read directly from this map. For question 30, simply try tracing a few alternative routes for visiting every building. You'll quickly see that Z must be visited twice every time, since L is an "outlying" building that can only be reached by passing through Z.

31. **The correct answer is (C).** If we start at G and take path IV toward Z, the shortest complete tour will run this way: G, Z, G, R, G, Z, L, Z, X, B. It's not very efficient, since we must double back through our starting point, G, to hit building R. But under the rules stated, this is the best we can do. It takes a total of nine paths = 900 yards.

32. **The correct answer is (E).** It's possible to make a complete tour by walking on six paths if we start at B or L; it can be done in 7 paths starting at G or X. But if you start at Z, the minimum number of paths required is 8.

33. **The correct answer is (D).** If you modify your map, it's possible to make the complete tour taking just five paths, starting at either L or R. There are two ways to do it: L, Z, X, B, G, R, or R, G, B, X, Z, L. Doubling back through any building is now unnecessary. Good move, campus groundskeepers!

34. **The correct answer is (D).** The conclusion drawn in the passage is that businesspeople today demand speedy delivery merely because it is available. All the answer choices except choice (D) challenge this conclusion in one way or another, whereas choice (D) strengthens it.

35. **The correct answer is (D).** The factors that influence the attitudes of non-American employees toward their CEOs aren't directly relevant to the present argument, which focuses completely on explaining the resentment of American employees toward their bosses.

SECTION 5

1. **The correct answer is (B).** Since 64 is divisible by 4, so is 3,458,064. Thus, the remainder is zero when dividing by 4. However, 5,559,063 is not divisible by 9, because its digits do not sum to a number divisible by 9. Hence, there is some remainder, which must be greater than 0.

2. **The correct answer is (D).** In 5 hours, 4 ounces $(7 - 3)$ have dripped. Therefore, the "drip rate" is $\frac{4}{5}$ of an ounce per hour. From 5:00 p.m. on Sunday until 2:00 a.m. on Monday is 9 hours, causing the total to be $7 + \frac{4}{5} \times 9 = 7 + \frac{36}{5} = \frac{71}{5}$.

3. **The correct answer is (D).** This depends entirely upon what x is. If x is zero, the two are equal. If x is positive, $2x > x$, and if x is negative, $2x < x$.

4. **The correct answer is (D).** The prime factorization of 24 is $2^3(3)$; hence, if $24AB$ is a perfect square, then AB must have a factor of 2 and a factor of 3. This means, first of all, that both A and B cannot be odd. So I cannot be possible. II also cannot be possible, because if AB were a perfect square and $24AB$ were also a perfect square, then 24 would be a perfect square, which it is not. Of course, if, for example, A were 6 and B were 36, $24AB$ would be a perfect square with both A and B divisible by 6, so III is possible. Hence, the correct answer is (D).

5. **The correct answer is (B).** Since the diameter is 10, OA and OB, being radii, both have a length of 5. Since the perimeter is 16, we see that AB has a length of 6. Hence, $\angle O$ is the largest angle in the triangle. Since the other two angles are base angles of an isosceles triangle, they must be equal and have measure x. Hence, x must be less than 60, or the three angles would total more than 180°.

6. **The correct answer is (C).** To find the largest possible value of $\frac{a}{b}$, you certainly want a positive number, which you can get in two ways: a positive divided by a positive, or a negative divided by a negative. The largest fraction you can form using positive numbers from A and B is $\frac{3}{4}$. However, using the negative possibilities, we have $\frac{-6}{-4} = \frac{3}{2} = 1.5$. Hence, the two quantities are equal.

7. **The correct answer is (E).** If $n^2 < 2n$, that means that $n^2 - 2n < 0$, or $n(n - 2) < 0$. Clearly, if n is any positive number less than 2, then n will be positive and $(n - 2)$ will be negative, making the result true.

8. **The correct answer is (C).** The arithmetic mean of x and y is $\frac{x + y}{2} = m$, which means that $x + y = 2m$ and $x + y + z = 4m$. Dividing by 3 to get the arithmetic mean of x, y, and z, we have $\frac{x + y + z}{3} = \frac{4m}{3}$.

9. **The correct answer is (B).** Substituting $y = \frac{1}{2}$ in Column B, we have $\left(\frac{1}{2}\right)^0 + \left(\frac{1}{2}\right)^2 = 1 + \frac{1}{4} = 1.25 > 1.2$.

10. **The correct answer is (D).** Looking first at $\triangle ABC$, we have a right triangle with one angle 90° and another 27°. Thus, m$\angle A$ must be 63°. Hence, m$\angle BAC$ is one-third of that or 21°. So, looking at $\triangle ABC$, m$\angle BCA$ must be 180° − 21° − 27° = 132°. Since x is the supplement to that angle, $x = 48$.

11. **The correct answer is (C).** In 1995, the lowest price for the stock was over 10.

12. **The correct answer is (E).** The highest price in 1992 was between 5 and 6. In every year subsequent to that except 1998, the lowest price was higher. Hence, there were 5 years that meet the criterion described.

13. **The correct answer is (B).** The low in 1994 was 8. The high in 1998 was 2. The ratio of these two values is 4:1 or 400%. Hence, the difference was choice (B), 300%.

14. **The correct answer is (B).** The sales figures were 2.8, 3.8, 5, 7, 4, 2, and 1. Arranged in increasing order, they were 1, 2, 2.8, 3.8, 4, 5, and 7. The median was 3.8.

15. **The correct answer is (E).** All three statements refer to the year of highest sales, which was 1995. The stock reached its high (about 19) in 1996. So, I is true. The steepest decline in sales was from 1995 to 1996, so II is true. The greatest spread in stock prices was in 1996 (from a low of 8 to a high of 19). Hence, III is also true.

16. **The correct answer is (C).** $\frac{1}{3}$ of 42 is 14, and $\frac{1}{6}$ of 42 is 7. Thus, 21 horses are black or white, leaving 21 brown horses.

17. **The correct answer is (A).** Five more than twice n is $2n + 5$. Thus, $2n + 5 = 17$, which we solve to get $n = 6$. Three less than 6 is 3, and 2 less than $\frac{1}{2}$ of 6 is 2 less than 3, or 1. Since $3 > 1$, the correct choice is (A).

18. **The correct answer is (D).** The area of a circle with a diameter of 8 is $\pi 4^2 = 16\pi$, since its radius is 4. Let the width of the rectangle be w. Its length is $2w$ and its area is $2w^2$, which must equal 16π. Thus:

    $$2w^2 = 16\pi$$
    $$w^2 = 8 \text{ and } w = \sqrt{8} = 2\sqrt{2\pi}$$

    Therefore, $L = 4\sqrt{2\pi}$. The perimeter is $2L + 2W = 8\sqrt{2\pi} + 4\sqrt{2\pi} = 12\sqrt{2\pi}$.

19. **The correct answer is (B).** The square with an area of 36 has a side of 6 and a perimeter of 24. A circle with a radius of 6 has a circumference of $2\pi(6) = 12\pi$. Since $\pi > 3$, the circumference is greater than 36.

20. **The correct answer is (A).** By the Pythagorean Theorem, $x = \sqrt{7^2 - 3^2} = \sqrt{40} = 2\sqrt{10}$. The area of the triangle is $A = \frac{1}{2}bh = \frac{1}{2}(3)2\sqrt{10} = 3\sqrt{10}$. Since $\sqrt{10} > 3$, the area is greater than 9.

21. **The correct answer is (D).** Since $x + 6 > 7$, we know that $x > 1$. Since $7 > 2x$, we know that $3.5 > x$. Therefore, x is a number between 1 and 3.5, and that is all we can say.

22. **The correct answer is (C).** Calling the numbers x and $(x + 2)$, the negative of the sum is $-[x + (x + 2)]$, and this should be less than -35. That is, $-[2x + 2] < -35$. Solving the inequality:

    $$-2x - 2 < -35$$
    $$-2x < -33$$

    Dividing by -2 reverses the inequality: $x > 16.5$. Of course, 18 and 16 are both even, and we need an odd number. $x = 15$ will work, because $(x + 2) = 17 > 16.5$.

23. **The correct answer is (B).** $m_{\overline{PQ}} = \dfrac{5 - 2}{3 - (-1)} = \dfrac{3}{4}$, $m_{\overline{QR}} = \dfrac{5 - 3}{3 - 2} = \dfrac{2}{1} = 2$.

24. **The correct answer is (A).** The lengths of $\overline{OQ}$ and $\overline{OP}$ are the same: $\sqrt{2^2 + 1^2} = \sqrt{5}$. The length of $\overline{PQ}$ is $\sqrt{1^2 + 1^2} = \sqrt{2}$. The perimeter is $2\sqrt{5} + \sqrt{2}$.

25. **The correct answer is (D).** Although it seems unlikely that there are fewer blue marbles in the bag, you cannot know for sure. Purely by chance, a blue marble could be drawn three times in a row even if blue marbles are outnumbered by another color.

26. **The correct answer is (A).** Since $P = M + 1$, $N = 3^P = 3^{M + 1} = 3(3^M)$, and $\dfrac{3}{N} = \dfrac{3}{3(3^M)} = \dfrac{1}{3^M}$.

27. **The correct answer is (D).** If $x = 0$, Column A is 0, and Column B is 1. If $x = -3$, Column A is 3, and Column B is $-\dfrac{1}{2}$.

28. **The correct answer is (B).** We know that the average of x and -1 must be 2. That is, $2 = \dfrac{x + (-1)}{2}$, or $4 = x - 1$, and $x = 5$. Similarly, we know that the average of y and 3 must be 6. Thus, $6 = \dfrac{y + 3}{2}$, or $12 = y + 3$, and $y = 9$. Since $2x = 10$, $2x > y$.

Part IV

Making It Official

Chapter 14

Scheduling and Taking the Test

Get the Scoop On . . .

- Choosing the test date and location that's best for you
- Saving time and money when you register for the exam
- Obtaining any special test accommodations you may need to do your best
- Which ETS services are worth buying—and which ones to skip
- How to ensure you'll feel good and perform well the day of the exam

DECIDING HOW AND WHEN TO TAKE THE GRE

The GRE CAT is administered year-round, Monday through Saturday, at Prometric Test Centers throughout the United States and Canada, as well as at a few other locations (including some universities and ETS offices). So to begin with, you have a lot of flexibility in picking your test date. But when you start factoring in graduate school application deadlines and other considerations, your options rapidly begin to narrow. Here are some of the main points to consider in choosing a test date.

Check the Application Deadlines for Your Program(s) of Choice
Most schools set a single date by which they want to receive all the supporting data they need—not only test scores but also college transcripts, your personal statement, letters of recommendation, etc. Determine which program you are applying to sets the *earliest* deadline, and count back six weeks from that date. (This allows enough time for your score report to be received; ETS aims to send reports out within three weeks of the test, but four to five weeks is more common.) The date you count back to should be your *latest* date for taking the GRE.

Allow Yourself the Option of Retaking the GRE
Suppose that, working backward from your earliest graduate school deadline, you determine that you must take the GRE no later than early November. Don't simply apply for that test date. Instead, if you can, we recommend that you take the exam at least two months earlier. That means applying for an early September test or, better still, a test in April or May of the previous year.

Why the hurry? In the event your GRE scores don't hit your personal targets, you'll want to have the opportunity to take the exam at least once more before your application deadline hits.

Most students find that their test scores rise the second time they take the GRE, and if you prepare in a focused and disciplined way before your second exam, you'll have the opportunity to achieve a significant score increase. (For more information about whether and how to plan on retaking the exam, see Chapter 15.) But this will be impossible if you schedule your exam during the final pre-deadline window.

Plan Carefully so You Can Avoid Having to Cancel and Reschedule Your Test Appointment

Only a partial refund is available when you do this, so each change in schedule will cost you money.

Don't Forget to Schedule Your GRE Analytical Writing Measure and/or Subject Test

The new GRE Analytical Writing Measure sections may be required by the schools to which you're applying. The Analytical Writing Measure is offered separately from the core GRE, and you have to register—and pay for it—as a separate exam. If you need to take the Analytical Writing Measure, don't forget to schedule it. If you take the Analytical Writing Measure at a Prometric Test Center, you'll take it as a computerized exam. If you schedule the exam at a university testing center (most offer it on the days when the Subject Tests are administered) you may have the option of taking it in pencil-and-paper format.

Most graduate programs will require a score on the GRE Subject Test in your field of study (if the test exists). These are administered at university testing centers on Saturday afternoons in December and April and are given in the traditional paper-and-pencil format only (not computerized).

FYI

If you are interested in applying for scholarships, fellowships, or other special programs, an earlier deadline may apply. Don't forget to take that into consideration.

REGISTERING FOR THE EXAM

ETS supplies colleges with plentiful stacks of GRE bulletins and registration forms, so one easy way to get the forms you need is to stop by the guidance office and ask for them. If you prefer, you can call ETS at 609-771-7670 and have them send you the materials. You can also download the information from the GRE Web site (*www.gre.org*).

When you register by mail, you'll fill in a fairly lengthy (four-page) computerized form that requires you to blacken in ovals using a #2 pencil. Take your time filling out the form; it's easier than a tax return, but not much. Be especially careful when looking up and transferring the code numbers for the test center where you want to take the exam and the code numbers for the universities you're listing to receive your test scores. Mistakes are easy to make.

FYI

If you take the GRE in October, it'll be possible to retake the exam in November—but just barely. ETS currently allows you to retake the CAT only once per month. Plan ahead, and check the current policy by calling ETS or visiting www.gre.org.

If you have access to the Internet and the use of a Visa, MasterCard, or American Express Card (to pay the fees), you can also register on line.

In any case, you'll need to register well in advance of your chosen test date. Regular registration deadlines are about four weeks prior to the exam. You can register late for an extra fee, but this gives you only a few more days. So don't put off registration.

Once you've registered, you can use the phone to do things like register for subsequent tests, request a change in your test center, or add universities to your score report list. Expect a fee for each service you request.

THE INSIDER'S REPORT: KNOW YOUR OPTIONS

Choosing the Best Location

You'll probably want to schedule a test-taking appointment at the Prometric Test Center nearest to you. However, the conditions at these centers vary. Some are more spacious, less noisy, cleaner, and better organized than others. If two or more centers are located reasonably close to you, consider visiting them both before you select your test location. Or ask a classmate about her experience in taking the GRE.

If you pick a testing center located some distance from your usual stomping grounds, make sure you know exactly how to get there and how long it will take. You don't want to arrive late or experience a long, anxiety-producing drive in search of the right street address on the morning of your exam. If necessary, make a preliminary visit the week before, just to be sure you can get there with a minimum of fuss.

Taking the Test for Free

Taking the GRE isn't cheap. Currently, the minimum fee to register for the general exam is $105 (it's even more costly outside the United States). And if you request a few additional score reports beyond the four you get "free," buy one or two of the official GRE publications, and throw in one or two other services, the cost can easily climb to $150 or more. If you register for the GRE Analytical Writing Measure, you'll need to pay an additional $50 fee.

If your personal finances make GRE fees a problem, visit your college financial aid office and ask for information about getting the fees waived.

Generally, you must be on financial aid and meet certain specific criteria based on the financial need analysis report developed by your college when you most recently applied for aid. Your college counselor should have a booklet explaining the process; if not, she can call ETS for information.

You'll need to get a fee-waiver form from your college's financial aid office, which must be enclosed with your registration form when you send it in. Be sure to check in with your college at least two weeks before the registration deadline so there'll be plenty of time to get the necessary paperwork completed.

Special Testing Arrangements

Some students need special accommodations when they take the GRE. For example, a student in a wheelchair or a student whose sight or hearing is impaired may need special seating arrangements, the use of a Braille or large-print test booklet, or a sign-language interpreter for the proctor's spoken instructions.

In addition, if you have a learning disability or any physical or psychological condition that would make it impossible or unfair for you to complete the GRE exam under the same time limits as other students, you may be able to take the test with special extended timing.

If you fall into a category like these, speak to a counselor at the office of your college that provides services for students with disabilities. You'll need him to complete a form called the Certification of Eligibility for Nonstandard Testing Accommodations. You'll fill out another form, the Applicant's Request for Nonstandard Testing Accommodations; it appears in the GRE Bulletin.

If for any reason you can't get a Certification of Eligibility Form from your college, you'll need a letter from the physician or other professional involved in treating your condition. The letter must describe the accommodation needed, explain the reason for it, and document the need through diagnostic test results or other medical records. You'll enclose this letter with your regular test registration form.

ETS is strict about demanding authentication of your need for special testing arrangements. If your need is real, stick to your guns! Just be sure to begin the registration process early, so that any letters, forms, or documents ETS requires can be submitted in plenty of time.

Score Reporting

When you register for the GRE, you'll be allowed to pick four universities to receive reports of your scores. Even if you're not yet completely sure to which schools you'll be applying, take advantage of this opportunity to name four of your most likely choices. Additional reports will cost you money (currently $13 per school).

You can add to the list of programs that will receive your scores in several ways:

- Space for up to four additional reports is provided on the test registration form. The $13 fee will be charged for each college listed there, of course.

- You can fill out and mail an Additional Report Request Form, which you'll receive with your test admission packet.

- You can request additional reports online at the GRE Web site (*www.gre.org*).

- You can request additional reports by phone using a credit card. Dial 800-GRE-SCORE.

See Chapter 15 for more information about your score reports.

Selecting Other Services

At the time you register for the GRE, you'll have the opportunity to select other ETS services. Here's a rundown of your options, with our explanation and recommendation concerning each one:

- **GRE Search Service.** If you opt for this service, your name and personal profile, based on the information you provide in the questionnaire that is part of your registration form, will be given to interested universities. As a result, they may add you to their mailing lists to receive brochures and ads about their programs. Our recommendation: sign up. There's no fee, and you may find it interesting to hear from universities whose programs you may not have considered.

- **GRE Publications.** You'll have the option of ordering several GRE publications, including their directory of graduate programs, test preparation software packages, and books containing actual past GRE exams. Appendix C of the book you're now reading lists these and other useful resource guides you may want to own; the GRE books are fine, but there are competing books you may like better. (The fact that the GRE Board is an "official," university-sponsored organization makes their publications a little less revealing and more stodgy than other books, we think.) Our recommendation: check out the GRE Board books in a bookstore first. If you like them, go ahead and order them.

- **GRE Forums.** Each fall, the GRE Board sponsors a series of daylong meetings about graduate education in cities around the U.S. These are the GRE Forums. In 2000, they were held in Boston, San Francisco, New York, Dallas, and Chicago. The Forums feature booths manned by representatives of various universities and workshops on admissions, financial aid, GRE preparation, and other topics. A GRE Forum is worth attending if it's conveniently located; we wouldn't travel any great distance to attend one. The registration fee is modest (currently $5, but free if you have a coupon), so sign up if you're interested.

WHEN TEST TIME COMES

The big day is here. You're about to face one of the most important challenges of your academic life, comparable to the final exam of a crucial course or your oral presentation of an honors thesis. If you've used this book (and other resources) effectively, you can be confident that you're well prepared for the GRE exam. Here are some last-minute reminders and suggestions that will help you handle the stress of "game time" gracefully.

The Night Before

1. Don't cram. Last-minute study isn't likely to make much difference in your skills or knowledge, but it can elevate your levels of anxiety and fatigue needlessly.

2. Lay out everything you'll want to bring with you to the test center. This includes your official admission ticket, a photo ID (driver's license, passport, etc.), a pen and a pencil (or two pencils for a paper-and-pencil exam), and a small snack, like a granola bar or a piece of fruit.

3. If the weather is cool, lay out a sweater or two—dressing in layers will let you adjust to conditions in the test room. If you're traveling to an unfamiliar test site, put out the map or directions you'll be following.

4. Set your clock, and if possible have a backup system in place to wake you if the clock fails. (The best such system is a truly reliable roommate, friend, or relative.) You need to arrive at the test center at least thirty minutes prior to your scheduled starting time, so plan accordingly.

5. Get to sleep early. Remember that the GRE—three and a half to four and a half hours long—is a physical as well as a mental challenge.

FYI

If you requested any special test accommodations, try to arrive early. You may need to find or be directed to a different room or building from your fellow test-takers, and the test administrators may have to do some last-minute scrambling to get all the details in place.

The Morning of the Test

1. Wake up early and have your usual breakfast. If you normally skip breakfast, consider having something light this day—cereal or fruit. You'll be needing more energy than usual.

2. Leave plenty of time for travel, so you can arrive at the testing site early and relaxed, not late and frazzled.

3. Don't listen to the predictions and advice of the students around you. If you've prepared with the help of this book, you know exactly what to expect—probably better than your fellow test-takers. Last-minute speculation can only fuel needless worry.

See Appendix D, "The Insider's Stress-Busting Guide," for more proven techniques for managing and minimizing anxiety when you take your exam.

During the Test

1. Make sure your accommodations are appropriate and comfortable. You should have a comfortable chair, an adequate writing surface, plenty of light, and a space that is reasonably quiet, well-heated or cooled, and pollution-free. If any of these conditions is lacking, raise your hand and ask for help.

2. Work through the computer tutorial material patiently and make sure you are completely comfortable with the software before tackling the real test questions. Make sure your computer, monitor, and mouse are all functioning properly. Above all, use the CAT strategies explained in Chapter 3, especially taking the time you need with the earliest questions to start each section with a bang.

3. You'll have at least one short (ten-minute) break during the test. Use it to eat your snack and to relax. The three-minute relaxation routine described in Appendix D will help you feel refreshed before you tackle the next test section.

After the Test

1. If you encountered any problems with the test or the testing procedures—a mistake by the administrator, incorrect timing, a disruptive environment, or a computer malfunction—make detailed notes about it immediately after the test. A letter of complaint should be faxed to ETS at 609-406-5360 no later than seven days after your test. Though such difficulties are rare, they do happen. Putting the facts on record as soon as possible is the best way to protect your rights and to guarantee that

you'll have another opportunity to take the exam, under fair conditions, at no additional expense.

2. If you're convinced that you bombed on the exam, consider cancelling your scores. See Chapter 15 for details on how this works and how to decide whether this option is right for you.

3. If you think you encountered an erroneous or flawed test question, consider mounting an official challenge to the item. Chapter 15 tells how.

4. Now go party. You've earned it.

JUST THE FACTS

- Pick a testing date based on your graduate school application deadlines, but leave yourself a chance to retake the test if needed.

- Find a test center that's comfortable and close to home.

- Be sure to request any test-taking accommodations you need and deserve.

- Some—not all—of the products and services offered by ETS and the GRE Board are worthwhile investments.

- Manage your energies the day of the exam to minimize anxiety and maximize performance.

Chapter 15

Understanding Your Scores

Get the Scoop On . . .

- What your score report really means
- How graduate schools interpret your GRE scores
- How and when to consider cancelling your scores
- What to do if you think your score is wrong or the test was flawed
- How to decide whether to retake the GRE

You've taken the GRE . . . congratulations! Getting this far hasn't been easy. We hope you found that your study-and-practice program prepared you well for the challenge of the exam.

You may be pleasantly surprised by your test scores. Students who think they did poorly often get surprisingly high scores. (This happens more often than the reverse.) Here's why: as you took the exam, you spent more time puzzling over the hardest questions—the ones you may have gotten wrong—than over the easy ones, which you whizzed through. So when you think about the test later, your main memory is of struggling to figure out the toughest problems. That selective recall isn't necessarily an accurate gauge of how you did overall.

Even after you receive your official score report in the mail, however, your "GRE work" may not be done. It's time now to analyze your scores and what they mean, which may be a little more complicated than you realize. And you may have some important decisions to make—especially about whether to try taking the exam again. In this chapter, we'll explain what you need to know to win this phase of the great GRE game.

YOUR GRE SCORE REPORT

Getting Your Scores

As soon as you complete the CAT, you'll have the option of seeing your scores, both on-screen and in the form of a simple printout that the test administrator can give you. These are "unofficial" scores, but they are generally accurate. Your Analytical Writing Measure scores, of course, are not included. Go ahead and view your scores, *unless* you want to cancel them (see upcoming "Cancelling Your Scores" section).

Despite ETS's use of computers to score their exams, it has always taken quite a while for students to receive their official score reports in the mail. Two weeks is what ETS predicts, but students say that three to four weeks isn't unusual. The wait can be inconvenient, so be sure to take the exam early enough to get score reports to all the schools that need them.

ETS now offers a score-by-phone service to alleviate the waiting game. It allows you to get your GRE scores about two weeks after the date of your computerized test. There's an extra charge (currently $10) for this service. (You've probably noticed a recurring theme: almost anything you might want ETS to do for you will cost you something. The fact that ETS is a "not-for-profit" organization doesn't make them a "not-for-money" organization.) To take advantage of the score-by-phone option, call 888-GRE SCORE after 8:00 a.m. eastern time.

Understanding Your Score Report

The printed score report you'll eventually get in the mail offers more information than you can get by phone. However, even savvy test-takers don't always find it clear. Here's a point-by-point description and explanation of what your score report will tell you.

FYI

Mean GRE scores also vary from one discipline to another. As you might guess, engineering students tend to earn high Quantitative scores (recent average: 690), while humanities students earn high Verbal scores (average: 580). Data on most recent averages by discipline will be included in the information packet you receive with your scores.

- **Your Verbal, Quantitative, and Analytical Scores.** These are your three-digit scaled scores, computed as we explained in Chapter 3. Each score ranges between 200 (low) and 800 (high). Average or mean scores vary from year to year and even from test to test. However, in recent years, the average Verbal and Analytical scores have been around 540, while Quantitative scores have averaged around 560.

- **Your Percentile Scores.** You'll also receive three percentile scores—Verbal, Quantitative, and Analytical. These compare your performance to that of all students who took the exam during the last three years. The percentile score indicates what percentage of these students scored *lower* than you on the test. So if you have a verbal percentile score of 70 (for instance), it means that you did better than 70 percent of the students who took the test. Obviously, the higher your percentile scores, the better.

- **Your Scores on Other GRE Tests.** Your score report will also list your scores on past GRE General Tests (up to five years old) as well as Subject tests. It's handy to have all these numbers in one place.

HOW UNIVERSITIES INTERPRET GRE SCORES

The graduate programs to which you ask ETS to send your scores will receive reports containing all the information from your own score report. What do universities look for in reading your score report? Naturally, it varies from school to school. However, here are some general observations that apply to most programs.

FYI

Students are often surprised to learn what the GRE is supposed to show. The "psychometricians" (test experts) at ETS are frankly modest in their claims. They tell universities that GRE scores—in combination with college grades— are supposed to help predict the performance of students in first-year graduate school classes. That's all. The GRE cannot predict who will successfully complete the graduate degree— let alone who will achieve success in later life. Don't take your GRE scores too seriously. The test-makers themselves don't!

- **Universities look to GRE scores to amplify their picture of you.** In combination with your college grades, GRE scores are supposed to help graduate departments measure your academic abilities and achievements. Did you pursue a challenging college program and earn grades that were good but not great? Or were your classroom grades hampered by difficult personal circumstances—loss of a parent, for instance, or the need to work throughout college? In cases like these, good GRE scores could help confirm that you are brighter than your grades alone suggest.

- **Different departments emphasize different scores.** If you're applying to a program in engineering or the natural sciences, the Quantitative score is likely to be the most important one, while the Verbal score may rank third. The reverse is true for most programs in the humanities, such as art history, music, or language studies. A psychology major needs to perform well in all three areas. Check with the schools to which you're applying for a specific breakdown of which scores they scrutinize most closely.

- **Universities generally focus on your *best* GRE scores.** If you take the exam twice or more, most schools will evaluate you on the basis of your highest score. A sizeable minority—up to 40 percent—will even combine your highest Verbal, Quantitative, and Analytical scores if those occurred on different days. Just a few insist on considering only your most recent scores—even if those were lower than some earlier scores. The department will generally tell you its policy.

- **Universities evaluate you against this year's pool of applicants.** Your graduate school application—not only your test scores but all your credentials—will never be considered in a vacuum. You are always being measured against the other students who've applied to a particular program. As the size and quality of this applicant pool rises and falls from one year to the next, a particular set of credentials may look better or worse by comparison.

Luck and fashion play a huge role in this process. For reasons that are often hard to fathom, some programs get "hot" at particular times; everybody and their brother decides to apply to University *X*, and the happy faculty there gets a chance, for a time, to skim off the very best students. An applicant who might have waltzed through the door two years earlier may not make the cut now. And the opposite happens when a school falls out of vogue. Bear this in mind if you're tempted to apply to this year's fashionable program: although the education probably hasn't improved, getting in has gotten a lot harder.

THE INSIDER'S REPORT: KNOW YOUR OPTIONS

Now you know how universities look at your GRE scores. What can you do about it all? Are there ways of managing the posttest part of the GRE process to make it work better for you?

Absolutely. Let's look at some of the options you have *after* your exam to minimize the damage from a bad day in the testing arena and to maximize your chances of getting your best possible scores.

Cancelling Your Scores

FYI

If you merely feel you may have done poorly on the exam, you should probably go ahead and allow the test to be graded. Then examine your scores to deter-mine which areas need most work and which ones are fairly strong. This will help you a lot in preparing to do better next time—and it's an option that's not available if you cancel your scores.

Occasionally, a student knows on the day of the test that he has truly bombed. Most often, the problem is physical: people do get ill, sometimes unexpectedly, and the stress of a three- to four-hour exam can worsen the early symptoms of a flu bug or stomach virus. Once in a great while, a student simply freezes up and is psychologically or emotionally unable to finish the test. And sometimes an ill-prepared student realizes, in despair, that he really should have studied and practiced before sitting down on test day. (If you've read the previous chapters in the book you're holding, you're not a candidate for this problem.)

If any of these calamities befalls you, there is an option—score cancellation. ETS will wipe clear your score slate for a particular day at your request; your test won't be graded, and neither you nor any school will know how well (or poorly) you did.

However, these caveats exist:

- You must request score cancellation immediately. A screen is provided for this purpose on the CAT. Cancelling your scores is as simple as clicking a couple of buttons.

- The request is irrevocable. Once you cancel your scores, they can never be reinstated. And you can't cancel just your Verbal or just your Quantitative score: the entire General Test must be wiped out.

- You won't receive any refund of your testing fee.

Obviously, cancelling your scores is a fairly serious step. Probably most significantly, it will put you in a position where you must retake the exam several weeks or months later, by which time application deadlines may be looming. The sense of pressure you feel on this subsequent test date may be even greater than before.

Therefore, you should cancel your scores only if you really must—illness being the most likely culprit.

If Your Scores Are Delayed

On rare occasions, a student's official GRE score reports are delayed. A simple glitch in mail delivery may be to blame. We suggest that, if you haven't received your scores by six weeks after the test date, you take advantage of the score-by-phone service (described above) to make sure your scores have been recorded. If they have, call the admissions offices of the universities to which you are applying and ask whether they've received your score report. If they have, the problem on your end is with the mail. Send a fax to ETS at 609-771-7906 to request a duplicate of your score report.

If neither you nor your universities have received a report by six weeks after the test date, try to find out whether other students are experiencing delays. Once in a while, computer or other problems at ETS cause general delays for all students who took a particular test. It's rare but frustrating, and there's not much you can do except sit tight.

Finally, if it appears that the score delay involves you alone (or only a handful of other students), it's possible that ETS may be investigating an apparent testing irregularity or a test security problem.

A *testing irregularity* is a problem with the way the test was administered. It could be due to an administrator's error (test-takers were given incorrect instructions, for example), an ETS error (faulty test items were used), or circumstances beyond anyone's control (a test center is disrupted by fire or flood, or a computer malfunctions).

A *test security problem* means, quite specifically, a suspicion that students had access to the test beforehand; used books, calculators, or other forbidden aids during the exam; took the test under false names; passed answers to one another; or otherwise cheated.

If you fall under suspicion of cheating, you'll be in for an unpleasant experience, whether or not you are guilty. Although ETS makes an effort at "due process," the adjudication of such cases is basically an internal process controlled by the test-makers.

This doesn't mean, however, that you are helpless, much less that you should meekly accept a "guilty" verdict if you are really innocent. Here is some advice as to what to do if you find yourself accused of misconduct on the GRE.

- Insist on understanding the accusation and the process. When an investigation is started, you should receive a copy of the ETS booklet *Why and How Educational Testing Service Questions Test Scores.* Read it thoroughly. Then make sure that the test-makers inform you as to exactly what misconduct is supposed to have occurred, so that you can marshal evidence in your defense.

- Enlist the help and advice of a college counselor, professor, or other trusted adviser. This is an important problem that can seriously affect your graduate school prospects, and the bureaucracy at ETS can be intimidating. Don't try to handle it alone.

- Communicate with ETS clearly and in writing. Use registered mail and keep copies of all your communications with the test-makers. Make sure that you "admit" nothing that is not completely true.

- As soon as you can, make detailed notes of everything you remember about your test-preparation and test-taking experience. In particular, if you remember anything "odd" that happened on the day of the exam, jot it down. (A mistake by an administrator, for example, may innocently explain some discrepancy ETS thinks is sinister.) Be sure to be as complete and accurate as possible. The sooner you make these notes, the clearer and more convincing your memory of events is likely to be.

- Provide the test-makers with any facts that could help to clear you. If you know why you're suspected of wrongdoing, you may be able to resolve the dispute by responding with information. For example, if you're suspected of cheating because you left the test room several times during the exam, you may want to ask your doctor to provide a letter confirming that you were suffering from a stomach complaint on the day of the test (if that was the case).

Sometimes, ETS will investigate a test-taker solely because of a dramatic score increase—200 points or more over a previous test. If you're in this category, be prepared to explain (and document, if possible) how you prepared for your second test. Describe your use of coaching, tutoring, books, software, and any other test-prep tools, and estimate the number of hours you devoted to study before the exam. A convincing account of your significant test-prep effort can go a long way toward showing that your score increase was produced not by trickery but by good, old-fashioned hard work.

- Consider enlisting legal help. In America, of course, final recourse in disputes between groups and individuals is to the law. Most wrangles with ETS don't require the help of a lawyer, but you may want to consider this option if you've been unjustly accused, if the test-makers refuse to resolve the dispute quickly and fairly, and if the cost is not a major problem for you and your family.

■ If the dispute is not resolved within a reasonable time (say, four to six weeks), insist on your right to retake the exam as soon as possible, at no charge to you. ETS is supposed to provide this service to give an innocent test-taker the chance to demonstrate his abilities again without penalty and free from any cloud of suspicion.

If You Think Your Scores Are Wrong

On rare occasions, a student becomes convinced that one or more of her test scores is inaccurate. Here's what to do if this happens to you.

■ **Request rescoring of your GRE Analytical Writing Measure.** Sometimes, a student feels that the scoring of his or her essays is inaccurate or unfair. This is not unlikely; as we explained in Chapter 12, the holistic grading system used by ETS puts a premium on speedy judgments, not detailed or authoritative ones. It's entirely possible that a good essay could be misinterpreted by a hasty or exhausted reader.

Your best option in this case is to request rescoring of your essays. You can do this up to six months after taking the exam by either fax or phone. (As you probably guessed, there's a fee for this service.) You'll get a new score report within three to five weeks. If it's found that your test *was* misgraded, ETS will send a notification letter to all of your universities. Note, however, that the revised scores will stand—whether they are higher or lower!

■ **Challenge a test question or procedure.** A more complicated problem arises if you become convinced that you were harmed either by some unfair procedure on the day of the test or by an inaccurate and flawed test question. There's a system for appealing such problems, but be prepared for a fairly lengthy process.

If you feel burned by a test procedure or question, write down all the details you can remember as soon as possible. Then send a registered letter to the test-makers at this address:

Graduate Record Examinations
Educational Testing Service
P.O. Box 6000
Princeton, New Jersey 08541-6000

Include your name, address, phone number, birth date, social security number, and test registration number; and mention the name of the test you took, the date, and the name, number, and address of the test center you used. In your letter, explain what happened and why you think it was unfair.

ETS will investigate and respond. In most cases, they will defend their procedure or test question (and often they are right to do so). If you aren't satisfied, there are several further levels of appeal you can request, culminating in a formal review by an independent panel. It's up to you to decide how significant your complaint is, how strongly you feel about it, and how much time and effort you want to invest in this process.

ETS is obviously not perfect. Over the years, they have been forced to admit errors in over a dozen test questions, increasing the scores of hundreds of thousands of students.

So don't hesitate to challenge the test-makers if you're convinced it's appropriate. The only way powerful institutions like ETS can be kept responsive to human concerns is if individuals hold them accountable for their actions, right and wrong.

FairTest, the nonprofit organization dedicated to fair and open testing, may be able to help you with information and referrals if you have a complaint or dispute about the GRE. Contact them at:

FairTest
342 Broadway
Cambridge, Massachusetts 02139-1802
617-864-4810
617-497-2224 (fax)
fairtest@aol.com

The Decision to Retest

Should you retake the GRE if you're not satisfied with your scores? In many cases, the answer is yes. Here are some of the factors to consider in making this decision.

- How do the scores you've already received match the credentials wanted by the graduate program(s) of your choice? You'll need to establish target GRE scores based on the admission requirements of the schools you want to attend, as well as the other credentials you bring to the table—your college grades, etc. If the test scores you've already earned fall outside the range in which most students at your ideal school score—or if they are at the lower end of that range—you should strongly consider retaking the test.

- How often have you already been tested? If you've taken the GRE twice or more previously—and especially if you prepared beforehand—you may have already tapped most of your potential for improvement. However, if you've been tested just once before—and especially if your preparation in the past was superficial—there's every reason to believe your score can go up, perhaps a lot.

FYI

Most students who take the GRE a second time enjoy at least a modest score increase, due to sheer familiarity with the exam. If you retake the test following a serious preparation program tailored to the weaknesses revealed by your first score report, the effects of that preparation, combined with the "familiarity effect," should give you a great shot at a significant score increase.

FYI

Universities differ in their policies about which GRE scores they look at when a student has been tested more than once. Before you decide to retake the GRE, call your top three graduate school choices and check their policies. Make sure you'll get the full benefit of any score increase you may obtain.

- Can you identify test areas with potential for improvement? You're an especially strong candidate to retake the exam if your practice tests reveal specific areas of weakness. For example, if you perform well on all the Verbal areas except analogies, where you get most of the items wrong, a targeted practice program focusing on analogies may boost your overall score significantly. Similarly, if a particular math area gives you trouble, work with a review book, teacher, or tutor to master that topic, and the chances are good that your Quantitative score will rise on test number two.

- Do you have time to invest in preparing for another test? Look realistically at your plans for school, work, and other activities. Before you schedule another exam, make sure you can block out hours during the weeks prior to the exam for study and practice. If you take the second test cold, without any real preparation or warm-up, you may wind up spinning your wheels, earning scores no higher than your first scores.

A final tip about retaking the exam: Don't forget to review *every* test area, at least briefly, before your second or later GRE. Although you may need to focus the bulk of your study on algebra (for example), it's important to keep your verbal skills and your knowledge of other math areas sharp, too. You don't want to gain points on one end while losing them on the other.

JUST THE FACTS

- Study your score report carefully, and make sure you understand what each number means.

- Evaluate your performance as universities will—against the credentials of their pool of applicants.

- If you think you completely bombed on the exam, consider cancelling your scores.

- If you think your GRE was unfair for any reason, you have ways to complain and be heard.

- Consider retaking the exam if your scores fall below the targets you need to achieve.

- If you do retake the test, focus your preparation on areas where you need the most improvement.

Chapter 16

The Insider's Tip Sheet

Get the Scoop On . . .

- The most important test-taking strategies to review just before taking the GRE

It's the night before you'll be taking the GRE—or maybe the very morning of the exam. You've been studying, practicing, and preparing for days, weeks, even months, and you're about as ready to take the test as you'll ever be.

Trouble is, the strategies, techniques, and methods you've learned from this book feel as if they're lodged in dozens of separate compartments scattered throughout your overloaded brain. A few weeks may have passed since you last tried your hand at a particular question type; you've probably become a little fuzzy about exactly how to tackle it. But you don't have time now—hours before the test—to review hundreds of pages covering strategies for nine separate question types. If you try, you may just intensify that gnawing sense of anxiety in the pit of your stomach—and maybe even develop a full-blown case of panic.

That's where this chapter comes in. It's a concise recap of the most important tips, strategies, warnings, and techniques from the entire book, organized for easy study during the final day before your exam. You may want to tear these pages out of the book and carry them with you in the car, bus, or train that takes you to the test center for a true last-minute review. It's even better to read them the night before—that way, if any one or two ideas don't ring a bell, you can look them up in the relevant chapters and refresh your memory.

OVERALL STRATEGIES FOR THE COMPUTERIZED GRE

- **Work your way patiently through the tutorial materials at the start of the exam.** Don't begin work on the real test until you're sure you're comfortable with all of the mechanics of the computerized test. Time spent mastering the computer tutorials does *not* affect your test-taking time.

- **Remember, answering the first five questions in each test section correctly is crucially important.** Take your time! Read and reread the questions, double-check your work, and consider every answer choice carefully. Getting these questions right will have a disproportionate effect on your overall scores.

- **The question types will be interspersed, seemingly at random, throughout a given test section.** An antonym may be followed by a sentence completion or a reading comprehension passage, unpredictably. Be prepared to adjust frequently from one type of question to another.

- **After spending as much time as you need to on the first five questions, speed up slightly.** The computerized GRE is fairly generous with time, but you shouldn't dawdle or get bogged down on a single, unusually tough question. If you work at a steady pace, you should have ample time to answer every question.

- **Use scrap paper freely—to perform computations, outline reading passages, diagram logical puzzles, and outline your essays.** If you run out of paper, don't be shy about asking for more.

- **Guess selectively.** Use what you know to eliminate answers that are clearly wrong, then pick the best answer from among those that remain. Chances are you'll gain points by following this method.

- **Expect one or two test sections made up of unscored questions for experimental or research purposes.** One of these sections may be labeled as a research section; the other may not. Any section not clearly labeled as experimental *may* count in your score and should be taken seriously. But if a test section is made up of "weird" questions of a type you've never seen before, don't fret about it—it is almost certainly experimental and will not affect your score.

VERBAL STRATEGIES

On All Verbal Questions

Read every answer choice. In the verbal section, there are degrees of right and wrong; the first answer may be partially correct, while the second answer is a little better, and the third answer is better still. Don't jump to select the first answer that appears tempting.

Antonyms

- Try to anticipate a possible answer before looking at the answer choices.

- When in doubt, check your answer backward by asking, "What would be the opposite of the answer I've chosen?"

- Use word roots and context clues to help you remember the meanings of tricky words.

- Don't forget that connotations (the feelings of words) and secondary meanings may make a difference in choosing between two tempting answers.

Analogies

- Build a bridge to define the relationship between the two words in the stem pair, and narrow the definition as needed to eliminate potential answer choices.

- Use the analogy relationship to help you guess the meanings of words you're not sure about.

- Don't be afraid to draw analogies between concrete, physical relationships and abstract ideas.

Sentence Completions

- Focus on how the ideas in the two parts of the sentence are related to one another—this usually offers a crucial clue to the meaning of the missing word(s).

- Try to anticipate a possible answer before you look at the answer choices.

- Avoid answers that are inconsistent with the rest of the sentence or that introduce new ideas.

- When necessary, eliminate answers where one word or the other doesn't work and guess from among the answer choices that remain.

Reading Comprehension

- Use the three-stage method (previewing, reading, reviewing) to get the most out of each reading passage.

- Focus on the big ideas in each passage, not the small details.

- Look for the connections among the ideas in each passage.

- Review the passage as often as necessary to locate the answer for a specific question.

- Don't pick an answer just because it sounds familiar, seems to be true, or reflects information that actually appears in the passage— the answer must also accurately respond to the question being asked.

QUANTITATIVE STRATEGIES

On All Quantitative Items
As soon as you've found the right answer, mark it and move on—there are no "degrees of rightness" to be considered.

Multiple-Choice Problems
- The questions are designed to focus primarily on the underlying relationships among the numbers presented, not your ability to perform calculations—therefore, if you find yourself spending too much time doing figuring, you've probably overlooked a simple shortcut.

- Feel free to round off and guesstimate, using approximate values.

- When in doubt about how to get started on a problem, try something—anything! This will often lead you toward a solution.

Quantitative Comparisons
- Remember, you usually *don't* have to calculate exact values for the two columns—you only need to be able to tell which column is greater when approximate values will suffice.

- Work on one or both columns to make them look as much alike as possible.

- Eliminate whatever the two columns have in common.

- When stymied, try plugging in possible values for x or any other unknown—but remember to try zero, a fraction, and a negative number unless they are specifically ruled out.

- When there *is* no unknown quantity, don't pick choice (D), "It cannot be determined."

ANALYTICAL STRATEGIES

Logical Reasoning
- Start by looking for the key elements of any argument (the conclusion, the evidence, the hidden assumptions)—most of the questions will turn on the relationship among them.

- Then look for any fallacy (a logical flaw or weakness) contained in the argument.

- Always read all the answer choices before selecting the best one—there are "degrees of correctness" in logical reasoning.

Analytical Reasoning

- Start by reading the puzzle conditions to get an overview of the situation.

- Then sketch a simple diagram that reflects the puzzle rules as clearly and completely as possible.

- Don't be concerned if the diagram seems incomplete or if there are pieces of the puzzle that don't immediately fit together—that's normal.

- Be prepared to alter the diagram from one question to the next, depending on new information presented—but don't carry the new information over to the next question unless you're expressly told to do so. (Do the basic diagram in pen; alter it as needed in pencil, which can be erased.)

- Work your way through the answer choices methodically—in alphabetical order, for instance—so you won't overlook any.

- As soon as you've found the right answer, mark it and move on—there are no "degrees of rightness" to be considered.

STRATEGIES FOR THE ANALYTICAL WRITING MEASURE

- Use the four-step writing process to organize your work—brainstorm (3 minutes), outline (2 minutes), write (20–30 minutes), revise (5 minutes). Use the scrap paper provided to brainstorm and outline, then write and revise on the computer.

- Keep your outline simple, and use the paragraph as the unit of organization—one big idea, fully developed, to each paragraph you write.

- Use signpost words (*nonetheless, similarly, next, consequently*) to guide your reader through the essay.

- Be as specific as possible when offering examples or evidence to back up your ideas.

- Vary the length of your sentences, using short sentences to state ideas you want to emphasize.

- Proofread carefully, looking for errors in spelling, grammar, and word choice. When in doubt, rephrase to make the sentence correct.

Part V

Appendices

Appendix A

The Insider's GRE Word List

WHY STUDY VOCABULARY?

If you're a native speaker of English, you already know thousands of words. (The average person has a working vocabulary of over 10,000 words—and is probably capable of at least recognizing thousands more.) After four years of college, you probably have an extensive vocabulary of words drawn from many fields of study, to say nothing of the words you hear, see, and use in everyday life. Is it really necessary for you to study vocabulary in preparation for the GRE?

For most people, the answer is Yes.

The test-makers consider vocabulary so important that they test it in several ways on the GRE.

1. As you know, the verbal sections of the exam include antonym questions, which require you to pick a word whose meaning is the opposite of some other word. In Chapter 4, we provided you with a number of hints and strategies for tackling these items effectively.

   Then there are *indirect* and *hidden* vocabulary questions—of which there are plenty.

2. Your ability to fully understand reading comprehension passages will often turn on your knowledge of vocabulary. The broader, more varied, and more accurate your vocabulary knowledge, the better your chances of answering the questions that cover these passages quickly and correctly.

3. Analogy questions obviously depend to a large extent on vocabulary. It's difficult—though not impossible, as we discussed in Chapter 5—to decipher the analogy relationships unless you understand the words that are involved. One typical group of analogy items includes the words *proficiency, embellish, carping, reclusive, tactile, criterion, intransigent,* and *strenuous,* among others. (How many of these can you define?) You don't have to throw up your hands in despair if an analogy item contains a word or two you don't know; there's more than one way to skin that cat. But the process will be a lot easier and faster if you know most of the words used, or at least have a nodding acquaintance with them.

4. The better your vocabulary knowledge, the easier you'll find it to understand the sentence completion items (which are, in effect, mini-reading passages, each one sentence long). Even an occasional math item is made a little more complicated by the use of a challenging vocabulary word.

5. Your performance on the Analytical Writing Measure will be aided by vocabulary knowledge that is both broad and deep: broad, in the sense that you have a relatively large and varied pool of words to draw upon; deep, in the sense that your understanding of individual words is accurate and sophisticated. The words you use in your essays will have a significant impact on the grades you receive. Reliance on rudimentary or narrow vocabulary makes you sound "less smart"; so does misusing words.

So vocabulary knowledge makes a clear and significant difference in your performance on the GRE. Fortunately, the kinds of words that regularly appear on the GRE—as with so much else on the exam—fall into definite patterns.

The GRE is basically a test of "book learning." It's written and edited by bookish people for the benefit of the other bookish people who run universities. It's designed to test your ability to handle the kinds of bookish tasks graduate students usually have to master: reading textbooks, finding information in reference books, deciphering scholarly journals, studying research abstracts, writing impressive-sounding papers, etc.

So the hard words on the GRE are hard words of a particular sort: bookish hard words that deal, broadly speaking, with the manipulation and communication of *ideas*—words like *ambiguous, amplify, arbitrary,* and *arcane.* The better you master this sort of vocabulary, the better you'll do on the exam.

Happily, you don't need to find these words on your own. We've done the spadework for you. By examining actual GRE exams from the last several years, we've been able to list the words most commonly used in reading passages, antonyms, analogies, and sentence completions, including both the question stems and the answer choices. This list became the basis of the Insider's GRE Word List. It includes about 500 primary words that are most likely to appear in one form or another on your GRE exam. It also includes hundreds of related words—words that are either variants of the primary words (*abrasion* as a variant of *abrade*, for example) or that share a common word root (like *ample, amplify,* and *amplitude*).

If you make yourself acquainted with all the words in the Insider's GRE Word List, you will absolutely learn a number of new words that will appear on your GRE. You'll earn extra points as a result.

THE SIX BEST VOCABULARY-BUILDING TIPS FOR THE GRE

Study Vocabulary Daily

There are some topics you can easily cram. Vocabulary isn't one of them. Words generally stick in the mind not the first or second time you learn them but the fourth or fifth time. Try to begin your vocabulary study several weeks before the exam. Take fifteen or twenty minutes a day to learn new words. Periodically review all the words you've previously studied; quiz yourself, or have a friend quiz you. This simple regimen can enable you to learn several hundred new words before you take the GRE.

Learn a Few Words at a Time

Don't try to gobble dozens of words in one sitting. They're likely to blur into an indistinguishable mass. Instead, pick a reasonable quantity—say, ten to fifteen words—and study them in some depth. Learn the definition of each word; examine the sample sentence provided in the word list; learn the related words; and try writing a couple of sentences of your own that include the word. Refer to your own dictionary for further information if you like.

Learn Words in Families

Language is a living thing. Words are used by humans, innately creative beings who constantly twist, reshape, invent, and recombine words. (Think of the jargon of your favorite sport or hobby, or the new language currently blossoming in cyberspace, for some examples.) As a result, most words belong to families in which related ideas are expressed through related words. This makes it possible to learn several words each time to learn one.

In the Insider's GRE Word List, we've provided some of the family linkages to help you. For example, you'll find the adjective *anachronistic* in the word list. It means "out of the proper time," as illustrated by the sample sentence: *The reference, in Shakespeare's* Julius Caesar, *to "the clock striking twelve" is anachronistic, since there were no striking timepieces in ancient Rome.*

When you meet this word, you should also get to know its close kinfolk. The noun *anachronism* means something that is out of its proper time. The clock in *Julius Caesar*, for example, is an anachronism; in another way, so are the knickers worn by modern baseball players, which reflect a style in men's fashions that went out of date generations ago. When you learn the adjective, learn the noun (and/or verb) that goes with it at the same time.

Become a Word Root Tracer

The two words we just discussed—*anachronistic* and *anachronism*—are like brother and sister. Slightly more distant relatives can be located and learned through the Word Origin feature you'll find near many of the words in the list. The Word Origin for *anachronistic* connects this word to a source from another language: The Greek word *chronos* = time. Ultimately, this is the root from which the English word *anachronistic* grows.

As you explore the Word Origins, you'll find that many words—especially bookish GRE words—come from roots in Latin and Greek. There are complicated (and interesting) historical reasons for this, but the nub is that, for several centuries, learned people in England and America knew ancient Latin and Greek and deliberately imported words from those languages into English.

They rarely imported just one word from a given root. Thus, many word roots can enable you to learn several English words at once. The Word Origins for *anachronistic* tells you that *chronos* is also the source of the English words *chronic, chronicle, chronograph, chronology, synchronize.* All have to do with the concept of time:

> *chronic* = lasting a long time
> *chronicle* = a record of events over a period of time
> *chronograph* = a clock or watch
> *chronology* = a timeline
> *synchronize* = to make two things happen at the same time

Learning the word root *chronos* can help you in several ways. It will make it easier to learn all the words in the *chronos* family, as opposed to trying to learn them one at a time. It will help you to remember the meanings of *chronos* words if they turn up on the exam. And it may even help you to guess the meaning of an entirely new *chronos* word when you encounter it.

Use the Words You Learn

Make a deliberate effort to include the new words you're learning in your daily speech and writing. It will impress people (professors, bosses, friends and enemies) and it will help solidify your memory of the words and their meanings. Maybe you've heard this tip about meeting new people: if you use a new acquaintance's name several times, you're likely never to forget it. The same is true with new words: use them, and you won't lose them.

Create Your Own Word List

Get into the habit of reading a little every day with your dictionary nearby. When you encounter a new word in a newspaper, magazine, or book, look it up. Then jot down the new word, its definition, and the sentence in which you encountered it in a notebook set aside for this purpose. Review your vocabulary notebook periodically—say, once a week. Use the words you learn this way. It's a great way to supplement our Insider's GRE Word List, because it's personally tailored—your notebook will reflect the kinds of things you read and the kinds of words you find most difficult. And the fact that you've taken the time and made the effort to write down the words and their meanings will help to fix them in your memory. Chances are good that you'll encounter a few words from your vocabulary notebook on the exam.

THE WORD LIST

Word Origin

Latin brevis = *short. Also found in English* brevity.

abbreviate (verb)   To make briefer, to shorten. *Because time was running out, the speaker was forced to abbreviate his remarks.* abbreviation (noun).

aberration (noun)   A deviation from what is normal or natural, an abnormality. *Jack's extravagant lunch at Lutece was an aberration from his usual meal, a peanut butter sandwich and a diet soda.* aberrant (adjective).

abeyance (noun)   A temporary lapse in activity; suspension. *In the aftermath of the bombing, all normal activities were held in abeyance.*

abjure (verb)   To renounce or reject; to officially disclaim. *While being tried by the inquisition in 1633, Galileo abjured all his writings holding that the Earth and other planets revolved around the sun.*

Word Origin

Latin abradare = *to scrape. Also found in English* abrasive.

abrade (verb)   To irritate by rubbing; to wear down in spirit. *Olga's "conditioning facial" abraded Sabrina's skin so severely that she vowed never to let anyone's hands touch her face again.* abrasion (noun)

abridge (verb)   To shorten, to reduce. *The Bill of Rights is designed to prevent Congress from abridging the rights of Americans.* abridgment (noun).

abrogate (verb)   To nullify, to abolish. *During World War II, the United States abrogated the rights of Japanese Americans by detaining them in internment camps.* abrogation (noun).

abscond (verb)   To make a secret departure, to elope. *Theresa will never forgive her daughter, Elena, for absconding to Miami with Philip when they were only seventeen.*

accretion (noun)   A gradual build up or enlargement. *My mother's house is a mess due to her steady accretion of bric-a-brac and her inability to throw anything away.*

adjunct (noun)   Something added to another thing, but not a part of it; an associate or assistant. *While Felix and Fritz were adjuncts to Professor Himmelman during his experiments in electrodynamics, they did not receive credit when the results were published.*

adroit (adjective)   Skillful, adept. *The writer Laurie Colwin was particularly adroit at concocting love stories involving admirable and quirky female heroines and men who deserve them.*

adulterate (verb)   To corrupt, to make impure. *Unlike the chickens from the large poultry companies, Murray's free-roaming chickens have not been adulterated with hormones and other additives.*

adversary (noun)   An enemy or opponent. *When the former Soviet Union became an American ally, the United States lost its last major international adversary.* adverse (adjective).

aesthete (noun)   Someone devoted to beauty and to beautiful things. *A renowned aesthete, Oscar Wilde was the center of a group that glorified beauty and adopted the slogan "art for art's sake."* aesthetic (adjective)

affability (noun)   The quality of being easy to talk to and gracious. *Affability is a much-desired trait in any profession that involves dealing with many people on a daily basis.* affable (adjective).

affected (adjective)   False, artificial. *At one time, Japanese women were taught to speak in an affected high-pitched voice, which was thought girlishly attractive.* affect (verb), affectation (noun).

affinity (noun)   A feeling of shared attraction, kinship; a similarity. *When they first fell in love, Andrew and Tanya marveled over their affinity for bluegrass music, obscure French poetry, and beer taken with a squirt of lemon juice. People often say there is a striking affinity between dogs and their owners (but please don't tell Clara that she and her bassett hound are starting to resemble each other).*

aggrandize (verb)   To make bigger or greater; to inflate. *When he was mayor of New York City, Ed Koch was renowned for aggrandizing his accomplishments and strolling through city events shouting, "How'm I doing?"* aggrandizement (noun).

agitation (noun)   A disturbance; a disturbing feeling of upheaval and excitement. *After the CEO announced the coming layoffs, the employees' agitation was evident as they remained in the auditorium talking excitedly among themselves.* agitated (adjective), agitate (verb).

alias (noun)   An assumed name. *Determined not to reveal his upper-class roots, Harold Steerforth Hetherington III went under the alias of "Hound Dog" when playing trumpet in his blues band.*

allegiance (noun)   Loyalty or devotion shown to one's government or to a person, group, or cause. *At the moving naturalization ceremony, 43 new Americans from 25 lands swore allegiance to the United States.*

Word Origin

Latin vertere = to turn. Also found in English adversary, adverse, reverse, vertical, and vertigo.

---

allocate (verb)   To apportion for a specific purpose; to distribute. *The president talked about the importance of education and health care in his State of the Union address, but, in the end, the administration did not allocate enough resources for these pressing concerns.* allocation (noun).

amalgamate (verb)   To blend thoroughly. *The tendency of grains to sort when they should mix makes it difficult for manufacturers to create powders that are amalgamated.* amalgamation (noun).

ameliorate (verb)   To make something better or more tolerable. *The living conditions of the tenants were certainly ameliorated when the landlord finally installed washing machines and dryers in the basement.* amelioration (noun).

amortize (verb)   To pay off or reduce a debt gradually through periodic payments. *If you don't need to take a lump sum tax deduction, it's best to amortize large business expenditures by spreading the cost out over several years.*

amplify (verb)   To enlarge, expand, or increase. *Uncertain as to whether they understood, the students asked the teacher to amplify his explanation.* amplification (noun).

Word Origin

Greek chronos = *time. Also found in English* chronic, chronicle, chronograph, chronology, *and* synchronize.

anachronistic (adjective)   Out of the proper time. *The reference, in Shakespeare's* Julius Caesar, *to "the clock striking twelve" is anachronistic, since there were no striking timepieces in ancient Rome.* anachronism (noun).

anarchy (noun)   Absence of law or order. *For several months after the Nazi government was destroyed, there was no effective government in parts of Germany, and anarchy ruled.* anarchic (adjective).

animosity (noun)   Hostility, resentment. *During the last debate, the candidates could no longer disguise their animosity and began to trade accusations and insults.*

anomaly (noun)   Something different or irregular. *The tiny planet Pluto, orbiting next to the giants Jupiter, Saturn, and Neptune, has long appeared to be an anomaly.* anomalous (adjective).

antagonism (noun)   Hostility, conflict, opposition. *As more and more reporters investigated the Watergate scandal, antagonism between the Nixon administration and the press increased.* antagonistic (adjective), antagonize (verb).

Word Origin

Greek pathos = *suffering. Also found in English* apathy, empathy, pathetic, pathos, *and* sympathy.

antipathy (noun)   A long-held feeling of dislike or aversion. *When asked why he didn't call for help immediately after his wife fell into a coma, the defendant emphasized his wife's utter antipathy to doctors.*

apprehension (noun)   A feeling of fear or foreboding; an arrest. *The peculiar feeling of apprehension that Harold Pinter creates in his plays derives as much from the long silences between speeches as from the speeches themselves. The policewoman's dramatic apprehension of the gunman took place in full view of the midtown lunch crowd.* apprehend (verb).

arabesque (noun)   Intricate decorative patterns involving intertwining lines and sometimes incorporating flowers, animals and fruits. *Borders of gold and fanciful arabesques surround the Arabic script on every page of this ancient edition of the* Koran.

Word Origin

Latin arbiter = judge. *Also found in English* arbiter, arbitrage, *and* arbitrate.

arbitrary (adjective) Based on random or merely personal preference. *Both computers cost the same and had the same features, so in the end I made an arbitrary decision about which one to buy.*

archaic (adjective) Old-fashioned, obsolete. *Those who believe in "open marriage" often declare that they will not be bound by archaic laws and religious rituals, but state instead that love alone should bring two people together.* archaism (noun).

ardor (noun) A strong feeling of passion, energy, or zeal. *The young revolutionary proclaimed his convictions with an ardor that excited the crowd.* ardent (adjective).

arid (adjective) Very dry; boring and meaningless. *The arid climate of Arizona makes farming difficult. Some find the law a fascinating topic, but for me it is an arid discipline.* aridity (noun).

Word Origin

Latin articulus I = joint, division. *Also found in English* arthritis, article, *and* inarticulate.

articulate (adjective) To express oneself clearly and effectively. *Compared to George Bush, with his stammering and his frequently incomplete sentences, Bill Clinton was considered a highly articulate president.*

asperity (noun) Harshness, severity. *Total silence at the dinner table, baths in icy water, prayers five times a day—these practices all contributed to the asperity of life in the monastery.*

assail (verb) To attack with blows or words. *When the president's cabinet members rose to justify the case for military intervention in Iraq, they were assailed by many audience members who were critical of U.S. policy.* assailant (noun).

assay (verb) To analyze for particular components; to determine weight, quality etc. *The jeweler assayed the stone pendant Gwyneth inherited from her mother and found it to contain a topaz of high quality.*

assimilate (verb) To absorb into a system or culture. *New York City has assimilated one group of immigrants after another, from the Jewish, German, and Irish immigrants who arrived at the turn of the last century to the waves of Mexican and Latin American immigrants who arrived in the 1980s.*

assimilated (adjective) *Unlike her sister, Sook Lee is thoroughly assimilated to southern California; she speaks more like a valley girl than a Korean and dismisses such traditional notions as respect for one's elders as "boring."*

assuage (verb) To ease, to pacify. *Knowing that the pilot's record was perfect did little to assuage Linnet's fear of flying in the two-seater airplane.*

audacious (adjective) Bold, daring, adventurous. *Her plan to cross the Atlantic single-handed in a twelve-foot sailboat was an audacious, if not reckless one.* audacity (noun).

authoritarian (adjective) Favoring or demanding blind obedience to leaders. *Despite most Americans' strong belief in democracy, the American government has sometimes supported authoritarian regimes in other countries.* authoritarianism (noun).

authoritative (adjective) Official, conclusive. *For over five decades, American parents regarded Doctor Benjamin Spock as the most authoritative voice on baby and child care.* authority (noun) authorize (verb).

avenge (verb)   To exact a punishment for or on behalf of someone. *In Shakespeare's tragedy* Hamlet, *the ghost of the dead king of Denmark visits his son, Prince Hamlet, and urges him to avenge his murder.*

aver (verb)   To claim to be true; to avouch. *The fact that the key witness averred the defendant's innocence is what ultimately swayed the jury to deliver a "not guilty" verdict.*

avow (verb)   To declare boldly. *Immediately after Cyrus avowed his atheism at our church fund-raiser, there was a long, uncomfortable silence.* avowal (noun), avowed (adjective).

barren (adjective)   Desolate; infertile. *The subarctic tundra is a barren wasteland inhabited only by lichens and mosses. Women who try to conceive in their 40s are often barren and must turn to artificial means of producing a child.*

belligerent (adjective)   Quarrelsome, combative. *Mrs. Juniper was so belligerent toward the clerks at the local stores that they cringed when they saw her coming.*

belligerent (noun)   an opposing army, a party waging war. *The Union and Confederate forces were the belligerents in the American Civil War.*

Word Origin

Latin bene = well. Also found in English benediction, benefactor, beneficent, beneficial, benefit, *and* benign.

benevolent (adjective)   Wishing or doing good. *In old age, Carnegie used his wealth for benevolent purposes, donating large sums to found libraries and schools around the country.* benevolence (noun).

berate (verb)   To scold or criticize harshly. *The judge angrily berated the two lawyers for their childish and unprofessional behavior.*

boggle (verb)   To overwhelm with amazement. *The ability of physicists to isolate the most infinitesimal particles of matter truly boggles the mind.*

bogus (adjective)   Phony, a sham. *Senior citizens are often the target of telemarketing scams pushing bogus investment opportunities.*

bombastic (adjective)   inflated or pompous in style. *Old-fashioned bombastic political speeches don't work on television, which demands a more intimate, personal style of communication.* bombast (noun).

boor (noun)   Crude, insensitive and overbearing. *Harold was well-known to be a boor; at parties he horrified people with stories of his past sexual exploits and old, off-color jokes.* boorish (adjective)

brazenly (adverb)   Acting with disrespectful boldness. *Some say that the former White House intern brazenly threw herself at the President, but the American public will probably never know the full truth.* brazen (adjective).

broach (verb)   To bring up an issue for discussion, to propose. *Knowing my father's strictness about adhering to a budget, I just can't seem to broach the subject of my massive credit-card debt.*

burgeon (verb)   To bloom, literally or figuratively. *Due to the extremely mild winter, the forsythia burgeoned as early as March. The story of two prison inmates in Manuel Puig's play* The Kiss of The Spiderwoman *is testimony that tenderness can burgeon in the most unlikely places.*

burnish (verb)   To shine by polishing, literally or figuratively. *After stripping seven layers of old paint off the antique door, the carpenter stained the wood and burnished it to a rich hue. When Bill Gates, the wealthiest man in the country, decided to endorse the Big Bertha line of Golf Clubs, many suggested that he was trying to burnish his image as a "regular guy."*

buttress (noun)   Something that supports or strengthens. *The endorsement of the American Medical Association is a powerful buttress for the claims made on behalf of this new medicine.* buttress (verb).

cacophony (noun)   Discordant sounds; dissonance. *In the minutes before classes start, the high school's halls are filled with a cacophony of shrieks, shouts, banging locker doors, and pounding feet.* cacophonous (adjective)

cadge (verb)   To beg for, to sponge. *Few in our crowd want to go out on the town with Piper, since he routinely cadges cigarettes, subway tokens, and drinks.*

calibrate (verb)   To determine or mark graduations (of a measuring instrument); to adjust or finely tune. *We tried to calibrate the heating to Rufus's liking, but he still ended up shivering in our living room.* calibration (noun).

castigate (verb)   To chastise; to punish severely. *The editor castigated Bob for repeatedly failing to meet his deadlines.* castigation (noun).

catalytic (adjective)   Bringing about, causing, or producing some result. *The conditions for revolution existed in America by 1765; the disputes about taxation that arose during the following decade were the catalytic events that sparked the rebellion.* catalyze (verb).

Word Origin

Greek kaustikos = *burning. Also found in English* holocaust.

caustic (adjective)   Burning, corrosive. *No pretensions were safe when the famous satirist H. L. Mencken unleashed his caustic wit.*

chaos (noun)   Disorder, confusion, chance. *The first few moments after the explosion were pure chaos: no one was sure what had happened, and the area was filled with people running and yelling.* chaotic (adjective).

charisma (noun)   Dynamic charm or appeal. *Eva Peron was such a fiery orator and had so much charisma that she commanded an enormous political following.* charismatic (adjective).

chary (adjective)   Slow to accept, cautious. *Yuan was chary about going out with Xinhua, since she had been badly hurt in her previous relationship.*

chronology (noun)   An arrangement of events by order of occurrence, a list of dates; the science of time. *If you ask Susan about her two-year-old son, she will give you a chronology of his accomplishments and childhood illnesses, from the day he was born to the present. The village of Copan was where Mayan astronomical learning, as applied to chronology, achieved its most accurate expression in the famous Mayan calendar.* chronological (adjective).

churlish (adjective)   Coarse and ill-mannered. *Few journalists were eager to interview the aging film star, since he was reputed to be a churlish, uncooperative subject.* churl (noun).

Word Origin

Latin circus = *circle. Also found in English* circumference, circumnavigate, circumscribe, *and* circumvent.

circumspect (adjective) Prudent, cautious. *After he had been acquitted of the sexual harassment charge, the sergeant realized he would have to be more circumspect in his dealings with the female cadets.* circumspection (noun).

cleave (verb)   NOTE: A tricky verb that can mean either to stick closely together or to split apart. (Pay attention to context.) *The more abusive his father became, the more Timothy cleaved to his mother and refused to let her out of his sight. Sometimes a few words carelessly spoken are enough to cleave a married couple and leave the relationship in shambles.* cleavage (noun).

coagulant (noun) Any material that causes another to thicken or clot. *Hemophilia is characterized by excessive bleeding from even the slightest cut and is caused by a lack of one of the coagulants necessary for blood clotting.* coagulate (verb).

coalesce (verb) To fuse, to unite. *The music we know as jazz coalesced from diverse elements from many musical cultures, including those of West Africa, America, and Europe.* coalescence (noun).

coerce (verb)   To force someone either to do something or to refrain from doing something. *The Miranda ruling prevents police from coercing a confession by forcing them to read criminals their rights.* coercion (noun).

cogent (adjective) Forceful and convincing. *The committee members were won over to the project by the cogent arguments of the chairman.* cogency (noun).

Word Origin

Latin mensura = *to measure. Also found in English* measure, immeasurable, immense, *and* mensuration.

commensurate (adjective) Aligned with, proportional. *Many Ph.D.s in the humanities do not feel their paltry salaries are commensurate with their abilities, their experience, or the heavy workload they are asked to bear.*

commingle (verb)   To blend, to mix. *Just as he had when he was only five years old, Elmer did not allow any of the foods on his plate to commingle: the beans must not merge with the rice nor the chicken rub shoulders with the broccoli!*

complaisant (adjective)   Tending to bow to others' wishes; amiable. *Of the two Dashwood sisters, Elinor was the more complaisant, often putting the strictures of society and family above her own desires.* complaisance (noun).

compound (verb)   To intensify, to exacerbate. *When you make a faux pas, my father advised me, don't compound the problem by apologizing profusely; just say you're sorry and get on with life!*

conceivable (adjective)   Possible, imaginable. *It's possible to find people with every conceivable interest by surfing the World Wide Web—from fans of minor film stars to those who study the mating habits of crustaceans.* conception (noun).

concur (verb)   To agree, to approve. *We concur that a toddler functions best on a fairly reliable schedule; however, my husband tends to be a bit more rigid than I am.* concurrence (noun).

condensation (noun) A reduction to a denser form (from steam to water); an abridgment of a literary work. *The condensation of humidity on the car's windshield made it difficult for me to see the road. It seems as though every beach house I've ever rented features a shelf full of Reader's Digest condensations of b-grade novels.* condense (verb).

condescending (adjective)   Having an attitude of superiority toward another; patronizing. *"What a cute little car!" she remarked in a condescending fashion. "I suppose it's the nicest one someone like you could afford!"* condescension (noun).

condone (verb)   To overlook, to permit to happen. *Schools with Zero Tolerance policies do not condone alcohol, drugs, vandalism, or violence on school grounds.*

congruent (adjective)   Coinciding; harmonious. *Fortunately, the two employees who had been asked to organize the department had congruent views on the budget.* congruence (noun).

Word Origin

Latin jungere = *to join. Also found in English* injunction, junction, *and* juncture.

conjunction (noun)   The occurrence of two or more events together in time or space; in astronomy, the point at which two celestial bodies have the least separation. *Low inflation, occurring in conjunction with low unemployment and relatively low interest rates, has enabled the United States to enjoy a long period of sustained economic growth. The moon is in conjunction with the sun when it is new; if the conjunction is perfect, an eclipse of the sun will occur.* conjoin (verb).

consolation (noun)   Relief or comfort in sorrow or suffering. *Although we miss our dog very much, it is a consolation to know that she died quickly, without much suffering.* console (verb).

consternation (noun)   Shock, amazement, dismay. *When a voice in the back of the church shouted out, "I know why they should not be married!" the entire gathering was thrown into consternation.*

convergence (noun)   The act of coming together in unity or similarity. *A remarkable example of evolutionary convergence can be seen in the shark and the dolphin, two sea creatures that developed from different origins to become very similar in form and appearance.* converge (verb).

Word Origin

Latin vivere = *to live. Also found in English* revive, vital, vivid, *and* vivisection.

conviviality (noun)   Fond of good company and eating and drinking. *The conviviality of my fellow employees seemed to turn every staff meeting into a party, complete with snacks, drinks, and lots of hearty laughter.* convivial (adjective).

convoluted (adjective)   Twisting, complicated, intricate. *Income tax law has become so convoluted that it's easy for people to violate it completely by accident.* convolute (verb), convolution (noun).

Word Origin

Latin volvere = *to roll. Also found in English* devolve, involve, revolution, revolve, *and* voluble.

cordon (verb)   To form a protective or restrictive barrier. *Well before the Academy Awards ceremony began, the police cordoned off the hordes of fans who were desperate to ogle the arriving stars.* cordon (noun).

corral (verb)   To enclose, to collect, to gather. *Tyrone couldn't enjoy the wedding at all, since he spent most of his time corralling his two children into the reception room and preventing them from running amok through the Potters' mansion.* corral (noun).

corroborating (adjective)   Supporting with evidence; confirming. *A passerby who had witnessed the crime gave corroborating testimony about the presence of the accused person.* corroborate (verb), corroboration (noun).

corrosive (adjective)   Eating away, gnawing, or destroying. *Years of poverty and hard work had a corrosive effect on her strength and beauty.* corrode (verb), corrosion (noun).

cosmopolitanism (noun)   International sophistication; worldliness. *Budapest is known for its cosmopolitanism, perhaps because it was the first Eastern European city to be more open to capitalism and influences from the West.* cosmopolitan (adjective).

covert (adjective)   Secret, clandestine. *The CIA has often been criticized for its covert operations in the domestic policies of foreign countries, such as the failed Bay of Pigs operation in Cuba.*

covetous (adjective)   Envious, particularly of another's possessions. *Benita would never admit to being covetous of my new sable jacket, but I found it odd that she couldn't refrain from trying it on each time we met.* covet (verb).

craven (adjective)   Cowardly. *Local Gay and Lesbian activists were outraged by the craven behavior of a policeman who refused to come to the aid of an HIV-positive accident victim.*

credulous (adjective)   Ready to believe; gullible. *Elaine was not very credulous of the explanation Serge gave for his acquisition of the Matisse lithograph.* credulity (noun).

cryptic (adjective)   Puzzling, ambiguous. *I was puzzled by the cryptic message left on my answering machine about "a shipment of pomegranates from an anonymous donor."*

culmination (noun)   The climax. *The Los Angeles riots, in the aftermath of the Rodney King verdict, were the culmination of long-standing racial tensions between the residents of South Central LA and the police.* culminate (verb).

culpable (adjective)   Deserving blame, guilty. *Although he committed the crime, because he was mentally ill he should not be considered culpable for his actions.* culpability (noun).

curmudgeon (noun)   A crusty, ill-tempered person. *Todd hated to drive with his Uncle Jasper, a notorious curmudgeon, who complained non-stop about the air-conditioning and Todd's driving.* curmudgeonly (adjective).

cursory (adjective)   Hasty and superficial. *Detective Martinez was rebuked by his superior officer for drawing conclusions about the murder after only a cursory examination of the crime scene.*

debilitating (adjective)   Weakening; sapping the strength of. *One can't help but marvel at the courage Steven Hawking displays in the face of such a debilitating disease as ALS.* debilitate (verb).

Word Origin

Latin celer = *swift. Also found in English* accelerate *and* celerity.

decelerate (verb)   To slow down. *Randall didn't decelerate enough on the winding roads, and he ended up smashing his new sports utility vehicle into a guard rail.* deceleration (noun).

decimation (noun)   Almost complete destruction. *Michael Moore's documentary* Roger and Me *chronicles the decimation of the economy of Flint, Michigan, after the closing of a General Motors factory.* decimate (verb).

decry (verb)   To criticize or condemn. *Cigarette ads aimed at youngsters have led many to decry the unfair marketing tactics of the tobacco industry.*

defamation (noun)   Act of harming someone by libel or slander. *When the article in* The National Enquirer *implied that she was somehow responsible for her husband's untimely death, Renata instructed her lawyer to sue the paper for defamation of character.* defame (verb).

defer (verb)   To graciously submit to another's will; to delegate. *In all matters relating to the children's religious education, Joy deferred to her husband, since he clearly cared more about giving them a solid grounding in Judaism.* deference (noun).

deliberate (verb)   To think about an issue before reaching a decision. *The legal pundits covering the O.J. Simpson trial were shocked by the short time the jury took to deliberate after a trial that lasted months.* deliberation (noun).

demagogue (noun)   A leader who plays dishonestly on the prejudices and emotions of his followers. *Senator Joseph McCarthy was a demagogue who used the paranoia and biases of the anti-communist 1950s as a way of seizing fame and considerable power in Washington.* demagoguery (noun).

Word Origin

Greek demos *= people. Also found in English* democracy, demographic, *and* endemic.

demographic (adjective)   Relating to the statistical study of population. *Three demographic groups have been the intense focus of marketing strategy: baby boomers, born between 1946 and 1964; baby busters, or the youth market, born between 1965 and 1976; and a group referred to as tweens, those born between 1977 and 1983.* demography (noun) demographics (noun).

demonstratively (adverb)   Openly displaying feeling. *The young congressman demonstratively campaigned for reelection, kissing every baby and hugging every senior citizen at the Saugerties Chrysanthemum festival.* demonstrative (adjective).

derisive (adjective)   Expressing ridicule or scorn. *Many women's groups were derisive of Avon's choice of a male CEO, since the company derives its $5.1 billion in sales from an army of female salespeople.* derision (noun).

derivative (adjective)   Imitating or borrowed from a particular source. *When a person first writes poetry, her poems are apt to be derivative of whatever poetry she most enjoys reading.* derivation (noun), derive (verb).

desiccate (verb)   To dry out, to wither; to drain of vitality. *The long drought thoroughly desiccated our garden; what was once a glorious Eden was now a scorched and hellish wasteland. A recent spate of books has debunked the myth that menopause desiccates women and affirmed, instead, that women often reach heights of creativity in their later years.* desiccant (noun), desiccation (noun).

despotic (adjective)   Oppressive and tyrannical. *During the despotic reign of Idi Amin in the 1970s, an estimated 200,000 Ugandans were killed.* despot (noun).

desultory (adjective)   Disconnected, aimless. *Tina's few desultory stabs at conversation fell flat as Guy just sat there, stony-faced; it was a disastrous first date.*

deviate (verb)   To depart from a standard or norm. *Having agreed upon a spending budget for the company, we mustn't deviate from it; if we do, we may run out of money before the year ends.* deviation (noun).

diatribe (noun)   Abusive or bitter speech or writing. *While angry conservatives dismissed Susan Faludi's* Backlash *as a feminist diatribe, it is actually a meticulously researched book.*

diffident (adjective)   Hesitant, reserved, shy. *Someone with a diffident personality is most likely to succeed in a career that involves little public contact.* diffidence (noun).

digress (verb)   To wander from the main path or the main topic. *My high school biology teacher loved to digress from science into personal anecdotes about his college adventures.* digression (noun), digressive (adjective).

dirge (noun)   Song or hymn of grief. *When Princess Diana was killed in a car crash, Elton John resurrected his hit song "Goodbye Norma Jean," rewrote it as "Good-bye England's Rose," and created one of the most widely heard funeral dirges of all time.*

disabuse (verb)   To correct a fallacy, to clarify. *I hated to disabuse Filbert, who is a passionate collector of musical trivia, but I had to tell him that the Monkees hadn't played their own instruments on almost all of their albums.*

disburse (verb)   To pay out or distribute (funds or property). *Jaime was flabbergasted when his father's will disbursed all of the old man's financial assets to Raymundo and left him with only a few sticks of furniture.* disbursement (noun).

discern (verb)   To detect, notice, or observe. *With difficulty, I could discern the shape of a whale off the starboard bow, but it was too far away to determine its size or species.* discernment (noun).

discordant (adjective)   Characterized by conflict. *Stories and films about discordant relationships that resolve themselves happily are always more interesting than stories about content couples who simply stay content.* discordance (noun).

discourse (noun)   Formal and orderly exchange of ideas, a discussion. *In the late twentieth century, cloning and other feats of genetic engineering became popular topics of public discourse.* discursive (adjective).

Word Origin

Latin credere = to believe. Also found in English credential, credible, credit, credo, credulous, *and* incredible.

discredit (verb)   To cause disbelief in the accuracy of some statement or the reliability of a person. *Although many people still believe in UFOs, among scientists the reports of "alien encounters" have been thoroughly discredited.*

discreet (adjective)   Showing good judgment in speech and behavior. *Be discreet when discussing confidential business matters—don't talk among strangers on the elevator, for example.* discretion (noun).

discrete (adjective)   Separate, unconnected. *Canadians get peeved when people can't seem to distinguish between Canada and the United States, forgetting that Canada has its own discrete heritage and culture.*

disparity (noun)   Difference in quality or kind. *There is often a disparity between the kind of serious, high-quality television people say they want and the low-brow programs they actually watch.* disparate (adjective).

Word Origin

Latin simulare = to resemble. Also found in English semblance, similarity, simulacrum, simultaneous, *and* verisimilitude.

dissemble (verb)   To pretend, to simulate. *When the police asked whether Nancy knew anything about the crime, she dissembled innocence.*

dissipate (verb)   To spread out or scatter. *The windows and doors were opened, allowing the smoke that had filled the room to dissipate.* dissipation (noun).

dissonance (noun)   Lack of music harmony; lack of agreement between ideas. *Most modern music is characterized by dissonance, which many listeners find hard to enjoy. There is a noticeable dissonance between two common beliefs of most conservatives: their faith in unfettered free markets and their preference for traditional social values.* dissonant (adjective).

distillation (noun)   Something distilled, an essence or extract. In chemistry, a process that drives gas or vapor from liquids or solids. *Sharon Olds's poems are powerful distillations of motherhood and other primal experiences. In Mrs. Hornmeister's chemistry class, our first experiment was to create a distillation of carbon gas from wood.* distill (verb)

diverge (verb)   To move in different directions. *Frost's poem "The Road Less Traveled" tells of the choice he made when "Two roads diverged in a yellow wood."* divergence (noun), divergent (adjective).

diversify (verb)   To balance by adding variety. *Any financial manager will recommend that you diversify your stock portfolio by holding some less-volatile blue-chip stocks along with more growth-oriented technology issues.* diversification (noun), diversified (adjective)

divest (verb)   To rid (oneself) or be freed of property, authority, or title. *In order to turn around its ailing company and concentrate on imaging, Eastman Kodak divested itself of peripheral businesses in the areas of household products, clinical diagnostics, and pharmaceuticals.* divestiture (noun).

divulge (verb)   To reveal. *The people who count the votes for the Oscar awards are under strict orders not to divulge the names of the winners.*

dogmatic (adjective)   Holding firmly to a particular set of beliefs with little or no basis. *Believers in Marxist doctrine tend to be dogmatic, ignoring evidence that contradicts their beliefs or explaining it away.* dogma (noun), dogmatism (noun).

dolt (noun)   A stupid or foolish person. *Due to his frequent verbal blunders, politician Dan Quayle was widely considered to be a dolt.*

Word Origin

Latin dormire = to sleep. Also found in English dormitory.

dormant (adjective)   Temporarily inactive, as if asleep. *An eruption of Mt. Rainier, a dormant volcano in Washington state, would cause massive, life-threatening mud slides in the surrounding area. Bill preferred to think that his sex drive was dormant rather than extinct.* dormancy (noun)

dross (noun)   Something that is trivial or inferior; an impurity. *As a reader for the Paris Review, Julia spent most of her time sifting through piles of manuscripts to separate the extraordinary poems from the dross.*

dubious (adjective)   Doubtful, uncertain. *Despite the chairman's attempts to convince the committee members that his plan would succeed, most of them remained dubious.* dubiety (noun).

dupe (noun)   Someone who is easily cheated. *My cousin Ravi is such a dupe; he actually gets excited when he receives those envelopes saying "Ravi Murtugudde, you may have won a million dollars," and he even goes so far as to try claiming his prize.*

eccentricity (noun)   Odd or whimsical behavior. *Rock star Michael Jackson is now better known for his offstage eccentricities—such as sleeping in an oxygen tank, wearing a surgical mask, and building his own theme park—than for his onstage performances.* eccentric (adjective).

edifying (adjective)   Instructive, enlightening. *Ariel would never admit it to her high-brow friends, but she found the latest self-help best-seller edifying and actually helpful.* edification (noun) edify (verb).

Word Origin

Latin facere = *to do. Also found in English* facility, factor, facsimile, *and* faculty.

efficacy (noun)   The power to produce the desired effect. *While teams have been enormously popular in the workplace, there are some who now question their efficacy and say that "one head is better than ten."* efficacious (noun).

effrontery (noun)   Shameless boldness. *The sports world was shocked when a pro basketball player had the effrontery to choke the head coach of his team during a practice session.*

elaborate (verb)   To expand upon something; develop. *One characteristic of the best essayists is their ability to elaborate ideas through examples, lists, similes, small variations, and even exaggerations.* elaborate (adjective), elaboration (noun).

elegy (noun)   A song or poem expressing sorrow. *Thomas Gray's "Elegy Written in a Country Churchyard," one of the most famous elegies in Western literature, mourns the unsung, inglorious lives of the souls buried in an obscure, rustic graveyard.* elegiac (adjective).

embellish (verb)   To enhance or exaggerate; to decorate. *The long-married couple told their stories in tandem, with the husband outlining the plot and the wife embellishing it with colorful details.* embellished (adjective) *Both Salman Rushdie, of India, and Patrick Chamoiseau, of Martinique, emerged from colonized countries and created embellished versions of their colonizers' languages in their novels.*

embezzle (verb)   To steal money or property that has been entrusted to your care. *The church treasurer was found to have embezzled thousands of dollars by writing phony checks on the church bank account.* embezzlement (noun).

emollient (noun)   Something that softens or soothes. *She used a hand cream as an emollient on her dry, work-roughened hands.* emollient (adjective).

empirical (adjective)   Based on experience or personal observation. *Although many people believe in ESP, scientists have found no empirical evidence of its existence.* empiricism (noun).

emulate (verb)   To imitate or copy. *The British band Oasis is quite open about their desire to emulate their idols, the Beatles.* emulation (noun).

encomium (noun)   A formal expression of praise. *For many filmmakers, winning the Palm d'Or at the Cannes Film Festival is considered the highest encomium.*

enervate (verb)   To reduce the energy or strength of someone or something. *The stress of the operation left her feeling enervated for about two weeks.* enervation (noun).

engender (verb)   To produce, to cause. *Countless disagreements over the proper use of national forests and parklands have engendered feelings of hostility between ranchers and environmentalists.*

enhance (verb)   To improve in value or quality. *New kitchen appliances will enhance your house and increase the amount of money you'll make when you sell it.* enhancement (noun).

enigmatic (adjective)   Puzzling, mysterious. *Alain Resnais' enigmatic film* Last Year at Marienbad *sets up a puzzle that is never resolved: a man meets a woman at a hotel and believes he once had an affair with her—or did he?* enigma (noun).

enmity (noun)   Hatred, hostility, ill will. *Long-standing enmity, like that between the Protestants and Catholics in Northern Ireland, is difficult to overcome.*

ensure (verb)   To make certain; to guarantee. *In order to ensure a sufficient crop of programmers and engineers for the future, the United States needs to raise the quality of its math and science schooling.*

Word Origin

Latin aequus = equal. Also found in English equality, equanimity, *and* equation.

equable (adjective)   Steady, uniform. *While many people can't see how Helena could possibly be attracted to "Boring Bruno," his equable nature is the perfect complement to her volatile personality.*

equivocate (verb)   To use misleading or intentionally confusing language. *When Pedro pressed Renee for an answer to his marriage proposal, she equivocated by saying, "I've just got to know when your Mercedes will be out of the shop!"* equivocal (adjective), equivocation (noun).

epicure (noun)   Someone who appreciates fine wine and fine food, a gourmand. *M.F.K. Fisher, a famous epicure, begins her book* The Gastronomical Me *by saying, "There is a communion of more than bodies when bread is broken and wine is drunk."* epicurean (adjective).

epithet (noun)   Term or words used to characterize a person or thing, often in a disparaging way. *In her recorded phone conversations with Linda Tripp, Monica Lewinsky is said to have referred to President Clinton by a number of epithets including "The Creep" and "The Big He."* epithetical (adjective).

Word Origin

Latin radix = root. Also found in English radical.

eradicate (verb)   To destroy completely. *American society has failed to eradicate racism, although some of its worst effects have been reduced.* eradication (noun).

erudition (noun)   Extensive knowledge, usually acquired from books. *When Dorothea first saw Mr. Casaubon's voluminous library she was awed, but after their marriage she quickly realized that erudition is no substitute for originality.* erudite (adjective).

esoterica (noun)   Items of interest to a select group. *The fish symposium at St. Antony's College in Oxford explored all manner of esoterica relating to fish, as is evidenced in presentations such as "The Buoyant Slippery Lipids of the Escolar and Orange Roughy" or "Food on Board Whale Ships—from the Inedible to the Incredible."* esoteric (adjective).

espouse (verb)   To take up as a cause; to adopt. *No politician in America today will openly espouse racism, although some behave and speak in racially prejudiced ways.*

estimable (adjective)   Worthy of esteem and admiration. *After a tragic fire raged through Malden Mills, the estimable mill owner, Aaron Feuerstein, restarted operations and rebuilt the company within just one month.* esteem (noun).

eulogy (noun)   A formal tribute usually delivered at a funeral. *Most people in Britain applauded Lord Earl Spencer's eulogy for Princess Diana, not only as a warm tribute to his sister Diana but also as a biting indictment of the Royal Family.* eulogize (verb).

euphemism (noun)   An agreeable expression that is substituted for an offensive one. *Some of the more creative euphemisms for "layoffs" in current use are: "release of resources," "involuntary severance," "strengthening global effectiveness," and "career transition program."* euphemistic (adjective).

Word Origin

Latin acer =
sharp. Also found
in English
acerbity, acrid,
and acrimonious.

exacerbate (verb)   To make worse or more severe. *The roads in our town already have too much traffic; building a new shopping mall will exacerbate the problem.*

excoriation (noun)   The act of condemning someone with harsh words. *In the small office we shared, it was painful to hear my boss's constant excoriation of his assistant for the smallest faults—a misdirected letter, an unclear phone message, or even a tepid cup of coffee.* excoriate (verb).

exculpate (verb)   To free from blame or guilt. *When someone else confessed to the crime, the previous suspect was exculpated.* exculpation (noun), exculpatory (adjective).

executor (noun)   The person appointed to execute someone's will. *As the executor of his Aunt Ida's will, Phil must deal with squabbling relatives, conniving lawyers, and the ruinous state of Ida's house.*

exigent (adjective)   Urgent, requiring immediate attention. *A two-year-old is likely to behave as if her every demand is exigent, even if it involves simply retrieving a beloved teddy bear from under the couch.* exigency (noun).

expedient (adjective)   Providing an immediate advantage or serving one's immediate self-interest. *When the passenger next to her was strafed by a bullet, Sharon chose the most expedient means to stop the bleeding; she whipped off her pantyhose and made an impromptu, but effective, tourniquet.* expediency (noun).

Word Origin

Latin tenere = to
hold. Also found
in English retain,
tenable, tenant,
tenet, and tenure.

extant (adjective)   Currently in existence. *Of the seven ancient "Wonders of the World," only the pyramids of Egypt are still extant.*

extenuate (verb)   To make less serious. *Karen's guilt is extenuated by the fact that she was only twelve when she committed the theft.* extenuating (adjective), extenuation (noun).

extol (verb)   To greatly praise. *At the party convention, one speaker after another took to the podium to extol the virtues of their candidate for the presidency.*

extraneous (adjective)   Irrelevant, nonessential. *One review of the new Chekhov biography said the author had bogged down the book with far too many extraneous details, such as the dates of Chekhov's bouts of diarrhea.*

extrapolate (verb)   To deduce from something known, to infer. *Meteorologists were able to use old weather records to extrapolate backward and compile lists of El Niño years and their effects over the last century.* extrapolation (noun).

extricate (verb)   To free from a difficult or complicated situation. *Much of the humor in the TV show* I Love Lucy *comes in watching Lucy try to extricate herself from the problems she creates by fibbing or trickery.* extricable (adjective).

facetious (adjective)   Humorous in a mocking way; not serious. *French composer Erik Satie often concealed his serious artistic intent by giving his works facetious titles such as "Three Pieces in the Shape of a Pear."*

facilitate (verb)   To make easier or to moderate. *When the issue of racism reared its ugly head, the company brought in a consultant to facilitate a discussion of diversity in the workplace.* facile (adjective), facility (noun).

fallacy (noun)   An error in fact or logic. *It's a fallacy to think that "natural" means "healthful"; after all, the deadly poison arsenic is completely natural.* fallacious (adjective).

fatuous (adjective)   Inanely foolish; silly. *Once backstage, Elizabeth showered the opera singer with fatuous praise and embarrassing confessions, which he clearly had no interest in hearing.*

fawn (verb)   To flatter in a particularly subservient manner. *Mildly disgusted, Pedro stood alone at the bar and watched Renee fawn over the heir to the Fabco Surgical Appliances fortune.*

feckless (adjective)   weak and ineffective; irresponsible. *Our co-op board president is a feckless fellow who has let much-needed repairs go unattended while our maintenance fees continue to rise.*

feint (noun)   A bluff; a mock blow. *It didn't take us long to realize that Gaby's tears and stomachaches were all a feint, since they appeared so regularly at her bedtime.*

ferret (verb)   To bring to light by an extensive search. *With his repeated probing and questions, Fritz was able to ferret out the location of Myrna's safe deposit box.*

finesse (noun)   Skillful maneuvering; delicate workmanship. *With her usual finesse, Charmaine gently persuaded the Duncans not to install a motorized Santa and sleigh on their front lawn.*

florid (adjective)   Flowery, fancy; reddish. *The grand ballroom was decorated in a florid style. Years of heavy drinking had given him a florid complexion.*

Word Origin

Latin fluere = to flow. Also found in English affluent, effluvia, fluid, and influx.

flourish (noun)   An extraneous embellishment; a dramatic gesture. *The napkin rings made out of intertwined ferns and flowers were just the kind of flourish one would expect from Carol, a slavish follower of Martha Stewart.*

fluctuation (noun)   A shifting back and forth. *Investment analysts predict fluctuations in the Dow Jones Industrial Average due to the instability of the value of the dollar.* fluctuate (verb).

foil (verb)   To thwart or frustrate. *I was certain that Jerry's tendency to insert himself into everyone's conversations would foil my chances to have a private word with Helen.*

foment (verb)   To rouse or incite. *The petty tyrannies and indignities inflicted on the workers by upper management helped foment the walkout at the meat-processing plant.*

forestall (verb)   To hinder or prevent by taking action in advance. *The pilot's calm, levelheaded demeanor during the attempted highjacking forestalled any hysteria among the passengers of Flight 268.*

fortuitous (adjective)   Lucky, fortunate. *Although the mayor claimed credit for the falling crime rate, it was really caused by a series of fortuitous accidents.*

foster (verb)   To nurture or encourage. *The white-water rafting trip was supposed to foster creative problem solving and teamwork between the account executives and the creative staff at Apex Advertising Agency.*

fracas (noun)   A noisy fight; a brawl. *As Bill approached the stadium ticket window, he was alarmed to see the fracas that had broken out between a group of Giants fans and a man wearing a Cowboys jersey and helmet.*

functionary (noun)   Someone holding office in a political party or government. *The man shaking hands with the governor was a low-ranking Democratic Party functionary who had worked to garner the Hispanic vote.*

gainsay (verb)   To contradict or oppose; deny, dispute. *Dot would gainsay her married sister's efforts to introduce her to eligible men by refusing to either leave her ailing canary or give up her thrice-weekly bingo nights.*

garble (verb)   To distort or slur. *No matter how much money the Metropolitan Transit Authority spends on improving the subway trains, the public address system in almost every station seems to garble each announcement.* garbled (adjective).

garrulous (adjective)   Annoyingly talkative. *Claude pretended to be asleep so he could avoid his garrulous seatmate, a self-proclaimed expert on bonsai cultivation.*

Word Origin

Latin genus = *type or kind; birth. Also found in English* congenital, genetic, genital, genre, genuine, *and* genus.

generic (adjective)   General; having no brand name. *Connie tried to reduce her grocery bills by religiously clipping coupons and buying generic brands of most products.*

gist (noun)   The main point, the essence. *Although they felt sympathy for the victim's family, the jurors were won over by the gist of the defense's argument; there was insufficient evidence to convict.*

gouge (verb)   To cut out, to scoop out with one's thumbs or a sharp instrument; to overcharge, to cheat. *Instead of picking the lock with a credit card, the clumsy thieves gouged a hole in my door. The consumer watchdog group accused the clothing stores of gouging customers with high prices.*

guile (noun)   Deceit, duplicity. *In Margaret Mitchell's* Gone With the Wind, *Scarlett O'Hara uses her guile to manipulate two men and then is matched for wits by a third, Rhett Butler.* guileful (adjective).

gullible (adjective)   Easily fooled. *Terry was so gullible she actually believed Robert's stories of his connections to the Czar and Czarina.* gullibility (noun).

hackneyed (adjective)   Without originality, trite. *When someone invented the phrase, "No pain, no gain," it was clever and witty, but now it is so commonly heard that it seems hackneyed.*

harrow (verb)   To cultivate with a harrow; to torment or vex. *During grade school, my sister was harrowed mercilessly for being overweight.* harrowing (adjective) nerve-wracking, traumatic. *Jon Krakauer's harrowing book* Into Thin Air *chronicles the tragic consequences of leading groups of untrained climbers up Mt. Everest.*

haughty (adjective)   Overly proud. *The fashion model strode down the runway, her hips thrust forward and a haughty expression, something like a sneer, on her face.* haughtiness (noun).

hierarchy (noun)   A ranking of people, things, or ideas from highest to lowest. *A cabinet secretary ranks just below the president and vice president in the hierarchy of the government's executive branch.* hierarchical (adjective).

Word Origin

Greek homos = same. Also found in English homologous homonym and homosexual.

homogeneous (adjective) Uniform, made entirely of one thing. *It's hard to think of a more homogenous group than those eerie children in* Village of the Damned, *who all had perfect features, white-blond hair, and silver, penetrating eyes.*

hoodwink (verb) To deceive by trickery or false appearances; to dupe. *That was my cousin Ravi calling to say that he's been hoodwinked again, this time by some outfit offering time shares in a desolate tract of land in central Florida.*

hone (verb) To improve and make more acute or affective. *While she was a receptionist, Norma honed her skills as a stand-up comic by trying out jokes on the tense crowd in the waiting room.*

iconoclast (noun) Someone who attacks traditional beliefs or institutions. *Comedian Dennis Miller relishes his reputation as an iconoclast, though people in power often resent his satirical jabs.* iconoclasm (noun), iconoclastic (adjective).

idolatry (noun) The worship of a person, thing, or institution as a god. *In communist China, admiration for Mao resembled idolatry; his picture was displayed everywhere, and millions of Chinese memorized his sayings and repeated them endlessly.* idolatrous (adjective).

idyll (noun) A rustic, romantic interlude; poetry or prose that celebrates simple pastoral life. *Her picnic with Max at Fahnstock Lake was not the serene idyll she had envisioned; instead, they were surrounded by hundreds of other picnickers blaring music from their boom boxes and cracking open soda cans.* idyllic (adjective).

illicit (illegal, wrongful) *When Janet caught her thirteen-year-old son and his friend downloading illicit pornographic photos from the World Wide Web, she promptly pulled the plug on his computer.*

illuminate (verb) To brighten with light; to enlighten or elucidate; to decorate (a manuscript). *The frosted-glass sconces in the dressing rooms at Le Cirque not only illuminate the rooms but make everyone look like a movie star. Alice Munro is a writer who can illuminate an entire character with a few deft sentences.*

immaterial (adjective) Of no consequence, unimportant. *"The fact that your travel agent is your best friend's son should be immaterial," I told Rosa; "If he keeps putting you on hold and acting nasty, just take your business elsewhere."*

immaculate (adjective) Totally unblemished, spotlessly clean. *The cream-colored upholstery in my new Porsche was immaculate—that is, until a raccoon came in through the window and tracked mud across the seats.*

Word Origin

Latin mutare = to change. Also found in English immutable, mutant, and mutation.

immutable (adjective) Incapable of change. *Does there ever come an age when we realize that our parents' personalities are immutable, when we can relax and stop trying to make them change?*

impartial (adjective) Fair, equal, unbiased. *If a judge is not impartial, then all of her rulings are questionable.* impartiality (noun).

impassivity (noun) Apathy, unresponsiveness. *Dot truly thinks that Mr. Right will magically show up on her door step, and her utter impassivity regarding her social life makes me want to shake her!* impassive (adjective).

imperceptible (adjective)   Impossible to perceive, inaudible or incomprehensible. *The sound of footsteps was almost imperceptible, but Donald's paranoia had reached such a pitch that he immediately assumed he was being followed.*

imperturbable (adjective)   Marked by extreme calm, impassivity, and steadiness. *The proper English butler in Kazuo Ishiguro's novel* The Remains of the Day *appears completely imperturbable even when his father dies or when his own heart is breaking.*

impetuous (adjective)   Acting hastily or impulsively. *Ben's resignation was an impetuous act; he did it without thinking, and he soon regretted it.* impetuosity (noun).

implacable (adjective)   Unbending, resolute. *The state of Israel is implacable in its policy of never negotiating with terrorists.*

Word Origin

Latin placare = *to please. Also found in English* complacent, placate, *and* placid.

implosion (noun)   To collapse inward from outside pressure. *While it is difficult to know what is going on in North Korea, no one can rule out a violent implosion of the North Korean regime and a subsequent flood of refugees across its borders.* implode (verb).

incessant (adjective)   unceasing. *The incessant blaring of the neighbor's car alarm made it impossible for me to concentrate on my upcoming Bar exam.*

inchoate (adjective)   Only partly formed or formulated. *At editorial meetings, Nancy had a habit of presenting her inchoate book ideas before she had a chance to fully determine their feasibility.*

Word Origin

Latin caedere = *to cut. Also found in English* concise, decide, excise, incision, *and* precise.

incise (verb)   To carve into, to engrave. *My wife felt nostalgic about the old elm tree since we had incised our initials in it when we were both in high school.* incisive (adjective) *Admirably direct and decisive. Ted Koppel's incisive questions have made many politicians squirm and stammer.*

incongruous (adjective)   Unlikely. *Art makes incongruous alliances, as when punk rockers, Tibetan folk musicians, gospel singers, and beat poets shared the stage at the Tibet House benefit concert.* incongruity (noun).

incorrigible (adjective)   Impossible to manage or reform. *Lou is an incorrigible trickster, constantly playing practical jokes no matter how much his friends complain.*

incursion (noun)   A hostile entrance into a territory; a foray into an activity or venture. *It is a little-known fact that the Central Intelligence Agency organized military incursions into China during the 1950s. The ComicCon was Barbara's first incursion into the world of comic strip artists.*

indefatigable (adjective)   Tireless. *Eleanor Roosevelt's indefatigable dedication to the cause of human welfare won her affection and honor throughout the world.* indefatigability (noun).

indelicate (adjective)   Blunt, undisguised. *No sooner had we sat down to eat than Mark made an indelicate remark about my high salary.*

inevitable (adjective)   Unable to be avoided. *Once the Japanese attacked Pearl Harbor, U.S. involvement in World War II was inevitable.* inevitability (noun).

infer (verb)   To conclude, to deduce. *Can I infer from your hostile tone of voice that you are still angry about yesterday's incident?* inference (noun).

inimical (adjective)   Unfriendly, hostile; adverse or difficult. *Relations between Greece and Turkey have been inimical for centuries.*

inimitable (adjective)   Incapable of being imitated, matchless. *John F. Kennedy's administration dazzled the public, partly because of the inimitable style and elegance of his wife, Jacqueline.*

inopportune (adjective)   Awkward, untimely. *When Gus heard raised voices and the crash of breaking china behind the kitchen door, he realized that he'd picked an inopportune moment to visit the Fairlights.*

inscrutability (noun)   Quality of being extremely difficult to interpret or understand, mysteriousness. *I am still puzzling over the inscrutability of the package I received yesterday, which contained twenty pomegranates and a note that said simply "Yours."* inscrutable (adjective).

insensible (adjective)   Unaware, incognizant; unconscious, out cold. *It's a good thing that Marty was insensible to the titters and laughter that greeted his arrival in the ballroom. In the latest episode of police brutality, an innocent young black man was beaten insensible after two cops stormed his apartment.*

insipid (adjective)   Flavorless, uninteresting. *Most TV shows are so insipid that you can watch them while reading or chatting without missing a thing.* insipidity (noun).

insinuate (verb)   Hint or intimate; to creep in. *During an extremely unusual broadcast, the anchor man insinuated that the Washington bureau chief was having a nervous breakdown. Marla managed to insinuate herself into the Duchess of York's conversation during the "Weight Watchers" promotion event.* insinuation (noun).

insolence (noun)   An attitude or behavior that is bold and disrespectful. *Some feel that news reporters who shout accusatory questions at the president are behaving with insolence toward his high office.* insolent (adjective).

insoluble (adjective)   Unable to be solved, irresolvable; indissoluble. *Fermat's last theorum remained insoluble for over 300 years until a young mathematician from Princeton solved it in 1995. If you are a gum chewer, you probably wouldn't like to know that insoluble plastics are a common ingredient of most popular gums.*

insular (adjective)   Narrow or isolated in attitude or viewpoint. *New Yorkers are famous for their insular attitudes; they seem to think that nothing important has ever happened outside of their city.* insularity (noun).

intercede (verb)   To step in, to moderate; to mediate or negotiate on behalf of someone else. *After their rejection by the co-op board, Kevin and Sol asked Rachel, another tenant, to intercede for them at the next board meeting.* intercession (noun).

interim (noun)   A break or interlude. *In the interim between figure-skating programs, the exhausted skaters retreat to the "kiss and cry" room to wait for their scores.*

interpolate (verb)   To interject. *The director's decision to interpolate topical political jokes into his production of Shakespeare's* Twelfth Night *was not viewed kindly by the critics.* interpolation (noun).

intransigent (adjective)   Unwilling to compromise. *Despite the mediator's attempts to suggest a fair solution to the disagreement, the two parties were intransigent, forcing a showdown.* intransigence (noun).

intrinsically (adverb)   Essentially, inherently. *There is nothing intrinsically difficult about upgrading a computer's microprocessor, yet Al was afraid to even open up the hard drive.* intrinsic (adjective).

Word Origin

Latin unda = *wave. Also found in English* undulate.

inundate (verb)   To overwhelm; to flood. *When America Online first announced its flat-rate pricing, the company was inundated with new customers, and thus began the annoying delays in service.* inundation (noun).

invective (noun)   insulting, abusive language. *I remained unscathed by his blistering invective because in my heart I knew I had done the right thing.*

invigorate (verb)   To give energy to, to stimulate. *As her car climbed the mountain road, Lucinda felt herself invigorated by the clear air and the cool breezes.* invigoration (noun).

irascible (adjective)   Easily provoked into anger, hot-headed. *Soup chef Al Yeganah, the model for Seinfeld's "Soup Nazi," is an irascible man who flies into a temper if his customers don't follow his rigid procedure for purchasing soup.* irascibility (noun).

jeopardize (verb)   To put in danger. *Terrorist attacks on civilians jeopardize the fragile peace in the Middle East.* jeopardy (noun).

jocular (adjective)   Humorous, amusing. *Listening to the CEO launch into yet another uproarious anecdote, Ted was frankly surprised by the jocular nature of the "emergency" board meeting.* jocularity (noun).

labyrinthine (adjective)   Extremely intricate or involved; circuitous. *Was I the only one who couldn't follow the labyrinthine plot of the movie L.A. Confidential? I was so confused I had to watch it twice to see "who did it."*

laconic (adjective)   Concise to the point of terseness; taciturn. *Tall, handsome and laconic, the actor Gary Cooper came to personify the strong, silent American, a man of action and few words.*

lambaste (verb)   To give someone a dressing-down; to attack someone verbally; to whip. *Once inside the locker room, the coach thoroughly lambasted the team for their incompetent performance on the football field.*

Word Origin

Latin laus = *praise. Also found in English* applaud, laud, laudatory, *and* plaudit.

laudable (adjective)   Commendable, praiseworthy. *The Hunt's Point nonprofit organization has embarked on a series of laudable ventures pairing businesses and disadvantaged youth.*

lethargic (adjective)   Lacking energy; sluggish. *Visitors to the zoo are surprised that the lions appear so lethargic, but, in the wild, lions sleep up to eighteen hours a day.* lethargy (noun).

levy (verb)   To demand payment or collection of a tax or fee. *The environmental activists pushed Congress to levy higher taxes on gasoline, but the automakers' lobbyists quashed their plans.*

lien (noun)   A claim against a property for the satisfaction of a debt. *Nat was in such financial straits when he died that his Fishkill property had several liens against it and all of his furniture was being repossessed.*

limn (verb)   To outline in distinct detail; to delineate. *Like many of her novels, Edith Wharton's* The Age of Innocence *expertly limns the tyranny of New York's upper-class society in the 1800s.*

loquacity (noun)   Talkativeness, wordiness. *While some people deride his loquacity and his tendency to use outrageous rhymes, no one can doubt that Jesse Jackson is a powerful orator.* loquacious (adjective).

Word Origin

Latin lux = *light. Also found in English* elucidate, pellucid, *and* translucent.

lucid (adjective)   Clear and understandable. *Hawking's* A Short History of the Universe *is a lucid explanation of a difficult topic, modern scientific theories of the origin of the universe.* lucidity (noun).

magnanimous (adjective)   Noble, generous. *When media titan Ted Turner pledged a gift of $1 billion to the United Nations, he challenged other wealthy people to be equally magnanimous.* magnanimity (noun).

maladroit (adjective)   Inept, awkward. *It was painful to watch the young congressman's maladroit delivery of the nominating speech.*

malinger (verb)   To pretend illness to avoid work. *During the labor dispute, hundreds of employees malingered, forcing the company to slow production and costing it millions in profits.*

malleable (adjective)   Able to be changed, shaped, or formed by outside pressures. *Gold is a very useful metal because it is so malleable. A child's personality is malleable, and is often deeply influenced by things her parents say and do.* malleability (noun).

Word Origin

Latin mandare = *entrust, order. Also found in English* command, demand, *and* remand.

mandate (noun)   Order, command. *The new policy on gays in the military went into effect as soon as the president issued his mandate about it.* mandate (verb), mandatory (adjective).

marginal (adjective)   At the outer edge or fringe; of minimal quality or acceptability. *In spite of the trend toward greater paternal involvement in child-rearing, most fathers still have a marginal role in their children's lives. Jerry's GRE scores were so marginal that he didn't get accepted into the graduate schools of his choice.*

marginalize (verb)   To push toward the fringes; to make less consequential. *Hannah argued that the designation of a certain month as "Black History Month" or "Gay and Lesbian Book Month" actually does a disservice to minorities by marginalizing them.*

martial (adjective)   Of, relating to, or suited to military life. *My old teacher, Miss Woody, had such a martial demeanor that you'd think she was running a boot camp instead of teaching fifth grade. The military seized control of Myanmar in 1988, and this embattled country has been ruled by martial law since then.*

Word Origin

Latin medius = *middle. Also found in English* intermediate, media, *and* medium.

mediate (verb)   To reconcile differences between two parties. *During the baseball strike, both the players and the club owners expressed willingness to have the president mediate the dispute.* mediation (noun).

mercenary (adjective)   Doing something only for pay or for personal advantage. *People have criticized the U.S. motives in the Persian Gulf War as mercenary, pointing out that the U.S. would not have come to Kuwait's defense had it grown carrots rather than produced oil.* mercenary (noun).

mercurial (adjective)   Changing quickly and unpredictably. *The mercurial personality of Robin Williams, with his many voices and styles, made him a natural choice to play the part of the ever-changing genie in Aladdin.*

metamorphose (verb)   To undergo a striking transformation. *In just a century, book publishers have metamorphosed from independent, exclusively literary businesses to minor divisions in multimedia entertainment conglomerates.* metamorphosis (noun).

meticulous (adjective)   Very careful with details. *Watch repair calls for a craftsperson who is patient and meticulous.*

mettle (noun)   Strength of spirit; stamina. *Linda's mettle was severely tested while she served as the only female attorney at Smith, Futterweitt, Houghton, and Dobbs.* mettlesome (adjective).

mimicry (noun)   Imitation, aping. *The continued popularity of Elvis Presley has given rise to a class of entertainers who make a living through mimicry of "The King."* mimic (noun and verb).

minatory (adjective)   Menacing, threatening. *As soon as she met Mrs. Danforth, the head housemaid at Manderlay, the young bride was cowed by her minatory manner and quickly retreated to the morning room.*

mince (verb)   To chop into small pieces; to speak with decorum and restraint. *Malaysia's prime minister, Mahathir Mohamad, is not a man known to mince words; he has accused satellite TV of poisoning Asia and has denounced the Australian press as "congenital liars. "*

Word Origin

Greek anthropos = *human. Also found in English* anthropology, anthropoid, anthropomorphic, *and* philanthropy.

misanthrope (noun)   Someone who hates or distrusts all people. *In the beloved Christmas classic,* It's a Wonderful Life, *Lionel Barrymore plays Potter, the wealthy misanthrope who is determined to make life miserable for everyone, and particularly for the young, idealistic George Bailey.* misanthropic (adjective), misanthropy (noun).

miscreant (adjective)   Unbelieving, heretical; evil, villainous. *After a one-year run playing Iago in* Othello, *and then two years playing Bill Sikes in* Oliver, *Sean was tired of being typecast in miscreant roles.* miscreant (noun).

mitigate (verb)   To make less severe; to relieve. *There's no doubt that Wallace committed the assault, but the verbal abuse Wallace had received helps to explain his behavior and somewhat mitigates his guilt.* mitigation (noun).

monopoly (noun)   A condition in which there is only one seller of a certain commodity. *Wary of Microsoft's seeming monopoly of the computer operating-system business, rivals are asking for government intervention.* monopolistic (adjective) *Renowned consumer advocate Ralph Nader once quipped, "The only difference between John D. Rockefeller and Bill Gates is that Gates recognizes no boundaries to his monopolistic drive."*

monotonous (adjective)   Tediously uniform, unchanging. *Brian Eno's "Music for Airports" is characterized by minimal melodies, subtle textures, and variable repetition, which I find rather bland and monotonous.* monotony (noun).

morose (adjective)   Gloomy, sullen. *After Chuck's girlfriend dumped him, he lay around the house for a couple of days, refusing to come to the phone and feeling morose.*

mutation (noun)   A significant change; in biology, a permanent change in hereditary material. *Most genetic mutations are not beneficial, since any change in the delicate balance of an organism tends to be disruptive.* mutate (verb).

Word Origin

Latin frangere =
*to break. Also
found in English*
fraction, frac-
tious, fracture,
frangible,
infraction, *and*
refract.

nadir (noun)   Lowest point. *Pedro and Renee's marriage reached a new nadir last Christmas Eve when Pedro locked Renee out of the house upon her return from the supposed "business trip."*

nascent (adjective)   Newly born, just beginning. *While her artistry was still nascent, it was 15-year-old Tara Lipinski's technical wizardry that enabled her to win a gold medal in the 1998 Winter Olympics.* nascence (noun).

noisome (adjective)   Putrid, fetid, noxious. *We were convinced that the noisome odor infiltrating every corner of our building was evidence of a mouldering corpse.*

notorious (adjective)   Famous, especially for evil actions or qualities. *Warner Brothers produced a series of movies about notorious gangsters such as John Dillinger and Al Capone.* notoriety (noun).

Word Origin

Latin durus =
*hard. Also found
in English* durable
and endure.

obdurate (adjective)   Unwilling to change; stubborn, inflexible. *Despite the many pleas he received, the governor was obdurate in his refusal to grant clem-ency to the convicted murderer.*

oblivious (adjective)   Unaware, unconscious. *Karen practiced her oboe solo with complete concentration, oblivious to the noise and activity around her.* oblivion (noun), obviousness (noun).

obscure (adjective)   Little known; hard to understand. *Mendel was an obscure monk until decades after his death, when his scientific work was finally discovered. Most people find the writings of James Joyce obscure; hence the popularity of books that explain the many odd references and tricks of language in his work.* obscure (verb), obscurity (noun).

obsolete (adjective)   No longer current; old-fashioned. *W. H. Auden said that his ideal landscape would contain water wheels, grain mills, and other forms of obsolete machinery.* obsolescence (noun).

obstinate (adjective)   Stubborn, unyielding. *Despite years of government effort, the problem of drug abuse remains obstinate.* obstinacy (noun).

obtuse (adjective)   Dull-witted, insensitive; incomprehensible, unclear, or impre-cise. *Amy was so obtuse she didn't realize that Alexi had proposed marriage to her. French psychoanalyst Jacques Lacan's collection of papers,* Ecrits, *is notoriously obtuse, yet it has still been highly influential in linguistics, film theory, and literary criticism.*

obviate (verb)   Preclude, make unnecessary. *Truman Capote's meticulous accu-racy and total recall obviated the need for note-taking when he wrote his account of a 1959 murder,* In Cold Blood.

odium (noun)   Intense feeling of hatred, abhorrence. *When the neighbors learned that a convicted sex offender was now living in their midst, they could not restrain their odium and began harassing the man whenever he left his house.* odious (adjective).

opprobrium (noun)   Dishonor, disapproval. *Switzerland recently came under public opprobrium when it was revealed that Swiss bankers had hoarded the gold the Nazis had confiscated from their victims.* opprobrious (adjective).

orthodox (adjective)   In religion, conforming to a certain doctrine; conventional. *George Eliot's relationship with George Lewes, a married journalist, offended the sensibilities of her more orthodox peers.* orthodoxy (noun).

ossified (adjective)   In biology, to turn into bone; to become rigidly conventional and opposed to change. *His harsh view of co-education had ossified over the years so that he was now the only teacher who sought to bar girls from the venerable boys' school.* ossification (noun).

ostentatious (adjective)   Overly showy, pretentious. *To show off his new wealth, the financier threw an ostentatious party featuring a full orchestra, a famous singer, and tens of thousands of dollars' worth of food.* ostentation (noun).

ostracize (verb)   To exclude from a group. *In Biblical times, those who suffered from the disease of leprosy were ostracized and forced to live alone.* ostracism (noun).

paean (adjective)   A joyous expression of praise, gratitude, or triumph. *Choreographer Paul Taylor's dance "Eventide" is a sublime paean to remembered love, with couple after loving couple looking back as they embrace an unknown future.*

parody (noun)   An imitation created for comic effect; a caricature. *While the creators of the 1970s comedy series* All in the Family *intended Archie Bunker to be a parody of closed-mindedeness in Americans, large numbers of people adopted Bunker as a working-class hero.*

parse (verb)   To break a sentence down into grammatical components; to analyze bit by bit. *In the wake of the sex scandal, journalists parsed every utterance by administration officials regarding the President's alleged promiscuity. At $1.25 million a day,* Titanic *is the most expensive movie ever made, but director James Cameron refused to parse the film's enormous budget for inquisitive reporters.*

partisan (adjective)   Reflecting strong allegiance to a particular party or cause. *The vote on the president's budget was strictly partisan: every member of the president's party voted yes, and all others voted no.* partisan (noun).

pastoral (adjective)   Simple and rustic, bucolic, rural. *While industry grew and the country expanded westward, the Hudson River School of painters depicted the landscape as a pastoral setting where humans and nature could coexist.*

patron (noun)   A special guardian or protector; a wealthy or influential supporter of the arts. *Dominique de Menil used her considerable wealth to become a well-known patron of the arts; she and her husband owned a collection of more than 10,000 pieces ranging from cubist paintings to tribal artifacts.* patronize (verb).

peccadillo (noun)   A minor offense, a lapse. *What Dr. Sykes saw as a major offense—being addressed as Marge rather than Doctor—Tina saw as a mere peccadillo and one that certainly should not have lost her the job.*

pedantic (adjective)   Academic, bookish. *The men Hillary met through personal ads in the* New York Review of Books *were invariably pasty-skinned pedantic types who dropped the names of nineteenth-century writers in every sentence.* pedantry (noun).

pedestrian (adjective)   Unimaginative, ordinary. *The new Italian restaurant received a bad review due to its reliance on pedestrian dishes such as pasta with marinara sauce or chicken parmigiana.*

Word Origin

Latin fides =
*faith. Also found
in English*
confide, confi-
dence, fidelity,
and infidel.

perfidious (adjective)   Disloyal, treacherous. *Although he was one of the most talented generals of the American Revolution, Benedict Arnold is remembered today as a perfidious betrayer of the patriot cause.* perfidy (noun).

peripatetic (adjective)   Moving or traveling from place to place; always on the go. In *Barbara Wilson's* Trouble in Transylvania, *peripatetic translator Cassandra Reilly is on the road again, this time to China by way of Budapest, where she plans to catch the TransMongolian Express.*

permeate (verb)   To spread through or penetrate. *Little by little, the smell of gas from the broken pipe permeated the house.*

personification (noun)   The embodiment of a thing or an abstract idea in human form. *Many people view Theodore Kaczynski, the killer known as the Unabomber, as the very personification of evil.* personify (verb).

pervasive (adjective)   Spreading throughout. *As news of the disaster reached the town, a pervasive sense of gloom could be felt everywhere.* pervade (verb).

philistine (noun)   Someone who is smugly ignorant and uncultured. *A true philistine, Meg claimed she didn't read any book that wasn't either recommended by Oprah Winfrey or on the best-seller list.* philistine (adjective).

pith (noun)   The core, the essential part; in biology, the central strand of tissue in the stems of most vascular plants. *After spending seventeen years in psychoanalysis, Frieda had finally come face to face with the pith of her deep-seated anxiety.* pithy (adjective).

placate (verb)   To soothe or appease. *The waiter tried to placate the angry customer with the offer of a free dessert.* placatory (adjective).

placid (adjective)   Unmarked by disturbance; complacent. *Dr. Kahn was convinced that the placid exterior presented by Frieda in her early analysis sessions masked a deeply disturbed psyche.* placidity (noun).

plaintive (adjective)   Expressing suffering or melancholy. *In the beloved children's book* The Secret Garden, *Mary is disturbed by plaintive cries echoing in the corridors of gloomy Misselthwaite Manor.*

plastic (adjective)   Able to be molded or reshaped. *Because it is highly plastic, clay is an easy material for beginning sculptors to use.* plasticity (noun).

plausible (adjective)   Apparently believable. *The idea that a widespread conspiracy to kill the president has been kept secret by all the participants for over thirty years hardly seems plausible.* plausibility (noun).

platitude (noun)   A trite remark or saying; a cliché. *How typical of June to send a sympathy card filled with mindless platitudes like "One day at a time," rather than calling the grieving widow on the phone.* platitudinous (adjective).

plummet (verb)   To dive or plunge. *On October 27, 1997, the stock market plummeted by 554 points and left us all wondering if the bull market was finally over.*

polarize (adjective)   To separate into opposing groups or forces. *For years, the abortion debate polarized the American people, with many people voicing views at either extreme and few people trying to find a middle ground.* polarization (noun).

ponderous (adjective)   Unwieldy and bulky; oppressively dull. *Unfortunately, the film director weighed the movie down with a ponderous voice-over narrated by the protagonist as an old man.*

poseur (noun)   Someone who pretends to be what he isn't. *Gerald had pretensions for literary stardom with his book proposal on an obscure World War II battle, yet most agents soon realized that the book would never be written and categorized him as a poseur.*

positivism (noun)   A philosophy that denies speculation and assumes that the only knowledge is scientific knowledge. *David Hume carried his positivism to an extreme when he argued that our expectation that the sun will rise tomorrow has no basis in reason and is purely a matter of belief.* positivistic (adjective).

pragmatism (noun)   A belief in approaching problems through practical rather than theoretical means. *Roosevelt's attitude toward the economic troubles of the Depression was based on pragmatism: "Try something," he said; "If it doesn't work, try something else."* pragmatic (adjective).

precedent (noun)   An earlier occurrence that serves as an example for a decision. *In a legal system that reveres precedent, even defining the nature of a completely new type of dispute can seem impossible.* precede (verb).

precept (noun)   A general principle or law. *One of the central precepts of Tai Chi Ch'uan is the necessity of allowing ki (cosmic energy) to flow through one's body in slow, graceful movements.*

precipitate (verb)   To spur or activate. *In the summer of 1997, the selling off of the Thai baht precipitated a currency crisis that spread throughout Asia.*

preclude (verb)   To prevent, to hinder. *Unfortunately, Jasmine's appointment at the New Age Expo precluded her attendance at our weekend Workshop for Shamans and Psychics.* preclusive (adjective), preclusion (noun).

precursor (noun)   A forerunner, a predecessor. *The Kodak Brownie camera, a small boxy camera made of jute board and wood, was the precursor to today's sleek 35mm cameras.* precursory (adjective).

preponderance (noun)   A superiority in weight, size, or quantity; a major-ity. *In Seattle, there is a great preponderance of seasonal affective disorder, or SAD, a malady brought on by light starvation during the dark Northwest winter.* preponderate (verb)

presage (verb)   To foretell, to anticipate. *According to folklore, a red sky at dawn presages a day of stormy weather.*

prescience (noun)   Foreknowledge or foresight. *When she saw the characteristic eerie yellowish-black light in the sky, Dorothy had the prescience to seek shelter in the storm cellar.* prescient (adjective).

presumptuous (adjective)   Going beyond the limits of courtesy or appropriateness. *The senator winced when the presumptuous young staffer addressed him as "Ted."* presume (verb), presumption (noun).

prevaricate (verb)   To lie, to equivocate. *When it became clear to the FBI that the mobster had threatened the twelve-year-old witness, they could well understand why he had prevaricated during the hearing.*

Word Origin

Latin claudere = *to close. Also found in English* conclude, include, recluse, *and* seclude.

Word Origin

*Latin primus =
first. Also found in
English primate,
primitive,
primogeniture,
and primodial.*

primacy (noun)   State of being the utmost in importance; preeminence. *The anthropologist Ruth Benedict was an inspiration to Margaret Mead for her emphasis on the primacy of culture in the formation of an individual's personality.* primal (adjective).

pristine (adjective)   Pure, undefiled. *As climbers who have scaled Mt. Everest can attest, the trails to the summit are hardly in pristine condition and are actually strewn with trash.*

probity (noun)   Goodness, integrity. *The vicious editorial attacked the moral probity of the senatorial candidate, saying he had profited handsomely from his pet project, the senior-citizen housing project.*

procure (verb)   To obtain by using particular care and effort. *Through partnerships with a large number of specialty wholesalers, W.W. Grainger is able to procure a startling array of products for its customers, from bear repellent for Alaska pipeline workers to fork-lift trucks and toilet paper.* procurement (noun).

prodigality (noun)   The condition of being wastefully extravagant. *Richard was ashamed of the prodigality of his bride's parents when he realized that the cost of the wedding reception alone was more than his father earned in one year.* prodigal (adjective).

proliferate (verb)   To increase or multiply. *Over the past fifteen years, high-tech companies have proliferated in northern California, Massachusetts, and other regions.* proliferation (noun).

prolixity (noun)   A diffuseness; a rambling and verbose quality. *The prolixity of Sarah's dissertation on Ottoman history defied even her adviser's attempts to read it.* prolix (adjective).

prophetic (adjective)   Auspicious, predictive of what's to come. *We often look at every event leading up to a new love affair as prophetic—the flat tire that caused us to be late for work, the chance meeting in the elevator, the horoscope which augured "a new beginning."* prophecy (noun), prophesy (verb).

propagate (verb)   To cause to grow; to foster. *John Smithson's will left his fortune for the founding of an institution to propagate knowledge, leaving open whether that meant a university, a library, or a museum.* propagation (noun).

propitiating (adjective)   Conciliatory, mollifying or appeasing. *Management's offer of a five-percent raise was meant as a propitiating gesture, yet the striking workers were unimpressed.* propitiate (verb).

propriety (noun)   Appropriateness. *Some people expressed doubts about the propriety of Clinton's discussing his underwear on MTV.*

proximity (noun)   Closeness, nearness. *Neighborhood residents were angry over the proximity of the proposed sewage plant to the local elementary school.* proximate (adjective).

pundit (noun)   Someone who offers opinions in an authoritative style. *The Sunday morning talk shows are filled with pundits, each with his or her own theory about this week's political news.*

Word Origin

Latin pungere = *to jab, to prick. Also found in English* pugilist, punctuate, puncture.

pungency (noun)   Marked by having a sharp, biting quality. *Unfortunately, the pungency of the fresh cilantro overwhelmed the delicate flavor of the poached flounder.* pungent *(adjective)*

purify (verb)   To make pure, clean, or perfect. *The new water-treatment plant is supposed to purify the drinking water provided to everyone in the nearby towns.* purification (noun).

quiescent (adjective)   In a state of rest or inactivity; latent. *Polly's ulcer has been quiescent ever since her mother-in-law moved out of the condo, which was well over a year ago.* quiescence (noun).

quixotic (adjective)   Foolishly romantic, idealistic to an impractical degree. *In the novel* Shoeless Joe, *Ray Kinsella carries out a quixotic plan to build a baseball field in the hopes that past baseball greats will come to play there.*

quotidian (adjective)   Occurring every day; commonplace and ordinary. *Most of the time, we long to escape from quotidian concerns, but in the midst of a crisis we want nothing more than to be plagued by such simple problems as a leaky faucet or a whining child.*

raconteur (noun)   An excellent storyteller. *A member of the Algonquin round table, Robert Benchley was a natural raconteur with a seemingly endless ability to turn daily life and its irritations into entertaining commentary.*

rancorous (adjective)   Marked by deeply embedded bitterness or animosity. *While Ralph and Kishu have been separated for three years, their relationship is so rancorous that they had to hire a professional mediator just to discuss divorce arrangements.* rancor (noun).

rapacious (adjective)   Excessively grasping or greedy. *Some see global currency speculators like George Soros as rapacious parasites who destroy economies and then line their pockets with the profits.* rapacity (noun).

rarefied (adjective)   Of interest or relating to a small, refined circle; less dense, thinner. *Those whose names dot the society pages live in a rarefied world where it's entirely normal to dine on caviar for breakfast or order a $2,000 bottle of wine at Le Cirque. When she reached the summit of Mt. McKinley, Deborah could hardly breathe in the rarefied air.*

raucous (adjective)   Boisterous, unruly and wild. *Sounds of shouts and raucous laughter drifted out of the hotel room where Felipe's bachelor party was being held.*

reactionary (adjective)   Ultra conservative. *Every day, over twenty million listeners tune in to hear Rush Limbaugh spew his reactionary opinions about "feminazis" and environmental "fanatics."* reactionary (noun)

recede (verb)   To draw back, to ebb, to abate. *Once his hairline began to recede, Hap took to wearing bizarre accessories, like velvet ascots, to divert attention from it.* recession (noun).

reclusive (adjective)   Withdrawn from society. *During the last years of her life, Garbo led a reclusive existence, rarely appearing in public.* recluse (noun).

reconcile (verb)   To make consistent or harmonious. *Roosevelt's greatness as a leader can be seen in his ability to reconcile the differing demands and values of the varied groups that supported him.* reconciliation (noun).

recompense (noun)   Compensation for a service rendered or to pay for damages. *The 5% of the estate that Phil received as executor of his Aunt Ida's will is small recompense for the headaches he endured in settling her affairs.* recompense (verb).

recondite (adjective)   Profound, deep, abstruse. *Professor Miyaki's recondite knowledge of seventeenth-century Flemish painters made him a prized—if barely understood—member of the art history department.*

redemptive (adjective)   Liberating and reforming. *While she doesn't attend formal church services, Carrie is a firm believer in the redemptive power of prayer.* redeem (verb), redemption (noun).

refractory (adjective)   Stubbornly resisting control or authority. *Like a refractory child, Jill stomped out of the car, slammed the door, and said she would walk home, even though her house was ten miles away.*

relevance (noun)   Connection to the matter at hand; pertinence. *Testimony in a criminal trial may only be admitted to the extent that it has clear relevance to the question of guilt or innocence.* relevant (adjective).

reparation (noun)   The act of making amends; payment of damages by a defeated nation to the victors. *The Treaty of Versailles, signed in 1919, formally asserted Germany's war guilt and ordered it to pay reparations to the allies.*

reproof (noun)   A reprimand, a reproach or castigation. *Joe thought being grounded for one month was a harsh reproof for coming home late only once.* reprove (verb).

repugnant (adjective)   Causing dislike or disgust. *After the news broke about Mad Cow Disease, much of the beef-loving British public began to find the thought of a Sunday roast repugnant.*

requiem (noun)   A musical composition or poem written to honor the dead. *Many financial analysts think that the ailing typewriter company should simply say a requiem for itself and shut down; however, the CEO has other plans.*

repudiate (verb)   To reject, to renounce. *After it became known that Duke had been a leader of the Ku Klux Klan, most Republican leaders repudiated him.* repudiation (noun).

resilient (adjective)   Able to recover from difficulty. *A pro athlete must be mentally resilient, able to lose a game one day and come back the next with renewed enthusiasm and confidence.* resilience (noun).

resonant (adjective)   Full of special import or meaning. *I found the speaker's words particularly resonant because I, too, had served in Vietnam and felt the same mixture of shame and pride.* resonance (noun).

resplendent (adjective)   Glowing, shining. *In late December, midtown New York is resplendent with holiday lights and decorations.* resplendence (noun).

rite (noun)   Ceremony. *From October to May, the Patwin Indians of California's Sacramento Valley held a series of rites and dances designed to bring the tribe health and prosperity.*

rogue (noun)   A mischievously dishonest person; a scamp. *In Jane Austen's* Pride and Prejudice, *Wickham, a charming rogue, seduces Darcy's young sister Georgiana and later does the same thing with Kitty Bennett.*

Word Origin

Latin frangere = *to break. Also found in English* fraction, fractions, fracture, frangible, infraction, refract.

ruffian (noun)   A brute, roughneck or bully. *In Dicken's* Oliver Twist, *Fagin instructs his gang of orphaned ruffians on the arts of picking pockets and shoplifting.*

rumination (noun)   The act of engaging in contemplation. *Marcel Proust's semi-autobiographical novel cycle,* Remembrance of Things Past, *is less a narrative than an extended rumination on the nature of memory.* ruminate (verb).

sage (noun)   A person of great wisdom, a sagacious philosopher. *It was the Chinese sage Confucius who first taught what is now known the world over as "The Golden Rule."* sagacious (adjective), sagacity (noun).

Word Origin

Latin salus = health. *Also found in English* salubrious, salutation, *and* salute.

salutary (adjective)   Restorative, healthful. *I find a short dip in an icy stream to be extremely salutary, although the health benefits of my bracing swims are, as yet, unclear.*

sanction (verb)   Support or authorize. *Even after a bomb exploded on the front porch of his home, the Reverend Martin Luther King refused to sanction any violent response and urged his angry followers to love their enemies.* sanctify (verb), sanction (noun).

sap (verb)   To exhaust, to deplete. *The exhaustive twelve-city reading tour so sapped the novelist's strength that she told her publicist that she hoped her next book would be a flop! While Uganda is making enormous economic strides under President Yoweri Musevini, rebel fighting has sapped much of the country's resources.*

satiate (verb)   To fulfill to or beyond capacity. *Judging by the current crop of films featuring serial killers, rape, ritual murder, gunslinging, and plain old-fashioned slugfests, the public appetite for violence has not yet been satiated.* satiation (noun), satiety (noun).

saturate (verb)   To drench or suffuse with liquid or anything that permeates or invades. *The hostess's furious dabbing at the tablecloth was in vain, since the spilt wine had already saturated the damask cloth.* saturation (noun), saturated (adjective)

scrutinize (verb)   To study closely. *The lawyer scrutinized the contract, searching for any detail that could pose a risk for her client.* scrutiny (noun).

scurvy (adjective)   Shabby, low. *I couldn't believe that Farouk was so scurvy as to open up my computer files and read my e-mail.*

Word Origin

Latin sequi = *to* follow. *Also found in English* consequence, sequel, *and* subsequent.

sequential (adjective)   Arranged in an order or series. *The courses required for the chemistry major are sequential; you must take them in the prescribed order since each course builds on the previous ones.* sequence (noun).

sedulous (adjective)   Diligent, industrious. *Those who are most sedulous about studying this vocabulary list are likely to breeze through the antonyms sections of their GRE exam.*

sidereal (adjective)   Relating to the stars or the constellations. *Jacqueline was interested in matters sidereal and was always begging my father to take the dusty old telescope out of our garage.*

signatory (noun)   Someone who signs an official document or petition along with others. *Alex urged me to join the other signatories and add my name to the petition against toxic sludge in organic foods, but I simply did not care enough about the issue. The signatories of the Declaration of Independence included John Adams, Benjamin Franklin, John Hancock, and Thomas Jefferson.*

sinuous (noun)   Winding, circuitous, serpentine. *Frank Gehry's sinuous design for the Guggenheim Museum in Bilbao, Spain has led people to hail the museum as the first great building of the twenty-first century.* sinuosity (noun).

specious (adjective)   Deceptively plausible or attractive. *The infomercial for "Fat-Away" offered mainly specious arguments for a product that is, essentially, a heavy-duty girdle.*

spontaneous (adjective)   Happening without plan or outside cause. *When the news of Kennedy's assassination hit the airwaves, people everywhere gathered in a spontaneous effort to express their shock and grief.* spontaneity (noun).

spurious (adjective)   False, fake. *The so-called Piltdown Man, supposed to be the fossil of a primitive human, turned out to be spurious, though who created the hoax is still uncertain.*

splice (verb)   To unite by interweaving separate strands or parts. *Amateur filmmaker Duddy Kravitz shocked and angered his clients by splicing footage of tribal rituals into his films of their weddings and bar mitzvahs.*

squander (verb)   To use up carelessly, to waste. *Those who had made donations to the charity were outraged to learn that its director had squandered millions on fancy dinners, first-class travel, and an expensive apartment for entertaining.*

stanch (verb)   To stop the flow. *When Edison began to bleed profusely, Dr. Munger stanched the blood flow by applying direct pressure to the wound.*

stint (verb)   To limit, to restrain. *The British bed & breakfast certainly did not stint on the breakfast part of the equation; they provided us with fried tomatoes, fried sausages, fried eggs, smoked kippers, fried bread, fried mushrooms, and bowls of a cereal called "Wheatabix" (which tasted like cardboard).* stinting (adjective).

stolid (adjective)   Impassive, unemotional. *The popular animated television series* King of the Hill *chronicles the woes of a stolid, conservative Texan confronting changing times.* stolidity (noun).

subordination (noun)   The state of being subservient or treated as less valuable. *Heather left the naval academy because she could no longer stand the subordination of every personal whim or desire to the rigorous demands of military life.* subordinate (verb).

Word Origin

Latin poena = pain. Also found in English impunity, penal, penalty, *and* punishment.

subpoena (noun)   An order of a court, legislation or grand jury that compels a witness to be present at a trial or hearing. *The young man's lawyer asked the judge to subpoena a boa constrictor into court on the grounds that the police had used the snake as an "instrument of terror" to coerce his confession.*

subside (verb)   To settle or die down. *The celebrated lecturer had to wait ten minutes for the applause to subside before he began his speech.*

subsidization (noun)   The state of being financed by a grant from a government or other agency. *Without subsidization, the nation's passenger rail system would probably go bankrupt.* subsidize (verb).

substantiated (adjective)   Verified or supported by evidence. *The charge that Nixon had helped to cover up crimes was substantiated by his comments about it on a series of audiotapes.* substantiate (verb), substantiation (noun).

subsume (verb)   To encompass or engulf within something larger. *In Alan Dershowitz's* Reversal of Fortune, *he makes it clear that his work as a lawyer subsumes his personal life.*

subterranean (adjective)   Under the surface of the earth. *Subterranean testing of nuclear weapons was permitted under the Nuclear Test Ban Treaty of 1963.*

summarily (adverb)   Quickly and concisely. *No sooner had I voiced my concerns about the new ad campaign than my boss put her hand on my elbow and summarily ushered me out of her office.*

superficial (adjective)   On the surface only; without depth or substance. *Her wound was only superficial and required no treatment except a light bandage. His superficial attractiveness hides the fact that his personality is lifeless and his mind is dull.* superficiality (noun).

superimpose (verb)   To place or lay over or above something. *The artist stirred controversy by superimposing portraits of certain contemporary politicians over images of such reviled historical figures as Hitler and Stalin.*

supersede (verb)   To displace, to substitute or supplant. *"I'm sorry," the principal announced, "but today's afternoon classes will be superseded by an assembly on drug and alcohol abuse."*

supine (adjective)   prone. *One always feels rather vulnerable when wearing a flimsy paper gown and lying supine on a doctor's examining table.*

supposition (noun)   Assumption, conjecture. *While most climate researchers believe that increasing levels of greenhouse gases will warm the planet, skeptics claim that this theory is mere supposition.* suppose (verb).

surge (noun)   A gush; a swelling or sweeping forward. *When Mattel gave the Barbie Doll a makeover in the late eighties, coming out with dolls like doctor Barbie and astronaut Barbie, the company experienced a surge in sales.*

Word Origin

Latin tangere = *to touch. Also found in English* contact, contiguous, tactile, tangent, *and* tangible.

tangential (adjective)   Touching lightly; only slightly connected or related. *Having enrolled in a class on African-American history, the students found the teacher's stories about his travels in South America only of tangential interest.* tangent (noun).

tedium (noun)   boredom. *For most people, watching even a fifteen-minute broadcast of the Earth as seen from space would be an exercise in sheer tedium.* tedious (adjective).

temperance (noun)   Moderation or restraint in feelings and behavior. *Most professional athletes practice temperance in their personal habits; too much eating or drinking and too many late nights, they know, can harm their performance.*

temperate (adjective)   Moderate, calm. *The warm gulf streams are largely responsible for the temperate climate of the British Isles.*

tenuous (adjective)   Lacking in substance; weak, flimsy, very thin. *His tenuous grasp of the Spanish language was evident when he addressed Señor Chavez as "Señora."*

terrestrial (adjective)   Of the Earth. *The movie* Close Encounters of the Third Kind *tells the story of the first contact between beings from outer space and terrestrial creatures.*

throwback (noun)   A reversion to an earlier type; an atavism. *The new Volkswagen beetle, with its familiar bubble shape, looks like a throwback to the sixties, but it is actually packed with modern high-tech equipment.*

tiff (noun)   A small, almost inconsequential quarrel or disagreement. *Megan and Bruce got into a tiff when Bruce criticized her smoking.*

tirade (noun)   A long, harshly critical speech. *Reformed smokers, like Bruce, are prone to delivering tirades on the evils of smoking.*

torpor (noun)   Apathy, sluggishness. *Stranded in an airless hotel room in Madras after a 27-hour train ride, I felt such overwhelming torpor that I doubted I would make it to Bangalore, the next leg of my journey.* torpid (adjective).

tout (verb)   To praise highly, to brag publicly. *A much happier Eileen is now touting the benefits of Prozac, but, to tell you the truth, I miss her witty, self-lacerating commentaries.*

Word Origin

Latin tractare = to handle. *Also found in English* intractable, tractate, *and* traction.

tractable (adjective)   Obedient, manageable. *When he turned three, Harrison suddenly became a tractable, well-mannered little boy after being, quite frankly, an unruly little monster!*

tranquillity (noun)   Freedom from disturbance or turmoil; calm. *Seeking the tranquillity of country life, she moved from New York City to rural Vermont.* tranquil (adjective).

transgress (verb)   To go past limits; to violate. *If Iraq has developed biological weapons, then it has transgressed the UN's rules against manufacturing weapons of mass destruction.* transgression (noun).

transmute (verb)   To change in form or substance. *Practitioners of alchemy, a forebear of modern chemistry, tried to discover ways to transmute metals such as iron into gold.* transmutation (noun).

treacherous (adjective)   Untrustworthy or disloyal; dangerous or unreliable. *Nazi Germany proved to be a treacherous ally, first signing a peace pact with the Soviet Union, then invading. Be careful crossing the rope bridge; parts of the span are badly frayed and treacherous.* treachery (noun).

tremor (noun)   An involuntary shaking or trembling. *Michael still manages to appear calm and at ease despite the tremors caused by Parkinson's disease. Brooke felt the first tremors of the 1989 San Francisco earthquake while she was sitting in Candlestick Park watching a Giants baseball game.*

trenchant (adjective)   Caustic and incisive. *Essayist H. L. Mencken was known for his trenchant wit and was famed for mercilessly puncturing the American middle class (which he called the "booboisie").*

Word Origin

Latin trepidus = alarmed. *Also found in English* intrepid.

trepidation (noun)   Fear and anxiety. *After the tragedy of TWA flight 800, many previously fearless flyers were filled with trepidation whenever they stepped into an airplane.*

turbulent (adjective)   Agitated or disturbed. *The night before the championship match, Martina was unable to sleep, her mind turbulent with fears and hopes.* turbulence (noun).

turpitude (noun)   Depravity, wickedness. *Radical feminists who contrast women's essential goodness with men's moral turpitude can be likened to religious fundamentalists who make a clear distinction between the saved and the damned.*

tyro (noun)   Novice, amateur. *For an absolute tyro on the ski slopes, Gina was surprisingly agile at taking the moguls.*

unalloyed (adjective)   Unqualified, pure. *Holding his newborn son for the first time, Malik felt an unalloyed happiness that was unlike anything he had ever experienced in his 45 years.*

undermine (verb)   To excavate beneath; to subvert, to weaken. *Dot continued to undermine my efforts to find her a date by showing up at our dinner parties in her ratty old sweat suit.*

unfeigned (adjective)   Genuine, sincere. *Lashawn responded with such unfeigned astonishment when we all leapt out of the kitchen that I think she had had no inkling of the surprise party.*

univocal (adjective)   With a single voice. *While they came from different backgrounds and classes, the employees were univocal in their demands that the corrupt CEO resign immediately.*

unstinting (adjective)   Giving with unrestrained generosity. *Few people will be able to match the unstinting dedication and care that Mother Theresa lavished on the poor people of Calcutta.*

urbanity (noun)   Sophistication, suaveness and polish. *Part of the fun in a Cary Grant movie lies in seeing whether the star can be made to lose his urban-ity and elegance in the midst of chaotic or kooky situations.* urbane (adjective).

Word Origin

Latin urbs = *city. Also found in English* suburb *and* urban.

usurious (adjective)   Lending money at an unconscionably high interest rate. *Some people feel that Shakespeare's portrayal of the Jew, Shylock, the usurious money lender in* The Merchant of Venice, *has enflamed prejudice against the Jews.* usury (adjective).

validate (verb)   To officially approve or confirm. *The election of the president is formally validated when the members of the Electoral College meet to confirm the verdict of the voters.* valid (adjective), validity (noun).

Word Origin

Latin validus = *strong. Also found in English* invalid, invaluable, prevail, *and* value.

vapid (adjective)   Flat, flavorless. *Whenever I have insomnia, I just tune the clock radio to Lite FM, and soon those vapid songs from the seventies have me floating away to dreamland.* vapidity (noun).

venal (adjective)   Corrupt, mercenary. *Sese Seko Mobuto was the venal dictator of Zaire who reportedly diverted millions of dollars in foreign aid to his own personal fortune.* venality (noun).

veneer (noun)   A superficial or deceptive covering. *Beneath her folksy veneer, Samantha is a shrewd and calculating businessperson just waiting for the right moment to pounce.*

venerate (verb)   To admire or honor. *In Communist China, Mao Tse-Tung is venerated as an almost godlike figure.* venerable (adjective), veneration (noun).

veracious (adjective)   Truthful, earnest. *Many people still feel that Anita Hill was entirely veracious in her allegations of sexual harassment during the Clarence Thomas confirmation hearings.* veracity (noun).

verify (verb) To prove to be true. *The contents of Robert L. Ripley's syndicated "Believe it or Not" cartoons could not be verified, yet the public still thrilled to reports of "the man with two pupils in each eye," "the human unicorn," and other amazing oddities.* verification (noun).

veritable (adjective) Authentic. *A French antiques dealer recently claimed that a fifteenth-century child-sized suit of armor that he purchased in 1994 is the veritable suit of armor worn by heroine Joan of Arc.*

vindictive (adjective) Spiteful. *Paula embarked on a string of petty, vindictive acts against her philandering boyfriend, such as mixing dry cat food with his cereal and snipping the blooms off his prize African violets.*

viscid (adjective) Sticky. *The 3M company's "Post-It," a simple piece of paper with one viscid side, has become as commonplace—and as indispensable—as the paper clip.*

viscous (adjective) Having a gelatinous or gooey quality. *I put too much liquid in the batter, and so my Black Forest cake turned out to be a viscous, inedible mass.*

vitiate (verb) To pollute, to impair. *When they voted to ban smoking from all bars in California, the public affirmed their belief that smoking vitiates the health of all people, not just smokers.*

vituperative (adjective) Verbally abusive, insulting. *Elizabeth Taylor won an award for her harrowing portrayal of Martha, the bitter, vituperative wife of a college professor in Edward Albee's* Who's Afraid of Virginia Woolf? vituperate (verb).

volatile (adjective) Quickly changing; fleeting, transitory; prone to violence. *Public opinion is notoriously volatile; a politician who is very popular one month may be voted out of office the next.* volatility (noun).

volubility (noun) Quality of being overly talkative, glib. *As Lorraine's anxiety increased, her volubility increased in direct proportion, so during her job interview the poor interviewer couldn't get a word in edgewise.* voluble (adjective).

voracious (adjective) Gluttonous, ravenous. *"Are all your appetites so voracious?" Wesley asked Nina as he watched her finish off seven miniature sandwiches and two lamb kabob skewers in a matter of minutes.* voracity (noun).

wag (noun) wit, joker. *Tom was getting tired of his role as the comical wag who injected life into Kathy's otherwise tedious parties.* waggish (adjective).

whimsical (adjective) Based on a capricious, carefree, or sudden impulse or idea; fanciful, playful. *Dave Barry's* Book of Bad Songs *is filled with the kind of goofy jokes that are typical of his whimsical sense of humor.* whim (noun).

xenophobia (noun) Fear of foreigners or outsiders. *Slobodan Milosevic's nationalistic talk played on the deep xenophobia of the Serbs, who after 500 years of brutal Ottoman occupation had come to distrust all outsiders.*

zenith (noun) Highest point. *Compiling the vocabulary list for* the Insider's Guide to the GRE *was the zenith of my literary career: after this, there was nowhere to go but downhill.*

Appendix B

The Insider's GRE Math Review

Perhaps more than any other subject, math creates a gulf between classes of students. Generally, speaking, there are students who think of themselves as "good at math," who do well in all the usual math subjects and often take advanced classes in their junior and senior years of high school. They may go on to major in math-intensive college subjects like chemistry, biology, economics, or engineering.

Then there are the others, more numerous, who are a little afraid of math. In high school they take only those math classes they are required to take and breathe a sigh of relief when they pass. They're more likely to major in the humanities, history, or any other field where the only numbers involved are the prices of textbooks.

Here's the good news. The test-makers know that the GRE will be taken by hundreds of thousands of students in both categories. *They've deliberately designed the exam to be fair to both.* As a result, many of the math topics that some students find most intimidating—such as trigonometry and calculus—do not appear on the test. Since many students are never exposed to these subjects, the test-makers wouldn't consider it fair to test them. Instead, they restrict their questions to topics that virtually all high school students study in the ninth and tenth grades.

This doesn't mean that all of the GRE math questions are easy. But it does mean that it's highly unlikely that you'll be tested on any topic you never learned in high school. Of course, if you haven't studied math in the years since then, you may have some serious catching up to do. But at least you have this comfort: You knew all this stuff once; now all you have to do is remember it. This appendix is designed to help.

In the Insider's GRE Math Review, we've selected the fifty math topics most frequently tested on the exam. For each, we've created a mini-lesson reviewing the basic facts, formulas, and concepts you need to know. We've also provided an example or two of how these concepts might be turned into test questions.

You'll probably find that you are comfortable with many of the topics included in the "Nifty Fifty" that follow. If so, great. Make a note of the other topics—the ones you find confusing, tricky, or difficult. Perhaps you never quite mastered those concepts when they were presented in class, or you've forgotten the details in the intervening years. In your study between now and the day of the GRE, concentrate on reviewing and practicing these topics. You can boost your GRE math score significantly by mastering as many of your personal "math demons" as possible.

ARITHMETIC

FYI

When a number line is shown on the GRE, you can safely assume that the line is drawn to scale and that any numbers that fall between the markings are at the appropriate locations. Thus, 2.5 is halfway between 2 and 3, and −0.4 is four-tenths of the way from 0 to −1 (closer to 0). However, always check the scale, because the "tick marks" do not have to be at unit intervals!

Topic 1. Numbers and the Number Line

We can think of the real numbers as points on a line. Usually, we draw a horizontal line, with one point chosen to represent zero. All the positive numbers are to the right of zero, and all the negative numbers are to the left. The numbers get larger as you go from left to right.

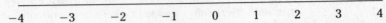

The further you get from zero, the larger the *absolute value* of a number. The absolute value of a number is the number without its sign; it can be thought of as the number's distance from zero. So numbers far to the left on the number line are negative numbers with large absolute values. Remember, in comparing negative numbers, the one with the *larger* absolute value is the *smaller* number!

Example 1

On the number line shown below, where is the number that is less than D and half as far from D as D is from G?

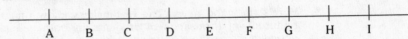

Solution

First, any number less than D must lie to the left of D. (Get it? Left = Less!) The distance from D to G is 3 units. Thus, the point we want must be $1\frac{1}{2}$ units to the left of D; that is, halfway between B and C.

Example 2

On the number line shown below, which point corresponds to the number 2.27?

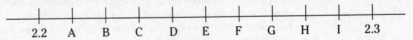

Solution

Since the labeled end points are 2.2 and 2.3, the ten intervals between must each represent one tenth of the difference. Hence the "tick marks" must represent hundredths. That is, $A = 2.21$, $B = 2.22$, and so on. Thus, we know that $G = 2.27$.

Topic 2. Laws of Arithmetic and Order of Operations

In carrying out arithmetic or algebraic operations, you should use the famous mnemonic device Please Excuse My Dear Aunt Sally. The operations of Powers, Exponents Multiplication, Division, Addition, and Subtraction should be carried out in that order, reading from left to right. If we want to indicate a change in the order of operations, we place the operation in parentheses, creating one number. In other words, calculate the number in parentheses first.

Thus, $16 - 3 \times 4 = 16 - 12 = 4$, because we multiply before adding. If we want the number $16 - 3$ to be multiplied by 4, we must write $(16 - 3) \times 4 = 13 \times 4 = 52$.

The basic laws of arithmetic were defined for whole numbers but carry over to all numbers. You should know all of them from past experience. They are:

- **The commutative law.** This says that it doesn't matter in which order you add or multiply two numbers. That is, $a + b = b + a$ and $ab = ba$.

- **The associative law** (also called *the Regrouping law*). This law says that it doesn't matter how you group the numbers when you add or multiply more than two. That is, $a + (b + c) = (a + b) + c$, and $a(bc) = (ab)c$. Remember, enclosing the numbers in parentheses indicates that the operation within the parentheses should be done first.

- **The distributive law** for multiplication over addition. This law can be stated as $a(b + c) = ab + ac$, which means that you can add first and then multiply, or multiply each term in the sum by a and then add the results. It doesn't matter which you choose—the value of the answer will be the same.

- **The properties of zero and one.** Zero times any number is zero. Zero added to any number leaves the number unchanged. One times any number leaves the number unchanged. Finally, it is very important to know that if the product of several numbers is zero, at least one of the numbers must be zero.

- **The additive inverse** (or opposite). For every number n, there is a number $-n$ such that $n + (-n) = 0$.

- **The multiplicative inverse.** For every number n except 0, there exists a number $\frac{1}{n}$ such that $\left(\frac{1}{n}\right)(n) = 1$. Division by n is the same as multiplication by $\frac{1}{n}$, and *division by zero is never allowed*.

Example

What is the value of $\frac{3 + B}{4 \cdot 3 - 3B}$ if $B = 3$? What value may B NOT have?

Solution

The fraction bar in a fraction acts as a "grouping symbol" like parentheses, meaning that we should calculate the numerator and denominator separately. That is, we should read this as $(3 + B) \div (4 \times 3 - 3 \times B)$. When $B = 3$, the numerator is $3 + 3 = 6$ and the denominator is $12 - 3 \times 3 = 12 - 9 = 3$. Therefore, the fraction is $\frac{6}{3} = 2$. Since we cannot divide by zero, we cannot let $4 \times 3 - 3 \times B = 0$. But in order for this to be zero, $4 \times 3 = 3 \times B$. By the commutative law, $B = 4$. Thus, the only value that B cannot have is 4.

Topic 3. Divisibility Rules

A *factor* or *divisor* of a whole number is a number that divides evenly into the given number, leaving no remainder. For example, the divisors of 24 are 1, 2, 3, 4, 6, 8, 12, and 24 itself. A *proper divisor* is any divisor except the number itself. Thus, the proper divisors of 24 are 1, 2, 3, 4, 6, 8, and 12.

If you want to know whether k is a divisor of n, just try to divide n by k and see whether there is any remainder. If the remainder is zero, then n is divisible by k. However, there are several useful rules for testing for divisibility for certain small numbers. These are summarized in Table B.1.

Appendix B

Table B.1
Rules for Testing Divisibility

Number	Is Divisible by a Number N if . . .
2	N is even; that is, its last digit is 2, 4, 6, 8, or 0.
3	The sum of the digits of N is divisible by 3.
4	The last two digits form a number divisible by 4.
5	The number's last digit is 5 or 0.
6	The number is divisible by 2 and 3.
8	The last three digits form a number divisible by 8.
9	The sum of the digits of N is divisible by 9.
10	The number's last digit is 0.

For example, consider the number 7,380. It is divisible by all the numbers in the table except 8. Do you see why? To start, 7,380 is divisible by 10 and 5 because the last digit is 0. It is divisible by 2 because it is even, and by 4 because 80 is divisible by 4. However, it is not divisible by 8 because 380 isn't. In addition, the sum of its digits is 18, which is divisible by 3 and by 9. Since it is divisible by both 2 and 3, it is also divisible by 6.

Example
Which numbers in the following list are divisible by 3, 4, and 5 but not by 9?

    15,840
    20,085
    23,096
    53,700
    79,130

Solution
The easiest thing to look for is divisibility by 5. Is the last digit 5 or 0? By inspection, we eliminate 23,096, whose last digit is 6. We want the number to be divisible by 4, which means it must be even and its last two digits must form a number divisible by 4. That knocks out the one ending in 5 (which is odd), and 79,130, because 30 is not divisible by 4. This leaves 15,840 and 53,700. The digits of 15,840 add up to 18, while those of 53,700 total 15. Both are divisible by 3, but 15,840 is also divisible by 9. Therefore, only 53,700 meets all the conditions.

Topic 4. Divisibility in Addition, Subtraction, and Multiplication

If you add or subtract two numbers that are both divisible by some number k, then the new number formed will also be divisible by k. Thus, 28 and 16 are both divisible by 4. If you take either their sum, 44, or their difference, 12, they too are divisible by 4.

If you multiply two numbers together, any number that divides either one divides the product. If j divides M and k divides N, then jk divides MN. If both have a common divisor, then the product is divisible by the square of that number. Thus, $21 \times 15 = 315$ is divisible by 7, because 7 divides 21, and by 5, because 5 divides 15. It is also divisible by $35 = 5 \times 7$, and by 9, because $9 = 3^2$, and 3 divides both 21 and 15!

Peterson's ■ *The Insider's Guide to the GRE CAT*

Example 1
If *m* is divisible by 5, what is the largest number that divides 5*m* + 25?

Solution
Since *m* is divisible by 5, 5*m* can be divided by 25. Therefore, the sum 5*m* + 25 can be divided by 25.

Example 2
If *a* and *b* are whole numbers, and 3*a* = 2*b*, which of the following must be true?

    I.   *a* is divisible by 2
    II.   *b* is divisible by 2
    III.   *b* is divisible by 3

    (A)   I only
    (B)   II only
    (C)   III only
    (D)   I and II only
    (E)   I and III only

Solution
If 3*a* equals 2*b*, then 3*a* must be divisible by 2, which means *a* must be divisible by 2, since 3 is not. Similarly, 2*b* must be divisible by 3, which means *b* must be divisible by 3, since 2 is not. Thus, the correct answer is (E)—both I and III must be true. Notice that II need not be true; since *b* = 3, *a* = 2 is a perfectly satisfactory solution.

Topic 5. Even Numbers and Odd Numbers

Even numbers are those that are divisible by 2: 0, 2, 4, 6, ... *Odd numbers* are those that are not divisible by 2: 1, 3, 5, ... Certain simple results follow from these definitions, and they can be very useful. They are as follows:

- If you add or subtract two even numbers, the result is even.
- If you add or subtract two odd numbers, the result is even.
- Only when you *add or subtract* an *odd number* and an *even* number is the result odd. Thus, 4 + 6 is even, as is 7 − 3. But 4 + 3 is odd.
- When you multiply any whole number by an even number, the result is even.
- Only when you *multiply two odd numbers* will the result be odd. Again, (4)(6) and (4)(7) are both even, but (3)(7) is odd.

Example 1
If 3*x* + 4*y* is an odd number, is *x* odd or even—or can't you tell?

FYI

Notice—you should think of zero as an even number.

Solution
4*y* must be even, so for the sum of 3*x* and 4*y* to be odd, 3*x* must be odd. Since 3 is odd, 3*x* will be odd only if *x* is odd. Hence, *x* is odd.

Example 2
If $121 - 5k$ is divisible by 3, can k be odd?

Solution
The fact that a number is divisible by 3 does not make it odd. (Think of 6 or 12.) Therefore, $121 - 5k$ could be either odd or even. It will be odd when k is even and even when k is odd. (Do you see why?) Thus, k could be odd or even. For example, if $k = 2$, $121 - 5k = 111$, which is divisible by 3; if $k = 5$, $121 - 5k = 96$, which is divisible by 3.

Topic 6. Comparing Fractions

Two fractions $\frac{a}{b}$ and $\frac{c}{d}$ are defined to be equal if $ad = bc$. For example, $\frac{3}{4} = \frac{9}{12}$ because $(3)(12) = (4)(9)$. This definition, using *cross-multiplication,* is very useful in solving algebraic equations involving fractions. However, for working with numbers, the important thing to remember is that multiplying the *numerator* (top) and the *denominator* (bottom) of a fraction by the same number (other than zero) results in a fraction equal in value to the original fraction. Thus, by

multiplying the numerator and the denominator by 3, we have $\frac{3}{4} = \frac{(3)(3)}{(3)(4)} = \frac{9}{12}$.

Similarly, dividing the numerator and denominator of a fraction by the same number (other than zero) results in a fraction equal in value to the original fraction. It is usual to divide through the numerator and the denominator by the greatest common factor of both the numerator and the denominator to "simplify the fraction to simplist form." Thus, by dividing numerator and denominator by

5, we have $\frac{15}{25} = \frac{15 \div 5}{25 \div 5} = \frac{3}{5}$.

For positive numbers, if two fractions have the same denominator, the one with the greater numerator is greater. If two fractions have the same numerator, the one with the least denominator is the greater one. For example, $\frac{5}{19}$ is less than

$\frac{8}{19}$, but $\frac{8}{17}$ is greater than $\frac{8}{19}$.

Example 1
If b and c are both positive whole numbers greater than 1, and $\frac{5}{c} = \frac{b}{3}$, what are

b and c?

Solution
Using cross-multiplication, $bc = 15$. The only ways 15 can be the product of two positive integers is as $(1)(15)$ or $(3)(5)$. Since both b and c must be greater than 1, one must be 3 and the other 5. Trying both cases, it is easy to see that the only possibility is that $b = 3$ and $c = 5$, and both fractions are equal to 1.

Example 2
Which is greater, $\frac{4}{7}$ or $\frac{3}{5}$?

Solution

The first fraction has a greater numerator, but it also has a greater denominator, so we rewrite both with the common denominator 35 by multiplying the numerator and denominator of $\frac{4}{7}$ by 5 and the numerator and denominator of $\frac{3}{5}$ by 7, to yield $\frac{20}{35}$ and $\frac{21}{35}$, respectively. Now it is easy to see that $\frac{3}{5}$ is the greater fraction.

Example 3

Which is larger, $\frac{-6}{11}$ or $\frac{13}{-22}$?

Solution: First of all, it does not matter where you put the negative sign—numerator, denominator, or opposite the fraction bar; if there is one negative sign, the fraction is negative. Remember, in comparing negative numbers, the one with the greater absolute value is the least number. So start by ignoring the signs, and compare the absolute values of the fractions. If the two fractions had a common denominator (or numerator), it would be easy. So multiply the numerator and denominator of $\frac{6}{11}$ by 2 to yield $\frac{12}{22}$ and it is easy to see that $\frac{13}{22}$ is the greater fraction. Hence, $\frac{-6}{11}$ is the greater number.

Topic 7. Multiplication and Division of Fractions

FYI

In word problems, of can usually be interpreted to mean times *(that is, multiply).*

When multiplying two fractions, the result is the product of the numerators divided by the product of the denominators. In symbols, $\frac{a}{b} \cdot \frac{c}{d} = \frac{ac}{bd}$. Thus, $\frac{3}{7} \cdot \frac{2}{5} = \frac{6}{35}$. Don't forget that the resulting fraction can be simplified to simplest form by dividing common factors in both the numerator and denominator, such as $\frac{3}{5} \cdot \frac{10}{9} = \frac{2}{3}$.

Example 1

Jasmine earns $\frac{3}{4}$ of what Sidney earns, and Sidney earns $\frac{2}{3}$ of what Paul earns. What fraction of Paul's salary does Jasmine earn?

Solution

Using J, S, and P to stand for the people's earnings respectively, we have:

$$S = \frac{2}{3}P; J = \frac{3}{4}S$$

Thus, $P = \frac{3}{2}S$, and $S = \frac{4}{3}J$. So $P = \left(\frac{3}{2}\right)\left(\frac{4}{3}\right)J$; $P = \left(\frac{12}{6}\right)J$, which means that P is twice J. Hence, Jasmine's earnings are one-half Paul's.

When dividing fractions, simply multiply by the reciprocal of the divisor. Remember, the *divisor* is the number you are dividing by (usually the second one named), or the denominator in a "built-up" fraction. In symbols:

$$\frac{a}{b} \div \frac{c}{d} = \frac{a}{b} \cdot \frac{d}{c} = \frac{ad}{bc}$$

or:

$$\frac{\dfrac{a}{b}}{\dfrac{c}{d}} = \frac{a}{b} \cdot \frac{d}{c} = \frac{ad}{bc}$$

For example:

$$\frac{3}{5} \div \frac{4}{11} = \frac{3}{5} \cdot \frac{11}{4} = \frac{33}{20}$$

Example 2

Patty has half as many pairs of jeans as Alfred has, and Marco has $\frac{3}{5}$ as many pairs of jeans as Alfred. What fraction of Marco's number of pairs does Patty have?

Solution

Using P, A, and M to stand for the number of jeans each person owns respectively, we have

$$P = \frac{1}{2}A; \; M = \frac{3}{5}A$$

thus,

$$\frac{P}{M} = \frac{\dfrac{1}{2}A}{\dfrac{3}{5}A} = \frac{1}{2} \cdot \frac{5}{3} = \frac{5}{6}$$

Thus, Patty has $\frac{5}{6}$ as many pairs as Marco.

Topic 8. Addition and Subtraction of Fractions

FYI

If you are rushed, you can always find a common denominator by just taking the product of the two denominators. For example, to add fractions whose denominators are 12 and 8, multiply: 12 × 8 = 96 is a common denominator. Maybe not as efficient—but guaranteed to work!

To add (or subtract) fractions with the same denominator, simply add (or subtract) the numerators. For example, $\frac{5}{17} + \frac{3}{17} = \frac{8}{17}$ and $\frac{5}{17} - \frac{3}{17} = \frac{2}{17}$. However, if the denominators are different, you must first rewrite the fractions so they will have the same denominator. That is, you must find a *common denominator*. Most books stress that you should use the *least common denominator* (LCD), which is the least common multiple (LCM) of the original denominators. This will keep the numbers smaller. However, any common denominator will do!

To find the least common denominator, you must first understand what a least common multiple is. Given two numbers M and N, any number that is divisible by both is called a *common multiple* of M and N. The least common multiple (LCM) of the two numbers is the least number that is divisible by both. For example, 108 is divisible by both 9 and 12, so 108 is a common multiple—but the LCM is 36.

For small numbers, the easiest way to find the LCM is to mentally, or in writing, list the multiples of each until you find the first common (or shared) multiple. For example, for 9 and 12 we have:

$$9 \quad 18 \quad 27 \quad \underline{36} \quad 45 \quad \dots$$
$$12 \quad 24 \quad \underline{36} \quad 48 \quad 60 \quad \dots$$

We see that the first number that appears in both lists is 36. However, the traditional method, which is really the method that translates most readily into algebra, requires that you find the *prime factorization* of the numbers.

Every whole number is either *prime* or *composite*. A prime is a whole number greater than 1 which has exactly two factors (divisors) namely 1 and the number itself. All numbers that are not prime are composite. Every composite number can be factored into primes in a unique way.

To find an LCM by the method of prime factorization, you must find the least number that contains all the factors of both numbers. Thus, 9 factors as (3)(3), and 12 factors as (2)(2)(3). The least number to use all the prime factors of both has to have factors (3)(3)(2)(2) = 36.

This process can also extend to sets of more than two numbers. Thus, the LCM of 12, 15, and 20 must contain all the prime factors of all three numbers: (2)(2)(3), (3)(5), (2)(2)(5). That is, (2)(2)(3)(5) = 60.

Example 1
Find the LCM for 18 and 30.

Solution
Using prime factorization, 18 = (2)(3)(3); 30 = (2)(3)(5). Since the factors of 2 and 3 are common to both numbers, we need only multiply in one extra 3 to get the factors of 18, and a 5 to get the factors of 30. Thus, the LCM = (2)(3)(3)(5) = 90.

Example 2
Mario figures that, working every day, he could finish a certain task in 20 days. Angelo figures that, working every day, he could finish the same task in 25 days. What fraction of the task could they get done by working on it together for seven days?

FYI

In Example 2, we have to add two fractions that have the same numerator. Can we add them directly by just summing the denominators? No! To add directly, it is the denominators that must be the same!

Solution

In 7 days, Mario would do $\frac{7}{20}$ of the entire task. In the same week, Angelo would do $\frac{7}{25}$ of the entire task. Therefore, together they do $\frac{7}{20} + \frac{7}{25}$ of the entire task.

To add these two fractions, we must find a common denominator. Find the LCD, which is 100. Thus, $\frac{35}{100} + \frac{28}{100} = \frac{63}{100} = 0.63$ or 63%.

Do you understand those last two equalities? If not, read the next section carefully.

Topic 9. Fractions, Decimals, and Percents

Every fraction can be expressed as a decimal, which can be found by division. Those fractions for which the prime factorization of the denominator involves only 2s and 5s will have terminating decimal expansions. All others will have repeating decimal expansions. For example, $\frac{3}{20} = 0.15$, and $\frac{3}{11} = 0.27272727 \ldots$

To rename a number given as a decimal as a fraction, you must know what the decimal means. In general, the decimal represents a fraction with denominator 10, or 100, or 1000, . . . , where the number of zeros is equal to the number of digits to the right of the decimal point. Thus, for example:

$$0.4 \text{ means } \frac{4}{10} = \frac{2}{5};$$

$$0.52 \text{ means } \frac{52}{100} = \frac{13}{25}; \text{ and}$$

$$0.103 \text{ means } \frac{103}{1000}.$$

Decimals of the form 3.25 are equivalent to *mixed numbers*, thus, $3.25 = 3 + \frac{25}{100} = 3 + \frac{1}{4} = 3\frac{1}{4}$. For purposes of addition and subtraction, mixed numbers can be useful, but for purposes of multiplication or division, it is usually better to rename a mixed number as an *improper fraction* (one whose numerator is larger than its denominator). That is, $2\frac{3}{20} = \frac{43}{20}$.

How did we do that? Formally, we realize that $2 = \frac{2}{1}$, and we add the two fractions $\frac{2}{1}$ and $\frac{3}{20}$ using the common denominator 20. More simply, we multiply the whole number part (2) by the common denominator (20), and add the numerator of the fraction (3) to get the numerator of the resulting improper fraction. That is, $(2)(20) + 3 = 43$.

FYI

Any repeating decimal can be written as the repeating portion divided by an equal number of 9s. Thus,

$0.333333\ldots = \dfrac{3}{9} = \dfrac{1}{3}$,

$0.279279279\ldots = \dfrac{279}{999} = \dfrac{31}{111}$,

$2.636363\ldots = 2 + \dfrac{63}{99} = 2\dfrac{7}{11} = \dfrac{29}{11}$.

FYI

To rename a number given as a percent as decimal form, simply move the decimal point two places to the left. To rename decimals as percents, reverse the process, that is, move the decimal point two places to the right. To avoid confusion, keep in mind that, written as a percent, the number should look greater. Thus, the "large" number 45% is 0.45, and the "small" number 0.73 is 73%.

Example 1

If $\dfrac{0.56}{1.26}$ simplified to simplest form is $\dfrac{a}{b}$, where a and b are positive whole numbers, what is b?

Solution

Rewriting both numerator and denominator as their fractional equivalents, $0.56 = \dfrac{56}{100} = \dfrac{14}{25}$, and $1.26 = 1 + \dfrac{26}{100} = 1\dfrac{13}{50} = \dfrac{63}{50}$. We now accomplish the division by multiplying by the reciprocal of the divisor. Thus, $\left(\dfrac{14}{25}\right)\left(\dfrac{50}{63}\right) = \dfrac{4}{9}$ and $b = 9$.

Of course, you could also do this example by renaming the numerator and denominator of the original fraction as whole numbers. That is, multiply numerator and denominator by 100 to move both decimal points two places to the right, thus: $\dfrac{0.56}{1.26} = \dfrac{56}{126}$. Now you can divide out the common factor of 14 in the numerator and the denominator to simplify the fraction to $\dfrac{4}{9}$.

Notice that by using long division or dividing on a calculator you will find that $\dfrac{0.56}{1.26} = 0.4444444\ldots$, which you might recognize as $\dfrac{4}{9}$.

Remember, per *cent* means per *hundred* (from Latin *centum* = hundred). So, for example, 30% means 30 per hundred, or, as a fraction, $\dfrac{30}{100}$, or, as a decimal, 0.30.

Example 2

In a group of 20 English majors and 30 history majors, 50% of the English majors and 20% of the history majors have NOT taken a college math course. What percent of the entire group have taken a college math course?

Solution

Start with English. Since 50% = 0.50, 50% of 20 = (0.50)(20) = 10. For history, 20% = 0.20, 20% of 30 = (0.20)(30) = 6. Hence, a total of 16 out of 50 people in the group have not taken math, which means that 34 have. As a fraction, 34 out of 50 is $\dfrac{34}{50} = 0.68 = 68\%$.

ALGEBRA

Topic 10. Addition and Subtraction of Signed Numbers

To add two numbers of the same sign, just add them and attach their common sign. So $7 + 9 = 16$, and $(-7) + (-9) = -16$. You could drop the parentheses and instead of $(-7) + (-9)$ you could write $-7 - 9$, which means the same thing. In other words, adding a negative number is the same thing as subtracting a positive number!

When adding numbers of opposite sign, temporarily ignore the signs, subtract the lesser from the greater, and attach to the result the sign of the number with the greater absolute value. Thus, $9 + (-3) = 6$, but $(-9) + 3 = -6$. Again, we could have written $9 + (-3) = 9 - 3 = 6$, and $(-9) + 3 = -9 + 3 = -6$.

When subtracting, change the sign of the "second" number (the *subtrahend*), and then use the rules for addition. Thus, $7 - (-3) = 7 + 3 = 10$, and $-7 - 3 = -7 + (-3) = -10$.

Example

Evaluate $-A - (-B)$ when $A = -5$ and $B = -6$.

Solution

All the negative signs can be confusing. However, if you remember that "minus a negative is a plus", you can do this in two ways. The first is to realize that, if $B = -6$, then $-B = +6$, and if $A = -5$, then $-A = 5$ Thus, $-A - (-B) = 5 - 6 = -1$. Alternatively, you can work with the variables first: $-A - (-B) = -A + B = -(-5) + (-6) = 5 - 6 = -1$.

Topic 11. Multiplication and Division of Signed Numbers

If you multiply two numbers with the same sign, the result is positive. If you multiply two numbers with opposite signs, the result is negative. Furthermore, the exact same rule holds for division. Thus, $(-4)(-3) = +12$, and $(-4)(3) = -12$.

For division, it doesn't matter which is negative and which positive, thus $(-6) \div (2) = -3$ and $(6) \div (-2) = -3$, but $(-6) \div (-2) = +3$.

This also means that if you have a string of multiplications and divisions to do, if the number of negative factors is *even*, the result will be *positive*; if the number of negative factors is *odd*, the result will be *negative*. Of course, if even one factor is zero, the result is zero, and if even one factor in the denominator (divisor) is zero, the result is undefined.

Example 1

If $A = (234{,}906 - 457{,}219)(35)(-618)$ and $B = (-2356)(-89{,}021)(-3125)$, which is greater, A or B?

Solution

Don't actually do the arithmetic! 457,219 is greater than 234,906, so the difference is a negative number. Now, you see that A is the product of two negative numbers and a positive number, which makes the result positive. B is the product of three negative numbers and must be negative. Any positive number is greater than any negative number, and so A is greater than B.

Example 2

If $\dfrac{AB}{MN}$ is a negative number, and N is negative, which of the following are possible?

    I. A is positive, but B and M are negative.
    II. A, B, and M are all negative.
    III. A, B, and M are positive.

    (A)   I only
    (B)   II only
    (C)   I and II only
    (D)   I and III only
    (E)   II and III only

Solution

To determine the sign of the fraction, just think of A, B, M, N as four factors. Knowing that N is negative, the product of the other three must be positive in order that the result be negative. The only possibilities are that all three are positive, or one is positive and the other two are negative. This corresponds to cases I and III. Thus, the correct answer is (D).

Topic 12. Laws of Exponents

In an expression of the form b^n, b is called the *base* and n is called the *exponent* or *power*. We say, "b is raised to the power n." Notice, $b^1 = b$, and hence the power 1 is usually omitted.

If n is any positive integer, then b^n is the product of n number of b's. For example, 4^3 is the product of three 4s, that is, $4^3 = 4 \times 4 \times 4 = 64$. Certain rules for operations with exponents are forced upon us by this definition. They are:

- $b^m \times b^n = b^{m+n}$. That is, when multiplying powers of the same base, keep the base and add the exponents. Thus, $3^2 \times 3^3 = 3^{2+3} = 3^5 = 243$.

- $(ab)^{(n)} = a^n b^n$ and $\left(\dfrac{a}{b}\right)^n = \dfrac{a^n}{b^n}$.

  That is, to raise a product or a quotient to a power, raise each factor to that power, whether that factor is in the numerator or denominator. Thus,

  $$(2x)^3 = 2^3 x^3 = 8x^3$$

  and

  $$\left(\frac{2}{x}\right)^3 = \frac{2^3}{x^3} = \frac{8}{x^3}$$

- $(b^m)^n = b^{nm}$. That is, to raise a power to a power, retain the base and multiply exponents. Thus, $(2^3)^2 = 2^6 = 64$.

- $\dfrac{b^n}{b^m} = b^{n-m}$ if $n > m$, and $\dfrac{b^n}{b^m} = \dfrac{1}{b^{m-n}}$ if $n < m$.

That is, to divide powers with the same base, retain the base and subtract exponents. For example,

$$\frac{4^5}{4^2} = 4^3 = 64$$

and

$$\frac{4^2}{4^5} = \frac{1}{4^3} = \frac{1}{64}$$

Topic 13. Zero and Negative Exponents

FYI

Commit to memory small powers of small numbers that come up in many questions. For example: The powers of 2: 2, 4, 8, 16, 32, . . . ; The powers of 3 : 3, 9, 27, 81, . . . and so on.

For various technical reasons, $x^0 = 1$ for all x except $x = 0$, in which case it is undefined. With this definition, one can define b^{-n} in such a way that all the laws of exponents given above still work even for negative powers! The definition is one that you should not only know but know how to use. It is: $b^{-n} = \dfrac{1}{b^n}$. Now you have the choice of writing $\dfrac{x^3}{x^5}$ as $\dfrac{1}{x^2}$ or as x^{-2}.

Example
Which is greater, 1.10 or $x^0 + x^{-4}$, if $x = 2$?

Solution
If $x = 2$, $x^0 = 2^0 = 1$; and $x^{-4} = 2^{-4} = \dfrac{1}{2^4} = \dfrac{1}{16} = 0.0625$. Hence, $x^0 + x^{-4} = 1.0625$, which is less than 1.10.

Topic 14. Even Powers and Odd Powers

Even powers of real numbers cannot be negative. Thus, x^2 is positive, except for $x = 0$, when it is zero. Note that -3^2 means $-(3^2) = -9$. If you want the square of -3, which equals $+9$, you must write it $(-3)^2$.

Odd powers are positive or negative depending upon whether the base is positive or negative. Thus, $2^3 = 8$, but $(-2)^3 = -8$. Zero to any power is zero, except that zero to the zero is undefined.

Example 1
If $x < 0$ and $y > 0$, what is the sign of $-4x^4y^3$?

Solution
x^4 is positive, because it has an even power. y^3 is positive because y is, and -4 is obviously negative. The product of two positives and a negative is negative. Thus, $-4x^4y^3$ is negative.

Example 2
If $x^4 + 3y^2 = 0$, what is the sign of $2x - 6y + 1$?

Solution
Since neither x^4 nor $3y^2$ can be negative, the only way their sum can be zero is if both x and y are zero. Therefore, $2x - 6y + 1 = +1$, which is positive.

FYI

The average does not have to be a number in the set. Notice, also, that to find an average, you don't have to know the individual numbers—just their total.

Topic 15. Averages

There are three common measurements used to define the predominant value—loosely thought of as the average—of a collection of numbers. However, when you see the word *average* with no other explanation, it is assumed that what is meant is the *arithmetic mean*. The average in this sense is the sum of the numbers divided by the number of numbers in the collection. In symbols, $A = \dfrac{T}{n}$.

So, for example, if on four math exams you scored 82, 76, 87, and 89, your average math score at this point is $(82 + 76 + 87 + 89) \div 4 = 334 \div 4 = 83.5$.

Example 1

At an art show, Eleanor sold six of her paintings at an average price of $70. At the next show, she sold four paintings at an average price of $100. What was the overall average price of the ten paintings?

Solution

You can't just say the answer is 85, the average of 70 and 100, because we do not have the same number of paintings in each group. We need to know the overall total. Since the first six paintings sold for an average price of $70, the total received for the 6 was $420. Do you see why? $70 = \dfrac{T}{6}$; this means $T = (6)(70) = 420$. In the same way, the next 4 paintings must have brought in $400 in order to average $100 apiece. Therefore, we have a total of 10 paintings selling for $420 + $400 = $820, and the average is $\dfrac{\$820}{10} = \$82$.

Example 2

Erica averaged 76 on her first four French exams. To get a grade of B for the course, she must have an 80 average. What grade must she get on the next exam to bring her average to 80?

Solution

If Erica's average is 76 on four exams, she must have a total of $(4)(76) = 304$. In order to average 80 on five exams, her total must be $(5)(80) = 400$. Therefore, she must score $400 - 304 = 96$ on her last exam.

The other two quantities that are sometimes used in ways similar to the average are the *median*, or the middle number when the numbers are arranged in increasing order, and the *mode*, the most common number.

Example 3

Which is greater, the mean minus the median or the median minus the mode, for the set of nine integers {1, 2, 2, 2, 3, 5, 6, 7, 8}?

Solution

The median (middle number) is 3, the mode is 2, and the mean is $(1 + 2 + 2 + 2 + 3 + 5 + 6 + 7 + 8) \div 9 = 4$. Thus, the mean minus the median is $4 - 3 = 1$. And the median minus the mode is $3 - 2 = 1$. Thus, the two quantities are equal.

Topic 16. Measures of Dispersion

In analyzing data, in addition to trying to measure average value, it is also important to measure the dispersion or "spread" of the numbers. The two sets A = {11, 12, 12, 12, 13} and B = {1, 2, 12, 17, 28}, both have the same average (12), but they have considerably different spreads. The amount of dispersion clearly has a major impact on how one interprets the significance of the data.

The simplest way to measure the dispersion is to look at the *range*. The range is the difference between the greatest and least values in the set. Thus, for set A, the range is 13 − 11 = 2, while for B it is 28 − 1 = 27.

A more complicated and more widely used measure is the *standard deviation*, which is the square root of the average squared deviation from the mean. To compute the standard deviation, follow these steps:

1. Find the mean.
2. For each data point, subtract the mean from the data value and square the result.
3. Average the squares you have just found.
4. Take the square root of the result.

Example
Find the standard deviations for sets A and B above.

Solution
For set A, the average is 12. For the five values, the differences when you subtract 12 from each are −1, 0, 0, 0, and 1. Their squares are 1, 0, 0, 0, and 1. The average of these numbers is 2 ÷ 5 = 0.4, and the standard deviation is about 0.63 (since the square root of 0.4 is close to 0.63).

For set B, the average is also 12, but the differences when you subtract 12 from each data point are −11, −10, 0, 5, and 16. Their squares are 121, 100, 0, 25, and 256. The average of these numbers is 502 ÷ 5 = 100.4, and the standard deviation is around 10.02. Quite a difference!

Topic 17. Ratio and Proportion

A fractional relationship between two quantities is frequently expressed as a *ratio*. It can be written as a fraction or in the form *b:a* (read "*b* is to *a*"). A *proportion* is a statement that two ratios are equal. To say, for example, that the ratio of passing to failing students in a class is 5:2 means that if we set up the fraction $\frac{P}{F}$ it should simplify to $\frac{5}{2}$. If we write this statement as *P:F* :: 5:2, we read it "*P* is to *F* as 5 is to 2," and it means $\frac{P}{F} = \frac{5}{2}$.

Often, a good way to work with information given in ratio form is to represent the actual numbers as multiples of the same number.

Example

The ratio of Democrats to Republicans in a state legislature is 5:7. If the Legislature has 156 members, all of whom are either Democrats or Republicans (but not both), what is the difference between the number of Republicans and the number of Democrats?

(A) 14
(B) 26
(C) 35
(D) 37
(E) 46

Solution

Let the number of Democrats be $5m$ and the number of Republicans be $7m$, so that $D{:}R :: 5m{:}7m = 5{:}7$. The total number of members is $5m + 7m = 12m$, which must be 156. Therefore, $12m = 156$, and $m = 13$. Of course, the difference is $7m - 5m = 2m = 2(13) = 26$. Hence, the answer is choice (B).

Topic 18. Solving Linear Equations

To solve a linear equation, remember these rules:

- You can add or subtract the same quantity from both sides of an equation and the equation will still be true and have the same roots (i.e., possible values).

- You can multiply or divide both sides of an equation by any number *except zero* and the equation will still be true and have the same roots.

Use these two properties to isolate the unknown quantity on one side of the equation, leaving only known quantities on the other side. This is known as *solving for the unknown.*

Example 1

If $14 = 3x - 1$ and $B = 6x + 4$, what is the numerical value of B?

Solution

From the first equation, $3x - 1 = 14$. Adding 1 to both sides:

$$
\begin{array}{r}
3x - 1 = 14 \\
1 = 1 \\
\hline
3x \quad\; = 15
\end{array}
$$

Dividing both sides by 3: $x = 5$.

Of course, the question asked for B, not x. So we substitute $x = 5$ into $B = 6x + 4$ and get $B = 6(5) + 4 = 34$.

Example 2

If $\dfrac{2x}{3} + 2 = a$, and $y = 2x + 6$, find an expression for y in terms of a.

Solution

How do we solve this? We realize that, if we knew what x was in terms of a, then we could substitute that expression for x into $y = 2x + 6$ and have y in terms of a.

In other words, we want to solve $\dfrac{2x}{3} + 2 = a$ for x.

Multiply both sides by 3 to clear the fractions. Be careful: when you multiply by 3, be sure to use the distributive law and multiply *every term* on both sides by 3. You should now have $2x + 6 = 3a$. Now add -6 to both sides of the equation:

$$\begin{aligned} 2x + 6 &= 3a \\ -6 &= -6 \\ \hline 2x &= 3a - 6 \end{aligned}$$

Now divide by 2:

$$x = \frac{3a}{2} - 3$$

Substituting:

$$y = 3a - 6 + 6$$
$$y = 3a$$

Topic 19. Solving Linear Inequalities

If a number M is less than another number N, this means that $N - M$ is positive. That is, when you subtract a lesser number from a greater number, the result is positive. In symbols, $M < N$ or $N > M$. Notice that the "sense arrow" always points towards the *lesser* number.

Another way of saying this is to note that, on the number line, M lies to the left of N. This means, in particular, that any negative number is less than any positive number. It also implies that, for negative numbers, the one with the greater absolute value is the lesser number.

To solve *linear inequalities* (also called *inequations*), remember these rules:

- You can add or subtract the same quantity from both sides of an inequation, and the inequation will still be true in the same sense. Thus, $14 > 7$, and $14 - 5 > 7 - 5$.

- You can multiply or divide both sides of an inequation by any positive number and the inequation will still be true in the same sense. Thus, $3 < 8$ and $(6)(3) < (6)(8)$.

- You can multiply or divide both sides of an inequation by any negative number and the inequation will still be true, *but with the sense reversed*. Thus, $4 < 9$; but if you multiply by (–2), you get $-8 > -18$. Remember, for negative numbers, the one with the greater absolute value is the lesser number.

Notice that these rules hold whether you are working with $<$ (is less than) and $>$ (is greater than) or $\leq$ (is less than or equal to) and $\geq$ (is greater than or equal to). You can use these rules to isolate the unknown quantity on one side of the inequality, leaving only known quantities on the other side. This is known as *solving for the unknown*.

Example 1
For what values of x is $12 - x \geq 3x + 8$?

Solution
We solve this just like an equation. Start by adding the like quantity $(x - 8)$ to both sides in order to group the x terms on one side and the constants on the other; thus:

$$12 - x \geq 3x + 8$$
$$\underline{x - 8 = x - 8}$$
$$4 \geq 4x$$

Now divide by 4, which does not change the sense of the inequality, yielding:

$$1 \geq x$$

Hence, the inequality will be true for any value of x less than or equal to 1 and false for any number greater than 1. For example, for $x = 3$, $12 - x = 9$, and $3x + 8 = 17$, and the inequality is *not* satisfied.

Example 2
If $A < 2 - 4B$, can you tell how large B is in terms of A? Can you tell how small B is?

Solution
We are really being asked to solve the inequality for B. To start, we add -2 to both sides, thus:

$$A \quad\quad < 2 - 4B$$
$$\underline{-2 = -2}$$
$$A - 2 < -4B$$

Next, divide by -4, remembering to reverse the inequality, thus:

$$\frac{(A - 2)}{-4} > B$$
$$\frac{(2 - A)}{4} > B$$

Notice two things here. When we changed the denominator on the left side from -4 to $+4$, we also changed the sign of the numerator by changing $(A - 2)$ to $(2 - A)$. Of course, what we really did, in effect, was to multiply numerator and denominator by -1.

Also, this tells us what B is *less than* but tells us nothing about what B might be *greater than*. For example, if A were 6, then $B < -1$, but B could be -100 or -1000 or anything more negative.

Topic 20. Solving Two Linear Equations in Two Unknowns

Many word problems lead to equations in two unknowns. Usually, one needs as many equations as there are unknowns to solve for all or some of the unknowns, but there are exceptions.

You should know two methods for solving two equations in two unknowns. They are the *method of substitution* and the *method of elimination by addition and subtraction*. We shall illustrate both methods by example. The first example uses the method of substitution.

Example 1

Mrs. Green and her three children went to the local movie. The total cost of their admission tickets was $14. Mr. and Mrs. Arkwright and their five children went to the same movie and had to pay $25. What was the cost of an adult ticket and what was the cost of a child's ticket?

Solution

Expressing all amounts in dollars, let x = cost of an adult ticket, and let y = cost of a child's ticket. For the Greens:

$$x + 3y = 14$$

For the Arkwrights:

$$2x + 5y = 25$$

The idea of the method of substitution is to solve one equation for one variable in terms of the other, and then substitute this solution into the second equation. So we solve the first equation for x, because that is the simpler unknown to isolate:

$$x = 14 - 3y$$

And substitute this solution into the second equation:

$$2(14 - 3y) + 5y = 25$$

This gives us one equation in one unknown that we can solve:

$$28 - 6y + 5y = 25$$
$$-y = -3$$
$$y = 3$$

Now that we know that $y = 3$, we put this into $x = 14 - 3y$ to get:

$$x = 14 - 3(3) = 5$$

Thus, the adult tickets were $5 each, and the children's tickets were $3 each.

Following is an example using the method of elimination.

Example 2

Paula and Dennis both went to the bakery. Paula bought 3 rolls and 5 muffins for a total cost of $3.55. Dennis bought 6 rolls and 2 muffins for a total cost of $3.10. What is the price of one roll?

Solution

Let us express all amounts in cents. Let r = cost of a roll; let m = cost of a muffin. Paula paid $3r + 5m = 355$; Dennis paid $6r + 2m = 310$.

The idea of the method of elimination is that adding equal quantities to equal quantities gives a true result. So we want to add some multiple of one equation to the other one so that, when we sum the two equations, one variable will be eliminated. In this case, it is not hard to see that if we multiply the first equation by -2, the coefficient of r will become -6. Now, if we add the two equations, r will drop out.

-2 times the first equation is:

$$-6r - 10m = -710$$

The second equation is:

$$6r + 2m = 310$$

Adding the two equations:

$$-8m = -400$$

Dividing by -8: $m = 50$. We now substitute this value into either of the two equations. Let's use the second:

$$6r + (2)(50) = 310$$
$$6r = 210$$
$$r = 35$$

Thus, muffins are 50¢ each and rolls are 35¢.

Topic 21. Word Problems in One or Two Unknowns

There are word problems of many different types. Some require special knowledge. Others, like age or coin problems, involve only common sense. For example, for *consecutive integer problems*, you need to remember simply that consecutive integers differ by 1, so a string of such numbers can be represented as $n, n + 1, n + 2, \ldots$

Consecutive even integers differ by 2, so a string of such numbers can be represented as $n, n + 2, n + 4, \ldots$ *Consecutive odd integers* also differ by 2! So a string of such numbers can also be represented as $n, n + 2, n + 4, \ldots$

Rate-time-distance problems require you to know and use the formula $d = rt$; that is, distance equals rate times time.

Here are some examples of various kinds of word problems.

Example 1

Sally is 6 years older than Manuel. Three years ago, Sally was twice as old as Manuel. How old is Sally today?

Solution

If you have trouble setting up the equations, try plugging in numbers. Suppose that Sally is 20. If Sally is 6 years older than Manuel, how old is Manuel? He is 14. You get from 14 to 20 by adding 6. So if S is Sally's age and M is Manuel's, $S = M + 6$. Three years ago, Sally was $S - 3$, and Manuel was $M - 3$. So, from the second sentence, we see that $S - 3 = 2(M - 3)$, or $S - 3 = 2M - 6$, or $S = 2M - 3$.

Now, substituting $S = M + 6$, $M + 6 = 2M - 3$, and $M = 9$; which means Sally is $9 + 6 = 15$.

Example 2

Three consecutive odd integers are written in increasing order. If the sum of the first and second integers and twice the third integer is 46, what is the second integer?

Solution

Calling the smallest number x, the second is $x + 2$, and the third is $x + 4$. Therefore:

$$x + (x + 2) + 2(x + 4) = 46$$
$$x + x + 2 + 2x + 8 = 46$$
$$4x + 10 = 46$$
$$4x = 36$$
$$x = 9$$

Hence, the middle number is $9 + 2 = 11$.

Example 3

It took Andrew $1\frac{1}{2}$ hours to drive from Aurora to Zalesville at an average speed of 50 miles per hour. How fast did he have to drive back in order to be home in 80 minutes?

Solution

The distance from Aurora to Zalesville is given by $d = rt = (50)(1.5) = 75$ miles. Since 80 minutes is 1 hour and 20 minutes, or $1\frac{1}{3}$ hours, we must solve $75 = \frac{4}{3}r$. Multiplying by 3, we have $225 = 4r$, and dividing by 4, we get $r = 56.25$ miles per hour.

Topic 22. Monomials and Polynomials

When we add a collection of algebraic and arithmetic expressions, each expression is called a *term*. *Monomial* means one term. For example, we might say that $2x + 3y^2 + 7$ is the sum of three terms or three monomials.

Technically, if we enclose an algebraic expression in parentheses, it becomes one term, so that we could say that $(x + 2y) + (3x - 5y^2)$ is the sum of two monomials. But usually when we talk about a monomial, we mean a term that is just the product of constants and variables, possibly raised to various powers. Examples might be 7, $2x$, $-3y^2$, and $4x^2z^5$. The constant factor is called the *coefficient* of the variable factor. Thus, in $-3y^2$, -3 is the coefficient of y^2.

If we restrict our attention to monomials of the form Ax^n, the sums of such terms are called *polynomials* (in one variable). Polynomials with two terms are called *binomials,* and those with three terms are called *trinomials*. Expressions like $3x + 5$, $2x^2 - 5x + 8$, and $x^4 - 7x^5 - 11$ are all examples of polynomials.

The highest power of the variable that appears is called the *degree* of the polynomial. The three examples just given are of degrees 1, 2, and 5, respectively.

In evaluating monomials and polynomials for negative values of the variable, the greatest pitfall is keeping track of the negative signs. Always remember that, in an expression like $-x^2$, the power 2 is applied to the x and the negative sign in front should be thought of as (-1) times the expression. If you want to have the power apply to $-x$, you must write $(-x)^2$.

Example

Find the value of $3x - x^3 - x^2$, when $x = -2$.

Solution

Substitute -2 every place you see an x, thus:

$$3(-2) - (-2)^3 - (-2)^2 = -6 - (-8) - (+4) = -6 + 8 - 4 = -2$$

Topic 23. Combining Monomials

Monomials with identical variable factors can be added or subtracted by adding or subtracting their coefficients. So $3x^2 + 4x^2 = 7x^2$, and $3x^4 - 9x^4 = -6x^4$. When you multiply monomials, take the product of their coefficients and take the product of the variable parts by adding exponents of factors with like bases. So we have $(-4xy^2)(3x^2y^3) = -12x^3y^5$.

Monomial fractions can be simplified to simplest form by dividing out common factors of the coefficients and then using the usual rules for subtraction of exponents in division.

Example

Combine into a single monomial $9y - \dfrac{(6y^3)}{(2y^2)}$.

Solution

The fraction simplifies to $3y$, and $9y - 3y = 6y$.

Topic 24. Combining Polynomials and Monomials

Polynomials are added or subtracted by just combining like monomial terms in the appropriate manner. Thus, $(2x^2 + 5x - 3) + (3x^2 + 5x - 12)$ is summed by removing the parentheses and combining like terms, to yield $5x^2 + 10x - 15$.

If there is a negative sign in front of a polynomial within parentheses, be careful to change the signs of all the terms within the parentheses when you remove the parentheses. Consider:

$$(2x^2 + 5x - 3) - (3x^2 + 5x - 12) = 2x^2 + 5x - 3 - 3x^2 - 5x + 12$$
$$= -x^2 + 9$$

Did you notice that $2x^2 - 3x^2 = -1x^2$, but the "1" is not shown?

To multiply a polynomial by a monomial, use the distributive law to multiply each term in the polynomial by the monomial factor. For example, $2x(2x^2 + 5x - 11) = 4x^3 + 10x^2 - 22x$.

When multiplying a polynomial by a polynomial, you are actually repeatedly applying the distributive law to form all possible products of the terms in the first polynomial with the terms in the second. The most common use of this is in multiplying two binomials, such as $(x + 3)(x - 5)$. In this case, there are four terms in the result: $x \times x = x^2$; $x(-5) = -5x$; $3 \times x = 3x$; and $3 \times (-5) = -15$; but the two middle terms are added together to give $-2x$. Thus, the product is $x^2 - 2x - 15$.

This process is usually remembered as the FOIL method. That is, form the products of First, Outer, Inner, Last, as shown in the figure below.

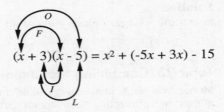

$$(x + 3)(x - 5) = x^2 + (-5x + 3x) - 15$$

Be sure to remember the special cases:

$$(x + a)^2 = (x + a)(x + a) = x^2 + 2ax + a^2$$

And:

$$(x - a)^2 = (x - a)(x - a) = x^2 - 2ax + a^2$$

Example
If m is an integer, and $(x - 6)(x - m) = x^2 + rx + 18$, what is the value of $m + r$?

Solution
The product of the last terms, $6m$, must be 18. Therefore, $m = 3$. If $m = 3$, then the sum of the outer and inner products becomes $-6x - 3x = -9x$, which equals rx. Hence, $r = -9$, and $m + r = 3 + (-9) = -6$.

Topic 25. Factoring Monomials

Factoring a monomial from a polynomial is simply reversing the distributive law. For example, if you are looking at $3x^2 - 6xy$, you should see that $3x$ is a factor of both terms. Hence, you could just as well write this as $3x(x - 2y)$. Multiplication using the distributive law will restore the original formulation.

Example
If $x - 5y = 12$, which is greater, $15y - 3x$ or -35 ?

Solution
We can see that $15y - 3x = -3(x - 5y)$; hence, it must equal $-3(12) = -36$, which is less than -35.

Topic 26. Trinomial Factoring and Quadratic Equations

When you multiply two binomials $(x + r)(x + s)$ using the FOIL method, the result is a trinomial of the form $x^2 + bx + c$, where b, the coefficient of x, is the sum of the constants r and s, and the constant term c is their product.

Trinomial factoring is the process of reversing this multiplication. For example, to find the binomial factors of $x^2 - 2x - 8$, we need to find two numbers whose product is -8 and whose sum is -2. Since the product is negative, one of the numbers must be negative and the other positive. The possible factors of 8 are 1 and 8, and 2 and 4. In order for the sum to be -2, we must choose -4 and $+2$. Thus, $x^2 - 2x - 8 = (x - 4)(x + 2)$.

This technique can sometimes be used to solve *quadratic equations*. If you have an equation like

$$x^2 - 7x + 6 = 0$$

you can factor the trinomial. You need two numbers whose product is $+6$ and whose sum is -7. Since the product is positive, both numbers must have the same sign, and since the sum is negative, they must both be negative. It is not hard to see that -6 and -1 are the correct options. Thus, the equation becomes

$$(x - 1)(x - 6) = 0$$

The only way a product of numbers can be zero is if one of the numbers is zero. Thus, either:

$$x - 1 = 0 \quad \text{or} \quad x - 6 = 0$$
$$x = 1 \quad \text{or} \quad x = 6$$

Example

The area of a rectangle is 60 and its perimeter is 32. What are its dimensions?

Solution

As you probably know, the area of a rectangle is calculated by multiplying its length by its width (see Topic 36). Calling the dimensions L and W, we have $LW = 60$, and $2L + 2W = 32$. Dividing by 2: $L + W = 16$. Therefore, $L = 16 - W$, which we substitute in $LW = 60$, giving us:

$$(16 - W)W = 60$$
$$16W - W^2 = 60$$

Grouping everything on the right side, we have:

$$0 = W^2 - 16W + 60$$

Now, factoring:

$$0 = (W - 10)(W - 6)$$

yields $W = 10$ or $W = 6$. Of course, if $W = 6$, $L = 10$, and if $W = 10$, $L = 6$. So, the dimensions are 6×10.

Topic 27. The Quadratic Formula

Some quadratic equations are not solvable by factoring using rational numbers. For example, $x^2 + x + 1$ has no factors using whole numbers, so $x^2 + x + 1 = 0$ has no rational roots (solutions.) In other cases, rational roots exist but they are difficult to find. For example, $12x^2 + x - 6 = 0$ can be solved by factoring, but it is not easy to see that:

$$12x^2 + x - 6 = (3x - 2)(4x + 3)$$

Setting each factor equal to zero:

$$3x - 2 = 0 \quad \text{or} \quad 4x + 3 = 0$$

yields $x = \dfrac{2}{3}$ or $x = -\dfrac{3}{4}$. What can you do when faced with such a situation? You use the quadratic formula: For any equation of the form $ax^2 + bx + c = 0$, the roots are $x = \dfrac{-b \pm \sqrt{b^2 - 4ac}}{2a}$

Topic 28. The Difference and the Sum of Two Squares

When you multiply $(a - b)$ by $(a + b)$ by the FOIL method, the middle term exactly cancels out, leaving just $a^2 - b^2$. Thus, the difference of two squares, $a^2 - b^2 = (a - b)(a + b)$.

For example, $x^2 - 16$ can be thought of as $x^2 - 4^2 = (x - 4)(x + 4)$.

This makes it easy to find $101^2 - 99^2$ as $(101 - 99)(101 + 99) = 2(200) = 400$. However, binomials such as $x^2 + 16$, which are the sum of two squares, cannot be factored.

Example 1

If x and y are positive integers, and $x - 2y = 5$, which of the following is the value of $x^2 - 4y^2$?

   (A)   0
   (B)   14
   (C)   45

Solution

Since $x^2 - 4y^2 = (x - 2y)(x + 2y) = 5(x + 2y)$, $x^2 - 4y^2$ must be divisible by 5. Therefore, 14 is not possible. If the result is to be zero, $x + 2y = 0$, which means $y = -2x$, so that both numbers cannot be positive. Hence, the expression must equal 45, which you get for $x = 7$ and $y = 1$.

Example 2

If x and y are positive integers, and $y^2 = x^2 + 7$, find y.

Solution

If we rewrite the equation as $y^2 - x^2 = 7$ and factor, we have $(y - x)(y + x) = 7$. Thus, 7 must be the product of the two whole numbers, $(y - x)$ and $(y + x)$. But 7 is a prime number that can only be factored as 7 times 1. Of course, $(y + x)$ must be the larger of the two, hence, $y + x = 7$, and $y - x = 1$. Adding the two equations gives us $2y = 8$; $y = 4$. (Of course, $x = 3$, but we weren't asked that.)

Topic 29. Operations with Radicals

The *square root* of a number N, written $\sqrt{N}$, is a number that when squared produces N. Thus, $\sqrt{4} = 2$, $\sqrt{9} = 3$, $\sqrt{16} = 4$, and so on. You should be aware that $\sqrt{0} = 0$ and $\sqrt{1} = 1$. Square roots of negative numbers are not real numbers.

The symbol $\sqrt{}$ is called a *radical,* and many people refer to $\sqrt{N}$ as "radical N." When we write $\sqrt{N}$, it is understood to be a positive number. So when you are faced with an algebraic equation like $x^2 = 4$, where you must allow for both positive and negative solutions, you must write $x = \pm\sqrt{4} = \pm 2$, where, as you know, $\pm$ is read "positive or negative."

All positive numbers have square roots, but most are *irrational numbers*. Only numbers that are *perfect squares* like 4, 9, 16, 25, 36, . . . have integer square roots.

If you assume that you are working with non-negative numbers, you can use certain properties of the square root to simplify radical expressions. The most important of these rules is $\sqrt{AB} = \sqrt{A} \cdot \sqrt{B}$.

This rule can be used to advantage in either direction. Reading it from right to left, we may write $\sqrt{3} \cdot \sqrt{12} = \sqrt{36}$. But you should also know how to use this rule to simplify radicals by extracting perfect squares from "under" the radical. Thus,

$$\sqrt{18} = \sqrt{9 \cdot 2} = 3\sqrt{2}$$

The key to using this technique is to recognize the perfect squares in order to factor them out in a sensible manner. Thus, it would do you little good to factor 18 as 3×6 in the preceding example, since neither 3 nor 6 is a perfect square.

Example

If $\sqrt{5} \cdot \sqrt{x} = 10$, which is larger, $\sqrt{x}$ or $2\sqrt{5}$?

Solution

Since $10 = \sqrt{100}$ and $\sqrt{5} \cdot \sqrt{x} = \sqrt{5x}$, we know that $5x = 100$ and $x = 20$. But $20 = 4 \times 5$, so $\sqrt{20} = 2\sqrt{5}$. Hence, the two quantities are equal.

GEOMETRY

Topic 30. Angles, Complements and Supplements

An *angle* is formed when two *rays* originate from the same point. Angles are usually measured in *degrees* or *radians*. We shall use only degree measure, which is customary on the GRE.

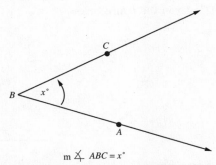

$$m \angle ABC = x°$$

A *straight angle* has a degree measure of 180°. Any two angles that sum to a straight angle are called *supplementary*. Thus, 80° and 100° are supplementary. Two equal supplementary angles are 90° each, and a 90° angle is called a *right angle*. Two angles that sum to a right angle are called *complementary*. Thus, 25° is the complement of 65°.

Angles less than 90° are called *acute,* and angles between 90° and 180° are called *obtuse.* The sum of all the angles around a given point must total to 360°.

Straight Angle, m∠ *ABC* = 180°

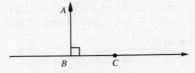

Right Angle, m∠ *ABC* = 90°

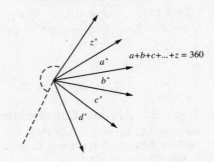

$a+b+c+\ldots+z = 360$

Example 1
Find *x* in the figure below.

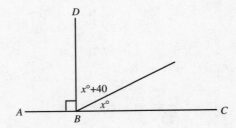

Solution
Since ∠*ABD* is a right angle, so is ∠*DBC*. Thus, $x + (x + 40) = 90$. Removing parentheses:

$$x + x + 40 = 90; 2x = 50; x = 25$$

Example 2
Find x in the diagram below.

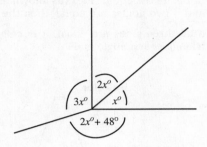

Solution

$$8x + 48 = 360$$
$$8x = 312$$
$$x = 39$$

Topic 31. The Angles in a Triangle

The sum of the measures of the three angles in any triangle is 180°, which is the measure of a straight angle. This fact is usually combined with other properties in the solution of geometric problems.

Example

In triangle ABC, m$\angle B$ is 30° more than twice m$\angle A$, and the degree measure of $\angle C$ is equal to the sum of the other two angles. How many degrees are there in the smallest angle of triangle ABC?

Solution

Calling the degree measure of $\angle A$ x, we have the following:

$$x = \text{number of degrees in } \angle A$$
$$2x + 30 = \text{number of degrees in } \angle B$$
$$x + (2x + 30) = 3x + 30$$
$$= \text{number of degrees in } \angle C$$

Summing, we have $x + 2x + 30 + 3x + 30 = 180$. Combining like terms:

$$6x + 60 = 180$$
$$6x = 120$$
$$x = 20$$

Clearly, $2x + 30$ and $3x + 30$ are larger than x, so the smallest angle is 20°.

Topic 32. Isosceles and Equilateral Triangles

A triangle with two sides of equal length is called an *isosceles triangle*. The angles opposite the equal sides (as shown in the following figure) are equal in measure, and if two angles are equal, then the triangle is isosceles.

If all three sides are equal, it is called an *equilateral triangle*. In an equilateral triangle, each angle is 60°.

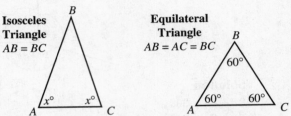

Here is a good example of how this fact can be used in a problem.

Example

If in triangle ABC as shown below, $AC = BC$ and $x \leq 50$, what is the smallest possible value of y?

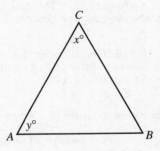

Solution

Since the sides AC and BC are of equal length, the two base angles, $\angle A$ and $\angle B$, must also be equal. The three angles must total 180°. Hence, $x + 2y = 180$, which means that $y = \dfrac{(180 - x)}{2} = 90 - \left(\dfrac{1}{2}\right)x$. The smallest possible value for y is achieved when x is as large as possible; that is, when $x = 50$, for which $y = 65$.

Topic 33. Other Triangle Properties

In a triangle, the sum of the lengths of any two sides must exceed the third. Thus, you cannot draw a triangle with sides of lengths 3, 6, and 10, because $3 + 6 < 10$. In addition, in comparing any two sides of a triangle, the longer side will be opposite the larger angle.

Example 1

A triangle has sides of 5, 12, and x. If x is an integer, what is the minimum possible perimeter of the triangle?

Solution

In order to form a triangle, the sum of any two sides must exceed the third. Therefore, $x + 5 > 12$, which means that $x > 7$. The smallest integer greater than 7 is 8. Hence, the minimum possible perimeter is $5 + 12 + 8 = 25$. (Can you see why the maximum length of the perimeter is 33?)

Example 2

In the triangle shown below, $AB = BC$. Which is longer, AC or AB?

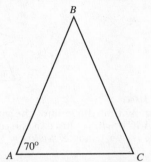

Note: Diagram not drawn to scale

Solution

Since the triangle is isosceles, the base angles are equal. Thus, $m\angle A = m\angle C = 70°$. This implies that $m\angle B = 40°$, in order to reach the full 180° in the triangle. And that means that $AB > AC$, because it is the side opposite the larger angle.

Topic 34. Vertical Angles

When two lines intersect, two pairs of *vertical angles* are formed (see the following figure). The "facing" pairs are equal and, of course, each pair on one side of the line add up to 180°.

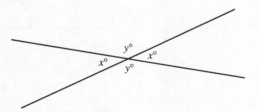

Example

In the diagram below, which is larger, $x + y$ or $w + z$?

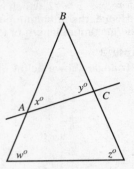

Solution

We know that the sum of the angles in any triangle is 180°. Letting the measure of $\angle ABC$ be m, we have in the upper triangle $x + y = 180 - m$. Similarly, looking at the larger triangle, we know that $w + z = 180 - m$. Therefore, $x + y = w + z$.

Topic 35. Parallel Lines and Transversals

If you start with two lines *parallel* to one another (that is, running in the same direction), and draw a line that crosses them, the crossing line is called a *transversal*. The intersections of the transversal with the parallel lines create several sets of related angles. In particular, the *corresponding angles*, labeled B in the diagram below, and the *alternate interior angles*, labeled A in the diagram, are equal.

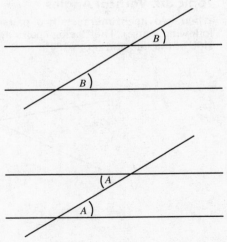

Combining these properties with your knowledge about vertical angles and the angles in a triangle can lead to interesting examples.

Example 1

In the diagram below, l_1 is parallel to l_2. Find x.

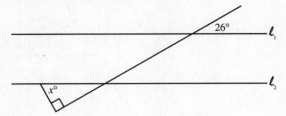

Solution

Label the diagram as shown below:

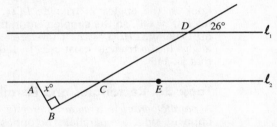

We see that m∠DCE = 26°, which makes m∠ACB = 26°. Since triangle ABC is a right triangle, x is the complement of 26°, or 64°.

Example 2

In the diagram shown below, l_1 is parallel to l_2. Find x.

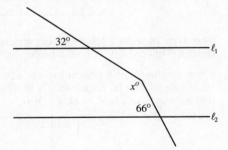

Solution

Extend the line *AB*, as shown in the following diagram.

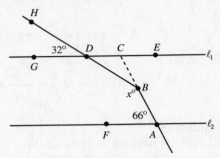

Look at the angles in triangle *BCD*. As alternate interior angles, m∠*BCE* = m∠*BAF* = 66°, so the supplement in the triangle, ∠*C* = 114°. As vertical angles, m∠*CDB* = m∠*HDG* = 32°. Therefore, in the triangle, m∠*D* = 32°. Since the three angles in the triangle must sum to 180°, m∠*B* = 34°. *x* is the supplement to 34°, that is, 146°.

Topic 36. Rectangles and Parallelograms

A *parallelogram* is a *quadrilateral* (a four-sided figure) in which the pairs of opposite sides are parallel. The opposite angles will be equal, and the opposite sides will be of equal length (see the figure below).

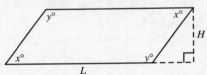

The area of a parallelogram is calculated by multiplying the length times the height. That is, $A = LH$, as labelled in the diagram.

If the angles in the parallelogram are right angles, we have a *rectangle*. For a rectangle of length *L* and width *W*, the area is $A = LW$, and the *perimeter* (the distance around) is $P = 2L + 2W$.

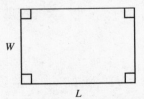

For example, the area of a rectangular garden that is 20 yards long and 10 yards deep is $(20)(10) = 200$ square yards. However, to put a fence around the same garden requires $2(20) + 2(10) = 60$ running yards of fencing (the perimeter of the rectangle).

These relatively easy formulas can lead to some tricky questions.

Example 1

If sod comes in 4 × 4 foot squares costing $3.50 per square, how much will it cost to sod the lawn shown in the figure below?

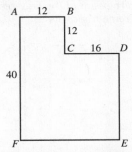

Distances are in feet. You may assume that all angles that appear to be right angles are right angles.

Solution

Complete the rectangle as shown in the figure below.

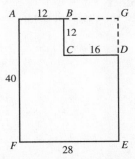

We see that the large rectangle *AGEF* is 40 × 28 = 1120 square feet. The smaller rectangle *BGDC* is 12 × 16 = 192 square feet. Hence, the area that must be sodded is 1120 − 192 = 928 square feet. Each 4 × 4 piece of sod is 16 square feet. Therefore, we need 928 ÷ 16 = 58 squares of sod at $3.50 each. (58)(3.50) = $203.

Example 2

Rectangle 1 has an area of 64, and Rectangle 2 has an area of 16. Which rectangle has a larger perimeter?

Solution

You can't tell! For Rectangle 1, $LW = 64$. If it were a square, each side would be 8 and the perimeter would be 32, but the length could be any number greater than zero if W is $\dfrac{64}{L}$. Thus, you could make its perimeter (virtually) as large as you wish! For example, the rectangle could be 64 × 1, with a perimeter of 130.

For Rectangle 2, $LW = 16$. If it were a square, each side would be 4 and the perimeter would be 16, but, again, the length could be any number greater than zero if W is $\dfrac{16}{L}$. For example, the rectangle could be 16 × 1, with a perimeter of 34, which is less than 130 but greater than 32.

Topic 37. The Pythagorean Theorem

FYI

You should remember some well-known Pythagorean triples, that is, sets of whole numbers such as 3–4–5 for which a² + b² =c². You'll encounter right triangles with these dimensions on the GRE. Other less easily recognized Pythagorean triples are 5–12–13, 8–15–17, and 7–24–25. In addition, look for multiples of these, such as 6–8–10 or 15–20–25.

The *Pythagorean Theorem* is probably the most famous geometric relationship. It tells us that the square on the *hypotenuse* (the longest side) of a right triangle is equal to the sum of the squares on the other two sides (or *legs*). In symbols, we usually remember this as:

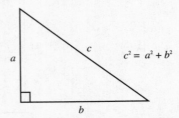

$$c^2 = a^2 + b^2$$

There are other important cases that yield non-integer solutions for the Pythagorean Theorem. For example, the hypotenuse of a triangle with one leg of length 1 and the other of length 2 can be found by computing $c^2 = 1^2 + 2^2$, that is, $c^2 = 5$ and $c = \sqrt{5}$.

Example 1

Find x in the diagram below.

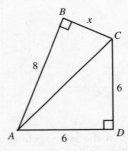

Solution

Using the Pythagorean Theorem, in triangle ACD, the theorem tells us that $6^2 + 6^2 = c^2$. Hence, $c^2 = 72$. In triangle ABC, if we let x represent the length of BC, $72 = c^2 = x^2 + 8^2$. That is, $x^2 = 72 - 64 = 8$. Thus, $x = \sqrt{8} = 2\sqrt{2}$.

Example 2

A rectangle has one side with a length of 6 and a diagonal with a length of 10. What is its perimeter?

Solution

Notice that the diagonal of a rectangle divides the rectangle into two identical right triangles. Hence, the other side can be found by the Pythagorean Theorem. We recognize that a side of 6 and a diagonal of 10 imply that we have a 6–8–10 right triangle, so the unknown side is 8. The perimeter of the rectangle is, therefore, $2(6) + 2(8) = 28$.

Topic 38. The Area of a Triangle

FYI

Remember that for a right triangle, you can use the two legs as base and altitude. For example, the area of a 5–12–13 right triangle is

$A = \dfrac{1}{2}(5)(12) = 30$

square units.

In any triangle, you can construct a line from any vertex perpendicular to the opposite side, although sometimes that side may have to be extended outside the triangle, as shown in the second illustration below. This line is called the *altitude* or *height* of the triangle; the side to which the altitude is drawn is called

the *base*. The area of a triangle is given by the formula $A = \dfrac{1}{2}bh$, where b = length of the base and h = the length of the altitude.

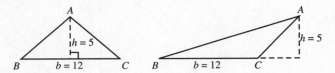

Both triangles shown above have the same area: $A = \dfrac{1}{2}(12)(5) = 30$.

Example

In triangle *ABC*, *AB* = 6, *BC* = 8, and *AC* = 10. Find the altitude from vertex *B* to *AC*.

Solution

Since the sides are 6–8–10, the triangle is a disguised 3–4–5 right triangle, with *AC* being the hypotenuse. Drawing the triangle (see the diagram below), we see that, by using the two legs as base and height, the area of the triangle must be

$A = \dfrac{1}{2}(6)(8) = 24$. By using the hypotenuse and the unknown altitude, the area

must be $A = \dfrac{1}{2}(10)(h) = 5h$. Therefore, $5h = 24$ and $h = 4.8$.

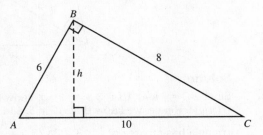

Topic 39. Special Right Triangles

There are two special right triangles whose properties you should be familiar with. The first is the *isosceles right triangle*, also referred to as the *45°–45°–90° triangle*. By definition, its legs are of equal length, and its hypotenuse is $\sqrt{2}$ times as long as the leg.

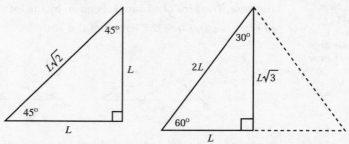

The other important right triangle is the *30°–60°–90° triangle*. You can see by dropping an altitude that this is half of an equilateral triangle. Hence, the shorter leg is half the hypotenuse, and the longer leg (the one opposite the 60° angle) is $\sqrt{3}$ times the shorter leg.

Example

Find the area of the region shown in the diagram below.

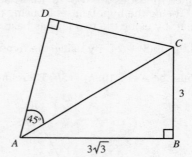

Solution

Since $BC = 3$ and $AB = 3 \times \sqrt{3}$, we know that triangle ABC is a 30°–60°–90° right triangle. Hence, we know that $AC = 6$, and taking half the product of the legs, the triangle has an area of $\frac{1}{2} \times 3 \times 3\sqrt{3} = \left(\frac{9}{2}\right)\sqrt{3}$. Since triangle ADC is an isosceles right triangle with a hypotenuse of 6, each leg must be $\frac{6}{\sqrt{2}}$. Again, taking half the product of the legs, the triangle has an area of $\left(\frac{1}{2}\right)\left(\frac{6}{\sqrt{2}}\right)\left(\frac{6}{\sqrt{2}}\right) = \frac{18}{2} = 9$.

Adding the two areas, we have $9 + \left(\frac{9}{2}\right)\sqrt{3}$.

Topic 40. Other Polygons

Any geometric figure with straight line segments as sides is called a *polygon*. To find the perimeter of a polygon, simply add together the lengths of all the sides. Of course, it may require some thinking to figure out each length. To find the area of a polygon, connect the vertices by line segments to divide the polygon into triangles and sum the areas of these triangles.

Example

Find the area of figure *ABCDE* shown in the diagram below.

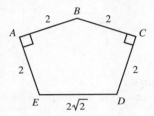

Solution

Drawing $\overline{BE}$ and $\overline{BD}$ divides the region into three triangles as shown in the diagram below.

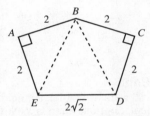

Triangles *ABE* and *BCD* are both 45°–45°–90° right triangles, making $BE = BD = 2\sqrt{2}$. This makes the central triangle an equilateral triangle. The area of each of the two outer triangles is $\frac{1}{2}(2)(2) = 2$; so the two together have area 4. The center triangle has a base of $2\sqrt{2}$. If you draw the altitude, you get a 30°–60°–90° right triangle with a shorter leg of $\sqrt{2}$, which makes the height $\sqrt{3}$ times that, or $\sqrt{6}$. This gives an area of $\frac{1}{2}(2\sqrt{2})(\sqrt{6}) = \sqrt{12} = 2\sqrt{3}$. Hence, the total area of the polygon is $4 + 2\sqrt{3}$.

Topic 41. Basic Properties of Circles

A line segment from the center of a circle to any point on its circumference is called a *radius*. All radii of the same circle are equal in length. A line segment that passes through the center of the circle and cuts completely across the circle is called a *diameter,* and it is, of course, twice as long as any radius. Thus, $d = 2r$.

Any line cutting across a circle is called a *chord,* and no chord can be longer than the diameter. Any portion of the circle is called an *arc.* The degree measure of an arc is the measure of the *central angle* subtended by it, as shown in the following diagram.

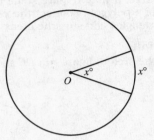

Example 1

If the arc *PS* in the diagram below has a degree measure of 62°, is the chord *PS* longer or shorter than the radius of the circle?

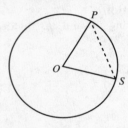

Solution

Since all radii are equal, triangle *OPS* is isosceles, and the angles at *P* and *S* must be equal. Suppose each is *x*. Now, $2x + 62 = 180$. Hence, $x = 59$. Therefore, *PS* is opposite the largest angle in the triangle and must be the longest side. Therefore, *PS* is longer than a radius.

Topic 42. The Area and Circumference of a Circle

For a circle of radius *r*, the *circumference* (the distance around the circle) is given by the formula $C = 2\pi r$. The area of the circle is given by the formula $A = \pi r^2$. In both formulas, π (the Greek letter pi) is a constant, a number whose value is approximately 3.1416 (or about $\frac{22}{7}$).

Example 1

Find the area of the shaded region shown in the figure below. The curved side is a semicircle.

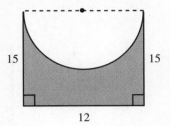

Solution

The dotted line completes the rectangle, which is $12 \times 15 = 180$ square units. The radius of the circular arc must be 6, since its diameter is 12. The area of the whole circle would be $\pi r^2 = \pi(6^2) = 36\pi$. Hence, the area of the semicircle is half of that, or 18π. Subtracting, the area of the shaded region is $180 - 18\pi$.

Example 2

The larger circle shown in the figure below has an area of 36π. Find the circumference of the smaller circle.

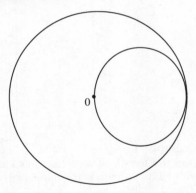

Solution

The larger circle has an area of $A_L = \pi(r)^2 = 36\pi$. This means that $r^2 = 36$ and $r = 6$. The diameter of the smaller circle equals the radius of the larger one, so its radius is $\frac{1}{2}(6) = 3$. Its circumference must be $C_S = 2\pi(3) = 6\pi$.

Topic 43. Volumes of Solid Figures

A solid figure with straight-line edges and flat surfaces is called a *polyhedron*. The surfaces bounding the solid are called *faces*. Thus, edges have lengths and surfaces have areas, and the solid has a *surface area*, which is the sum of the areas of all its faces.

A solid figure also has a *volume*, expressed in cubic units. You should be familiar with the following formulas for volumes of regular figures:

- A *rectangular solid* is a polyhedron with rectangular faces at right angles to one another.

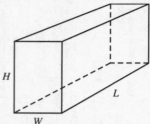

$$V = LWH = \text{Length} \times \text{Width} \times \text{Height}$$

- A *cube* is a rectangular solid with all edges of equal length s; that is, $L = W = H = s$. Therefore, $V = s^3$.

- A *right circular cylinder* is a solid with a circular base and a side perpendicular to the base (like a soda can). The volume is the area of the base times the height, or $V = \pi r^2 h$.

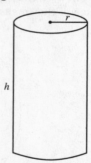

Example 1

Find the length of a rectangular solid of height 6 that is twice as long as it is wide, if its volume is the same as that of a cube with a total surface area of 864 square inches.

Solution

Let x = the width. Now $2x$ = length. The volume of the rectangular solid is $V = 6(x)(2x) = 12x^2$. Since the cube has six square faces, its total surface area is 6 times the area of one face. In symbols, $6s^2 = 864$. Dividing by 6, $s^2 = 144$; $s = 12$. Hence, the volume of the cube is $12^3 = 1728$. Since the two solids have the same volume, $12x^2 = 1728$; $x^2 = 144$; $x = 12$. The length, which is twice the width, is thus 24.

Example 2

Which has a greater volume, a rectangular solid that is 6 feet long and has a square base of side 4, or a cylinder with a length of 7 feet and a diameter of 4?

Solution

The volume of the rectangular solid is $V = (4)(4)(6) = 96$. The radius of the cylinder is 2, so its volume is $V_C = \pi(2)^2(7) = 28\pi$. Since π = about $\frac{22}{7}$, 28π = about 88. Therefore, the rectangular solid is larger.

COORDINATE GEOMETRY

Topic 44. The Midpoint Formula

Given two points $P(x_1, y_1)$ and $Q(x_2, y_2)$, the midpoint M of the $\overline{PQ}$ has coordinates: $x_M = \dfrac{x_1 + x_2}{2}$; $y_M = \dfrac{y_1 + y_2}{2}$

Expressing the same idea in words: To find the coordinates of the midpoint, simply average the coordinates of the end points. For example, the midpoint between (3,4) and (2,–2) is $x_M = \dfrac{3+2}{2} = \dfrac{5}{2}$; $y_M = \dfrac{4+-2}{2} = \dfrac{2}{2} = 1$.

Hence, the midpoint is $\left(\dfrac{5}{2}, 1\right) = (2.5, 1)$.

Example 1

If (2,6) is the midpoint of the line segment connecting $(-1,3)$ to $P(x,y)$, which is larger, $2x$ or y?

Solution

We know that the average of x and -1 must be 2. That is, $2 = \dfrac{(x-1)}{2}$, or $4 = x - 1$; $x = 5$. Similarly, we know that the average of y and 3 must be 6. Thus, $6 = \dfrac{(y+3)}{2}$, or $12 = y + 3$; $y = 9$. Since $2x = 10$, $2x > y$.

Example 2

If $b < 6$, is (3,b) closer to $P(0,2)$ or to $Q(6,10)$?

Solution

We see that (3,6) is the midpoint of $\overline{PQ}$. Therefore, in the x-direction, (3,b) will be equidistant from both P and Q. However, if $b < 6$, then b must be closer to 2 than to 10. Therefore, (3,b) is closer to (0,2) than to (6,10).

Topic 45. The Distance Formula

Given two points $P(x_1, y_1)$ and $Q(x_2, y_2)$, the distance from P to Q is given by the formula:

$$d = \sqrt{(x_1 - x_2)^2 + (y_1 - y_2)^2}$$

In words, the distance is the square root of the sum of the change in x squared plus the change in y squared . For example, the distance from (6,2) to (3,−1) is:
$$d = \sqrt{(6-3)^2 + (2-(-1))^2}$$
Thus: $d = \sqrt{3^2 + 3^2} = \sqrt{9+9} = \sqrt{18} = 3\sqrt{2}$

Example 1

The point $(t,-1)$ lies on a circle with a radius of 5 and its center at $(4,2)$. What are the possible values of t?

Solution

Since every point on the circle must be 5 units from the center, we know that $(t,-1)$ must be 5 units from $(4,2)$. Using the distance formula,

$$\sqrt{(t-4)^2 + (-1-2)^2} = \sqrt{t^2 - 8t + 16 + 9} = \sqrt{t^2 - 8t + 25} = 5$$

Squaring both sides, we have $t^2 - 8t + 25 = 25$. We subtract 25 from both sides to yield $t^2 - 8t = 0$, which factors as $t(t-8) = 0$. This gives us two possibilities: $t = 0$ or $t = 8$.

Example 2

The point $(4,t)$ is equidistant from $(1,1)$ and $(5,3)$. What is the value of t?

Solution

Since the distances from the two given points are the same, we use the distance formula twice and equate the results, thus:

$$\sqrt{(4-1)^2 + (t-1)^2} = \sqrt{(5-4)^2 + (3-t)^2}$$

$$\sqrt{9 + (t^2 - 2t + 1)} = \sqrt{1 + (9 - 6t + t^2)}$$

$$\sqrt{10 - 2t + t^2} = \sqrt{10 - 6t + t^2}$$

Squaring both sides:

$$10 - 2t + t^2 = 10 - 6t + t^2$$

Subtracting $t^2 + 10$ leaves $-2t = -6t$; $4t = 0$; $t = 0$.

Topic 46. The Slope of a Line

Given two points $P(x_1, y_1)$ and $Q(x_2, y_2)$, the slope of the line passing through P and Q is given by the formula:

$$m = \frac{y_1 - y_2}{x_1 - x_2}$$

In other words, this says that the slope is the change in y divided by the change in x. For example, the slope of the line passing through $(6,4)$ to $(3,-1)$ is:

$$m = \frac{(4 - [-1])}{(6 - 3)} = \frac{5}{3}$$

Example

The points $(-1,-1)$, $(3,11)$, and $(1,t)$ lie on the same line. What is the value of t?

Solution

Since the slope of a line is the same for any two points on the line, using $(-1,-1)$ and $(3,11)$, we must have a slope of:

$$m = \frac{11 - [-1]}{3 - [-1]} = \frac{12}{4} = 3$$

Now, using the pair $(-1,-1)$ and $(1,t)$:

$$3 = \frac{t - [-1]}{1 - [-1]} = \frac{(t + 1)}{2}$$

Multiplying by 2, $6 = t + 1$; $t = 5$.

COUNTING AND PROBABILITY

Topic 47. The Addition Principle for Counting

If a set A has m elements, and a set B has n elements, and the two sets have no elements in common, then the total number of elements in the two sets combined is $m + n$. But if there are k elements common to the two sets, then the total in the combined set is $m + n - k$. That is, you must take into account the double counting of elements common to both groups.

This kind of situation is usually handled most easily by displaying the given information in a *Venn Diagram*.

Example 1

Helena applied to 12 colleges for admission. Sergei applied to 10 colleges. Between them, they applied to 16 different colleges. How many colleges received applications from both students?

Solution

We let H be the set of colleges to which Helena applied, and S be those to which Sergei applied. Letting x be the number that are common to both sets, the following Venn diagram displays the data.

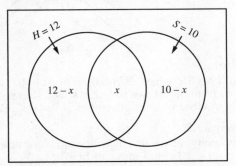

The central region includes the colleges common to both groups, and we can see that the total is $(12 - x) + x + (10 - x) = 16$. Removing parentheses and combining like terms, we have $22 - x = 16$; $x = 6$.

Sometimes problems of this type can involve more than two sets.

Example 2

A survey of voters shows that 43% listen to radio news reports, 45% listen to TV news reports, and 36% read a daily newspaper. What is the maximum percentage of voters surveyed that do all three?

Solution

If the three sets were totally *disjoint*, that is, had no overlap, the sum of the percentages would be 100%. The extent of various kinds of overlap will show up as an excess over 100%. Everyone in two of the three categories will be counted twice, and everyone common to all three will be counted three times.

If we total 43 + 45 + 36, we find that we have accounted for 124% of the voters, a 24% overcount. Therefore, the number common to all three cannot be greater than one-third of that, or 8%. This maximum of 8% is reached only if no one falls into two out of three categories, so that the entire overcount is the result of people in all three.

Topic 48. The Multiplication Principle for Counting

If a process can be broken down into two steps, and the first step can be performed in m ways; and if, for each of those ways, the second step can be performed in n ways; then the total number of ways of performing the complete process is $T = mn$. This is known as the *multiplication principle* for counting.

For example, suppose that a jar contains five blocks of five different colors. We pick a block, record the color, and then pick a second block without replacing the first. The number of ordered color combinations is $(5)(4) = 20$.

This process extends to more than two steps in the natural way.

Example 1

The following diagram is a road map from Abbottsville to Cartersburg. How many different routes can you follow to drive from Abbottsville to Cartersburg if you go through Batestown only once?

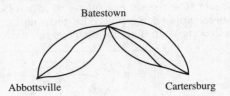

Batestown

Abbottsville   Cartersburg

Solution

You have 3 choices of roads from Abbottsville to Batestown and 4 choices of roads from Batestown to Cartersburg. Hence, by the multiplication principle, the total number of possible routes is $3 \times 4 = 12$.

Example 2

How many different 3-digit license plate numbers can be produced if the first digit on any license may not be 0?

Solution

By the natural extension of the multiplication principle to a three-step process, we see that we have 9 choices for the first digit, 10 choices for the second, and 10 choices for the third. Thus, the total is $9 \times 10 \times 10 = 900$.

Topic 49. Permutations (Arrangements)

As a natural extension of the multiplication principle, it is not hard to show that the number of distinct *permutations,* or arrangements of n distinguishable objects in a row, is n *factorial*; that is:

$$n! = n(n-1)(n-2) \times \ldots \times 2 \times 1$$

For example, there are $4! = 4 \times 3 \times 2 \times 1 = 24$ ways of arranging the four symbols #, *, @, and % in a straight line.

Example 1

If the five starting members of a basketball team are lined up randomly for a photograph, what is the chance that they will appear in order of height from shortest to tallest, left to right?

Solution

There are 5 distinguishable people in the group, who can be arranged in $5! = 5 \times 4 \times 3 \times 2 \times 1 = 120$ ways. In only one of these ways will they be in the correct size order. Therefore, the chance is $\dfrac{1}{120}$.

Example 2

In how many ways can 3 men and 3 women be seated in theater seats if the seating must alternate men and women, starting with a woman?

Solution

The 3 women can be arranged in the first, third, and fifth seats in $3! = 6$ ways. However, for each of these six possibilities, the 3 men can be seated in the remaining seats in $3! = 6$ ways. Hence there are really $6 \times 6 = 36$ ways altogether.

Topic 50. Probability

To find the probability of any random event, divide the number of outcomes favorable to the event by the total number of possible outcomes. For example, if a bag contains 12 blue marbles and 9 red marbles, the probability that a marble selected at random is blue is the number of blue marbles divided by the total number of marbles:

$$\frac{12}{21} = \frac{4}{7}.$$

Example

A box contains five blocks numbered 1, 2, 3, 4, and 5. Johnnie picks a block and replaces it. Lisa then picks a block. What is the probability that the sum of the numbers they picked is even?

Solution

Since each person had 5 choices, there are 25 possible pairs of numbers. The only way the sum could be odd is if one person picked an odd number and the other picked an even number. Suppose that Johnnie chose the odd number and Lisa the even one. Johnnie had 3 possible even numbers to select from, and for each of these, Lisa had 2 possible choices, for a total of $(3)(2) = 6$ possibilities. However, you could have had Johnnie pick an even number and Lisa pick an odd one, and there are also 6 ways to do that. Hence, out of 25 possibilities, 12 have an odd total, and 13 have an even total. The probability, then, is $\dfrac{13}{25}$.

Appendix C

Resources for Further Study

We hope you've found the information in this book to be a valuable aid in pursuing admission to the graduate school of your choice. Here are some other sources we recommend to help you with other phases of this challenging and exciting process.

PRACTICE TESTS

When you've taken the Insider's tests in this book, your next source of practice exams should be the test-makers themselves. Look for the most recent compilation of GRE exams published by the GRE Board. It will contain some test-taking advice, a collection of actual recent tests, answer keys, and scoring instructions. However, explanatory answers are not provided for most of the test questions. As of this writing, the current books are:

GRE Practicing to Take the General Test, 9th Edition. The GRE Board, 1994. 499 pages, $15.00.

(Contains six actual full-length GRE exams, plus test-taking advice and strategies.)

GRE General Test—The Big Book. The GRE Board, 1997. $30.00.

(A compendium of 27 sample tests, including a total of over 5,000 questions. Enough to choke even a very large horse.)

GRADUATE SCHOOL GUIDES

There are many reference books that can give you basic information about the thousands of graduate programs in the United States. Most are available at public libraries or in your college guidance office. Each offers a slightly different arrangement and selection of information, so browse through a few to find the one you like best. Three that are quite complete and useful are:

Peterson's Decision Guides: Graduate Schools in the U.S. Peterson's, 2001. 714 pages, $19.95.

(Profiles of colleges and universities offering graduate degrees. The publisher also produces a series of specialized volumes with profiles of programs in specific subject areas.)

The Official GRE/CGS Directory of Graduate Programs, 16th Edition. ETS, 1997. Four volumes, each 415–483 pages, each $20.00.

(Graduate school guides in four volumes by speciality. Volume A: Natural Sciences. Volume B: Engineering and Business. Volume C: Social Sciences and Education. Volume D: Arts, Humanities, and Other Fields.)

Guide to American Graduate Schools by Harold R. Doughty. Eighth Edition. Penguin Books, 1997. 635 pages, $24.95.

(An attractive single-volume guide with profiles of 1,200 universities offering graduate degrees.)

APPLYING TO AND SURVIVING GRADUATE SCHOOL

Game Plan for Getting into Graduate School by Marion B. Castellucci. Peterson's, 2000. 184 pages, $14.95.

(A basic once-over-lightly covering the graduate admission process.)

Grants for Graduate and Postdoctoral Study, Fifth Edition. Peterson's, 1998. 566 pages, $32.95.

(Lists 1,400 fellowships, grants, internships, and awards for graduate students.)

The Real Guide to Grad School: What You Better Know Before You Choose—Humanities & Social Sciences. Edited by Robert E. Clark and John Palattella. Lingua Franca Books, 1997. 511 pages, $24.95.

(A feisty, well-written guide to the graduate school experience, with chapters giving the inside scoop on all the major disciplines in humanities and social sciences. A remarkable appendix shows which graduates were hired by which academic institutions—*tremendously* valuable info.)

Working for a Doctorate: A Guide for the Humanities and Social Sciences. Edited by Norman Graves and Ved Varma. Routledge, 1997. 202 pages, $20.00.

The Complete Guide to Graduate School Admission: Psychology and Related Fields by Patricia Keith-Spiegel. Laurence Erlbaum, 1991. 373 pages, $18.50.

(Two somewhat academic guides. The first focuses on the experience of working toward the Ph.D., the second on the admission process.)

SPECIALIZED STUDY GUIDES—MATH

Most bookstores have a math shelf containing a selection of review and study guides covering specific topics. If you want to review and practice math in greater depth than the information in this book permits, browse the shelf at your local store and find a book that interests you.

Be careful, though: most math books will cover topics that are *not* included on the GRE! If you are interested in focusing your study specifically on test-related topics, be guided by the Insider's GRE Math Review in this book (Appendix B). Any topic not listed there will *not* appear on the GRE.

Here's a worthwhile math review book you may want to consider.

Math Review for the GRE, GMAT, and MCAT. Peterson's, 2000. 316 pages, $16.95.

SPECIALIZED STUDY GUIDES—VERBAL

As with math, most bookstores will have a shelf containing books that can be helpful in preparing for the verbal portions of the GRE (including the Analytical Writing Measure). The following list includes books dealing with three major verbal skill areas: vocabulary building, reading, and writing.

Merriam Webster's Vocabulary Builder by Mary Wood Cornog. Merriam Webster, 1994. 558 pages, $4.95.

1000 Most Important Words by Norman Schur. Ballantine, 1982. 245 pages, $4.99.

(These two books are small, "mass-market" sized paperbacks that focus on vocabulary building. Neither is specifically focused on the GRE exam; however, both are interesting and well written and include many words that are highly appropriate for GRE preparation.)

Triple Your Reading Speed by Wade E. Cutler. Arco, 1993. 206 pages, $12.95.

(These two books will help you improve your reading skills. Neither is focused specifically on the GRE, but the techniques they teach can easily be applied to the exam.)

Grammar for Grownups by Val Dumond. Harper Perennial, 1993. 245 pages, $11.00.

(Two easy-to-read books that can help clarify tricky grammar topics. If this is a weakness of yours, reviewing grammar before tackling the Analytical Writing Measure can be helpful.)

The Elements of Style by William Strunk, Jr. and E. B. White. Third Edition. Allyn & Bacon, 1979. 92 pages, $5.95.

(The classic brief guide for writers. If you truly master the rules and concepts presented here, all your writing—including the essays you write for the GRE Analytical Writing Measure—will benefit greatly.)

SPECIALIZED STUDY GUIDES—ANALYTICAL

Unlike math and verbal skills, analytical skills have no true home in the bookstore—just as most students never take a high school or college course in which they learn the reasoning skills tested on this section of the exam. If you want additional reading to help you hone your knowledge in this area, books are available, but it'll take a bit of doing to find them. They may be shelved under reference, math, philosophy, psychology, games—or all of the above!

Here are a few titles that we recommend.

The Art of Deception: An Introduction to Critical Thinking by Nicholas Capaldi. Prometheus Books, 1987. 222 pages, $16.95.

Informal Logic: A Handbook for Critical Argumentation by Douglas N. Walton. Cambridge University Press, 1989. 292 pages, $19.95.

(Two books that deal with logical fallacies and other topics tested in the logical reasoning questions on the GRE. The former title is more lively, the latter more comprehensive.)

The Power of Logical Thinking by Marilyn Vos Savant. St. Martin's/Griffin, 1997. 204 pages, $11.95.

(An entertaining book about clear thinking by a popular newspaper columnist and TV commentator.)

The Dell Book of Logic Problems by Erica L. Rothstein. Dell, 1996. 175 pages, $10.99.

(One of a series of books collecting puzzles from a game-lovers' magazine. Written for fun, but does a good job of walking you through the logic of puzzles that resemble those on the GRE.)

The Ultimate Book of Puzzles, Mathematical Diversions, and Brainteasers by Erwin Brecher. St. Martin's/Griffin, 1996. 271 pages, $14.95.

Puzzles 4 Pleasure by Barry R. Clarke. Cambridge University Press, 1994. 118 pages, $10.95.

(The contents of these two books only resemble the GRE puzzles in part. Both, however, offer mental workouts that are interesting and fun and that are appropriate as "stretching exercises" for the GRE.)

Appendix D

The Insider's Stress-Busting Guide

by Mary-Jo D. Weber, M.S.
Psychiatric Nurse Practitioner

THE ROLE OF STRESS IN PEAK TEST PERFORMANCE

Let's face it—if you're like most people, you're not really looking forward to taking the GRE. In fact, the very thought of the test might make your stomach queasy and your neck and shoulders tight. You might become aware of your heart beating, and your hands might get clammy. You might even feel restless and be tempted to close this book right now and get a snack!

All these physical responses to the stress of test-taking can work for you or against you. Conditioned by millions of years of evolution, your body has developed a complex natural reaction, sometimes called the *fight or flight* response, that comes into play whenever you feel physically or psychologically threatened. This reaction has a very real value in getting you ready to meet whatever challenge you face, whether it's a menacing stranger on a dark street, an auditorium full of people waiting to hear you deliver a speech, or a standardized exam.

The adrenaline and other hormones that are released when you are under stress can get you ready for peak performance. They arouse your senses to increased sensitivity, alert your brain cells to pay attention, sharpen your mental focus, increase the amounts of energizing oxygen delivered to all parts of your body, and raise the levels of glucose available to fuel your brain. These chemical processes account for the sense of excitement you feel when you're under stress. Some people—artists who thrill to public applause, for example, or world-class athletes—actually relish this state of physical and mental arousal, and even the average person finds it exhilarating, though perhaps scary, too.

The problem comes when these responses get out of control, freezing your thoughts and leaving you feeling uncomfortably tense or anxious. When that happens, you may develop "tunnel vision," a narrowing of perception that hampers your awareness of what's around you; you may even feel that your mind is "going blank," as if your brain is on overload and is starting to shut down.

Fortunately, you *can* manage your stress so that the natural stress response will sharpen your focus without limiting your perspective or closing off your options, making you more creative and imaginative and helping you to retrieve more of the useful information stored in your memory.

This appendix will give you specific, scientifically tested techniques to use in the weeks before the exam, while you are studying, and on the very day you take the GRE. If you practice these methods, you may find yourself almost looking forward to the opportunity to tackle the test—and beat it!

PREPARING FOR PEAK PERFORMANCE

Top athletes find that mental preparation is as important to their success in competition as practicing their specific athletic skills. The field of sports psychology has taught us a lot about how you can best prepare for your test. Practicing your academic skills is something like a basketball player working on his foul shot or a swimmer perfecting her stroke: it's essential, but it's not enough. The best performers don't stop there. They also use relaxation and visualization techniques to ensure that they'll be able to apply their skills and to respond effectively and creatively to the challenges that game day will bring their way.

Similar relaxation and visualization techniques can help keep you from freezing up and allow you to efficiently handle whatever comes your way in the test-taking situation. They can also help you experience the test as a positive challenge, not a looming source of terror. You will maintain a degree of comfort and be able to manage the unpleasant symptoms of anxiety without letting them overwhelm you.

Learning to Relax

First, you'll need to learn to relax whenever you decide you want to. Yes—for most people, it's a skill that must be learned. If you're like most people, you probably tend to keep going—with work, play, or just hanging around—until you're physically exhausted, and then you crash. It's not the most efficient way to harness the energy in your body and mind. Instead, if you learn to relax whenever you want to, you'll be able to modulate your stress responses so that you'll feel only the amount of anxiety you need to wake up your brain cells and perform your best.

The following exercise is a good way to start. If you're feeling any sense of tiredness or anxiety—after a couple of hours of studying, for example—this is a better way to refresh yourself than napping or taking a TV break. It takes only a few minutes and will leave you feeling energized and alert. You can either read through this suggested exercise and then try it, or, even better, get a friend with a pleasant voice to read it aloud to you while you try it. (Later, you can return the favor.) As you go through the exercise, feel free to alter it in any way that seems pertinent to your individual situation.

Relaxation Exercise

Start by sitting comfortably with both feet flat on the floor. Take some time to notice how the floor is supporting your feet. Allow the surface on which you are resting to support you completely. Take all the time you need to notice the comfort and security of this.

Next, turn your mind toward your breathing. Don't try to change it; just observe it. Observe how effortless your breathing is, realizing that, with every exhalation, the tension of the day is flowing out, and, with every inhalation, revitalizing oxygen is flowing in to nourish all parts of your body.

Turn your attention again to your feet. Notice that they are comfortably resting on the floor. Notice that feeling of comfort spreading up to your ankles, calves, and knees. Feel how securely the chair is supporting your thighs, your buttocks, your lower back, and your upper back.

Your hands may be in your lap or at your sides. Allow them to open, and as you continue to breathe comfortably and naturally, experience any tension flowing down from your shoulders to your arms and out your finger tips. You will notice that, the more relaxed you can keep your hands, the more relaxed and alert you will be.

Notice whether your eyes are open or closed. Either way is fine. Take some time now to notice the muscles around your eyes, in your cheeks, and around your mouth. Notice whatever expression you naturally have on your face, whether it's frowning, neutral, or smiling. Don't feel you need to change it. Allow these muscles to soften. Close your eyes if you wish. Feel the heaviness of your jaw, and don't try to hold it up.

As you continue to notice the comfort in your body, pay attention to your neck and scalp. If you perceive any tension there, allow it to flow out with your next breath. Scan your body now, and if you find any areas of discomfort or tension, notice that, as you breathe, any tension or discomfort flows out with each exhalation, while energy flows in with each inhalation.

Now, as you continue to enjoy the comfort of your body securely supported by the chair and energized by your breathing, imagine that you are in a special, favorite place. It may be the beach, or the mountains, or your room, or just inside yourself. Notice how comfortable and alert you are to all the things that make that place pleasurable for you. Notice the sights, sounds, smells, and feelings that make the place so nice.

Take your time enjoying your special place. When you are ready to return to the room in which you are sitting, gently reorient yourself, experiencing your calm alertness and renewed enthusiasm for all your endeavors.

Now that you're back from your special place, notice how revitalized you feel.

With practice, this process of relaxation will become easier and quicker, but you already have noticed that from the very first attempt. You can recharge your batteries in a way that is even better than a nap because your alertness will be increased and your focus will be sharpened. Try using this method of relaxation whenever the pressure of studying is making you feel exhausted or tense. You'll find yourself learning more—and enjoying it more, too.

Visualizing Success

The next step is to add visualization of the test-taking situation and your desired successful outcome. It's a favorite preparation strategy of many successful athletes and entertainers; they find that visualizing themselves hitting the perfect tennis stroke or playing a difficult piano concerto with fluency and ease makes it much easier to actually perform that way.

It works for test-takers, too. In preparing for the computerized GRE, it'll help if you visit the testing center beforehand, so you'll know what to expect; but you can use our visualization exercise even if you don't have a chance to make such a visit. Here's how it works.

Visualization Exercise

Repeat the relaxation exercise. This time, however, after you've imagined your special place and while you're alertly and attentively noting the sights, sounds, and feelings that you experience there, imagine that you are entering the test room. Notice the rows of cubicles and the computer monitor and keyboard at each location.

Take your seat, noting how comfortably your feet are supported by the floor, how your body is supported by the chair, and how your breathing is energizing your body and mind. You see that the computer monitor contains the directions for the GRE exam. You review them and you begin your work, knowing that you have prepared for this test and that you will correctly answer all the questions you need to in order to achieve your desired goal.

You experience just the right amount of anxiety you need to feel in order to achieve your peak performance. As you work, the questions appear familiar and interesting to you. You look forward to reading each question because you know you will find it to be an interesting challenge to the skills you've been learning and practicing. You work efficiently, and, when you come to the end of the test, you experience the sense of a job well done.

At this time, reorient to the room.

You may also use this exercise before going to sleep, perhaps after a strenuous study session. If you do the exercise in bed, when it's completed, simply allow yourself to drift into a refreshing sleep.

During the weeks while you are studying for your exam, you can ensure peak performance by practicing relaxation and visualization every day. The best time for many people is at night, just before sleep. This will help your learning because your mind is working even while you sleep. Thus, if you practice visualizing test-taking success before you go to sleep, your brain will probably continue to process that information while you sleep, reinforcing the positive message.

Some people find it effective to make an audiotape of the relaxation and visualization exercises, to be played while they fall asleep.

TECHNIQUES OF POWER STUDYING

If you're an athlete, a musician, or an actor, you know how important your physical condition is to your training. What you eat or drink before practice will influence how effective your training will be. The same is true of test preparation.

Physical Conditioning for Effective Study

Everyone knows his or her own best time of the day for studying. For some people, it's early in the morning, before class or work; for others, it's late at night. Whatever time you favor, make sure you're in peak condition before you hit the books. Any alcohol intake within the past twelve to twenty-four hours (depending upon the amount) will decrease your mental functioning. Other mood-altering chemicals can interfere with your ability to learn and think critically for a much longer time, sometimes for as long as a month after use. A word to the wise, or to those who want to be: lay off drinking and drugs when preparing for a crucial exam.

Nutrition is just as important for studying as it is for athletic training, because thinking and learning are physical functions of your body, carried out by the cells of your brain. It so happens that your brain cells work on glucose (sugar) only. That said, it would be incorrect to deduce that your diet while studying should consist of candy bars and sodas. But you do learn and think best when your brain has a steady stream of glucose.

The best way to ensure this is to eat high-protein and so-called "complex carbohydrate" foods before studying and about every three hours during studying. Fruit, lean meat and fish, vegetables, pasta with low-fat sauce, cereal, crackers, bread, and legumes (such as peas and beans) are the foods associated with high mental performance. These foods will keep your blood sugar steady at an optimal level.

Avoid greasy or fatty foods; the work of digesting them actually pulls oxygen-rich blood away from your brain and toward your digestive system. (So pizza, although you may love it, is really not the best study food. Wait till after the exam, and then treat yourself to a pie with your favorite toppings—as a reward for the high score you've earned.)

Rest is often neglected when people are studying very hard, but this is a mistake. Research has shown that people who are in a state of chronic sleep deprivation just don't think or perform very well. When hospitals shorten the working shifts of their medical residents, the doctors suffer fewer mental lapses and make better treatment decisions. The same applies to anyone working with his or her brain. The optimal amount of sleep varies from one person to another, but few people do well on less than six hours a night over any extended period of time, and most people thrive on seven or eight hours a night. Don't pull an all-nighter; get the sleep you need, and you'll find yourself learning more, and more easily, the next morning.

Reducing Stress When You Study

When you sit down to study, you can improve your memory and creativity by practicing the relaxation and visualization exercises earlier in this chapter. If you don't want to spend that much time, there is a brief technique that can be used just before studying or as needed during breaks in your study sessions. It takes only a few minutes. It works best if you have already experienced the longer exercise, and the more familiar you become with the long exercise the better this short one will work.

The Three-Minute Relaxation Technique

Sit comfortably wherever you like, with your feet flat on the floor. Rest your hands on your lap or desk. Place the thumbs and index fingers of each hand together.

Close your eyes. Take a moment to notice your breathing. After a few seconds, turn your attention to the pressure of your thumbs on your index fingers. The pressure can be light or firm. Notice that pressure as you inhale and exhale several times; really notice how your fingers feel.

Then, as you exhale, release the pressure, relaxing your hands, feeling your tension and fatigue flowing out with your exhalation and melting down your arms and out your fingertips.

Continue to focus on your breathing for a few minutes. When you are ready, open your eyes and reorient yourself to your surroundings.

This quick exercise will enable you to capture a sense of calm alertness whenever you need it.

Music to Learn By

Many people enjoy listening to music while they are studying. There is nothing wrong with music as long as you like it and don't find it distracting, but there are some things to consider when you choose music for your study sessions.

Music can help you to concentrate by filtering out extraneous sounds or thoughts. For this purpose, it is helpful if the music is familiar, so listening to a selection of favorite CDs would help you to study more efficiently than listening to the radio (which will probably play both familiar and unfamiliar selections, as well as interjecting a stream of chatter and commercials that may well be distracting).

Music can also set a helpful mood while you're studying. It's a very personal choice, but in certain recent studies, when research subjects listened to classical music, particularly the works of Mozart, just before and during cognitive (mental) tasks, their performance on those tasks improved. You might want to experiment with different kinds of music to see which help you to concentrate best.

STRESS-BUSTING STRATEGIES FOR TEST-DAY AND TEST-DAY MINUS ONE

Hopefully you're not reading these suggestions for peak performance for the first time the day before your test. Ideally you'll have used the ideas we've presented for developing your personal test-preparation plan and you will be following it, more or less closely, in the weeks leading up to the exam. In particular, repeatedly visualizing success in the weeks before the test will motivate you to study and to view the test as a challenge you can meet, not a disaster in the making.

The Night Before

On the day before the test, make sure you have your admission form, your identification, a pen and pencil, and your directions to the test site ready and available for the morning. Make sure you know how to get to the test center and how long it will take you to get there given the expected weather conditions and traffic patterns. If you control these "petty" details, they won't inject an unnecessary note of anxiety or uncertainty on the morning of the exam.

It's really helpful if you can do something pleasant and relaxing the night before the test. Avoid alcohol and other mood-altering chemicals, and get into bed early. If you've made a tape of your relaxation and visualization exercises, have it playing as you drift off into a refreshing sleep.

However, if you're going to be worrying about that one last math rule or analogy technique while you're watching that movie—or if you're feeling that you haven't suffered enough yet to appease the testing gods so they'll allow you to get your highest score—here are some tips for last-minute studying.

Don't try to reread this book or do any kind of comprehensive review. At this point that will only increase your anxiety and convince you, incorrectly, that all the studying you have already done was inadequate and futile. Instead, decide how long you can study while still getting a good night's sleep. If you need nine hours to feel rested, your score will be boosted more by getting the full nine hours than by another few hours of studying.

Then pick a few topics you can comfortably cover in the amount of time you have left. Choose topics you are good at but feel can use a little more polishing, keeping in mind that you don't need a "perfect" score or to get every question correct.

Always remember, it is really all the previous study you've done that will determine your score; you're only reviewing the night before to appease the testing gods. When it's time to go to sleep, set your alarm clock to give you plenty of time to get ready, eat breakfast, and get to the testing site without rushing. Then practice your relaxation and visualization exercises, and have pleasant dreams of test-taking victory.

The Morning of the Exam

In the morning, eat something. Yes, we know that you never eat breakfast—but just take our word on this one. Study after study has demonstrated that people perform better on tests when they have eaten about thirty to sixty minutes beforehand. The foods you should eat are the same as those recommended during studying—high protein, low fat, and complex carbohydrate. Bring a piece of fruit or a power bar to the test center to eat during the brief mid-exam break.

During the exam itself—especially during the short breaks provided between test sections—you might try using the Three-Minute Relaxation technique if you feel fatigued or stressed.

All these tips, if practiced along with the study outlined in this book, will ensure your optimal performance on the GRE. They'll also help you attain an even higher goal: to feel balanced and sane before and after the test.

NOTES

NOTES

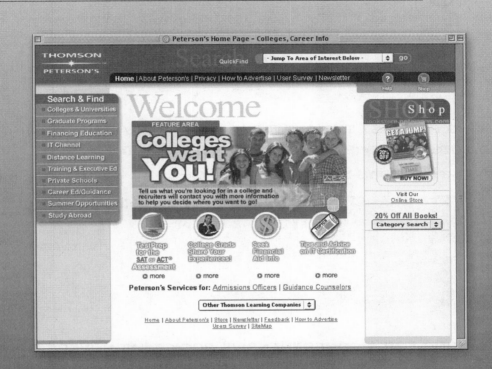